France

AN APPLIED GEOGRAPHY

France

AN APPLIED GEOGRAPHY

J. W. HOUSE

METHUEN & CO LTD

First published 1978
by Methuen & Co Ltd
11 New Fetter Lane
London EC4P 4EE

Photosetting by Thomson Press (India) Ltd., New Delhi
and printed in Great Britain by
J. W. Arrowsmith Ltd, Bristol

ISBN 0 416 15080 2

To Jean Labasse

Contents

Part two Growth, change and reconversion: the context for public policies

Part three Spatial management policies

Figures

xii *Contents*

Tables

Acknowledgements

Permission to reproduce the following figures is gratefully acknowledged:

Association Ouest Atlantique, fig. 73
DATAR, figs 55 and 75
EPA Cergy-Pontoise, fig. 64
IAURP, fig. 62
INSEE, *Statistiques et Indicateurs des Régions Françaises*, figs 3, 17, 33, 34 and 35
La Documentation Française, figs 15, 26 and 60
OREAM Nord, fig. 71

Preface

Geographers in postwar Britain have found fresh professional outlets in urban and regional planning. Applied geography has grown as a result, to serve the needs of society, economy and polity, and through the feedback from such commitment to contribute in its turn to the teaching of the discipline. With such an applied experience in mind this book looks critically at the distinctively different world of postwar planning in France. Both France and Britain are currently passing through difficult and politically sensitive years, following postwar rehabilitation and a long phase of rapid economic growth. The time may thus be particularly ripe for a stock-taking and evaluation of resources and prospects, and the contribution which planning in all its forms has made and continues to make to the transformation of postwar France. Geography too has been changing and any regional writing must seek an accommodation between older and newer traditions, just as planning flatters to deceive unless it takes fully into account the subtle but elusive continuity of character and heritage in people and place.

In acknowledging the profound debt which British geographers owe to generations of their French colleagues this book seeks to interpret the contemporary state of France through the perspectives of a British applied geographer. In so doing the hope is to strengthen the geographer's role and potential in planning in France, whilst not forgetting that the ultimate purpose of any regional study is to serve the educational needs of all. Tribute is due and gratefully extended to those who have aided this work, over several years: to the cartographers, John Knipe, Olive Teasdale and Eric Quenet, at Newcastle; Penny Timms, Ursula Miles and Margaret Loveless at Oxford; to the secretaries, Jane Potts at Newcastle and Dinah Wood-Mallock at Oxford. I particularly wish to acknowledge the outstanding contribution by Dinah, as both research assistant and secretary, especially over the last critical stages.

University of Oxford   *J. W. House*
July 1977

Part one

---

*Environment and man:
the regional setting*

1 Regional geography: changing perspectives

To write of regional geography nowadays may call for courage; to write of France, the traditional home of the art, doubly so. To write of France, not being a Frenchman, adds to the risks, not least since other Englishmen have charted the course in recent years (Scargill 1968; Thompson 1970; Clout 1972). To write of France as an entity, a nation state yet member of the EEC, is less likely to be controversial, least of all as seen from within that country. To interpret France to the English, European nearest neighbours, is a rewarding, testing but never-ending task.

The objectives of regional study have been variously defined through time, with widely differing purpose, selectivity and emphasis. The list of ingredients is less open to question, though shortened on the environmental side and greatly expanded through statistics and systems in contemporary studies. A fresh regional interpretation should clarify its objectives, state priorities, justify the coverage and logical sequence; and be placed in the context of other contributions, both past and present.

The most characteristic purpose of regional geography has become that of coherent, concise presentation of essential information, spiced with an individual interpretation, and blended for distinctive levels in the educational system. Therein lies its justification but also the built-in weakness which has led many to preach the decadence of the art. As a disciplined and explanatory overview of nation, region, area and place, of location, environment, people and other resources, the regional perspective makes a unique contribution to the prime geographical task — 'to make sense out of the globe'. Yet to do so comprehensively risks the tedium and seeming sterility of endless evidence, of catalogue and classification, of fact piled upon fact, of arid generalization and regionalization. No amount of literary interpretation, cartography or case study can wholly offset these risks, as already every student may have learnt to his cost. The elegance of statistical précis may play its part but more than card index or calibration are involved in the search for a full and sensitive understanding of space and place.

Significance and scale are keynotes in a simplified and ordered regional interpretation. In traditional work tests for significance are applied through the evaluation, priority ordering and study of relationships between a range of factors, from those directly environmental to those historical, economic, social or political. From such an assessment the major themes of the interpretation emerge systematically. Following upon or in parallel with this stage a regionalizing synthesis regroups the evidence by significant spatial units, with many types of region for many differing purposes. Just as it is impossible to discern an elegant and universally ordered symmetry in human affairs expressed spatially, so too is the search for universal geographical regions doomed to disappointment. Yet convenience and common sense in regional analysis yield practical results, though often stopping short of final solutions to problems or proofs for policies. For this reason interpretation is necessarily many-sided and neither total nor ever complete. New evidence may constantly be brought to light, old evidence reworked and rethought. Measurement becomes more precise, the models more elegant, the techniques more sophisticated, but as in planning so in regional geography there is no end, rather the prospect of a rolling review, monitoring and reinterpretation.

Significance requires selectivity, and scale conditions the range of evidence used and the level of generalization attempted. First steps in regional geography start with single or predominant factor explanations, a tendency to seek physical causes for distributions of people, resources or settlement whenever and wherever possible. There is also an inclination to study either very small or very large areas, but at both extremes to derive generalizations broad, even diffuse, in character. With greater sophistication the range of evidence widens alarmingly, the dangers of an information explosion loom increasingly large. Faced with such a situation there are alternative ways forward: on the one hand by the more intuitive search for regional personality, on the other through the systems approach with statistical tests for significance, scale and linkages. In each case the range and types of region defined and used are apt to be distinctive, and indeed the purposes of regional study are likely to be divergent.

The classical French school of regional geographers sought to identify the collective traits of regional personality. Though disciplined in its analysis and synthesis, such a perspective relates rather to that of the regional novelist or the landscape painter. It has traditionally been a less technical view, less statistical, less comprehensive and focused primarily upon natural units as regions. Within these, the subtle interacting relationship between man and his environment is interpreted with a measure of subjective judgement. The time scale of such studies is conventionally longer, perhaps spanning many centuries, and there is emphasis on enduring qualities and less on the dynamics of economic and social change. Ironically perhaps this type of regional study has passed out of fashion among professional geographers at the very time when there is widespread and growing public concern for the environment and its resources; when mass tourism is creating greater interest in the topography and history of overseas countries; and when there is rising sensitivity to the cultural heritage imprinted on landscape and townscape.

The alternative view, more fashionable nowadays, highlights economic, social and perhaps even political change, interpreting such trends over shorter-run but formative periods. The approach is of necessity more heavily statistical and relies upon a loose framework of interrelated data time series, expressed spatially and analysed through a network or hierarchy of regions. These regions may tend to the ephemeral, the theoretical, the abstract, but they are also often units of convenience, for management or administration. Such studies are orientated towards ventilation of problems, concern for policies or for action, and in this work, as in all planning, the geographer joins other specialists. In the past decade indeed the burgeoning growth of regional science, regional planning and regional economics, to name only three fresh disciplines whose vital concern also is with space, has wrested the monopoly of regions from their lifelong guardian, the geographer. Yet during the same period the geographer has himself become more applied in outlook and also more professionally involved directly in the plan process. His objectives, techniques and presentations today thus have much in common with those of other social scientists.

Some might say, and say increasingly, that the preoccupation with short-run trends of economic or social change is not without its debit side when the results of regional interpretation are assessed. Gone is the balanced view of environment, restricted are many of the systematic insights, short indeed is the sense of history, difficult to discern are the enduring themes in the face of what may prove to be ephemeral statistical change.

The stage is thus set and the time may be ripe to attempt a fresh synthesis and perspective through an applied regional geography. The broadly educational purpose will always condition the extent of change from past traditions, but among potential clients today must also be numbered decision-takers and policy-makers, both public and private. Theirs is a course directed to action and important as such, but the wider interests of the general public should not be totally ignored. Both the pure and the applied geographer thus have persisting and vital concern for the regional view and its projection; indissolubly they are bound in, with others, to serve the educational, cultural and practical needs of their times.

REGIONAL GEOGRAPHIES OF FRANCE

The collective inheritance of previous works needs to be assessed, both those from the distant and the more recent past, for in the regional geographies of France this heritage has been incomparably rich and diverse (Thibault 1972). Such an assessment has the benefit of hindsight and, in making it, it must be remembered both that the authors were men of their times, contributing to the development of their subject as it then stood, and also that they wrote of a France different in many ways, in degree or in kind, from that of today. Philosophies evolve, intellectual fashions change, the faces of economy, society or polity have become transformed, but it would be as false to imagine that each succeeding interpretation annulled all that had gone before as it would to attempt to interpret the present with too much dependence on the findings, the lessons or the methods of the past.

Some of the principal differences between interpretations relate to the range of factors reviewed, the extent to which measurement is used rather than descriptive evaluation, the balance between systematic and regional treatment, the place of landscape in the study, or the emphasis laid upon the static picture at a point in time, in contrast to a dynamic perspective on the kaleidoscope of change. In many cases the true worth of the result is greater than the sum of the parts, since regional geography, like the parent subject, is no less a craftsman's art than a science.

Books, monographs and learned journals all help to chart the course. That there has been a French school of regional geography may be confidently asserted for the period from the 1870s until almost the Second World War (Harrison Church 1951; Meynier 1969). In the UK there was no such school during the same period, though isolated works on British regional geography indicated some influence from across the Channel (Mackinder 1908) and, indeed, one of the most masterly texts on the British Isles was by a celebrated French author (Demangeon 1927).

The pioneer works on French regional geography were those by Reclus (1877) and Vidal de la Blache (1903). The wide-ranging perspectives, the structuring around key themes and the encyclopaedic attention to small regions by Reclus matched the magisterial synthesis of regional personality, the sense of history, and the search for the permanent, underlying formative traits of man-environment relationships by Vidal de la Blache. Though interwar France was becoming more industrialized, rural France was slow to change, and these trends were reflected in the regional geographies of the times (Bruhnes 1926; Demangeon 1939, but not published until 1942 and 1946). Bruhnes interpreted the complex interaction between man and habitat through the physical environment to the cultural landscape, supremely the careful observer, recorder and analyst. Demangeon wove economic as well as social themes into a regional geography in which man was both producer and consumer, yet he followed tradition also in a classical focus upon natural and cultural landscapes. Ormsby (1931) drew inspiration from the French masters, adding meticulous subregional interpretation, keyed to the topographical map, to the sense of history in geographical controls and influences.

The regional work of Pierre George (1938, 1964, 1967) links interwar and postwar changes in French economy and society, and their interpretation by geographers. Gone was the attempt to interpret a static situation or to rely upon a long historical, evolutionary perspective. In their place a forward-looking assessment of problems and forces for change, a critical evaluation of strengths and weaknesses: an altogether more appropriate approach to the dynamism of economic, social and political change in postwar France, and an indication of the merits and potential of an applied perspective in geographical work. After 1945 it becomes difficult to perceive a French school of regional geography. Systematic topics are emphasized, the historical perspective is shortened and studies become less literary and more problem-oriented. Furthermore, in France more than in Britain the geographer has lost his near monopoly in the study of space and place (Perroux 1950, Boudeville 1961). The economist's regions are more abstract, ephemeral or administrative, concerned with homogeneity, nodality or polarization. In the study of spatial management policies (Part III) with few exceptions (George 1964, Phlipponneau 1960) it is the economists rather than the geographers in France who have been in the forefront of planning at both the national and regional levels. During the 1970s there has been some harmonization in objectives, methodology, and application between geographers and economists (Cazes and Reynaud 1973, Noin 1976). Prior to that time only the work of Chardonnet (1958–9) had equal acceptance within both disciplines.

The 1960s were a period of high productivity in regional studies on France by French authors (Pinchemel 1964, Le Lannou 1964, Chabot 1966, George 1967) and also by Britons (Scargill 1968, Ardagh 1968, Thompson 1970, Clout 1972). Pinchemel was concerned to interpret the organization of the national space, the origins of the inequalities and differentiation within France; three geographical milieux were postulated: the countryside, the industrial environment and the towns. There was a total lack of

regional chapters and regional character emerges rather from the cumulative review of systematic aspects. In strong contrast, as an act of faith in
traditional regional method, Chabot had not a single systematic chapter.
He extolled the pedagogic merits of regional study, but also the significance
of a rising political and cultural identity at regional level, the proper base
for planning at less than national level. The 8-volume series on the regions
of France (Closon and George 1959–65) carries such a purpose further, but
unfortunately the regions chosen correspond neither with ZEAT nor
planning regions (fig. 4).

The works by English authors share a common preoccupation with the
dramatic changes in social and economic life in postwar France, their
spatial impact and its interpretation. Scargill (1968) has an avowedly
economic approach, through patterns of production and their explanation.
Thompson (1970) has a principal theme in the problems of economic and
social organization, set against the physical background as a variable
resource base. Population is seen as a key indicator of change at both
national and regional levels. The theme of regional disparity and the
planning policies to reduce it introduces an interpretation of each of the 22
planning regions, justified as 'possessing both an internal potential and an
external relationship to the optimum organization' of the national space.
Clout (1972) concentrated upon urban and regional planning measures and
their spatial impact, deliberately eschewing full treatment of the background features of the French economy. None of the three English
authors sums up, and no advice is offered to the regional or the urban
planner.

Two recent works (Cazes and Reynaud 1973, Noin 1976) logically
complete a transformation in regional methodology from the times of
Reclus and La Blache scarcely less dramatic than the evolution of France
herself over the past 100 years. Cazes and Reynaud focus on the dynamics
of short-run economic or social change: its momentum, the fears of change,
the importance of mobility and of modernization. Though regional
interpretation as such is absent it is admitted that nationwide generalizations about France are hard to sustain. Noin's analysis has some affinity
with the regional economists in the treatment of growth poles, development axes and territorial or structural disequilibria. Yet the context of space
is kept firmly geographical and differentiated rather than abstract, but the
emphasis is practical, upon the contribution of the geographer to an
understanding of the dynamic processes underlying spatial management.

THE PRESENT WORK

The purposes are to review resources, both natural and human, identifying both potentials and constraints of development; to analyse the dynamics of change in habitat, economy, society *and* polity, emphasizing the past three formative decades; to assess the spatial impact and implications of these changes within the context of policies and their achievements; and to interpret the balance of forces for further change in the light of national and regional circumstances, and policies and plans active in the public and private sectors.

Three additional purposes will be borne in mind: to seek to harmonize traditional with newer perspectives in geographical thought within a specifically regional context; to interpret contemporary France through an applied perspective, related to planning in all its forms; to compare when relevant the British and French problems of today, and the experience and achievements of geographers in considering and helping to deal with them (House 1973).

Part one, 'Environment and Man: the regional setting', concerns the role and status of France within Europe and the world, contrasting both short- and long-run perspectives. The interpretation of a changing balance of internal and external forces, of centripetal vying with centrifugal tendencies, contrasts traditional cohesion in France with the manifest diversities and inequalities (ch. 2). The recent growth in disparities indeed underlines the rising strength of regionalism within the unitary nation-state. There follows an analysis of the forces acting upon landscape and resource patterns, arising from economic, social or political change, leading to some assessment of the yield from growth policies (to the end of the VIth Plan 1971–5) and the price to be paid for implementing them. The analysis of natural resources (ch. 3) has a twofold purpose: to draw up a budget of strengths and weaknesses, assets and liabilities for France, stressing resources critical in the development equation. Part I is completed by a closer examination of people and work (ch. 4), in terms of structure, distribution and trends, in order to identify and evaluate growth, stabilization and decline tendencies in particular sectors or individual regions.

Part two covers 'Growth, change and reconversion in the French economy', in the light of public location policies and their spatial impact. A stock-taking is made of the potential and actual growth elements (ch. 1) in the French economy, stressing the role of communications, energy, growth manufacturing and growth services. The range of public location policies is reviewed (ch. 2) and their content, impact and effectiveness are assessed. Part three is concerned with spatial management policies (ch. 1), their theoretical justification and the way they have been developed and applied. Management of the urban system (ch. 2) is distinguished from management of the regions (ch. 3), though both are fundamentally interrelated themes.

Scale levels of the urban network are seen to have distinctive roles and particular related policies, whilst industrial growth complexes, corridor growth and the problems of smaller towns illustrate innovatory features of French regional planning. Treatment of the planning regions is limited to a comparative evaluation of their regional strategies and, finally, there is consideration of more diffused policies for rural areas and for industrial or mining problem localities.

Part four considers the present state of France and her prospects in the light of political policies and planning intentions, looking with difficulty through the uncertain short-term future to the potentials for 1985 and towards the end of the century.

References

Where no place of publication is given, the work was published in Paris.

Ardagh, J. (1968) *The New France*, Harmondsworth.
Boudeville, J. R. (1961) *Les espaces économiques.*
Bruhnes, J. (1926) 'Géographie humaine de la France', in Hanotaux, G. (ed.) *Histoire de la nation française*, II.
Cazes, G. and Reynaud, A. (1973) *Les mutations récentes de l'économie française.*
Chabot, G. (1966) *Géographie régionale de la France.*
Chardonnet, J. (1958–9) *L'économie française. Etude géographique d'une décadence et des possibilités de redressement*, 2 vols.
Closon, F.-L. and George, P. (eds) (1959–65) *France de demain*, 8 vols.
Clout, H. D. (1972) *The Geography of Post-war France*, Oxford.
Demangeon, A. (1927) 'Les Iles Britanniques' (1942, 1946) 'La France économique et humaine', 2 vols in Vidal de la Blache, P. and Gallois, L. (eds) *Géographie universelle.*
George, P. (1938) *Géographie économique et sociale de la France*, (2nd edn 1946).
    (1964) *La géographie active.*
    (1967) *La France.*
Harrison Church, R. J. (1951) 'The French school of geography' in Taylor, G. (ed.) *Geography in the Twentieth Century*, London: 70–90.
House, J. W. (1973) 'Geographers, decision-takers, and policy-makers' in Chisholm, M. and Rodgers, H. B. (eds) *Studies in Human Geography*, London: 272–305.
Le Lannou, M. (1964) *Les régions géographiques de la France*, 2 vols.
Mackinder, H. J. (1908) *Britain and the British Seas*, Oxford.
Meynier, A. (1969) *Histoire de la pensée géographique en France.*
Noin, D. (1976) *L'espace français.*
Ormsby, H. (1931) *France. A Regional and Economic Geography*, London.
Perroux, F. (1950) 'Economic space: theory and applications', *Q. J. Econ.*, LXIV: 89–104.

Phlipponneau, M. (1960) *Géographie et action. Introduction à la géographie appliquée.*

Pinchemel, P. (1964) *Géographie de la France*, 2 vols.

Reclus, E. (1877) 'La terre et les hommes', *Nouvelle Géographie Universelle.*

Scargill, D. I. (1968) *Economic Geography of France*, London.

Thibault, A. (1972) 'L'analyse des espaces régionaux en France depuis le début du siècle', *Annls Géogr.*, 8, (444): 129–70.

Thompson, I. B. (1970) *Modern France. A social and economic geography*, London.

Vidal de la Blache P. (1903) 'Tableau de la géographie de la France', in Lavisse, P. (ed.) *Histoire de la France*, I.

2 State, nation and region

There is general agreement among recent geographical writers, both French and British, that France has experienced remarkable economic and social development during post-war years. To some, demographic revival lies at the heart of the matter; to others, the breakthrough from 'living in a closed circuit' (President Pompidou) to full participation in the European and international market economy provided the engine for growth. The sophisticated mechanisms of national sector planning, regional planning and urbanization policies have also undoubtedly played a leading role in stimulating change, applied through what is by long tradition a remarkably centralized national administration.

Most interpretations by geographers consider the impact of change upon basic resource patterns and structures, upon the interaction of production and exchange in the economic planning regions. Economists and planners lay greater emphasis upon process, upon time series of change, upon the variable mix of policies or management objectives and achievements, in both the public and the private sectors. All writers agree that change has been substantial and structural, with an occasional reference to an 'economic miracle' (Part II, Introduction), but there is divergence among the interpreters as to the extent to which traditional life styles in town, countryside or region have really been fundamentally altered. The long-run economic and social characteristics of the regional geography of France provide a back-cloth against which to measure and put these changes into context. Certainly such change cannot be assessed merely at its surface statistical values and not all planning measures, however impressive their mechanisms, have realized their intended achievements. Indeed, change has at times been fitful, uneven in its incidence, spatially or sectorally, productive of tensions and dislocations as well as of dramatic growths and transformations in habitat, economy, society or polity. Nor has change yet run its full course. If 1958 and 1968 indicated marked shifts in direction and tempo in French national life, it is equally certain that the future will give rise to its own unpredictabilities. In their report to the French government shortly before the 1973 General Election, the Hudson Institute forecast a further dramatic realization of French resource potential, with emphasis on the major assets represented by a youthful and growing population, ample reserves of land, under-utilized natural resources, and a markedly favourable location in relation to Europe and its adjacent seas. To this may be added the confident prediction by President Pompidou in 1972 that from a position fifty per cent below the industrial production of W. Germany (BRD) France was in a position to achieve parity within ten years.

During the 1970s the tempo of economic expansion in France slackened abruptly, partly but not exclusively due to the oil crisis of 1973–5. Demographic growth rates also began to decline, but it is still too early to assess if the check to confident growth is likely to be only temporary or perhaps more permanent in character, requiring further adjustment in economy and society. Contemporary with such enforced changes there has been a transformation in the planning approach to growth itself. Under the VIIth Plan (1976–80) the accent is less upon growth for its own merits, but rather in its significance for redistributive social justice, including justice for regions as well as for deprived social classes. The Giscardian image of a future France (Part IV) is one harking back to older cultural virtues, firmly set against large-scale developments, and with highest priority for improvement in the quality of life and for greater democratic participation in decision-taking.

During the post-war period France, like the UK, has had to make an agonizing reappraisal of her world, European and national roles, a task of structural readjustment which for both countries still has some way to go. In interpreting the spatial outcomes in resource distributions, regional characteristics, population and work patterns, the regional geographer must have regard to the spectrum of forces at work, the balance between external and internal influences bearing upon French policies and the course of development and change. He must also put short-run changes firmly into the longer time perspective and review the change at all the significant scale levels, namely those of the world, the French community, Europe and the nation state itself. As in Britain, the great issues for post-war France have been concerned with: adjustment to a post-imperial role, which still carries important responsibilities for some of what were once dependent territories; redefinition of a national identity within the embryonic conception of a supra-national EEC; the pursuit of national policies in a world of change, in which nation states have at times seemed powerless in the face of world economic forces; and the security of the West and its constituent nation states in world power politics. That world events and outside influences have pressed in so strongly upon France has not prevented, and indeed has contributed in some measure to, the rapidity and scale of change within the network of her cities and regions, and the extent of inequalities and differences in her already diverse economic and social fabric.

The long-run perspective

Vidal de la Blache (1903) and Demangeon (1942) both interpreted the context of France within her European setting, balancing the influences, the importations and the exchanges from the Mediterranean world through history with those emanating from the European continent and, for Demangeon, also from the Atlantic face of France. For Vidal the questions concerned how, when and along which channels there was diffusion of ways of life throughout France, to interact with the diversity of adjacent areas; for Demangeon the focus was rather upon the paradoxical interpretation of France as one of the least isolated, geographically least closed of European states, yet one which had by tradition the most independent national consciousness and autarchic tendencies. Both authors ranged widely in their search for the enduring realities behind the implantation and growth of a distinctive civilization in France.

France and the Mediterranean. There has been a complete revaluation, even reversal of relationships, through history between France and the Mediterranean lands. From the Mediterranean came the early contacts with graeco-roman civilization, the colonization of Roman Gaul, the diffusion into the celtic lands of agrarian practices including cultivation of the olive and the vine, the siting of towns along the trading axes radiating from the Midi to the eastern Bassin Parisien, the Rhine, the North Sea shores, and even the Danube. The influences upon forms of production, ways of life, trading exchanges and administration were subtle, widespread and lasting. The impact was most marked in the coastal lands of Languedoc and Provence, limited inland by the highlands of the Cévennes and the Alpes. The Rhône-Saône corridor then as now offered the major routeway northwards, an axis of trade along which there developed the great commercial cities of Marseille and Lyon. The subsidiary coastal axis linking Catalonia in Spain to Lombardy in Northern Italy did not, and still does not, offer the same prospect for exchanging complementary products.

During the Middle Ages French trading spread throughout the Mediterranean, to the commercial cities of Venice, Genoa and Naples, the Levant States, and even beyond to India. The French kingdom was in course of consolidation, the incorporation of Provence in 1481 completing possession of the coastlands of the Midi (with the exception of Roussillon), whilst closer political contacts with Italy stimulated the fruitful introduction into France of artists, workers and entrepreneurs. Lyon developed into a major textile centre and commercial town, nodally situated on the Rhône-Saône and at a focus of routeways through the Alps from Piedmont and Lombardy. Many small, specialized industrial towns were implanted throughout southern France. The trading role of the Mediterranean face of France persisted through the seventeenth and eighteenth centuries, with a developing interchange of the products of French industry, particularly silks and, later, cotton textiles, for bulk imports from the Mediterranean or tropical products from the overseas possessions of France in India, the West Indies or along the West African coast.

By the end of the Napoleonic period the French empire overseas had been reduced to fragments, but during the nineteenth century it was reestablished on a vastly expanded scale (1814: 7000 km², 1 million popn; 1914: 10 million km², 50 million popn), throughout West and Central Africa and in Indo-China. The momentum started with the occupation of bases on the Algerian coast in 1830, followed by penetration inland during the mid-century; the seizure of Saigon (Indo-China) in 1859 and the establishment of Brazza (Gabon) in 1875. During the colonial scramble for Africa in the last decades of the nineteenth century, France established a major equatorial and savanna lands empire, linked to her colonial expansion throughout the North African Maghreb, from Morocco to Tunisia, by the seizure and pacification of the Sahara and northern savanna lands (1900–14).

Mediterranean France directly profited from close and steadily growing trading with the Maghreb states and, after the opening of the Suez Canal (1869), Marseille also enjoyed some positional advantage in direct seaborne trade with the French possessions in India and SE Asia. This overseas trading vocation with the French empire was at once a cause of major stimulus to the economy and cities of the Midi, but equally became a reason for its dramatic vulnerability in the decolonizing era after 1945. The striking asset of an intermediate position between France and her major overseas possessions had then to be reinterpreted in the light of a peripheral position within France when her economic destiny was seen to lie more within continental Europe.

The Atlantic and North Sea. The Atlantic and North Sea vocations of France have seen less dramatic changes through history. Western France had early been peopled partly by northward movements from Iberia and there has also been an intermittent diffusion of ideas and practices across the Pyrénées, including the arts of copper working, the introduction to France of the cider apple, and, during the Spanish colonial period, of maize and the potato (Demangeon 1942). A close affinity has remained between Aquitaine and northern Spain, but it is an orientation towards the world oceans that has been, and still remains, paramount for the Atlantic face. Like those of Mediterranean France, the fortunes of coastal provinces in the Ouest have been bound up with the course of overseas expansion in trading. It was rather to the New World possessions of France that trade from Bordeaux, Rouen or Nantes was turned. By the early sixteenth century Breton fishermen were exploiting the Grand Banks off Newfoundland, and until the loss of French Canada (1763) there was a classical mercantilist trade with the mother country. The sugar and cotton trade from the Antilles, and the trade in slaves to the West Indies, were important for the coastal cities, together with French exports of textile goods and industrial products, a trade also carried on with the Spanish and Portuguese possessions.

Rivalry with Britain was a perennial theme, both for influence in Europe and in overseas expansion, a clash involving naval aspirations to dominate the oceans and commercial policies to exploit the ocean sea-lanes. Britain had possessions in France throughout the Middle Ages, in Guyenne, and later in Poitou, Périgord and in the northern cities of Calais and Cherbourg. For some two hundred years the wine trade of Bordeaux was orientated to the English market. Yet the influence of Britain on French life, or on the regional geography of that country, was remarkably limited for many centuries. It was not until the diffusion of scientific farming and factory organization in industry, both from the late eighteenth century onwards, that British influence began to change the cultural landscape of France. Even then the effects were localized, with the impact on farming strongest in the northern Bassin Parisien, and that on mechanization of industry at its most apparent in the Nord, Lorraine, Rouen and to a lesser extent in Calais, the locations of heavy metallurgical and factory-based textile industries. During the twentieth century traditional rivalries and antagonisms across the Channel have given place to mutual support and cooperation in two world wars, though without a very close *rapprochement* being sustained.

The Atlantic vocation of France today is that of world trading, but apart from the rising inflow of foodstuffs, fuels and industrial raw materials, compensated for only partly by return flows of manufactured goods, it is of lesser importance for her economic destiny than the orientation towards the European continent, within which she occupies a strategically-placed western peninsula.

France and Continental Europe. The interaction between France and continental Europe has always been more complex and, to this day, more difficult to evaluate. Vidal interpreted Europe as the open frontier of France, the source of countless human migrations channelled by the few natural routeways: along the drier loess-covered southern border of the North European Plain, along the coastal plain from Flanders, up the Meuse and Moselle and across the few passes through the Vosges. The peopling of France was achieved largely along these routes, her ethnic characteristics early established. In reality there were constant two-way fluctuations and interchanges, crystallizing out in the frontier zone between Frank and Teuton. Political reality was given to this borderland as early as the division of the Kingdom of Charlemagne (843 AD), with the creation of the buffer Kingdom of Lotharingia (Burgundy), including a broad belt of the eastern Bassin Parisien, Burgundy and Provence.

Demangeon (1942) interpreted differently the influences from the north through Flanders and those from the east across the Rhine. As one of the so-called 'natural limits' of France the Rhine has often been looked on as a barrier, a defensive line, but through history it has been, and continues to be, the main north-south routeway through Europe. Across the Rhine into France came the waves of settlers who brought the kind of agricultural production, settlement and land-holding practices so formative in the creation of rural landscapes through the eastern Bassin Parisien. Throughout the Middle Ages the close contacts between France and the trading cities of the Rhinelands and South Germany diminished the national contrasts in the disputed borderlands, but political instability was endemic until the mid-twentieth century. From Germany, during the Middle Ages, mining techniques were introduced into the Vosges, metal-working and porcelain manufacture were established but, as in the case of economic diffusion from Britain, it was from the eighteenth century that the major impact was seen. Though Germany experienced the late-eighteenth century industrial revolution rather later than Britain, her industrial areas were more closely in touch with adjacent areas in France and had a greater influence as a result, upon both agriculture and industry. The impact would no doubt have been even greater but for political claims and counter-claims to Alsace-Lorraine, though to some degree the sovereign transfers of these territories in 1871 and 1914 reflected major contributions by both France and Germany to their economic development.

Diffusions from Germany (Prussia) into France during the nineteenth century included technologies and products from the chemical industries, particularly dyestuffs and fertilizers, and machinery manufacture of many types. This traditional relationship between a less and a more industrialized economy has been strikingly strengthened since 1958, with the emergence of W. Germany (the BRD) as the dominant industrial partner in the EEC. The economic interaction between France and Germany for more than a century, particularly in northward flows of iron ore and semi-finished steel, lay until recently at the base of the close integration between the French border industrial regions of the Nord, Lorraine and Alsace and their nearest neighbours of the Saar, the Rhine-Main and Ruhr industrial nodes in Germany.

Economic relationships between Northern France and adjacent Belgian Flanders have also been traditionally strong and were early established. Mediaeval Flanders was perhaps the most urbanized sub-region of Europe at that time, with a close pattern of trading cities engaged in commerce, woollen manufactures and metal-working. To supply the food needs of these cities the practice of intensive farming was early essential throughout the Low Countries. The metal industries became specialized in Belgium, with arms manufacture a distinctive trait. The diffusions into France were threefold: first, the spread of the pattern of industrial towns into the Nord-Pas-de-Calais and Picardie; secondly, the introduction of intensive farming in the coastal lowlands, including flax for linen, the essential practice of fertilization, and the growing of sugar beet and vegetables; and, thirdly, the transplanting of specialized metal manufactures to individual French towns, for example armaments manufacture to St Etienne.

The long perspective on external influences shows that France was in a position to benefit, and for many centuries did benefit, from her cumulative relationships with the Mediterranean lands, the Atlantic and North Sea countries and Central Europe, and that she made a distinctive contribution to each in her turn. The exchanges and diffusions were neither wholly one-way nor unchanging through time. As the balance of forces changed, resources were revalued and different policies were implemented from within and from without France. There is no fatal or deterministic logic behind all this and George (1967) expressly made the point that French culture and civilization, and indeed the entire course of French history, represent an achievement in which geography as such may have had no clearly or simply discernible role. Nevertheless, the nodal location of France within Europe endowed her with great strategic potential and equipped her to receive, assimilate, and in her turn diffuse the main currents of European economic, social and political exchanges. In so doing the characteristics of French society, economy and the nation state were both created from within, and influenced from without, with an early and persistent identity as for many centuries the leading nation within Europe.

Table 1   Selected economic indicators. France, 1876–1974

	1876†	1909†	1935	1974
Population (million)	36.9	39.2	41.9	52.6[2]
Paris (city)	2.2	2.7	2.8	2.2
Ile-de-France	4.1[1]	5.3	6.7	9.8
Marseille	0.3	0.5	0.9	1.0
foreign-born	0.8	1.4	2.4	3.0
Wheat (million quintals)	71.3	86.1	98.0	191.4
(qu. per ha.)	10.5	13.1	19.4	46.1
Wine (million hectolitres)	36.0	54.6	68.3	52.8
(million ha.)	2.0	1.6	1.4	1.1
Iron ore (million tonnes)	2.3	10.0	33.1	54.2
Coal (,, ,,)	19.0	36.3	46.5	25.7
Steel (,, ,,)	1.4	2.3	7.8	27.0
Railways (1000 km)	23.4	40.0	41.7	34.8
Rivers (navigable) and canals (1000 km)	10.4	11.3	9.6	7.0
Imports (1000 million frs)	5.9	5.6	46.3	250.1
Exports (,, ,, ,,)	4.7	5.0	31.2	217.1
unadjusted for prices				
No. of communes with > 100,000 popn		13	17	39[2]

† excluding Alsace-Lorraine
[1] 1891
[2] 1975
Source: Annuaires Statistiques

The balance between centrifugal and centripetal forces within France during this process is touched upon later, but suffice it to say that an economically strong, highly centralized nation state was fashioned in France already by the seventeenth century. This nation had been created and progressively strengthened from a rich diversity of natural endowment, a selective and somewhat retarded development of a wide range of natural resources, and a variety of regionalist aspirations. The centralizing tradition in government had its origins as far back as the eleventh century, but it was most powerfully expressed in lasting form during and after the Napoleonic period. Counterbalancing in some measure her relative loss of economic status within nineteenth century Europe, France assumed a major imperial role overseas. The trauma of two world wars, the major shifts of economic as well as political power within Europe in the twentieth century and the dissolution of her overseas empire since 1945, have enforced a fundamental revaluation of her position and prospects. It is, however, in relation to the long perspective of history and the enduring traits of regional geography, that more recent and short-run policies and achievements must be judged.

Post-1945. The age of planning

In some respects the scale and urgency of problems facing successive post-war governments in France have been similar to those faced in Britain: the need to recover from the ravages of war, to re-equip, modernize, and diversify the economy; to achieve greater balance between the regions and to sustain national economic growth in the longer term without unacceptable levels of inflation or dislocation; to adjust to a changed and initially to a diminished world trading status, and to reorientate political as well as economic policies to the realities of a post-imperial era. Additionally, both countries sought to promote full employment and social justice at home and were open and active in aid policies for the developing world, particularly in those areas for which they had earlier had a colonial responsibility. Both were foundation partners in the defence of the West, though in this as in other matters France came in time to play a more independent national role.

Yet there were major differences in the basic geographical situations and the fundamental resource problems of the two countries, as also in the prescriptions and policies adopted and the priorities accorded. Post-war France had to achieve economic recovery from a narrower resource base more effectively dislocated, in greater need of modernization, and with widespread and enduring rural and agrarian traits. Her population numbers increased dramatically in the decades after 1945, creating their own special urgencies, which led to prescriptions for massive urbanization and industrialization to provide the necessary economic growth momentum, the range and diversity of jobs, and yet also a much-needed improvement in the quality of the living environment. A sophisticated system of national sector planning was set up, which later came to have an increasingly important spatial dimension.

In Britain post-war reconstruction (House 1977) was concerned mainly with industrial reconversion, from declining to growth industries, and the need to set to rights the unfavourable industrial revolution legacy in landscape and townscape. Population grew but at a slower rate than in France and migration flows were from the less prosperous to the more affluent regions, rather than from the countryside to the towns. There was already a well-developed, even in some places an over-expanded, urban hierarchy. Policies for the redistribution of the industrial population included those to decongest the great city clusters by the planning of New and expanded towns. The promotion of regional economic balance developed from pre-war policies of economic 'first-aid' to distressed areas, and the need to reduce the rate of growth in the Midlands and the South East. Planning was, however, much more strongly land use in character and, when compared with French practice, was less preoccupied with the comprehensive management of space through manipulation of the urban system, or by resource allocations of public services among the regions.

Four phases may be distinguished in postwar planning in France, broadly corresponding with successive plans, but also taking into account the changing political equilibrium at home and abroad: 1947–57 Ist and IInd Plans; 1958–70 IIIrd, IVth and Vth Plans; 1971–5 the VIth Plan; and 1976–80, the VIIth Plan.

Ist and IInd Plans (1947–57). Between 1947 and 1957 the major problems facing France related to starting up production after wartime destruction, during which two million buildings had been destroyed or damaged, the railway system had been dislocated over wide areas, and some 12,000 bridges had been blown up. Priority was given to six basic sectors: coal mining, electricity production, steel, transport, agricultural machinery and cement. During the Ist Plan (1947–53) industrial production rose seventy-one per cent, that of agriculture twenty-one per cent, and there was a thirty per cent rise in the standard of living. The IInd Plan (1954–7) was more comprehensive, extending to all sectors of production and also including housing targets. It covered a more difficult economic and political period, in which there was economic recession following the Korean war, the granting of independence to Tunisia and Morocco (both in 1956), the withdrawal of the French expeditionary force from Indo-China in the same year, and a new balance to be struck with the rise of political and economic power in the BRD. In 1956, for example, France and Germany signed a twenty-five year agreement to supply coal from the Warndt mines (Saarland) to France. The IInd Plan was more strikingly 'indicative', flexible and non-compulsory, characterized by a sharp acceleration in production, but also greater emphasis on productivity. The rapidity of growth produced its own problems, increasing the imbalance between regions and among sectors of production. Chardonnet (1958–9) underlined the continuing weaknesses illustrated by French foreign trade: a lag in exports when compared with the growth rate of total production; a marked tendency to export goods in semi-finished state, e.g. steel ingots, textile materials or intermediate manufactures; a deficit in overseas trade and an excessive concentration on trade with the franc zone (24 per cent French imports by value, 35 per cent exports, 1957). Certainly France experienced many physical scarcities, including solid fuels, heavy non-ferrous metals, non-temperate foodstuffs, textile raw materials, but in significant measure her trade problem arose from her own industrial shortcomings.

IIIrd Plan (1958–61). 1958 was a momentous year for France, both politically and economically. It was the year of the signing of the Treaty of Rome inaugurating the EEC, the year in which General de Gaulle returned to power and the Fifth Republic was created. It was also the occasion for the establishment of the post-imperial French Community, comprising former colonial possessions overseas, and furthermore the first year of the Third Economic Plan. France urgently needed to restore balance, both sectorally and regionally, within her economy, to reorientate her production and trade to face the challenge and the opportunities to be offered by the EEC, and not least to pave the way for full employment of the large young generation about to reach working age. The period of the Third Plan was a troubled one, with devaluation and sharp fluctuations in economic growth rates and a very unsettled situation in Algeria.

IVth Plan (1962–5). The IVth Plan covered years of remarkable changes in France. In 1962 Algeria became independent following upon the Evian Agreements, which led to the massive and rapid repatriation of one million Frenchmen. This added substantially to capital and labour in the mother country, especially in the Midi, and helped to fuel a phase of rapid economic growth (24 per cent target over four years). Relations with other former French states of the Maghreb were unsettled by land nationalization or expropriation, whilst elsewhere in Africa France was drawn into military intervention in Gabon (1964) and to a diplomatic break with Guinea (1965). France had withdrawn her Mediterranean fleet from NATO in 1960 and withdrew entirely from that organization in 1966. Yet during the same period of the early 1960s trading treaties were concluded by France with: several states of the Socialist World; Latin America; and countries in the Middle East. In Europe France opposed British entry to the EEC (1963), and struck out along firm nationalist lines in her dealings with fellow member states of the EEC of the Six.

At home, under the IVth Plan, France moved both towards a fuller market economy, with in-depth market surveys of every sector of production, and also towards greater social justice. The Plan sought to promote equality and had measures in favour of low wage earners, students, old people and large families, for example. The priority given to promoting exports followed traditional British practice, in attempts to profit from the liberalization of international trade and also, a politically desirable objective, to stimulate more trade with the Third World.

Infrastructure improvement was emphasized strongly, and included remedial policies for housing, the creation of more hospitals, schools, roads and utilities. This basic regard for a better living environment led to proposals for more effective and interrelated town and country planning and a policy of reducing the growing imbalance and disparity between the regions of France. Expansion was to be encouraged by government action in the great agrarian realm of the Ouest, diversifying its economy by urbanization and the introduction of industries. In the older industrial regions of the Nord and Lorraine reconversion operations were intensified, to change the industrial structure by introduction of new growth elements, and through the retraining of manpower redundant from declining coalmining, textiles and heavy metal industries.

Vth Plan (1966–70). The Vth Plan covered a further stage of movement towards a mass consumption society, with a strong emphasis upon a fairer distribution of the benefits of expansion and a gradual elimination of existing inequalities as between the classes of society, town and countryside, and among the regions. It spanned a period of political ferment at home and abroad. Within the French Community relations deteriorated, with the Congo, the Central African Republic, and also with Algeria; during the years 1968–72 there was continuing French military intervention in Chad. The EEC moved through stages of tariff reduction and closer economic cooperation, but there continued to be clear reservations by France to defend her national interests; in particular the introduction of the Common Agricultural Policy (CAP) was delayed for two years. Within France the political and social upheavals of 1968 had been traumatic and there was a rising current of political and cultural regionalism, focused by the protests in Lorraine (1969) and Brittany (1966–8). These arose from a sense of deprivation, as well as of cultural identity, but also included the fears of a centralizing bureaucracy in Paris, plus the uncertainties for peripheral regions within the EEC. Regional reforms were canvassed during 1968 but narrowly rejected at the time of the referendum in that year, almost certainly because reform of the Senate complicated the issue.

The Vth Plan sought to improve living conditions, with heavy expenditure on schools, hospitals and communications; a rise of one-third in investment in new-housing programmes, and a differentially high increase in farm incomes. Its geographical outcome was striking. The setting up of the SAFER (*sociétés d'aménagement foncier et d'établissement rural*) gave impetus to agricultural restructuring as part of a wide-ranging farm modernization programme. The balance of the rural economy was to be improved by afforestation of underutilized or poor-grade land and by diversification of the economy through the implanting of manufacturing or service activities. Policies were developed for safeguarding and bettering the environment, including the establishment of national (since 1960) and regional parks, the fight against pollution (Ministry of the Environment created 1971, changed to Quality of Life 1974), and a comprehensive management programme defining priorities in the use of water resources. Controls were introduced to combat land speculation but they were variously effective (pp. 77–8).

In promoting regional balance the Vth Plan was far-reaching in its implications. The Paris region was to be remodelled by creating new 'cities in the suburbs' in the outlying areas but industrial location measures, later extended to include service industries, aimed to decentralize further economic growth to less privileged regions and in particular to eight counterbalancing metropoli (*métropoles d'équilibre*) which were to act as major growth poles within a more balanced urban hierarchy. Growth policies for problem areas such as the Nord, Lorraine and the Vosges were intensified. These regions were undergoing industrial reconversion operations to graft growth employment on to localities of declining mining or industrial activity. For the first time tourism was identified as a major growth prospect and large-scale programmes for tourist investment were promulgated for Languedoc and the Aquitaine coastlands. The joint public-private development company concept was also introduced into schemes for regional agricultural and hydraulic development in: the lower Rhône-Languedoc; Gascogne; wastelands of the Est (*friches*); Auvergne and the Limousin.

VIth Plan (1971–5). With the inauguration of the VIth Plan the objectives for France were changed. Now firmly a member of an EEC showing all the indications of fast and coherent growth, the major preoccupation for French planners became that of increasing the competitiveness of national firms and industries, opening the economy to a foreign trade increasingly dominated by her European partners, and focusing orderly growth upon a major industrialization programme. Hand in hand with such a policy went a commitment to social progress and to the increase in opportunities for all sections of society. Social priorities were not to be sacrificed to the needs of economic progress, where these may have been in conflict. The greater preoccupation with Europe should not disguise some continuing deterioration in relationships with former colonial territories. Only six of the original member states of the 1958 French Community continue in membership, with Community participation agreements. Six further states continued to enjoy special relationships with the erstwhile mother country ouside the Community, but of these six Mauritania (1972) and the Malagasy Republic (1973) have since decided to leave the franc zone, the latter decision potentially weakening French naval strategy in the Indian Ocean. On the other hand, the French government during the early 1970s strengthened its overseas links by trade, cultural and scientific agreements with socialist countries and the Third World. It is, however, within the EEC that the immediate economic destiny of France is being worked out, notably within the context of developing economic, industrial, scientific and technical cooperation with the BRD (1973 Agreement).

The VIth Plan laid down twenty-five objectives, which may be regrouped and briefly reviewed geographically. Manufacturing industry was to provide the means for fast economic growth, with at least 250,000 new industrial jobs to be created by 1975. Investment in mechanical engineering, chemicals and electronics was to spearhead industrial expansion, with an objective of replacing imports and enabling France to retain at home a greater part of the value added by manufacture. The introduction of such new growth industries into the regions undergoing industrial restructuring, the Nord and Lorraine in particular, was to be given special emphasis, with approximately one-third of all new jobs created in mechanical engineering, car manufacture and chemicals going to the designated problem areas. The impact of fast growth upon the larger cities and coastal complexes was to be programmed through comprehensive land use strategies and infrastructural provision for the Paris region, Dunkerque, the Basse Seine, the Lyon region and Marseille-Fos.

The securing of adequate energy supplies for the period of the Plan and the maximization in the use of those available on national territory were seen as important priorities. The nuclear power station programme was to be stepped up, massive underground storage for petroleum provided, and the capacity of transmission systems for all types of energy steadily increased. Similarly, better communications were seen to be a further vital priority, to promote growth and to disseminate balance among the cities and the regions. The major targets included: increase in the capacity of the national road network, with the extension of motorways and dual carriageway roads; inter-urban transport schemes; the third Paris airport (Charles de Gaulle-Roissy); the improvement of telephone, telex and data transmission facilities; and completion of the massive port development schemes at Dunkerque, in the Basse Seine and at Marseille-Fos. In both the energy and communications programmes French national needs have to be interpreted and set against those of her EEC partners.

The rural economy continued its transformation under the VIth Plan. It needed protection in some measure against the potential adverse effects of the massive industrialization and urbanization policies. The economically less developed and more isolated rural regions in the Massif Central, the Ouest and Aquitaine were given special priority for new job provision. Meanwhile adjustments to the requirements of the CAP continued, with restructuring of farms and change in the balance of crops and stock production.

The environmental protection programmes of the Vth Plan were greatly expanded and strengthened, with a full water resource and anti-pollution policy in the forefront. Urban development was to be controlled with objectives to: offer freedom of choice in types of dwellings; improve the workplace-residence relationship and the community basis of housing layouts; allow for more green open spaces in urban development; redefine and promote the functional role of small and medium-sized towns (*villes moyennes*); and improve the distribution of urban functions throughout the country. Four New Towns were to be developed in the provinces (Villeneuve d'Ascq at Lille, Le Vaudreuil near Rouen, L'Isle d'Abeau near Lyon and at the Etang de Berre near Marseille), in addition to the five New Towns planned for the Paris region.

Policies for controlled social improvement were also prominent in the VIth Plan: of the 510,000 new homes planned, two-thirds were built and 250,000 housing units were modernized by 1975; a guaranteed minimum wage system (SMIC) was introduced; overall social benefits increased by almost one-half; and priority was given to the underprivileged in the national community.

VIIth Plan (1976–80). The VIIth Plan ushered in a new era. The deep-seated economic depression of the mid-1970s coincided with a deliberate shift in emphasis away from the primacy of economic growth. Though continuing growth was to be fostered as a means of achieving and sustaining full employment and an improvement in the balance of trade, there was to be a more determined attack upon inequalities of all kinds, an overriding emphasis on quality of life and on fuller democratic partici-pation. Though spatial inequalities at regional level were still seen to be important, there was to be greater preoccupation with the broader realms of the underprivileged, still largely agrarian, Ouest and the 'mono-industrial' conversion regions of the Nord, Lorraine and Alsace. The region as a planning level was put under suspended sentence in favour of greater participation by *départements* and *communes*. A similar concern for planning to be at more human scales underlined the attack upon *gigantisme*, the large-scale, impersonalized phenomenon of the large city, the port-industrial complex, monolithic structures in industry. This further turning against the unacceptable face of growth maximization was pointed firmly in the direction of priorities for the provincial smaller towns (*villes moyennes*) and rural settlements, with their agricultural hinterlands (*contrats de pays*, local rural development schemes 1975). Dissemination of growth, the tempering of growth by greater concern for environmental management, and greater concern for the merits of small-scale operations, led to greater devolution of responsibilities, but not of political power, to regional bodies and local authorities. To the 25 priority action programmes of central government were to be added regionally-inspired programmes, funded at least in part from locally-derived revenues.

A review of the successive Plans for French economy and society provides the framework of policies and intentions, the geographical outcome of which is the basis for the interpretations in Part III of this book. Major transformations in region, landscape and townscape have been achieved and others are in train. Increasingly, the EEC dimension has intruded into purely nation-based intentions, not without some conflict of purpose and need for harmonization, even at times for an agonizing reappraisal. As a result of the Plans thus far, France is well-placed to strengthen her role in the EEC, founded upon a massive transformation in the use and redeployment of her resources. It remains, however, true that there are continuing tensions between France and her EEC partners and within France herself. These tensions are often expressed as the result of continuing inequalities, of the uneven incidence of growth and development, even the outcome of antagonisms to change. In any full geographical appraisal the balancing of these constraints and retardations needs to be set against the more dramatic achievements of the Plans themselves. As Ardagh (1968) put it, 'France is in a sense making a leap straight from the late eighteenth into the twentieth century' (p. 24), or 'With each year that passes France can afford less and less the luxury of its remaining built-in weaknesses' (p. 64).

Foreign trade. An indicator of externalities
Fig. 1 shows in diagrammatic form the essentials of the sources, destinations and structure of French foreign trade early in the VIth Plan. France was then, as she had long been, the fourth in rank among trading nations of the world, with approximately five per cent of both world imports and exports. Foreign trade contributed less to GNP (about one-quarter for France) than in the case of the UK (about two-fifths to one half), but by 1973 France had moved far from the description of her foreign trade by Demangeon in the late 1930s as that of 'an agricultural country whose

FRENCH FOREIGN TRADE 1973 in milliard francs

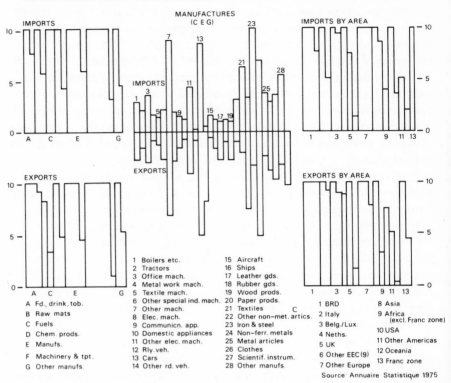

Figure 1   Foreign trade, 1973.

production is slightly lower than her consumption and whose specialized exports include textiles, metal objects and luxury goods'. She has also improved the general structure of her trade, achieved a major reorientation towards Europe and the EEC in particular, and greatly diminished the traditional deficit in visible trade earnings, when compared with the critical findings by Chardonnet (1958–9).

In the structure of her import trade France shows certain similarities with that of the UK for the same year: a strong representation of foodstuffs and raw materials, particularly those from the tropics and sub-tropics; and a major importation of fuels, notably crude petroleum, and by France to a lesser extent natural gas and coal. Differences lie in the greater proportion of manufactured imports into France, particularly those of machinery, machine tools and the products of the light and electrical engineering industries. Among exports France has a markedly different structure from that of the UK. For both countries it is true that manufactured goods are the most important sector, but the composition is altogether different. The most significant category of French manufactured exports is that of cars (21.9 milliard francs worth exported, 11.1 milliard francs imported 1974), but there is a net deficit on almost all trade in engineering products, with the exception of some electrical manufactures. On the other hand, semi-finished iron and steel products figure more strikingly among French exports, whereas for the UK, as for the BRD, engineering products dominate the export trade. A further particular feature of French exports lies in the importance of food and drink, of wheat, wine, fruit and vegetables, one of the major reasons for her strong nationalist interventions in the formation of EEC agricultural and trade-liberalizing policies.

EEC trade. French foreign trade is now increasingly with her EEC partners of the Nine (54 per cent of French exports, 48 per cent of imports by value, 1974) and decreasingly with the countries of the franc zone (1949, 41 per cent French exports, 26 per cent imports; 1974, 9 per cent and 7 per cent respectively). The remainder of Europe, including the socialist states, is France's second most important trading region, but otherwise trading is worldwide but on a limited scale. The net deficit on trading with the USA has been a traditional feature of French overseas trade in postwar years.

French trade with her neighbours in Europe has been analysed in detail by Weigt (1969). He drew attention to the strong and rising trade between contiguous countries in Western Europe, most of which were industrializing with a rapid economic growth momentum. The links between France and West Germany (BRD) were, and continue to be, outstandingly the most important, with strong two-way flows emphasizing the measure of complementarity which the locations, resources, disposition of production and patterns of employment strongly indicate. The BRD is the dominant partner in trading not only with France but with all other states in the original EEC of the Six. Many flows of exports and imports between France and the BRD are almost in balance, but the detailed composition often shows significant differences. French exports of grain, wine and meat, of iron ore, bauxite and sulphur, are of long-standing importance, with only coal and coke among raw materials flowing in the reverse direction. France has traditionally sent semi-finished products to Germany, including for example steel ingots, rolling mill products, woollens or synthetic fibres, and finished textile products. She has received in return machinery imports from the BRD, cars, electrical equipment and machines, chemicals, textile goods and precision manufactures, all the vast and proliferating range appropriate to the exchange between industrial nations, in which the BRD has had markedly the more advanced stage of industrialization until recent times.

Trade with Belgium and Luxemburg (UEBL) is second in importance for France within the EEC. The UEBL is a highly urbanized, industrialized region with an intensive agricultural economy, located nodally at the gateway to the affluent heartland of the EEC. Trading between the two countries is nearly in balance, with intensive complementary flows in each direction: to the UEBL, grain, feeding stuffs, wine and sugar, with vegetables, meat, cattle and tropical products in return; iron ore and wool, with diminishing supplies of coal in return; rolling mill products to UEBL with hot and cold rolled strip and steel scrap returning for French electric arc furnaces. In machinery and equipment France has a slight trade surplus, sending cars, mining and steel-making plant and textile machinery in return for transport equipment, agricultural machinery, machine tools, weapons and dyestuffs.

Italy is third in rank in French trade in the EEC and perhaps surprisingly at first sight it is industrial products which dominate the interchanges. Chemical products and textiles flow in both directions, woollens to Italy, whilst clothing and silks figure prominently in return trade. France sends steel scrap for electric furnaces in northern Italy together with semi-finished iron and steel products, receiving sheet steel for car bodies in return. Car exports to Italy exceed imports and there is a complex and growing two-way trade in machinery (office machinery, refrigerators, washing machines and knitting machinery to France; machine tools, textile and agricultural machinery to Italy). French agricultural exports to northern Italy include animal products, barley and specialized wines; the return flow of fruit and vegetables comes from the Italian south, but is supplemented by maize and rice from Piedmont and Lombardy.

French trade with the UK probably contains the greatest growth potential, to mutual benefit. As recently as 1970 it was small in scale, scarcely more than one-third by value the trade of France with the UEBL, and it is France which had the slight trading deficit in the exchanges. The UK is the main customer for surplus foodstuffs within the EEC and France is potentially the most efficient grower and exporter. Hitherto the Commonwealth has had preferences in the British market, and Denmark too has been a competitor with France for the supply of dairy products. Already France has important wine and grain exports to the UK, followed by butter, cheese and vegetables. There is today little import of coal from Britain and little interchange of iron and steel products. The French and British chemical industries exchange products, starting with the net exports of crude petroleum to Britain from refineries on the Basse Seine;

Table 2 France and the EEC of the Nine. Selected economic indicators 1971

1971	France	UK	BRD	Italy	EEC of the Nine	France as % EEC
Area (1000 sq. km)	551	244	248	301	1,524	36
Population (millions)	51	55	61	53	253	20
Population, density per sq. km	93	228	247	179	217	43
Employment, % agricultural	13.5	2.9	8.2	19.3	13	–
industrial	40.5	46.6	48.6	43.7	44	–
services	46.0	50.5	43.2	37.0	43	–
Wheat harvest (million t.)	12.9	4.2	5.6	9.6	34.7	37
Coal prodn (,, ,,)	33	109	117	0.3	280	12
Petroleum refined (million t.)	110	99	114	123	556	20
Electricity prodn (TWh)	149	248	242	119	857	17
Steel output (million t.)	23	28	45	17	138	17
Motor car output (millions)	2.6	1.7	3.6	1.7	8.4	31
Rail goods traffic (milliard ton km)	70	26	72	18	200	35
Air traffic (milliard passenger km)	13	19	8	8	57	23
Foreign trade (milliard $): imports	18	21	30	15	117	15
exports	17	19	34	13	113	15

Source: CEE Statistiques Générales; Annuaire Statistique (France) 1972

UK exports include the more sophisticated petrochemical products such as terylene and polyethylene, or pharmaceuticals, with a strong return flow of fertilizers and first-stage chemical products. Britain is today a net importer of cars from France, and has been on a rising scale over recent years, with net exports of electrical products and a complex range of machinery and engineering goods. The limited nature of Franco-British trade is perhaps its most dramatic feature and the greatest single prospect for development to the advantage of both countries.

France and the EEC of the Nine

Table 2 shows orders of magnitude in the economic characteristics of France and her three most significant partners in the EEC of the Nine. Fig. 2 shows the spatial pattern of states, the location of conurbations with more than 500,000 population, the planning regions and the areas designated as 'peripheral' for 1975–8, and the major growth zones within the EEC. Both strengths and weaknesses in the situation of France come to light. She has the reserves of space to 'present her planners with some of the exciting challenge of a virgin land' (Ardagh 1968, 184) and her substantial population has a strongly youthful structure, a further reservoir of potential. Her food base is well-established and she could more readily pursue autarchic policies if she chose to do so. Her steel production and most particularly her motor car output are further great sources of continuing economic strength. On the debit side her energy sources on national soil are inadequate, and she has proved to be particularly vulnerable to the risks of political interruption in her supplies of petroleum. She has an employment structure in which the agrarian sector is still substantial, conservative to change in many areas, and she still lags behind in manufacturing employment; service occupations show a ratio above the EEC average but are often poorly organized and with too much inefficient labour. Foreign trade per capita continues to lag behind the EEC average, and the structure of industry still includes a higher ratio of small or medium-sized firms than is the case in, say, the UK or the BRD.

Location potentials. An interpretation of the potential offered and the constraints imposed by geographical location of France within the EEC of the Nine is more difficult to define unambiguously. It is true that she lies in an intermediate peninsular position between the Mediterranean-Iberia, the Atlantic-UK-North Sea, and the Continental European realms. This position has conferred fluctuating but cumulative economic, social, cultural and political benefits in the past (ch. 1), but must be effectively revalued in contemporary terms. France's ability to profit from, indeed to

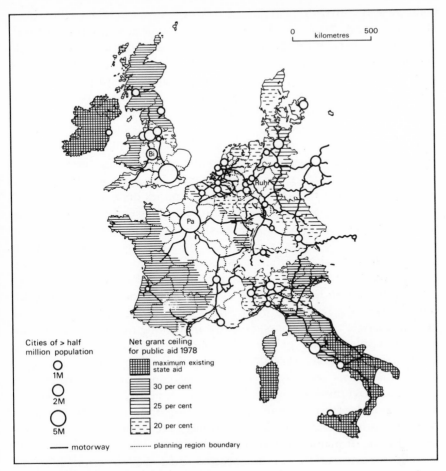

Figure 2   The EEC of the Nine, 1975–78.

capitalize upon, the assets of her position, has always been conditioned by the variable sum of her own strengths, as a nation and state and in more recent times through the vitality of her economy and the resilience of her society. Today France is stronger and more coherent in her role within an EEC which has extended its limits to include the UK, Eire and Denmark. She lies, however, somewhat peripheral to the great economic axes of the European continent: north-south from the mouths of the Rhine-Maas to the Rhine-Main, Switzerland and northern Italy; east-west from Berlin through the Ruhr to the Sambre-Meuse industrial region, Flanders and the Channel coast. Nevertheless France lies sufficiently close to the economic heartland of the EEC for almost half the country to be included within the concept of the growth quadrilateral linking Manchester-Marseille-Milan-Hamburg, and Paris lies at an apex of the inner 'golden triangle', Birmingham-Paris-Ruhr. Furthermore the most intense traffic of world sea-lanes skirts the northern shores of France, linking the North Sea lands with the world oceans. France's basic problem is to maximize her advantages of proximity to the EEC heartland, whilst at the same time increasingly developing the potential which her intermediate position within the European peninsula indicates to be possible.

To develop and implement the necessary policies will be neither simple nor speedy. Fig. 2 shows that some conflict of interest may arise between French national and EEC supranational interests in the process. Management of the French national space implies diffusion of growth to achieve regional balance, working through policies of influencing industrial and services location and the establishment of the eight regional growth metropoli. Paris has a crucial role in the process for it is a part of her growth which must be diffused, at least in the short term. In her EEC context, on the other hand, it is at least logical for Paris and for the more prosperous eastern half of France to attract and concentrate all available economic growth and to link more closely to other growth areas within the 'golden triangle'. It is of course true that in defining the peripheral regions for the supplementing of national policies of regional aid, the EEC Commission (1973) accepted that the reduction of regional inequalities in all member states was also a supranational commitment. Furthermore, individual governments would continue to have the right to determine their regional priorities, but in time the operation of a freer market economy would tend to polarize European life upon the more nodally located areas of major growth potential.

In 1975 (House 1976) four categories were defined for permissible levels of national aid within the EEC. The areas of France receiving industrial development grants (fig. 55) fell within the second priority, to have a ceiling of 30 per cent upon public investment in any regional development programme. The mainly agrarian Ouest and Sud-Ouest were the major potential beneficiaries but, in addition, there were many localities in frontier industrial regions where unfavourable economic structure rather than structure plus inaccessibility was the determinant for scheduling EEC aid.

French hopes for a more balanced use of her national space within EEC strategies must have particular relevance to closer trading with the UK, in which the Channel tunnel would have played a part, and an enhanced European gateway function for the Atlantic and Channel ports of France, to add to the already exciting and economically powerful secondary growth axis of the Rhône-Saône corridor inland from Marseille-Fos.

Fig. 3 shows the extent of participation by each economic planning region in the foreign trade of France by value, classified by origin of imports and destination of exports. The predominant role of Paris in virtually all categories is clearly apparent, but the importance of trans-frontier trade into the EEC from the northern and eastern regions of France is also striking. This is the more intriguing in that the Nord and Lorraine are two of the national problem regions, currently undergoing industrial reconversion programmes. They are peripheral in the sense of an unfavourable economic structure, yet locationally close to the major growth centres of the EEC. The roles of the Nord and Provence-Côte

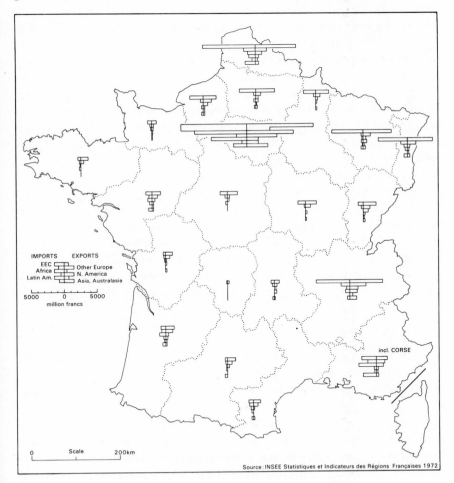

Figure 3   Foreign trade, by economic planning regions, 1971.

d'Azur in bulk imports from most world trading areas contrast with the export surpluses in manufactured goods most marked from the Rhône-Alpes region. The general impression is that much of the foreign trade of France originates and has destinations in the coastal and landward frontier zones, but is overall most strongly represented nodally in the Paris region. The orientation of French foreign trade towards the EEC has strengthened the economic growth prospects of regions to the north, east and south-east of Paris, but has weakened the momentum of the Ouest, Aquitaine and the ports of Provence-Côte d'Azur which have traditionally had closer relationships with overseas territories.

These trans-frontier linkages between adjacent economic regions are much more than simply the effects of closer proximity and rest upon complementarity of products. They are beneficial for those regions which have specialized products, lower costs of production, or a better representation of industrial growth sectors. Disadvantages may set in if the nearest foreign neighbour region is the more prosperous and dynamic, draining people and resources out of the less favoured areas. In France, Alsace and Lorraine have been overshadowed in this way but on balance have gained by diffusion of the benefits of fast growth from Switzerland and South Germany (Regio Basiliensis). The Nord, on the other hand, has greater similarity in structure and prosperity with the adjacent region of Belgium. The regions of the Ouest and Sud-Ouest will not capitalize upon all the advantages inherent in their maritime location until the UK and Iberia respectively are more intimately bound into trading with their nearest neighbour regions in France. The entry of the UK into the EEC (1973) opened up to mutual advantage the potential for trading with ports from Bordeaux to Dunkerque; the prospects for enhanced trading between Aquitaine and the trans-frontier Spanish economic growth-poles of Zaragoza and Pamplona have not yet been adequately realized.

UNITY AND DIVERSITY

Vidal de la Blache (1903) referred to the geographical personality of France as that of 'a medal struck in the effigy of a people', the outcome of a centuries-long evolution and complex interaction between habitat conditions, quality of resources, technology, and policies for social, economic or political development. More recently and more dynamically, but in not dissimilar terms, Boudeville (1968) defined spatial planning as the daily exercise by a community which is determined not to suffer from the fatal logic of geography. Injecting a political comment, Pisani (1969) emphasized that France had become a state before she became a nation, and that in the face of uniquely great and long-established internal diversities, geographical, social, economic and political in character, she has constantly had to preserve in peacetime the national consciousness forged in periods of invasion or conquest. Vidal de la Blache, on the other hand, had seen positive merits in an innate diversity as an essential ingredient of an even stronger national unity.

As important as dramatic economic growth in postwar France have been the dynamic changes in society and in political life, highlighted in the troubles of 1958 and 1968. The tensions then generated have not been entirely submerged and are not likely to be, since some of the ingredients have been deeply geographical, both in their origins and in the spatial outcome. It thus seems appropriate to attempt an interpretation of the contemporary balance of forces, broadly contrasting centripetal with centrifugal forces for change in French economy, society and polity. Clearly not all change may be even indirectly linked to geography and it has certainly been claimed, for example, that class differences in habits, living standards and aspirations within any region of France characteristically outweigh those between the regions. Nevertheless, with regionalism in all its forms a live and growing issue in the French state, the planning of resources within a spatial framework ever more significant, and the role of nationalism in a supranational EEC under continuing and critical scrutiny, an evaluation of the sum total of forces at work is an essential preliminary to considering their effects on space and place. The balance of forces must be interpreted in terms of the extent of diversity, the degree of cohesiveness, the range and effectiveness of public policies in advancing the objectives of the French state, its component groups and sub-groups in society and economy, and the constituent regions and sub-regions of the national territory. In a sense the interpretation is that of the genesis of power, political, administrative, social and economic, its distribution and dynamics, and the spatial impact at national, regional and local levels. Such a budgetary stock-taking contributes to an understanding of post-war change in France but, no less significantly, offers pointers to the future in the light of the trends of the present. It further should enable a considered opinion to be formed on the search for a new regional equilibrium in France 'fluctuating between denying every geographical constraint and seeking an absolute balance (and harmony) within the country' (Monod and Castelbajac 1971).

Centripetal forces. Underpinning the cohesion and homogeneity of France, centripetal forces have traditionally been strong, and have been reinforced in recent times. They are well-founded in the 'state-idea' of the

French people, with Great Power status in Europe since the days of Charlemagne; the characteristically strong and long-established central administration of power and its carefully limited devolution at *échelons* lower than the national level; the quantitative and status significance of Paris as the capital city, uniquely dominant throughout the country; the policies of large firms which, in practising economies of scale, concentrate on fewer, more nodal centres of decision-taking, usually in Paris; the urban hierarchy, impoverished at all levels below that of Paris and with many towns directly dependent upon the capital city, rather than upon second-rank provincial cities; the interregional linkages, again conventionally stronger centripetally with Paris than with other economic regions; the unifying force arising from the increasing mobility of persons, freight, energy, transport, and telecommunications; and the cumulative effects of spatial management of the French economy, promoting its greater integral cohesion through six successive economic plans. In such planning the proposals to energize and interlink the urban hierarchy by the designation of eight metropolitan 'countermagnet' growth cities, (Part III, ch. 2), and the concept of promoting at the same time greater regional balance, are the most formative elements.

Centrifugal forces. To almost every centripetal force there is a countervailing centrifugal tendency. Equilibrium is thus difficult to establish, is likely to be differently interpreted according to the perspective of the observer, and is often unstable in a rapidly-developing economy and society such as that of postwar France. Even within the consensus on the state idea of France there was in the late 1970s an almost equal polarization between Left and Right. Occasionally dissident minority voices are heard, not only those of political ideology or class interest, but also those of ethnic groups–the primary nations of France as they have been termed (Pisani 1969). In this as in other ways the voting patterns throughout the national space afford a general barometer of the cohesion of French society and the extent of its alignment behind current national policies. The increasingly articulate and widespread claims for more devolution of powers and decision-taking to the regions are also concerned not only with deconcentration of activities from the centre but also with real decentralization of authority. The strength of trans-frontier linkages into other states of the EEC, the tardy and limited growth of supranational thinking, confined to the economic and social fields, are among the important externalities which continue to influence the meaning of nationalism within the French state.

The most formative centrifugal forces may, however, arise rather from the basic geographical diversity of the national space, its physical characteristics and their disposition, the historical evolution of economy, society and polity, variegated in their spatial forms. Perhaps most important of all today is the continuing imbalance within France at the regional level, the variable extent of prosperity, adequacy of living standards, social conditions or total expectations. These contrasts are deep-seated, difficult to remove even in the longer term, but they have given strong impetus to a regionalism which has added claims for social justice to those for equal participation in national prosperity. The contrasts are subtle and widespread, with differences between regions vying with those between city and countryside, capital city and the provinces, Est with Ouest. Indeed the diverse and shifting scale levels of difference are perhaps the most difficult to identify and evaluate. Finally, in the late 1970s there is a growing resistance to further centralized planning, either by the state or by large-scale industry, and an increasing wish for fuller participation and local expression of democracy. Though the basic task of French planning may continue to be 'to master space' (Teneur and Di Qual 1972) it must not be at the expense of the diversities within French national life. These have been the long-term and enduring strengths from which unity was fashioned and has since been sustained, though not without recurrent difficulties throughout history.

A politico-geographical assessment

Historical perspectives. The iconography of the French state, its essential Frenchness, has been cumulatively built up through the centuries to form one of the more powerful, enduring nation-states of Europe. Such political strength was generated by the harnessing of the innate diversity of people and place through the medium of a highly-centralized administration, penetrating to the furthest corners of the national territory. The Great Power status of France was nurtured within a well-defined geographical space, nodally located within Europe to absorb and benefit from the currents of civilization and trade, and to suffer and surmount the tides of war and conquest. These external forces helped to forge the coherent nation-state, whose sovereignty was organized from within and pro-gressively spread towards the so-called 'natural frontiers' of the Rhine, the Alpes, the Pyrénées and the Ardennes. The most formative of these periods of French political geography (NID Handbook 1943) started with the monarchical centralization under the Capetian kings, with a power base in the small, compact but centrally located territory including Paris and Orléans. For three centuries after 978 AD the nominal feudal superiority of the Capetians was converted to direct sovereignty over an expanding kingdom. This spread of sovereignty encountered resistance in the south (Albigensian crusade; conflicts with Aragon; the suzerainty of the bishoprics of the Rhône valley), the west (the celtic lands of Brittany; the dukedom of Normandy; the country of the 'langue d'oc' and the English possessions in Aquitaine and Poitou) and the east (the fragmented feudal territory of the Dukes of Burgundy, included within France by the end of the Middle Ages; the fluctuating northern frontier in Flanders and Artois).

The centralizing process was carried further under Louis XI (1461–83) with the intensification of economic life and the establishment of a network of postal roads. The growth of an absolute monarchy through the centuries did not however create a unification of peoples or altogether diminish built-in geographical diversities (Gravier 1970). France remained fundamentally divided and during the sixteenth and seventeenth centuries religious conflicts threatened to disintegrate the state. During the seventeenth century, however, the administrative reforms of Richelieu opened the path to the further centralizing policies under Louis XIV (1643–1715). Yet even by the time of the French Revolution (1789) the country retained many local autonomies and anomalies, relict features of early centuries; differences in administration, law and commercial practice persisted. The Revolution swept these away and established a centralization uniquely powerful and penetrating. It is, however, important to distinguish the centralization of French sovereignty, which became a revolutionary principle in which the individual vested his authority in a national unity at the level of a collective contract (Lafont 1967), from the establishment of a highly-centralized administrative bureaucracy, which once created spread its tentacles downwards to the most remote localities. The leaders of the Revolution reproached the *ancien régime* for the abuse of power, not for the use of a centralized bureaucracy. The Napoleonic period powerfully reinforced the centralized administration (p. 42), and this has persisted through the five republics of France with little modification or alleviation, multiplying and ramifying the vertical links between Paris and the provincial centres at the expense of horizontal links within the provinces themselves (Pisani 1969).

Hand-in-hand with the growth of the nation-state, and indeed further cementing the bonds between nation and state, there was a great flowering of French civilization and culture. This took place both in literature and in the arts, spreading culture by the French language, thereby helping to diminish the cultural and regional differences throughout France. French civilization reached a zenith during the eighteenth century at a time when she was also the dominant Great Power in Europe. As seen by some the strength of the French heritage is thus the most powerful of all the icons behind her deeply-engrained State Idea; to others (Pisani 1969) the driving force in contemporary nationalism is generated by the sense of participation in a common destiny.

Yet there continue to exist, even to grow, counter-arguments to a unitary outlook on French society and sovereignty. Stress is laid (Sérant 1965, Lafont 1967) upon the continuing and underlying differences which have not been totally eradicated by the powerful central administration. Seen from the political perspective of regionalists, the territorial consolidation of French sovereignty through the centuries was achieved by the military or diplomatic annexation of lands inhabited by ethnic or primary sub-nations (Bretagne 1532; Alsace and French Flanders under Louis XIV; Corse 1768). The regionalist movement throughout the nineteenth century (Flory 1966) was more cultural than political, and had a strong sense of nostalgia for the provincial identities of the *ancien régime*. Insofar as the regionalist movement was political it reflected traditional and conservative attitudes on the political Right, and for this reason was viewed by many as contrary to the institutions and the political ideals handed down from the French Revolution (Phlipponneau 1968).

Post-1945. Since 1945 the ferment of regionalism has only loosely been concerned with older ethnic or historical traditions of provincial identity or autonomy. It has rather had its origins in the demands for economic and social justice and for a setting to rights of the profound regional imbalances within France, a situation described as that of 'home-based colonialism' (Lafont 1967). To some extent this has involved 'depoliticizing and demystifying' the concept of regionalism (Flory 1966) and economic priorities have replaced political dogma in the pressures for regional reform. The relationship between a regional sense of deprivation and the political will to manifest and to seek a greater degree of autonomy in regional affairs is complex, but not entirely lacking in respect for earlier ethnic or historical antecedents. Brogniart (1971) asserted that only Bretagne and Corse had strongly-founded or deeply-felt ethnic sub-nationalisms (Sérant 1965), and that in all other areas of France regionalist feeling is rather a reaction against the dominance of Paris than a constructive manifestation in its own right. Nevertheless the issue of languages other than French being sustained in local education (Hassold 1971), for example, is felt to be increasingly important in Bretagne (Phlipponneau 1968) and is not without continuing significance in Alsace-Lorraine. In the Pyrénées, agitation by the Basque people has spread from the Spanish to the French side of the watershed, leading to the banning of the ETA party in France in 1972, whilst during 1969 and again in 1977, the protests in Meurthe-et-Moselle were more localized expressions of economic dissatisfaction. It is, however, virtually certain that should there be a French version of the recent Kilbrandon Commission on the British Constitution (1973), it would show no support in France for federal-type government on the West German (BRD) model. The real enemy is bureaucratic over-centralization rather than the coherence of sovereignty itself.

Central administration and regional powers

Any geographical consideration of the relationships between government and territory must be concerned both with the network of units for administration at various scale levels, their interrelationships, and the powers and functions which are devolved to the representative bodies at each hierarchical level among these units. The patterns of units may be manipulated, often with a view to optimizing their accordance with contemporary economic, social or political realities, or the apportionment of powers and functions may be altered, increased or diminished. The history of administrative regionalism in France as elsewhere has shown that it is easier and thought more convenient to propose changes in the network of units, at least at the intermediate regional level, than to reapportion powers from the centre to any effective extent. The 'units-powers' mix is thus less flexible than might be thought necessary, has not a few relict features built-in, and tends to evolve in a gradualist manner with many compromises inevitably limiting radical change. Among the most fundamental of the compromises is that between efficiency, whose promotion favours fewer, larger territorial units to achieve economies of scale and the full advantages of mobility in the factors of production and in the design of flexible regional strategies for growth and change, and democratic representation, which on all available evidence is strongest at the level of micro-units, at which scale the citizen recognizes those he deals with in day-to-day affairs, and whereby he conventionally defines his 'home area'.

The basic units of local government in France, the *commune* (36,394 in 1975) and the *département* (96 since the division of Corse (1975)), were created during the French Revolution and have persisted little changed for more than 180 years (Boucher 1973). It is these units rather than the regions, defined in post-war years for planning purposes, which are the underlying administrative realities against which all proposed division of powers must be calibrated. As M. Pompidou put it–'The region is another matter. In the first instance it is a group of *départements*'. As recently as the reforms of July 1972, the twenty-two planning regions (fig. 4) were seen in central government eyes as having a strictly limited functional role, not as

Figure 4 Planning regions and ZEAT regions, 1973.

the platform for extended political powers (La Documentation Française (La DF) 1974). The regional reformers, on the other hand, have never ceased, since the rebirth of regionalism as a cultural and political movement during the nineteenth century, to press for greater devolution of powers to some regional level. Furthermore, such devolution should not only be the fuller representation of central government at regional level (*déconcentration*) but should involve the vesting of worthwhile powers in regionally-elected bodies (*décentralisation*). Geographers have perhaps been too prone to extol the merits of planning at the regional level, to advance and advocate many alternative regional networks for particular functional purposes, without adequate recognition that powers in France (as in Britain) at the regional level continue to be minimal, in comparison to those in *départements* and *communes*. Yet it remains true that the regional reforms advocated, and in principle accepted, by the French government after the events of 1968 envisaged realistic devolution of powers to the twenty-two regions, which presently have planning functions limited to the review of economic and social development. Even the 1972 reforms, instituted October 1973, represent but a cautious first step in the direction of greater regional powers of decision-taking.

The commune. The commune persists as the level at which 'grass-roots' democracy has tangible recognition and, for this reason perhaps, the fragmented mosaic of communes covering France has proved resistant to many attempts at reform or rationalization. Unlike the prefect, executive head of the *département* appointed by central government, the local mayor is directly elected by his constituents and thus more responsive to local needs and aspirations. The myriad communes may readily be shown to be an anachronism and potentially the most inefficient of patterns for administration. At the time of their creation all communes were declared to be sovereign equals in the eyes of the nation (1789), irrespective of size, shape, population or resources. During the past 180 years this juridical equality has been exposed as something of a myth and the pattern of communes has been seen to be increasingly out-of-touch with economic and social realities. Of the 36,394 communes in 1975, no fewer than 23,000 had less than 500 inhabitants, a further 6,300 under 1,000. There were more communes in France than equivalent units in all five of the other EEC members of the original Six, although the French population was only one-quarter that of the then EEC (Boucher 1973). Particularly serious problems arose in large cities and towns, in which the division into communes for administration made effective planning very difficult, and in rural areas where steady depopulation had depleted residents below the numbers at which minimum services or economic and administrative viability could be sustained. Moreover, the inequalities in the geographical endowment of communes became even more seriously apparent as the costs of fulfilling their local responsibilities outstripped their capacity to finance them from local population and resources. The richer communes were able to reduce local taxes, whilst an increasing number of poorer communes had to levy unreasonably high rates.

Advocates of reform at the level of the communes have never been lacking. Some prefer to reduce the number of communes drastically by amalgamation (Club Jean Moulin 1968), but gradualist change has more supporters. Already in 1890 intercommunal syndicates could be formed for a specific purpose, e.g. water supply, electrification. In 1959 the urban district was instituted to tackle problems arising from the fragmentation of towns into communes. The legislation of 1966 reinforced this important planning notion by creating the possibility of forming 'urban communities' (*communauté urbaine*) for cities and towns with more than 50,000 inhabitants. Lyon, Bordeaux, Lille and Strasbourg have established 'urban communities' and these have also been introduced spontaneously by Dunkerque, Creusot-Montceau-les-Mines, Le Mans, and Cherbourg. In 1971 Commissions were created in each *département* to further the process of amalgamation of communes or cooperation between them (SCA, SIVOU), by the consent of either their municipal councils or the local electorate. Two years later some 9,761 communes had shown an interest in amalgamation proposals, but in a country still somewhat wedded to the 'spirit of the belfry' progress has inevitably been slow.

The Guichard report (1976) on local powers and responsibilities favoured further decentralization to a local level. As M. Fourcade put it–'the framework of daily life is above all a local responsibility. No centralized technical competence, however expert, can replace the advantages of a locally-placed authority living in the midst of the problems.'

The département. Whereas the communes created in 1789 had in many cases had some earlier expression in ecclesiastical parishes or municipalities, the higher *échelon* of administrative units–the *canton*, the *arrondissement*, and most notably the *département*–were deliberate breaks with any earlier political identities. In particular there was to be no possible continuity with the provinces of the *ancien régime*, which in their rich diversity had sustained political individualities in spite of the centralizing intentions by successive monarchs and the administration of the provinces by *intendants* appointed by the king. Nevertheless it is argued by some that the 83 *départements* created by 1800, and even more so their constituent *arrondissements*, corresponded well with the original Gallic *pays* or 'pagi' (Boucher 1973). They were thus far from the 'technocratic abstractions' condemned by Mirabeau when the original intentions were to divide France into 80 square units each of about 324 square leagues. The pattern adopted was in fact a compromise. The area of each *département* was approximately the same, the population of a similar size, and in every case it was possible to travel from the central place to the outermost border within a day. Yet modifications were made in the light of local circumstances, the distribution of resources, local customs, traditions and affiliations.

The prefect in the *département* is the representative of central government, and he continues to have considerable powers, advised in his role by the elected *conseil général*. During the past 150 years the *département*, by its very existence, and its legal personality, has come to have greater popular recognition and through time a greater attribution of responsibilities, particularly in the economic and social fields. Not all *départements* have gained a like degree of acceptability and, as in the case of the communes, the poorer *départements* have suffered most as their responsibilities grew more rapidly than their means of financing desirable developments. From 1871 to 1939 there was some stagnation at the administrative level of the *département*, with minimum budgeting and reduction in expenditures. Provision of electricity, water supply, roads, and intervention in the local economy have been among the more important responsibilities with a geographical outcome. To these have been added since 1945 participation in national programmes of planning, urbanization and industrialization, in addition to increasing involvement in the extension and implementation of the welfare state. From being merely a political and administrative entity in the nineteenth century, the *département* has become a major agent in economic and social change. The Vth Plan recognized the important role of the *département* in assessing needs and in making provision for an increasingly wide range of public investments, which could not be as expeditiously or as sensitively directed from the national level. Furthermore the system of *départements* offered the most effective prospect for maintaining a satisfactory balance between rural regions and the rapidly-urbanizing areas of France. The 1972 regional reforms confirmed and strengthened the powers at *département* level, the only legitimate authority intermediate between the nation and the commune, but crucial to the interests of both.

The région. With the powers of the *département* thus strengthened, those of the *région*, at the next higher level in the administrative hierarchy, may be thought to have been weakened. Such powers at regional level have always been limited, however, and the regions themselves have only recently had a clear identity. France is today divided into twenty-two regions for planning purposes (fig. 4), eight ZEAT (*zone d'études et d'aménagement du territoire*) regions for the preparation of the VIth Plan, or three regions (Paris, Est, Ouest) for more general planning and longer-term forecasting purposes. There is additionally a tentative division of France into Euro-regions (the ZEAT network) for policy-making in the EEC and, no less than in the UK, there is also a great proliferation of regional networks for particular functional purposes. Though it is possible for geographers and others to discuss indefinitely the number of units, their territorial disposition, or the allocation of functions between levels of the regional hierarchy, the reality is that there are in effect twenty-two planning regions for the French national space (the twenty-second was Corse, 1970).

The twenty-two planning regions had their origins in the regionalizing which took place in the mid-1950s to give an embryonic regional dimension to national planning. There had been earlier attempts to regionalize: Clemenceau (1919), fifteen regions based upon the territories of Chambers of Commerce; Vichy (1940–4), nineteen regions each under a regional prefect concerned with the maintenance of law and order; the postwar IGAME system (*inspecteurs généraux de l'administration en mission extraordinaire*); 1947, eight military regions, concerned with law and order. It was, however, the planning legislation of 1955 establishing 'regional action programmes' that led in the following year to the definition of twenty-one programme regions (*régions de programme*). These corresponded in many cases closely with the regions within which mixed development commissions (*comités régionaux d'expansion économique*) had been working since the 1940s. In 1958 legislation was introduced requiring regional plan documents to be prepared, under the authority of a coordinating prefect and an interdepartmental conference, and in 1960 the twenty-one planning regions were renamed (*circonscriptions d'action régionale*), without changes either in frontiers or in composition. During the 1960s there were further positive steps towards greater regionalization in planning: in 1964, the creation of regional prefects (*préfets de région*) with powers to 'implement economic and planning policies of central government in the region', assisted by a cabinet (*mission régionale*), a board of senior civil servants (*conférence administrative régionale*), and a consultative council (CODER, *commission de développement économique régionale*). This stage of regional reform merely formulated the necessary political liaison between central government and the *départements*; it did not create new powers at the regional level. Nevertheless, the regions formulated for planning purposes began to attract and polarize political forces concerned to advance regional devolution of powers.

The growing political pressures behind regionalism played their part in the 1968 troubles. In the referendum of the following year, the outcome of which was complicated by the linking of reform of the Senate with that of the regions, there was a slight majority against these combined reforms. The 1969 proposals for reform envisaged the region as a body possessing legal authority (*collectivité territoriale*), with powers over equipment, public aid to building, and town planning. These proposals were probably too strong and premature in a society with grass roots pressures strongest at more parochial levels. In 1970 a market research study (SOFRES) revealed that a great majority of Frenchmen supported the general idea of regional reforms in spite of the negative vote of the previous year, and it was thus entirely logical that the regional reform legislation of 1972 should carry the process a stage further.

With effect from October 1973 the twenty-two former *circonscriptions d'action régionale* became *régions*. There were no changes of boundary when the new *régions* came into being, each defined as having 'a corporate juridical and financial personality' (EPR–*établissement public régional*) with unchanged tasks, i.e. 'to contribute to economic and social development'. None of the powers or prerogatives of the constituent local government units (*départements, communes*) were transferred to the *régions*. The regional bodies nevertheless had an augmented role by comparison with their predecessors, the CODER: the principle of joint action with central government was accepted; major investments could no longer be imposed on the regions; and consultation was to be more detailed and regular on development and planning issues, particularly those concerned with elaboration and execution of the National Plan. Greater decision-powers were conferred at regional level, for investments of regional significance or appropriate to each constituent *département*. Modest funds might now be raised to finance equipment projects at the choice of the region: from the revenue on driving licences, supplementing of state taxes on property transfers and vehicle registration documents, supplementing local fiscal resources (*centimes*), up to a ceiling budget. For a large region the ceiling might be 100 million francs per annum, for a small region 20 million (1974).

The regional prefect continues to hold the powers to instruct and execute, and he is directly responsible to central authority (*Ministère de l'Intérieur*). He is assisted by two assemblies: *conseil régional*, a deliberative body of parliamentarians and representatives of local government; and *comité économique et social*, a consultative body including representatives of economic, social, cultural, scientific and sporting organizations.

This latest accommodation of the forces of regionalism is uncertainly regarded. To some it represents a step in the direction of more worthwhile regional powers in the future, but to others the powers of the regional prefect on the one hand and of the constituent local government units on the other remain entrenched. In particular, the maintaining of the twenty-two planning regions is arguable in the face of EEC requirements for fewer, larger planning regions.

This then is the present equilibrium of powers between the centre, the regions, and local government, but the region is the weakest among the partners. Behind lie the deepening issues of regional imbalance, inequality and sense of deprivation (Part III, ch. 3). These introduce further distortions into a pattern in which centrifugal forces tend to be rising and yet centripetal forces have succeeded for so long and so effectively in limiting real regional devolution of powers.

Political perspective
A quick but not unambiguous check on regionalist attitudes may be made by looking at recent voting patterns (fig. 5). The evidence is at best indicative and not entirely clear-cut in its implications. There are indeed

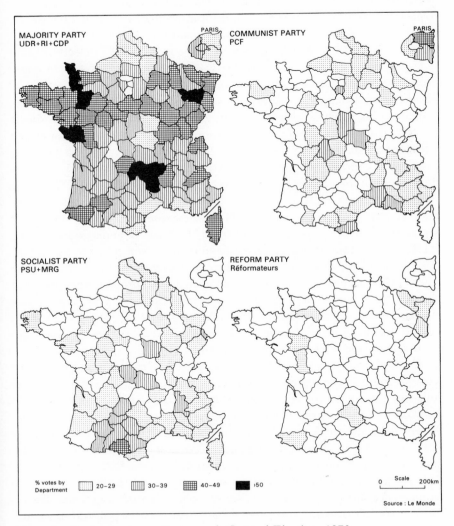

Figure 5   Voting patterns, first round, General Election, 1973.

those who argue that the class differences, attitudes and aspirations upon which voting is thought customarily to depend in the first instance, are greater within any locality or region than spatially distributed across France. On the other hand, the social and economic mix differs spatially, the range and intensity of problems is also differentiated markedly within the national space, and for these reasons alone voting patterns should shed some light on the strengths and distribution of regionalism. The evidence may be clearer by studying votes for the opposition parties since the principal government party in 1973 (UDR, *Union des démocrates pour la République*) had a broader spectrum of opinion than any of its opponents, and moreover was associated with coalition elements (*Républicains indépendants*, CDP–*Centre Démocratie et Progrès*) in the 1973 election.

Fig. 5 shows that the majority party (UDR 184, RI 54, CDP 23 seats) polled well in 1973 in its traditional strongholds within a broad zone across France from Bretagne through the southern Bassin Parisien to Alsace-Lorraine. There were islands of voting strength in the southern Massif Central, the western Pyrénées, the Hautes Alpes and Corse. Compared with the landslide of 1968 in favour of the majority party, ground had been lost in the central Bassin Parisien in particular. In Paris the UDR was dominant but lost the north-east of the city to the communists (PC); in the Petite Couronne (Hauts-de-Seine, Seine-St Denis, Val-de-Marne) the majority party was entrenched in Hauts-de-Seine and Val-de-Marne but seats were lost in the latter district in 1973. In the Grande Couronne the UDR was the dominant party, but less so than in 1968. The voting pattern for the majority party thus showed it to be strong in the more affluent and middle-class sections of the city suburbs but also in problem regions, both those with agrarian as well as those with industrial problems, where working-class votes are predominant. The patterns cut vertically through society and were also differentiated horizontally over France; there was no clear correlation with the forces of regionalism.

The communist party (PC), 73 seats in 1973, had scattered islands of voting strength, concentrated in the north-east quarters of inner Paris, the adjacent suburbs of St Denis and Bobigny, and in Essonne in the Grande Couronne. In provincial France there were strongholds in the Marseille-Rhône delta area, in Auvergne and the Somme. The socialist coalition, 100 seats in 1973, had its greatest support in Greater Toulouse, the Pyrénées, and Auvergne but had lost ground even in those areas. Its voters tend to be located in the less-privileged regions south of the Loire and it is no coincidence that political regionalism is constantly surfacing there. The reform party (*Réformateurs*) occupied central ground in the political spectrum, 31 seats in 1973, but was nowhere strong, though with support scattered over individual *départements* as diverse as Orne, Aveyron, Haut-Rhin. The opposition parties thus have very divided territorial allegiance and this tends to be fragmented. There is perhaps a clearer identification between opposition voting and problem areas, but it is evident that political regionalism, though in general a course currently espoused by the moderate Left, has no coherent party-political following, at least in national elections.

The presidential election of 1974 (Denis 1974) saw a loss by the Right both in its more traditional strongholds of the Ouest, the Est, the heart of the Massif Central and other mountain areas, but also in those areas of greatest weakness. This seemed to indicate a trend to greater spatial uniformity in voting patterns, with sociological factors taking precedence over regional issues. By contrast with the patterns of 1946, those of 1974 were almost the inverse and in many respects marked a return to longer-term trends, perhaps the reflection of underlying perennial cultural traits. In the 1977 municipal elections there was a marked swing to the Left throughout France (control of 96 towns 1971, 153 in 1977); within the Left the socialist party (PS) increased its control from 45 to 82 towns, the communist party (PC) from 51 to 71. Only Quimper and Cambrai were lost by the Left to the Centre-Right (UDR-RPR). The greater political weight of the socialist party within the Left was underlined in the outer Parisian ring, in the mining and industrial towns, and even in the deep countryside. In traditionally catholic areas of the agrarian Ouest, the Est and parts of the Massif Central, the socialist party made notable gains, perhaps an indication of a declining influence of the clergy on voting behaviour.

Imbalance: national, regional and local.
At the heart of a consideration of the interplay of centrifugal and centripetal forces within French economy and society lies a deep-seated and unstable imbalance, of many kinds and at several scale levels. It is an imbalance reflected in relative economic health or deprivation, in differences of living standards, the social environment, problems encountered, aspirations and expectations, and an overall sense of grievance or satisfaction. Though it may be argued that differences in wealth, education, housing, or social habits transcend all others at the level of the individual citizen it remains true that to a sense of social injustice there must be added a growing recognition of regional or spatial injustice. Political reformers (Durrieu 1969) wish to see the fortunes of each region equalized and an economic and institutional equilibrium established, with harmonized regional development promoted and supported when need be by public funds. To others the imbalance is more fundamental, and the objective must rather be

limited to seeing that each region is enabled to fulfil its 'natural vocation' (Pisani 1969). Lafont (1967) was anxious to stress that regional under-development was not an unchangeable natural catastrophe, resulting from the fatal logic of geography. Monod and Castelbajac (1971) were more cautious, pointing out that regional disequilibrium in the distribution of economic activities tends to be self-perpetuating, independently of the causes which originally provoked it.

Correcting of imbalances is the central issue towards which remedial planning had been directed throughout the 1960s. Some assessment of the forces at work and the current state of the game is essential to a full interpretation of contemporary unity and diversity in France. Imbalances are of many kinds: between the centre and the periphery, more directly postulated in France as Paris v. the provinces; between the regions or localities themselves, in terms of spatial equilibria; contrasting large towns with small towns, or all towns with rural areas; or the major dichotomy between east and west in France.

In his classic work *Paris and the French desert* Gravier (1947, 1972) identified, highlighted and analysed the most substantial and crucial of all the imbalances, that resulting from the long-standing and continuing polarization of French life upon the capital city. The unique degree of dominance by Paris as a primate city is without parallel elsewhere in Europe. The population of the Paris conurbation (8.5 millions in 1975) includes the city and 221 adjacent communes and is eight times greater than that next in size, Greater Lyon (1.0 millions). The Paris planning region (Ile-de-France), the city plus the seven neighbouring *départements*, has almost exactly double the numbers (9.8 millions in 1975) of those in the next largest planning region, that of Rhône-Alpes. By comparison Greater London has only twice the population of the second largest conurbation in the UK; in Italy the capital city has scarcely more people than the city next in line, Milan.

The power of Paris. Table 3 illustrates the importance of the Paris region in France by a wide diversity of economic and social criteria. Collectively these underline the concentration of power and decision-taking in the capital (Beaujeu-Garnier 1974), but they present only a partial picture. Reinforcing the national role of Paris as capital city is the wide range of political and economic functions it fulfils as an international centre. In this latter role Paris suffers from the competition of London and Brussels as a potential EEC capital, and London emerges clearly as the more significant banking, insurance, financial and commodity dealing centre; furthermore, in commercial terms Paris is rivalled by Frankfurt and Zurich (La DF 1973). Nevertheless the French capital derives strength from the very

Table 3 Economic and social indicators: Paris region and France

	units	Paris	France	Paris as % France	Date
Population	millions	9.7*	50.7	19	1971
	% change p.a.	+0.7	+0.5		1962–8
Employment					
Owners in indus. and commerce	thou.	339	1,955	17	1968
Liberal professions/snr management	,,	386	994	39	,,
Researchers and R and D engineers: public	,,	30	51	60	,,
private	,,	17	26	67	,,
Indus. and Commerce					
Establishments with 1000 employees		263	813	32	1971
Consumptn indus. energy	{ million tonnes coal equivalent	8.8	98.2	9	1970
Indus. constrn permits > 500 sq.m.	thou. sq.m.	628	7,867	8	1969
Investments in mechan. and elec. indus.	million frs	3,182	7,881	40	,,
Business receipts	milliard frs	615	1,160	53	,,
,, turnover, commerce/services	,,	124	381	32	1966
Imports	,,	38	117	33	1971
Exports	,,	31	112	27	,,
Communications					
New cars registered	thou.	371	1,468	25	,,
Passengers at airports	millions	13.2	20.3	65	,,
Telephone traffic	milliard frs tax	6.5	17.4	38	,,
University students	thou.	221	701	31	1971–2
Hotel rooms	,,	219	803	27	1966
Budgetary receipts	milliard frs	83.6	173.8	48	1969
Bank deposits	,,	111.2	266.3	42	1971

*Ile-de-France
Sources: Annuaire Statistique and INSEE

diversity of its functions (George 1968A). It has already been seen that the centralization of government decision-taking in Paris is uniquely great, including the executive and the legislature, the Ministries, the embassies of more than thirty foreign nations, together with the administrative HQ of many public corporations (PTT, SNCF, Electricity, Gas, Coal), trade unions and employers' federations (Rochefort 1972). Around this core there have agglomerated information and press services; banks, consultancy groups; research and developmental bodies; financial and commercial institutions. The polarizing process was further added to by concentration in Paris of the higher education institutions of the university and the *grandes écoles*; congress, trade and exhibition centres.

To a degree Paris grew independently as an industrial as well as a commercial centre. In 1971 53 per cent of national employment in printing, 40 per cent in electrical engineering and 32 per cent in general engineering and vehicles were concentrated in and around Paris. The 42 per cent of the national workforce in manufacturing in the Paris region is to be compared with only 35 per cent in London or 30 per cent in New York. Moreover, the Paris workforce has a higher ratio in growth industries than other French regions, enjoys mean wage and salary levels about 50 per cent above those of the provinces, and has a greater proportion of managerial and skilled high-grade workers; 38 per cent of those with university diplomas, 41 per cent of higher civil servants and 54 per cent of artists lived in Paris in the late 1960s (Kayser 1971). Employment in the tertiary sector, not surprisingly, is higher in the Paris region (59.9 per cent in 1973) than nationally (53.4 per cent) and is growing more rapidly in the capital city conurbation. This tertiary activity is partly induced by the cumulative needs of the resident and transient populations but it also includes the full range of international cultural institutions as well as those of government. The most recent manifestation has been seen in the location in Greater Paris of the head offices of international companies and conglomerates. These contribute to the rising office population, already seriously inflated by the many headquarters of national companies located in Paris (47 per cent of all those registered in France in 1969). Furthermore, in 1969 62 per cent of all company taxes in France were paid in through offices in the Paris region.

The process of agglomeration around Paris has seemed to be geographically logical, even inevitable, though the momentum of growth has slowed during the past twenty years. George (1968A) emphasized the long-term, fundamental and continuing assets of location enjoyed by Paris, her nodality within the Bassin Parisien and the natural routeways radiating to the borders of France. He showed how these advantages were early capitalized upon by the timely centralization of political power, and the progressive and calculated build-up of radial communications from Paris, by road and later by rail. Paris thus became ever more confirmed as the heart of the state, socially, economically and politically. The capital city interpreted each region to every other, and lay at the hub of almost all internal transit routes.

A questionnaire study of foreign businessmen's attitudes to Paris (1973, unpublished) favoured the advantages rather than stressing the demerits of the city. The advantages, in order of importance, were listed as: the quality of intellectual and cultural life; the business climate; the potential arising from the location of the city; its beauty; attitudes to foreigners; the quality of services and infrastructure; and manpower availability. On the debit side were mentioned: official attitudes to foreigners; the language barrier; tax controls and policies; the poor quality of intra-urban transport; the housing problem; and the scarcity of offices. Nevertheless many trends indicate that since the mid-1950s the growth rate of Paris has fallen to about the national mean. This is true in respect of growth in total employment, jobs in large factories, consumption of energy, or building permits issued. It is also the case in the rate of growth in the tertiary sector of employment, perhaps the most sensitive of all indicators (Quelennec 1973). This slowing-down of growth was reflected in the fall in net in-migration to the Ile-de-France (Région Parisienne), from 87,500 p.a. 1954–62, to 52,800 p.a. 1962–8, and 12,400 p.a. 1968–75.

The reduced growth momentum in Paris over the past twenty years has been in part the instinctive reaction to urban congestion and overcrowding, on the part of both firms and individual citizens, and in lesser part the outcome of deliberate government policies to decentralize activities from the capital city conurbation. The 'diseconomies of scale' are difficult to prove but their effects are clear. Increasingly the high social costs of further agglomeration are borne by the community at large. Public expenditure rises and returns upon it fall, whilst higher costs of living proliferate. The environmental problems resulting from great city life become more apparent: congestion and claustrophobia, longer journeys to work (some 20 million individual movements in Greater Paris every working day), costly and unsatisfactory housing conditions for many, pollution, social anonymity, with rising crime and delinquency rates. In 1965 INED (*Institut national d'études démographiques*) discovered in a survey that only two in every five Parisians were satisfied with life in their city, and the majority would have preferred to live in the provinces.

Dispersal policies. French government policy since the mid-1960s has sought to limit the growth of the Paris agglomeration by redistributing manufacturing and services to promote regional balance elsewhere in France (Part II, ch. 2). Restrictions on growth have been operated by levies on office and factory development in Paris, inducements (*indemnités de décentralisation*) to decentralize from the Lyon (1966–70) as well as the Paris conurbations. As a positive measure regional development premiums, with tax reliefs in addition, are offered on a complicated pattern throughout France (fig. 55) to assist in the decentralization process. To date, such decentralization has been only a partial success, and that mainly to sites within the Bassin Parisien, but it is hoped to accelerate the policy with a view to restricting population growth in the Paris region by the year 2000 to 14 millions rather than the 18 millions which market forces might otherwise generate or attract. The extent to which the growth pressures from EEC economic integration may so stimulate the Paris region as to frustrate the intention of the French planners remains to be seen.

The linkages between Paris and the extremely diverse characteristics of other parts of France are through the urban network (*armature urbaine*) and by interchange with the planning regions and their constituent areas. The liaison is sustained by means of the total communications system, which links city to city, region to region, and all to Paris. The assessment of imbalances is complex and must be interpreted at several scale levels (Glayman 1971). At the micro-level of the *pays* or the *arrondissement* France is almost certainly the most variegated in its landscapes and traditional ways of life. The mosaic of mountain, hill, scarpland or plain has been interpreted through a long history of rural and small town development. The late arrival of large-scale industry and urbanization has not had the effect of creating the greater uniformity in ways of life found, for example, in Britain. Apart from the differences in local habitat there are inequalities in economic and social conditions, the mainsprings of a sense of deprivation and of nascent regionalism. These inequalities may be reviewed at the levels of the *département* and the twenty-two economic planning regions.

Well-being. Fig. 6 shows the pattern of economic and social well-being in France during the late 1960s. The criteria which have been ranked and correlated include: mean earnings per household; persons per doctor; new cars; unit of low tension electricity consumption; telephone traffic; business receipts; tax revenues. At first sight the pattern appears lacking in regularities; furthermore, within almost every *département* there exists further differentiation as between town and country, principal centre and smaller towns, and within each town between the classes and socio-economic groups. Nevertheless certain generalizations emerge: first, the

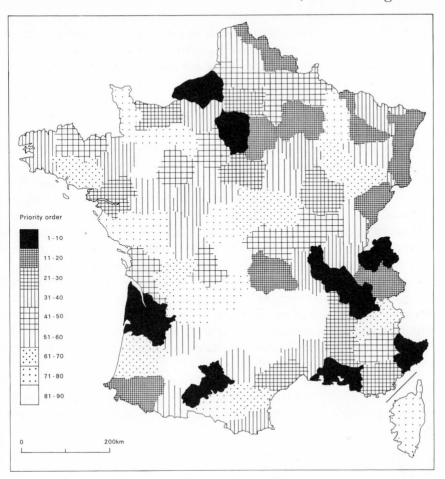

Figure 6 Index of well-being, by *départements*, 1966.

higher the composite ranking (1–10) the greater the correlation with the
major economic growth centres; secondly, the broad contrasts between the
low ranking of most of western France (west of a line linking the Basse
Seine with the Rhône delta) and the higher, though far from homogeneous,
ranking of eastern and northern France; thirdly, the concentrated zone of
deprivation westwards from Lozère through the Causses to the middle
Garonne valley; fourthly, even the industrial regions of the Nord and
Lorraine, undergoing reconversion, rank high in some aspects of economic
and social well-being.

A recent study (Knox and Scarth 1977) analysed 41 indicators of the quality of life, similarly at the *département* level. Rank-ordering of aggregate standardized scores produced a marked latitudinal zoning, with quality of life improving steadily from the north and west towards the south and east. Using cluster analysis, followed by a seven-fold multiple discriminant iteration, nine groups of *départements* were identified. Direct comparison with fig. 6 is constrained by the difference in date of information, the range of variables used, and in particular the significance attached to economic as against social conditions; Knox and Scarth included many more social variables, and notably a set of indicators of social pathology. Nevertheless, for the extreme cases there are salient contrasts with fig. 6. The northern and eastern zones of France score lowest in the Knox and Scarth study, but very variably on fig. 6. By contrast, the southern Massif Central, an outstanding economic and social problem region on fig. 6, is broken into diverse categories in the other study. The high scores for the Alpes generally, for the Midi, and for the Bassin Parisien, correlate well in both studies, but fig. 6 shows a clearer positive achievement by the regional counter-metropoli. Knox and Scarth find no correlation with traditional geographical subdivisions of France. and none with the twenty-two economic planning regions; fig. 6, on the other hand, admits of diversity within the planning regions but correlates better with economic growth centres, and the traditional contrasts between a deprived western and more variably prosperous eastern France.

With the importance attached to promoting the quality of life (Min. de la Qualité de la Vie 1974; VIIth Plan), variations in well-being are likely to be no less significant than economic conditions in future spatial management policies.

Planning region classification

Table 4 classifies the twenty-two *planning regions*, by fifteen attributes, into five economic trend categories. Quelennec (1973) reached similar conclusions after carrying out a principal components analysis based on: index of disposable earnings per capita, index of capital per person, density of population, per cent employed in agriculture and in industry, productivity per worker in industry, ratio of growth industries, and extent of urbanization. The most striking feature of table 4 is the extent to which the Paris region dominates in almost every respect; differences among other regions are almost invariably less than those between every region and Paris. Within any category there are differences comparing one region with another, but the overall mix of economic and social conditions identifies each group. The pattern might be clearer if all regions had approximately similar populations, space, and traditional recognition for their identities.

Table 4 Planning regions, classified by economic trends

	Popn 1975 (million)	Popn density 1971 per km²	% rural popn 1968	Popn change 1962-8, % p.a.	Energy consumption 1969, mill. t. coal equiv.	Business receipts 1967, milliard frs	Indus. estab. <1000 empl. 1966	% out of work monthly mean 1970	Mean household inc. <% national 1965	Mean ann. male earnings as % national 1968	% serious over crowding, households 1970	% houses without water in dwelling 1968	% households with cars 1970	Telephone traffic, tax per cap. as % national mean	FIAT aid as % national 1963-71
Paris	9.86	803	3	+1.5	8.9	473	132	1.4	146	135	9.7	4.2	54	202	0
Growth															
Champagne	1.33	51	40	+1.0	2.5	16	10	0.6	97	88	7.4	7.4	53	74	1.3
Picardie	1.67	84	44	+1.1	3.4	13	19	0.9	90	88	8.4	11.4	56	62	0.1
H. Normandie	1.60	126	31	+1.2	3.5	15	18	0.9	98	96	8.6	15.3	62	82	1.0
Franche-Comté	1.05	63	43	+1.1	2.1	10	12	0.4	89	89	6.4	4.8	54	61	1.3
Rhône-Alpes	4.78	105	25	+1.6	12.1	66	49	1.0	100	97	8.8	4.7	62	94	7.6
Provence-C.d'Azur	3.67	108	12	+2.6	4.7	38	12	3.0	102	96	8.8	2.8	57	117	6.4
Growth potential															
Centre	2.15	53	44	+1.2	2.0	17	12	0.8	84	87	9.5	11.6	59	77	0.6
Bourgogne	1.56	49	47	+0.7	2.0	13	12	0.6	83	84	8.5	10.8	61	72	1.4
Aquitaine	2.54	60	41	+1.0	3.9	22	13	1.6	83	85	7.3	15.1	61	90	6.6
Languedoc	1.78	63	34	+1.6	2.0	13	1	3.4	87	84	7.2	4.2	59	69	7.5
Reconversion															
Nord	3.91	312	14	+0.7	14.2	51	60	1.8	93	88	6.1	9.3	50	59	11.5
Lorraine	2.33	99	29	+0.7	19.3	27	32	0.8	97	88	6.3	3.3	55	67	4.4
Alsace	1.51	175	30	+1.2	3.0	20	22	0.3	100	91	4.2	1.9	58	87	2.3
Developing															
Auvergne	1.33	51	48	+0.5	1.4	11	16	1.0	72	84	9.2	11.2	54	66	5.5
B. Normandie	1.30	73	52	+0.7	1.8	9	6	1.1	76	83	10.1	22.5	66	64	2.5
Poitou-Charentes	1.52	58	56	+0.4	1.4	11	6	1.0	72	81	10.1	17.1	62	67	2.8
Pays de la Loire	2.76	82	46	+0.8	2.2	21	18	1.3	77	83	12.1	17.8	62	65	5.5
Bretagne	2.59	92	51	+0.5	1.3	17	11	1.2	74	82	15.0	23.6	57	61	12.6
Limousin	0.73	44	56	+0.1	0.5	5	3	1.2	69	78	8.0	19.6	56	66	3.1
Midi-Pyrénées	2.26	49	45	+1.0	4.7	17	17	1.3	78	82	7.9	10.6	62	69	13.1
Corse	0.2	25	54	−0.3	0.1	0.6	—	1.1	—	—	12.8	0.9	—	61	2.8
France	52.58	94	30	+1.1	97.1	894	481	1.3	100	100	8.9	9.2	57	100	100

Source: INSEE data

In reality, fifteen regions have populations below 2.5 millions, the desirable lower threshold for regional strategy formulation in the UK; the small size of the populations of Limousin (0.73) and Corse (0.2 millions) in particular are serious impediments to planned growth. Fifteen regions have population densities below the national mean, itself low among west European states, and sixteen regions have proportions of rural dwellers higher than those for France as a whole.

By definition the planning regions have had no more than an administrative significance. In their original selection (1956) the influence of large towns, the future pattern of universities, agricultural specialization and heritage were taken into account and, in principle, the minimum threshold for population was set up at one million. Only limited regional consultations took place and the task of regional definition lasted only one year. Older provincial entities were resurrected for the first time since 1789, though often with different boundaries: Bretagne, Picardie, Alsace, Aquitaine, Franche-Comté, for example. The outcome in terms of regional identity or iconography was very uneven (Gravier 1970). Rhône-Alpes, united in the late 1950s, emerged well-integrated and economically strong (Kayser 1971), as did Provence-Côte d'Azur. Bretagne and Corse (after 1970) alone represented corporate ethnic personalities. Normandie was split, perhaps to accommodate the rivalry between Rouen and Caen, whilst Franche-Comté was separated from Bourgogne. Some regions were difficult to justify other than on grounds of administrative expediency. A 1968 survey in Pays de la Loire showed that 88 per cent of those interviewed were dissatisfied with its definition; all five constituent *départements* preferred association with another region. The Centre (Verrière 1968) remains difficult to justify, as do Poitou-Charentes, Midi-Pyrénées and Limousin. Gravier (1970) looked on Picardie as the least coherent of the regions, on an economic watershed between the Bassin Parisien, Reims and the Nord.

It has, however, been said (Claval 1975, 215) that the network of regions is perhaps the least unfair that could have been drawn, accepting the built-in constraints of medium-sized space and regularity of shape within the national hexagon. The regions often correspond with older iconographies, frequently contain a major city, and their councils permit arbitration to take place among towns and between towns and rural areas. The significant inequalities present in the regions are nevertheless so great, and in some measure arbitrary as the result of boundary definitions, that 'polarization is confirmed rather than equilibrium promoted' (Glayman 1971). Nevertheless, there are clustering traits for each category: the growth regions have faster population growth; higher levels of energy consumption, business receipts, representation of large firms, mean household income and male earnings; and lower unemployment or sub-standard housing conditions. By contrast, the developing regions have high ratios of rural population, slow population growth, low business momentum; higher than average unemployment and poorer housing conditions. The high ratio of rural car ownership, as in the UK, is a surface anomaly, to be explained as the vital need for personal mobility in areas where public transport has seriously deteriorated.

The regions with growth potential have fewer positive attributes than the growth regions, but are either well-placed to benefit from growth spreading from the Ile-de-France (Centre) or along the Paris-Lyon axis (Bourgogne), or have undeveloped potential (Aquitaine, Languedoc). The industrial reconversion regions are distinguished by the high ratio of employment in declining or stagnant activities, a frontier province location, and a high rate of energy consumption per capita (excluding Alsace); mean household income approaches the national average, and in spite of urban dereliction household utilities are generally well provided for.

To some writers (Lafont 1967, Phlipponneau 1968, 1970) the less-favoured regions are 'underdeveloped', the result of neglect, even of policies of neo-colonialism within the French state. Though accepting the disparities Kayser (1971) rejects the charge of underdevelopment. He is, however, pessimistic on two counts: the prospect of achieving a fuller regional equilibrium and the likelihood of effective political powers being devolved to regional level.

When grouped into the eight ZEAT regions (fig. 4), for longer-term planning, or to match EEC-scale regions, the generalizations about homogeneity are even more difficult to sustain. The Bassin Parisien in particular has growth regions in Haute-Normandie, Picardie and Champagne, potential growth in Centre and Bourgogne and a developing region in Basse-Normandie. The ZEAT Ouest, on the other hand, is uniformly composed of developing regions, and Sud-Ouest similarly with exception of the potential growth region of Aquitaine. Franche-Comté and Auvergne fit into their ZEAT regions rather as exceptions, and show trends more characteristic of the Ouest or Sud-Ouest. Languedoc emerges as a greater problem province when compared with its partner in Méditerranée, Provence-Côte d'Azur.

The urban network
Given the importance of urban growth as an instrument of regional and national planning policy the features, structure and trends of the *urban*

network need to be briefly reviewed (Pumain and Saint-Julien 1976). Early studies by geographers focused on urban spheres of influence, implying a gravity model of concentric zone relationships defined in terms of time rather than cost-distance. The classic study by Carrière and Pinchemel (1963) reviewed the French urban system, classifying and categorizing its component structures and trends. Subsequently, studies have become more systematically specialized, concerned with typologies and hierarchies of towns (Le Guen 1960, Charlet 1967, George 1968B) according to: dominant or diverse employment, concerned with equilibrium or growth potential as elements which might be manipulated by planning; balance of basic/non-basic activities (economic base theory), in terms of the potential for induced growth or multiplier effects (Noin 1974); and general functional structure (La DF 1970, Noël and Pottier 1973). Other studies dealt rather with the urban network in terms of space relations between units, and the hierarchical hinterland concept (Hautreux *et al.* 1963, Piatier 1968). Dalmasso (1975) considered the functional levels of the urban hierarchy, in both quantitative and qualitative terms, whilst others (Coppolani 1959, Juillard 1961, Le Fillâtre 1964) sought to identify the command structures appropriate to each urban level. This trend to analysis of urban dynamism led in turn to the studies by Hautreux and Rochefort (1964, 1965) and OTAM (*Omnium Technique d' Aménagement*) (La DF 1970). The theoretical base of urban network analysis has been drawn as much from economics as from geography; geographers, on the other hand, have also studied the totality and uniqueness of particular urban centres or sub-regions (Brunet 1972).

Three studies are of particular importance, though none derives its data later than the 1962 census. First, the OTAM (La DF 1970) study investigated 191 urban centres of more than 20,000 population, taking 195 indicators for each. The indicators were consolidated by principal components analysis to six factors: general importance of the town; economic and demographic balance; role of the environment on this equilibrium; crude growth in population and employment terms; equilibrium between demographic dynamism and stagnation of employment; importance of environment to development. A further factor analysis identified ten clusterings and on the basis of these thirteen categories of urban centre were established: A & B, strong regional centres; C & D, well-balanced medium-sized towns; E, F, G, towns with varying degrees of centrality in the tertiary sector; H, tourist centres, with residential character and an ageing population; I, ancient towns with vigorous economic activity; J, mining towns, often with weak manufacturing, a youthful population and individual housing; K, manufacturing towns; L, mainly ports; and M, manufacturing centres with significant female employment.

The classical interpretation of the French urban network remains that by Hautreux and Rochefort (1964). Given the dominance of the Paris agglomeration, it is not surprising that they found no regional capitals with a sufficient range of services and functions to supply adequately the complete needs of a region. Even Lyon, the second city in rank after Paris, lacked adequate decision-taking powers, either in local government, industry, or in banking (Rochefort, Bidault, Petit 1970). Hautreux and Rochefort analysed urban functions through the employment structure, services to the economy (banks, professions, specialized commerce), personalized services and the internal-external roles of each of 208 towns.

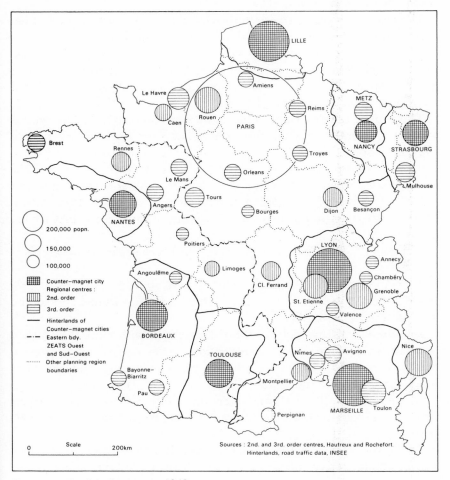

Figure 7   Regional centres, 1968.

A threefold hierarchy was identified (fig. 7): first, eight provincial cities which had the greatest range of functions, albeit incomplete, to serve as full regional metropoli. These cities were Lyon, Marseille, Bordeaux, Lille-Roubaix-Tourcoing, Toulouse, Strasbourg, Nantes and Metz-Nancy. All are located near the periphery of the French state and with possible exception of Metz-Nancy are closely linked into trading across the national frontiers. In 1964 these eight cities were designated as metropolitan counter-magnets (*métropoles d'équilibre*) and planning policy has since sought to stimulate growth there, particularly by inducements to develop tertiary activities. In turn, growth at these second-rank centres was to be diffused through the next stage of the network, the towns described as relay-centres (*centres relais*).

The second tier below the eight provincial cities was represented by ten regional towns, capable of furnishing many regional services but fewer than the metropoli. These towns were Dijon, Grenoble, St Etienne, Nice, Montpellier, Clermont-Ferrand, Limoges, Rennes, Caen and Rouen. Their distribution is either within the proximity hinterlands of the regional metropoli, or in a ring around Paris.

Third-order centres, twenty-four in number, were classified as 'centres with an incomplete regional function'. They were unevenly distributed over the national space, often with specialized functions complementary to each other or to a larger regional town. This category blends into the medium-sized towns (*villes moyennes*) so widely represented in France and indeed the basis of a planning policy (VIth and VIIth Plans) complementary to that for the metropolitan counter-magnet cities (Part III, ch. 2).

Gravier (1970) outlined the criteria for the lesser-order urban centres as follows:

prefectoral seats, 3000–10,000 km² hinterland with 150,000–200,000 population. Minimum town size 20,000, with 8000 in workforce (including 4000 in tertiary activities);

arrondissement towns, 600–3000 km² hinterland, with more than 60,000 population. Though many *arrondissement* towns satisfy these criteria, many others are located in the shadow of larger cities and are limited solely to an administrative function;

cantonal towns, 100–400 km² hinterland, with 4–5000 population. Great diversity in small town size: in Alsace 2–10,000; elsewhere often 800–2000 persons.

At the lower orders in the urban hierarchy the linkage between the town and an administrative unit is close (Thibault 1976). As Gravier put it 'The départemental network has permitted sociological space to be modelled on administrative space much more frequently than in Great Britain or Germany'. The relationship between the higher orders and the twenty-two planning or the eight ZEAT regions is notably less regular. Some regions, including Bretagne, Auvergne, Picardie, or the Centre are not polarized by any major town; in others the central town dominates the region, as in Alsace, Rhône-Alpes or even Limousin.

The French planning mechanism works both through regions, as collections of *départements*, and also in complementary fashion, through management of the urban hierarchy. The hierarchy of towns is uneven and regions very diverse in characteristics and problems; towns and regions alike are still often more directly linked with Paris than with neighbouring units. For perhaps four only of the planning regions is there likely to be a clash of interest between regional growth and urban priorities; elsewhere the two programmes may be harmonized. Characteristically urban growth is the major propulsive force for regional growth. Cardinal to both is the improved communication network analysed later, by road, rail, air, waterway, telephone and telex. The models by which the growth process may be simulated include both central place networks, the centre-periphery formulation, and balanced regional equilibrium frameworks. For the moment such models are embryonic (Courbis and Prager 1973), inputs are inadequate and the integration into a family of national and sub-regional models poses particular problems. There is, however, no doubt but that the search for growth and equilibrium must take into account a regional dimension in national planning, if not necessarily for efficiency then in response to increasing social and political pressures manifested at levels less than that of the nation.

References

General
Demangeon, A. (1942) 'La France économique et humaine', 2 vols in Vidal de la Blache, P. and Gallois, L (eds) *Géographie Universelle*.
George, P. (1967) *La France*.
Vidal de la Blache, P. (1903) 'Tableau de la géographie de la France' in Lavisse, P. (ed.) *Histoire de France,* I.

Regions
Ardagh, J. (1968) *The New France*, Harmondsworth.
Boucher, M. (ed.) (1973) 'La région', *Cahiers Français*, 158–9.
Boudeville, J.-R. (1968) *L'espace et les pôles de croissance*.
Brogniart, P. (1971) *La région en France*.
Chardonnet, J. (1958–9) *L'économie française*, 2 vols.

Claval, P. (1975) 'Planification régionale et aménagement du territoire', *Revue géogr. Est,* XV: 169–216.

Club Jean Moulin (1968) *Les citoyens au pouvoir, 12 régions, 2000 communes.*

Courbis, R. and Prager, J.-C. (1973) 'Analyse régionale et planification nationale: le projet de modèle "Régina"', *INSEE R* 12, 93.

Denis, N. (1974) 'Du mai 1946 au 19 mai 1974', *Revue fr. Sci. politique,* XXIV, (5): 893–910.

Durrieu, Y. (1969) *Régionaliser la France. Capitalisme ou socialisme.*

Flory, T. (1966) *Le mouvement régionaliste français.*

Glayman, C. (1971) *Liberté pour les régions. Bretagne et Rhône-Alpes.*

Gravier, J.-F. (1947) *Paris et le désert français.*

(1970) *La question régionale.*

(1972) *Paris et le désert français en 1972.*

Guichard, O. (1976) *Vivre ensemble.*

Hassold, J. J. (1971) 'La langue bretonne', *Aménagement du territoire et développement régional,* IEP, Grenoble: 421–49.

House, J. W. (1976) 'UK marginal regions in the context of EEC policies' in Lee, R. and Ogden, P. E. (eds) *Economy and Society in the EEC,* Farnborough: 194–216.

(ed.) (1977) *The UK space: resources, environment and the future,* London.

Kayser, B. and J. L. (1971) 95 *régions.*

Knox, P. L. and Scarth, A. (1977) 'The quality of life in France', *Geogr.,* 62: 9–16.

La Documentation Française (1974) 'La réforme régionale. Loi du 5 juillet 1972', *Notes et Etudes Documentaires,* 4064.

Lafont, R. (1967) *La révolution régionaliste.*

Monod, J. and Castelbajac, P. de (1971) *L'aménagement du territoire.*

Naval Intelligence Handbook (1943) *France.* Vol. II, *History and Administration,* London.

Phlipponneau, M. (1968) *La gauche et les régions.*

(1970) *Debout Bretagne,* St Brieuc.

Pisani, E. (1969) *La région . . . pour quoi faire?*

Quelennec, M. (1973) 'Différences et ressemblances entre régions économiques', *INSEE R* 12, 93.

Rochefort, M., Bidault, C. and Petit, M. (1970) *Aménager le territoire.*

Sérant, P. (1965) *La France des minorités.*

Teneur, J. and Di Qual, L. (1972) *Economie régionale et aménagement du territoire.*

Verrière, J. (1968) 'Réflexions sur la région dite du Centre', *Norois,* 15(60): 503–15.

Weigt, E. (1969) 'Die Integration Europas', *Nurnberger Wirtschafts-und Sozialgeographische Arbeiten,* 9.

The urban system

Beaujeu-Garnier, J. (1974) 'Place, vocation, et avenir de Paris et de sa région', *Notes et Etudes Documentaires,* 4142–3.

Brunet, R. (1972) 'Organisation de l'espace et cartographie de modèles: les villes du Massif central', *L'Espace géogr.,* 1(1): 43–8.

Carrière, F. and Pinchemel, P. (1963) *Le fait urbain en France.*

Charlet, J. C. (1967) 'Les agglomérations françaises de plus de 100,000 habitants: quelques aspects de leur croissance', *Hommes et Terres du Nord*, 2: 49–64.

Coppolani, J. (1959) *Le réseau urbain en France*.

Dalmasso, E. (1975) *La géographie urbaine en France depuis* 1945, SSRC, London.

George, P. (1968A) 'Paris. Présentation d'une capitale', *Notes et Etudes Documentaires*, 3463.

    (1968B) *Les villes métropoles*, IEP, Grenoble.

Hautreux, J., Lecourt, R. and Rochefort, M. (1963) *Le niveau supérieur de l'armature urbaine française*, Minist. de la Construction.

Hautreux, J. and Rochefort, M. (1964) *La fonction régionale dans l'armature urbaine française*, Minist. de la Construction.

    (1965) 'Physionomie générale de l'armature urbaine française', *Annls Géogr.*, LXXIV (406): 660–77.

Juillard, E. (1961) *Essai de hiérarchisation des centres urbains français actuels*, Minist. de la Construction.

La Documentation Française (1970) 'Composante de la fonction urbaine: essai de typologie des villes', *Travaux et Recherches de Prospective*, 3.

    (1973) 'Paris. Ville internationale', *Travaux et Recherches de Prospective*, 39.

Le Fillâtre, P. (1964) 'La puissance économique des grandes agglomérations françaises', *Etudes et Conjoncture*, 1: 3–40.

Le Guen, G. (1960) 'La structure de la population active des agglomérations françaises de plus de 20,000 habitants', *Annls Géogr.*, LXIX (374): 355–70.

Noël, M. and Pottier, C. (1973) *Evolution de la structure des emplois dans les villes françaises*.

Noin, D. (1974) 'Les activités spécifiques des villes françaises', *Annls Géogr.*, LXXXIII (459): 531–44.

Piatier, A. (1968) 'Les villes où les Français achètent', Supplément au no. 1229 des *Informations*.

Pumain, D. and Saint-Julien, T. (1976) 'Fonctions et hiérarchie des villes françaises', *Annls Géogr.*, LXXXV, (470): 385–440.

Rochefort, M. (1972) 'La localisation du pouvoir de commandement économique dans une capitale: les sièges sociaux des entreprises dans Paris et la région parisienne', *Revue Géogr.alp.*, LX, (2): 225–44.

Thibault, A. (1976) 'La structure économique des espaces locaux en France: dépendance et domination', *L'Espace géogr.*, 5 (4): 239–50.

3 An environmental appreciation

REGIONAL GEOGRAPHY AND ENVIRONMENTAL MANAGEMENT

Concomitant with the growth of quantification in geography and the rising preoccupation with urban and spatial networks there has been a sharp decline in the attention paid to the physical environment in regional study. Traditionally, the systematic analysis of physical characteristics was regarded as important in its own right (Martonne 1942), and both a fitting and an essential prelude to the interpretation of human geography in any area. The regrettable separation between the physical and the human attributes of place is the more surprising at a time when studies of the total environment and its planned management have come into high fashion (Groupe Interministériel 1976), and there has emerged the possibility of a fresh and compelling harmonization or closer synthesis between Nature and Man.

It is not intended to review the environment of France in order to explain the processes working in systematic physical geography, but rather to attempt an interpretation of the physical attributes in terms of resources, both actual and potential. The economic significance of resources must be balanced by proper regard for the role of resources in environmental management and conservation. The viewpoint must be dynamic since all resources need to be flexibly assessed. A resource has certain finite characteristics, but may have been variably utilized through time in response to demand, price and available technology. It may have potential for further, fuller or alternative uses, or its use may be static, even declining in absolute or in relative terms in the light of demand or the possibility of replacement by a substitute. There is no fatal and unchangeable geographical logic about the resource endowment of a country, but the physical elements set a framework of options, contribute to defining the division of labour, the 'vocation' of place, and offer constraints as well as providing opportunities for development. A stocktaking of natural assets and liabilities is thus a much-needed preliminary to an evaluation of contemporary economy and society. To some extent the stock-taking must be personal, since any resource may be valued differently according to policy perspectives. This has surely been one of the major revelations of the rising environmental debate, in France as well as in the UK. One of the main tasks of public planning, indeed, is to define the range of options in the use of resources, to assess the extent of conflict, assign priorities among potential alternative uses, or promote conservation, in the public interest, with least disturbance to the individual. Conventionally nowadays the maximization of profit motive, or more realistically the pursuit of sufficient satisfaction (satisficing) for the entrepreneur (Plans I — VI), may clash with environmental or ecological management objectives (Plan VII). What is economically profitable may or may not be socially desirable or politically feasible. To aid the planner in resolving these issues a clear picture of available resources and the state of their use is thus a necessary prerequisite.

Natural resources include those arising from position (Part II, ch. 1), the atmosphere, surface of the earth, soil and subsoil. Thus selectivity and some priority ranking is important. Land in its broadest economic connotation, water, and other key minerals, are outstanding natural resources by any criterion. In shaping policies to programme these and other resources certain concepts and methods of assessment need to be formulated. First is that of critical volume, mass or area, together with some measurement of uniqueness, abundance or scarcity, translated through the price mechanism on the one hand and within the framework of public resource-using policies on the other. Related to critical characteristics is the notion of demand or supply thresholds, representing an equilibrium position in terms of use-non use, fuller or lesser use, defined in terms of quality, or accessibility in the widest sense, as well as with reference to quantity. In the case of dynamically-changing resources, such as those of climate or water availability, an evaluation of mean conditions needs to be supplemented by regard for rhythm, regime and amplitude of change, periodic or non-periodic variations, extremes or random catastrophic occurrences, together with some assessment of the total environmental complex both in place and time.

In the narrower economic context, marginal pricing is a valid general-purpose indicator of the trends in resource use. For the wider purposes of planning, cost-benefit techniques are more appropriate for the determination of alternative uses when arbitration may be needed in the public interest. In a broader sense still there needs to be some budgetary assessment of the use of natural resources, involving consideration of the trends towards improvement, conservation or deterioration. Such an overall stocktaking helps to define ground-rules for environmental management policies, by pointing up the most serious trends and problems, and the extent of success or failure in benefiting from or accommodating to the natural heritage.

Environmental management policies

Public policies to safeguard environmental resources and promote the quality of life have come to prominence in both France and Britain only effectively during the 1970s. Unlike Britain, France has had no widespread industrial and urban dereliction to contend with, the legacy from fast economic growth in the nineteenth century. She inherited instead the benefits of extensive, thinly-peopled rural space and the historic character of many provincial centres and small towns. As the result of two decades of burgeoning industrialization and urbanization in France, however, with growth a priority almost without regard for social cost, her precious landscape and townscape heritage came under ever more menacing threat. From long-standing but limited policies of minimum intervention to safeguard public health in the towns and cities, a wide-ranging set of environmental measures were formulated within a surprisingly short space of time (Antoine and Duret 1972). Policy discussions during 1969 led to a new Ministry for the Protection of Nature and the Environment (MDPNE) two years later; in 1974 the Ministry was retitled 'for the Quality of Life' (*qualité de la vie*), with an even wider remit (Groupe Interministériel 1976).

Responsibility of the Ministry covers the entire field of environment management, from research to policy-making, execution and monitoring, together with the coordination of the work of other agencies with environmental interests. To finance such wide-ranging involvement a 'pump-priming' fund was created (FIANE — *Fonds d'intervention et d'action pour la nature et l'environnement*). In its first year of operation the percentage allocation of funds was as follows: anti-pollution and nuisance measures 52 per cent, including air 11, water 28, oceanic 3, dumping of cars 6, sand and gravel 2; protection of nature 31 per cent; and improvement of the urban environment in New Towns 17 per cent. This initial programme indicates the balance between protective measures against the most unacceptable levels and forms of pollution, on the one hand, and the deliberate introduction of better living conditions on the other. As used in environmental management the term environment has thus come to have a variety of meanings (Margant 1973). There is the more limited but increasingly significant ecological approach (Tarlet 1977), focusing upon ecosystems (Delpoux 1972). Alternatively, an economic approach to the management of resources (Boudeville 1973) leads directly to cost-benefit studies and the formulation of investment programmes for the living environment of cities (IAURP 1972, Coulaud 1975), regions (Berquin and Perrin 1973), or recreational and nature conservation zones (Préau 1972). In the preparation of the VIIth Plan (1976–80) environmental management became a more deliberate preoccupation and priority, with control measures and conservation set within a more comprehensive framework (*cadre de vie*) for improving the quality of life (Groupe Interministériel 1976).

After a preliminary assessment of land use the review of natural resources follows the sequence: geology, morphology, topography, the characteristics of the major physiographic provinces and the implications of economic geology; climate in the service of man, environmental factors in the use of land, tourism and recreation, water resources generally and also their implications for energy and transport; the problems of pollution and its environmental management; general conservation issues; and, finally, a summing-up on the problems and prospects for natural resources.

An outline of land use

A broad classification of land, in terms both of present use and further potential, is perhaps the most valid general purpose indicator of natural assets and the extent of their realization. Potential is a many-sided term but it certainly includes measurements of productivity, flexibility for alternative uses, the implications of public as well as private land-using policies. The present pattern of land classification (fig. 8) defines the general framework within which to measure directions and tempo of change. A full explanation of such change involves land values and public policies (p. 77), but consideration at this stage is limited to a general interpretation of the pressures for change, both positive and negative, in response to economic growth or decline tendencies. France as yet lacks an overall public land-using strategy and, furthermore, there are few of the characteristic British physical planning controls over the use of land, in either town or country. Any assessment of the desirable ingredients for a land-use programme must thus be general and related to levels of scarcity or abundance of particular land resources, the priorities to be exercised wherever and whenever competition or conflict in land use arises, and the extent of conservation measures which may be needed.

The basic facts on both land use and its classification are no less difficult to ascertain in France than in the UK. Data is scattered, if available, and has to be gleaned from diverse sources; information on the total area of urban land, in particular, is calculable only with great difficulty. Table 5 shows the structure of land use in 1969, together with trends of change in France since 1920. Comparable data is provided for the UK (1971) and for the annual rates of land use change since the early 1950s in both countries.

With more than double the land area of the UK, France has a greater proportion of her land under improved agricultural uses (arable,

Table 5   Land use change: France 1920–69, UK 1971 and 1950–65

million ha.	France			% total area 1969	UK 1971	% total area 1971	Ann. rates of change France 1952-69	UK 1950-65
	1920	1952	1969					
Arable	25.32	21.15	19.83	36.0	7.22	29.6		
Permanent grass	10.87	12.31	13.81	25.0	4.96	20.3		
Rough grazing	—	—	—	—	6.67	27.3		
Non-cultivated	4.64	5.57	3.58	6.5	—	—		
Other	—	—	—	—	0.28	1.1		
Total agricultural	40.83	39.03	37.22	67.5	19.11	78.3	− 0.3	− 0.2
Forest	10.32	11.40	13.01	23.6	1.85	7.6	+ 0.8	+ 1.2
Urban/site uses	1.43	2.78	3.12†	5.7	2.14	8.8	+ 0.7	+ 1.0
Other	1.78	1.92	1.78	3.2	1.30	5.3		
Total	54.36	55.13	55.13	100.0	24.40	100.0		

(† non-agricultural area minus non-registered land)
Sources: Annuaires Statistiques; Statistique Agricole; A. G. Champion 1974

permanent grass) and almost three times the British proportion under forest. On the other hand much land classified presently as non-cultivated (*friche*) in France might come partly under the heading of rough grazing in the UK. Certainly much more land of marginal quality has been afforested in France and that over a longer period than in Britain. The assessment of land in urban or site uses (communications, industry, public open space etc.) is likely to have been overestimated for France, even though the Paris region alone had 1.0 million ha. urban land in 1962. The French area of urban land seems nevertheless to be some fifty per cent above that of the UK, a surprising statistic indeed. Since the early 1950s the tempo of decrease in the agricultural area has been more rapid in France than in Britain, even though the ratio of non-cultivated land had been reduced, mostly by afforestation. Within the agricultural area there has been a sharp long-term decline in arable land and a rise in the area under permanent pasture, trends characteristic also of the UK during the same period. The rate of growth in both the urban and forest areas was slower in France, but in each case from a larger initial base total. In general terms, with a population rather less than that of the UK, the pressures on the greater land space of France are less intense and prospective conflicts more localized and less severe.

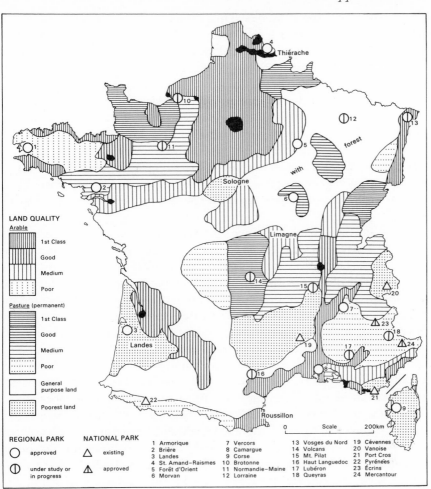

Figure 8   Outline land classification.

First-class land. Fig. 8 shows an outline land classification, based in part upon existing use, in part upon land values, and lastly upon the physical potential of the land. First-class land is irregularly distributed but more prominent to the north of the Loire. The largest compact area of the highest grade land for arable cultivation occupies the centre and north of the Bassin Parisien. At this macro-scale a great deal of internal diversity is obscured, but the physical characteristics are very favourable to intensive, sustained and flexible production of a wide range of crops. This is an area for the most part of large-scale, profitable commercial farming, based on wheat, barley and sugar beet as staple crops, raised on loam (*limon*) soils overlying calcareous rocks, in a longish, moderately intensive growing season. A similar, but very localized area is the Plaine de Caen, set within the first-class pasturelands of Normandie. Other first-class arable lands are found in the plains of Alsace, on well-drained terrace gravels and loam, under a shorter, intensive continental growing season; apart from the vine, the main crops are exceedingly diverse under systems of *polyculture* (multiple cropping on individual farms, or even in particular fields). The Breton coastlands, especially the northern shores, benefit from the mild all-year climate, with an almost continuous growing season, capable of 'early' production of vegetables (*primeurs*). To sustain such intensive fertility on leaching soils heavy fertilizer inputs are necessary, phosphates and lime in particular.

In the southern half of France first-class arable land is mainly under intensive cultivation of specialized crops, including the vine, vegetables and flowers. The main natural asset in most areas lies in the volume of incoming radiation, the higher annual temperatures and the intensive summer growing season. Precipitation often needs to be supplemented by irrigation and most soils are light in texture and lose soil moisture easily. Once again, high fertilizer inputs are necessary to sustain fertility. In Aquitaine the plains and terraces of the Garonne valley have a high ratio of land under arable with a strong representation of vine cultivation and steadily spreading areas under maize. In Roussillon and pockets of coastal land between Marseille and the Italian frontier, land is under specialized crops such as flowers, vegetables and tree-fruit; the broad plains and shallow plateaux of coastal Languedoc are well-known for the high volume production of lower-grade wine, with some diversification to other agricultural uses since the late 1940s. The lower and Middle Rhône valley, with a sheltered climate disturbed only by the chilling local wind, the *mistral*, also has intensive arable cultivation of cereals, fruit crops, the vine, and vegetables.

The first-class permanent pasturelands occupy three types of area: the coastal zone of the north-west, parts of the Hercynian massifs, and the lower and middle slopes of the Jura. The term pastureland in France should be extended to include artificial grasslands (2.7 million ha.) classified under arable, whilst permanent pasture needs subdivision into hay meadows (5.2 million ha.), grazed pasture (4.7 million ha.) and drier alpine-type grasslands (3.8 million ha.). The major regions of first-class permanent pasture are in Normandie west of the Seine, the Thiérache district of the Ardennes fringe, the lime and phosphoric acid rich lands of Auvergne in the Massif Central, and the slopes of the Jura mountains. There is a close correlation between first-class pasture and intensive and traditional dairy farming on the lowlands, cattle rearing or cheese production in the uplands, though stall-fed cattle in arable areas are of increasing importance.

Pressures for alternative uses of high grade arable or grassland are fortunately low and on the whole localized. Table 5 showed that permanent grassland has been increasing during this century at the expense of the arable surface, a characteristic sign of industrializing-urbanizing economies, with rising demand for animal products. It is also indicative of a lessening in the labour-intensiveness of farming. The pressures of urbanization in the Bassin Parisien, both in the growth and outward extension of the metropolis, with its satellite New Towns, and also in the peripheral additions of the high-rise estates (*grands ensembles*), bear directly on first-class farmland. For example, in the Paris planning region the area of farmland fell by 21,780 ha. (3.3 per cent) between 1962 and 1968 (Mission d'Etude 1971). Urban pressures were strongest southwards and westwards, whereas fortunately the first-class farmland lay to the east; additionally, pressures for recreational use spread rapidly into the forested areas on the more sterile tertiary sandstone country. The forward projection of loss of farmland in Ile-de-France (1966–86) indicates a requirement for a further 24,700 ha. for housing and an additional 24,700 ha. for other site uses, making a loss of 7.7 per cent in all. The loss of high grade land around the towns of the Bassin Parisien is an unavoidable outcome of the policy of accepting short-to-medium-distance industrial decentralization and its accompanying urbanization. It underlines the fact that high-grade farmland cannot compete with even the more extensive forms of urban land use, unless there is a firm policy of conservation.

Fortunately the problems of land use conflict on the Greater Paris perimeter are not found to a similar extent elsewhere. Indeed, by comparison with the UK, first-class land in France is much less subject to non-agricultural competition. In the alluvial and silt plains of the Nord coal mining and industry have traditionally intruded upon high grade farmland, with a marked incidence of derelict land; to a lesser extent the same is true locally in Lorraine. It is important in regional land-using strategies that industrial reconversion, the attraction of new industry, should take place either upon existing urban areas, or that industrial sites should preferably be directed to reclaimed derelict land. Along the Côte d'Azur the competition for land is locally intense, with land values high and growing still higher. With a population of 760,000 on 110,000 ha. the forward projection for expansion of the urban area is calculated at 4100 ha. by 1986, even at high densities (ODEAM 1971). Facing such intensive competition, and with an almost astronomical gradient of land values, farming on limited high grade land is consistently squeezed out, unless protected by zoning ordinances. The suburban perimeter of Greater Lyon is also subjected to great growth pressures affecting first-class farmland.

Medium-quality land. Land of intermediate quality for arable usage is found in a narrow zone from the mouth of the Loire eastwards along the southern and eastern borders of the Bassin Parisien (including the lands south of the Sologne), in the tertiary basin of the Limagne (Massif Central), and in the immediate hinterland of the Côte d'Azur. Pastoral zones of medium quality characterize the middle and lower slopes of the Alpes (*basse et moyenne montagne*), the hills of the eastern Massif Central, and a zone from the Seine through southern Normandie to the southern coastlands of Bretagne.

Intermediate-quality land grades into general purpose land, flexible in conversion from arable to pastoral uses. In the eastern Bassin Parisien and in Lorraine this land contains an above average forest cover, located on the poorer siliceous soils of the sandstones (Vosges), clays (Argonne) or limestone skeletal soils (Lorraine, Plateau de Langres). General purpose land is also strongly represented in Poitou-Charentes and in Aquitaine. Conflicts for alternative uses are infrequent, and indeed in any reduction of the agricultural areas of France under the implementation of schemes such as the Mansholt Plan (Common Agricultural Policy of the EEC), the zones of general purpose land are likely to be affected no less than the accelerated withdrawal of cultivation from marginal land.

Low-grade land. Poor-quality land is of three types: the sterile or barren lowlands such as the Landes or the Sologne, the higher surfaces of the Hercynian massifs, or the land above even pasturage potential in the Alpes. The podsolized soils and hydromorphic drainage conditions largely explain the poor quality of the Landes and the Sologne. The shortened growing season and increasing exposure, coupled with skeletal soils, account for the deterioration of land class with rising altitude. Upper cultivation limits have fluctuated through history but are around 1200–1400 m in the Pyrénées, 1200 m in the northern Alpes and as high as 2000 m in the Queyras (Pinchemel 1964). Above these levels are the seasonally utilizable summer pastures, with thin soils and grass growth often insufficient for the cutting of hay. Afforestation of the Landes and the Sologne, the latter especially since 1945, has led to profitable commercial use of low-grade land. The sylvo-pastoral economy of the upper Massif Central, Vosges and Alpes has added to yields from agriculture, but it is a form of economy in decadence over wide areas of marginal land.

Land management policies

French environmental management policies include the promotion of national parks and regional nature parks (Antoine and Duret 1972). These are shown on fig. 8 and their location correlates well with land of modest or poor agricultural value. There are five national parks (Vanoise 1963, Port Cros 1963, Pyrénées occidentales 1967, Cévennes 1971, Ecrins 1973) and from 1967 eighteen designated regional nature parks (*parcs naturels régionaux*), the latter covering two million ha. (four per cent of the national territory) in sixteen of the planning regions. A further national park (Mercantour) and six additional regional nature parks are envisaged (Vosges-du-Nord, Lorraine, Volcans, Lubéron, Queyras, and Normandie-Maine). Forested land has a particular role and representation in French parks, and there is also a well-developed policy for conservation and protection of wild life.

There is, furthermore, a measure of public control over designated areas of *urban land* ripe for development and where land prices might escalate unreasonably. The designation of control areas is by the *département* prefect, not the municipal authorities, and the state undertakes most of the financing. From 1958–67 ZUP (*zones à urbaniser par priorité*, zones for priority urbanization) might be designated, each with no fewer than 500 dwellings and associated infrastructure. All housing schemes for more than 100 new dwellings initially had to be located in a ZUP if public service provision was required (Biarez 1973), though this constraint was later relaxed. The ZUP legislation is often linked to the growth of the *grands ensembles*, the mass housing projects, which provided housing quickly but at a sociological cost that was only realized later. In 1962 ZAD (*zones d'aménagement différé*, deferred development zones) were instituted for two purposes: the purchase of land for major public projects, or for residential development. The ZAD legislation was intended to limit land speculation and contained reserve compulsory purchase powers in the public interest. The more comprehensive ZAC (*zones d'aménagement concerté*, concerted development zones) have been a major instrument of land price control in an area of urban redevelopment since the Outline Land Act (LOF) (p. 326) of 1967. In a ZAC the builder may be absolved from local construction taxes if he finances certain infrastructure. If the local authority delays permission to develop, it may be statutorily required to buy the land. In 1976 the ZIF (*zones d'intervention foncière*, land value intervention zones) were instituted, giving local authority the right to pre-emption, i.e. a priority in land purchase. These land use controls have proved essential, but have been only partially successful in a period of rapid urbanization, permitting the purchase of land ahead of the large-scale housing or industrial schemes which have grown on the perimeter of many French towns since the mid-1950s.

The 1967 Outline Land Act (*loi d'orientation foncière*) established a land use control mechanism closer to the physical planning legislation of post-war Britain. Structure plans (SDAU—*schémas directeurs d'aménagement et d'urbanisme*) and land use plans (POS—*plans d'occupation des sols*) became a statutory requirement (Part III, ch. 2). Yet comprehensive land-using policies by government are still lacking. Public intervention in the land market is to prevent abuse in urban areas and to promote conservation in areas of natural beauty or recreational appeal. The safeguarding of agricultural land from urban encroachment is seen as less of a problem in France than in Britain, though in Provence-Côte d'Azur it is a major issue in the coastal strip and around the Etang de Berre. Nor is there in France a derelict land problem on the scale of that of Britain, yet both countries share a growing realization that pressures for recreational space are mounting rapidly and will in time spread land-use competition and demand careful multi-purpose use even in remote areas of marginal land.

THE PHYSIQUE OF FRANCE

Solid geology and superficial deposits reflect the complex morphological evolution of the physical landscape to its present range, characteristics and diversity of surface forms, drainage and soil-forming qualities as far as these relate to parent materials, and the lithology of rock which denotes the resource base for economic geology and in its turn for the tourist appreciation of scenery. In a regional interpretation the interaction between geology, morphology and surface form is studied for its resource differentiation of the surface and subsurface, rather than for its manifest intrinsic scientific interest.

Geology

An outline comparison between a relief and a geology map of France (fig. 9; *NB*, numbers in the text are keyed to those on the figure) highlights seemingly close relationships between structure and topography within the highly-differentiated mountains and uplands of the southern half of France (II). In the northern half (I), composed rather of plateaux, basins and plains, the relationship is more subtle, overall less clear-cut, and perhaps the least determinate in a broad zone of undulating and shallow plateaux from Bretagne through Normandie to Artois and Flandres. Confirming this initial observation Pinchemel (1964) drew attention to the outstandingly important structural and topographical dividing line between a Hercynian

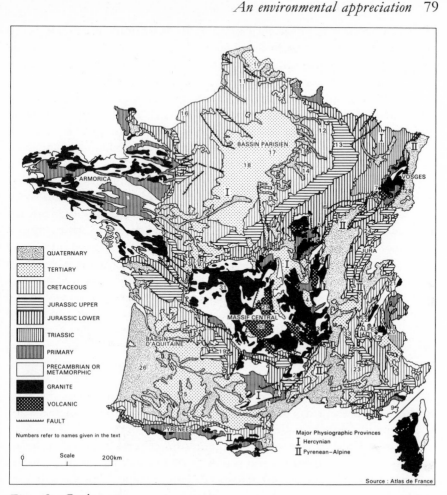

Figure 9   Geology.

and a Pyrenean-Alpine France. The divide runs from the central Pyrénées through the Montagne Noire[1], the Cévennes[2], Monts du Lyonnais[3], Beaujolais[4], Côte d'Or[5], Plateau de Langres[6] to the Vosges[7] and the western rim of the upper Rhine rift valley. For much of its course the divide follows escarpments or fault-lines, along the dislocated southern and eastern border of the Massif Central and the outermost zone of the eastern Bassin Parisien.

The terms Hercynian and Pyrenean-Alpine refer both to differences in geological structure and to the distinctive topographical outcome of its complex morphological evolution. The two major physiographic provinces so defined, reminiscent in some respects of Mackinder's Highland and Lowland Britains, are internally very diverse. To understand both the major differences between the provinces, and to point up the intricate variety within, a brief evolutionary account may be helpful.

The physiographic evolution of France may be interpreted in terms of the structural controls exerted by rafts of hard, resistant rock material underlying much of the country during successive phases of earth movement and mountain-building. The relative stability of these platforms, whose surface expression today is mostly in the Hercynian massifs, led to relief of crustal tension for the most part by uplift, tilting, fracturing or subsidence of sections of the rock rafts. By contrast, the area to the south and east of the rafts, in Pyrenean-Alpine France, was more dramatically affected by complex rippling, folding, churning up and overthrusting of rock masses. Sedimentation during stillstand periods was more rhythmical and less disturbed within the area of rock rafts and their included basins. In the more contorted areas of Pyrenean-Alpine France the sedimentary rhythm was disturbed and complicated during the fashioning, erosion and refashioning of the mountain systems. Through the long geological periods of relative stability denudational processes reduced uplifted surfaces towards base-levels of peneplanation. These resulting erosional surfaces were themselves locally or regionally deformed by subsequent earth movement, but planations across rock material of different age and lithology help to explain morphologically the discrepancies between geology and present-day relief. This is particularly true for the plateaux and the plains of Hercynian France.

The geological basement material composing France has limited surface expression, but it underlies and stabilizes the greater part of the country north and west of the major structural dividing line. This ancient rock material contains pre-cambrian metamorphosed sediments and a wide range of igneous and metamorphic rocks from the early primary period; with exception of the Ardennes[8] there is very limited surface distribution in France of sedimentary rocks of primary age. For the most part the primary rocks are crystalline, resistant to erosion, and contain mineralized veins locally; they tend to poor, thin or skeletal soils in terms of parent rock materials. The present surface patterning of these rocks is that of the roots or ridges of denuded Hercynian mountain chains, bevelled or peneplaned during succeeding erosion cycles or part-cycles.

There is in France no clear representation of the caledonian (siluro-devonian) earth movements, with the north-east to south-west structural trend-lines so characteristic of much of Highland Britain. The first major mountain-building phase important to present scenery was that of the hercynian (armorican) orogeny during permo-carboniferous times. This created complex, but for the most part tightly-structured, east-west axes of folding and dislocation. These east-west trend-lines are most clearly to be seen in the armorican massif of Bretagne and western Normandie, but they reappear in the Pyrenean axis and the small Maures-Esterel[9] massifs in Provence. In the Massif Central the structural roots lie in the south and the trend-lines are rather fan-shaped, north-westwards and northwards. In the Vosges a more ancient north-south axis may have been exhumed, repeated in the backbone of Corse, perhaps an exhumed Malvernian trend-line; in the Ardennes the east-west armorican structural direction is again paramount.

The exposed hercynian massifs have been successively planed-off with widespread removal of the sediments of primary age which once covered them. The most characteristic erosion surface is that of late hercynian times, modified by the later eocene (early tertiary) and the much more fragmented miocene surfaces. Only the Ardennes still have a thick cover of primary age sediments, reminiscent of central Wales or the Southern Uplands of Britain. In Bretagne and Manche the primary sediments have been locally preserved from erosional removal as structural depressions in downfolds, whilst in the much-dislocated structure of the eastern and northern Massif Central primary sediments are very localized and virtually absent over the vast plateaux of the western and southern massif. The igneous rocks of the Massif Central, Bretagne-Manche, and the Vosges contain massive granitic intrusions, further diversifying the structure and surface form. In some areas the granites stand out as rounded uplands, whilst in others they have decayed and afford softer relief.

During the long stillstand era of sedimentation from the permo-carboniferous period to the dramatic Alpine mountain-building period of tertiary times (oligocene and miocene phases) there was rhythmical but not always regular deposition of beds in the two major down-warped basins: the Bassin Parisien and the Bassin d'Aquitaine; along the northern border of France there is localized representation of the Bassin de Flandres[10]. The Bassin Parisien is much the larger of the two principal basins, with a shallow ellipsoid, saucer-like shape and cross-section. The alternance of hard and softer strata in the sedimentary succession is well-marked, with a predominance of limestones and chalk, separated mostly by shales, clays, or marls. The symmetry of deposition was disturbed by the variable depth of down-warping of the basin, so that the chalk and overlying later tertiary rocks are much thicker in the Paris region at the heart of the basin and along the axis of the English Channel. They thin out within the broad zone of north-west to south-east anticlinal flexures stretching from Normandie to

Artois[11] (Pinchemel 1964). Furthermore, the locus of maximum sedimentation migrated through the Bassin Parisien, affecting the thickness of deposits and the range of representation of strata. Subsequently, as a result of the Alpine (tertiary) orogeny, the Bassin Parisien was tilted with its south-eastern rim uplifted. This gave renewed strength to erosional forces, etching out the lithological differences among the exposed rocks and giving prominence to limestone or chalk scarps and uplands. At the same time the major drainage network of the Seine and Loire systems was established, flowing down the 'glacis' towards the Atlantic coast.

The rich diversity of limestones and chalk are the major land-form builders of the Bassin Parisien, occurring in all parts of the geological successions from the trias (muschelkalk) upwards through the jurassic and cretaceous to the tertiary beds. In a secondary role the sandstones are also scarp- or plateaux-building sediments, particularly those of the permian (*grès bigarré*), the lower cretaceous (Argonne) and the tertiary (Fontainebleau sands). The principal limestones are those in the trias (the shell limestone of the muschelkalk), the jurassic (the bajocien of the Côtes de Moselle, the corallian of the Côtes de Meuse[13], and the Portlandian of the Barrois[14]), the cretaceous (the chalklands of Champagne[15], the Pays de Caux[16], Artois) and the tertiary (Brie[17] and Beauce[18]). In the eastern arc of the Bassin Parisien the limestones, chalk and sandstones give rise to a succession of cuestas with westward dip-slopes; near the centre of the Bassin more level bedding leads to residual, flat-topped plateau fragments; along the western flank the chalklands are more widespread, with undulating summits capped with tertiary, or later superficial deposits (*limon*). The economic resources of the basin sediments are referred to later, both as building stone, as a basis for soils, or as industrial salts and minerals including iron ore, salt and gypsum.

Drained axially by the Garonne system, the Bassin d'Aquitaine is smaller and less symmetrical. It has fewer limestone beds and generally softer sediments, with a fuller presence of sands and clays; the karstic surfaces of Quercy[19] and Périgord (jurassic), on the other hand, more closely resemble the dry, barren Causses region of the south-western Massif Central. The tertiary infilling of the Bassin d'Aquitaine was the more widespread but with a higher ratio of sterile or low-grade sediments spreading across the Pyrenean piedmont foreland.

Pyrenean-Alpine France has more dramatic and complex relief, the product of the tertiary and later geological periods. Both the Pyrénées and the Alpes contain remnants of earlier mountain-building periods and both are thus composite chains, but the major orogeny reflected in present physiography was that of eocene-oligocene in the Pyrénées and oligocene-miocene times in the Alpes. The Pyrénées, trending east-west, have a core of hercynian type rocks, igneous and metamorphosed, with less representation of sediments from the secondary or tertiary eras. The Alpes, on the other hand, have a markedly arcuate patterning of zones resulting from the pressures of mountain-building in waves, breaking against the resistant rock rafts of the Massif Central, the underlying basement of the Bassin Parisien, and the Vosges. Pinchemel (1964) drew attention to the marked zoning in Alpine structure and relief. The inner, eastern core is made up of crystalline massifs, with the contorted ancient sediments of the roots of earlier earth movements. Around this core lies the inner-Alpine zone, with an intricate structure of nappes and overthrusts, subdivided into the areas of the lustrous schists succession, and the complex sedimentary areas of the Brianconnais[20]. More clearly differentiated, within the outer western zone, are three further rings: an inner series of crystalline massifs including Mont Blanc[21], Belledonne, Pelvoux and Mercantour, offering some of the finest tourist scenery of the Alpes; a central sweep of the structural subalpine depression[22] (*sillon alpin*); and an outer subalpine zone of folded jurassic and cretaceous sediments, including thickly-bedded massive limestones. This outer alpine zone broadens considerably southwards into a region of domes and depressions (Baronnies, Dévoluy, Diois[23]) with a more marked east-west trend-line. In the central and northern Alpes, on the other hand, dissection has led to more compartmented massifs, separated by deep valley-trenches (*cluses*).

The Jura mountains[24] continue the Préalpes northwards but are structurally independent, with more regular folding of jurassic and, to a lesser extent, cretaceous sediments. The adaptation of the drainage system to the Jura type of structure is a classical example of trellis-patterning, with deep *cluses* trenching across the anticlines and strike-vale streams in the synclinal floors.

Fronting both the Pyrénées and the Alpine system there is a piedmont zone of great diversity. In the Bassin d'Aquitaine the structure is simpler with great tertiary outwash aprons, notably that of the Plateau de Lannemezan[25], composed of gravels and sands. In the south-west apex of France is the great triangular lowland of the Landes[26], composed of quaternary sands. At the eastern end of the Pyrénées the structural basin of Roussillon[27] is the first of a chain which stretches through Languedoc and the Rhône-Saône corridor to the Rhine rift valley in upper Alsace. These basins were formed by faulting along the edges of the resistant rock rafts of the Massif Central, the basement of the Bassin Parisien, and the Vosges. The phases of relative depression were complicated by differential uplift and there were periods of marine transgressions laying down jurassic, cretaceous and pliocene sediments, interrupted by deposition of gravel spreads and deltas from the Alpine province to the east. The plains of upper Alsace[28] show the simplest surface conditions, with river terraces, gravel spreads and the alluvium of the Rhine valley floor. The plains of Languedoc are more complex, with more fragmented outliers of jurassic and cretaceous limestones set within tertiary and quaternary plateaux, gravel spreads and terrace levels. The Rhône-Saône corridor is the most complicated of all, with a succession of basins flanked by tertiary plateaux or hills and floored with a great diversity of quaternary sediments, including the moraines and outwash materials from the quaternary ice age in the Alpes.

The Alpine orogeny had the direct effect of creating, or in part exhuming and refolding the Pyrénées and the Alpes, with the associated Jura chains. The indirect effects were less dramatic but more widespread, affecting the faulted basins of the foreland province of the Alpes, tilting the basement rafts of the Massif Central and the Bassin Parisien-Vosges, causing tensional movements along their lines of structural weakness, and creating the massive volcanic outpourings of the regions of Auvergne[29] and Cantal[30]. Vulcanicity expressed itself in diverse forms: the shield volcanoes of Cantal and Mont Dore, the acid lava cones of the Puys-de-Dôme, and lava sheet flows such as that of Coiron (pliocene). These volcanic areas give potential for soils rich in mineral nutrients, but this is somewhat combatted by the marginal conditions of climate.

Since the Alpine orogeny the sculpturing of the land surface has been modified by limited coastal marine transgressions in the pliocene period, and the localized direct effects, both erosional and depositional, of the four advance and retreat phases of the quaternary ice age. This affected directly the Alpine province, the Pyrénées on a lesser scale, the higher ground of the Massif Central and the Vosges, but France lay beyond the great ground moraine belts of Northern Europe. The overdeepening of Alpine valleys, the moraine-damming of lakes, the valley shoulders and hanging valleys are a scenic topographical heritage from this period. Elsewhere in France periglacial conditions were widespread, affecting ground-water percolation, slope deformation and the denudational work of the river systems. Of outstanding importance in late-glacial or post-glacial times was the wind-blown deposition of the fine loess-like material known as *limon*, derived from the moraine and outwash materials further north. The *limon* caps many of the plateaux and undulations of the northern and central Bassin Parisien. It is also found along parts of the northern coastlands of Bretagne.

The present land surface of France, its altitudes, relief, slopes, country rocks or superficial deposits, its drainage or soil-forming qualities, is in the first instance the product of a long and varied geological evolution. This has differentiated hercynian from Pyrenean-Alpine France and has created the considerable diversity of land-forms and resources within each. It remains to comment briefly upon relief and topography, and upon the hydrological conditions for ground-water, before considering the other economic resources inherent in the geology.

Relief and topography

Almost by way of summary for the preceding section it is clear that regional mean altitudes rise generally south-eastwards through France. The human significance of altitude and of critical thresholds of height varies according to latitude, land-sea relationships, aspect and exposure. North and west of a line joining the mouth of the Gironde with the Ardennes there are only very localized tracts above 250 m in altitude, scattered through the central parts of Bretagne and in southern Normandie. Indeed much of north-western France and the major river valley network of the Bassin Parisien lies below 100 m above sea-level. The Jurassic scarplands of the eastern Bassin Parisien rise to 350–400 m, increasing altitude thus adding to the extremes of regional climate introduced by more continental interior location; the Plateau de Langres[6] rises to 512 m. The Massif Central has well-marked summit-levels, but a general increase in altitude south-eastwards, from 750–1000 m in the Plateau de Millevaches[31], to summits of above 1700 m along the Cévennes[2] escarpment; the former volcanic areas of Auvergne and Cantal rise to more than 1850 m. Within the Jura mountains, on the other hand, summit altitudes are between 500 and 1000 m for the most part and the valley floors of the Rhône-Saône corridor and the Rhine rift valley never rise more than 200 m above sea-level.

The culminating heights of the Alpine province are around Mont Blanc (4807 m) and in the Pelvoux massif[32] (4101 m), both cloaked with glaciers and perpetual snow. The Préalpes[33] rise to over 2300 m but average altitudes throughout the dissected southern Alpes rarely reach 1000 m, with large tracts between 500 and 750 m. The Pyrénées show greater regularity and accordance of heights, rising to 3298 m at Vignemale, but summits of 2500–2900 m are more characteristic. In Corse the central mountain backbone rises to heights of 2710 m and 2625 m respectively. In all these mountain systems the relief amplitude between peak and valley floor is very considerable. Even within the more limited zone of resource use the relief difference between summer pasture and base village or, more recently of importance, between highest winter ski-slopes and ski resort, poses difficult resource management problems.

Water-bearing capacity

The problems and policies of water resource management are treated later. Attention in this section is confined to the location of the principal aquifers, or underground storage areas, and secondly to the geological possibilities of storing water in barrage-reservoirs. Characteristically, these two types of water-resource are found in different areas and are complementary to each other.

The most substantial underground reserves of water are to be found below the Bassin Parisien and the Bassin d'Aquitaine (La DF 1965). Outside these basins there are important ground-water supplies available from the alluvium of the major river valleys, including the upper Rhine, the Rhône-Saône and the coastal valleys of Languedoc and Roussillon. The alluvial water-tables near the great cities suffer, either actually or prospectively, from serious pollution, notably in the Seine valley from Greater Paris to the sea. Moreover the water-table surface is falling disturbingly near several major consuming areas, since underground supplies are renewed only by slow percolation or filtration. Among the most readily-replenished and accessible underground reserves are those in the sands and sandstones of the lower trias (Vosges sandstone), lower cretaceous (greensand formation), tertiary (Fontainebleau sands) and quaternary (Landes sands; sands of Gers and Périgord). The reserves in the tertiary sandstones and limestones (Champigny) of the northern Ile-de-France are of particular importance for the supply of the metropolis. The Paris region draws forty per cent of its water supplies from underground sources (one million cubic metres per diem), of which one-half comes from the chalk succession (senonien beds), and one-quarter from tertiary water-tables. The greensand formation lies at 500–600 m below Paris, but is tapped with difficulty and yields only 100–200 m³ per hour.

Deeper and longer-term water reserves are located in the fissured rocks, especially limestones and chalk, wherever these outcrop and pass below other formations. In the Nord-Pas-de-Calais, for example, the chalk beds (senonien and upper turonien) are the principal source of a regular supply, though the water-table is unevenly distributed. It is a well-stocked aquifer below the valleys, thinner under the plateaux, and almost absent whenever there are impermeable cappings. The carboniferous limestone formations are tapped for 50–60 million m³ per annum to supply the coalfield conurbations, but these reserves are being steadily over-exploited. Some 400–500 million m³ of underground supplies are consumed annually in the Nord-Pas-de-Calais, including 150 million m³ for domestic purposes. Elsewhere in the Bassin Parisien the lower cretaceous (greensand formation), the chalk (cenomanien), the tertiary limestones (Beauce, Brie) and the alluvial water-tables of the upper Seine, the Yonne and the Marne hold the major underground reserves. In striking contrast to the Bassin Parisien the Loire drainage basin has few underground supplies and most of these are from alluvial water-tables below the valley floors.

The Lorraine industrial region draws upon underground water from the alluvium of the Moselle, now fully exploited (19 million m³ per annum); the limestone beds of the ore-mining basin, including some 200 million m³ pumped from the mines annually and used for both domestic and industrial supplies; the lower trias (Vosges sandstone), which also supplies water pumped from the coal mines (130 million m³ per annum); and the suballuvial limestone water-table of the Meuse valley (200 million m³ p.a.). Alsace, on the other hand, is supplied very largely from the massive alluvial water-table of the Rhine rift valley, replenished by the precipitation falling on the Vosges and the Black Forest, and by percolation from the river. Presently less than twenty per cent of the potential 1.3 milliard m³ yield of this water-table is being utilized, but it supplies three-quarters of the water requirements of Alsace.

The principal aquifers in the Bassin d'Aquitaine are of three types: jurassic and cretaceous limestones, in broad zones along the northern and eastern borders; the alluvial water-tables of the Gironde, Dordogne and Adour; and the sands of the Landes region. The reserves from limestone formations are distant from the main urban centres and within the Pyrenean zone the beds dip steeply for the most part and the reserves may be at inaccessible depths. The greatest underground supplies come from alluvial water-tables, both for the supply of water to the larger towns, and for irrigation. The Bordeaux region additionally draws water from artesian aquifers in the limestones and sandstones of the tertiary succession.

Impermeable terrain is widespread within the hercynian massifs of Armorica, the Massif Central, the Ardennes and the Vosges, the non-limestone areas of the Alpes, the Pyrénées and Corse. Within these regions underground reserves are limited, confined for the most part to the alluvial spreads, with local discontinuous water bodies elsewhere. In the Massif Central, for example, the Allier alluvial water-table supplies 2.5 million m³ p.a. to Clermont Ferrand. The volcanic massifs of Auvergne supplement the underground supply and have an estimated potential yield as high as 100 million m³ p.a.

Although underground supplies are limited below impermeable beds there is usually the compensating possibility of frequent potential surface storage sites, at many of which barrage reservoirs have been constructed. In Pyrenean-Alpine France the location and pattern of aquifers is very complicated. Throughout limestone areas such as the karstic Jura or the coastal massifs (Gardiole, Corbières) there are underground supplies, but in most component subregions there is high precipitation and the run-off is rapid and substantial. Percolation to the ground-water table builds up considerable supplies in the gravels and alluvium of the principal river valleys. The Rhône-Saône corridor, with its associated flanking limestone formations, is a major reserve of great importance for almost all the industrial cities along its course. The Durance valley and the barren Crau in the immediate Marseille hinterland offer further prospects for underground supplies. With the rapid urbanization and industrialization of the Rhône-Alpes region in particular, an overall water resource management policy becomes of vital importance.

Other economic geology
In a full evaluation of natural assets the availability of mineral resources of all types is a central issue. Since France is unusually endowed with a great, but markedly uneven, diversity of such resources, some selection and priority ordering are essential. The principle behind selectivity of treatment is two-fold: contribution to the French national economy, and the planning problems associated with the use and aftermath in the use of mineral wealth. For convenience, minerals may be grouped into the following major categories: fuel and power, metallic, non-metallic, and quarry products. Of these categories fuel and power are treated later (Part II, ch. 1), and comment here is limited to the assessment of indigenous resources in the light of national needs.

Table 6 shows in outline form the relationship between the annual French output of key minerals and their role in the total consumption needs of the national economy. The value of output indicates the individual contributions to GDP and also their significance within the balance of payments. The scarcity of fuel and power is part of a much more complex and growing energy problem with a deficit of 8.6 milliard francs in 1969 and 13.7 in 1971. Suffice it here to draw attention to certain salient facts. First, that in spite of a decline in output from 60 Mt at the peak in 1958 to only 33 Mt in 1971 and 25 Mt in 1974, coal is still the most valuable French mineral resource. Yet today almost one-third of French coal requirements continues to be met by imports. Secondly, and in the light of the events of 1974 adding greatly to the vulnerability of the French economy, crude petroleum imports supply 98 per cent of national needs. The French output of crude petroleum is still small in scale (in 1938 only 72,000 t, in 1974, 1,100,000 t), and there are no known offshore oil prospects comparable to the bonanza in the North Sea. Prospecting is active in the Mer d'Iroise off Bretagne, but problems of contested sovereignty remain to be resolved with

Table 6   Mineral resources, 1971

1971 million tonnes	*a* Production	*b* value million frs	*c* Imports	*d* Exports	Imports as % national need *c* as % (*a*+*c*−*d*)
Fuel and power					
Coal	33.0 ⎫		13.6	0.8	29
Lignite	2.7 ⎬	3,280	0	0	—
Crude petroleum	1.8	219	108.8	0	98
Natural gas (milliard m³)	10.8	616	4.2	0	28
Uranium ore	0.7		x	x	x
Metallic minerals					
Iron ore	55.8	749	9.3	18.3	20
Bauxite	3.2	86	0.5	0.1	14
Lead ore	0.04	55	0.14	0	78
Zinc ore	0.02	19	0.38	0	95
Non-metallic minerals					
Salt, rock	4.5	107	x	x	x
Salt, sea	1.1	44	x	x	x
Potassium, salts	12.1	—	0.3	1.2	3
Potassium, K$_2$O content	2.0	320	x	x	x
Sulphur	2.2[1]	168	0.4	0.9	31
Iron pyrites	0.18	6	0.24	0	57
Fluorine	0.11[2]	16	0.12	0	52
Quarry products					
Sand and gravel	205.2	1,485			
Clay, brick	10.8	67			
Clay, cement	13.9	65			
Chalk	30.0	196			
Limestone, building	2.4	129			
Granite, ,,	0.9	98			
Glass and ceramic sands	2.4	96			

[1] including 1.8 from natural gas
[2] from mine stocks
x not known
Source: Statistique de l'Industrie Minérale 1971

Britain in a division of the Atlantic approaches. Natural gas output from home sources has risen sharply since the war (1938 274,000 m³; 1952 276 million m³; 1971 10,281 million m³). Production now meets four-fifths of French requirements, but the ratio of imports from the Dutch fields is rising.

Among metallic minerals vital to modern industry availability is exceedingly uneven and there are marked deficiencies. Iron ore production has fluctuated (1938 34, 1950 30, 1960 62, 1974 54 Mt) but today shows a considerable surplus over French needs; 96 per cent of French production, however, comes from the low-grade Lorraine ore-fields (30.9 to 31.6 per cent Fe content). Bauxite, lead and zinc ores are other significant metallic mineral resources, but of these only bauxite output largely covers French ore requirements and even so there are heavy imports of aluminium. Bauxite production rose from 0.6 Mt in 1938, to 1.1 in 1952 and 3.0 in 1974. There is an absence of copper (imports about 370,000 refined tonnes in 1974), of manganese (1.4 Mt of ore imported 1974) and of virtually all ferro-alloy metals.

There is a variety of non-metallic minerals but none of outstanding importance, or capable of meeting all French needs, with the possible exception of industrial and table salt. Potash is the most significant resource in this group, with a 1971 production (12.1 Mt) almost double that of twenty years earlier. Rock salt production has risen since pre-war days: 1938 1.5, 1952 2.1, 1974 4.9 Mt. Output of sea-salt from evaporation pans, on the other hand, has fluctuated considerably: 1938 0.5, 1970 0.3, 1974 1.0 Mt. Among deficiencies, that of calcium phosphates ranks high, with 3.9 Mt imported in 1971, mainly from N. Africa, Togo and the USA. Sand and gravel extraction dominates as the source of building materials, even though France is moderately rich in building stones; granite or limestone quarries are located to some extent in complementary fashion regionally. Yet it is sand and gravel, clay for bricks or cement, and chalk for cement that provide the most substantial, freely-available, flexible, and fastest-growing raw materials for the building industry.

Fig. 10 shows the distribution of the principal French mineral resources, excluding those of fuel and power (see figs. 38–42). The low-grade *minette* iron ores in Lorraine have already been referred to. They are located within the jurassic succession, above the lias formations and at the base of the bajocien limestone. The ore body is contaminated by phosphorus and had to await the Thomas-Gilchrist purifying process (1878) before being brought into large-scale commercial production. It is worked by mining and open-casting on the flanks of the Côtes de Moselle and in the tributary valleys west of the main escarpment. Output has become stabilized during the past few years at about 54 Mt of ore, containing 16 Mt Fe content. Almost two-thirds of the output goes to French blast furnaces, mostly locally, one-quarter goes by rail to Belgium and Luxemburg, and seven per cent is exported to the adjacent Saar steelworks. Although large reserves exist, estimated at six milliard tonnes, the future of the low-grade Lorraine ores is uncertain in the face of cheaper, higher-quality foreign ores landed at the major coastal steel complexes of the EEC.

Other French iron ore bodies are small in scale, but the Fe content is higher. The Normandie and Anjou-Bretagne ores occur in primary age sandstones or schists and vary from 41.8 to 56.0 per cent Fe content, with

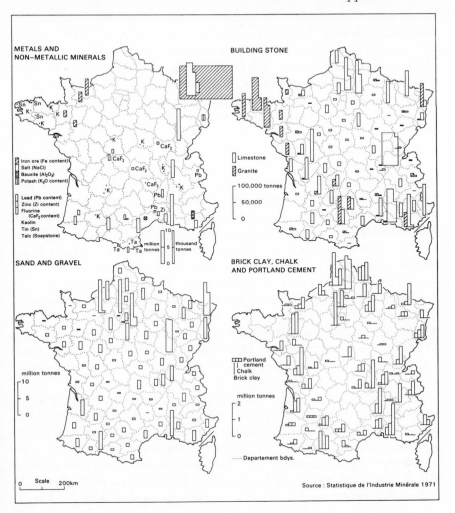

Figure 10   Mineral resources (other than fuel and power).

an output falling from a peak of 2.5 Mt (1967) to 2.2 Mt in 1974; 78 per cent of production is consumed in French steelworks, 11 per cent goes to the Saar and 6 per cent to Belgium or Luxemburg. The remaining small iron ore deposit in Pyrénées-Orientales is of high-grade ore (48.3 per cent Fe content), producing 89,000 t in 1974, all of which was exported.

The decomposition product of cretaceous limestone, bauxite deposits, are found entirely within the Midi, three-quarters of national production coming from the Var *département* and much of the remainder from Hérault

(Bédarieux, Villeveyrac). The bauxite is processed mainly for anhydrous alumina, an intermediate stage in the extraction of aluminium metal; in 1974 one million tonnes of anhydrous alumina were produced. The major alumina-processing plants are in Var (Gardanne, La Barassé), Gard (Salindres), the Pyrénées and the northern Alps. Lead, zinc and silver deposits occur on a small scale within the southern border of the Massif Central; tin is found at three sites in western Bretagne, whilst uranium ores are worked in small, scattered deposits in both the Massif Central and southern Armorica.

Fortuitously, none of the French deposits of metallic minerals are worked within areas of high amenity or priority for landscape conservation. Derelict ore-mining land in Lorraine is, perhaps, the major problem involving large-scale landscape restoration. A similar but more limited restoration or conservation problem affects also the principal non-metallic mineral workings. Localized subsidence may be a problem in the triassic deposits of the Lorraine salt-field, from which 2 Mt of salt are removed annually by the brining process, and a further 1 Mt in solid form. Furthermore, there is seepage into the water-table and sterilization of underground water-supplies over a wide area. Other rock salt deposits are worked in the Jura, in northern Drôme (Hauterives) and in the western Pyrénées. Sea-salt extraction by evaporation from coastal salt-pans has had a chequered history, but today 98 per cent of production comes from the Mediterranean coast, particularly from Bouches-du-Rhône.

Output of potash is concentrated in Alsace, near Mulhouse. Five per cent is exported and of this two-thirds goes to other member-states of the EEC. Kaolin for china clay is worked in the decayed granites of western Bretagne and Dordogne, but without giving rise to a landscape restoration problem on the scale of the Cornish pits. A small but economically significant area of talc extraction (298,000 t in 1974) is located in the eastern Pyrénées.

Building raw materials are in ever more voracious demand. Fig. 10 shows the pattern of sand and gravel extraction, emphasizing the importance of alluvial gravel spreads in valley bottoms within economic transportation distance of the major city markets. The Seine valley within and downstream from Paris is yielding almost 40 Mt per annum and almost 20 Mt are being extracted in the upper Bassin Parisien, from the Yonne valley and its tributaries. Some 60 ha. of alluvial land are being sterilized annually, and on estimated rates of continuing extraction the reserves will be exhausted by 1980. Other significant extraction areas include the Rhine rift valley (17 Mt), the Rhône delta (7.7 Mt) and the upper Garonne valley (5.6 Mt). Almost one-half the French sand and gravel output is from wet pits, or directly from river beds. The restoration problems near cities are the more difficult in that urban wastes cannot be dumped without risks of polluting the underground water-table. Chalk quarrying, on the other hand, produces great terraced open-cast workings, which often remain as major scars on the landscape. The areas principally affected are in Yvelines (west of Paris), the northern Bassin Parisien, eastern Lorraine, the Jura, Bouches-du-Rhône, and Mayenne.

Clay for bricks is worked in most parts of France, but there are concentrations of pits near the major urban areas, though not notably so in the Paris region. Clay for cement is produced in areas in which chalk also is readily available as in Pas-de-Calais, Lorraine, Alpes-Maritimes or Bouches-du-Rhône. Clay pits also produce planning problems, since they are virtually all wet and there is commonly a measure of conflict with continuing use for farming. Manufacture of portland cement is centred in Pas-de-Calais (2.5 Mt), the western Ile-de-France (3.0), west of Lyon (1.7), Mayenne (1.2), the Alpes Maritimes (0.6) and Bouches-du-Rhône (0.7). Finally, fig. 10 also shows the distribution of limestone and granite quarries for building stone. These are often of long standing and also contribute to the scarring of the landscape. Such building stones are increasingly expensive by comparison with bricks, concrete, or synthetic stone. Furthermore, production sites are often distant from the major urban markets and transport costs are high on such bulky materials.

CLIMATE AS A RESOURCE

Together with the physique and structural characteristics of the land surface climatic conditions help to explain the prime differentiation in the use of a wide range of resources, and the framework of a natural division of labour based upon biological productivity. The full economic implications of climate cannot easily be isolated and unambiguously measured, even among other environmental characteristics. Nor can they be readily evaluated within the context of non-environmental factors affecting production or profitability. Nevertheless climatic conditions are often paramount in setting flexible limits to the range of options in the use of many natural resources. These limits may be ecological in absolute terms, in the sense of what is possible up to the finite frontiers of cultivation, afforestation, settlement, the storage or extraction of water, or the location of some high-altitude recreational facility. Much more commonly, however, are the less-determining climatic limits defining the relative profitability of exercising any particular option. Such marginal conditions of profitability among alternative uses, or mixes of uses, are even more difficult to establish and measure, for a number of reasons. First, profitability differences between entrepreneurs in any one region may transcend those arising from climatic conditions varying over either space or time. Secondly, there are usually so many complicating economic or social considerations affecting productivity or profitability that its biological or ecological fundaments are not easily costed. Thirdly, profitability is a rapidly-changing concept, rarely applicable for more than one season, and perhaps for even less if public policies on pricing are changed in the short term.

Notwithstanding these or other qualifications on the economic meaning or potential of climatic conditions, it is possible to make a threefold interpretation: as the basis for a selective use of resources for either specialized or balanced production, on grounds of natural comparative advantage; in respect of the competitive assets which may be conferred by particular features of climate in individual areas over a given period of time; and in relation to resource-conserving or sustained yield-managing policies. In an increasingly environment-conscious age it seems right that there should be the closest accord with the natural basis of productivity in the use of resources and, furthermore, that conservation should have precedence over profitability wherever and whenever these may be in conflict.

The resources most directly influenced by climatic conditions concern the use, productivity and potential of land under farming or forestry. Secondly, there are the implications for the rapidly growing industry of tourism, with its proliferating use of recreational space. Thirdly, there follows a consideration of water supply, its distribution and multiple-purpose usage. Some reference is then made to the potential for generating hydro-electricity, and it is also necessary to look briefly at the relationship between climate and transport in France. Climate and human health is a further not very well-known dimension (Besancenot 1975).

It is not intended to analyse French climatic conditions in a systematic manner in their own right, but rather to select and comment upon those elements which have the most direct economic connotation and influence in respect of each major resource use. Nevertheless, a brief summary of essential climatic characteristics and their regional variations may be a helpful preliminary.

An outline of climate

By comparison with the UK France occupies more southerly latitudes (43–51°N, Corse 41°) and has a position more clearly intermediate between maritime-oceanic, continental and Mediterranean climatic influences. The total incoming solar radiation is thus greater, and the plateaux, basins and plains of hercynian France offer few obstacles to the free-flow and interchange of maritime-oceanic and continental conditions. Mediterranean climatic characteristics are for the most part confined to the narrow coastal lands of Languedoc-Roussillon and Provence-Côte d'Azur, with limited extensions into the Rhône-Saône corridor. The Alpes, Massif Central and, to a lesser extent, the Pyrénées thus create important climate divides and nurture their own mountain or high-plateau climates. As in the UK the influence of maritime-oceanic conditions is most prominent during the winter months, with a general north-south orientation of mean isotherms (more than 6°C mean January temperatures in a coastal strip from the Spanish frontier to the mouth of the Seine; 0°C from the Lorraine plateaux to the Plateau de Langres, the Jura, Alpes, Massif Central and the Pyrénées). During summer the influences of latitude and altitude predominate (18°C mean July isotherm links southern Bretagne, Paris and the plains of Alsace), with an approximate fall of 0.6°C mean temperature for every 100 m increase in altitude.

Even more than altitude, slope and exposure are the dominating influences upon mean annual precipitation (fig. 12). Westward-facing slopes universally receive heavier precipitation whilst the total amount diminishes eastwards through the Bassin Parisien and Bassin d'Aquitaine until increasing elevation causes higher totals in the Vosges and the Massif Central (Brest 1,129 mm, Paris 619 mm, Nancy 712 mm). Precipitation regimes vary from the characteristically maritime-oceanic (Brest), with a summer minimum in June and late autumn-early winter maxima, to the modified continental (Strasbourg) with a pronounced midsummer maximum and a minimum in early spring (fig. 11). Intermediate between these opposites is the Paris regime with an early spring minimum and a tendency to a slight maximum in late summer, whilst at Dijon the spring minimum is more accentuated and there is a secondary minimum in July. In Mediterranean France the characteristic midsummer and the late autumn maximum are well-known, whilst in the Massif Central there is an early summer maximum with a winter minimum, and a secondary minimum during July. There is great complexity of regime among Alpine stations, but February is characteristically the month of minimum precipitation.

Finally in this brief introductory outline a consideration of air-mass controls and characteristics confirms that France shares with the UK, though to a less marked extent, the day to day weather and seasonal variations arising from the fluctuating sway of air-masses with different characteristics. During the winter months the dominant air-masses are the high-pressure centres over eastern Europe, the Azores, Scandinavia and, less importantly, Greenland. Over the northern Atlantic lies an interrupted

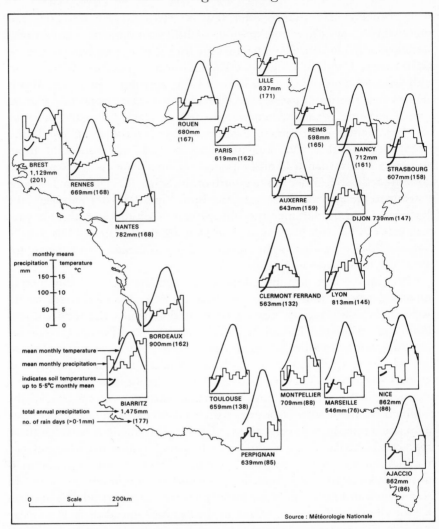

Figure 11   Mean monthly temperature and precipitation, 1931–60 means. Representative stations.

belt of low-pressure systems, with centres passing south of Iceland in broad tracks north-eastwards towards the Arctic ocean. Less frequently, the depression tracks pass over the UK, into the Baltic, or southwards across France to the Mediterranean. The average frequency of air-masses over France is as follows (per cent): cold and very cold, polar continental (Pc) 35, polar maritime (Pmk) 30, arctic continental (Ac) 6, arctic maritime (Am) 6;

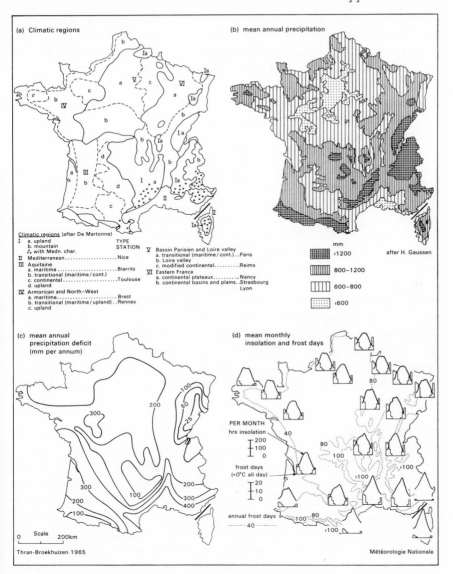

Figure 12   Climatic regions; mean annual precipitation; mean annual precipitation deficit; mean monthly insolation and frost-free period.

warmed polar maritime (Pmw) 20; tropical maritime (Tm), much more common over the UK, 3. In summer the depression tracks pass further north and fewer low-pressure systems affect France. There are high-pressure centres over the Azores and south-east Europe, with low pressures over the north European plains. The frequency of air-mass dominance shows: arctic maritime 3 per cent; polar continental 33, cold polar maritime 26, warm polar maritime 24; tropical maritime 6; and Mediterranean warm air 7 (Reader's Digest 1969).

Regional differentiation of climatic conditions within France (Bénévent 1926, Estienne 1956, Pédélaborde 1957) is more clearcut at the extremes, in the definition of maritime-oceanic, mountain, Mediterranean or modified-continental climatic regions, but there are many intermediate gradations (fig. 12). This is particularly true of the principal farming belt from Aquitaine through Bretagne and the Bassin Parisien. Martonne (1942) stressed the importance of even localized differences in topography in modifying climatic conditions marginally but significantly. He distinguished four subregions in Aquitaine: an oceanic strip, a transitional zone, a more continental inner zone, and an eastern upland margin. In Bretagne and Normandie he differentiated the inland hill and plateau country from the coastal margins. Within the Bassin Parisien he identified the transitional zone around Paris, a distinctive subregion of the Middle Loire, and three zones of increasing continentality in Champagne, the plateaux of Lorraine, and the Vosges-Alsace.

Thus far climatic conditions have been reviewed in regional or macro-terms, the generalized basis for evaluating economic potential. In the following sections, on particular resources, it will be necessary to consider meso- and micro-scales as affecting the growth of plants or the well-being of humans.

Climate and farming
The process of crop or grass production involves the conversion of the environmental inputs of solar energy, water and soil nutrients into a wide range of economic end-products (Wareing and Cooper 1973). In determining the best return from available natural resources, economic or political considerations may dictate the type of farm system or the selection of crop, but choice should as far as possible be based upon biological principles of productivity. In this respect it has been said that climate influences choice of crop, whilst weather governs the yield. Crops should be reasonably tolerant of climatic variations and be consistently productive from year to year. As far as possible those crops should be avoided which yield well only under the most favoured conditions. On the other hand, and most notably so in the case of vines, the highest quality product may be grown close to the ecological margins of cultivation. Within reason, man has been able to breed plants to get the maximum from locally available environmental conditions.

The annual cycle of incoming solar radiation is the dominant control upon photosynthesis and evaporation, measured in k cal/cm² for unit periods of time. In France the total annual solar radiation, governed mainly by latitude but modified by cloud cover, varies from about 100 k cal/cm² in the north to 140 along the Mediterranean coast. During July at the height of the growing season the mean monthly range is from 12 k cal/cm² in the Nord-Pas-de-Calais to 20 in Languedoc, but in January the gradient diminishes (2 to 6 k cal/cm²). Budyko (1968) illustrated the importance of radiation budgets by a comparison of yields for Golden Delicious apples as between the Rhône valley and south-east England. In the former area, with 40 per cent higher midsummer radiation totals, the yield was 40,000 kg per ha.$^{-1}$ compared with 27,000 kg per ha.$^{-1}$ in England. Furthermore, cereal yields are closely correlated with total effective radiation during the growing season.

Radiation measurement is still patchy and, though less directly useful, temperature data is normally used in its place. The critical considerations in temperature relate to the length, rhythm and intensity of the growing season, which is often defined either as the period of frost-free days or the period during which diurnal temperatures are higher than 6°C for more than three hours. Fig. 12 shows the regional variations in frost-free period from more than 345 days along the coastal strips of Bretagne and Manche and the entire Mediterranean shores to around 275 to 300 days in the central Bassin Parisien, 240 to 275 in Lorraine and less than 265 days in the Massif Central, the Vosges, the Alpes and the Pyrénées. A clear correlation has been established between milk yields and the number of grass-growing days.

The air and soil temperatures in the early weeks of the growing season are critical for the onset of growth. Fig. 11 has an indication of calculated soil temperatures for the first four months of the year and the rate of increase at each station. This data reinforces the sharp contrast between the long slower-growing season with an early but slow onset in the western coastal areas, and the short more intensive growing season in the east; the quality of soils for early warming in the east is critical for the starting of plant growth. Finally on temperature, the distribution of average air temperatures through the period of 150 days after the mean diurnal temperature first exceeds 5°C shows variation from 10 or 11°C on the western coast to 13°C in the central Bassin Parisien, and 14°C in Lorraine and the Mediterranean coastlands (Thran and Broekhuizen 1965).

Fig. 12 shows total annual precipitation and fig. 11 the monthly incidence and rhythm at individual stations. Precipitation during the growing season (April—September) is critically important, particularly the proportion which falls during the spring months. The Mediterranean coastlands have low summer season totals (200 to 300 mm) and rarely more than one-third of annual precipitation during the growing season. Western coasts have very variable summer totals (Biarritz 655 mm, Brest 425 mm, Rouen 335 mm), representing between one-third and one-half the annual amount. Within most of the Bassin Parisien about 330 mm fall between April and September, one-half of the annual total. Under more continental conditions further east growing season rainfall is about 400 mm and almost two-thirds of the yearly contribution. With increasing altitude the total precipitation increases but a smaller proportion falls during the shortening growing season. Generally speaking rainfall during spring (March—May) is less than 130 mm throughout the major arable farming lands of the Bassin Parisien. The incidence of summer storms over the same areas is variable but with from 40 to 150 storm days between June and August there are additional hazards to successful cropping.

The value of precipitation to plant growth depends upon the evapotranspiration rates and the availability of soil moisture. Fig. 12 shows the annual maximum precipitation deficits in mm, varying from less than 50 mm in Alsace, to 200–300 mm over much of the Bassin Parisien, and between 300 and 400 mm in the south of France. The deficit in the Bay of Biscay coastlands (about 300 mm) is greater than from Bretagne to the Belgian frontier (less than 200 mm). These deficits are calculated by deducting the average annual potential evapotranspiration (Turc's formula) from the mean annual total precipitation. A negative residual indicates the scale of the need to supplement precipitation by irrigation or water conservation. Between 500,000 and one million ha. are presently irrigated in France and the irrigated area is increasing at almost 50,000 ha. per annum.

Climate and tourism

The tourist appeal of an area will normally be based at least in part upon certain positive climatic elements; conversely, unfavourable or unreliable climatic conditions are likely to affect tourism somewhat adversely. Positive elements include duration and seasonal incidence of sunshine, particularly in coastal areas; availability, quality and depth of snow in winter sports areas, emphasizing conditions over Christmas and Easter; reliability of mean temperatures during the holiday periods, and diurnal variations, especially land-sea breezes at coastal resorts. Negative aspects relate to excessive precipitation, number of rain-days, storms, cloudiness and low temperatures in coastal areas. In the mountains the unreliability and poor quality of snow cover, or its absence at either Christmas or Easter, are unfavourable features; the cool damp summer conditions in uplands surprisingly seem readily discounted by holiday-makers.

The highest insolation figures during summer (April to September) are found along the Mediterranean (about 1800 hours); by comparison Atlantic coast figures are much lower (Biarritz 1231, Brest 1191, Rouen 1151 hrs.). Alpine and high altitude stations elsewhere conventionally enjoy between 1300 and 1500 hrs of summer insolation. The sunshine advantage of the Mediterranean coast is confirmed by the 800 to 1000 hrs of insolation during the autumn and winter months, justifying the year-long tourist season. Further adding to the climatic assets of the coast from Roussillon to the Côte d'Azur is the long, dry summer with slight risks of precipitation; Corse enjoys a comparable range of advantages. Summer precipitation risks are higher along the Atlantic and Channel coasts, e.g. Biarritz 86 rain days (more than 0.1 mm fall) between April and September, Brest 87, Rouen 75. At all these stations the likelihood of rain increases as the summer holiday season progresses. The risks of the occasional torrential downpour are, however, confined mainly to the mountains, plateaux and lowlands of the southern half of France.

Snow cover is notoriously uneven and variable from year to year. Ten-year averages indicate 30 to 99 days per annum with snow lying in much of the Massif Central, the Préalpes, the Vosges and the lower slopes of the Pyrénées. At higher altitudes up to 2000 m the snow cover is usually 100 to 149 days. Mountain life has for many centuries become attuned to the severity of winter and the length of the snow cover has long governed the agricultural year. The date of the disappearance of the snow cover is more significant than that of the last frost in the onset of both ploughing and pastoralism. The *alpage* season is limited by snow cover, e.g. to only eighty days in Beaufortin, and the period of stall-feeding of cattle and sheep may vary from as little as three months to as much as eight months in the highest Alpine valleys (Val de Tignes, Haute-Maurienne).

At all altitudes above 1000 m snow cover poses a problem not only in limiting the farming year, but also in the temporary or seasonal interruption of communications, particularly by road (Boisvert 1955). To sustain the escalating winter sports industry a strategy of road clearance has been developed, but it is expensive. In the Briançon area, even as far back as the early 1950s, snow clearance was costing 50,000 frs per km during the winter and spring. Several of the Alpine cols are normally open only for a limited season: e.g. Petit St Bernard, on average 1 June—5 November; Iséran, 1 July—1 November; Izoard, 5 July—10 October. Others such as the Cols du Lautaret, de Porte and de la Croix Haute are kept open all the year round.

The mean snowfall in the northern Alpes is 3 m and above at 1500 m altitude, but only 2.50 m in the southern Alpes at a comparable height. In the Préalpes many winter sports stations are below 1200 m and though they may receive more than three metres of snow in an average year there is likely to be considerable variation from year to year. The deficiency of snow at middle-altitude stations is offset in part by the development of ski-lifts to open up the more substantial and reliable snowfields at or above 2000 m, e.g. at Villard de Lans or Isola. Newer stations have been created at these higher altitudes (p. 296).

WATER SUPPLY, DISTRIBUTION AND MANAGEMENT

Since on average 1.5 per cent of the total French GDP is expended on the use of water as a public resource, from supply to sanitation, it represents an economic good of steadily rising and increasingly critical significance. The distribution and seasonal incidence of precipitation has been outlined, and also the location and characteristics of the major underground aquifers. It remains to consider run-off and its implications, the possibilities of storage, the principal features of water distribution and usage, and the strategies for the most effective coordination of available water resources in each of the major drainage basins. Soil water requirements for plant life are discussed later.

As in the UK so in France an integrated approach to river basin management came late (1965–6) and is still in the early stages of implementation (La DF 1973). The problem of budgeting for the most effective use of water resources is complex and involves balancing availability of supplies with a demand rising among a multiplicity of potential users. This is a question of quantities in the first instance, but increasingly also of quality of supplies. It is also a matter of supplies adequate in quantity and quality at the right place at the right time. Since water is a universal resource, capable of multiple uses, management policies must increasingly assign priorities among alternative possible users and in so doing may need to sustain the public interest against would-be unilateral private users. Hitherto considered an abundant resource in most areas, water has rarely been charged for at economic cost and thus market forces have so far played a limited role in regulating usage. With an increasing realization of the relative scarcity of supplies in certain places, and during periods of low-water flow almost everywhere, the costing of usage becomes an important means of assuring that priority needs are met, and that users contribute an appropriate share of the costs of making supplies of the right quantity and quality available. In such an allocation of costs the pollution of supplies during and after use must also be increasingly taken into account. Conversely, where policies for the protection of nature involve limitation upon abstraction of supplies, or upon certain uses of water, it is appropriate that public authority should contribute to the marginal costs of modifying some economic parameters.

The global water budget of France starts from the 440 milliard m³ of precipitation over the land surface. Of this quantity, which varies from year to year, 260 milliard m³ are lost by evaporation or evapotranspiration. The annual surface flow is thus 180 milliard m³, of which 70 to 90 milliard m³ are contributed by direct run-off and 110 to 90 milliard m³ come from underground water-tables. Unfortunately there is great seasonal fluctuation in gross surface flows, from a median January figure of 9800 m³/sec down to 2800 m³/sec in August; at least once in every hundred years the low season flow may be as low as 1000 m³/sec throughout France (La DF 1965). Furthermore, conditions vary markedly from river basin to river basin and, since water management policies are presently related to individual major catchments, the problems of supply must be examined at basin level. As yet there are very limited intercatchment bulk water exchanges, other than those needed to sustain inland navigation over summit levels (perhaps 200 to 300 million m³ per annum for twenty summit sections).

For the assessment of natural supply and replenishment, regional climatic conditions need to be interpreted in terms of the characteristics of river regimes (Martonne 1942). These relate in turn to the total annual precipitation, its seasonal incidence and long-term reliability, the levels of evaporation or evapotranspiration, the ratio of run-off to storage (either surface in the form of snowfields or reservoirs, or by percolation to underground water-tables), and the configuration of both the river channel and the catchment basin.

Martonne distinguished four regional hydrological regimes: the Atlantic plains, broadly corresponding to Pinchemel's hercynian France less the Massif Central and the Vosges; the uplands; the Alpes; and the Mediterranean. Over the basin and plateaux north of a line from the Basque country to the Vosges less than one-third of precipitation runs off directly. Two-thirds percolates to the underground water-tables and is released more regularly, evening-out the river regimes. In summer run-off may fall to less than ten per cent of precipitation; in the heaviest precipitation, through the winter, run-off rises to two-thirds and yet the underground water-tables are largely restocked during this period.

In the uplands of the Massif Central, the Vosges, the Préalpes and the Jura run-off rates are characteristically higher than 50 per cent. Winter precipitation is in the form of snow, held for several months and then melted in large quantities over short periods. Two subtypes of river regime may be recognized: the snow-rain (*nivo-pluvial*) and the rain-snow (*pluvio-nival*). The former is characteristic of the Préalpes, the latter of the Massif Central and the Jura. Both show double maxima and double minima in river flow patterns: maxima in autumn, due to reduction in evaporation and increase in precipitation, and spring, caused by the snow-melt; minima in summer, due to low precipitation and high evaporation, and in mid-winter due to freezing and retention of precipitation in the form of snow or ice. The snow-rain variant has a delayed spring secondary maximum. The Alpine regime (*nival*, or glacial) covers very localized high mountain tracts. With up to six months of snow-lying there is a steady melting through spring and summer with high flow in the rivers and torrents. Winter is the period of minimum flow. The Mediterranean regime has the reverse pattern of autumn-winter maximum flow and summer drought when local river-beds may be dry.

The principal rivers of France rise in areas of upland or Alpine regimes and flow through plateaux and plains with different regime characteristics (fig. 13). Their flow patterns are thus composite and complex. That of the Seine system is the most regular and least influenced by an upland headwaters regime; flooding is usually due to precipitation from winter low-pressure systems rather than the effects of snow-melt. The Loire, on the other hand, is perhaps the least stable in regime, with two-thirds of total annual flow coming off the impermeable Massif Central. Heavy flooding from the upper reaches contrasts with the marked low-season flow in the middle course, with its broad, flattish bed subject to heavy summer evaporation. Underground aquifers are largely lacking and the river regime is thus more fluctuating and directly dependent upon precipitation over the catchment. The Garonne system has very low summer season flow with a composite regime, snow-rain as far as Montauban and rain-snow downstream under the influence of the major tributaries from the Massif Central. Flooding may be destructive, particularly in spring and autumn, but the most frequent flood period is during the winter months. The Rhône catchment experiences virtually all the types of regime, combining Alpine with upland, snow-rain with rain-snow, and partaking also of the Mediterranean regime for the tributaries joining in the lower reaches. Above Lyon the Saône has a regular flow (*pluvial* type, with summer minimum and spring and winter maximum); the Isère has an Alpine regime (*nival*, with summer maximum and winter minimum); the Durance has a regime with both Alpine and Mediterranean characteristics. Thus by Beaucaire the composite Rhône has low season flow in August-September

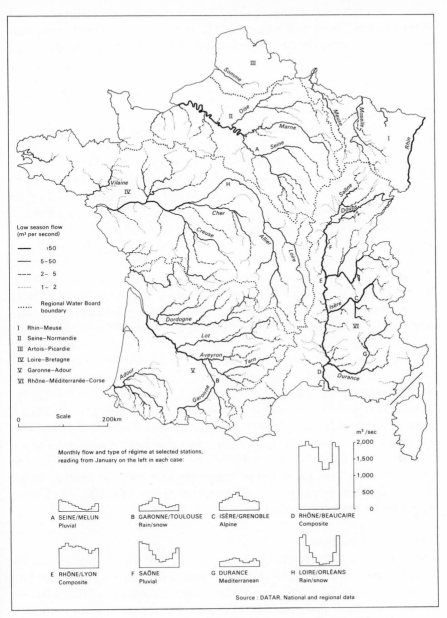

Figure 13 Regional Water Boards. Low season flow and seasonal regimes.

(7 litres per second per km² of catchment during 10 consecutive days of minimum flow), but a well-maintained flow throughout the rest of the year (45 l/sec km² during 10 days of maximum flow; 18 l/sec km² under mean discharge conditions). By way of summary it may be noted that a comparison of low season discharge of the major rivers near the mouth shows: Seine 80, Loire 180, Garonne-Dordogne 210, Rhône 650 m³ per second.

Figures for global *water consumption* are notoriously difficult to establish. A survey during the mid-1950s (La DF 1965) suggested the following proportions among French consumers in milliard m³: domestic public distribution 3.5, including 2.5 urban; agricultural, including irrigation, 10 to 15; industry 10.4, of which 6.8 was for power station use. The per capita consumption per annum for all purposes has been variously estimated and clearly differs considerably according to both regional economic structure and living standards: Paris 194 m³, Lyon 146 m³, Marseille 354 m³. Water use for domestic purposes varies from 5 to 15 m³ per person per annum in rural areas, to 10–40 m³ in the towns, 20–50 m³ at seaside resorts, and up to 350 m³ for resident population on the Côte d'Azur with its very large seasonal population variations. Water needs differ markedly within and between the major drainage basins (table 7) but demand for water is rising steadily, though not uniformly, among the many users. It is estimated that between now and the end of the century domestic requirements in France will increase by a factor of 2.3 and the needs for power station cooling and process water by 5.7. On the other hand recycling and re-use of water has already led to great economies in its industrial use. Presently, to produce 1 tonne of pig-iron 250 m³ of water are required, but within thirty years this may be down to 2 m³. Comparable reductions may be envisaged for 1 tonne of sugar (from 100 m³ down to 10 m³), or paper (200 m³ to 60 m³). The washing of wool and the use of industrial process water in textiles, on the other hand, is unlikely to reduce markedly the demand for 1000 m³ of water per tonne of manufactured cloth.

Regional water strategies

The publication of river-basin strategies (La DF 1971) emphasized the crucial importance for regional development programmes of the effective harnessing and most efficient use of water resources. The pollution problem is mentioned later (p. 112), and for the moment attention is confined to the policies and strategies for each major drainage basin. Unlike the UK where inter-basin bulk transfers of water are more common, regional water strategies in France, even for the supply of Ile-de-France, are largely internal to each major catchment.

Table 7   Water supply and demand, major drainage basins

River basin	Area 1000 km²	Popn 1968 millions	Total ann. precipn	Usable ann. precipn	Surface flow	Water-table ann. potential	Low season flow at estuary m³/sec
			milliard m³				
Rhine-Meuse	31.5	3.8	29	13	13[1]	2	—
Seine-Normandie	95.5	15.0	x	x	18	4.5	80
Artois-Picardie	20.0	4.5	14	4	x	x	x
Loire-Bretagne	154.7	10.3	x	x	x	x	180
Adour-Garonne	115.0	5.8	x	x	x	x	210
Rhône-Med.	130.0	11.0	x	x	70	x	650

Water usage (milliard m³)

	Ann. abstraction	Drinking water	Industry	Power stns	Agric.	Canal links
Rhine-Meuse	3.5	0.3[2]	1.2[3]	1.6[4]	0.01	0.15
Seine-Normandie	6.7[5]	1.2	1.8	3.5	1.0	—
Loire-Bretagne	3.0	0.5	1.7	0.6[6]	0.2	—
Rhône-Med.	9.4(est.)	0.9	3.0	2.5[7]	3.0[8]	—
[9]						

[1] 47 including Rhine
[2] 80 per cent from underground
[3] 70 per cent from surface water
[4] 100 per cent from surface water
[5] 27 by year 2000
[6] nuclear power only (June-September)
[7] barrage storage capacity
[8] incl. 1.5 irrigation
[9] no inf. for Artois-Picardie and Adour-Garonne
x no information
Source: Aménagement du Territoire. 'Projets de Livre Blanc' for each drainage basin (see La DF 1971)

   The *Rhine-Meuse* system uniquely lacks unity on French soil, with the three parallel basins (Rhine, Moselle, Meuse), all of which discharge outside the boundaries of France. Since France exercizes sovereignty only in the upper tracts of Moselle and Meuse and is but a riparian power on the Rhine her water management strategy in this region is constrained by her international obligations; these obligations are particularly important in respect of pollution control. In terms of water availability the problems concern the marked low season flow on rivers west of the Vosges, the risks of winter flooding in towns along the principal valleys, and the limited availability of pure underground water supplies outside the plains of Alsace with their massive water-table below the Rhine. As importantly, there is an urgent need to safeguard most water supplies from pollution, a more serious issue in the Rhine-Meuse than in other French catchment basins.

Regional water policy has three subregional objectives: first, to ensure an adequate supply to the 'critical' areas of the regional metropolis (*Métropole Lorraine*) and the Lorraine coal basin; secondly, to protect the high quality of major reserves, including those of the Rhine and Meuse alluvial water-tables; and thirdly, over the rest of the catchments to conserve and preserve the water environment. The high concentration of heavy industry in Nancy-Toul-Lunéville, in Metz-Thionville and in other steel-making towns makes heavy and rising demands upon water supply and creates serious pollution problems. Total demands for water are likely to increase in the regional metropolis, but not dramatically, from 700 million m³ to 1300 million m³ per annum by the year 2000. Meeting these demands will involve strengthening the low season flow on the Moselle by selectively 'feeding' the alluvial water-table at times of maximum flow and drawing upon it during the summer. The Lorraine coal basin is heavily dependent upon the Vosges sandstone water-table and almost all surface flow is seriously polluted. Both here and in the regional metropolis it may be necessary to seek water supplies from further afield, perhaps from the Saarland.

The Rhine alluvial water-table in Alsace may seem to have an inexhaustible potential for supplying the towns and industries of the upper rift valley. Serious localized threats are, however, posed by saline pollution from the potash mines, and the spreading rash of gravel-workings. The Rhine itself is subject to serious pollution, but not on the scale of its lower course in which it is justly named 'the sewer of Europe'.

The *Seine-Normandie* system has the advantage of a more sustained surface flow regulated by the discharges from underground water-tables. On the other hand the rate of growth in regional water demand (1970 6.7, estimated year 2000 27 milliard m³ per annum) makes water an increasingly scarce resource. Furthermore, pollution in and downstream from the Paris region is both serious and increasing. The major projected increase in water consumption is for power station use (1970 3.5, est. 2000 20 milliard m³ per annum). Part of this water will later be returned to the river system, but the problem is rather that at the localized level even a 500 Mw power station may require to use for cooling purposes the total low season flow of a river such as the Oise; 4000 Mw combined capacity in a chain of power stations will evaporate 150,000 m³ of water per diem. The ensuring of an adequate water supply for all purposes has already necessitated a complex pattern of storage reservoirs in the upper reaches of the main tributaries of the Seine, and a well-developed distribution network to the major urban and industrial centres. Because of the purity of underground supplies these are to be reserved wherever possible for drinking water.

The water supply of Ile-de-France (Paris region) requires 3.8 million m³ per diem, of which 1.1 million m³ are drawn from the water-table and the remainder from barrage reservoirs in the Seine basin head-waters, or by direct abstraction from surface flow. To meet the estimated demand of 6 million m³ per diem in 1985 underground supplies will need to be stepped up to 2 million m³. In 1972 a protection order was placed on the 850 surface ha. of the Montereau water-table, a resource capable of producing 0.6 million m³ per diem in due course. The greater part of increased supplies for the Paris region, however, will come from increased surface storage and abstraction. In 1966 the 'Seine' reservoir (205 million m³) was completed and the 'Marne' reservoir (365 million m³) was being flooded in mid-1977; other reservoirs are planned on the Yonne, the Aube and the Oise.

The Seine-Normandie system well illustrates the need to harmonize coherent water management policies for the entire catchment with the sometimes conflicting objectives of regional planning organizations. Apart from the Paris region planning authority there are: the OREAM (*Organisme d'études d'aménagement d'aire métropolitaine*) Basse-Seine; OREAV (*Organisme régional d'études et d'aménagement des vallées de l'Oise et de l'Aisne*, until its demise); ZANC (*zone d'appui Nord-Champenoise*, a subregional growth area); and the planning groups for the regional growth centres at Caen and Troyes. Though water management does not impose binding constraints on regional planning it is of increasing significance in appraising subregional investment allocations, or the siting and development of towns or industrial plants.

The composite catchments of *Artois-Picardie* include the major asset of the chalk aquifer, for water storage and regular supply, but the disadvantage north of Artois of extensive pollution throughout the industrial and urban districts of Nord-Pas-de-Calais. Faced with the probability of a fourfold increase in both domestic and industrial demand for water by the end of the century, management policy is concerned with quantity, quality and availability of water at the right place and the right time. The Lille-Roubaix-Tourcoing conurbation poses some of the most serious problems of existing pollution and future population growth. Surface flow in the conurbation will continue to be heavily polluted, but will increasingly be used for industrial cooling-water. Some of the pollution will move by gravity along the canal system towards the coast; pollution on the rivers flowing into Belgium poses a delicate international problem. With a major port-industrial complex in course of rapid creation, and build-up in the Calais-Dunkerque coastal zone, water demands are escalating. In part these demands may be met by massive use of processed sea-water for cooling purposes, but large-scale transfers along the Dunkerque-Valenciennes canal system will also be necessary. Pumping from the water-table in the winter period of maximum precipitation provides supplies for agriculture, but there is always a risk of the infiltration of saline waters in the coastal tracts.

The *Loire-Bretagne* system is less densely settled (67 persons per km², France 92), with a more scattered population, and has a level of urbanization below that for France as a whole (53 per cent in towns, France 69 per cent, 1968). Industrial activity is concentrated: in the upper reaches (e.g. at Clermont Ferrand), and around the Loire estuary (Nantes-St Nazaire). Nevertheless, during the 1960s population rose more rapidly than was the case nationally, and the proportion living in towns in the Loire-Bretagne catchments has shown a similar differentially-greater increase. Regional water management problems are already serious by reason of the unstable river regime and lack of regulating underground aquifers; summer drought and winter flooding are ever-present hazards. Not the least of the problems is that created by the peak summer demand for domestic water in tourist areas around the Breton peninsula, for the most part an impermeable massif with virtually no underground storage.

At the heart of catchment management policy lies a priority for increasing reservoir storage as a means of increasing the critical low-season flows on the Loire-Allier and of contributing at the same time to effective flood-control. Around the Breton peninsula the creation of many small reservoirs for local peak needs is envisaged. Since the heaviest coastal consumption does not correspond with the pattern of potential reservoir sites, inter-basin water transfers will become increasingly important. Along the main Loire system the objective is to raise low-season flow to a sustained level: 70 m³/sec at Orléans, 180 m³/sec at Nantes in the middle-term, which represents three times the present 10-year lowest flow. To do this an increased reservoir capacity (to 1300 million m³) in the upper basins of the Loire and Allier will be necessary. Of the nine new reservoirs required, that at Naussac (Allier) is under construction and will eventually impound 200 million m³.

The *Garonne-Adour* catchments supply a region described conventionally as 'underdeveloped'. It has a traditional out-migration of young people and an economy too narrowly-based upon an agriculture itself too defined by an inefficient 'polyculture' (subsistence-type farming, with diverse but small-scale products on either each farm, or in some cases each field). Only 54 per cent of the population lives in towns and there are only seven towns with more than 50,000 inhabitants; the two urban agglomerations of Bordeaux and Toulouse dominate an under-equipped urban hierarchy. Industrialization remains limited and backward, though there is great potential from locally-available resources. Regional development programmes are concerned with modernization of agriculture, including commercialization and extension of irrigation; industrialization, including both growth manufacturing and tourism; and concentration of growth upon axial corridors, particularly that along the Garonne valley.

The most significant constraint on regional water policy is that of summer drought and low-season flow. This seasonal scarcity is more pronounced than in any other French catchment and is aggravated by the rising demands from tourism and irrigation. Overall there is growing and serious competition between alternative users for the annually available supplies. Pollution is, furthermore, a most marked problem, intensified during the summer season by low river flow. Irregularities in river regime on the Garonne have been mentioned earlier, with a high flooding risk at all seasons other than summer. Catchment management gives priority to evening-out the seasonal flows to achieve a sustainable minimum season discharge (DMA). The numerous barrage-reservoirs for hydro-electric power along the tributaries coming off the Massif Central will need to be used more for river-regulation and less for maximum power production, as nuclear-powered stations elsewhere make an increasingly vast contribution to the French energy budget. Hydro-electric power production has hitherto had first priority in planning the use of the Garonne catchment. Today there is the need for a basin-wide multiple purpose water plan to: improve navigation on the Garonne for standard European barges; supply direct hydro- or indirect thermal-power; service industrial plants; irrigate increasing agricultural acreages; and, at the same time, provide for increased recreational use of water.

The *Rhône-Méditerranée-Corse* river basins are distinguished by the volume of surface water flow: along the Rhône at all times of the year; in the Mediterranean coastlands and Corse with seasonal irregularities in flow and a sharply-pronounced summer minimum. In much of the region public bodies have a uniquely great responsibility for water management: Electricité de France, for the network of reservoirs, particularly those in the Alpes; CNR (Compagnie Nationale du Rhône) for integral management of the Rhône system; CNABRL (Compagnie Nationale d'Aménagement du Bas-Rhône-Languedoc) and Société du Canal de Provence, for distribution of Rhône and Verdon waters for irrigation purposes; and finally SOMIVAC (Société de la Mise en Valeur de la Corse) concerned with rural management policies.

The basis of regional water policy is to effect multiple use of the Rhône waters with minimizing of pollution, and to distribute surplus water throughout as much of the deficit areas of the Mediterranean coastlands as possible. Flood control is another major preoccupation, notably so in the steep catchment basins of the Midi with their pronounced irregularities of regime. Among all French catchments, however, the main Rhône system is the most abundantly provided in volume and regularity of flow. In an economic growth region such as Rhône-Alpes the security of water supplies is a major asset, but the problems of pollution of both the waters and the environment are among the most intense in France.

ENVIRONMENTAL POLLUTION

Water pollution
Action against pollution of rivers and water-tables was initiated in the legislation of 1964 concerned with river basin management (Antoine and Duret 1973 B). Some forty-five parameters are regularly monitored, covering physical, chemical, biochemical, hydrobiological, bacteriological and radioactive contents in surface water. Fig. 14 shows the most serious forms of pollution to be in scattered locations, but generally widespread in the Rhine-Meuse, Artois-Picardie and Seine-Normandie catchments. Water pollution is measured in person-equivalents and in 1970 amounted to 76 millions, including 47 millions from towns and industries linked to purifying systems and 29 millions from industries on isolated sites; presently only some 10 million persons are served by effluent purifying

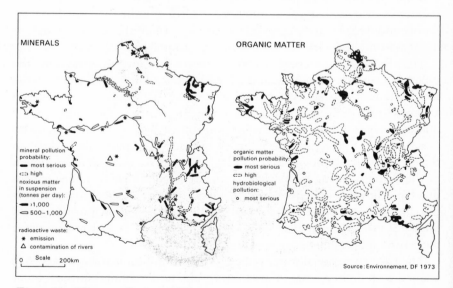

Figure 14   Water pollution, 1971.

plants. The rate of pollution is increasing, partly due to the rise in population, since each additional person pollutes 150 litres of water a day and adds 50 gr of oxydizable matter and 90 gr of matter in suspension. The greater volume of pollution, however, is contributed by manufacturing industry, a proportion likely to increase in the estimated 100 million persons-equivalent of total pollution to be produced annually by 1985. The ratio at which pollution is cleansed varies greatly among the regions, e.g. in the Paris region 16 per cent for the public system, 24 per cent for isolated industries. Comparable data for the Nord shows 15 and 40 per cent; Lorraine 21 and 58 per cent; Rhône-Alpes 8 and 9 per cent; Provence-Côte d'Azur 11 and 8 per cent respectively.

Pollution by mineral elements is most severe in the Rhine-Meuse catchment and along the canals and rivers of the Nord-Pas-de-Calais (fig. 15). In part this pollution is natural, as in the case of sulphates from the

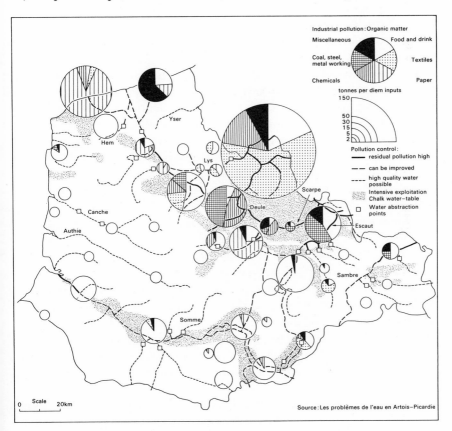

Figure 15   Water pollution, Artois-Picardie.

gypsum or pyrites beds of the Saar and Moselle, the chlorides from the triassic salt-beds of Lorraine, or the potash wastes of Alsace. It is considerably augmented by industrial effluent from soda-works, mines, salt-pans or the petroleum industries. Particularly serious pollution occurs along the river Ill in Alsace with 500 to 1000 mg/litre of chlorine ions, some two to four times a maximum acceptable threshold level. Some 16- to 18,000 tonnes of salt wastes are discharged daily into the Rhine and 3000 tonnes of chlorides into the Meurthe, the latter creating pollution levels of 1200 mg/litre of chlorine ions at Nancy and 550 mg/l at Metz. The Rhône system receives 3 Mt of salt effluents per annum and this pollutes 75 milliard m³ of water. Pollution by solids in suspension varies with the size of the river and the extent of urbanization or industrialization in the catchment. The major rivers carry the heaviest load, including the Seine at Rouen, the Garonne after Agen, the Rhône at Avignon and the Isère below Grenoble. Yet the heaviest pollution is along some secondary rivers such as the Var, Aude, Tarn, Aveyron and Allier. Oil waste products are among the most serious pollutants with some 60,000 tonnes entering the Rhône system each year and polluting 100 milliard m³ of water.

The most troublesome forms of water pollution, however, are those concerned with organic matter. Under favourable conditions rivers may be self-cleansing from certain organic pollutants, since an adequate volume of oxygen dissolved in water degrades and mineralizes the organic matter rendering it harmless. The oxygen levels in water are also of paramount importance for the fish life. The lowest levels tend to coincide with the regions of mineral contamination in surface flow, particularly in the Rhine-Meuse and Artois-Picardie catchments. The river Deule is among the most polluted and the length of sections without any fish life doubled between 1954 and 1964. In the Rhône system phenol pollutants contaminate an estimated 700 milliard m³ of water every year, 2500 tonnes of detergent effluent pollute 5 milliard m³, and 1000 tonnes of pesticide residues contaminate a further 100 milliard m³.

Policies for reducing water pollution are directed to increasing the number of treatment works, causing the polluters to bear both the direct and the social costs of their actions, and to classifying all surface flow in each catchment according to pollution level and risks. Good management of water resources requires close collaboration with regional planners and participation in decisions on siting and growth of both towns and industries.

Some of the most severe water pollution is caused by the proliferation of massive coastal oil refineries and petrochemical complexes, whilst in a more general sense oil pollution of coastal waters, out to the 320 km mark, and

Table 8   Marseille-Fos. Water pollution management, 1972–75

	COD		BOD5		Suspended solids	
tonnes/per diem	1972	end 1975	1972	end 1975	1972	end 1975
Petroleum refineries	31.0	8.5	8.7	2.8	16.4	1.2
Petrochemicals						
(Lavéra and Berre)	132.0	64.5	55.0	22.4	65.0	47.0
	163.0	73.0	63.7	25.2	81.4	48.2

COD = chemical oxygen demand
BOD5 = biological oxygen demand after 5 days

the high seas beyond, is becoming a disturbing international problem. In July 1976, indeed, the French government set up a coordinating body (GICAMA) to review the further control measures which may be necessary to limit pollution of the sea. In the meantime there have been impressive results from the coordinated attack on mounting coastal pollution. By its very size and rapidity of growth, the Marseille-Fos industrial complex led to heavy water and air pollution, potentially the more serious in view of the relatively still waters and the high quality natural environment of the setting. A pollution control organization was set up in 1971 (SPPPI) to limit emissions, from the refineries and petrochemical plants in particular. As table 8 shows, there had been a 50 per cent improvement 1972–5 and by the end of 1977 a 90 per cent reduction was to be achieved; the costs of the programme for the first four years have already amounted to 300 M frs.

Air pollution

With smaller and fewer concentrations of either coal-burning industries or nineteenth-century industrial towns than in the UK, France has traditionally had lower levels of air pollution. Most of the larger urban and industrial areas, however, show levels which may rise to unhealthy or even dangerous proportions for short periods (Antoine and Duret 1973C). Air pollution may come from physical, chemical or biological sources, but two measures are most commonly taken: sulphur dioxide (SO_2) content, an assessment of strong acidity when more than 150 $\mu g/m^3$ are present; and black smoke, measured in $\mu g/m^3$ dust content. Some 2 Mt of SO_2 and 1 Mt of dust are emitted over France in an average year. To these must be added the most recent pollutants, carbon monoxide from cars and lorries (5 Mt per annum) and nitric oxide (0.5 Mt from high temperature furnaces and 0.4 Mt from vehicle exhausts).

   Though pollution conditions vary among French industrial regions and cities there has been some improvement during the 1960s, particularly in

Table 9   Air pollution: acid (SO_2) content and smoke emission, selected stations

μg/m³ per diem 1972	Paris 1961/2	Paris 1971/2	Lyon mean ann.	summer	winter	Lille	Marseille	Petit-couronne (refin.)	Sheffield 1971	London 1971
SO_2, acid content	154	144	108	50	167	120	117	164	167	151
smoke content	82	58	57	28	87	63	104	29	64	46

Source: Antoine and Duret (1973) for France

respect of reduced smoke emission (table 9). The SO_2 content on the other hand has remained over several cities at about the same level as in the early 1960s. This has, however, been stabilized in spite of up to forty per cent more fuel being consumed during the decade. With the increasing substitution of oil for coal as the prime fuel the nature of residual hydrocarbons in the atmosphere has changed and there have been shifts among localities with the most intense air pollution. Conditions over coalmining areas have improved but there has been deterioration around the major oil refineries. Smoke emission by power stations has been strictly controlled.

Air pollution varies markedly according to meteorological or seasonal climatic conditions. For the most part pollution maxima occur during the winter months, with minima during the month of August. SO_2 concentrations vary from 250–320 μg/m³ per diem in the most polluted month down to 30–40 in the least polluted; comparable figures for smoke concentration vary from 120–140 down to 30–37 μg/m³ per diem. Winter pollution levels have been more effectively reduced at the peak, but summer levels continue little changed. Daily concentrations injurious to health may occur within the winter peak period. For example, at Lille the mean annual SO_2 content is 120 μg/m³ per diem, but this rises to 232 μg/m³ as the mean for December, and 935 μg/m³ as the maximum daily concentration. Comparable figures for smoke concentrations are 63, 80 and 735 μg/m³ per diem respectively. Though Marseille-Fos has the highest concentration of petrochemicals, normal air pollution (Marseille 120 μg/m³, Fos 70 μg/m³) is lower than for Paris — 150 μg/m³ (1975). In still air conditions, on the other hand, daily concentrations of pollution may reach 1000 μg/m³ (from observations at the town of Martigues in 1973) for short peak periods.

Within the Paris agglomeration (table 9) there is a variation in mean air pollution levels from as low as 80 per cent in the outer suburbs to 125 per cent in the inner eastern industrial districts. A further measure of air pollution is that of solid deposits (μg/m²/per diem). This has been diminished only slowly in most places during the past decade, though the number of days with heavy dust deposit has diminished. In Paris, for example, the 1959 mean showed 310 $\mu g/m^2$/per diem and that for 1970 271 $\mu g/m^2$/per diem. The heaviest concentration of solid deposits occur in Lorraine (160–9,000 $\mu g/m^2$/per diem) with an exceptional monthly maximum of 33,000 $\mu g/m^2$/per diem at Homecourt. Other high mean annual concentrations in 1970 were recorded at Le Havre 457, Caen 259 and Châlon-sur-Saône 220 $\mu g/m^2$/per diem.

An interesting experiment in environmental planning is being carried out at the New Town of Le Vaudreuil, near Rouen, the first town for which anti-pollution and anti-nuisance measures are being instituted from the very start (Antoine and Duret 1973A).

SOILS

To realize their maximum potential soils require optimal supplies of water, mineral nutrients and oxygen. Depth, texture and structure of soils are other important characteristics affecting fertility, both directly and also indirectly in facilitating the movement of elements in the soil. Soil management can considerably improve soil characteristics, by manuring or fertilizing, ploughing, drainage, or choice of cropping system. Yet the inherent qualities of soils are persistent and good soil management increasingly works closely in harmony with these natural assets, rather than risk incurring additional on-costs of production by transforming the soil habitat. Ultimately however it is climate rather than soil which is dominant in the range of crops which may be grown, or the yields which may be realized. The characteristics of soil which most directly influence productivity are those of texture, depth and permeability. Soil organisms or soil organic matter, on the other hand, affect crop growth only indirectly.

Soils are created by the interaction of the elements of climate and organisms upon a wide, but initially passive, range of parent rock materials. Among the infinitely varied possible classifications of soils the most directly applicable is perhaps that which considers how far the interaction has progressed in different areas of France and with what outcome in terms of inherent fertility, to be exploited by selective management systems. Fig. 16 shows an outline classification and distribution of soils for this purpose. Broadly speaking, in France the interaction of climate and organisms upon rock mantle has progressed variably far and has thus produced a range of zonal soil types, from brown forest or red brown Mediterranean to podzolic in process and character. Nevertheless the influence of the great diversity of parent rock materials is still very strong and differentiates the soil map quite clearly with azonal characteristics. These relate, for example,

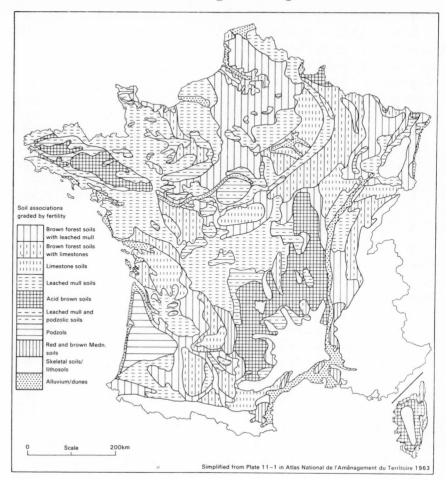

Soil associations
graded by fertility

Brown forest soils
with leached mull

Brown forest soils
with limestones

Limestone soils

Leached mull soils

Acid brown soils

Leached mull and
podzolic soils

Podzols

Red and brown Medn.
soils

Skeletal soils/
lithosols

Alluvium/dunes

0   Scale   200km

Simplified from Plate 11–1 in Atlas National de l'Aménagement du Territoire 1963

Figure 16   Soil types.

to the limestones, sandstones, granites, loess, alluvium or other parent
materials which dominate in the formation of soils from their regolith. Fig.
16 shows a very generalized pattern of soils and even so the boundaries
between the orders are necessarily indistinct, both by definition and on the
ground. This is particularly true for the lower plateaux and plains of the
more fertile areas of France. In the mountains the soils are mostly skeletal
(lithosols or regosols) and correspond more directly and closely with the
local rock materials.

The zonal soils in France reflect very largely the regional climatic
variations already described. There are few perfectly developed brown

forest soils and equally true podzols are very localized, other than where soil permeability is particularly favourable to podzolization. Intermediate grades between brown forest soils and podzols, on the other hand, are very widespread and cover most of the fertile areas. Furthermore, the characteristics of the zonal soils are much influenced by the underlying parent material. Variants of brown forest soil are widespread through the central and northern Bassin Parisien, the Lorraine plateaux and the plains of Alsace, and also in the eastern Bassin d'Aquitaine and the Rhône valley east of Lyon. These variants blend with leached mull soils (*sols lessivés*) but there is great diversity in drainage conditions. Parent material varies from the loess (*limon*) capping of the central and northern Bassin Parisien, to the marls of Lorraine and the tertiary 'mollasse' of Aquitaine and the Rhône. In the Bassin Parisien and Alsace these soils support intensive cereal-growing and in some localities also vines, but equally provide the base for very diverse farming systems; in Lorraine there are large areas of forest on such soils. Where jurassic limestones outcrop, but are covered by marls or decomposition products, the brown forest soils have a higher calcareous content. In Lorraine and the Jura these are cattle-rearing areas or forested; upon such soils in Poitou or Aquitaine mixed farming is more characteristic. There are smaller areas of brown forest-limestone soils in the Plaine de Caen and along the flanks of the Somme valley. Where the limestone beds outcrop in the 'Champagne' country (Troyes-Reims, Cognac, Berry) the soils are often thin and dry, but, as in comparable areas of the UK, pastoralism has been greatly diversified by cereal-farming, made possible by the sustained application of fertilizers.

The leached mull soils are widespread in western France. Where they occur above the plateaux loams of the Bassin Parisien their rich constituents, the limited degree of leaching, the good texture and depth all contribute to the intensive farming systems, based upon wheat, sugar beet, potatoes, or orchards. Upon the more acidic rocks of Armorica the leached mull soils are well-watered but mainly under grass. Along the northern coast of Bretagne, however, the plateaux loams nurture the intensive cultivation of spring vegetables, even though such soils are derived from acidic rocks.

At higher altitudes the quality of both brown forest and leached mull soils deteriorates. Over wide areas of the Massif Central, the Ardennes, central Armorica and upland Corse the acidic brown soils predominate upon parent materials which include granites, quartzites, schists, or sandstones. Land is principally under pastoral or forest cover. In less-favoured upland areas leached mull soils degenerate through increased leaching and podzolization. Precipitation tends to be high and washes out the mineral or humus constituents on sandy or thin acidic soils. Areas particularly affected include upland Bretagne, the Plateau de Millevaches (Massif Central) and Perche. Pastoralism, marginal arable cultivation, or forestry tend to be the characteristic land uses. The gradation to true podzolic soils occurs with a further increase in altitude, deterioration in drainage, or greater permeability on sands or gravels. The most extensive true podzol occurs in the Landes, where hydromorphic conditions produce seasonal waterlogging and lead to the creation of hardpan layers. Other podzols occur in the tertiary sandstones of the Bassin Parisien (Fontainebleau sands), and in the hydromorphic area of the Sologne sands in the middle Loire valley.

The Mediterranean zone of France has small but distinctive areas of brown or red-brown earths. The red-brown soils may occur over limestones, but more commonly on terraces or gravel-spreads. Soil-water conditions govern the agricultural value of these soils, from the dry *garrigue* to the moderate productivity of localities with irrigation or a higher annual precipitation. Brown-earths are found at moderate altitudes on the flanks of Corse. Derived from varied parent materials they are usually well-drained and capable of sustaining the characteristic Mediterranean arable systems.

The highest uplands and mountain tracts have poorly-developed or skeletal soils. The skeletal soils are found at altitudes of more than 2000 m in the Alpes and 1800 m in the Pyrénées, and they have negligible agricultural value. The lithosols derived from acidic rocks tend to occur between 1200 and 1800 m in the Alpes and Pyrénées and 800–1200 m in the Massif Central. These altitudes correspond fairly closely with the zone under coniferous forest. Lithosols derived from calcareous rocks are found in the Alpes and the Jura in particular. They tend to be clayey or mixed in character (grumosols) and are characteristically either forested or under pasture.

The most fertile soils in ecological terms are those of the zonal order, particularly the brown forest soils admixed with leached mull, but also the limestone-based brown forest soils of Lorraine, the Caen-Alençon area of Normandie, and the Charollais. Alluvial soils are very varied in quality but with good drainage are usually capable of flexible and intensive cropping under good management. Local soils of high quality escape mention in a general assessment, such as the black-earths of the tertiary Limagne basin east of Clermont-Ferrand, suited for intensive arable farming, or the basaltic slopes of Auvergne for intensive pasturing of cattle.

Management may conjure and sustain fertility from unpromising natural circumstances, but there has also been degradation of soils, erosion and other man-induced losses. Some of these are of long standing, such as the deforestation of the Mediterranean shorelands and the production of *garrigue* by overgrazing and burning. Other damage is more recent and includes the reversion of improved lands to waste since the mid-nineteenth century, the alteration of underground water-levels as at the barrage site of Donzère-Mondragon (Pinchemel 1964), or the effects of over-cropping leading to sheet or gully erosion. Pédélaborde and Dupuis (1969) estimated that 4 to 5 million ha. were then suffering from some form of soil erosion. They instanced the heavy cropping practices including those for maize, the cutting of hedgerows and the absence of natural manuring as contributing to soil instability and declining fertility.

IN CONCLUSION

Ardagh (1968, 184) commented that 'France today presents her planners with all the exciting challenge of a virgin land'. Her land surface is more than double that of the UK and contains no less diversity of natural habitat conditions. Furthermore, her densities of urbanization and of population nation-wide are lower and developed later than in Britain. In particular, there is in France no extensive landscape legacy from the industrial revolutions during the past 150 years. Scarred areas such as the coalfields of the Nord-Pas-de-Calais or the Lorraine coal- or iron ore fields are localized and even then set within little-changed rural hinterlands.

Fortuitously, but fortunately for France, the strong economic growth pressures since 1945 have been manifested through the spread of towns and the implanting of industries in areas where the high quality of natural resources has not been at widespread risk. Even around Greater Paris the losses of high-grade farmland have been limited in scale, though it is true that the growth of towns in the outer Bassin Parisien would threaten the reserves of first-class soils. However, there is ample first-class agricultural land and it is likely indeed that the areas under cultivation may be rationalized and concentrated between now and the end of the century.

Apart from the reserves of high-grade farmland, France possesses some of the finest tourist scenery in Europe. Recreational and tourist pressures are building up on a vast scale, for winter sports as well as for the peak summer season. The need to plan for safeguarding water resources is another objective with important landscape and siting implications. Additionally, the demands upon France's prime mineral resources: coal, natural gas, iron ore, bauxite and sand and gravel, produce further conservation and landscaping problems. Hitherto these planning issues have been treated in piecemeal fashion very much as in the UK, in spite of our comprehensive post-war town and country planning legislation. Since the establishment of the French Ministry of the Protection of Nature and the Environment (MDPNE) in early 1971, and its successor the Ministry of the Quality of Life (1974), there has been for the first time the assurance that the total environment will be investigated, policies for integrated land uses formulated, costed, and the course of their execution monitored. This is all in the future, but comes not too soon if France is to safeguard and utilize most effectively her rich range of natural resources for the benefit of future generations.

References

Natural resources
Bénévent, A. (1926) *Le climat des Alpes françaises.*
Besancenot, J.-P. (1975) 'Premières données sur les stress bioclimatiques en France', *Annls Géogr.*, LXXXIII (459): 497–529.
Biarez, S. (1973) *Une politique d'urbanisme: les ZUP*, Grenoble.
Boisvert, J.-J. (1955) 'La neige dans les Alpes françaises', *Revue Géogr. alp.*, 43 (1): 357–434.
Budyko, M. I. (1968) 'Solar radiation and the use of it by plants', *UNESCO Symp. Natural Resources Res.*, 7 (Reading): 39–53.
Champion A. G. (1974) 'An estimate of the changing extent and distribution of urban land in England and Wales, 1959–71', *Centre for Environ. Stud. Res. Pap.* 10.
Estienne, P. (1956) *Recherches sur le climat du Massif Central français.*
Martonne, E. de (1942) *Géographie physique de la France.*
Pédélaborde, P. (1957) *Le climat du bassin parisien.*
Pédélaborde, P. and Dupuis, M. (1969) *Atlas économique et sociale pour l'aménagement du territoire*, II Agriculture, Les Données Naturelles: 1–8.
Pinchemel, P. (1964) *Géographie de la France*, I, Les conditions naturelles et humaines.
Reader's Digest (1969) *Grand Atlas de la France*: 100–3.
Thran, P. and Broekhuizen, S. (1965) *Agro-climatic Atlas of Europe*, I.
Wareing, P. F. and Cooper, J. P. (1973) *Potential Crop Production*, London.

Environmental management
Antoine, S. and Duret, A. *Collection Environnement*:
    (1971) 3 'La sauvegarde du milieu naturel et urbain'.
    (1972) 4 'La politique française de l'environnement'.
    (1973A), 14 'La ville nouvelle du Vaudreuil'.
    (1973B), 16 'Inventaire du degré de pollution des eaux superficielles, rivières et canaux'.
    (1973C), 17 'La pollution de l'air en France.
Ardagh, J. (1968) *The New France*, Harmondsworth.
Berquin, A. and Perrin, A. (1973) 'Le cas de l'Aire Métropolitaine Marseillaise, Analyse de l'Environnement', *Revue écon. Sud-Ouest*, 1: 139–55.

Boudeville, J.-R. (1973) 'La gestion de l'environnement', *Revue écon. Sud-Ouest*, 1: 13–33.

Coulaud, D. (1975) 'Les espaces verts publics urbains et péri-urbains', *Moniteur Trav. publ.*, 38: 35–7.

Delpoux, M. (1972) 'Ecosystème et paysage', *Revue géogr. Pyrénées Sud-Ouest*, 43. (2): 157–74.

Groupe Interministériel d'Evaluation de l'Environnement (1976) *Vers une évaluation du cadre de vie.*

IAURP (1972) 'Environnement et pollution', *Bull. Information Rég. Parisienne*, 6.

La Documentation Française (1965) 'Le problème de l'eau en France', *Notes et Etudes Documentaires*, 3219.
  (1971) *Projets de Livre Blanc:*
  15 'L'eau en Seine-Normandie'.
  16 'Les problèmes de l'eau en Artois-Picardie'.
  18 'Bassin Rhin-Meuse: eau et aménagement'.
  21 'L'eau en Adour-Garonne'.
  22 'Les problèmes de l'eau dans le Bassin Rhône-Méditerranée-Corse'.
  27 'L'eau dans le bassin Loire-Bretagne'.
  (1973) *Le Livre Blanc de l'eau en France.*

Margant, H. (1973) 'L'environnement, signification et portée du concept', *Aménagement du territoire et développement régional*, IEP, Grenoble, VI: 121–46.

Mission d'Etude d'Amenagement Rural (1971) *Eléments pour un schéma d'aménagement rural de la Région Parisienne.*

Organisation Départementale d'Etudes des Alpes Maritimes (ODEAM) (1971) *Schéma d'aménagement de la Bande Côtière des Alpes-Maritimes*, 3 vols, Nice.

Préau, P. (1972) 'De la protection de la nature à l'aménagement du territoire: l'expérience caractéristique du parc national de la Vanoise', *Aménagement du territoire et développement régional*, IEP, Grenoble, V: 119–72.

Tarlet, J. (1977) 'Milieu naturel et aménagement. Les méthodes de planification écologique', *Annls Géogr.*, LXXXVI (474): 164–200.

4 People and work

Alike in consideration of the past, the interpretation of present relationships and as a basis for measuring future prospects the study of
population, its characteristics, structure, distribution and trends, offers
perhaps the most useful general-purpose yardstick or barometer of changes
in economy or society. Population is a major resource in its own right,
dynamic, flexible and mobile, but it is in its relationships to other resources,
including the land, that its interpretation becomes most significant. Such
relationships are neither simple nor static, nor may they be fully understood
using economic criteria alone. Though there is a detectable and important
set of economic linkages to be established between man and resources by
study of the workforce, its deployment and structure, it is the setting of
people within the total environment which must more significantly be
taken into account. Quality of life and total satisfactions must be
considered, together with more pragmatic issues of measuring human
needs and the means of achieving material objectives. Furthermore,
biological characteristics form a substratum to population change, and
behavioural attitudes or perceptions also help to condition family size,
social values and forms of social organization or expression. All in all, the
relationships between population and resources, complex and unstable as
they may be, nevertheless continue to afford the most useful generally
available indicators of change.

For the purposes of planning it is possible to identify certain objectives
concerning population. In the first place, the planner is seeking to
harmonize or to optimize man-land ratios and that at several scale levels,
from local, through regional to national. He is also seeking to influence
mobility of people, particularly by affecting interregional or countryside-
town movements in the interests of economic balance or the conservation
of spatial identities or communities. The management of the urbanization
process is perhaps the most powerful of all planning controls in terms of
town size, housing, or provision of facilities of many kinds. In more
general public policies attempts to influence family size or vital trends are
among the most important issues. The wish to counteract social segre-

gation introduces the political dimension into social and economic planning.

The people

Most recent studies on the population of France (Armengaud 1965, Huber, Bunle and Boverat 1965, Beaujeu-Garnier 1969, Clarke 1963) emphasize the dynamism of post-war growth in numbers and underline the sharp contrasts this implies with the stagnant or slow growth of the interwar years. Never far from the surface lie the trauma of two major world wars which undermined the vitality of the country. Reviews of postwar population characteristics, structure and trends tend to the euphoric, with stress upon the potential for economic growth, better living standards, and social dynamism in a youthful age structure now that man has for the most part ceased to be a scarce resource in France.

The 1975 census showed that, discounting the sudden and exceptional influx of North African repatriates 1962–8, the population increase rate for France (+0.80 per cent p.a.) was sustained, but the underlying causes had shifted in balance. 1968–75 there was a birth surplus of 295,000 p.a., lower than 1962–8 (320,000 p.a.) by reason of an acceleration in the fall of the birth rate. During the same period a net inflow of 115,000 migrants took place each year (cf 70,000 p.a. from N. Africa, 1962–8), the product of the fast growth of the French economy and its demand for labour. Already in the late 1970s some fears are being expressed about the falling birth rate and its social, economic, or political implications, awakening echoes of the feeble demographic dynamism of the interwar years.

FRANCE AND THE EEC OF THE NINE

First, France needs to be placed briefly in the context of the population of the EEC of the Nine. Some of the characteristics have already been seen in table 2; others are illustrated by table 10. 52.59 million Frenchmen (February 1975) today represent 20 per cent of the EEC population, compared with only 18.6 per cent for the same countries of Europe in 1938, but 26.7 per cent as far back as 1850. By 1985 France is expected to contain 21 per cent of the then EEC population. The French population density is markedly the lowest among the major EEC partners, but the annual rate of population increase matches that of the BRD, even during the past decade. On the other hand the 1968 figures for crude birth and death rates showed France as having a greater annual rate of natural increase (+5.7 per cent) than the UK (+5.2 per cent) or the BRD (+4.2 per cent), but less than that

Table 10   Population characteristics, France and the EEC of the Nine

	Population (million)				Density per km² 1971	Ann. rate increase 1963/70	Crude rates per 1000 1968		% Age-groups Years		
	1850	1938	1968	1985 (est.)			Births	Deaths	<15	15–64	>65
France	35.6	42.0	49.9	57.7	93	0.9	16.7	11.0	25.1	62.5	12.4
UK	23.2	47.5	55.2	60.0	228	0.5	17.1	11.9	23.6	64.1	12.3
BRD	35.3 †	68.6 †	60.1	61.9	247	1.0	16.1	11.9	23.0	64.5	12.5
Italy	25.0	43.6	52.7	59.9	179	0.8	17.6	10.1	22.9	66.9	10.2
EEC(9)	133.2	225.9	248.5	274.0	217	—	—	—	—	—	—

† *all* Germany.
Sources: UN Demographic Yearbook; Annuaire Statistique etc.

for Italy (+7.5 per cent). The higher French percentage in the under fifteen age groups related directly to the sustained birth rate of the period since 1945, the reinforcements for the rising numbers in the national workforce.

Apart from the sustained population growth rates in postwar France the structural changes in her economy, particularly those of industrial concentration and rural out-migration, have been reflected in the patterns and structure of urbanization. The French urban hierarchy shows both similarities and differences when compared with those of her larger EEC neighbours (table 11). Such a comparison underlines the contrasts in degree and stage of industrialization achieved, the relative significance of the rising services sector, and the varying structure of the urban networks in course of formation.

Highlighting the rapid postwar urbanization of France is the fact that as far back as 1930 50 per cent lived in towns and this had risen to only 54 per cent twenty years later. During the next two decades, however, the figure rose sharply to 70 per cent. Though more urbanized than Italy, France

Table 11   Urban population. France and her neighbours

	% urban popn		Popn in towns (millions)			% change 1962–8 in these categories (1,000s)		
	1950	1970	>500	100 500	20–100	>500	100–500	20–100
France	54.5	70.6	11.7	8.9	7.1	17.4	19.1	13.6
UK	80.5	78.0	18.7	8.5		−0.2	14.9	
BRD	70.9	76.0	10.6	8.9	11.4	−0.03	13.6	67.6
Italy	42.0	54.0	8.3	6.6	12.7	18.6	17.8	12.4

Source: Les Villes Moyennes, Aménagement du Territoire, 1972

remains markedly less so than either the UK or the BRD, both mature industrialized urban economies. By comparison with the UK, in which almost one-third of the population lives in eight conurbations of more than 500,000, five of which have more than 1,000,000 people, France has scarcely one in four of her population in such large cities. One Frenchman in six, however, lives in the Greater Paris conurbation, but there are only two other cities with around 1 m (Lyon, Marseille). In the group of towns with 100,000–500,000 population France has about the same total numbers of people as in the UK or the BRD (France 48 towns containing 9.0 million people; BRD 45 towns with 8.9 and in the UK 50 towns with 8.5 millions). The medium-sized group of towns has shown the greatest growth dynamism in most of the EEC countries since 1945, with those between 100- and 200,000 developing particularly rapidly. The reasons for such differential expansion are both negative, in the sense of a reaction against life in the great cities and a search for a more satisfying life style in medium-sized towns, but also positive in respect of the profitability of industrial development in such centres, the economies to be made in public service provision, and their role within both the urban network based upon the regional metropoli, and in service to a rural hinterland.

POPULATION GROWTH AND CHANGE

Evolution 1871–1946

Fig. 17 shows the essentials of population change during the past hundred years expressed regionally. As a backcloth to these patterns it is important to interpret briefly the national demographic trends and their relationship to the changing social structure, economy, political character and status of France.

Already by the mid-nineteenth century France had lost demographic momentum when compared with her European neighbours (INSEE, 1965). In 1871 her crude birth rate was lower (25.4 per 1000, cf. UK 35.4) and the death rate was higher (23.7 per 1000, UK 21.4). Beaujeu-Garnier (1969) attributed the differences to the strength of individualism in France, the influence of women ('more Malthusian than men'), the laws of primogeniture in the inheritance of property and the dominance of the bourgeois outlook in nineteenth-century France. Prior to the Franco-Prussian war France still cherished the leadership role in Europe, but this was increasingly belied by economic as well as demographic facts and trends. Although on the threshold of great colonial expansion France remained essentially an agrarian country to which the commercial revolutions in agriculture had not yet come; furthermore, she lacked large-

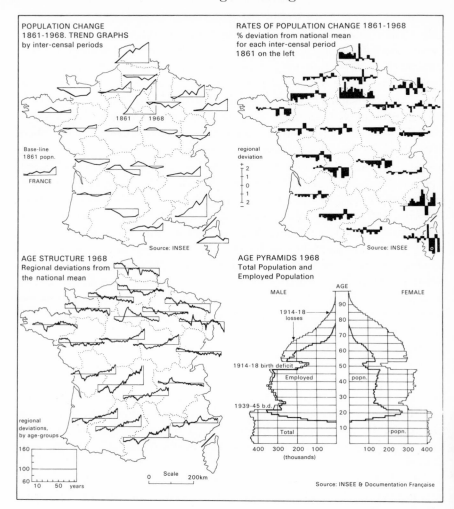

Figure 17   Population change, 1861–1968; age structure, France and planning regions.

scale factory industry and even in railway development started late and lagged behind. The Franco-Prussian war administered a severe shock and added domestic political troubles to those of slow economic development.

These unfavourable trends continued in one form or another through two world wars to the transformations post-1945. Their broad and cumulative effects may be assessed first systematically and then regionally. The birth rate continued to fall (France 1891–1900 22.2, 1931–40 15.5 per

1000; UK figures respectively 29.9 and 14.9) and with it the net reproduction rate and general fertility rates. Fall in the death rate was tardy in France (1901–10 19.5, 1935–9 15.7 per 1000; cf UK 15.4 and 12.0 respectively) and thus the population grew even more slowly. Thompson (1970) reported that in only four years for the entire period 1890–1936 did the net reproduction rate rise above unity, and that though the increase in life expectancy did contribute to a rise in numbers, the low fertility levels meant that the population became weighted towards old age. The first world war traumatically intensified French population problems. 1.3 million men were killed between 1914 and 1918, deaths were higher than normal among the civilian population (1.3 million), and there was a substantial deficit of births estimated at 1.0 million (Beaujeu-Garnier 1969). Even though the provinces of Alsace-Lorraine were returned to France in 1919 (1.1 million), the population of the country had actually fallen between 1911 and 1921, in spite of a net immigration of 300,000 during the same period.

The years between the two world wars were years of demographic stagnation and of rising fears of population decline. A short period of birth surpluses faded after 1923 and during the years 1934–9 there were actually more deaths than births in France. The economic depression of the early 1930s did not bite so deeply as in the UK and in particular there was no French counterpart of the great tides of inter-regional migrations. The immigrations into France, which so powerfully contributed to industrial and urban labour needs in the earlier part of the interwar period, fell away and the demographic problem became a cause of increasing public concern. The economy continued its slow momentum of growth. No less than one-third of the labour force continued to work on the land, the industrial structure remained traditional in character and organization, and urbanization outside Paris did little to disturb the patterns of peacefulness of small and medium-sized provincial towns. Though the second world war did not cause such devastating manpower losses as in 1914–18 (200,000 military deaths; 730,000 civilian deaths beyond those expected; 205,000 deficit in births between 1939–45) the net total population loss was estimated as 1.5 million, including 420,000 emigrants leaving the country by 1946 (Beaujeu-Garnier 1969).

The regional effects of population changes 1861–1946 (Fontanel and Peseux 1976) were complex, not only because vital trends were not uniform over the national space, but also because of the differential volume and incidence of migration currents. Townward movements off the land were widespread, strong and persistent. Flows from all parts of France to Paris were both striking and cumulative, and the urbanization of mining and industrial areas drew in migrants in search of work. Fig. 17 shows the course of population change both in absolute terms and in respect of the regional rates of change interpreted as a ratio of the national rates at each stage. It must be remembered that natural increase rates were higher throughout rural France in the nineteenth century, though progressively falling away after 1871. During the twentieth century it has been northern France (Armorica and the Bassin Parisien) which has had the higher birth rates, and this trend has become even more pronounced since 1945.

The trend graphs show numerous rhythms of change. In the rural west the rapid growth in some country areas in the first half of the nineteenth century was replaced by a high level of out-migration loss after 1861. Bretagne was a classic case with four of its *départements* collectively losing more than 700,000 by outmigration between 1900 and 1954, affecting all rural population and not solely that dependent on agriculture. In Aquitaine generally the rates of rural loss were moderate between 1861 and 1891 but accelerated thereafter; between 1891 and 1921 more than 700,000 were lost in thirty years; from 1921 to 1946 the regional population was maintained with immigration of foreigners offsetting the continuing departure of local people. Puy-de-Dôme and Cantal showed a slow but steady population decline from 1861 to 1946, but in Limousin and Auvergne generally the main towns succeeded in stabilizing migration within the region, notably so after the severe agricultural depression of 1846–56. After 1921 however the rural exodus from even these areas grew in momentum. Rural migration from French Lorraine and the Jura, especially to the Paris region, continued little abated from 1861 to 1946. Alsace, on the other hand, with its higher quality farmland and viable small farm units, held its rural population better, and the flows to the growing city of Strasbourg remained within the region. Natural increase rates were traditionally higher in eastern France, and there was a greater surplus of people who could leave the land without detriment to the rural economy. The Rhône-Alpes region showed a remarkable population stability from 1861 to 1946, increasing in numbers by only two per cent over the entire period. There was, however, considerable internal redistribution, with the mountain tracts depopulating and the regional metropolis, Lyon, trebling its population within a century.

The concentration of population upon Paris was the most striking positive effect during the eighty-five years 1861–1946. The city of Paris experienced its most rapid growth rates in the first half of the nineteenth century, thereafter slowing down towards 1914, with only a brief flourish after 1921. The suburban zones around the capital, on the other hand, continued to expand, with persistent massive attraction of young immigrants from the provinces. The Nord and Lorraine showed the characteristic rising population curves of all mining and heavy industrial centres, the product of immigration to meet high labour demands and the social response through the larger families of native-born. Though the rhythm of overall population growth was similar to that of the nation, between 1861 and 1946 the Provence-Côte d'Azur region showed very sharply contrasting internal trends: the coastal towns grew as tourist and retirement centres with a deepening economic and social gradient of decline towards the depopulating, sparsely-settled interior of the Basses-Alpes (Alpes-de-Haute-Provence).

Postwar change (1945 to date)
The remarkable acceleration in postwar population growth in France and her transformation in demographic structure have been widely remarked upon. By any criterion the trends represent a major revitalization in national society and the basis for a rising labour force to power economic growth momentum. France has become more urbanized, the population more freely mobile, and the range of jobs more diversified, particularly with the proliferation of service industries. Economic growth has lain at the root of demographic growth, but in its turn the larger population has fuelled further advances in production and GNP. Social attitudes have changed, notably so among young married couples who clearly decided to have more than the customary single child of prewar years. Furthermore, the marriage rate recovered (8.0 per 1000 in 1950, 7.0 in 1960, but 7.5 in 1974) and with it a lowering of the average age on marriage (1931–5, males 28.7 years, females 25.7; 1974, 25.9 and 23.7 respectively), all of which stimulated an increase in the crude birth rate in early postwar years (table 12).

The postwar milieu has led to a greater sense of adventure, to more mixing of the social classes, and wider possession of a proliferating range of consumer durables. In demographic terms the national population has

Table 12 Vital statistics, 1946–74

France *Crude rates per* 1000	1946	1954	1961	1971	1974
Births	20.8	18.5	18.1	17.1	15.0
Deaths	13.4	12.1	10.8	10.8	11.0
Natural incr.	7.4	6.4	7.3	6.3	4.0
Total popn (millions)	40.1	42.7	46.2	51.4	52.6

Source: INSEE

been renewing itself in each generation (net reproduction rate greater than unity), in striking contrast to the stagnation and even decline of the interwar period. Public policy has had a formative influence, both direct and indirect, upon individual decisions on family size. In a direct way the creation of a Ministry for Population in 1946 gave official recognition to the importance of the family, reinforced in a practical way by welfare aid, tax concessions, and family allowances; large families (*familles nombreuses*) with more than three children received many reductions, as for example in travel or on certain retail products. Medical services also were improved and in total it has been estimated (Beaujeu-Garnier 1969) that French aid to the family since 1945 has been at the highest and most comprehensive levels among comparable countries in the West. Greater medical investment and more freely available medical care led to a lowering of the crude death rate, but the increasingly youthful age structure of the national population also played its part in this statistic.

Not quite two-thirds of the postwar population increase in France (1954–71) was attributable to indigenous surplus of births over deaths (62 per cent), but net immigration into the country has also made a great contribution, in two respects: first, the repatriation of Frenchmen from North and West Africa and from Indochina, amounting to 1.3 millions between 1954 and 1965, including 710,000 in 1962 alone after Algerian independence (McDonald 1965); and, secondly, the influx of foreign workers and their dependants, 1.8 millions 1954–70. The number of foreign-born living in France in 1970 was estimated at 3 millions (1968 2.6 millions).

The positive demographic budget for the French nation over virtually the past three decades has been dramatic overall, though by the late 1960s there was already some indication of a slight waning of demographic vitality. From a geographical point of view the *regional differentiation* of postwar growth and change is no less important, not least in its implications of the development and planning of French economy and society (Carrère and Muguet 1972). The intercensal phases 1954–62, 1962–8 and 1968–75 are briefly reviewed, to bring out regional trends and also the shifting balance between rural and urban populations. A third dimension of change is structural, in the contrasts of trends among socio-economic groups in any one locality. These are referred to later under social structure.

1954–62.   During this period there was a striking contrast, which was to persist, between the trends in the planning regions west of a line from the mouth of the Seine to that of the Rhône and those to the east; the Paris region was a third distinctive component. To the west, the mean annual population increase rates were lower (e.g. Bretagne +0.2, Poitou-Charentes +0.4, Limousin even −0.2) and there was characteristically a net loss by outmigration over the eight years (in 1000s: Bretagne −67, Poitou-Charentes −27, Limousin −7). To the east, though the pattern of greater growth was uneven it was regionally widespread. The highest annual rates of growth were found in Provence-Côte d'Azur (+2.0), the product of postwar revival in tourism, the move to retirement, and the enlivening of the industrial economy of the lower Rhône; the net in-migration was as high as 343,000 into the planning region, a rate of 1.7 per cent per annum sustained over eight years. In second place, Greater Paris continued to be attractive as a place to work and to live (+1.7 per cent per annum total growth rate, of which +1.2 per cent represented persisting in-migration). Between 1954 and 1962 the heavy metallurgical industries of Lorraine were prospering, population was rising (+1.5 per cent p.a.) faster than the national average, and there was a net inflow of people (0.3 per cent p.a.). The Nord, Haute-Normandie, Alsace and Franche-Comté all increased in population at about the national average, but to some extent all four regions were living upon their population capital. In-migrant rates were less than the mean for the nation and, indeed, from the Nord there was even a slight net outward loss during the period.

Between 1954 and 1962 urbanization gained momentum strongly, not only by in-migration from the countryside but also because the town populations became more fecund. Whereas in the years 1936 to 1954 the population of urban communes increased by only 2.1 millions, the figure rose to a further 3.9 millions 1954–62, plus 400,000 who had been in communes classified as rural in the 1954 census. As another indication of the urban momentum, the figures for the annual increase in town populations 1861–1936 were 130,000, but from 1954–62 this rose to plus 540,000 each year, the equivalent of adding a town the size of Lyon every twelve months. By 1962 two out of every three Frenchmen lived in towns, compared to only two in five in 1900. Though the Paris agglomeration continued to increase in absolute numbers more rapidly than any other size category of towns, the rates of growth throughout the urban hierarchy became more even than they had been in the period 1946–54. The medium-sized towns (*villes moyennes*), 20–100,000 in population, increased most rapidly, whilst the provincial metropolitan centres had almost exactly the same growth rate as Greater Paris (+2.0 per cent p.a.). Provincial towns generally succeeded in intercepting part of the tide of out-migrants who might otherwise have flooded to the capital; indeed the coefficient of rural migrants moving to the towns of their region correlates closely with the degree of urbanization of the region (INSEE 1965).

The loss from the rural areas was but the continuation of a long-standing trend of townward movement. The smaller communes directly and wholly dependent on agriculture lost most heavily, but fertility differentials ensured that the rural communities were more effectively sustained in Lorraine, Alsace and Bretagne for example. Furthermore, the haemorrhage of young people from Bretagne was slowed by improvement in the local economic situation and by the vigour of the smaller towns. In Auvergne and Limousin a low natural increase rate compounded with poor agricultural prospects accelerated the rural loss.

1962–8. During these years the momentum of national population growth increased, by +0.1 per cent per annum compared with the 1954–62 rate, but the increase was unevenly shared among the planning regions (Calot *et al.* 1970). The threefold division of France into Ouest, Est and Région Parisienne, mentioned earlier, continued to reflect different growth trends, but there was greater internal diversity by individual planning regions. The annual population growth rate in the Ouest was 0.8 per cent p.a., but this varied from 1.2 per cent in Centre, down to 0.5 per cent in Bretagne, and even 0.1 per cent in Limousin; Aquitaine and Midi-Pyrénées (1.0 per cent p.a. each) experienced a sharply increased growth momentum by comparison with 1954–62, the outcome of industrialization and urbanization, particularly around Toulouse, Bordeaux and Lacq. In both these SW planning regions there was an in-migration rate (+0.7 per cent p.a.) higher than the national average (+0.5 per cent). From most of the Ouest, however, the net out-migration continued for the six years (fig. 18): e.g. 1962–8 Bretagne –12,000, Poitou-Charentes –19,000, Limousin –4800. It was, however, on a much reduced scale when compared with the 1954–62 outflow.

The Est, which stretches from the Nord-Pas-de-Calais in an arc through Alsace-Lorraine to Provence-Côte d'Azur showed both mixed and novel trends. Provence-Côte d'Azur (+2.7 per cent p.a.), Rhône-Alpes and Languedoc-Roussillon (both +1.6 per cent) had higher growth rates than the Paris region (+1.5 per cent). For all three southern regions in-migration currents were strong (Provence-Côte d'Azur +2.2 per cent p.a., Rhône-Alpes +0.9 per cent, and Languedoc-Roussillon +1.3 per cent). This was in part due to the repatriation of French nationals from overseas and the rate of in-migration was well above the national average (+0.5 per cent) and even that for the Paris region (+0.7 per cent). Indeed the momentum of inflow into Paris was only about half what it had been in 1954–62 (+1.2 per cent p.a.). The Paris population grew only a little more

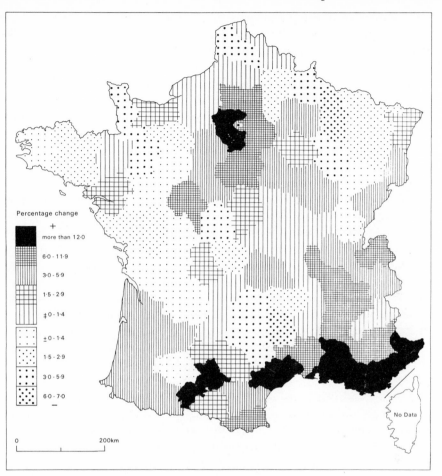

Figure 18   Migration balance, 1962–8, by *départements*.

slowly, however, as the result of higher levels of fecundity in the more youthful age structure. Apart from the rising population vigour of Alsace and parts of the Bassin Parisien (Picardie, Champagne-Ardennes) it was sharply-changed demographic trends in the Nord and Lorraine which deserve particular mention. Both planning regions had slower demographic growth rates than in 1954–62 (Nord, down from +0.9 to +0.7 per cent p.a.; Lorraine from +1.5 to +0.6 per cent p.a.) and both became substantial net exporters of population, whereas in 1954–62 Lorraine still had a slight net annual inflow. The reasons for the changes in trends are not hard to find and relate to the difficult industrial reconversion problems experienced in the coal and iron mines, and in the steel, metallurgical and textile industries. In all these activities rationalization of production took place and the labour force was considerably reduced, with only partial replacement of jobs by introduction of new forms of employment.

Two principal trends may be detected in the urbanization of France between 1962 and 1968: the differentially rapid growth of medium-sized towns (La DF 1972), and the centrifugal movement of suburbanization around the larger cities. To these may be added the invigoration of growth in satellite towns in some city regions and the fortunes of particular cities where economic growth has been rapid. The definition of medium-sized town (*ville moyenne*) in France conventionally refers to one with 20,000 to 200,000 inhabitants, though 20,000–100,000 has become a statutory planning definition (VIth and VIIth Plans). 1962–8 the population in medium-sized towns (20–100,000) increased by 30 per cent, compared with only 17 per cent for towns with more than 500,000 persons. Many such medium-sized towns reflected in their growth the dynamics of the economic region in which they were situated. Those in the Bassin Parisien grew vigorously, but such towns in the Nord or Lorraine showed only weak growth. Medium-sized towns in rural areas played an important role in intercepting and stabilizing rural migrants within their own region.

The core communes of most large cities lost population 1962–8, whilst the suburbs gained, often dramatically (e.g. Lyon −0.2 per cent core, +1.6 per cent per annum suburbs; Rouen −0.1 per cent and +3.3, Nancy −0.7 and +5.0, and Bordeaux −0.7 and +5.2 per cent p.a. respectively. Not surprisingly, the Paris conurbation (*agglomération*) shows the most striking evidence (table 13). The loss of population from the city is a combined product of low demographic vitality in an ageing population and an outward movement to the suburbs. The suburbanization process shows the centrifugal forces to be stronger in the outer than in the inner suburbs, and differentially greater in the southern (Essonne, fig. 22) and in the northern sectors.

1968–75. In the most recent period, demographic growth has been slowing (1954–62, +1.1; 1962–8, +1.2; 1968–75, +0.8 per cent p.a.). It must, however, be remembered that during the two earlier intercensal periods there had been major influences from overseas. Even so, the slackening momentum of population growth is further illustrated by the decline in the natural increase rate from +0.7 (1962–8) to +0.6 (1968–75) per cent per annum. Three-quarters of the growth in numbers between 1968 and 1975 was due to natural increase, a higher proportionate contribution than during the previous two intercensal periods.

Table 13   Population change, 1962–75. Zones of the Ile-de-France

| (1,000s) | 1975 | annual change rates | | | | | |
		1968/75 Total	Natural	Migration	1962/8 Total	Natural	Migration
Paris (City)	2,290	− 1.74	+ 0.38	− 2.12	1.22	+ 0.44	− 1.67
Inner ring							
Hauts de Seine	1,437	− 0.24	+ 0.71	− 0.95	+ 0.94	+ 0.82	+ 0.11
Seine St Denis	1,322	+ 0.79	+ 0.95	− 0.15	+ 2.43	+ 1.04	+ 1.38
Val de Marne	1,217	+ 1.18	+ 0.87	+ 0.31	+ 2.35	+ 0.82	+ 1.52
Outer ring							
Yvelines	1,080	+ 3.40	+ 1.20	+ 2.19	+ 3.67	+ 1.07	+ 2.59
Essonne	921	+ 4.58	+ 1.31	+ 3.26	+ 5.85	+ 1.13	+ 4.71
Val d'Oise	838	+ 2.74	+ 1.02	+ 1.72	+ 3.98	+ 1.05	+ 2.93
Seine-et-Marne	755	+ 3.23	+ 0.78	+ 2.45	+ 2.39	+ 0.72	+ 1.66
Total (IdF)	9,863	+ 0.92	+ 0.79	+ 0.12	+ 1.48	+ 0.77	+ 0.70

Though there was a general slowing of growth rates in most economic regions, it was the regions with the strongest economic potential which showed the least loss of momentum (Provence-Côte d'Azur, +1.5 per cent p.a.; Rhône-Alpes and Corse, +1.1). The lowest growth rates in population were found in the Massif Central (Limousin < 0.1; Auvergne + 0.2), in the Nord and in Lorraine (+ 0.3). Somewhat surprisingly at first sight, some of the traditionally deprived regions of the Ouest: Bretagne + 0.7; Poitou-Charentes + 0.4; and Pays de la Loire + 1.0, reversed their decline trends and actually increased their demographic momentum between 1968 and 1975. Though this no doubt owed something to the degree of success of planning at the regional and national levels, it is likely also to be due both to a high natural increase rate and also a slackening in out-migration towards the growth regions. With slower national economic growth and rising unemployment, jobs would not have been available there to attract in-migrants. There is even an indication of a net return flow of migrants to Bretagne 1968–75, + 41,000 and Pays de la Loire, + 30,000. Franche-Comté and Centre showed stability in positive trends, the former mainly by natural increase, three-quarters of total change, the latter with fifty per cent of growth due to in-migration.

Fig. 19 shows a more detailed pattern of total population change 1968–75. Fast growth is concentrated in an arc south of the Paris conurbation (suburban spread), around Etang de Berre (industrial growth complex), and in the prosperous immediate hinterland of Geneva (Bonazzi

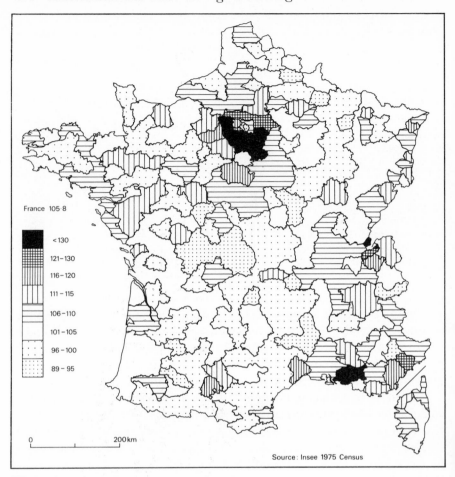

France 105·8

<130
121–130
116–120
111–115
106–110
101–105
96–100
89–95

0   200 km

Source: Insee 1975 Census

Figure 19   Population change, 1968–75, by *arrondissements*.

1972). The most serious declines occurred in a rural arc north of Limoges (Creuse, Haute Vienne), not previously a problem area, in the Cévennes around Alès (severe decline 1962–8 also), in the upper Arc valley (industrial decline, Chabert 1972, 1975), and in scattered pockets elsewhere.

Urban population grew more rapidly than total population, + 1.0 per cent per annum compared with + 0.8, and 80 per cent of the French people were located in settlements of more than 2000 in 1975 (37.3 millions); 71 per cent lived in urban communes. With the exception of the Paris conurbation (growth rate down from 1.31 per cent p.a. 1962–8 to 0.51 1968–75) there was much greater similarity in annual urban growth rates by size category than in the preceding inter-censal period: 20–100,000, + 1.5; 100–200,000, + 1.4; 200,000 − 2M, + 1.0 per cent p.a. As Bouchet (1976) put it, 'the aggregate town population of centres with less than 100,000 received each year the equivalent of a town of 75,000 people'. Nevertheless, there continued to be great regional variety even within the same urban size categories. Regional urban networks usually reflected the growth trends of their economies, though often with a better growth rate than the region, indicating continuing polarization of life on to the towns. Bouchet (1976) drew attention to a broad corridor of deprivation, not flanking the Caen-Marseille line of tradition, but a swathe of non-urbanized country stretching from Tarbes-Carcassonne through the Massif Central to Bourgogne and the Meuse-Ardennes.

Within the Région Parisienne (Ile-de-France) the urban growth trends were remarkably diverse. Declining population in the city of Paris (− 1.5 per cent p.a., 1968–75) down to the level of 1880 was matched by many slight decreases throughout the inner suburbs. Only in parts of the eastern and south-eastern inner suburban rim were there sharp increases in population, linked to the growth pole policy (Pt III, ch. 2). In the outer suburban ring there were many rapid growth communes, whilst in the direction of St Germain most centres grew only at about the national rate.

Fig. 65 shows the diversity of population change in urban communes for four of the growth metropoli. Characteristically, there has been a decline in numbers living in and around the city centre (Strasbourg is an exception, but the growth rate in the centre is notably lower than elsewhere in the urban area; Lille has the extraordinary contrast of a declining traditional core offset by rapid growth in the adjacent new core of Villeneuve d'Ascq, the New Town). The inner cores are surrounded by a zone of slow decline or stability in numbers, but further out the pattern of change, by commune, is already extremely variegated, but with some very fast growth localities of new integral housing estates.

Bouchet (1976) further drew attention to the tendency of urban clusters to fuse together, citing the areas surrounding the growth metropoli, the Sillon Alpin (north-east from Grenoble), the middle Loire valley, and the Poitiers-Châtellerault axis. He indicated the diffusion effects of population growth from the Bassin Parisien towards the Ouest, along the two corridors: Le Mans—Laval—Rennes; Val de Loire—Nantes.

Overall there was remarkable stability of population in rural communes at the national scale, but underlying this there was a continuing polarization into the small towns and a slight net loss by migration from rural hinterlands. Concealed within these broad national indications are the severe localized rural problem areas already referred to. Throughout rural

France the ageing population structure betokens a long-term serious social and welfare problem.

Having considered the formative phases of postwar population change in terms of regions and towns it is next appropriate to look at present distributions of people and the structure and dynamics of on-going changes, particularly in their implications for planning.

Population distribution

France has already been seen to have a lower population density than her EEC neighbours (table 10). To this essential characteristic must be added a marked irregularity of population distribution within the national he-

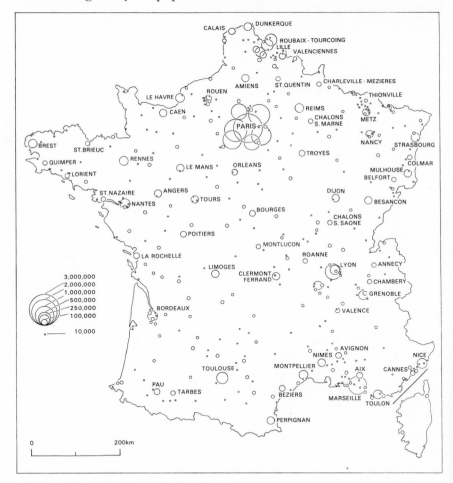

Figure 20   Towns of over 10,000, 1968.

xagon. Ile-de-France (9.8 millions in 1975, 18.7 per cent of the national population) is eccentrically positioned, towards the northern (c. 200 km) and eastern (c. 350 km) frontiers. 40 per cent of the French population is located in either frontier (6.1 millions) or coastal (15.5 millions) *départements* and the urban hierarchy (fig. 20) is uneven both in distribution and in balance of size categories.

Population density and patterns reflect the relationships between man and milieu, but in no simple, static or unambiguous way. It is rare for such relationships to persist unchanged for long, since vital trends evolve, man is mobile and his occupational patterns and structure change in adjustment to the interpretation of resources and their potential. Nevertheless, within broad limits rural densities give a crude man-land ratio, qualified by the proportion of the population which is not farm-based. In towns the densities in ward or neighbourhood highlight housing standards and the general quality of life. Densities also give a useful indication of the distances over which services have to be provided for a given number of people. The patterns and hierarchy of nucleated settlements from hamlets, through villages and towns to cities permit a further valuable insight into the relationships between people, place and space.

Four contrasting sections of France have been chosen (figs 21–4) to illustrate these relationships. More general comment can thus be correspondingly brief, both on densities and urban pattern. The lowest densities (less than 20 persons per km²) by *département* are found in a broad zone from the Ardennes southwards through the eastern and southern Bassin Parisien to include much of the Massif Central. In southern France there are detached pockets of low density on the least fertile land in the Landes, the Cévennes and in Alpes-de-Haute-Provence. Within the low density *départements* there is, of course, local variety in the distribution of population. Valley floor or scarp-foot ribbons of villages contrast with very sparsely-settled areas of sterile soils, of plateau or mountain tract. It is from many of these low density areas that the most massive rural depopulation has taken place during the past hundred years, leaving many communities reduced to barely adequate social threshold levels.

Higher rural densities (up to 150 persons per km²) characterize the western flank of France from Normandie, through Bretagne to northern Aquitaine; the lowlands of Languedoc and the basins of Provence; and the plains of Alsace. Along the western flank there has traditionally been a high density of rural population based on small family farms; in Bretagne and Normandie, furthermore, the higher than average natural increase rates have replenished the rural manpower reservoir. Languedoc has a close pattern of rural settlements related to the earlier labour-intensive monoculture of the vine, whilst in Alsace the high densities arise from the small family farms practising intensive commercial *polyculture*.

The urban hierarchy (fig. 20) is better interpreted by compact agglomerations (*unités urbaines*) than by urbanized communes. The functional pattern of submetropolitan and regional centres (fig. 7) has been referred to in Part I, ch. 2. The uniquely high degree of primacy of the Paris conurbation (8.5 millions in 1976) has already been mentioned, eight times the next in size (Lyon). Marseille (0.9) and Lille-Roubaix-Tourcoing (0.8) are the only other city clusters with pretensions to million-city status, and below them in size there is a gap down to Bordeaux (0.5) and Toulouse (0.4 millions); other core cities for regional metropoli (*métropoles d'équilibre*) are even smaller: Nantes (0.30), Strasbourg (0.38) and Nancy (0.25 millions). Given that management of the urban network is a major objective of regional planning in France (Part III, ch. 2), as part of the attempt to achieve greater balance in the economy and society, the present structure and pattern of the major city regions should be considered.

The city region pattern is irregular in shapes, degree of dominance by one or more cities in each, and in composition by categories of towns. The dominance of the Paris conurbation within the Bassin Parisien is outstanding, with only three other towns having more than 175,000 people (Rouen 388,000, Le Havre 264,000 and Caen 181,000 in 1975). Bordeaux-Toulouse illustrates a bipolar city region within an unusually concentrated

Table 14 City-region structure, by urban agglomeration sizes, 1968

Urban agglomerations 1968 *(thou.)*	20–49.9	50–99.9	100–174.9	175–249.9	325–400	450–499	500–1074	>8 000
population (millions)	3.9	3.1	3.0	2.3	2.8	0.9	2.9	8.1
no. of towns	59	43	24	11	8	2	3	1
City regions (no. of towns)								
Paris (Bassin Parisien)	10	7	6	2	1	—	—	1
Lyon	6	4	—	—	2	—	1	—
Marseille	8	2	—	1	2	—	1	—
Lille	5	4	3	2	1	—	1	—
Bordeaux-Toulouse	7	3	2	—	—	2	—	—
Nantes	4	3	3	1	1	—	—	—
Strasbourg	5	2	2	1	1	—	—	—
Nancy	3	2	3	1	—	—	—	—
Montpellier	6	3	4	—	—	—	—	—
Central France (Tours-Clermont F.-Dijon)	5	13	1	3	—	—	—	—

Source: Calculated from Recensement 1968

urban hierarchy, whilst the Lyon, Lille and Nancy regions have a more 'federal' or balanced network. The Strasbourg, Nantes, Marseille and Montpellier regions are more linear in character, whilst in a broad tract of central France from La Rochelle to Dijon there exists perhaps the most balanced of all urban regions and the nearest to the symmetry beloved of central place theorists. The Rhône-Alpes region has a balanced first and second order hierarchy, whilst the Mediterranean coastal region shows little hierarchy at all.

Four specimen areas. Figs 21–24 illustrate the detailed distribution of population (1968), by size category of settlements and on a common scale, for four contrasting areas of France: Dunkerque-Lens/Arras (fig. 21); Paris-Orléans (fig. 22); Côte d'Azur (Cannes-Fréjus and hinterland) fig. 23; and Aurillac-Rodez-Villefranche de Rouergue (fig. 24). Table 15 indicates the proportionate importance in total population and by size category of settlements in each area. Dunkerque-Lens is a traditional coalmining and intensive agricultural area in course of economic reconversion, including the major growth pole at the port of Dunkerque. Paris-Orléans illustrates the spreading suburban impact of fast population growth upon former rural areas with their market town economy. The most striking feature of Cannes-Fréjus is the sharp population gradient from the rapidly growing resort and tourist towns along the coast to the sparsely-settled, depopulating hinterland. Aurillac-Rodez, on the other hand, shows a rural tract of the south-western Massif Central with a diversity of middle-sized service towns (Aurillac, Rodez, Villefranche) but also the depressed mining town of Décazeville, set within a region of rural decline.

The main features on fig. 21 are: the dense clustering of coalfield towns from Bruay (1) and Béthune (2) to Lens (3), total ZPIU *zone de peuplement*

Table 15   Size categories of settlements 1968, four selected areas

| | Total popn 1968 1000s | | settlement size % total popn | | | | | |
| | | | Nucleated | | | | | |
		Dispersed	<100– 399	400– 999	1000– 1999	2000– 4999	5000– 9999	>10,000
Dunkerque-Lens	996	10.8	6.4	6.4	5.2	13.5	14.9	42.8
Paris-Orléans	950	7.2	4.5	4.2	5.8	7.6	10.9	59.7
Cannes-Fréjus	371	14.8	2.7	4.7	3.5	5.4	1.7	67.2
Aurillac-Rodez	148	52.9	7.5	6.5	2.7	4.2	10.4	15.9

Source: Population de la France 1968

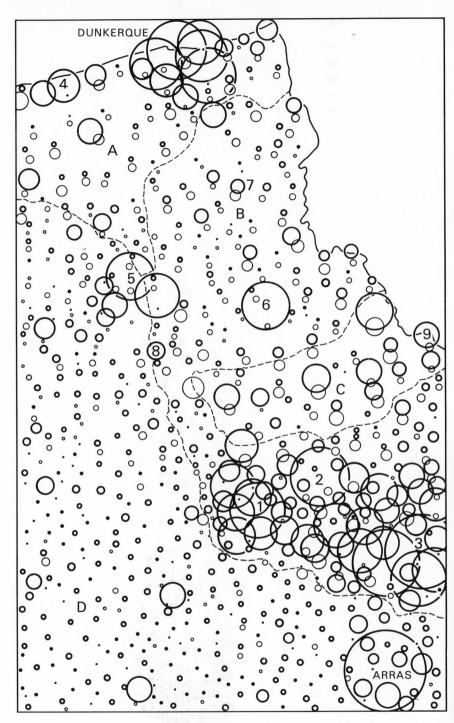

Figure 21   Population distribution, 1968: Nord (Dunkerque-Lens).

industriel ou urbain) population 652,000 (1968), virtually static since 1962 with higher than average natural increase rates now declining, and persisting out-migration since the mid-1950s; the complex of urban communes of the Dunkerque ZPIU (195,000 in 1968), from the Belgian border to Gravelines (4), with a strikingly youthful population and rapid in-migration since 1954, though slackening in the mid-1960s. The Arras ZPIU (84,000 in 1968) has also shown vigorous growth over the past twenty years, both by natural increase and by in-migration. Between the coalfield and the littoral, the so-called 'intermediate zone' contains St Omer (ZPIU 64,000) (5) and Hazebrouck (22,600) (6), both with above-average natural increase rates, but St Omer in particular today has only a bare balance of net in-migration. Contrasts in the detailed patterns of rural settlement are striking: the larger market centres and dispersed population of the clay lowlands behind the coast (A); the small market towns and sparser settlement of hilly interior Flanders (B) (e.g. Wormhout (7)); the industrial towns along the Lys valley (C) from Aire (8) to Nieppe (9). The close and regular pattern of small nucleated villages and open network of market centres on the chalk uplands of Artois (D) stand out clearly, in

KEY TO FIGURES 21, 22, 23, 24

DUNKERQUE-LENS/ARRAS
A Flemish clay lowlands
B Hilly interior Flanders
C Lys valley
D Chalk uplands of Artois
1 Bruay　　2 Béthune　　3 Lens
4 Gravelines 5 St. Omer　6 Hazebrouck
7 Wormhout 8 Aire　　9 Nieppe

PARIS-ORLÉANS
A Seine valley
B Hurepoix
C Beauce
D Gâtinais
E Forêt de Fontainebleau
F Forêt d'Orléans
1 Corbeil

CÔTE D'AZUR (CANNES-FRÉJUS)
A Mountains of Upper Var
B Crêts et plans
C Maures massif
D Esterel massif

AURILLAC-VILLEFRANCHE DE
ROUERGUE-RODEZ
A Cantal volcanic upland
B Xaintrie
C Châtaigneraie
D Bassin d'Aurillac
E Bassin de Décazeville
F Ségalas
G Causse de Comtal
1 Rodez　　　　　　　2 Aurillac
3 Villefranche de Rouergue　4 Décazeville

SETTLEMENTS 1968

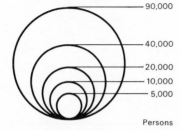

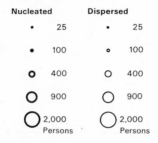

	Nucleated	Dispersed
	• 25	• 25
	• 100	◦ 100
	○ 400	○ 400
	○ 900	○ 900
	○ 2,000 Persons	○ 2,000 Persons

90,000
40,000
20,000
10,000
5,000
Persons

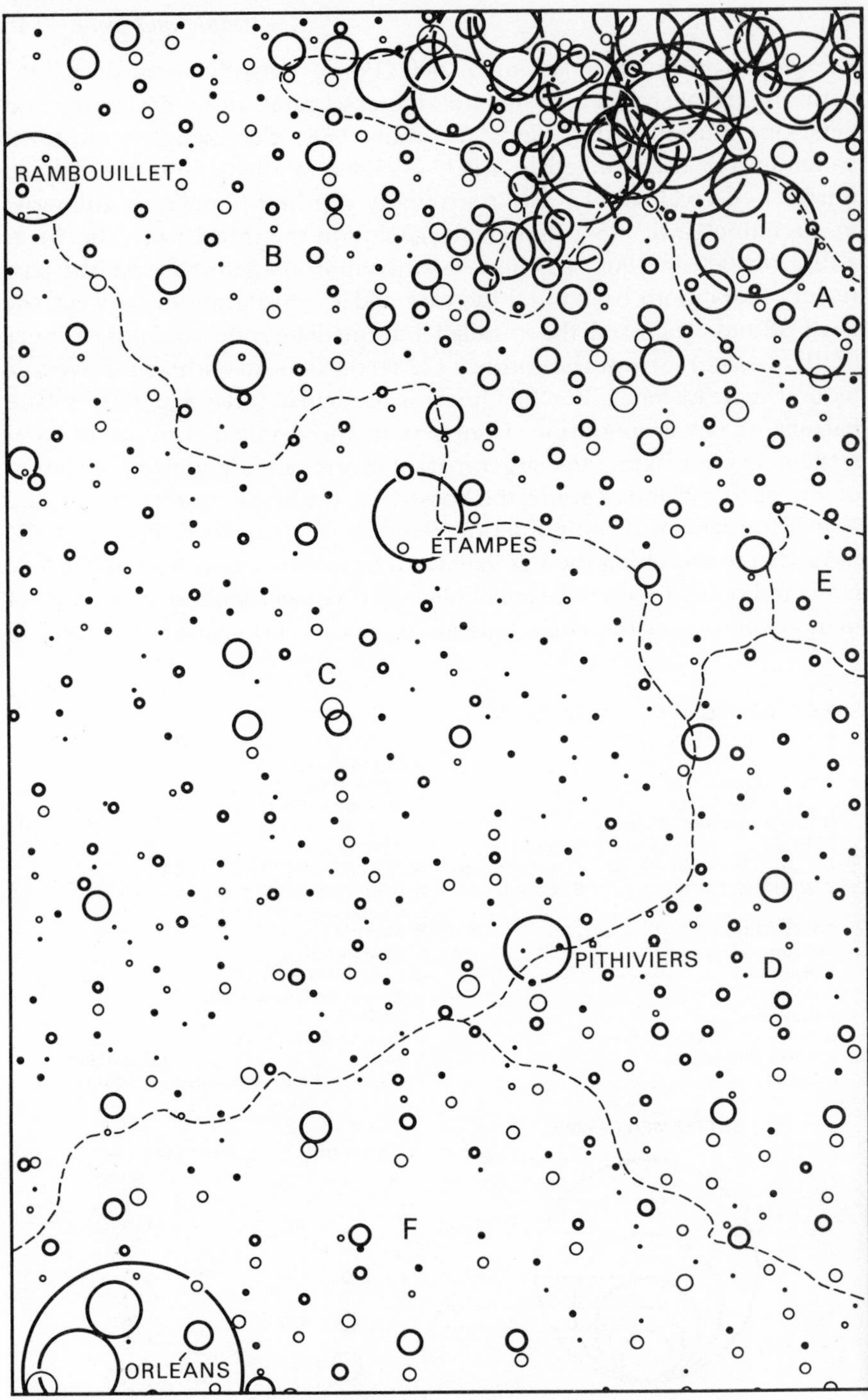

Figure 22 Population distribution, 1968: South of Paris (Essonne).

contrast to the irregular impact of mining and urbanization in other parts of the area.

The Paris-Orléans area (fig. 22) illustrates a belt of very rapid population increase during the past twenty years (Paris ZPIU in Département of Essonne 550,200–1968), + 47 per cent on 1962, which in turn was + 48 per cent on 1954; in-migration contribution to inter-censal growth rate in each period was + 39 per cent). The urbanization southward from Paris has been perhaps the most dramatic growth in France during the period, with secondary impacts in the diffusion of commuter residences to smaller towns further out (e.g. Etampes + 16 per cent population growth 1962–8) and throughout the suburban countryside belt. Decentralization of industry has also played a part in invigorating the economy of the southern Bassin Parisien.

The spread of Paris was channelled in part along the Seine valley (A) through Corbeil (1) but also into the hilly and forested clay uplands of Hurepoix (B). The Beauce (C) is a *limon* (loam) covered plateau with large tenanted farms practising cereal agriculture; rural settlements are dispersed in groups of farms and hamlets, with few larger market settlements. This pattern shades eastwards into the clay-covered plateau of Gâtinais (D) and the Forêt de Fontainebleau (E), and southwards into the more sterile Forêt d'Orléans (F).

The Côte d'Azur section (fig. 23) shows extreme contrasts from the sparsely-settled mountain tract in the upper Var (A), through the barren *crêts et plans* (B) south of Puget Théniers to the coastal crystalline massifs of the Maures (C) and Esterel (D). The densest settlement is in the coastal band with two ZPIUs: Cannes-Grasse-Antibes (213,300 in 1968); and the Côte Varoise (80,000) including Fréjus (41,400). All the towns along this coast have shown a remarkable vigour in population growth over the past twenty years: e.g. Cannes-Grasse-Antibes, + 23 per cent 1954–62, + 13 per cent 1962–8; Fréjus, + 42 per cent and + 48 per cent in the same two periods. In-migration is the main source of growth; indeed the natural trend in Cannes was to show virtually no birth surplus at all over deaths, the product of an ageing structure of population in a retirement area.

By contrast with the coastal zone the rural interior has been a reservoir for incessant out-migration, reducing numbers in many villages and hamlets to levels at which social and community life is threatened with collapse. In recent years, however, at least along the main routes inland, the rapid development of 'second homes' is building up an adventitious population, not always contributing very much to the well-being of the rural community.

Fig. 24 shows the Aurillac-Villefranche de Rouergue-Rodez area of the

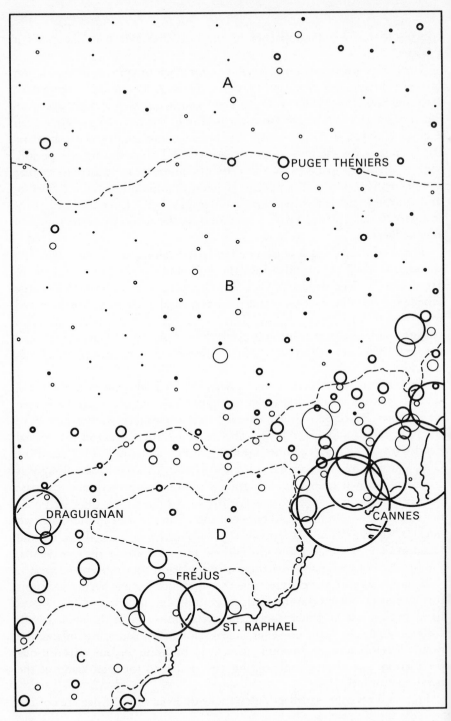

Figure 23   Population distribution, 1968; Côte d'Azur (Cannes and hinterland).

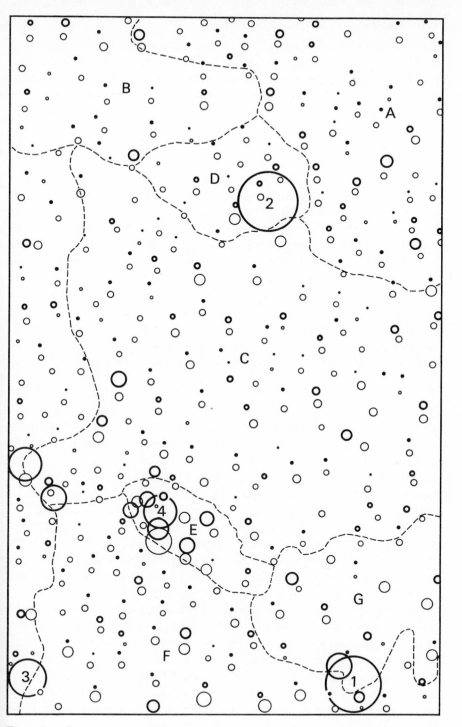

Figure 24   Population distribution 1968: SW Massif Central (Aurillac-Décazeville).

south-western Massif Central. The rural economy is diverse, from the cattle-rearing uplands of the volcanic Cantal upland (A), to the dairy-farming and forested tracts of the Xaintrie (B) and the Châtaigneraie (C), the basins of Aurillac (D) and Décazeville (E), the formerly poor arable lands of the Ségalas (F) and the grazing lands of the Causse de Comtal (G). The Ségalas rural economy has been revived by cooperative livestock farming for cattle and sheep, but for the most part the entire area on fig. 24 has been subject to steady and debilitating rural depopulation for the best part of a century. Towns are few and scattered but they have played a vital role in stabilizing part of the rural exodus within the region. Rodez, 29,900 in 1968 (1), has proved the most successful, + 17.7 per cent growth 1954–62, including + 11.9 per cent by migration; + 24.3 per cent 1962–8, including + 15.9 per cent by migration. Aurillac (2), 33,700 in 1968, has had a less favourable record with a decline in natural increase rate and even a net migration loss in 1962–8. Villefranche-de-Rouergue (3), 10,600 in 1968, has had a vigorous in-migration of + 11.9 per cent 1954–62, and 12.1 per cent 1962–8 to offset a stagnant trend of natural change. Décazeville (4), 35,000 in 1968, has lost population, and shows both a minimal natural increase and a disturbing net out-migration. This is due to the closure of coalmines and the lack of adequate replacement industries.

Population structure and prospects

For the purposes of planning, the characteristics and dynamics of present population structure, and the projection of salient demographic trends over the proximate future (to 1986), are equally important, both nationally and regionally. There are implications for prospective changes in GNP per capita, the size and structure of the labour force, the levels of health and welfare provision required, and the scale of housing and education programmes. The age and sex structure of the nation, its cities and regions, underlie current population dynamics, the trends in birth, fertility, marriage, death or natural increase rates. Furthermore and increasingly, migration and mobility must be taken into account, through an analysis of the volume, direction, structure and motivation of migrant flows, both internally at several scale levels and internationally.

In February 1975 the population of France was estimated to be 52.59 millions, with a sustained growth rate of + 0.8 per cent p.a. since 1968. The latest demographic forecasts for 1986 vary between 56.1 millions, assuming present rates of fertility and mortality and no migration, and 58.8 millions incorporating migration predictions (Cazin 1970). A notable diversity in regional and urban trends of change is forecast, and many of the recent trends of change are expected to continue. Natural increase rates will be greatest, as at present, in the ZEAT regions (fig. 4) of the Nord, the Bassin Parisien, the Est and the Ouest and below the national average elsewhere; the Méditerranée will show the lowest rate. Generally speaking, the natural increase rate will be greatest in the medium-sized towns (60–200,000 population) and least in Ile-de-France and the rural areas. On the other hand, prediction of migration flows by 1986 (fig. 25) shows that Ile-de-France will continue to be a considerable net importer of persons (1.8 millions in 18 years), with the Méditerranée (+ 0.6) and Centre-Est (+ 0.5 millions) next in rank. Somewhat surprisingly, the migration budget of the Bassin Parisien is expected to be virtually in balance 1968–86, whilst the Nord (− 0.2) and the Ouest (− 0.5 million) will continue to lose migrants, in spite of regional support policies by government. In other regions there will be small net inflows. Among ZPIUs the rate of population increase will vary little by size category of town. It is, however, the Paris agglomeration (+ 1.9 million migrants) and towns with more than 200,000 people (+ 1.6 millions) which would have both the greatest absolute and proportionate in-migration flows, had not planning constraints been so vigorously prosecuted.

Age and sex. Fig. 17 shows the 1968 age pyramid for France and also the regional deviations from the national mean of age groups. The national age pyramid is both irregular and asymetrical in shape. Females are more numerous at all ages above 53 years, the result of the heavy losses of men during the first world war and the naturally greater longevity of women. The sharp indentations on both sides of the pyramid for 48–53 years indicate the deficit of births due to the 1914–18 war, whilst the narrowing of the pyramid, 30–48 years, is to be explained by the low interwar birth rates, aggravated by the deficit of births when the smaller generation born 1915–19 reached the most fertile ages (22–30 years). The high and sustained birth rate between 1945 and 1965 gives the broader base to the lower part of the pyramid, for both sexes, but the post-1965 fall in births is also detectable in a further narrowing in the age-group 0–4 years.

The regional variations from the national pyramid are complex, and relate alike to differential natural trends and the effects of migration, both internal and international. The higher than average birth rates in northern and eastern France, from Bretagne to the Nord and Lorraine, show up in the higher representation of the 0–20 age groups, but the fall below the national mean for the 20–24 year group highlights the sharp peak of greatest out-migration. The counterpart may be seen in the above average representation of this latter group in Ile-de-France, Rhône-Alpes and Provence-Côte d'Azur, the areas of greatest affluence and growth potential.

Table 16   Age structures, ZEAT regions, 1973

ZEAT regions (fig. 4)	Total popn (millions) 1973	<20	20–4	25–44	45–64	>65 years
		(percentage deviations from national means)				
R. Parisienne	9.9	−2.9	+0.9	+4.3	−0.4	−1.8
Bassin Parisien	9.4	+2.2	±0	−1.3	−1.0	+0.2
Nord	3.9	+4.2	+0.4	−1.4	−1.5	−1.8
Est	4.8	+2.9	+0.2	+0.2	−1.6	−1.7
Ouest	6.6	+1.9	−0.3	−2.4	+0.4	+0.4
Sud-Ouest	5.4	−2.9	−0.6	−2.0	+2.3	+3.2
Centre-Est	6.0	−0.3	−0.2	+0.7	−0.1	−0.1
Méditerranée	5.4	−3.4	−1.0	−0.5	+2.3	+2.6
FRANCE	51.9	32.8	8.4	25.3	20.6	12.9

Source: Statistiques et Indicateurs, INSEE 1972

The regions of long-term out-migration and of slow economic growth, in the Massif Central, the Sud-Ouest, and Languedoc, have greater ratios of those over 40 years. The graphs for Limousin and Midi-Pyrénées show particularly unfavourable trends of deficit among the young and excess representation of the retired. Languedoc-Roussillon and Provence-Côte d'Azur are regions attracting the retired, but the secondary 'peaks' in age structure around 50 years almost certainly indicate those repatriated from Algeria and North Africa in the early 1960s. Rhône-Alpes and Franche-Comté most closely approximate the national means of age structure.

The most striking overall feature of age-group distributions in France is that in general the northern half of the country has the higher percentage today in the age groups up to 25 years; Paris is under-represented in groups to 15 years and Bretagne in the out-migrant age groups 15 to 24 years. On the other hand people over 25 years of age are proportionately more strongly represented in the southern half of France, with the highest ratios of those over retiring age (65 years) in the southern Bassin Parisien, the Massif Central, Côte d'Azur and Aquitaine.

Vital trends. The general course of postwar natural increase has already been commented upon. It remains to put the most recent trends into perspective and to discuss the principal regional variations. Since 1965 there has been a perceptible falling away in both the crude birth rate (15.0 per 1000 in 1974, cf. UK 16.2) and the latest crude reproduction rate at 1.22 (number of female children born per generation of mothers, subject to the birth rates of the years 1967–9 and discounting female deaths). The crude death rate has remained approximately static at about 11.0 per 1000 (cf. UK 11.6), whilst the marriage rate in France has increased slightly (7.5 per 1000 in 1974) (INSEE 1973).

Fig. 25 shows the regional differences in crude birth, death and reproduction rates. To some extent these reflect the age structures in each region (fig. 17), but they are also to be related to the socio-economic classes

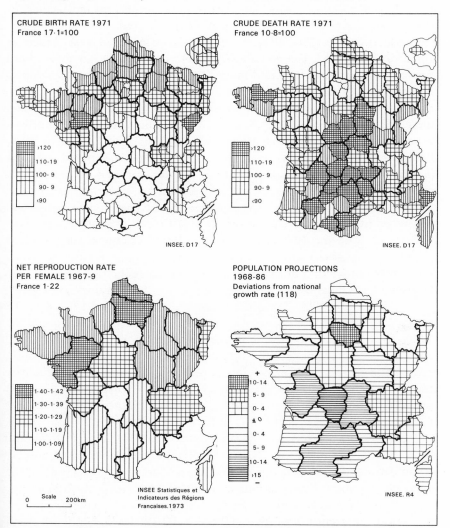

Figure 25   Population structure: crude birth- and death-rates 1971; net reproduction rates 1967–9; predicted population 1986.

and the extent of mobility, both geographically and occupationally. Birth rates are high in a broad 'fertile crescent' from the mouth of the Loire through Normandie and Picardie to the Nord and Lorraine, with an outlier in the *département* of Doubs (20.1 per 1000). The lowest rates are in the Massif Central and the Sud-Ouest, together with the southern Alpes, all areas with an ageing population and long-standing net out-migration trends of young people. The reproduction rate follows closely the pattern of birth rates, though it bears long-term implications for the replacement of the generations; exact replacement is indicated by unity (1.0). Reproduction rates (1967–9) are high in the Nord and the Ouest (Ardennes 1.57, Morbihan 1.51, Pas-de-Calais 1.49) and particularly low in southern France, Limousin and Ile-de-France (1.07 Haute-Garonne, 0.93 Alpes-Maritimes, 0.89 Paris).

Regional death rates are not quite a mirror image of birth rates, though there is a general inverse relationship. The highest rates are found in a broad zone southwards from Paris through the Massif Central to Midi-Pyrénées, with outliers in Alpes-Maritimes (12.7 per 1000) and Bretagne (Côtes-du-Nord 13.1). Low rates are more scattered, with general correspondence to *départements* with a youthful age structure (e.g. Doubs 8.2), but this generalization is to be qualified by adverse environmental and urban conditions in areas such as the Nord (10.7) or Lorraine (Meuse 11.6).

Between 1962 and 1975 large towns (> 100,000 popn) tended to show population dynamics similar to those of the economic regions in which they were situated, but often with rather more favourable features. Grenoble (+ 1.4 per cent p.a. natural increase, + 2.8 net migration 1962–8; + 1.2 and + 1.08 1968–75), Montpellier (+ 1.0 and + 4.8 1962–8; + 0.8 and + 2.0 1968–75), and Caen (+ 1.5 and + 2.6 1962–8; + 1.6 and 0.9 1968–75) showed the strongest combination of natural growth and attraction to migrants. At the other extreme large towns of the Midi, retirement centres with an ageing population, showed natural increase rates conventionally below the national average (+ 0.7 per cent p.a.), but positive net in-migration rates: Nice (± 0 natural increase and + 2.1 net migration 1962–8; − 0.1 and + 1.75 1968–75); Nîmes (+ 0.7 and + 3.0, + 0.5 and + 0.1 respectively). Several towns over 100,000 in Lorraine, and to a lesser extent in the Nord, illustrated the most unfavourable combination, of above average natural increase and net out-migration, the product of youthful populations and the problems of industrial reconversion: e.g. Hagondange-Briey (+ 1.5 per cent p.a. natural increase, − 0.4 per cent net migration 1962–8; + 0.9 and − 1.1 1968–75); Lens (+ 1.0 and − 1.0, and + 0.8 and + 1.4 respectively).

Immigration of foreigners

The 1968 census recorded 2.6 million foreigners in France, some 5.3 per cent of the total population (cf. UK figures 1.9 million and 3.5 per cent respectively). To these must be added those who have become naturalized French citizens (326,000 between 1962 and 1970 inclusive, for example), and have thus been more fully integrated and assimilated into society and economy. A 1974 figure showed 3.8 million foreigners (7 per cent total population). Since the first world war, indeed, France has had a higher ratio of foreign immigrants to total national population (515 per 100,000) than even the United States (492) (Armengaud 1965). The reasons are not hard to find: the serious manpower shortages resulting from losses during the two world wars and also the need for workers in a wartime economy; and the shortfall of labour in the interwar period when the effects of falling birth rates led to fewer workers in each succeeding generation. To these reasons must be added the need for adequate supplies of labour of the right quality, in the right place, at the right time. French workers tended to be more immobile and there were certain jobs that they preferred to leave to others, especially the low-paid, dirty, unhealthy or even dangerous jobs in manufacturing or urban services.

Ever since the first world war treaties with Poland, Czechoslovakia, Belgium and Italy, immigration of foreign workers has been closely supervised and controlled by French government agencies, with a view to regulating inflow and repatriation to correspond as far as possible with phases of the trade cycle and to protect French workers from 'unfair' competition (La DF 1964). Between 1921 and 1931 the numbers of foreigners in France rose from 1.5 to 2.7 million, with an annual net inflow of about 110,000 p.a. Twenty per cent were from Poland and came to work in either the coal or iron mines of the Nord-Pas-de-Calais or Lorraine; thirty-five per cent were Italians and fifteen per cent Spaniards, both national groups settling mainly on the land or in the towns of the Midi. The great world economic depression of the early 1930s led to repatriation of several thousand Poles and to a cut-back in all immigration. Even so, 1.7 million foreigners were recorded in France at the 1946 census and to these should be added 500,000 naturalized French citizens.

After the second world war both the labour demands of the economy and the need to revitalize the flagging population structure (Sauvy 1946) led to further mass immigration, controlled through the ONI (*Office National d'Immigration*) by the issue of both work and residence permits (McDonald 1969). The policy was to provide for the needs of agriculture, the mines, the steel industry and the building industry in particular and to do so by recruiting the right volume of labour with the necessary capabilities and attempting to sustain an ethnic mix which would keep in balance those coming from latin and germanic countries. In practice the policy had to be modified, and there were marked shifts in the source origins of immigrants (fig. 26) according to the state of the economy in their homelands and the demands also from other West European states. In the early postwar years the immigrants were mainly Italians, some Germans and displaced persons, but labour demands could not be met by adequate immigration (243,000 persons entered France 1946–9). From 1949–55 the French economy grew only slowly, and immigration was cut back to 173,000 in six years, including 129,000 workers. From 1956 the inflow increased sharply to replace the 400,000 Frenchmen sent to Algeria and to meet the needs of an accelerating national economy; 1958–60 was a further period of austerity and of decline in immigration. From 1960, however, the tempo of immigration has been better sustained though the composition has become more complex: from 1962–5 860,000 French citizens were repatriated, mainly from North Africa; the net inflow of Algerians has fluctuated, but on average has been + 30,000 per annum between 1962 and the end of 1971; other foreigners have entered at an average rate of + 100,000 per annum during the same period. Among other foreigners the proportion of Italians has fallen in recent years, whilst those of Portuguese and Spaniards have risen commensurately. In the 1968 census the nationality of foreigners showed: EEC 26.5 per cent (incl. Italy 21.8), Spaniards 23.2, Algerians 18.1. The 168,000 repatriated from North Africa and located in Ile-de-France in 1968 were mostly young white-collar workers, diffused through the city and in the newer housing developments of the inner suburbs (Guillon 1974).

Fig. 26 shows the distribution and proportionate significance of foreigners in France (1968). Two features stand out clearly: the dominance of particular groups in the frontier *départements* of France adjacent to their own countries; the attraction of the major regions of affluence (Ile-de-France, Rhône-Alpes). The rise of foreign-born in the city of Paris has been truly dramatic: 1921, 1 per cent, 1954 4, 1968 10, 1975 25 per cent of the total population. The main countries of origin are on the shores of the Mediterranean. The concentration in Lorraine includes Italians as one-half the foreigners, mainly in the iron mines and steel mills. By contrast, in the agrarian regions of the Ouest, the southern Massif Central and Limousin, there are few foreigners, the result of surplus indigenous rural populations and the limited economic prospects.

In 1972 two-thirds of all foreigners entering France took jobs in one of four sectors: agriculture 10 per cent, mechanical and electrical industry 14

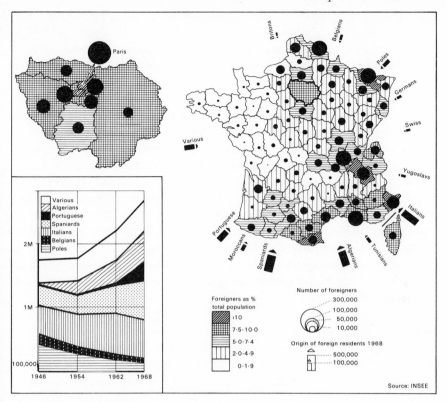

Figure 26   Foreigners in France, 1968.

per cent, building 27 per cent and personal service 13 per cent. The balance in jobs taken varied by the region: in Paris 26 per cent went into personal services; in Franche-Comté 67 per cent to mechanical and electrical industries; in Languedoc-Roussillon 47 per cent to agriculture, 29 per cent to building and public works.

The contribution of immigration by foreigners in postwar years has been both vital and considerable to French economy and society. On the positive side redeployment of labour throughout the expanding national economy has been facilitated, both territorially and occupationally. Furthermore, with rising affluence it has been possible to find workers for an increasing range of jobs disliked by Frenchmen. The aggregate net contribution of foreign workers to French GNP has been estimated at four milliard francs, even taking into account emigrants' remittances back to the home country. A particularly sharp stimulus was given to the towns of the Midi by the returning French families from North Africa in 1962–3 (Rognant and Schultz 1964).

Yet there have emerged serious and continuing social problems. Most of the foreign workers have been either unskilled or semi-skilled and there has been a constant fear among French trade unions that foreign workers might be used to depress wage rates or at least reduce their growth. The housing problem for foreign workers has proved acute, in the *bidonvilles* around the larger cities, in the *carons* of the Nord coalfield or the slums of Roubaix-Tourcoing. Social segregation in 'ghettoes' or single-culture neighbourhoods has sometimes been the preference of foreign workers, living cheaply in over-crowded conditions, whilst working on short-term labour contracts. Assimilation into French national culture has been slow and difficult, even at times unsought and unwanted. The problems of immigrant families relate to education and social services as well as to housing. They have proved to be as intractable in France as in the UK in postwar years. During 1975 economic depression led to a government policy for restricting foreign immigration; even voluntary repatriation was contemplated.

Population projections

The latest population projections for 1986 (Cazin 1970) envisage a France of 58.8 millions with migration assumptions, or 56.1 millions if these are not taken into account. The higher estimate would mean a growth rate of 0.65 per cent per annum over the years 1968–86, or 0.62 per cent by natural trends alone. As in the UK, and for the same reasons of perceptibly falling birth rates and economic uncertainty, it is likely that these forward estimates will be steadily revised downwards in due course. Yet both predictions are markedly lower than the annual growth rate ($+0.83$ per cent) between 1954–68.

Fig. 25 shows the regional deviations from the national growth rate projections 1968–86. The Ile-de-France shows the greatest positive deviation (the same annual excess rate as for the 1954–68 period), followed by Rhône-Alpes which is expected to increase its relative population position in the nation. Haute-Normandie, Picardie and Alsace are other regions with slightly higher than average growth rates, all more favourable than their relative rates 1954–68. The most markedly lower than average growth rates are expected for Limousin, Poitou-Charentes, Auvergne and Midi-Pyrénées, all with slightly worse relative positions than in 1954–68. The remaining regions of the Ouest and Sud-Ouest are to have lower than average growth rates, with the implication that regional or national policies can do little to correct fundamental economic or social imbalances within the next two decades. Corse will have lower growth rates, Languedoc will pass below the national growth average and Provence-Côte d'Azur, the fastest growth region of the 1960s, will have a momentum only in keeping with that for France as a whole.

Growth rates 1968–86 have been worked out for the ZPIUs, which are conventionally larger than the urban agglomerations (*unités urbaines*). All ZPIUs with more than 20,000 inhabitants are to grow faster than the national average (118): 20–60,000 (123); 60–100,000 (124); 100–200,000 (126); Paris (130). On the other hand ZPIUs with under 20,000 persons will increase only at about national tempo, whilst non-ZPIU units will show a marked negative deviation (92) and will actually lose population. The implications for regional policy must be that unless more decisive public interventions are made the disparities between regions will decrease only minimally and for the more remote agrarian regions will probably become even more acute; the urbanization of France will be intensified and the larger the town in general the greater the beneficiary in population terms. Under the VIIth Plan, however, positive steps are to be taken to restrain the growth of large conurbations, in favour of the priority development of small and medium-sized towns (Part III, ch. 2).

Migration and mobility

In classical economic theory the movement of labour and/or capital is the natural means of adjusting inequalities in both time and space, at the level of the firm, the locality or the employment sector (Beltramone 1966). Migration includes those changes of job which require a change of residence by the worker; mobility refers to change of job but not necessarily of residence. Within these definitions seasonal movement is a form of migration, but journey to work change is so only if the residence is changed in the process. Both migration and mobility are complex processes which may be explained only in part by economic motivations, though material betterment is the most common cause of an intention to move. Housing, quality of life, marriage, relatives and friends and retirement (Cribier 1975), are among the principal non-economic motivations. In pursuit of regional and social justice most West European states, including France, seek to reduce the level of gross migration flows and to take work to the worker whenever and wherever possible. Such guiding or manipulating of gross migration is attempted in a crude and at times indirect manner, through regional planning, industrial location or housing policies, or by programmes for improving differentially the quality of life in particular regions or localities. Achievement to date has stopped far short of any optimum equilibrium and indeed the case is often contested that all out-migration is damaging to the regions of loss or that in-migration is invariably beneficial. The movement of surplus farm-workers out of low-income, overpopulated rural tracts, as in parts of Bretagne, is clear evidence of the merits of out-migration in some cases. The diversion of would-be in-migrants from already congested districts of the metropolis is a further indication that in-migration may at times add to, rather than subtract from, social problems. A balanced assessment of migration must take into account the impact on both the locality of the out-migrants and also their reception areas (Courgeau 1970).

Two difficulties stand in the way of such an assessment: inadequate data, and imperfect understanding of the motivation of migrants. A further problem, somewhat ignored in many geographical studies, is that of measuring the true significance of a given volume or percentage of migration change over a fixed period, particularly when the data is of net or residual change rather than of gross two-way flows. Figs 18, 27, 28 and 29 illustrate both the possibilities and the limitations of the evidence. Fig. 18 shows the net migration balance of total populations for the period 1962–8, at the level of *départements*. There is general correspondence between economic growth and in-migration (Midi, Rhône-Alpes, Bassin Parisien), on the one hand, and decline and out-migration on the other (most rural areas, Lorraine, Pas-de-Calais). During the period the massive influx of Frenchmen from independent Algeria boosted the figures, especially in the Midi. Yet the very diversity of rates of net migration change stresses the complexity of the process and indicates the complicating influence of age and sex structures, net natural increase rate differences or the aggregate decisions of countless individual migrants. In terms of significance, it is likely that net rates of migration change of six per cent and above (in six years) will produce community level problems of absorption and assimilation of in-migrants, or social deterioration of a community from which such a rate of loss is sustained for any length of time.

Figs 27 and 28 show a fuller picture in one sense in that gross movements, both in and out, are measured, but are less complete in other respects in that units are the economic planning regions and the data refers to employed persons only. The period (1962–8) is the same as that of fig.18, but there is greater insight into the volume and direction of migrant flows. Even in the case of the major growth region of Paris there is a striking two-way flow of migrants, with a lesser return 'countertide' moving back to other planning regions. This countertide includes older or retired people, but also, as the diagrams show, many in employment, an indication of the migration flux which prosperity stimulates. The most striking countertide is to other economic planning regions which are themselves prosperous,

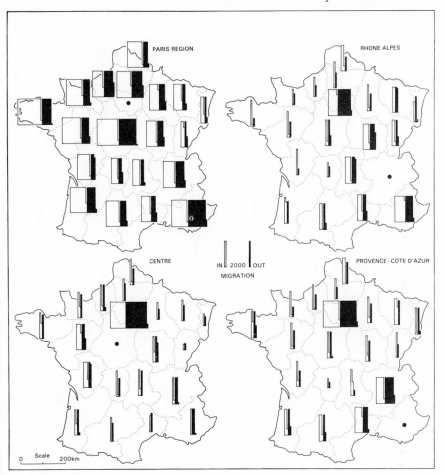

Figure 27   Interregional gross migration of employed, 1962–68; growth regions.

e.g. Paris to Provence-Côte d'Azur, or Paris to Rhône-Alpes. The gross migration to and from decline regions is more directly linked with the metropolis, but in respect of both growth and decline regions the block interchanges of workers with adjacent planning regions is very significant.

1968–75. Between 1968 and 1975 migration currents reflected the deteriorating economic situation, but also indicated changing spatial preferences among those with the means to greater mobility. The most prosperous regions attracted the greatest volume of net migrants (Provence-Côte d'Azur, +298,000; Rhône-Alpes, +147,000; Centre, +87,000; Ile-de-France, +87,000). Conversely, the industrial recon-

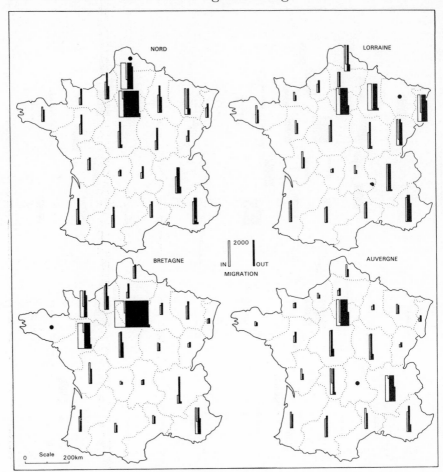

Figure 28   Interregional gross migration of employed, 1962–68: decline regions.

version regions and some rural regions suffered the most unfavourable trends, with an aggravation of out-migration (Nord − 112,000 compared with − 49,000, 1962–8; Basse-Normandie − 22,000 as against − 14,000). Lorraine had about the same momentum of loss as in the previous intercensal period (− 68,000 net out-migration). The Ile-de-France showed a marked fall in net in-migration (1954–62, + 700,000; 1962–8, + 377,000; 1968–75, + 87,000). Since 200,000 foreigners entered the Ile-de-France, 1968–75, there was clearly a strong countertide (about 110,000 persons) moving to the provinces and the smaller towns.

At a more detailed scale (fig. 29) the *départements* of Manche (peripheral

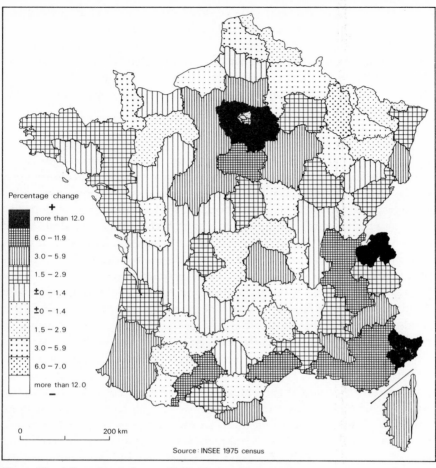

Percentage change
+
more than 12.0

6.0 − 11.9

3.0 − 5.9

1.5 − 2.9

±0 − 1.4

±0 − 1.4

1.5 − 2.9

3.0 − 5.9

6.0 − 7.0

more than 12.0
−

0   200 km

Source : INSEE 1975 census

Figure 29   Migration balance, 1968–75, by *départements*.

location, declining port of Cherbourg), Cantal (marginal agriculture, rural depopulation), Pas-de-Calais and Meuse (industrial reconversion) Ardennes and Haute-Marne suffered serious migration losses, aggravating a social situation which had already been apparent in the early 1960s. The strong attraction of migrants to Haute-Savoie, on the other hand, is a strikingly positive feature, together with the evidence of centrifugal, gravity model outward movement from the Ile-de-France. Alpes-Maritimes is the only *département* in the Midi to sustain its volume of in-migrant movement.

Even figs. 18, 27, 28 and 29 taken together conceal much migration since the time period is arbitrary and only those recorded at the censuses of 1962,

1968 and 1975 are identified, and even then only those who moved across the boundaries of the relevant administrative units. In reality most migration takes place over short distances and within the same administrative unit. Finally, the significance of migration trends over a short period (1962–75) needs to be set within the context of longer-term trends of change. Only in this way can the true impact of rural depopulation or rapid urbanization, for example, be adequately assessed.

Migration motivation and impact. Migration movements are conventionally classified by scale, time, distance and purpose. Traditionally the best-known, rural out-migration to the towns has for more than a century been widespread in France and has reached serious proportions over very sizeable areas (Merlin 1971). Rural populations have often been reduced to levels at which farming is less than intensive, even inefficient, and the fabric of community life is adversely affected. When the critical threshold equilibrium between man and resources is breached the situation progressively deteriorates thereafter. Geographers have characteristically taken a long-term view on rural out-migration, highlighting the dramatic flood-tides off the land in the later nineteenth century and the population rundown due to two world wars. More significantly, the relationship between present numbers in rural areas and the viability or the satisfactions felt in economic and social life at community level is the all-important issue. This is a matter of the farm-based population but also of the often larger proportions of people in rural areas who are employed other than on the land. We have already seen that not all rural out-migration is adverse in its effects, but the emotive implications of the term 'rural depopulation' are not inappropriate in many parts of France today. In Aquitaine between 1962 and 1968 (Duboscq 1972), for example, the poorer and more remote rural areas of most of Périgord and the north Pyrenean villages suffered serious depopulation, but so did rural communes in the vicinity of Bordeaux, denuded of farm-workers and even farmland by the rapidity of urbanization. On the other hand, the trend to commuting over longer distances and the desirability of living in smaller settlements vigorously revived some rural villages up to 50 km from Bordeaux. Yet, on balance, the great increase in personal mobility in the 1960s had been seriously at the expense of the rural communities. The general townward polarization of rural people was the more serious in that the longer-term rundown of people had already created serious economic and social problems, which rapidly became intensified.

Region to region exchanges of migrants are perhaps the most significant of all for public planners, concerned with regional balance and equilibrium.

These gross balances conceal diverse trends: town to town, country to town, small town to larger town and vice versa; the bulk exchanges with the Paris region usually dominate all others. For example, between 1962 and 1968 270,000 in-migrants went to the Centre, 13 per cent of all residents at the time of the latter census. 203,000 left the region in the same period, leaving a net residual of + 67,000, two-thirds of whom had come from other French regions, including 19,000 from Paris and its environs. Forty-five per cent of net in-migrants settled in the major central places in each *département*, 35 per cent in other urban *communes* and 20 per cent went to rural *communes*, In Auvergne (1962–8) 200,000 changed *commune* of residence, 15 per cent of the base population at the earlier date. 52,000 of these moved from rural areas to the towns and only 25,000 moved in the opposite direction; two-thirds of the net in-migrants moved to the six largest towns. Nevertheless the degree of population stability in some regions is well-illustrated by figures for Bourgogne (1962–8). Of every 100 persons resident in Bourgogne in 1968, 75 had been recorded in the same *commune* six years earlier, 15 in another *commune* within the region, only 7 in another planning region, and 3 abroad.

A study of migration in the Bassin Parisien, 1954–62 (DATAR 1968), illustrates both inter-urban movements and the attractive power of the metropolis. Of in-migrants into the Bassin from other regions a proportion were held in the towns whilst the remainder moved directly to Paris. For those from the Nord 53 per cent were intercepted by regional centres in the Bassin, from the Ouest 34 per cent and from the Midi only 20 per cent. Paris dominated the intra-Bassin flows of migrants, both as a centre for in-migrants and as a source of out-migrants. By comparison, other inter-urban movements within the Bassin were weak, although between towns of more than 70,000 population they were stronger. The rural zones of the Bassin sent double the number of migrants to other Bassin towns compared with those moving directly to Paris.

The migration process is both age- and sex-selective. The age groups 15–24 years are consistently the most mobile and in general young women are more mobile than men in these same groups. Propensity to migrate falls with increasing age, but over 65 there is a clear return tide towards rural areas and smaller towns, for retirement. For example, the Région du Centre (1962–8) lost 5900 by out-migration of the 15 24 year olds but gained 8800 by in-migration of those over 65 years. For Bourgogne in the same period the respective figures were − 10,588 and + 4240. The demographic consequences of continued out-migration of young, more active people are severe and lasting, with an ageing population, lack of replacement of the generations, and loss of morale.

Migration is also selective in terms of socio-economic groups, with the most mobile those at the two ends of the employment spectrum: the managers and professional men, as a migratory *élite*, and at the other extreme the landless peasants or unskilled labourers. In 1962–8, for example, Lorraine gained 101,000 (52,000 men, 49,000 women) by in-migration from other French regions and 74,000 (43,000 men, 31,000 women) from abroad. Numerically manual workers and unskilled men were in the majority, but the additions of relatively small numbers of managerial, professional and administrative workers were significant in representing scarce but critical categories.

Modelling of migration behaviour is an important tool both for its understanding and for the planning process (Courgeau 1970). The important variables are those of distance, actual and perceived, the power of the origin to repel and the power of the destination to attract. Analysis of the motives for migration is a central question and one not readily reduced to simple proportions. The hypothesis of the general primacy of economic motives (Chatelain 1960, Fielding 1966) is broadly tenable, but even in an explanation of rural out-migration cannot stand alone. The rural exodus certainly relates to the unfavourable gradient in living standards, earnings, housing and range of employment as between the countryside and the towns, but there are other issues. Agriculture has become more productive but less labour-intensive in many forms of production. Rural social provision has deteriorated and the taste for the urban ways of life has grown, among the young in particular.

Fielding (1966) saw a clear two-way relationship between internal migration and economic growth. His interpretation stressed the importance of employment, range of jobs and career prospects, but he saw the adjustment between supply and demand for labour to be very imperfect. Between 1954 and 1962, 56 per cent of in-migrants sampled in Paris (Pourcher 1964) gave job prospects as the prime reason for the move, compared with 50 per cent of a sample of migrants moving into provincial regions. Personal or family reasons were 27 per cent in Paris and 40 per cent in the provinces respectively. A further interesting finding by Fielding was that in-migrants to a region tended to take up different and often lower-grade jobs than those taken by natives of the region. This finding needs to be set in the context of the competition between French and foreign workers, which is strong at the unskilled level for a wide range of similar jobs, and at its height in industrial or frontier *départements*. On the other hand, movement of foreign workers into agricultural areas of the Sud-Ouest or the Midi is often complementary and in replacement of Frenchmen who have left for the towns. Some of this movement is

Table 17   Daily trip generation and composition: Paris, Rennes, London, Detroit

1965	Daily trips per household	to and from work	business	purchases	leisure	other	Total
			% *reasons for trips*				
Paris	3.51	43.9	34.5	7.7	4.3	9.6	100.0
Rennes	4.26	40.9	36.0	9.5	7.2	6.4	100.0
London (1962)	3.83	42.1	30.0	11.2	7.3	9.4	100.0
Detroit (1955–65)	6.16	39.4	23.3	14.9	14.3	10.1	100.0

Source: IAURP (1969) *volume* 17–18, *pt.* 1, *Table* 22

seasonal, for the peak of the agricultural year, but part represents permanent settlement (fig. 26).

Trip generation. Equally of importance to urban planners, the complex patterns of individual and aggregate daily trip generation give an insight into citizen behaviour, and afford the basis for formulating mathematical models for land use-transportation programming. Table 17 shows that, in comparison with London or Detroit, Paris in 1965 had fewer daily trips of all types per household, though Rennes had more than London. The reasons for trips varied somewhat among the four cities, with Paris having a distinctly lower proportion generated for shopping or leisure activities. The balance of reasons reflects different life-styles and also the socio-economic composition of the populations. In outer suburbs the journey to work element necessarily was greater, whilst trips generated for business purposes were fewer. In the more well-to-do quarters the ratio of trips for shopping and leisure was correspondingly higher. The size of household, its income and the level of car ownership are the critical parameters in trip generation.

Though journey to work represents only two-fifths of total trips, it is the most constant type of flow and productive of the most serious social problems. In 1969 there were 4.3 million daily trips (average time taken 30 mins) to and from work in Ile-de-France; in 1971 15.4 million trips of *all* types daily. The median time of daily travel varied according to direction, time of day, location within the region, and purpose of the trip. Thirty-two per cent of daily journeys to work were within 2.5 km (10 mins), 20 per cent within Paris but more than 2 km (32 mins average), 23 per cent Paris—suburbs or vice versa (55 mins average) and 25 per cent suburb to suburb (35 mins average). The flow patterns between residence and workplace were exceedingly complex with very unequal networks of transport, favouring the western and southern parts of the region against the districts north and east of Paris. In 1965 the mode of travel to work was: 30 per cent private car, 20 per cent *métro*, 15 per cent rail, 14 per cent two-wheeled, 12 per cent bus and 9 per cent by other means.

Data on trip generation in other regions and cities of France is patchy. As in Britain, the available evidence suggests that trips per household are increasing, as part of rising personal mobility for all purposes, but that distances between residence and workplace are not increasing much, and that the modal split between public and private transport is moving in favour of the latter, though it has not yet gone as far as in Britain. The Nord illustrates a traditional industrial region with well-established journey to work patterns. Some 500,000 workers in 1962 travelled daily to jobs outside the commune of residence (37.4 per cent of all workers); 231,900 travelled across commune boundaries within the fifteen principal towns and 122,671 came daily into these fifteen towns from neighbouring areas. The central conurbation (*métropole*) of Lille-Roubaix-Tourcoing has a journey-to-work hinterland stretching southwards to include the entire Nord coalfield, from which there is selective daily out-migration, particularly by women, to work in the conurbation textile factories or the service industries. Elsewhere in the Nord each town tends to have an independent journey-to-work catchment area, e.g. Arras, Dunkerque, Valenciennes. By contrast, the Marseille conurbation (1962) was almost entirely self-contained in journeys-to-work, only 6000 coming in and 5000 leaving to work elsewhere each day.

Study of the journey-to-work patterns in Bourgogne and Franche-Comté 1962–8 shows the effects of rapid urbanization and industrialization upon the hinterlands from which workers are drawn. Dijon illustrates a town with general balance between jobs and resident workers: in 1968 75,068 jobs and 76,240 workers. Thus, 1172 travelled to work outside the agglomeration, especially to three nearby communes which had more than 130 jobs for every 100 resident workers. Otherwise the characteristic pattern of journey-to-work at Dijon was from residential suburb to central workplace. At Montbéliard-Sochaux, on the other hand, an industrial centre including Peugeot car plants, urbanization during the 1960s outstripped the availability of local labour supplies: 53,184 jobs were matched by only 45,532 resident workers (1968). More than 8000 workers travelled daily from the Belfort region and firms were actively engaged in searching for additional labour, often using firm's transport, for distances up to 65 km. There is widespread evidence that the conventional, even the acceptable, maximum distance for journeys-to-work is around 20 km. The average commuting radius varies very little according to the size of the central town: Lyon 22–25 km, Grenoble 22 km, Montbéliard 24 km, Châlon-sur-Saône 15 km, Belfort 12 km, Besançon 11 km.

Migration and mobility is thus a highly complex and rising phenomenon with important planning implications, given that a demographic birthright is often assumed to include the right to live and work in a locality of one's choice and not to be obliged to move in search of betterment, or even a job at all.

THE GEOGRAPHY OF WELL-BEING

The measurement of well-being by a composite index of social and economic indicators has already been illustrated in fig. 6. The social indicators movement, concerned with identifying areas with distinctive traits or problem mixes, developed late in France, even though there has long been a rising public concern with questions of social justice. An assessment of the degree of well-being involves an examination of basic inequalities (Knox and Scarth 1977). These notably include social class and expectations (Marceau 1977), income, family budgets, housing and use of leisure time and they have both temporal and spatial manifestations. In spatial terms it must not be too readily assumed that the greatest inequalities are those between regions, though these may on accasion be dramatic. The differences within a single town as between adjacent neighbourhoods may be at least as notable, or even among individual households in the same street.

Inequalities: spatial and structural
Rapid economic growth in postwar France has increased general levels of affluence but has sharpened inequalities in both spatial and structural terms (Cazes and Reynaud 1973), and perhaps for this reason has given less than the anticipated widespread satisfaction. French GDP per capita (25,230 frs in 1974, at purchasers' prices) was 14 per cent above the mean level for the EEC of the Nine in that year and surpassed only by those for Western Germany (BRD), Luxemburg and Denmark. It has been estimated (Hudson Institute 1973) that by 1985 at the latest French GDP per capita will be the highest in Europe, assuming (now known to be false) that in the meantime no overriding priority has been given to improving the quality of life or to the fuller promotion of social justice, if necessary at the expense of the market economy. Furthermore, the real income enjoyed by the citizen and the living standards which may be generated depend upon that per capita part of the GNP which is available after deductions for

investment (about 21 per cent in France, 17 per cent in the UK), measured against costs of living traditionally 10 to 20 per cent above those of the UK.

The socio-professional structure of France may not readily be compared with that of the UK since classifications are essentially different. It is, however, clear that France has a higher proportion of farm-households (France 12, UK 1 per cent) and a lower proportion of those headed by manual workers (France 30, UK 41 per cent), whilst the ratio of unskilled labourers' households is the same for both countries (7.8 per cent). Class remains a somewhat nebulous concept (Ardagh 1968, Marceau 1977), more apparent in Britain but more divisive in France. During this century French society has proved conservative against change, with acceptance of well-defined social positions and roles as the means of reducing the risks of confrontation and conflict. The persistence of feudal attitudes in rural France has been matched by the aloofness of the traditional bourgeoisie in the towns. Britain has pushed the objectives of a more egalitarian society the more forcefully since 1945, perhaps for that reason among others avoiding the trauma of social ferment which swept France in 1958 and again in 1968. In both countries the middle class has lost both status and wealth over the past thirty years, but in France secondary and higher education, the pathway to social and economic advance, has remained much more a middle-class preserve; 68 per cent of the ruling élite are still recruited from the upper 5 per cent of French society. The gross disparities in income, opportunities, or life styles at both work and play have been increased rather than reduced in postwar France. Today the extremes are among the greatest in Western Europe: the gross income per household by socio-professional category showed a variation from 1 to 10 in 1965 (1 to 8.8 in 1956), though this was reduced to 1 to 5 after the redistributive measures of taxation and social aid. In individual cases the differences in gross income may rise to 1 to 40 or even 1 to 60, whilst in a particular industrial plant the manager may earn 25 times the wage of his poorest worker. The institution of a national minimum wage in 1950 (SMIC, *salaire minimum interprofessionel de croissance* since 1970) helped to reduce extremes. For example, between 1968 and 1971 the purchasing power of manual workers rose by 20 per cent, those of office workers by only 13 per cent and managers by only 12 per cent. In absolute terms, however, the workers received a lesser increase.

The inequalities cover far more than income. Working class households on average have more child dependants (2.8 for farmers, 2.7 labourers, 1.7 middle management, 2.0 higher management), their patterns of consumption are more restricted (if an index of 100 represents consumption by a worker's household then a higher manager's household consumes 135 for food, 245 for housing, 305 for transport and 390 for leisure pursuits), and workers command less space, time, and educational facilities. In respect of all major consumer durables (car, television, refrigerator, washing machine, vacuum cleaner) the national mean of appliances per 100 households was reached in 1971 at an income level of around 15,000 frs per annum. Below this level the provision fell away sharply, whilst above it rose quickly to virtual saturation level.

Below the standards of even manual workers' households lie those of the truly deprived groups: the aged, the single person female households, the foreign workers, and the sick and handicapped. In 1970 more than one million persons were classified as still living in 'shanty towns' (*bidonvilles*), slums or emergency accommodation, whilst in 1971 no fewer than 300,000 households still had an income of less than 3000 frs.

By reason of all these inequalities it is difficult to interpret broad regional differences in their true meaning (for towns see Pumain 1976). Fig. 30 shows deviations from the national means of socio-professional groups, classified by head of household and by economic planning region. In the key the socio-professional structure of households for all France is shown, similarly by occupation of the head of the household. Five categories of region may be distinguished, corresponding closely to development problems and prospects (see table 4). Ile-de-France is unique in the unusually high ratios of professional and managerial households, office employees and domestic service, but has only average proportions of manual workers or unoccupied heads of household. The growth regions generally (Champagne, Picardie, Haute-Normandie, Franche-Comté, Rhône-Alpes) have distinctly higher ratios of manual workers, for the most part lower than average proportions of farm households, and only a slightly less than average representation of professional or managerial households. Provence-Côte d'Azur stands out in this as in other social respects by the uniquely high representation of unoccupied heads of household, and by the marked under-representation of both manual workers' and farm-based households. The regions of growth potential (Centre, Bourgogne, Aquitaine and Languedoc) are marked by positive deviations in the representation of both unoccupied and farm-based household heads but equally by clear negative deviations in the proportion of managers, office workers and manual workers. Regions undergoing economic reconversion (Nord, Lorraine, Alsace) have high ratios of manual workers' households, and in the Nord and Alsace also of unoccupied heads of household. There are negative deviations in farm-based households and in the professional and managerial classes. 'Backward' or developing regions (Auvergne, Basse-Normandie, Poitou-

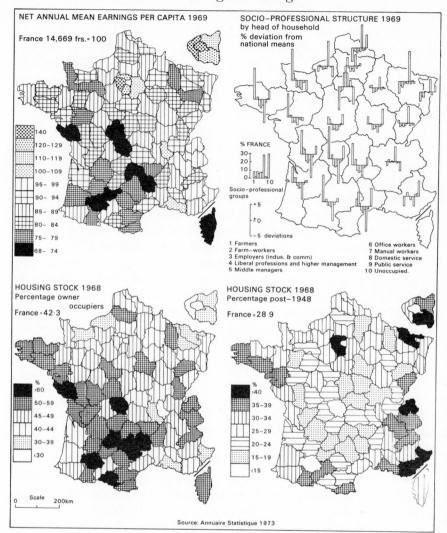

Figure 30   socio-professional structure; earnings per capita; age and tenure of housing.

Charentes, Pays de la Loire, Bretagne, Limousin and Midi-Pyrénées) distinctively show very high ratios of farm-based households, of small-scale employers in business and commerce, and also of households with an unoccupied head. There is a sizeable under-representation of managers, and of all types of office or factory worker.

These differing socio-professional structures are an essential ingredient in the diversity of annual incomes at regional level, and also indicate both the balance of various life styles and even, by implication, the range of attitudes to political questions. Fig. 30 shows that regional incomes are above the national mean only in Ile-de-France, Greater Lyon and Marseille-Bouches-du-Rhône. On the other hand, virtually all France west and south of a line from Le Havre to Marseille, with exception of Haute-Garonne and a few coastal *d'épartements*, has a level of mean earnings per capita 15 per cent or more below the national average. Other islands of lower income occur in the eastern Bassin Parisien, Somme, Hautes-Alpes and Corse. The correlation of low income with an agrarian society, low urbanization levels, and ageing populations is clear, and is perhaps the most important single reason for out-migration by the younger and more able.

Different levels of income, however, tell only part of the story. Just as in the case of industry and commerce, where it is the reinvestment level after tax which is critical to an appreciation of economic growth, so in domestic affairs net consumption patterns, after tax and the propensity to save, are the most important outcome of a consideration of gross incomes (Brousse 1969). Together these define living standards, once regional differences in price levels have been taken into account. Household consumption patterns generally have shifted with rising national affluence, less proportionately being spent on food and more on housing, fuel and power and personal transport. Public spending has lagged somewhat behind rates of private consumption and has at best mitigated rather than diminished regional differences by interregional cross-subsidization.

During the 1960s the relationship between gross regional revenues, salaries and wages, and consumption developed differently in various regions of France. The more prosperous regions had a great boost in consumption, followed by equalizing rates of revenues and salaries. In the regions undergoing reconversion and in regions of growth potential the rate of revenue increase was in balance with that of salaries and propensity to consume. The developing regions of the Ouest, on the other hand, showed two trends: either slackening in the rate of consumption with a marked rise in savings (Aquitaine, Poitou-Charentes, Pays de la Loire, Centre), or a sharp rise in salaries and wages ahead of an increase in consumption (Bretagne, Basse-Normandie, Limousin).

Housing
Two further key indicators of regional living standards are those of housing and possession of other consumer durables. Fig. 30 shows two characteristics of housing, by age and tenure. The French housing stock (in 1974, 43 per cent pre-1915, 16 1915–48, 26 1949–67, and 15 per cent post-

1967) is somewhat less favourable than for Great Britain (in 1969, 37 per cent pre-1919, 25 1919–44 and 38 per cent post-1944). The housing stock has deteriorated during this century as the result of rural out-migration, low levels of investment in the building industry, retarded urban development or redevelopment schemes, the persistence of rent controls between 1920 and 1948, and destruction during two major wars (1.3 million dwellings made unusable 1939–45). Frenchmen have traditionally devoted less of their income to housing expenditure, and public authorities by custom have been less involved in the housing market than in the UK.

Nevertheless, the rapid postwar population growth led to unprecedented levels of new household formation and thus to demand for accelerated housing programmes. The momentum of the national programme for new housing rose from completion of 215,000 dwelling units in 1955, to 316,000 in 1960 and 500,000 in 1974. 47 per cent of the units built in 1974 were grant-aided by the state but only 18 per cent represented social housing for letting (HLM, *habitations à loyer modéré*); only 43 per cent of dwelling units were owner-occupied, compared with 49 per cent in Great Britain. Furthermore, in France the flat, in Britain the semi-detached house, is the most characteristic dwelling.

Fig. 30 shows some correlation between a high proportion of older housing and a high representation of owner-occupiers, especially in the rural areas of the Ouest and the eastern Bassin Parisien. Conversely, in some of the most prosperous regions a strong proportion of housing built since 1948 coincides with a low rate of owner occupation. The differential growth of housing as between economic regions broadly corresponds to the thrust of government planning policies of reconversion or of the stimulation of growth in key towns or regions. Nevertheless market forces have played an important role in housing. In Provence-Côte d'Azur, for example, between 1962 and 1968 the housing stock rose by 25 per cent, including almost one-half of this new stock for second homes, a growth rate more than double even that for Ile-de-France. In the Nord and Lorraine, on the other hand, with much dilapidated housing and overcrowding, the stock rose by only 6 and 8 per cent respectively, though it is true that these figures conceal positive achievements in slum clearance and urban redevelopment.

Furthermore, the prosperous regions had higher than average numbers living in larger blocks of flats: France 3.5 per cent in blocks of more than 10 dwellings; Ile-de-France 9.4, Rhône-Alpes 3.6, and Provence-Côte d'Azur 3.9 per cent. Individual houses were more common in the Ouest and particularly also in the Nord. Not surprisingly, the proportion of dwellings with running water, interior WC, bathroom or shower, central heating or the telephone was markedly higher in the prosperous regions and low in the Nord, Bourgogne, and in a zone from Basse-Normandie through Bretagne to Pays-de-la-Loire. Statutory overcrowding was also more prevalent in the same regions of the Ouest, notably in Bretagne. Second homes have increased sharply during the 1960s to 1.25 million or 7 per cent of the total housing stock (Brier 1970). They are most strikingly to be found in the Sud-Est, the Ouest and the Massif Central with strong percentages as week-end homes; also in the regions surrounding Paris.

Housing is one of the most important tools of regional planning policy, essential in urban renewal programmes for new living environments, in town expansion, in creation of New Towns, or in suburban spread and sprawl. Social segregation by neighbourhoods is at least as characteristic in postwar France as in the UK, and the sociological and psychological problems of living in high-rise housing or the great postwar 'curtain-wall' housing projects (*grands ensembles*) are no less great.

Family budgets

The proportion of the average French family budget spent on housing has fluctuated since the war (1950 16.8, 1965 19, but 1974 only 10 per cent of all expenditure), whilst the purchase of consumer durables has shown a consistently upward trend. As in the UK, the provision of refrigerators and television sets is approaching saturation level; ownership levels for motor cars, vacuum cleaners and washing machines are not far behind. Curiously enough, there is no direct and simple correlation between regional prosperity and highest ownership ratios of consumer durables. In France as in Great Britain, for example, car ownership is of necessity higher in rural areas, where public transport has greatly diminished. Perhaps surprisingly, the highest proportion of households with both television and a washing machine is in the Nord. The truth of such regional differences, however, is likely to be concealed in varying socio-professional structures within any one region.

Successive French governments have proclaimed the need to diminish social inequalities. During the 1960s a rising proportion of French GNP has been committed to public investment, with one-half of such expenditure for directly social purposes. Furthermore, the state has emerged as a major direct employer, with 25 per cent of the labour force in central and local government, or nationalized industry. The total contribution by social expenditure to the mean gross family income is today about 20 per cent. However, the taxation system is not yet socially just. Indirect taxes (58 per cent) far outweigh direct personal taxation (18 per cent) in contribution to the national budget, and the poorer families pay the same taxes on consumption as the rich. Social payments have been increased and the national minimum wage has been raised, but great inequalities continue to persist in French society.

Work

THE SIGNIFICANCE OF EMPLOYMENT

The volume, structure and distribution of employment is the most useful general-purpose indicator of economic progress and prospects, both nationally and at regional level. Furthermore, it affords the best yardstick for assessing living standards and, at the same time, provides the prime explanation for most migration movements (figs. 27 and 28). Nevertheless it is not an unambiguous method of measuring economic growth, least of all for some branches of manufacturing industry. For example, between 1962 and 1971 the output of petroleum products in France rose in value by 135 per cent, but the labour force by only 28 per cent; that of electrical and electronic manufactures by 136 per cent with an addition to jobs of only 31 per cent. The value added through agricultural output rose by 1.9 per cent per annum, but employment fell by more than one-quarter during the same period. A more refined indicator of growth must thus include productivity of labour and real income earned, as well as the rise in numbers employed. If the interpretation of growth itself was to be the main issue, rather than its human implications, value added, turnover and profitability, and investment levels would also need to be taken into account (Carré, Dubois and Malinvaud 1972).

From a planning point of view, however, analysis of the workforce adds a significant dimension to the parameters of population already considered. It further defines the significant relationships between people and resources, and helps bring to light sectoral and spatial differences and the problems arising therefrom. Just as the national planner is primarily concerned with the management of aggregate demand in the economy, so the regional planner is preoccupied with the spatial manifestations, their monitoring and their manipulation. In postwar British economic planning there has been perhaps an excessively single-minded pursuit of the relief of unemployment, preferably as nearly as possible 'in situ'. By contrast, unemployment in France has remained low, at least until recently, and its relief has not been in the forefront of policies for public intervention. Much more regard has been paid to maintaining a general equilibrium, both nationally and regionally, between the rapid growth of population and the provision of work for the increased numbers entering the workforce on the one hand, and the need to accommodate the remarkable postwar economic transformation of France through industrialization and urbanization on the other. Maintenance of full employment has been a major objective in both Britain and France, the more effectively achieved in France by virtue of sustained national economic growth rates. In France the run-down in the agricultural workforce has been the most dramatic problem, in Britain the redeployment of labour out of declining mining and manufacturing industries. In France successive governments have remained less interventionist in the economy than in Britain, but in both countries the promotion of a better employment balance between the regions has become an increasingly acknowledged objective. In France government intervention in the management of employment has worked more closely with market forces, both sectorally and spatially, and less by policies of interdiction of growth in certain areas and at particular times. In both countries a nationwide equilibrium in the supply and demand of labour has been persistently sought, but there have remained significant distortions, alike in sectors and space. In the policies of both Britain and France there has continued to be a fundamental ambiguity as to how far increased mobility of people rather than jobs should be either promoted or allowed to develop, in preference to solving regional problems as far as possible within the region. Both countries presently share major uncertainties about the effects of EEC membership upon the continuance of effective national employment policies.

As in Britain (House 1977), it is important for regional economic policy to assess the balance between structural and specifically regional characteristics contributing to the trends of change in employment or production. Béaud (1966), for the period 1954–62, interpreted the changing structural component as firmly positive in only one region (Franche-Comté), whilst stagnation or depression characterized the Nord, Languedoc and Midi-Pyrénées. On the other hand, the regional component, seemingly a combination of regional attributes plus the effects of accessibility, was unfavourable only in Auvergne, and provoked very rapid growth in the Bassin Parisien. The Ile-de-France had a favourable economic structure, with very strong tertiary growth potential, counterbalanced in some measure by the strong policy for decentralization of manufacturing growth out of Paris.

EMPLOYMENT GROWTH AND CHANGE

In postwar France the rapid growth of population has vied with the dramatic transformation of the economy as an issue of major planning concern. Until the mid-1960s, however, it was the transformation of the economy which had pride of place. Thereafter the rapidly rising numbers of entrants to the labour force born since 1945 pre-empted public interest.

The rate of growth of the workforce has indeed been markedly uneven in postwar years (INSEE 1967). From 1954 to 1962 the total numbers in employment in fact fell by about 40,000 per annum, the product of men being taken into the Armed Forces, a general absence of overseas immigrants, and the raising of the school-leaving age. Between 1962 and 1967, on the other hand, there was a sharp growth phase, as repatriates from North Africa flooded into France, matched by equal numbers of net immigrant foreign workers; furthermore, men had been released from the Armed Forces, and an increasing number of young people and also more women were entering the workforce. After 1968 there was a more rapid rise in young entrants, even more women entered employment and the immigration of foreign workers was sustained (1965–70 +130,000 foreign workers p.a., 1974 +133,000). The VIth Plan, 1971–5, assumed a continuing employment growth rate of +0.9 per cent p.a., to which women and foreign workers continued to make a major contribution.

There has been a pronounced shift in the balance of employment sectors in the postwar French economy. The primary sector (agriculture, forestry, fishing) has fallen from 32 per cent of total employment in 1954 to 10 per cent in 1975; the secondary sector (energy, manufacturing, building and public works), on the other hand, rose barely perceptibly (1954 36, 1968, 39, 1975, 38 per cent of employment). It is, however, in the tertiary sector (transport; commerce; services; banks, insurance, finance; administration) that the greatest differential increases have taken place: 1954 36, 1968 46, 1975 52 per cent), a phenomenon common to all developed Western countries, but a rate of transformation unique to France.

Fig. 31 shows the structural changes in employment in more significant detail. The fast growth groups (more than 25 per cent employment increase 1954–71) covered two-thirds of all employment and included growth manufactures (machinery, electrical and electronic products, cars, chemicals, paper and petroleum) and the majority of services. The slower growth groups (up to 24 per cent employment increase) included 12 per cent of all jobs, and somewhat surprisingly the transport group, which is in secular slow employment decline in Britain. The slow decline groups (up to 25 per cent employment loss) were small, with only 5 per cent of all jobs. The faster decline groups, on the other hand, covered 18 per cent of the workforce, dominated by agriculture, but with coal and coke, textiles, clothing and leather well represented. Comparable data for the UK over a similar period showed: fast growth 56 per cent, slower growth 19 per cent, slower decline 10 per cent and faster decline 15 per cent.

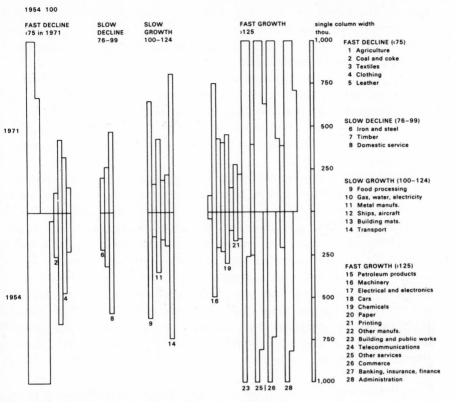

1954 100

| FAST DECLINE (‹75 in 1971) | SLOW DECLINE 76–99 | SLOW GROWTH 100–124 | FAST GROWTH ›125 | single column width thou. |

FAST DECLINE (‹75)
1 Agriculture
2 Coal and coke
3 Textiles
4 Clothing
5 Leather

SLOW DECLINE (76–99)
6 Iron and steel
7 Timber
8 Domestic service

SLOW GROWTH (100–124)
9 Food processing
10 Gas, water, electricity
11 Metal manufs.
12 Ships, aircraft
13 Building mats.
14 Transport

FAST GROWTH (›125)
15 Petroleum products
16 Machinery
17 Electrical and electronics
18 Cars
19 Chemicals
20 Paper
21 Printing
22 Other manufs.
23 Building and public works
24 Telecommunications
25 Other services
26 Commerce
27 Banking, insurance, finance
28 Administration

Figure 31   Employment. Structural change, 1954–71.

Regional impact

The regional impact of these changes in postwar employment structure was exceedingly varied (Commissariat du Plan 1966), the result of initial diversities of regional economy and the differential effects of government policies. Between 1954 and 1962, a period of general stability in the workforce overall, there were nevertheless important redistributions. Ile-de-France increased its proportion of the national labour force (1954 19 per cent, 1962 21 per cent), mainly at the expense of the Ouest (down from 39 to 37 per cent), whilst the Est remained little changed. On the other hand the Est suffered some of the heaviest losses of agricultural workers during this period, especially from Alsace, Franche-Comté, Rhône-Alpes and Lorraine. Such loss correlated well with the rates of national and regional development in the secondary and tertiary sectors, and poorly with the extent of agricultural overpopulation as an expulsive factor. The extent of agricultural overpopulation in the Ouest was estimated as an index of 157, compared with 131 in Ile-de-France and 141 in the Est. The highest rates were in Basse-Normandie (214), Bretagne (184), Limousin (174) and Auvergne (173); in the latter two regions the rapidly ageing population aggravated the already difficult rural problems. In Bretagne, Languedoc and Midi-Pyrénées in particular there was strong regional opinion in favour of reducing the out-migration rate, but at the same time of affecting an internal redistribution whereby surplus rural labour might be moved into the towns and employed there in industry or the services sector. In 1962 FASASA (*Fonds d'adaptation sociale pour l'aménagement des structures agricoles*) and in the following year the *Fonds national de l'emploi* were created to facilitate this process.

Manufacturing employment grew by only 5 per cent overall between 1954 and 1962, but this masked important regional variations. The fastest growth in industrial jobs took place in Ile-de-France and the Bassin Parisien (e.g. Centre + 15.7 per cent in manufacturing, Picardie + 18 per cent, Haute-Normandie + 11.4 per cent), an indication of the early effects of policies to deconcentrate the excessive industrial growth of the metropolis. Franche-Comté had the highest industrial growth rate of all, due to its concentration of fast-growth manufactures, machinery, electrical and mechanical apparatus, cars and cycles, and plastics. The Nord, on the other hand, was suffering from the early stages of a major industrial reconversion out of the declining coalmining and textile groups, and employment in the secondary sector fell by 5 per cent, 1954–62. Unemployment rose in the Nord and out-migration became heavy. In Lorraine, by way of contrast, the heavy metallurgical industries prospered, unemployment was low and out-migration on only a small scale. Both heavy industrial regions had low female activity rates (proportion of females in employment to the total in the employable age groups). There was also a slight fall in industrial employment in Languedoc and Aquitaine, agrarian regions which could least afford such a loss.

The growth of employment in the building industry and in the services sector, 1954–62, was fastest in the already prosperous regions, and contributed little to the needs of the regions overdependent on agriculture or on a narrow range of manufactures. The strong interregional migration currents were thus doubly stimulated by the polarizing forces of manufacturing jobs and service industry employment, and channelled into and around the prosperous and rapidly-growing larger urban areas. For example, the building industry of France grew by 23 per cent 1954–62, but by 66 per cent in Provence-Côte d'Azur, 40 per cent in Rhône-Alpes, and 37 per cent in Ile-de-France. Interregional population movements and the growth of the tourist industry were the major forces behind this disproportionate spread of building and services.

In the Vth Plan (1966–70) concern was already being expressed over the distortion of employment growth patterns, the resulting volume of interregional migration, and the social costs which were thereby increasingly incurred. There developed policies for restricting the rate of growth of both tertiary and secondary employment in Ile-de-France (Part II, ch. 2), and conversely of stimulating such development in the provinces, either as the means of furthering regional employment equilibrium or of building up designated regional growth poles or axes (figs 7 and 61). Some 35–40 per cent of new industrial jobs were to be created in the Ouest in 1965–70, compared with only 18 per cent in 1954–62. Nantes-St Nazaire, Bordeaux and Toulouse were to be developed as selected growth poles, a North Sea-Mediterranean axis of growth was envisaged, and within the Bassin Parisien growth was to be channelled along certain sectors, downstream towards Rouen, south to Orléans and north to Amiens and St Quentin. With exception of a measure of industrial development in the provinces, the other objectives have proved to be long-term in nature and general directions only for a spatial growth strategy.

Since 1962 the pattern of employment has thus changed markedly. Agricultural jobs have continued to decline, indeed at an even faster rate (− 3.6 per cent p.a. 1954–62, − 3.8 per cent 1962–8), but the total workforce in the national economy began to rise at a sustained rate of around one per cent p.a. The trend towards the tertiary sector has accelerated with the rise in the total population, the spread of affluence and the increased tempo of urbanization. Scientific and technical personnel, for example, increased by 50 per cent 1962–70, compared with 35 per cent 1954–62; health and social service workers have increased by 43 per cent, middle managers by 38 per cent, and teachers by 28 per cent. The tertiary sector has grown at double the rate of jobs in secondary employment. With such rising employment more skill and higher qualifications have become ever more necessary, the range of jobs in each sector has become much more diversified, and the rate of job turnover has increased. The proportion of those employed who are wage or salary earners has risen steadily (1954 65, 1968 76 per cent). Unemployment has fluctuated from 230,000 in 1962, to 270,000 in 1965, and 293,000 in 1970, to the dramatic proportions of 1,002,500 in March 1977. For employment structure changes 1968–76, see p. 186.

REGIONAL EMPLOYMENT STRUCTURE

Fig. 32 summarizes the essentials of regional employment structures. The deviations from the national means for each major subdivision of

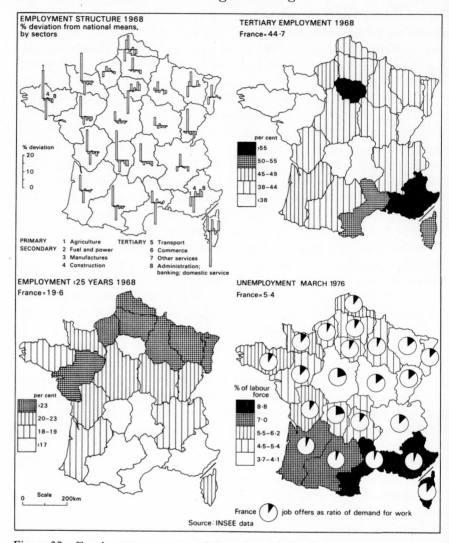

Figure 32 Employment structure 1968, regional deviations; tertiary employment 1968; employment under 25 years 1968; unemployment March 1976.

employment sectors illustrate implied growth-decline potentials for each type of region, and also the extent of employment equilibrium and balance attained. Ile-de-France is yet again unique in the strong under-representation of agriculture and the highest positive deviation for 'other services', and, with exception of Corse, for the banking, insurance, finance and administrative groups. Since Ile-de-France has such a notable proportion of the national workforce (21.4 per cent) it is not surprising that representation of most groups is close to the national norms. The other growth regions (p. 59) are distinguished by marked positive deviation in manufacturing (+13.4 per cent for Franche-Comté) and slight, but widespread deviations in all other respects. Provence-Côte d'Azur, however, emerges as a major anomaly in that it shares with Paris an above average representation of all tertiary activities, to which must be added building, but it is proportionately deficient in industry and also in agriculture. The regions of growth potential, Champagne, Bourgogne, Aquitaine and Languedoc, have modest positive deviations in agriculture, but not to a problem extent, and deficiencies in industry, marked however only in Languedoc and Aquitaine. The regions undergoing reconversion, Nord, Lorraine, Alsace, have positive deviations in manufacturing, and for the Nord and Lorraine also in the energy group, and negative deviations in the tertiary sector, particularly in 'other services'. The remaining, or 'developing' regions, have well-marked positive deviations in agriculture, noticeably negative in manufacturing (Corse −21.4, Bretagne −12.9 per cent), and general deficiencies throughout the tertiary sector.

Since the tertiary sector was the fastest-growing in the 1960s and 1970s, fig. 31 shows its proportionate importance in each planning region (1968): the positive correlation with metropolitan status and tourism is clearly apparent, as is the general under-representation of tertiary activities in the Ouest, or agrarian France. A further cartogram shows the proportion of the workforce under 25 years of age, with marked concentrations in the northern half of France and especially north of a line from the mouth of the Seine to southern Alsace. The younger workers thus identify areas in which the growth of the workforce is accelerating and will build up further momentum; during the VIth Plan it is estimated that the numbers in employment under 25 years of age increased by about 540,000 per annum. Corse is an anomaly in the Midi in that it has a more youthful workforce, though unfortunately a slow-growing economy.

Unemployment
The final cartogram on fig. 32 illustrates the distribution of unemployment. The point has already been made that unemployment levels in France have traditionally been low by British standards (House 1977, 185–91), and policies of unemployment relief have only very recently come to the forefront of French regional policy-making. It must, however, be admitted that the definition of unemployment in France differs from that in the UK and, furthermore, that in an economy with a still substantial agricultural

sector there is a considerable concealed underemployment in France which has no British counterpart.

The most common indicator of unemployment levels in France is that of requests for work related to job availability (fig. 32). In March 1977 1,002,500 persons were seeking work (5.8 per cent of the labour force), 538,200 were in receipt of state benefit (*aide publique*), whilst 538,000 were receiving supplementary benefit (ASSEDIC— *Association pour l'emploi dans l'industrie et le commerce*); the latter two categories are contained within the first but are not necessarily mutually exclusive. Another indicator occasionally used is that of persons available for work (PDRE—*population disponible à la recherche d'un emploi*), measured annually by INSEE (March 1974 = 782,000 persons) or at census time. Among those seeking work in March 1976, 39 per cent were under 25 years of age and 50 per cent of the total were women.

The distribution of unemployment among the economic planning regions (1976), fig. 32, shows the highest rates to be concentrated in the Midi and Sud-Ouest. The lowest were in Rhône-Alpes, central and eastern France (including, surprisingly, Lorraine), whilst the Nord, Basse-Normandie and Bretagne also showed disturbing levels. The availability of jobs within the same region was almost exactly the inverse of the requests for work: low when these were high, and conversely. The markedly unfavourable situation of the Midi relates to: the vulnerable nature of the high ratio of service employment, the continuing in-migration in search of work, the high ratio of foreigners and North African repatriates, and overpopulation on the land.

Within such broad regions there are undoubtedly small, localized pockets of deeper unemployment, as in coal and iron-ore mining communities of the Nord and Lorraine, or at Décazeville in the south-western Massif Central. High unemployment also characterizes the remaining *bidonvilles* and the run-down working class suburbs of the older industrial towns.

Women at work

The variety in female employment in France developed later but has since risen to a slightly higher level than in the UK (France 38 per cent females in the workforce in 1973, UK 35.9 per cent in 1970). The only regions with an above-average female employment ratio were Ile-de-France, with its large tertiary sector, and the predominantly rural areas of Bretagne, Basse-Normandie and Pays de la Loire. Curiously, in spite of the large tertiary sector in the Midi, female job ratios were there the lowest in France. Female employment has gathered momentum rapidly during the past decade, with one million female entrants to the labour force in ten years; in 1972 of 260,000 new entrants no fewer than 210,000 were women. This 'petticoat' revolution had its counterpart earlier in the UK and in both cases the development had profound social as well as economic consequences.

Female activity rates in France show an interesting variation according to age structure. The overall rate for the 15–64 age groups in 1968 was 43.6, compared with 41.7 in the UK in 1970, but for the 20–24 age group the rate was no less than 62.3 per cent; for the 45–54 group the rate was 45.0, after an intermediate fall for those in the major child-bearing years of 25 to 40. 55 per cent of all women in work in 1968 were married, and 29 per cent of all women with two children were gainfully employed in the same year. Indeed, between 1954 and 1968 the rate of married women entering non-agricultural occupations was double that for single women.

In socio-professional status 13 per cent of women were farmers, 25 per cent office workers, 22 per cent manual workers, 13 per cent in personal services and 11 per cent were employers; the remaining 16 per cent were scattered through the occupational structure. In terms of employment by sector 46 per cent of all tertiary, 22 per cent of all secondary, and 32 per cent of all primary jobs were held by women. The highest ratio of female employment in the tertiary sector was in private services (66.8 per cent) and in domestic employment (94 per cent). In manufacturing jobs the highest ratios of women were still in the traditional clothing (94 per cent) and textiles (52 per cent) branches, but each of these showed employment declines from 1962–8. In the newer growth industries female entrants were well-represented in printing and publishing (36 per cent), electrical and electronic manufactures (35 per cent) and chemicals (29 per cent).

This rising female participation in the workforce carries profound implications for the regional planner. By tradition migration movements have been sex- as well as age-selective. Women and girls have tended to migrate to the towns at an earlier age than men and to go to those towns with either a strong tertiary sector or that limited range of manufactures employing a high ratio of females. The rapid growth of labour-intensive service industries has multiplied the job opportunities for women and the policies of urbanization have added to the attractions for women to move in search of betterment. Finally, the industrial location policies favouring the rural areas or the industrial areas undergoing reconversion have led to the introduction of light manufacturing or assembly industries of the type employing women. The run-down in family workers on the farms has released women for employment in rural areas, whilst in mining or manufacturing towns there has always been a reserve of female workers and a dearth of adequate or remunerative employment.

REGIONAL EMPLOYMENT BALANCES AND PROSPECTS

The French government is now committed to the difficult task of establishing and sustaining regional employment balances, at a time when the national economy is becoming more 'open' to external influences and stimuli, including those generated within the EEC. The task is the more difficult in that conflicting objectives are involved: on the one hand, mobility and flexibility in the use of resources throughout the French national space are desirable, even essential ingredients in policies for maximizing national economic growth; on the other hand, the problems of particular regions often require that they should receive differentially higher levels of aid and that out-migration should be slowed down to promote greater balance spatially within France. Furthermore, apart from economic considerations of the wisest use of resources there are growing pressures for greater social justice, both for deprived sections of the community and for underprivileged regions.

Table 18 shows the employment projections over the VIth Plan and the actual changes which took place 1968–74. Though the general spatial redistributive policies under the VIth Plan were broadly achieved, there were significant departures, both by employment sector and regionally. Given the economic depression of the mid-1970s, the overall provision of new jobs fell well short of targets which were sometimes too ambitious in the first place. Job availability for young people and for the rising numbers of females seeking employment were important priorities. In the towns the need to provide jobs for those leaving the countryside and for foreign immigrants was paramount. The phasing of employment growth with changes in population is perhaps the most delicate and difficult planning task, whether migration forecasts are taken into account or not. Table 18 illustrates the degree of mismatch between regional labour reserves and the actual growth in jobs. Only in the Sud-Ouest, assuming no migration, and in the Ouest, taking migration into account, did employment growth harmonize almost exactly with demographic trends. In the Nord, and to a lesser extent the Est, there has been a serious shortfall, whilst Ile-de-France shows new jobs for residents doubly covered but scarcely half for the anticipated immigrants, many of whom did not in fact materialize. The Centre-Est and Méditerranée show a similar discrepancy, but the immigrants *did* arrive and had to be absorbed.

The loss of farm jobs matched VIth Plan expectations reasonably well; indeed in the most underprivileged agrarian regions the rural exodus from agriculture was sizeably less than had been anticipated. It is not yet clear if this indicates that more young people have stayed on the land or that older

Table 18 Estimated employment structure changes, 1968–76, and actual change 1968–74, by ZEAT regions (fig. 4)

| (*in 1000s*) | *Workforce* 1968 | *Employment change* | | *Expected 1968–76 (actual in brackets)* | | 1968–74 *Tertiary (incl. building)* | *Estimated workforce projections 1968–76* | |
		Expected 1968–76	*Actual* 1968–74	*Agric.*	*Industry*		*If no migration*	*With migration*
Région Parisienne (Ile-de-France)	4397	+420/430	+307	−12(−11)	+30(−34)	+400(+352)	+143	+560
Bassin Parisien	3713	+350/380	+249	−170(−181)	+160(+150)	+360(+280)	+290	+336
Nord	1372	+70/86	+48	−17(−19)	+4/−12(−7)	+101(+74)	+144	+131
Est	1818	+165/175	+105	−47(−48)	+58/70(+49)	+153(+104)	+151	+191
Ouest	2647	+96/113	+106	−213(−167)	+86/91(+86)	+223(+187)	+184	+109
Sud-Ouest	2151	+65/99	+59	−157(−121)	+41/49(+21)	+187(+159)	+60	+77
Centre-Est	2390	+210/260	+130	−106(−78)	+65/70(+34)	+256(+174)	+111	+231
Méditerranée	1906	+200/240	+100	−60(−51)	+39/42(+4)	+225(+147)	+55	+150

Source: *VIth Plan, Commission sur l'emploi,* 1971, INSEE

farmers have been disinclined to retire early (IVD—*indemnité viagère du départ*). The VIth Plan estimate was that the farm labour force would contain a higher proportion of farmers over 45 years by 1976 (49 per cent 1968, 56 per cent 1976). With few but significant exceptions, the provision of new jobs in manufacturing matched Plan expectations, most notably so in the critical region of the Ouest. The factory labour force in Ile-de-France actually fell. A major decentralization of jobs to the Bassin Parisien was successfully accomplished, but much of the increased factory employment there must have come from earlier transplantations. The Nord stagnated in overall industrial employment, as expected, and Lorraine fell short of the anticipated rate of development. The most marked shortfalls, however, were in the prosperous Centre-Est and in the Midi, the more serious in both areas in that the growth in tertiary employment was scarcely more than half the forecast rate.

In either an economic depression or more sharply competitive conditions, with an increasingly international dimension, industrialists are in a better position to resist government pressures or inducements. The needs of those regions which most need a growing, modernized and diversified manufacturing base are likely to be the least realized. Fortunately, the Ouest in particular has benefited from government location policies, not only in volume of new jobs, but also in the contribution made by propulsive industries (electronics, cars, chemicals). The programmed growth of the motor car industry in the Nord (4000 jobs in 1970, 12,600 at the end of 1974) and in the Est is likewise a tribute to industrial location policies. Unfortunately, as in Britain, the French car industry is undergoing a downturn at the very time it is most vulnerable in the midst of a major regional redeployment. The electronics industry (22,000 in the Ouest and 17,000 in the Sud-Ouest in 1968) has been the most successful of all in dissemination to formerly agrarian regions.

During the VIth Plan the tertiary sector grew faster than overall employment (+1.9 per cent p.a. 1968–74, compared with +0.9 per cent p.a. in all jobs). Particular tertiary activities grew even faster (e.g. banking, insurance and finance +4.3 per cent p.a.); domestic service, however, continued to decline (−2.3 per cent p.a.). In all regions there was nevertheless a shortfall in the even more ambitious forecasts under the VIth Plan, only 65 per cent of expectations being realized in the Méditerranée compared with 88 per cent in Ile-de-France.

The trends and problems at regional level may be sharply differentiated. In the Ile-de-France all employment growth 1968–74 was in tertiary activities, whilst the number of manufacturing jobs declined. The change in employment structure in the Bassin Parisien closely matched expectation in losses from agriculture, with an almost counterbalancing rise in manufacturing jobs; the increase in tertiary employment only slightly exceeded half the volume anticipated. With a vigorous population growth and a continuing, though regionally variable, net in-migration the problem continues to justify vigorous government measures for decentralization, most particularly of tertiary activities.

The Nord, and to a lesser extent the Est, illustrate the industrial reconversion problem, well-known in the Assisted Areas of the UK. In the Nord the continuing rundown in coalmining and traditional manufactures, especially textiles, has been almost exactly offset by the introduction of new industries. Unfortunately, even with a further 68,000 tertiary jobs in the Nord, 1968–74, there was insufficient employment to prevent a sharp rise in out-migration. Until the severe depression of the mid-1970s in the steel industry, the employment structure of the Est had progressed somewhat more favourably. The overall increase in jobs was only two-thirds of that forecast for 1968–76, but 49,000 additional jobs had been provided in manufacturing by the end of 1974. Out-migration (1968–75) continued at about the same rate as 1962–8 (− 0.5 per cent p.a.). The location close to the Rhine-Main industrial belt and the Saarland, the former continuously prosperous and economically more dynamic than the Est, has over-shadowed Lorraine and Alsace rather than conferring major benefits. Franche-Comté (p. 397) has had vigorous industrial growth during the mid-1960s, particularly in the car industry.

The other four ZEAT regions (Ouest, Sud-Ouest, Centre-Est and Méditerranée) face a similar type of employment balance problem, even though there is great diversity in their present economic structure. In the Ouest and Sud-Ouest decline in farm labour 1968–74 has been massive, though less than forecast (table 18); in the Ouest manufacturing growth offset half the loss, but in the Sud-Ouest only 17 per cent. The Centre-Est region covers the diverse and little-related regions of Rhône-Alpes and Auvergne. The rise in employment 1968–74 was compounded of a loss from agriculture, 40 per cent of which was offset by growth in manufacturing jobs, whilst tertiary employment added a further 174,000 jobs. The Méditerranée has one of the most complex employment structures: losses from agriculture were modest, 1968–74, there was almost no overall increase in manufacturing, whilst increases in the tertiary sector were only two-thirds of those forecast. Overall employment growth accommodated all the needs of residents, but fell short of full employment for the sizeable tide of in-migrants. Unemployment has remained at the highest level for French regions.

Two major uncertainties may affect the success of government in continuing to fine-tune the French regional economies. The 'openness' of the national economy makes internal policy objectives more subject to the vagaries of international trade and supranational decisions. The peripheral location of French problem regions adds to the vulnerability of purely national controls, whilst at the same time, on the positive side, contributing somewhat to the solution of employment balance by external stimuli. Direct EEC policies might theoretically set up entirely fresh rules for the regional game, but thus far their effects have been minimized in favour of national priorities.

The political and regionalist ferment within France might have the greater effects, in seeking regional development of a more socially just kind, with fuller diffusion of growth by more positive government policies for influencing industrial location decisions and for providing the modern infrastructure at regional level. As the French population grows in size, the economic growth rate slackens, and the employment structure is further transformed, it is difficult to resist the view that the regions will and should make their case more forcefully to central government.

References

The people

Ardagh, J. (1968) *The New France*, Harmondsworth.

Armengaud, A. (1965) *La population française au XXe siècle.*

Beaujeu-Garnier, J. (1969) *La population française.*

Beltramone, A. (1966) 'La mobilité géographique d'une population', *Tech. écon. mod.* 15, *Sér. Espace écon.* 6.

Bonazzi, R. (1972) 'Un problème urbain frontalier: l'influence de Genève sur le département de la Haute-Savoie', *Revue Géogr. alp.* LX: 359–86.

Bouchet, J. (1976) 'Enseignement du recensement et conditions nouvelles pour l'aménagement du territoire', *Futuribles*, 6: 193–209.

Brier, M. A. (1970) *Les résidences secondaires.*

Brousse, H. (1969) 'Le niveau de vie en France', *Que sais-je?* 371.

Calot, G., Mugnier, S. and Burs, M. (1970) 'L'évolution de la population au niveau régional et urbain 1962–1968', *INSEE D*1.

Carrère, J. and Muguet, J. (1972) 'Analyse statistique globale de l'évolution des régions françaises entre 1954, 1962 et 1968', *Annls INSEE*, 11.

Cazes, G. and Reynaud, A. (1973) *Les mutations récentes de l'économie française.*

Cazin, F. (1970) 'Projections totales pour les régions et les Z.P.I.U.', *INSEE* 4.

Chabert, L. (1972) 'L'industrie en Maurienne et en Tarentaise', *Revue Géogr. alp.*, LX: 75–100.

(1975) 'Les nouvelles orientations industrielles des Grandes Alpes de Savoie', *Revue Géogr. alp.*, LXIII: 77–102.

Chatelain, A. (1960) 'La géographie des salaires en France et son incidence sur les migrations de population', *Revue Géogr. Lyon*, 35 (4): 381–93.

Clarke, J. I. (1963) 'Demographic revival in France', *Geogr.*, 48 (3): 309–11.

Courgeau, D. (1970) 'Les champs migratoires en France', *Inst. natn. étud. démographiques, Trav. et Docums.*, Cah. 58.

Cribier, F. (1975) 'Retirement migration in France' in Kosinki, L. A. and Prothero, R. M. (eds), *People on the Move*, London: 361–73.

DATAR (1968) *Les migrations dans le Bassin Parisien de* 1954 *à* 1962.

Doboscq, P. (1972) 'La mobilité rurale en Aquitaine. Essai d'analyse logique', *L'Espace céogr.*, 1 (1): 23–42.

Fielding, A. J. (1966) 'Internal migration and regional economic growth. A case study of France', *Urb. Stud.*, 3 (3): 200–14.

Fontanel, C. and Peseux, C. (1976) 'Potentiel de population et résean urbain en France', *L'Espace géogr.*, 5 (4); 251–4.

Guillon, M. (1974) 'Les rapatriés d'Algérie dans la région parisienne', *Annls Géogr.*, LXXXIII (460): 644–75.

House, J. W. (ed.) (1977) *The UK Space: resources, environment and the future*, London (2nd edn).

Huber, M., Bunle, H. and Boverat, F. (1965) *Population de la France.*

Hudson Institute (1973) *France and its future*, 1973–85, Croton-on-Hudson.

INSEE (1965) *L'espace économique français*, Fasc. I, *Démographie générale.*

Knox, P. L. and Scarth, A. (1977) 'The quality of life in France', *Geogr.*, 62: 9–16.

La Documentation Française (1964) 'Les travailleurs étrangers en France', *Notes et Etudes Documentaires*, 3057.

(1971–2) 'Les Villes moyennes. Dossiers d'étude', *Aménagement du Territoire.*

McDonald, J. R. (1965) 'The repatriation of French Algerians', *Int. Migration*, 3: 146–56.

(1969) 'Labor immigration into France, 1946–65', *Annls Ass. Am Geogr.*, 59: 116–34.

Marceau, J. (1977) *Class and Status in France: Economic Change and Social Immobility*, 1945–75, Oxford.

Merlin, P. (1971) 'L'exode rural', *Inst. natn. étud. démographiques, Trav. et Docums*, Cah. 59.

[ND] 'La dépopulation des plateaux de Haute Provence', *La Documentation Française.*

Pourcher, G. (1964) 'Le peuplement de Paris', *Inst. natn. étud. démographiques*, Cah. 43.

Rognant, L. and Schultz, J. (1964) 'Les rapatriés d'Afrique du Nord dans l'Hérault', *Soc. Languedocienne Géogr.*, XXXV (34): 183–282.

Sauvy, A. (1946) 'Evaluation des besoins de l'immigration française', *Population*, 1: 91–8.

Thompson I. B. (1970) *Modern France: a social and economic geography*, London.

Work

Béaud, M. (1966) 'Une analyse des disparités régionales: composante régionale et composante structurelle de l'évolution de l'emploi régional en France', *Revue Econ.*, 17: 55–91.

Carré, J. J., Dubois, P. and Malinvaud, E. (1972) *La croissance francaise.*
Commissariat Genéral du Plan (1966) *Ve Plan. Rapport général de la commission de la main d'oeuvre.*
    (1971) *Rapports des commissions du 6e Plan*, 1971–1975, *Emploi,* 2 vols.
INSEE (1967) *L'espace economique français, Fasc, II, Population active.*
Pumain, D. (1976) 'La composition socio-professionelle des villes françaises: essai de typologie par analyse des correspondances et classification automatique', *L'Espace géogr.*, 5 (4): 227–38.

Part two

Growth, change and reconversion: the context for public policies

Introduction

In interpreting the course of postwar economic and social change in France (Carré, Dubois and Malinvaud 1972; Cazes and Reynaud 1973), it is difficult to disentangle the effects of market forces from the impact of public policies. The outcome has been imperfect and uneven, both spatially and in terms of particular sectors of the economy. Unlike Britain over the same period France has had a greater overall growth momentum. Indeed, 1949–69 the French economic growth rate was high (+ 5.0 per cent p.a.), but more remarkable in that it was sustained at such levels for so long a period. Although there was an element of catching up with other West European industrial economies, the quantum and rate of growth betokened an ongoing structural change in France (Guibert *et al.* 1975). In the 1950s this came from technological change and productivity increases, in the 1960s additionally from the sharp rise in numbers entering the labour force, and from the benefits of EEC membership. The 1970s, by contrast, have thus far been a time of consolidation, even of retrenchment in certain sectors. In more difficult, as in more prosperous times, industry remains the spearhead of growth. Though increases in consumption have led to greater investment and higher incomes, inflation has become serious and public investment has notoriously lapsed behind that in the private sector. Public planning in France has perhaps been more elegant than in Britain, but also more permissive and less comprehensive, to a greater degree aligned with market forces.

Part II interprets the structure and patterns of growth and reconversion in the French economy, both sectorally and spatially, and assesses the nature, role and significance of planning measures. Part III is concerned rather with the impact of public policies on the urban system and spatial strategies. There must necessarily be some overlap between the two Parts, since market forces and public policies are inextricably interwoven at all structural and spatial scale levels. Both Parts are a prelude to a prospective view, the substance of Part IV.

Almost all the factors, processes or forces at work in the French economy in recent decades have provoked some countervailing tendency, seeking to restrict or redirect the course of change. Some forces, however, have been consistently dominant, most notably those arising from the sustained postwar demographic momentum and the fortuitous coincidence of this dynamic trend with accelerating growth in certain key sectors of the national economy (Part II, ch. 1). Increased mobility, of people, jobs and other factors of production, has vied with technological developments in powering the course and spatial outcome of change. In almost all sectors, including industry, agriculture, mining, transport and retail trading, modernization has implied rationalization, with the advantages on the side of economies of scale, with fewer, larger, more nodally situated and better-financed units. Yet in all cases there has been a counteraction, sometimes politically-motivated, at others arising from a deep-seated reluctance to change. Such a counteraction has rarely changed the course of development, but has slowed down the rate of change and more so in some areas than others. Ardagh's observation (1968, 22) that in France 'two ways of life uneasily co-exist' is capable of widespread application, to a much greater extent than would be valid for postwar Britain. The tensions of change have scarcely abated in the 1970s, and disparities of all kinds have indeed increased, in employment structure, urban growth differentials, regional prospects, or for particular classes in society. The development plans of public policies have had increasingly to take these tensions into account, but it has been difficult to formulate models and theories which can adequately cater for both equity and efficiency, and the kind of trade-offs between them which would be widely if not universally acceptable.

Energy, mobility, industrialization and urbanization have been the keynotes of growth and reconversion in the French economy. French energy problems are in some respects better and in some worse than in Britain. France has traditionally been deficient in home-based coal output, but has had a better balance between thermal and hydro sources of electricity. Nevertheless the industrial reconversion of declining coalfields has produced difficult regional problems in both countries, whilst both have become overdependent on imported supplies of Middle Eastern oil. The small-scale production of natural gas in south-west France will not match the immense potential wealth of petroleum and natural gas in the British sector of the North Sea. Both countries have made a wise and timely investment in nuclear power capacity, but until recently at uneconomic costs. France intends a dramatic, even controversial, expansion of nuclear capacity between now and the end of the century.

Increased mobility in all its aspects has had overall beneficial effects, but an adverse impact in many less-favoured or remoter areas and localities. Life has been increasingly polarized into the larger, more accessible places, with islands of even greater deprivation than hitherto elsewhere. The centripetal, magnetic power of Paris has been in some measure diminished and new transport and traffic axes have been defined or strengthened: the Rhine, the Rhône-Saône or the Grand Delta (Rhône), and the Basse-Seine. New technologies in transport have spread rapidly, notably in pipelines, electrified rail traction, internal airlines and telecommunications; yet the telephone system has remained a laggard. Car ownership has soared, but public transport services, in rural areas at least, have atrophied. The greater personal mobility now available has been reinforced by the growth of a more educated population and by the pressures of a search for material and environmental betterment. Currents of migration (Part I, ch. 4) are today more from region to region, or town to town, rather than the traditional drift from the countryside to the town. A migratory *élite* may be defined, in contrast to the more static masses, but migratory currents are complex and few flows are without some compensatory countertide. Transport facilities, in ports, airports, freight yards, or market-depots (*marchésgares*) have become more concentrated, and flows are more and more directed along strategic traffic corridors linking the major urban centres.

The classical nineteenth-century industrial revolution based on coal, steam power, textiles and heavy engineering came late in France and has had an uneven and partial impact. As in Britain, the twentieth century has seen radical transformations, both in the structure and the locational patterns of industry. In France these transformations have been particularly concentrated into the postwar years. More freely available and more diverse energy sources, coupled with greater mobility of transport media, loosened many traditional ties to fuels or raw materials. Coastal sites, the larger towns, and the main communication axes exercised increasingly strong locational pulls. Improved production technologies led to a proliferation of new manufactured products, notably in light engineering, consumer durables, chemicals, vehicles and aircraft, or the electrical/electronics industries. Partly offsetting such rapid growths there were sharp declines of jobs in agriculture, small-scale commerce, and coalmining in particular. Over the past three decades the tertiary or services sector has grown rapidly, most notably so in business and professional services; banking, insurance and finance; and in government, both central and local. Tourism has been the fastest growth industry of all, with dramatic effects on the landscape and the economies of Languedoc, Aquitaine, the Alpes and the Pyrénées. Other services sectors have declined, in some aspects of transport and the retail trades for example.

The effects of such production and employment changes have been complex, widespread and, on occasion, traumatic. The Nord and Lorraine have had to undergo profound industrial restructuring and reconversion; Ile-de-France, the Rhône-Alpes and Provence-Côte d'Azur, on the other hand, have had the difficult problems of either accommodating or even restraining growth. Rural France has suffered its own transformations. Change there has often been slow, the continuation of long-established trends until the 1970s. Out-migration of the younger and more able had been a persistent phenomenon, the outcome of both push and pull factors. Demand for farm products from the growing towns has led to moves from a subsistence to a market economy, further stimulated by membership of the EEC. Mechanization and scientific farming have spread, but their incidence has been fragmentary and partial. Urban pressures have been diffused into the countryside and the traditional distinctions between town and country have become increasingly blurred.

The course of postwar urbanization in France has illustrated both the potential and the problems inherent in rapid and dramatic change. The greatest changes were concentrated in the large towns, with urban renewal of centres which had either decayed or been damaged in the war years, and the mushrooming of *grands ensembles* on the suburban perimeter. Public housing policies have notoriously fallen behind the tempo of employment growth, and the adequate provision of services has been laggard. By the mid-1980s three-quarters of all Frenchmen will be living in towns of more than 20,000 people (60 per cent only 1954), but in the VIth Plan a deliberate attempt was made to promote the medium-sized towns (*villes moyennes*), if necessary at the expense of the *métropoles d'équilibre*, or the large cities. Hitherto the starkest juxtaposition of growth and decay has occurred in the smaller towns, which have suffered often in the economic and social shadows of their larger, more affluent neighbours.

The search for a better equilibrium between regions and among towns has been a major justification for increasing the scope and the impact of public planning intervention. This intervention has been both sectoral and spatial, most recently concerned to promote equity as well as efficiency in national life. The quality of public intervention has been variable, stronger theoretically than in practical terms, more effective sectorally than spatially, and nationally than regionally. As in Britain, regionalist forces in France were more strongly manifested in the late 1960s and early 1970s, producing an increasingly powerful counterweight to centralizing or bureaucratic tendencies of national government.

Part II attempts a balanced assessment of the principal ingredients of growth and reconversion, in the light of market trends and their spatial effects, and the kind of problems posed to the regional and resources planner. In terms of growth potential transport, energy and the growth industries, both manufacturing and services, have been dominant; in reconversion the problems of farming, coalmining, certain declining manufactures and the role of marginal areas have been paramount. Planning policies seek to mobilize the potential for growth and to manipulate growth spatially, to offset, as far as economically feasible, the adverse effects of decline or stagnation in other regions or urban centres.

1 Key elements of growth

Communications

The interaction between the various modes of communication and all forms of economic or social development and change is both complex and fundamental. Rail, road, waterway, air, seaport, postal and tele-communications create their own networks, with routes and functions which may be independent, complementary or even downright com-petitive. In France, perhaps more than in any other western country, governments intervened earlier in guiding the investments in infrastruc-ture, with the spatial purposes of government administration well in mind at all times. Furthermore, until very recent times, public policy has strongly governed the conditions under which modes of transport competed, through licensing and influence on tariffs. Since 1945 communications planning has had a key role in successive economic and social plans. Traditional communications roles have been those of aiding in the production of goods and services, their dissemination and marketing; movements of people to work and for leisure; and public administration at national, regional and local levels. To these have been added new functions in an age of planned rapid industrialization and urbanization, of the maintenance of full employment, and of policies for promoting regional balance as well as sustained national growth momentum. The attack upon isolation through improved accessibility has been supplemented by deliberate environmental policies aimed at landscape conservation, sound ecology and improvement of the quality of life. Programmes for greater social justice have had spatial implications in both the inner cities and deprived marginal regions. Spatial interaction through use of com-munications infrastructure and services has proved to be a most important catalyst in planning for both economic and social improvements. Such enhanced roles for communications have developed at a time of unparal-leled technological change in almost every mode, and during a period when

France has become ever more open to interchange of all kinds across her borders. For all these reasons it is increasingly difficult to measure the success of communications facilities in straightforward economic rates of return, viability or profitability, without adequately taking into account the rising significance of social product maximization as a major new objective.

HERITAGE

The considerable extent of the French national space, the low overall density of population, its irregular distribution and traditionally low levels of urbanization, allied with the dominance of an eccentrically-placed national capital and frontier locations of major industrial areas and seaports, have inevitably posed transport planners with long-term difficult problems. Long hauls along thinly-trafficked routes have long been a characteristic feature at one end of the spectrum. Increasingly congested movements along certain corridors and within and around cities have posed problems at the other end of the scale.

The model for state intervention in the growing communications networks was set by the radial postal roads of the age of Louis XIV and the Napoleonic creation of the 'routes nationales', linking the provinces with Paris, with a more or less balanced secondary network between *préfectures* and *sous-préfectures*. Early railways were licensed, 33 companies under the 1842 Law, and there was public supervision over both construction and operation from the very outset. By the mid-nineteenth century a star-shaped rail net linked Paris to the Nord, Bâle (via Strasbourg), Nevers, Bordeaux and Le Havre; Lyon and Marseille had small local nets. Between 1859 and 1883 secondary and tertiary networks were defined, deliberately to penetrate and link up the most remote areas. The *Plan Freycinet* (1879), completed by 1914, attempted to link all *sous-préfectures* to the national rail system, but in the event it led to overequipment of the network. State policy of giving virtual regional monopolies to particular rail companies contributed nothing to competitiveness: in 1907 the Ouest company was purchased by the state; in 1918 the re-acquired Alsace-Lorraine net was added, and in 1937 SNCF was created, a national railway company with well-defined and constraining public obligations.

The waterway network had early antecedents under Louis XIV in the Canal des Deux Mers, but it received its major outlines after the Plan Freycinet which created 1300 km of canals and led to the deepening of a further 4000 km of rivers and canals to take the then standard barge (*péniche flamande*), of 280–350 tonnes capacity.

The heritage of the French communications system has proved to be a heavy legacy for planners since World War II. The network of each mode had grown up before the major policies of urbanization and industrialization, and there had been a strong non-economic, or administrative, influence in the layouts of rail, road and waterway. Concepts of regional monopoly were allied with that of the dominance of the railway in freight traffic. Already in 1934 road haulage licensing by carrying capacity of vehicle fleet had been introduced, to give protection to rail-borne freight.

POST-1945

Postwar planning in France has had to cater for a fast growth in demand for communications, derived from the rapidly rising numbers of people, and the location of expanding social and economic activities. Indeed the first postwar Plan (1947–53) gave high priority to restoration and development of the communications networks as an essential precursor to economic growth, a priority which has since been modified, but never lost. It was perhaps inadequately recognized by governments that the various modes of communication do not only adapt to economic growth, with provision of infrastructure and services to meet the needs of the times, they are also capable of creating economic growth on their own account. New facilities, faster, more direct, or cheaper services stimulate demand, and are capable of having multiplier effects on housing, jobs, social provision, and indeed upon quality of life generally. These powerful impacts may be for ill as well as for good since, ironically, better communications may be the means of decreasing the viability or vitality of areas through introduced competition, draining away people and resources to more favoured or more nodal areas.

The interaction between communications and the processes of economic and social change since 1945 has been strongly influenced by state intervention, both in the sanctioning of major infrastructural investment projects for all modes and through the regulation of traffic competitiveness, by capacity licensing and influence in tariff structures (Despicht 1964, 1969; Bayliss 1965). The spatial impact of such public intervention is difficult to measure, during a period when the structure of traffic was itself undergoing dramatic shifts, and when the technology of the individual modes was developing rapidly.

The principal forms of state intervention have been firstly through communications infrastructure, the need for prior approval of major railway investments, all motorway and trunk road proposals, and all programmes for the fully state-owned waterway facilities. To these must be added the government overview of airport and seaport strategies, and also the programmes for installing and developing telecommunications and computer networks. The attempt to regulate competition and define the functions of each transport mode in relation to the needs of the nation was by regulation of capacity and tariffs in the 1949 Transport Act, amended 1963. Railway freight rates had traditionally been 'ad valorem' and had thereby favoured disseminated regional development. Even so, the heavy metallurgical and coal industries had enjoyed some protected rates and there was more inequality in treatment of firms and regions than the legislation of 1949 seemed to permit. In 1955 variation in rail freight charges according to intensity of traffic at stations of origin or destination was permitted, leading La Rochelle, for example, to complain about a scheme which seemed to favour Nantes and Bordeaux. Road competition with rail had been constrained first by the tonnage restriction on the road haulage fleet (115,000 tonnes in 1934, confirmed in 1949); secondly, since 1938, by the introduction of some approved tariffs for long-distance haulage. The 1949 codification of road haulage tariffs, with minimum as well as maximum limits, was extremely complex and entered into effective force only in 1961. From 1949 also there was clarification of road haulage journeys by permitted zones: the local (*zone de camionnage*), one or two per *département* (3 for Allier), with radius of 30–40 km based on each capital town; the short-haul zone (100–200 km radius), which might be increased if geographical conditions were unfavourable for traffic; and the long-haul zone (more than 200 km). In theory vehicle tonnage quotas were laid down for each zone, but there were exceptions at the outset (e.g. transport on own account) and a gradual relaxation through time. In 1963 vehicle numbers rather than tonnage became the basis for licensing road haulage vehicles, and in 1965 licensing was suppressed for the short-haul zone. Between 1958 and 1966 the capacity of the long-distance haulage fleet rose by two-thirds.

Similarly, there was state control over the tonnage capacity of the waterways fleet. New vessels could be introduced only by the scrapping of old vessels, tonne for tonne, though double the tonnage of dumb-barges could be scrapped for each self-propelled vessel introduced. As for road haulage, the rota (*tour de rôle*) system long operated for waterways: on completion of a journey the haulier had to quote for the next, or return, consignment. Tariff structure on inland waterways was government-regulated, and until 1963 based on the costs of a drawn barge.

During the early 1960s it was clear that regulation by the state had not achieved its objectives: the railway system was in growing deficit, road haulage was expensive partly because it was constrained and partly because of the very numerous small entrepreneurs, whilst on the waterways barges were underemployed. It has been argued (Wolkowitsch 1959) that public involvement had done no more than reflect the strengths of conflicting modes of transport, rather than providing either an integrated or the cheapest transport service. Competitiveness among the modes of transport had been further affected by the changing structure of freight traffic, and by consumer choice. Freight traffic doubled within ten years, but the share of the railway fell (table 19), both proportionately and after 1964 also in absolute terms. The decline in such traditional rail freight as solid fuels or heavy metallurgical products was due in part to the declining coal output, its greater consumption in local power stations, the transfer of petroleum traffic to pipeline, and also to the trend towards coastal location of new heavy industries such as steelworks (using imported ore) or chemical plants. Waterway traffic also was affected, but road-hauled tonnage and that carried by pipelines grew steadily. Competition from the private car, and from internal air lines, increasingly affected adversely the earlier dominance of the railway in passenger traffic. In Great Britain during the same period similar trends had been even more dramatic. France remained a country with a more balanced modal mix in transport, with stronger representation of railways, pipelines and inland waterways.

The extent of competition or complementarity between transport modes is very much the product of geographical differentiation in both networks and traffics. To this degree the logical transport mix for a particular city or region is likely to be only modified rather than changed by state policies.

Table 19   Inland freight and passenger traffic, by transport mode, 1963 and 1973

(percentages) Freight	Rail		Road		Inld Water		Pipeline	
	1973	1963	1973	1963	1973	1963	1973	1963
France tonnes	12.6	18.9	77.0	72.9	5.1	5.7	5.3	2.5
tonnes/km	35.6	55.7	40.2	31.3	6.5	9.6	17.7	3.4
Gt Britn tonnes	9.6	15.1	88.8	83.4	0.2	0.6	1.4	0.9
tonnes/km	24.2	30.2	72.6	68.4	0.1	0.3	3.1	1.1

Passengers	Rail	Road		Air
		Private	Public	
France	16.0	78.2	5.3	0.5
Gt Britn	8.7	77.3	13.5	0.5

Sources: UN (1974) *Annual Bull. Transport Statistics for Europe* 1973

Table 20   Internal freight transport, by distance of journey, 1973 (in percentages)

line-haul in km	Rail		Inland water		Road	
	Tonnes	tonne/km	Tonnes	tonne/km	Tonnes	tonne/km
1–49	19.4	1.6	34.0	3.9	79.7	22.0
50–149	22.0	7.0	30.9	24.4	13.1	23.7
150–299	20.8	16.3	23.7	36.9	4.1	17.8
300–499	19.4	26.1	9.6	26.2	1.7	14.8
500–699	9.3	22.0	1.5	6.5	>500 1.4	21.7
700+	9.1	27.0	0.3	2.1		

Sources: UN (1974) *Annual Bull. Transport Statistics for Europe* 1973; *Annuaire Statistique des Transports* 1973

Furthermore there is differentiation between the modes according to economic distances of line-hauling (table 20). As expected, inland water journeys are concentrated in the shorter ranges (mean length of haul per tonne 126 km); road transport concentrates hauls within the local zone (*zone de camionnage*) but one-fifth of tonne/km hauls are longer than 500 km; the railway has a more even spread, but in tonne/km terms has the advantage at all distances over 300 km. The mean length of rail haul per tonne is 275 km in France, compared with 121 km (excluding National Carriers and Freightliners) in the UK.

Increasingly, the communications network is now regarded as a most powerful tool in regional and urban planning. Since the early 1960s government policy on transport has worked in the direction of liberalization, fairer and more equal competition between the individual modes. At the same time, there has been a policy of alignment and coordination of rail and road transport, through regional and national coordinating committees.

Under the 1962 tariff reforms rail freight per waggon load was to be based on the real costs of operating and maintaining individual lines. This seemed immediately to threaten the economic prospects of more distant or more economically marginal areas such as Bretagne or the Massif Central, whose limited exports might expect to have to bear higher freight charges on thinly-trafficked and expensively maintained lines. This was met by limiting the rise in freight rates in any one case to 30 per cent and by public compensation to SNCF for loss incurred as the result of special tariffs, e.g. on agricultural produce or for reduced passenger fares (in suburban or rural areas) imposed by the government. Indeed some special tariffs were kept for factories in the Alpes and Massif Central (e.g. for Décazeville). Furthermore, in the 1971 agreement with SNCF the government undertook to bear 60 per cent of the costs of maintaining the permanent way, and contributed also to the deficits on the railway pensions fund. Whilst permitting a sizeable increase in long-distance freight haulage by road, the state imposed an axle-tax to help align road haulage with railway conditions. At the same time the tariff system for long-distance haulage was relaxed, with a 20 per cent 'fork' tariff based on nine thresholds for particular goods. Relaxation on the waterways fleet permitted extra additions of 'pusher craft' operating north of Lyon. Furthermore, the *tour de rôle* system for allocation of traffic was not applicable to either international traffic or the operations of the large, modernized barge fleets or pusher-trains which were replacing the stock of individual barge owners.

French policy on transport has thus moved some way towards the 'transparency' principles inherent in the Common Transport policy of the EEC. The elements of public subsidy are more clearly to be seen and measured, whilst the economics of transport operation have tended to favour ever more concentration upon fewer, larger nodes, or upon major axes of circulation. These transport nodes and corridors do not always coincide with the major urban centres (Auphan 1975), but in spatial strategy formulation they possess both actual and potential significance for economic growth.

As integration within the EEC proceeds, flows of commodities and services are likely to be generated most strongly towards the trans-border regions of Flanders, the Randstad, Ruhr, Rhein-Main and Piedmont. French ports will feel stronger competition from those in the Low Countries, and perhaps also from Genoa. Fig. 3 shows the extent of participation in foreign trading by each of the French economic planning

Table 21   International traffic across the borders of France, by transport mode, 1973

	Entering		Leaving		International tonnage as % total freight
	million t	%	*million t*	%	
Rail	16.6	6.9	37.4	30.8	22.5
Road	24.4	10.0	28.8	23.6	3.2
Inland water	12.8	5.3	25.4	20.9	23.3
Sea	187.8	77.8	30.1	24.7	—
Total	241.6	100.0	121.7	100.0	

Source: UN (1974) *Annual Bull. Transport Statistics for Europe* 1973: *Annuaire Statistique des Transports* 1973

regions, with striking indication of the strength of cross-frontier exchanges with adjacent zones. The Atlantic facade of France and the interior south of Paris, on the other hand, have relatively little overseas trade by value and are ill-placed to benefit from the momentum of market forces generated in the EEC heartland.

The contribution of each transport mode to international freight traffic is shown in table 21. Though the seaports dominate in tonnage of imports they are only on an equal footing with rail, road and inland water for exports, even by tonnage. Had value been the criterion, the role of road haulage would almost certainly have been more dominant.

The role of each transport mode will be considered next, in the light of functions, potentials and constraints, together with some assessment of the context of urban and regional planning.

RAILWAYS (fig. 33)

Although SNCF has had the same obligation since 1974 as British Rail, that of balancing the financial budget, there are fundamental differences between the two systems, geographically, historically, and in terms of present economic functions (table 22). The greater size of the French national space, its compactness, and the continuous rail routes possible throughout the European continent, together with an economic pattern of concentrated and often peripheral industrial areas, an eccentrically-placed

Table 22   SNCF and British Rail, 1963 and 1973

System	SNCF			BR		
	1973	1963	1973 *as* %1963	1973	1963	1973 *as* %1963
Route (km)	34,435	38,550	89	18,224	27,330	67
Route freight only (km)	9,941	9,280		3,852	7,002	
Electrified (%)	27.0	20.2		19.0	9.4	

Traffic 1973	SNCF	BR	SNCF *as* %BR
Passenger train km (millions)	252	292	86
Passenger km (milliards)	44.7	29.7	150
Av. length of journey (km)	72.1	40.9	176
Freight train km (millions)	221	87	254
Freight tonne/km (milliards)	70.0	30.4*	230
Av. length of haul per tonne (km)	275	121	227

* excludes National Carriers and Freightliner
Source: UN (1974) *Ann. Bull. Transport Statistics for Europe* 1973; *SNCF Mémento de Statistique* 1973

capital, and vast rural hinterlands, have favoured the railway over its most economic operating distances, and with the types of traffic it was most suited to bear. The traditional dominance of the railway in France was, and continues to be, powerfully reinforced by government protection and in particular by the control over potentially competing transport modes. In Britain the railway system had no such protection and both the size and layout of the country, with short line-hauls from many ports to industrial centres, together with the earlier changes in national economic structure towards lighter, more valuable, more mobile products, conferred singular

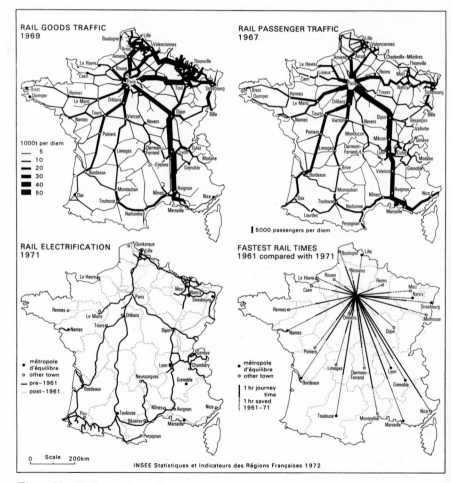

Figure 33   Rail goods traffic 1969; rail passenger traffic 1967; rail electrification 1971; fastest rail times 1961–71.

advantages on road transport. As table 22 shows, the shorter network of British Rail was less densely trafficked by passengers, though more so for freight, than that of SNCF.

Fig. 33 illustrates the network of passenger and freight flows. The general pattern of passenger traffic has long been predominantly radial to and from Paris, with a particularly dense traffic to Dijon, Lyon and Marseille. Journey times to and from the capital have been systematically reduced through electrification and other improved traction. Freight flows also have a strikingly radial component but there are much stronger linkages with the Nord and Lorraine, and also between these major heavy industrial regions. The polarization of the rail network on Paris was furthered by the policy of line closures since 1945 (Schnetzler 1967). Though the closures were much less dramatic than those in Britain under the Beeching Plan (1963) they affected many short feeder lines in the Massif Central, the Est, and in Bretagne and Normandie. The progressive definition of a mainline network has been accompanied by withdrawal of passenger services from almost one-quarter of the total route km; indeed, since 1930 the rail network for passengers has been reduced by almost one-half (52,000 to 24,494 km), with the withdrawal of passenger services not infrequently being the prelude to total closure.

Though total numbers of passengers carried and volume of freight transported by rail have been sustained since 1965, the railway has had a declining proportion of total traffic, particularly for goods. Competition, from the private car, pipelines and inland waterways, has played its part, but the structure of freight traffic has been changing, to the disadvantage of the railway. Coal and iron ore traffic has fallen abruptly: coal output has declined dramatically and more coal has been converted to power at coalfield thermal stations; the steel and chemical industries have sought coastal locations for new capacity, using imported ores or raw materials. Petroleum traffic has increasingly used pipelines, whilst there has also been a general tendency for all firms to locate with a view to minimizing both cost and time of transport.

SNCF has met competition by fullest use of modern technology (Devaux 1971) and by concentrating upon those services and traffics in which it has competitive advantage. State intervention in the transport market, referred to earlier, has aided the railway by increasingly requiring all modes of transport to meet full marginal and social costs, and to balance operating budgets without subsidy. Furthermore, SNCF has had the benefit of specific subsidies for urban and suburban commuter traffic, and for certain rural lines.

Electric traction now hauls three-quarters of total freight and passengers, and the tardy introduction of diesel locos finally eliminated steam traction in 1973. Newer electric locomotives (BB 15,000) permit sustained speeds of 200 km/h on suitable main lines, whilst the 'turbo-train' can sustain 160 km/h, and diesel traction 120 km/h on the secondary feeder-links. Rapid inter-city expresses (e.g. *Mistral*: Paris-Lyon: *Drapeau*: Paris-Bordeaux: *Capitole*: Paris-Toulouse) compete effectively in time and regularity with internal air services. A 'Tokkaido'-type fast transit rail link was envisaged between Paris and Lyon (VIth Plan), reducing the journey time to two hours, but the project was later deferred until the 1980s. On regional planning grounds it is argued that such a new line should be built on a more westerly trajectory to serve underprivileged regions better. Regular shuttle inter-city and intra-metropolitan services (*dessertes cadencées*) are being introduced, e.g. that linking Metz and Nancy (Métrolor) by an hourly departure, now operating on a reduced scale. In freight operation computerized marshalling, the use of integral trains (c.f. the British 'merry-go-round' system between coalfield and power station) and complete trains (> 480 tonnes capacity), together with belated spread of containers, is enhancing rail competitiveness (Minist. des Transports 1969).

The impact of the rail system upon regional and urban development in the past has been profound. Dissemination of economic development and the specialization of regions according to natural comparative advantage were both fostered. On the other hand, urbanization led to concentration of traffic at particular traffic nodes. In the era of state planning of the postwar economy, all modes of transport were regarded as instruments of change (Wickham 1962). On the one hand, the progressive introduction of 'transparency' or market principles into tariffs has inclined SNCF to close marginal routes, to concentrate on the primary inter-city network and the major nodes (Auphan 1975). This benefited the policy of regional growth centres (*métropoles d'équilibre*) but it threatened the prosperity or even the viability of widespread rural areas and small-town networks (Caralp 1967). Freedom to vary tariffs based on the real costs of operation on particular lines, together with the possibility of public subsidies, mitigated, but has not changed, the direction of such a traumatic rationalization. During the 1970s SNCF developed some important transverse links for passengers (e.g. Nantes-Tours-Lyon; Lille-Reims-Dijon; Bordeaux-Clermont Ferrand-Lyon), as part of the policy of strengthening the urban network (*armature urbaine*).

Under the Sixth Plan (1971–5) integrated transport was developed for three high-density zones (Basse-Seine, Nord, and the Rhône corridor), and intra-metropolitan and intra-urban transport systems were improved. The impact of the railway on suburbanization has been and continues to be considerable (Merlin 1966, 150 *et seq*). In the high-density inter-urban corridors rail carries most effectively the base passenger and freight load over medium distances, and affords the backbone for an integrated system.

ROADS (fig. 34)

Closely-spaced and regularly patterned, the French road network was centrally planned from the eighteenth century, at several scale levels: the national, with radial routes focusing on the capital; provincial, and later departmental, linking the chief town with its administrative hinterland;

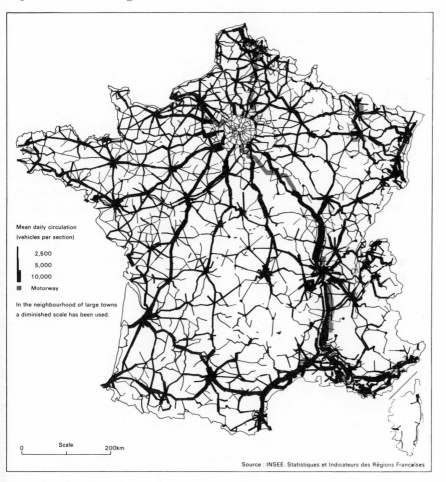

Figure 34   Road traffic in open country, 1968.

and locally within each *commune* (Sec. Gén. du Gouvernement 1964). Since the First World War the volume of road traffic has increased steadily, since 1960 meteorically: private cars, 5.5 million in 1960, 17.3 million in 1975; lorries over 20 tonnes, 11,900 in 1965, 26,826 in 1969. Rising density of road traffic is indicated by pressures on the *routes nationales*: in 1955, only 4 per cent of the network had 3000–5999 vehicles per day, in 1970 18.5 per cent; in 1955, 1.3 per cent had more than 6000 per day, in 1970 12.7 per cent. Tonne/kms of freight hauled on the roads rose from 9 milliards in 1934 to 22.5 milliards in 1955 and 72.5 milliards in 1969, with an increasing proportion by vehicles with 10 or even 13-tonne axle loading. Pressure on the road system has been uneven through time, and in space. Traffic flows can be disaggregated: radially to and from Paris, to a lesser extent into and out of regional cities; centrifugally to the coast in summer, and transversely by foreign tourist traffic, canalized into several axial corridors (Rhône-Saône; Mediterranean coast); in disseminated fashion down to individual communities. The commuting flows to and from urban centres represent a particular aggravation of the congestion and over-use problem. Between 1955 and 1968 the metropolitan areas of Marseille and Nantes had among the most difficult problems of traffic growth, together with many tourist regions (La DF 1962).

Recognition of the deteriorating road system coincided with the period of postwar planning. Indeed, because of the very flexibility of road transport and the ability of the state to influence flows and interconnections by a sensitive policy of infrastructure investment, the road system was seen as the prime transport mode to aid in restructuring and developing the urban network, and for both disseminating the policy of regional balance, and aiding isolated rural areas. It has been a difficult task to canalize this capacity of road transport to induce economic change, with the need to regulate competition between the transport modes, whereby the road should enjoy no competitive advantage.

In 1960 (*plan directeur routier*), 1967 (*projet d'aménagement du réseau routier*) and again in 1970 (*schéma directeur des grandes liaisons routières*) strategies were formulated for the road network, with particular regard for motorways (*autoroutes*) and priority *routes nationales* (RN). The 1960 Plan proposed 3558 km of motorways, later raised to 5000 km by 1980, of which 2629 km had been built by the end of 1974; there was also to be a 15-year programme for improvement of those *routes nationales* then bearing the heaviest traffic. Extrapolation of existing traffic trends led to an investment programme confirming and aggravating the radial-concentric pattern of major routes and offered no advantage for regional planning. The 1967 Plan retained the priority for linking all towns of more than 40,000 people effectively with their hinterlands, and with both the nearest metropolitan centre and the capital. The 'multiplier' effects of motorways and the impact on local or regional economies were taken more fully into account. Above all, the transport needs of regional planning were integrated, after full consultation at regional and metropolitan levels. Even so the DATAR criticised the 1967 Plan as spreading its investments excessively. The priorities should be: link-up of metropolitan counterbalancing centres with each other and with Paris; linkage of each four relay-towns with the adjacent metropolis and with Paris; international routes; and finally, coordinated road nets in the total hinterland of each regional metropolis. In 1971 the government accepted the third version of the Road Plan. This took into account the social and economic purposes of each route, and sought to integrate road strategy with other forms of public planning. Responsibility for national road strategy, particularly for the 15,000 km RN which carried 50 per cent of all road traffic, was to rest with the state. Regional and local government was to be responsible for planning second-order routes. Investment was to be concentrated on a basic network of 27,500 km RN, plus a deliberate choice of priority routes for regional planning purposes. These latter were to have a multiplier (*entraînement*) effect and be built or improved ahead of traffic justification. The national network was to have a broad grid pattern, to break down the concentric radials based on Paris. Three N-S interregional routes, and six E-W arteries are to be the framework for the new policy of regional equilibrium.

Geographers (Labasse 1971, Comby 1971) have been critical of the French motorway programme. It has been argued that the motorway plan reinforces the polarization of French life on to Paris, and a few other economically strong regions. Moreover, the tying of the French network into the European system: to Benelux 1974, to Germany via Metz and Strasbourg by the end of the VIIth Plan (1980), and to Italy by 1978 (via the coast) and later linking to the Mont Blanc tunnel, will confirm the star-shaped layout focused on the capital. By 1978 there will be only limited sections of motorway primarily of regional importance: Lille-Dunkerque, Lorraine, Dijon-Beaune, Bordeaux-Marseille, with tentative sections probing from Paris towards Poitiers, Le Mans and Caen.

Distinction must be drawn between urban access motorways (*autoroutes de dégagement urbain*) and interregional motorways (*autoroutes de liaison*). The latter have been toll-roads from the outset, financed by joint-companies (*compagnies mixtes*), like the Mont Blanc tunnel or the Tancarville bridge. Since 1971 private investment capital, from banks and insurance firms for example, has been sunk in new motorways to speed up and sustain continuity in development.

Labasse (1971) criticized the routes of various motorways. For example, Dijon is not served by the Paris-Lyon motorway; Orléans and Troyes are not yet linked, and there is no concept of motorway net to help industrial decentralization within the Bassin Parisien. Many motorways have dense traffic only near the extremities; other sections, as in the Rhône valley, have unnecessarily been routed through high-grade orchard land. On the other hand, he indicated the great importance of motorway interchange points as potential or actual economic growth centres on the American model. To achieve rational planning the regional interest must be fully consulted; otherwise haphazard or unbalanced development is likely.

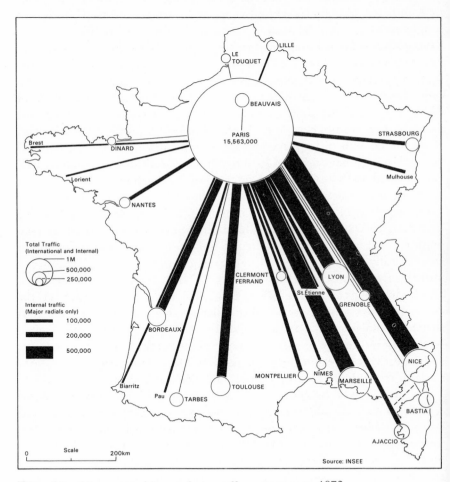

Figure 35   Airports and internal air traffic, passengers, 1972.

INTERNAL AIR SERVICES (fig. 35)

The spatial potential of airports and air services, and their implications for regional and urban planning, are only now becoming fully recognized (Labasse 1972, Spill 1973). The possible economic impact may relate to the international air network (e.g. competition between Roissy-Charles de Gaulle in Paris, and London-Heathrow, or Frankfurt-am-Main), or the national scale where a network strategy becomes an increasingly powerful tool for regional or urban planners. Between 1961 and 1975 passenger traffic through French airports rose from 6.6 to 25 millions, that attributable to the Paris airports from 57 to 72 per cent of the total traffic. Freight traffic increased from 260,000 tonnes (Paris 35 per cent) to 410,000 tonnes (Paris 69 per cent) during the same period. The rate of internal air traffic growth has exceeded that for international flights in recent years, but still is on a markedly lesser scale.

The most direct impact on urbanization and industrialization is that of the airport itself. Roissy-Charles de Gaulle (1973) is expected to provide 70,000 jobs when fully developed, with an indirect multiplier effect on perhaps 300,000 people overall. Such a massive potential economic impact will be a major regional growth generator, threatening to polarize migrants from Picardie at the expense of that region and even to disturb the industrial decentralization programme south and west from Paris. Already in 1968 Paris-Orly employed 25,000, whilst the new Lyon airport (Satolas) is expected to employ 4200 by 1985. Additional economic impetus is given by the flood of visitors to major airports: 4 millions to Orly in 1968, with a major contribution to retail turnover in a broad zone around (Labasse 1971). Decisions on national and regional airport strategy can thus be a powerful force in regional planning, affecting the city-region perhaps more than individual towns.

The effect of internal air service networks, directions, frequencies and hierarchical linkages, is less easily measurable but overall no less significant (Spill 1974). Seventy-five per cent of all French internal flights are for business purposes, with strong polarizing flows to and from Paris (fig. 35). The effects of this radial-concentric flight pattern upon the regions are debatable. In one sense the focal role of Paris means that centres of industrial and commercial decision-taking remain in the capital and only production units are decentralized to the provinces. Indeed there is some evidence of provincial firms establishing head offices in Paris, weakening even further localized powers of decision-taking.

The power of internal air services to influence the definition of French regions is limited, since these had already been laid out in response to land communications (Spill 1973). Furthermore, since air transport of passengers becomes competitive with first-class rail only beyond three hours rail journey time, it is in relations between the metropolitan growth centres that the commercial aircraft has a most clear-cut role to play. On the other hand, air transport is more flexible according to type of aircraft, and infrastructural investments once made are less expensive than those of other modes to alter.

Transverse links are weak in France, with only Lyon having strong interregional connections through the secondary airline network of Air Inter. A third-level private network is now filling in the gaps, both radially and transversely. An internal airlines plan (La DF 1972) proposed developing interconnections between regional metropolitan centres, and between each and its hinterland. Unfortunately, planning of air services has tended to follow demand rather than stimulate it. Already some transverse lines developed by Air Inter in 1960 have been given up. What is clearly needed is a deliberate attempt to break up the concentric radial pattern focused on Paris and to strengthen interregional connections, permitting larger and more economic aircraft to be used. Concentration of feeder services on the regional metropolitan airports would link to a rapid and frequent service to and from the capital. Presently DATAR offers subsidies to new transverse routes for three years and to new radials for one year. The air network of local flights within Auvergne shows what can be achieved by dynamic regional policy, even within a thinly-peopled rural region. FIAT (*fonds d'intervention pour l'aménagement du territoire*) subsidizes direct links with neighbouring European towns, and there is a further planning need to improve internal services to and from the major French ports to facilitate the interchange of crews.

The ideal plan for air services linking the regional metropoli is not to be adequately fulfilled this century. Lyon, Bordeaux, and Marseille are likely to be interlinked with all other metropoli by 1985, but there are also non-metropolitan centres with rapidly growing air services, e.g. Grenoble and Nice. Other towns, such as Cherbourg, are ill-placed for links to the metropoli and too great a detour would be involved to route traffic through such regional nodes (Spill 1973). In short, it is unlikely that the reorganized internal air service network will fulfil all the expectations of the regional planners, but through the channelling of business travel it will continue to have a strong influence upon the effectiveness of industrial and tertiary decentralization.

TELECOMMUNICATIONS

France is moving towards the post-industrial society, with 51.8 per cent of the workforce already in tertiary and quaternary employment. From an increasingly complex urbanized way of life and rising sophistication in manufacturing, the volume of data in circulation is growing at around 10 per cent p.a., or doubling every eight years (La DF 1973). Face-to-face contacts, by surface or air transport, have had to be supplemented by telephone, telex and most recently telecomputing networks. Analysis of telephone traffic has traditionally been used by geographers as an index of urban centrality, but it provides an uncertain indicator of purely business contacts. The backwardness of the French telephone network has probably constrained regional development in some measure (Paré 1974), even though density of telephones per 100 persons correlates well with the economic status of regions. Furthermore, during 1963–73, the most rapid development of telephone subscribers has been in Bretagne, Languedoc, Corse (and the Centre), all areas to which government priority economic aid has been directed.

The telex system is a better indicator of business traffic (Laborde 1973). Its flows are symptomatic of the industrial, commercial or administrative ranking of cities or regions, since the number of subscribers rather than some hierarchy of machines or technology is the true measure of significance. In 1963 Ile-de-France had 47 per cent of all subscribers, but ten years later only 35 per cent, in spite of a sevenfold increase in national subscribers during the same period. The most rapid increase rates were either in prosperous regions such as Rhône-Alpes or, more commonly, in hitherto deprived areas like Corse, Basse-Normandie, or Bourgogne. The measure of industrial decentralization throughout the Bassin Parisien is shown in the rapid increase rates in Picardie and the Centre. Telex traffic (1973) showed the Paris centre, at 43 per cent, more significant than for number of subscribers. Moreover, 48 per cent of messages to and from the capital were on the international network, with only Strasbourg (34 per cent) and Lille (32 per cent) matching even the national average for foreign messages. It seems clear that telex facilities have been a potentially significant support for decentralization of both manufacturing and services. Rapid circulation of decisions and information has been possible, but with the continuing, excessive centralization of head offices in Paris it is far from certain that plants or establishments in the provinces have had enhanced powers of decision-taking.

As the most recent technology, telecomputing (*téléinformatique*) is a potentially powerful instrument for the effective decentralization of tertiary and quaternary services. Telecomputing is a system of dependent communications, with terminals linked to computers and these to each other. The distribution of terminals is a fair indication of the level of regional development, and of the extent of integration into the national economy (Bakis 1975). In 1965 159 terminals were in use, in 1972 more than 8000. Terminals are more numerous at greater distances from Paris. Computers, on the other hand, are more concentrated, occurring outside Paris, in the Est, Rhône-Alpes, Midi-Pyrénées and the Nord. The ratio of computers to terminals is high in Paris, but generally low in the provinces. The latest developments in technology, the *Caducée* network, has its own cable system with an automatic changeover switch in Paris. This presently means that all messages between provincial subscribers must pass through Paris, but it is proposed to establish changeover switches also in the provinces, possibly at Lyon and Bordeaux. Long-distance interchange of data thus becomes possible, and the potential for greater decentralization of both manufacturing and tertiary activities to the provinces is thereby enhanced. In the mid-1970s 50 per cent of telecomputing was by banks, air control centres and scientific establishments, and the technology is in use mainly in large firms, especially multinationals. Only simple and largely unprofitable uses are yet being made of the new network and lack of demand outside Paris has hindered its expansion. The Cyclades project, linking Rennes, Grenoble, Toulouse and Paris in a network of mini-computers (1974), indicates the potential for the future.

INLAND WATERWAYS (fig. 36)

Tables 19 and 20 show the significance of inland waterway traffic in France, falling in proportion of total freight traffic but sustaining a similar tonnage of freight (109 Mt in 1974). The waterways carried 6.5 per cent of total tonne/km of freight in 1973, compared with 27.9 per cent in West Germany, but only 0.1 per cent in Britain. During 1974 waterway freight consisted of: loose construction materials (49 per cent); refined oil products (19 per cent), especially heavy oil; agricultural produce and food (13 per cent); solid mineral fuels (6 per cent); and various goods (metallurgical products, ores, fertilizers, cars, chemicals). The traditional bulk-carrying role of inland waterways is emphasized, competing strongly in such traffic with other transport modes up to distances of 300 km for tonnage and 500 km in tonne-km. During the past decade, indeed, water transport has competed effectively with rail, on certain sections, for both cereal and fuel traffic. Pipeline transport, on the other hand, has made serious inroads into potential waterway traffic, at least on the Rhône. On the Basse-Seine the waterway has maintained its competitiveness.

With improved technology, and given both the continuing state provision of infrastructure and the measure of freight rate protection, the

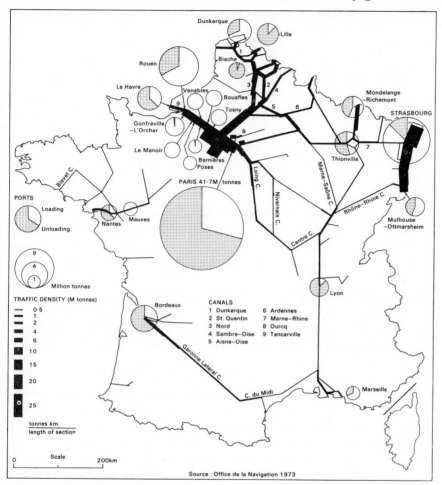

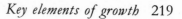

Figure 36   Inland waterways: ports and traffic density, 1972.

inland waterway is capable of remaining a competitive transport mode for a wide range of bulk commodities (Morice 1968). Fig. 36, however, shows all too clearly that the real constraints on waterway use in France lie in the layout, technical specification and carrying capacity of the system. Expensive works and maintenance have been necessary to maintain navigation at commercially acceptable limits on the Seine, the Rhine, and the Moselle. The canals interlinking these river systems date back in some cases to the *ancien régime,* in most others to the *Plan Freycinet* (1879). Of the 7028 km of navigable inland waterways in 1974, only 17 per cent were navigable by the largest Rhine barges (3000 t) or pusher-convoys, and only 21 per cent by the Euro-barge (1350 t). On the other hand, 67 per cent of the system can accommodate only 400 tonne craft, and 2000 km (23 per cent) are limited even to boats of less than 250 tonnes. The higher-capacity waterways, Basse-Seine, Dunkerque-Valenciennes, Moselle to Toul and the Rhine, are not effectively interlinked; furthermore, the Rhine and the Dunkerque-Valenciennes canal are parallel to the frontiers and the latter is inadequately linked into the international system. The watersheds from the Seine system are crossed by canals of limited capacity and with many locks; even the Canal du Nord, completed under the IIIrd Plan in 1958, is already a bottleneck, whilst the Seine above Montereau is virtually a cul-de-sac.

Inland waterway ports (fig. 36) are either large (more than 1 Mt loaded and unloaded) or small and scattered along the banks of rivers and canals. Few ports have a balance between loadings and unloadings, and there is specialization in traffic. For example, Paris handles one-quarter of the total national freight tonnage, but of this one-half is the unloading of construction materials or crude minerals. Strasbourg, on the other hand, handles 8 per cent, but of this 87 per cent is in loadings, almost equally divided between oil products and construction materials. Loading and unloading of oil products dominates the trade of the river port at Le Havre, whilst Dunkerque has the most balanced trade with considerable diversification of commodities.

Planning of the inland waterway network, and its integration into a national and European transport system, has been laggard, but the outlines of major selective investment programmes in infrastructure and technology are now clear. First priority under the VIth Plan was given to extending and coordinating the development of waterways in the hinterlands of the port-industrial complexes (Basse-Seine, Dunkerque and Marseille-Fos). The upper Seine was improved from Paris to Montereau, the Oise from Conflans to Compiègne (and by 1980 to Reims), whilst the Dunkerque-Douai canal was extended to Valenciennes. Later the Dunkerque-Valenciennes canal will be linked by a high-capacity section to the Belgian waterways, and the Seine system by upgraded waterways to the Escaut (Seine-Nord), and to the Moselle (Seine-Est), via Reims and the Argonne plateau to Toul.

The Moselle has already been improved for 1350 tonne barges by an international canalization project opened from Koblenz to Thionville and Metz in 1964 (Martin 1974), extended to Pompey in 1971, and to Neuves Maisons (1975). The Moselle scheme is multi-purpose, with power generation and flood-control important secondary purposes, but even in direct economic terms has fully justified French expectations of 10 Mt of

Table 23 Freight traffic by transport mode, 1966

	Rhône (*Dijon-Avignon*)	*Seine* (*Mantes-Le Havre*)	*Rhine* (*Mulhouse-Strasbourg*)
Total (Mt)	56–62	33–36	54
Rail	16–20	4–8	10
Water	1–3	6–13	13
Pipeline	31	20–7	28
Road	8	3–8	3

Source: Notes et Etudes Documentaires (1971) 3842–43, 54

traffic annually. Interestingly, French and German railways had to counter the competition from the canalized river through reduction of freight rates on Ruhr coal and coke destined for Lorraine by 30–39 per cent, almost down to the railways' marginal cost.

The Rhône-Saône corridor is one of the most densely trafficked in France by all transport modes (table 23). The dominance of the pipeline, for oil and oil products, and the significance of rail dwarf the contribution of river traffic. Nevertheless the potential for waterway development is considerable (Audant and Béthémont 1973). Since 1934 the Compagnie Nationale du Rhône (CNR), a mixed enterprise representing SNCF, EdF, local authorities and interests, and the Département de la Seine (for electricity supply), has been developing a multi-purpose programme of barrages for the river system: electricity generation from 19 hydro-stations, seven upstream and twelve downstream from Lyon, with total annual output of 16 milliards KWh (16 TWh); navigation channel improvement, to provide 3.5 m navigable depth accessible to 1350 t barges or pushed barge-trains of 3 to 5000 tonnes; creation of linear industrial zones linking greater Lyon and Marseille-Fos; agricultural improvement, on 200,000 ha, including irrigation and flood protection, restructuring of farms, and stabilization of the water-table; and, finally, tourist development (Séc. Général du Gouvernement 1971). Presently the sections near Caderousse, north of Avigon, and Vaugris-Péage de Roussillon, south of Vienne, remain to be improved to open the Rhône to major river traffic from the sea to Lyon. By 1978 the section north along the Saône to St Symphorien should be accessible; thereafter, the construction of the Rhône-Rhine canal must be awaited. Approval for this construction was given in late 1975, with a route via Belfort to Mulhouse on the Grand Canal d'Alsace (Séc. Général du Gouvernement 1962). There are, however, some doubts about the economic viability of an improved Rhône-Rhine canal. It has been estimated that 50 Mt traffic per annum would be a minimum commercial threshold, but only 10 Mt are projected for 1990. Many of the smaller French canals will be more useful for pleasure craft than for commercial purposes.

Finally, the improvement of the waterways fleet and its effective commercial organization are essential to competitiveness. In 1973 already one-quarter of waterways traffic was operated by pushed barge-trains or special-purpose craft, such as tankers. The *plan batellerie* (1971) aimed to extend the waterway networks accessible to pusher trains of two 2500 tonne targes. Barge-lifts (e.g. at Arzwiller on the Marne-Rhine canal), and roll-on/roll-off facilities, indicate the potential of new technology. Specialization of waterway haulage firms, e.g. in the movement of cars from Paris to Le Havre (Renault) and in the reverse direction (Ford), is a further development.

PIPELINES

Postwar development of a crude oil and products pipeline network in France (fig. 40) has been rapid. At the end of 1973 the length of the network was greater than that of the UK and was much more intensively used (table 24). The network links coastal refineries with major inland markets, and also ports with inland refineries. The Rhône valley carries the heaviest traffic: South European crude pipeline (PLSE); SPMR products pipeline.

Table 24   Pipeline network, France and the UK, 1973

		France	UK
Length operated (km)		5,943	4,094
crude oil	A	111,244	28,475
	B	37,503	3,966
oil products	A	28,285	11,331
	B	5,035	2,327

A = 1000 tonnes   B = million tonne km
Source: UN (1974) *Ann. Bull. Transport Statistics for Europe* 1973

PORTS (fig. 37)

Industrialization and urbanization in postwar France have greatly increased the role and status of her ports, and markedly changed the structure of their traffic (Séc. Général du Gouvernement 1966). Shifts in world trade and the altered relationship of France to her former colonies and possessions have contributed to further changes, notably so in ports such as

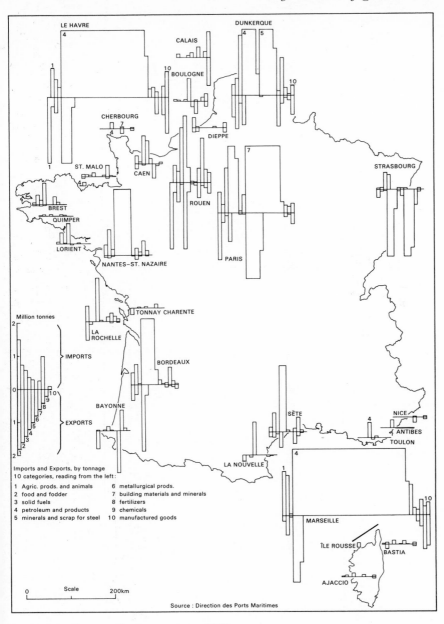

Figure 37   Port traffic, by tonnage, 1972.

Table 25 Ranking of major French ports, by tonnage and dominant traffic 1974

million tonnes	Imports				Exports			
	Total	oil and prods	non-oil	next group	Total	oil and prods	non-oil	next group
Marseille	93.2	84.0	9.1	1.3 agric. prods	15.8	10.6	5.0	0.2 chemicals
Le Havre	67.3	61.1	6.2	0.7 manuf. 0.6 cereals	16.7	11.8	4.9	0.7 agric. prods.
Dunkerque	29.7	10.2	19.5	9.4 iron ore	4.8	1.1	3.6	1.0 food
Nantes/St Nazaire	12.9	10.3	2.6	0.8 food	1.6	0.8	0.8	no signif. gp.
Rouen	8.0	1.9	6.1	1.7 coal	6.1	1.5	4.6	2.2 cereals
Bordeaux	10.6	8.7	1.8	0.6 food	2.9	1.4	1.5	0.4 agric. prods.
All other ports	24.6	9.0	15.6		10.8	0.3	10.5	
Total	246.6	185.5	61.1		59.0	27.9	31.1	

Source: Minist. de l'Equipement (1975), L'activité des ports maritimes français en 1974

Marseille, Bordeaux and Nantes. The progressive opening of the French economy to Europe since the Treaty of Rome (1958) has potentially enhanced the competitive advantage of the ports of Rotterdam and Antwerp at the expense of Dunkerque. It has also prospectively put the ports of the Atlantic facade of France into an even more marginal situation. On the other hand, Marseille-Fos at the mouth of the Rhône-Saône corridor is not without pretension to the title of 'Europort Méditerranéen', linked by pipeline to the EEC heartland.

A hierarchy of French ports may be defined in terms of either total traffic or degree of specialization (fig. 37 and table 25). Certain features are striking: the unbalanced trade with a heavy import surplus, though this is characteristic of all rapidly industrializing countries, and would be somewhat redressed if value of trade could be taken into account; the unusually high proportion of import tonnage represented by oil and oil products, and this heavily concentrated in two ports (Marseille and Le Havre), with three others of considerable significance; a diversity of import structures in the non-oil traffic, with Dunkerque iron ore and Rouen coal particularly noteworthy. In export traffic much lesser significance of oil products and a generally good correlation between the structure of traffic at individual ports and the economic nature of the regional, rather than the national, hinterland. Le Havre and Rouen as the ports of the Bassin Parisien have a diversified but complementary export structure, Rouen with foodstuffs, textiles, Le Havre featuring machinery, vehicles and engineering products in addition.

The secondary and minor ports of France (fig. 37) are either regional trans-shipment centres like Brest, Bayonne or Caen, or have specialized packet-boat or fishing functions: Calais, with 3.5 million arrivals and departures (1974), is traditionally the major passenger-handling port (next Boulogne 1.2 millions).

State policy towards the French ports has been elaborated through the series of four-year Plans. The most recent objectives have been to concentrate major infrastructural investments into the Basse-Seine (Le Havre, Rouen), Dunkerque and Marseille-Fos, to equip these port complexes for resisting the loss of traffic to Antwerp and Rotterdam (VIth Plan). All are above the threshold of 10 Mt of general merchandise traffic deemed necessary for ports of European stature. Approaches and quayside depths have been improved, large-scale and specialized handling-gear, storage areas and port exits landwards have been added to. Even so, given the limited inland transport networks discussed earlier it will be difficult for French ports to recover traffic already lost to Antwerp and Rotterdam, the more so if principles of 'transparency' pricing are introduced under EEC regulations to reflect true journey costs from ports through hinterlands.

It is not intended to neglect second-order ports, though it is necessarily accepted that major infrastructural investments must logically be ever more concentrated, if the fullest benefits of ship and harbour technology are to be exploited. Containerization, unit-load handling, roll-on/roll-off facilities came late in France, and landward transport of containers has not yet experienced the developments introduced, for example, by British Rail in the UK. In 1972 only 14.2 per cent of import tonnage, and 12.6 per cent of export tonnage were in unit-loads (pallets, small containers, etc.); the figures for containers more than 6 m long were 6.3 and 8.9 per cent respectively. Large container traffic is concentrated at Le Havre, Dunkerque and Marseille in that order of importance. In addition to these three ports unit-load cargoes are also important at Nantes, Boulogne, Bordeaux and Ajaccio.

Public policy has also focused on port organization and administration (June 1965), upon establishing selected free zones (*zones francs*) to encourage international transit traffic, and upon building up integrated industrial complexes at the major ports (Part III, ch. 2). Finally, the French merchant marine has been modernised and built up (*Plan Morin*), so that in future more than the present one-third of national trade will be carried in French ships. Subsidized shipbuilding has played its part in reinforcing the regional economies of the Atlantic face of France. Shipping companies have been reorganized to face foreign competition: CGT (French Line) and Messageries Maritimes have merged; CETRAMAR has been created from a merger of the principal bulk-handling companies, to offset competition from firms' private shipping; French participants have joined the Atlantic Container Line pool.

URBAN TRANSPORT

Rapid urbanization in postwar France has led directly to greater commuting flows over longer distances in search of urban jobs. At the same time the 'flight to the suburbs', which had never reached British proportions in prewar France, added to the daily flows in search of work, shopping, entertainment or public services (Part I, ch. 4, trip generation). City centres were already congested, the product of tradition, lack of renewal, and the tardy but dramatic impact of industrialization and commercialization of land uses.

The problems of planning and operating an integrated metropolitan transport network were first and most fully examined within the Paris region (Merlin 1966). The creation of particular transport infrastructure and services were progressively adapted to demand, at each succeeding technological phase. Such creations in their turn further stimulated demand, and were the means of decentralizing first residence and, later and to a lesser extent, workplaces. Major housing developments, the *grands ensembles*, were grouped near motorway interchanges, or scattered around the city perimeter wherever private transport was the dominant mode. Following the nineteenth-century tradition, suburban nuclei grew up around local commuter stations, and were progressively added to by housing sprawl. Unfortunately, the planning of transport, as in Britain, was too much divorced from city planning, and both lacked sufficient regional context.

Most recently, the growing unprofitability of public transport matched an increasing congestion caused by the motorcar. During the VIth Plan more deliberate public intervention was directed to metropolitan and large-scale urban traffic problems. The planning of metropolitan motorways improved mass accessibility for cars (inner urban expressways and the Paris *boulevard périphérique* 1973), but to an extent at the expense of the environment, producing parking scarcity, pollution and traffic hazard. The greater Paris planning scheme (Délégation Générale 1965) proposed the decentralization of metropolitan functions to new urban centres, within or beyond the suburbs (Part III, ch. 2). An essential corollary of such proposals was a coherent, extended and interrelated transport strategy. An ambitious programme was drawn up, for radial motorways and ringways, and public transport on its own tracks; the heaviest investment was to go into a high-capacity network based on the mainline railway stations. In 1971 a comprehensive transport plan confirmed many of these proposals, but modified others: regional planning was by then seeking to limit demand for transport, through a better relationship between residences and workplaces; greater priority was given to public transport. For town planning, financial and technical reasons, the scheme for regional fast transit (RER — *réseau express régional*) was to be cut back after completion of the major east-west link. Under the VIth Plan (1971–5) the link-up of the New Towns with Paris was started, but this meant deferring the essential infrastructure for the preferential growth axes (Part III, ch. 2) and the integration of the New Towns with their immediate hinterlands.

As the VIIth Plan (1976–80) develops, Ile-de-France is still served by dominantly radial-concentric transport links. Of the 280 km of motorways and expressways created during the Vth and VIth Plans 210 km were radials; the inner ringway (*boulevard périphérique*) round the city of Paris (37 km) was completed in 1973 and by the end of 1975 the outer ringway (A86) had 20 km of its 80 km in service. Nevertheless, a deliberate attempt is being made to use existing rail infrastructure more intensively, rather than create new facilities, further radial motorways have been abandoned and priority given to linking up the growth centres within the suburbs, with each other, with the New Towns and with Paris. In particular, the *métro* system is to be extended to the restructuring poles in the suburbs (about the distance to the A86 ringway). Links to the airports at Orly and Roissy are being improved and the national context of Paris further strengthened by long-distance motorways and electrified rail routes.

Lyon and Marseille are large enough economically to justify the provision of the new *métro* underground systems in construction in the mid-1970s, but with a line capacity much below that of the Paris network. Better integrated bus service networks, priority bus lanes, single manning of buses, and improved speed and comfort of public service vehicles have a familiar ring to British ears. Not so the intention to reintroduce tramways, on segregated tracks, in several of the larger cities. Lille, St Etienne and Marseille saved and modernized some of their original lines; Strasbourg, Toulouse and Bordeaux are seriously planning the installation of modern tramway networks (1976).

The great controversy affecting all transport planning in industrialized urbanized western countries remains unresolved. Shall overwhelming priority be given to state aid for public transport, on grounds of environmental conservation or social justice, or shall individual preference for using the motorcar be accommodated as fully as possible? It is hard to escape the conclusion that in France, as in Britain, the resolution of these irreconcilable differences will continue to be by a compromise which owes much to political expediency.

Energy

POLICY AND PLANNING

Like communication, energy is a key resource in all programmes for economic development. Indeed, consumption of energy in all its forms is the best single indicator of growth through urbanization and in-dustrialization, correlating well with increase in GNP. Curiously though, there is a wide discrepancy between France and her European neighbours in the consumption of energy per unit of GNP. This is ascribed to the more efficient use of energy, concentration upon the most efficient forms of generation with more modern (because more recent) technology, and a lower level of domestic consumption, related to traditionally lower overall living standards (Médina 1975). Successive energy crises, that for coal from

1958 onwards, and that arising from the tripling of oil prices 1973–5, caused a slackening in economic growth. Countries like France, which had traditionally and increasingly become dependent upon foreign sources of energy, proved to be particularly vulnerable to such disruptions. Given the geographical constraints upon resource availability and the time taken to switch major investment programmes among the potentially competing energy sources, it is not surprising that substitution of one source by another has proved to be very limited, at least in the short term.

Nevertheless, public intervention in both the supply of energy and its marketing has been profound and of long standing. The coal industry was nationalized in 1946 and has been centrally planned since that date: in 1974 only 1 Mt of a national output of 24.5 Mt came from other than state mines, mostly from EdF opencast pits in the Landes. The public sector gas company (Gaz de France) also was created in 1946, but it has increasingly become a treatment and distribution agency (115.6 out of a total sales of 144.3 billion tonnes thermies (th = 1 million calories) in 1974). Electricité de France (EdF) came into being in 1948. Though dominant in electric power generation and distribution (93 per cent production HEP, 75 per cent production thermal power in 1972), there are other important secondary producers: Compagnie Nationale du Rhône (CNR) and SNCF for HEP, Charbonnages de France and the private sector steel industry (blast furnace gas) for thermal power. EdF controls nuclear power generation and its contribution to the national grid network. The massive oil consumption of France, on the other hand, is almost entirely supplied by commercial oil corporations, with French companies (Total, Elf-Aquitaine-Antar) responsible for about 50 per cent.

The objectives of public planning of energy resources are to ensure an adequate supply of the right types in the right places at the right time. This involves programming the most effective mixes among energy sources and the development of regional energy budgets (Gautier 1968). In terms of regional and urban planning, public intervention is to be used to stimulate growth as well as to accommodate to it. Methods of energy planning include the control over investment programmes and their relationship with EEC as well as national policies; the provision of infrastructure, for generation and transmission, with important indirect relationships with housing, other utilities, manufacturing, and communications; and influence upon pricing through insistence upon marginal costs, thereby producing a more effective interplay of market forces than within transport. The significance of public intervention affects the cost of energy, itself a variable but not negligible part of production costs in a wide range of industries. For example, the transmission cost of electricity is often

12–13 per cent of its delivered price, as compared with 10 per cent of the price of coal delivered from the Nord to Paris. Inevitably, the high investment costs in providing energy, the rapidity of technical change, and the heavy legacy of past energy generation and distribution networks, limit the speed of adaptation to and stimulus of economic change (Commissariat Général du Plan 1971, 1972).

France was particularly, even uniquely, hard-hit by the energy crisis of the mid-1970s because she was in a critical stage of both industrialization and urbanization, excessively dependent upon foreign energy sources, and her national endowment of resources for fuel and power (Gamblin 1968) was ill-distributed in relation alike to markets and to serve the purposes of regional and urban planning. Since 1945 three phases in the demand for energy may be distinguished: 1945–60, a period of general scarcity; 1960–73, a phase of general abundance; and since 1973 the severe impact of the tripling of oil prices (table 26).

For fifteen years after World War II there was maximum exploitation of all energy potential in France, including even marginal and high cost sources and locations. In 1955 two-thirds of French energy needs were provided from coal, of which only one-quarter had to be imported. Hydropower covered about 8 per cent of all needs, also from indigenous resources, whilst imported oil already amounted to one-quarter of energy requirements. The national price of coal governed other fuel and power prices, and the total consumption of energy rose in parallel with GNP at about 4 per cent p.a. Between 1960 and 1973 there was increasing abundance of cheap oil, and by the late 1960s oil was providing for 55 per

Table 26   National energy mix, 1955–74

Mt coal equivalent (MTec)		1955	1965	1974	*est.* 1985	
					A	*B*
coal —	production	57.3	54.0	25.7	18.0	?
	imports	16.7	17.1	21.3	27.0	?
	consumption	69.8	69.0	47.0	45.0	25.0
oil —	,,	27.2	74.1	174.0	146.0	300.0
primary gas —	,,	0.4	8.0	26.0	56.0	55.0
hydro-electricity —	,,	8.7	15.0	18.0	20.0	20.0
nuclear power —	,,	0	0.3	4.3	90.0	50.0
Total		106.1	166.4	308.0	357.0	450.0

A.   Conseil de Planification, Jan. 1975; B. VIth Plan estimates 1971
Sources: CdF 1975; EdF 1974; *Gaz de France* 1974; *Comité du Pétrole* 1972

cent of French fuel and power needs. The coverage of energy needs from indigenous resources in France fell from 63 to only 37 per cent during the period. Coal production was largely sustained and imports were about stable. It was the sharp rise in oil imports, assisted in a secondary way by the virtual doubling of the HEP contribution, that permitted energy consumption to rise by 5.2 per cent p.a. Oil prices governed those of other fuel and power sources and the recession in the coal industry set in after 1958.

Since the tripling of oil prices in 1973–5, a revaluation of the entire French national energy strategy to 1985, and for the longer term, has been enforced. The prosperity and prospects of particular industries and regions have been threatened by the oil crisis. On the other hand, the prospects for the French coal-producing areas stand to be improved. To reduce her vulnerability, the 1975 French energy plan stressed the need to develop national resources as a first priority and, at the same time, to reduce consumption, with the ambition of only 50–60 per cent dependence on foreign energy sources by 1985, compared with 76 per cent in 1974. The coal industry is to be rehabilitated, and a massive nuclear power programme undertaken (pp. 243–6).

Within such planning, the spatial component is of vital importance. There is, and has long been, a mismatch between sites of energy production in France, the points of entry for imports (by land and sea), and the planning objectives of balanced provision of varied energy resources over the French national space (fig. 38). Regional energy budgets are as unbalanced as the distribution of industry itself, both in respect of energy mixes and also in the availability of particular sources of fuel and power at an acceptable price. Geographers have drawn attention (Gamblin 1968, 114–16; George 1973, 99–100) to the existence of what appear at first sight to be spatially complementary fuel and power provinces: in the Nord, Lorraine and Paris a region of thermal power generation, based principally on French coal (fig. 39) supplemented by imports of coal, and of oil through Dunkerque. Coal imports in recent years have come from Western Germany, by rail and the Moselle (10.8 Mt in 1974, mainly Ruhr coal and coke, but with 1.8 Mt from the Saar); from the USA (2.7 Mt), Poland (3.3 Mt) and the USSR (1.5 Mt), by sea into Dunkerque and Rouen. Traditional HEP producing regions such as the Alpes have diversified their energy sources since the mid-1950s by greater use of imported oil (fig. 40) and the exploitation of small but declining coal reserves in the uplands (fig. 39). In the Sud-Ouest the natural gas province, Lacq (fig. 41; Brunet 1958), serves the French market by pipeline, but has been increasingly supplemented in this role by imports of liquid methane gas from Algeria to Le Havre, and since 1973 to Fos, together with a rising volume of imported natural gas

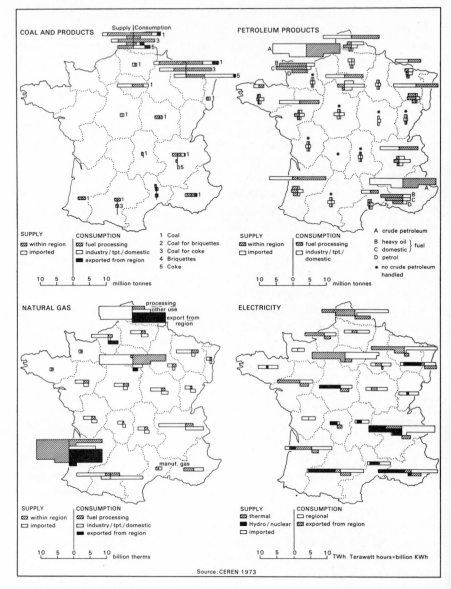

Figure 38   Regional fuel balances, 1971.

from Groningen. Elsewhere in western and central France, in a broad swathe flanking the Loire valley, there are no indigenous energy sources of significance. Perhaps for this reason, among others, there has been a concentration in this area of nuclear power generation sites, 1963–71. The

Loire estuary, the Gironde, and the Basse-Seine are important oil-importing centres.

The most striking feature of fig. 38 is the general importance of consumption of energy within its region of production or within a contiguous economic region. The block interregional interchanges of fuel and power are less than might have been expected, even within the electricity market. Movements of oil, petroleum products and natural gas, together with export of surplus hydro-power from the Massif Central, provide major exceptions to the generalization that regional energy production, plus imports, and regional consumption are somewhat surprisingly often in balance.

The ability of state planning to manipulate fuel and power production and the distribution of energy over the national space is conditioned, in the first place, by the weight of inertia in those solid fuel-based regions in which coal has had a traditional industry-locating role. Reconversion and diversification are the keynotes for both industrial restructuring and the provision of energy in the Nord and Lorraine. Steering of the distribution of oil, petroleum products and natural gas into the hinterlands of Marseille-Fos, the Basse-Seine, and to a lesser extent Bordeaux and Dunkerque, is potentially the most powerful short-term instrument of public energy policy, to serve mass markets in manufacturing, transport and domestic consumption. Substitution between energy sources, in time or place, is limited by the extent to which each source has particular suitability in certain markets (table 27).

At first sight, electricity appears to be the most flexible, fluid energy source (Félice 1958), interlinked virtually instantaneously in a nation-wide

Table 27   Energy consumption 1972, by energy source and market

MTec	Coal [†]	Oil	Gas	Electricity	Total
Iron and steel	16.0	3.5	2.0	3.4	24.9
Other manufactures	3.9	31.0	7.5	22.0	64.4
Domestic services	7.5	44.5	8.0	16.5	76.5
Mines and their power stations	9.1	—	—	—	9.1
EdF	6.6	—	—	—	6.6
Agriculture	—	4.0	—	—	4.0
Transport	0.1	41.0	—	2.0	43.1
Total	43.2	124.0	17.5	43.9	228.6

[†]1974

Sources: Various

grid network (fig. 42). In practice, although this is technically true, there are transmission costs to be borne. These are concerned with investments in, and maintenance of, power-lines, as well as the loss in transmission (1.2 per cent per 100 km in 1960, since reduced by about one-sixth) even with the high-tension networks (225 kV, 380 kV). Thus electric power generation is developed regionally to serve regional base and middle loads. Only peak loads are transferred over long distances through the grid network, and then under special circumstances. For example, HEP stations in the Alpes have a spring peak potential at which maximum turbining coincides with early morning and evening peak consumption in Paris, justifying large-scale long-distance transmission. The Massif Central exports half its HEP output, since the regional market in no way matches the capacity for generation.

During the mid-1970s, the principles of a new French energy policy were defined by the Conseil de Planification: a diminished role for home-produced coal; a deliberate reduction in oil imports, and economy in their use; maximum production of primary gas, including guaranteed imports; completion of HEP development, though this had almost been achieved by the end of the VIth Plan; and, finally, suspension of programmes for further conventional thermal stations and a very large-scale nuclear power programme. If achieved, nuclear power will supply 50 per cent of French electricity requirements by the end of the century.

COAL-BASED ENERGY

In contrast to the UK, and the EEC of the Nine, the oil crisis has not led to major new development proposals for the French coal industry. Indeed, any further development in coal-based energy will need to be derived from increased imports. The EEC, on the other hand, intends to build up the solid fuel contribution to overall energy consumption from 318 MTec (including 37 lignite) in 1974 to 360 MTec by 1985 (Charbonnages de France—CdF 1974).

Fig. 39 shows the decline in coal output in France and the extent to which falls have affected all coal basins. In 1974 output in Nord-Pas-de-Calais (9 Mt) was only 30 per cent of the 1952 and 36 per cent of the 1963 figure; for Lorraine (9 Mt) the declines were to 74 per cent and 68 per cent respectively; for Centre-Midi (6.4 Mt) to 44 per cent and 56 per cent. These declines and their prospective continuance to a national output of 21 Mt in 1980 and only 18 Mt in 1983 are the result of physical, economic and social constraints. The physical constraints on French coal resources are well-known (Novel 1970, CdF 1974). Many of the best and most accessible

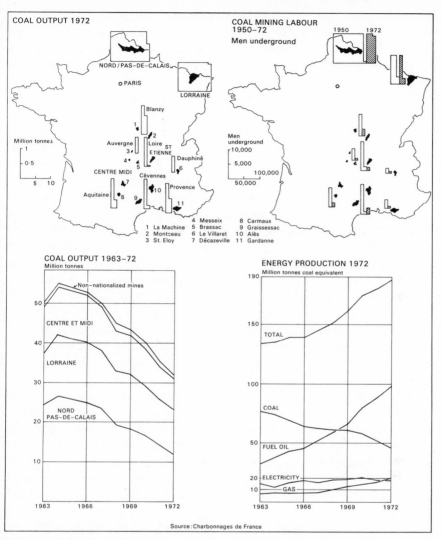

Figure 39   Energy production, coal output 1972; coal output 1963–72; coal mining labour 1950–72.

seams have been worked out, and the volume of proven reserves, though considerable, is unlikely to be intensively exploited at economic prices. Natural on-costs are high: mean depth of exploitation is 600 m (excluding opencast), compared with 60 m in the USA, and mean seam thickness 1.3 m (varying by coal basin from 1 m–4 m) compared with 1.3 m in the Ruhr and 1.27 m in the UK. The greatest physical disability lies in the contorted, faulted, or folded nature of coal-bearing strata, limiting mechanization and thus output per worker; only 20 per cent of output comes from seams with angles of less than 20°. The quality of coals includes a substantial ratio (68 per cent of output) of high volatile general purpose coals, with weak coking properties. This is particularly true for Lorraine, which thus had early recourse to imports from Belgium, later the Ruhr on a massive scale, and even the Netherlands, in preference to the Nord within France. Since electrification of the rail route from the Nord, more coke has been taken to Lorraine, whilst new technology is permitting some increase in Lorraine coals for coking purposes.

Government policies on coal pricing, at 3 centimes per thermie (th) energy value in the early 1970s, define the level below which pits and particular seams become unprofitable to work. During 1974 the coal market changed dramatically: the price of coking coal within the EEC doubled, imports of US coal increased three-fold, and coal from Poland and the USSR by 50 per cent. French coal prices were regionally aligned: coke in Nord-Pas-de-Calais was related to the import price of US and even Australian coal at Dunkerque; Lorraine-produced coke to the costs of that imported from the USA and Ruhr; coal supplied to EdF was price-controlled according to power station prices of the preceding year. In other words, free-market pricing, with little protection to the French producer, added to the problems of competing profitably against coal imports or other fuel sources.

Social constraints on French coal output relate to the poor underground working conditions in many pits, and the growing scarcity of mining labour arising from the dramatic run-down in numbers of those employed (112,000 1964; 42,100 1974). It is estimated that an additional 7–9000 miners are needed if output is to be sustained at anything near its present levels. In 1955 there were 22,000 Poles in the mining industry, reduced to 1471 in 1974; in 1964, almost 18,000 North Africans, but ten years later only 7113.

Given the collective constraints on French coal prospects, the 1975 Plan implies greater rationalization of production, on larger, more accessible reserves, particularly those in Lorraine. In marketing there will be concentration upon the needs of the steel industry and thermal power generation. Smaller outlying coalfields in the Massif Central and the Alpes will serve local needs, mainly for general-purpose coals, and production there will be limited by the scale of the regional market, and competitiveness with other locally-produced energy sources.

The social and economic problems arising from the run-down of

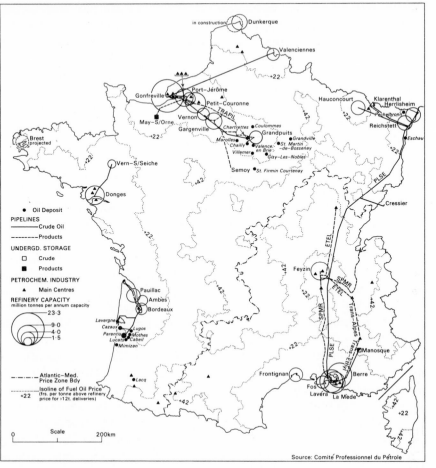

Figure 40   Oil production and distribution, 1973.

coalmining and the restructuring of coalfield economies (Thompson 1965A and B) are treated later (pp. 430–32).

REDUCTION IN OIL IMPORTS

Home production (fig. 40) is small in scale, about 1.5 Mt per annum, and known reserves are extremely limited. French exploration companies are actively seeking to diversify sources of oil supplies, including thus-far profitless prospecting in the western approaches to the Channel (Mer d'Iroise). Two-thirds of imported oil tonnage in 1972 came from the

Middle East, 16 per cent from North Africa and 11 per cent from Nigeria. Until 1958, Algerian oil had been within French sovereignty, but increasingly France became heavily dependent upon supplies which were vulnerable to political disruption (Comité du Pétrole 1972). By 1974, 56 per cent of the energy consumption in the country came from oil, and a massive investment had taken place in refineries, both coastal and inland, petrochemical plants and pipelines (fig. 40). Of 151 Mt of crude oil landed in 1974 (129 Mt for French markets), 55 Mt passed through Le Havre, 52 Mt through Lavéra (Etang de Berre)-Fos, plus 21 Mt in transit for the South European pipeline (PLSE), 6 Mt through Dunkerque and 5.5 Mt through Le Verdon (Gironde). For comparison, the largest UK refinery of that time, Fawley, processed only 16.2 Mt.

Inland distribution by pipeline includes the crude oil pipelines to Strasbourg and Karlsruhe (South European), with a branch to Lorraine: the local network in the Landes; the Basse-Seine-Paris; the Loire estuary (Donges-Vern sur Seiche); and Le Havre-Valenciennes. Products pipelines serve Lyon (SPMR, ETEL), the Alpes, and Basse-Seine-Paris (TRAPIL). The pipelines link coastal refineries to inland markets, but also to smaller satellite inland refineries, by the principle of 'refinery-clusters'. The mother refinery sends crude oil or products along the pipeline to satellites which have limited cracking facilities.

The boom in oil imports since 1961 has led to massive investments in infrastructure, all at commercial risk, with a profitability presently threatened by the high price levels for crude oil and the deliberate shift in national energy policy. Effects upon industrial location have been direct, in contribution to the creation of major coastal industrial complexes (Marseille-Fos-Etang de Berre; Basse-Seine; Dunkerque), see Part III, ch. 2. Indirectly, the availability of oil has permitted greater locational freedom for inland industrial siting, for the development of transport by rail, road, waterway and air, and for the domestic heating market. Nevertheless, there are clear pricing constraints on such locational freedoms. Crude oil at Strasbourg already costs 20 per cent more than at Marseille, whilst the zoning of fuel oil prices seen on fig. 40 clearly puts much of the Massif Central, the south-west Bassin Parisien and western Lorraine at some locational disadvantage. In general terms, the advent of oil has tended to confirm many industries in their industrial locations whilst giving a greater locational flexibility to some industries, but only in certain regions.

The effect of oil on the power station burn is seen in table 28. The rising contribution by oil is dramatic, whereas coal is now less important than primary gas plus nuclear-generated power. To gain maximum benefit from competing fuels, the power station mix varies regionally. Two-fuel or even

Table 28 Power station burn 1955–72

MTec	Total	Coal	Oil	Gas	Nuclear
1955	5.5	4.2	1.1	—	—
1965	13.2	7.0	4.3	1.4	0.3
1972	31.0	7.0	17.2	3.1	4.3

Source: EdF 1973

three-fuel stations are increasingly common to exploit regional energy budgets most effectively. For example, Bordeaux stations use refinery gas, fuel oil or natural gas; in other regions inputs of coal, fuel oil and/or natural gas are blended as appropriate during different periods.

Longer-term implications of oil costs and import limitations are likely to be most profound at the major coastal and industrial complexes, and in the more disseminated industrial sites and settlements fuelled by oil and reached by diesel rail or road transport.

MAXIMUM OUTPUT OF PRIMARY GAS

Natural gas is a very flexible cheap resource but, if it is to justify the major infrastructural investments of pipelines during what may be a short 30–40 year life of the fields in Aquitaine, it requires a mass consumption market with steady and continuous demand. Table 29 shows the switch from coal gas and refinery gas to natural gas during the past two decades. The Lacq discoveries in Aquitaine were made only in 1959 and have since had a profound effect on economic development in Midi-Pyrénées (Brunet 1958, Vanssay 1959). The gas exists at great depth (4000 m), with very high temperatures and pressures, and is contaminated by sulphur which nevertheless provides a valuable by-product. Since 1965 Algerian liquefied methane has been imported from the liquefaction centre at Skikda to the

Table 29   Consumption of gas, by origin, 1958–74

per cent	1958	1966	1974
coal gas	75.0	20.3	1.0
natural gas	12.8	51.8	94.5
refinery gas	11.6	27.9	4.5

Source: Gaz de France 1975

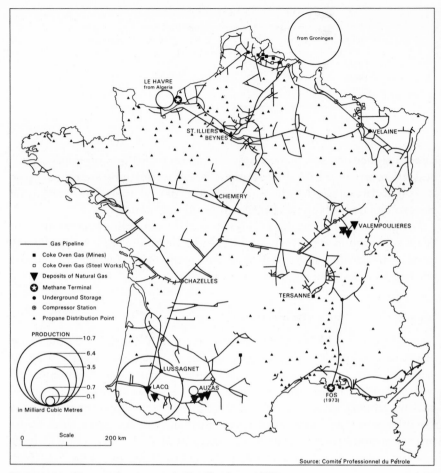

Figure 41   Gas production and distribution, 1973.

terminals at Le Havre and, since 1973, Fos, using specialized tankers. After the development of the major natural gas reserves in Groningen (Netherlands) there was a link-up by pipeline to the French network in 1966. In 1973, of 171 billion M cal consumed, 10 per cent of primary power in France, 69 came from Aquitaine, 82 from the Netherlands and 20 from Algeria (GdF 1974). Fig. 41 shows the natural gas system with its interconnected pipelines serving the major industrial and urban areas. Traditional gas sources in the Nord (coke-oven gas from the mines) and Lorraine (coke-oven gas from the steelworks) are indicated, together with the major underground storage reservoirs for natural gas in the Bassin

Parisien. The disseminated pattern of propane gas distribution points throughout rural France is a further striking feature.

In 1975 the energy planners programmed the contribution of natural gas to rise from 10 per cent to 15.5 per cent of national energy requirements within ten years. This necessarily involves most of the additional output coming from outside France. Already in 1975 long-term contracts had been signed with the USSR to raise the piped gas level from 2.5 to 4.0 billion m³, with North Sea producers (Ekofisk) for 2 million m³ from 1976 and a further 1 million m³ by 1978. The scale of the necessary investments is already so substantial that a European gas-purchasing consortium has been created to purchase long-term supplies from the Middle-East (Iran); in the meantime (1975) a pipeline from Algeria to Marseille has been agreed upon.

COMPLETION OF HEP DEVELOPMENT

Until about 1963 there was a general equilibrium between the power generated from thermal and hydraulic sources. The latter showed the greater year to year variation, dependent upon the precipitation and storage characteristics of the major upland and mountain catchments. In 1955 thermal power produced 25 TWh (Terawatt-hours), hydro power 25; in 1965 the figures were 55 and 47 respectively, but in 1972 115 and 49. This major growth in generation has been directly related to the satisfying of greatly increased demand by oil-fired power stations, and by a new technological generation of larger thermal stations with more powerful generating sets. In 1972 there were 10 conventional thermal stations plus 2 nuclear stations with installed capacities of more than 500 MW. In that same year, the most powerful hydro station, La Bâthie-Roselend, in the northern Alpes, had 522 MW installed, but Génissiat, the next most powerful, only 405 MW (EdF 1973).

Fig. 42 shows the electricity system of France with power stations classified by output in GWh (Gigawatt-hours, equal to 1/1,000th TWh), interlinked by the high tension transmission network at 225 kV and 380 kV. Monthly electricity flows show some expected and also some more surprising features. The flow of surplus power from the nuclear stations on the Loire to Paris is very striking, with an August minimum; blocks of power moving to Rhône-Alpes from the lower Rhône, with an autumn and winter peak, and from the northern Alpes towards Paris in the spring and autumn, are clearly to be seen. Short-term meeting of peak loads are, of course, concealed within the monthly figures. All-year balanced flows from Aquitaine towards Paris and the autumn and winter flows from Lorraine to Alsace are less expected. The virtual lack of any movement from the Nord-

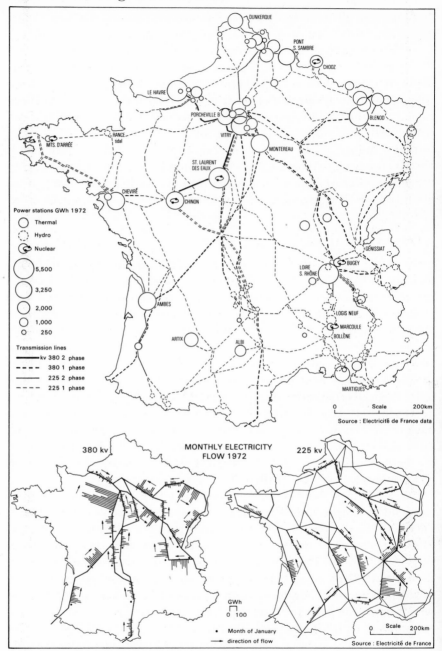

Figure 42   Electric power stations, more than 200 GWh output 1972, and transmission network; monthly electricity flow 1972.

Pas-de-Calais is striking confirmation of its self-contained electricity economy.

The geographical fundaments of the electricity economy and its progressive development are complex and cannot be adequately treated here (Rousseau 1970). Coal-based and port-orientated thermal power generation balanced the evolution of HEP generation which derived fullest benefit from the complementary nature of seasonal precipitation and snow-melt in the major upland provinces. In the Alpes and Pyrénées the spring snow-melt balanced the heavier autumn and early winter precipitation of the Massif Central. After a first generation of scattered small HEP stations in the Alpes and Pyrénées during the early twentieth century, attracting electro-chemical and electro-metallurgical plants to near the site of power production, there were two major advances: technical capacity to transfer electricity without unacceptable levels of loss in transmission; and the rationalization to a smaller number of larger-capacity hydro-stations as the power potential became exploited in a more rational fashion with higher levels of technology. After 1948, EdF systematically programmed the progressive realization of hydro-power potential within, and even be-tween, each catchment. Alpine and Pyrenean valleys were occupied by series of major storage reservoirs; in the Massif Central similar interlinked chains of reservoirs were built to exploit the principal westward-flowing rivers. The Rhine and Rhône (CNR) were harnessed by multi-purpose navigation, flood-control, power generation and, in the case of the lower Rhône, irrigation schemes (p. 408). Thus, by the end of the VIth Plan, virtually all large river sites had been exploited and suitable dam sites exhausted: on the Rhône the works at Péage de Roussillon (to be operational early 1978) and Vaugris (by 1980) remain to be completed. In spite of the interesting tidal power station on the Rance, this form of energy is unlikely to be competitive and, indeed, overall HEP is a relatively expensive energy source. HEP is likely to be a contributor to servicing base and middle load in its regions of generation and to meeting peak load in more distant areas at particularly favourable coincidence of supply and demand. For this reason installed turbining capacity is often greater than normal through-flow can exploit.

THE NUCLEAR POWER PROGRAMME

The generation of commercial nuclear power in France goes back to the IVth Plan (1962–5). What has been proposed in the 1975 energy plan is no less than to increase the contribution of nuclear power from 4.3 MTec in 1974 to as much as 90 MTec by 1984, or one-quarter of all energy then produced. Doubt has already been expressed as to the feasibility of such an immense investment programme, and also as to its technological prospects. Even if a fair proportion of the proposed 40 nuclear power stations is built, each of about 1000 MW installed capacity, the regional pattern of energy output will be radically transformed. The potential implications for sectoral development of the economy and for regional and urban planning are indeed dramatic. Geographical implications include the sources of supply, movement and processing of uranium, the fuel source; the distribution of nuclear power stations; the direct and indirect multiplier effects on localities and regions; environmental problems, including those relating to pollution of air and water; the cost competitiveness of alternative nuclear technologies, in respect of the unit costs of power produced and their relationships to conventional power costs.

With an annual output of about 60,000 tonnes metal content, from deposits in Vendée, Limousin and Forez, France commands about 5 per cent of known world reserves of uranium. The ore is concentrated on site, further treated at Malvesi (Aude), then to Pierrelatte, abroad, back to Pierrelatte and finally converted to fuel elements at Romans (Isère). After being burnt in the reactors, the spent elements travel to La Hague (Cotentin) for extraction of plutonium, which then goes to Cadarache in the Rhône valley for manufacture of further fuel elements. In 1974 a French-Belgian-Spanish-Italian factory was started at Tricastin (EURODIF) on the Rhône (adjacent to the Pierrelatte atomic centre) to produce enough enriched uranium by 1980 to fuel 100 power stations. For the present, however, enriched uranium is also imported from the USA and the USSR.

The location of first generation nuclear power stations was partly for strategic reasons, but the great demands for process water and regional planning interests were also important (Soumagne 1973). Apart from Marcoule (1956–9) in the Rhône valley, established primarily to produce plutonium for weapons, the principal commercial stations (also producing plutonium) in the first generation were located in the middle Loire valley: at Chinon, 3 stations 1963–6 (EdF 1 70 MW, EdF 2 200 MW, EdF 3 480 MW); at St Laurent-des-Eaux, 2 stations 1969, 1971 (combined capacity 995 MW). The Loire valley is remote from the major solid fuel producing areas and also the major hydro-power sites. Nuclear power generation there thus aids the policy of improving the balance of regional energy budgets and also provides some contribution to local professional and managerial employment. The Loire stations are based on natural uranium (238) in a gas-cooled graphite-moderated reactor, similar to the HTGR technology of UK nuclear stations. A further station was opened at Bugey

(540 MW) in the Alpes during 1972, an interesting indication that, with virtual maximum use of available hydro-power and its irregular peak availability, nuclear power generation may increasingly be needed for meeting the demands of local electro-chemical and electro-metallurgical industries. Experimental reactors are in production at Brennilis (1967, Bretagne) 70 MW capacity, using a heavy water process, Chooz (1967, Ardennes) 266 MW, using a light water-enriched uranium process. At Tihange in Belgium (1974) a joint French-Belgian project is to generate 870 MW, the first of the larger-scale plants.

In 1970 EdF was given authority to build nuclear power stations using enriched uranium (235). The new technology is a break with the past, using enriched uranium in either a pressurised water (Westinghouse), which is the most favoured, or boiling water (GEC) process. The 250 MW prototype fast-breeder reactor, Phénix, was connected to the national grid in 1974, but its technology remains experimental. The second generation of PWR and BWR is to be the basis for the remarkable proliferation of nuclear power stations envisaged in the 1975 energy plan. The proposal is to build 22 reactors, each of 1000 MW capacity, by 1981 (13 were to be started 1974–5), 18 of similar capacity by 1985, and an even larger programme by the end of the century. If fully achieved, this programme, estimated to save the equivalent of 65 million tonnes of oil, would produce 50 per cent of French electricity energy by the year 2000, on the assumption of a doubling of energy consumption. 40–50 sites would be developed and it is possible that their location could play a vital role in promoting regional energy balance, and also in the management of growth in the urban hierarchy. Of 22 regional economic councils, 10 have voted in favour of locating reactors in their regions, others have reservations on environmental grounds, and 3 have voted against (Languedoc-Roussillon, Provence-Côte d'Azur, and Port-la-Nouvelle (Aude)).

The short-term impact of nuclear power station building on local economies is considerable, during a 5–10 year construction period. 1500–2000 workers are needed on site, with important multiplier effects on the local job market and upon services. These effects are particularly pronounced in rural areas, as they had been at an earlier stage in the establishment of barrages and HEP stations in the Alpes, Pyrénées and the Massif Central. On completion of construction, the risk is that out-migration is stimulated, with local men moving on with the migrating gangs. The permanent resident labour-force required to operate the power station is perhaps 200–300, but it includes a high ratio of skilled and highly-paid staff. The multiplier effect on the regional economy in the longer term may not be great. There is little likelihood of industry being attracted to the

Table 30 Comparative costs of thermal power
generation, nuclear and fuel oil, 1975

price per kWh (centimes)	fuel oil	nuclear
Investment	1.83	3.15
Exploitation	1.11	1.18
Fuel	7.90	1.67
Total	10.84	6.00

Source: Le Monde, 9 *avril,* 1975

vicinity of the power station and tourism may even be repelled.

The relative economies of nuclear power generation vis-à-vis conventional thermal generation are constantly changing. Table 30 shows the 1975 comparison, but, significantly, the investment costs in building nuclear stations have been rising more rapidly than for conventional ones. Moreover, technological teething troubles have plagued nuclear power, as in the UK. On the other hand, the rises in oil prices and the continuing threat of political vulnerability introduce long-term uncertainties to the other side of the equation.

In short, French energy planning now relates to a slowing-down in national growth momentum, and intends a major shift within energy sources, developing indigenous nuclear power and natural gas to the maximum possible extent. The political and economic vulnerability of oil imports is to be diminished and the costs of such change to be borne by commercial firms in the oil industry. Energy availability is seen as a powerful stimulus to national, regional and local planning, down even to the provision of a low tension electricity network or propane gas supplies to rural areas. Location of nuclear stations, as in the USA, will in future have an important role in the management of the urban network. Increasingly, however, the French energy problems will have to be treated within long-term international agreements, in the EEC and in a wider framework of world suppliers. In the process, the traditional geography of energy and of economic development in France stands to be profoundly modified.

References

General
Ardagh, J. (1968) *The New France*, Harmondsworth.
Carré, J.-J., Dubois, P. and Malinvaud, E. (1972) *La croissance française. Un essai d'analyse économique causale d'après-guerre.*

Cazes, G. and Reynaud, A. (1973) *Les mutations récentes de l'économie française.*

Guibert, B. *et al.* (1975) 'La mutation industrielle de la France. Du traité de Rome à la crise pétrolière', *INSEE E* 31–2, 2 vols.

Communications

Audant, J. and Béthémont, J. (1973) 'La navigation rhodanienne en 1972: un constat en fin de siècle', *Revue Géogr. Lyon*, 48 (4): 317–29.

Auphan, E. (1975) 'Les noeuds ferroviaires, phénomène résiduel ou points forts de l'espace régional?', *L'Espace géogr.*, IV (2): 127–40.

Bakis, H. (1975) 'Téléinformatique et disparités régionales en France', *L'Espace géogr.*, IV (2): 141–8.

Bayliss, B. T. (1965) *European Transport*, London.

Caralp, R. (1967) 'Les tarifications ferroviaires de marchandise et les économies régionales', *Annls Géogr.*, LXXVI (415): 305–15.

Comby, J. (1971) 'Autoroutes, rivalités urbaines et régions de programme', *Norois*, 72: 724–9.

Délégation générale au District de la Région de Paris (1965) *Schéma directeur d'aménagement et d'urbanisme de la région de Paris.*

Despicht, N. (1964) *Policies for Transport in the Common Market*, Sidcup.
(1969), 'The Transport Policy of the European Communities', *PEP European Series* 12, London.

Devaux, P. (1971) *Les chemins de fer.*

Labasse, J. (1971) 'Le réseau autoroutier français', *Revue Géogr. Montr.*, XXV (3): 235–44.
(1972) 'L'aéroport et la géographie volontaire des villes', *Annls Géogr.*, LXXXI (445): 278–97.

Laborde, P. (1973) 'Le télex, un aspect mal connu de la vie des nations', *Annls Géogr.*, LXXXII (449): 193–207.

La Documentation Française (1962) 'Les grandes liaisons routières. Histoire d'un schéma', *Travaux et Recherches de Prospective*, 31.
(1972) 'Eléments pour un Schéma Directeur de l'équipement aéronautique', *Travaux et Recherches de Prospective*, 25.
(1973) 'Services nouveaux de télécommunications', *Travaux et Recherches de Prospective*, 42.

Martin, J. E. (1974) 'Some effects of the canalization of the Moselle', *Geogr.*, 59: 298–308.

Merlin, P. (1966) *Les transports parisiens.*

Minist. des Transports (1969) 'Où va la politique des transports?', *SNCF Eléments d'Information.*

Morice, L. (1968) 'Les transports fluviaux', *Que sais-je?* 494.

Paré, S. (1974) 'Les disparités régionales de l'informatique française', *Annls Géogr.*, LXXXIII (456): 173–89.

Schnetzler, J. (1967) 'Le chemin de fer et l'espace français', *Revue Géogr. Lyon*, 42 (1): 81–118.

Sec. Général du Gouvernement (1962) 'L'axe de transport par voie d'eau entre le Nord-Est de la France et la Méditerranée', *Notes et Etudes Documentaires*, 2874.

(1964) 'Les transports routiers en France', *Notes et Etudes Documentaires*, 3146.
(1966) 'Les ports maritimes de commerce en France', *Notes et Etudes Documentaires*, 3290.
(1971) 'L'aménagement du Rhône', *Notes et Etudes Documentaires*, 3842–3.
Spill, C. (1973) 'Le transport aérien et la région', *Annls Géogr.*, LXXXII, (451): 316–30.
Spill, J. M. (1974) 'Le réseau aérien complémentaire en France', *Acta géogr. Paris*, 14–15: 13–31.
Wickham, S. (1962) 'Development of French Railways under the French 4 year Plans', *Bull. Oxford Inst. Statistics*, 24 (1): 167–84.
Wolkowitsch, M. (1959) *L'économie régionale des transports dans le Centre et le Centre-Ouest de la France.*

Energy
Brunet, R. (1958) 'Lacq, le pétrole et le Sud-Ouest', *Revue géogr. Pyrénées et Sud-Ouest*, XXIX: 351–74.
Charbonnages de France (1974) *Rapport au gestion.*
(1975) *Statistique annuelle.*
Comité Professionel du Pétrole (1972) *Pétrole 1972.*
Commissariat Général du Plan (1971) *Rapport de la Commission: Energie.*
(1972) *L'Energie*, Plan et Prospectives.
Electricité de France (1973) *Statistiques de la Production et de la Consommation* 1972.
Félice, J de (1958) 'Energie électrique et aménagement du territoire', *Revue fr. Energ.*, 93: 155–61.
Gamblin, A. (1968) *L'énergie en France. Etude de géographie.*
Gautier, M. (1968) 'L'énergie dans la région de programme dite de Bretagne', *Norois*, 58: 253–67.
Gaz de France (1974) *Annual Report.*
George, P. (1973) *France — A Geographical Study*, London.
Médina, E. (1975) 'Consommations d'énergie, essai de comparaisons internationales', *Econ. et Statistique*, 66: 3–21.
Novel, P. (1970) 'Le charbon et l'énergie en France', *L'Administration Nouvelle.*
Rousseau, H. (1970) 'L'électricité en France', *Que sais-je?*, 59.
Soumagne, J. (1973) 'Problèmes géographiques de l'énergie nucléaire en France', *L'Information géogr.*, 37 (1): 43–51.
Thompson, I. B. (1965A) 'A geographical appraisal of recent trends in the coal basin of Northern France', *Geogr.*, 50 (3): 252–60.
(1965B) 'A review of problems of economic and urban development in the Northern coalfield of France', *Southampton Res. Ser. in Geogr.*, 1: 31–60.
Vanssay, R. de (1959) 'Le gaz de Lacq au service de l'économie du Centre-Est', *Revue Géogr. Lyon*, XXXIV (3): 285–90.

2 Employment location policies and the market

At the heart of regional planning policies and practice in France, as in Britain, lies the proposition that it is through action on the structure and/or the distribution of employment that progress may be most directly made and measured. This politically convenient assumption relates to the relief of unemployment (never as prominently a regional policy objective in France as in Britain), the influencing of interregional migration flows, the correcting of regional or urban/rural imbalances, or a better allocation of the benefits of growth among classes as well as between areas. A second underlying assumption is that a range of effective public policies can be devised, implemented, and monitored to achieve at least some part of all these objectives. In France there have now been two decades of such policy-making (Simonetti 1977), in contrast to just over forty years of comparable public involvement in British regional problems. Employment location policies by government action may be operated directly, through measures to control or to stimulate development and change at the level of individual firms, entrepreneurs or localities, or indirectly through fiscal or monetary measures, or the provision of an infrastructure of communications, energy sources, housing or other utilities. By contrast with Britain (House 1977), French government policies have stressed inducements far more than constraints upon entrepreneurs, logical in a more market-orientated economy, and there has been greater emphasis upon indirect rather than direct intervention. Such an orientation of policy in France recognized early that, to be effective, public policies needed to work within and not clean contrary to market forces. In classical economic theory market forces are working to restore equilibrium, through equalizing flows of capital and labour, reducing differences between regions and among towns and cities. On the other hand, the economic growth theories of Myrdal (1957) emphasize that though such equalizing flows, or 'spread' effects, may work towards equilibrium, they may be more than offset by adverse 'backwash' effects, further polarizing growth and accentuating differences. Hirschman (1958) disputed that regions become less equal through time.

Any assessment of the effectiveness or the geographical impact of public location policies faces many difficulties. What would have been the state of the urban and regional system without government intervention? What are the truly formative elements in urban and regional change and how do the roles of manufacturing and the tertiary sectors compare in these processes? In particular, do leading firms or leading industries or activities play a pioneering role (Marnet-Leymarie 1974)? What part does urbanization play in the course of regional or national economic change? Does it precede or follow upon such change? Of particular importance to geographers is the further question—does effective government location policy require spatial as well as structural (sectoral) mobility, i.e. is actual territorial movement of firms necessary and to what extent? If economic change can be promoted or steered through regional or urban management policies, what are to be the preferred forms for such allocations, and what is the role of growth centres, poles, axes, corridors, or 'anchor points' in all this? Apart from difficulties inherent in the available data, further distortions in interpretation are often introduced by the arbitrary nature of the areal units for which it is published. The final problem, well-known to British regional planners, is that of determining the relative importance of economic structure, and of location or accessibility as ingredients in regional problems.

Under the Vth Plan (1966–70) the government entered into planning agreements with groups of leader firms in certain key industries, as part of the policy of transforming the economic structure and aiding in the rationalization of firms. The principal agreements covered: steel (*Plan Acier*), computer manufacture (*Plan Calcul*), shipbuilding (1968), aircraft (Caravelle, Concorde, Airbus and Mercure projects), aerospace (European cooperation, *Programme Espace*). Such government-industry planning has continued through to the more difficult economic times of the mid- to late-1970s.

The analysis of public policies on location, in the context of the market, will be in the following stages: the structure of economic growth and change, and its spatial manifestation in patterns of entrepreneurial activity; secondly, a separation into mining and manufacturing (secondary sector), and tertiary activities, for convenience and for assessment of the different elements of public policy. In considering the secondary sector, correlations between growth, change and mobility are attempted; for the tertiary sector, in addition, the potential for mobility and attitudes to mobility will be stressed. Thereafter public policies on location and mobility will be reviewed and their geographical impact assessed through a separate consideration, for the secondary and tertiary sectors, before attempting a brief overall assessment.

Fig. 31 shows the structure of employment change, 1954–71, and its salient points have been outlined in Part I, ch. 4. It remains here to comment additionally that changes in employment, though perhaps the most useful general-purpose barometer of wider economic changes, may be misleading if divorced from other criteria for measuring such change. Such other criteria include floorspace occupied, value added, profitability and so forth. For present purposes it is sufficient to stress that 'growth' industries or tertiary activities are not necessarily, and perhaps decreasingly are, labour-intensive; conversely, not all additional employment gained by a city or region is necessarily beneficial if it is in labour-intensive but 'non-growth' activities. For example, among the fast-growth groups on fig. 31, petroleum products and chemicals are not labour-intensive, whilst vehicles, electrical and electronic manufactures, machinery and printing are variously so. On the other hand, and it is a characteristic regional policy-makers should not ignore, the fastest and most substantial growth in the tertiary branches involves almost exclusively labour-intensive activities. Unfortunately, but almost universally, the fast-decline employment groups, agriculture, coal and coke, textiles, clothing and leather goods, are all labour-intensive, with a correspondingly sharp impact upon local and regional unemployment. Among slow growth manufactures and services, most are disseminated geographically, and only shipbuilding (in the UK a fast decline industry) and aircraft manufacture are concentrated. On the other hand, the slow decline sectors include iron and steel, in which there have been major post-1945 relocations of capacity (fig. 51), and the labour-intensive domestic service group (long a fast decline group in Britain).

Figs. 43 to 53 (inclusive) illustrate the detailed patterns of location of the major branches of *manufacturing*. With exception of figs. 44, 46 and 51, all the diagrams are drawn at the same scale and with a common key to employment numbers, facilitating direct visual cross-comparison of the geographical patterns. These patterns are derived from the 1966 Industrial Census, the last to have such a detailed geographical breakdown. Since 1966 considerable further industrialization has taken place, but the series of figures provides a datum-plane from which later changes can be assessed. In the light of government policies for decentralizing activities from Paris, supporting the deprived western half of France and aiding reconversion of the industrial regions of the Nord, Lorraine and Alsace, the patterns shown illustrate the orders of magnitude in territorial employment mobility that might be necessary to fulfil these objectives. Finally, the patterns have been grouped so that each four diagrams indicate interrelated activities, linked by stages in processing, or by labour skills possessed in common. Attempts to decentralize employment or to reach a better regional balance of economic growth and diversification in structure must necessarily bear such linkages particularly in mind. Furthermore, in the light of such linkages, existing locational ties may be either weaker or stronger at the production stages. All such patterns and the possibility of modifying them through public policy must be related to concepts of marketing space, to differential transfer as well as to production costs which may arise from relocation of activities. In short, growth and change in employment may take place structurally 'in situ', by differential trends affecting particular localities, or spatially, involving diffusion of employment, perhaps transplantation of firms, or equally cases of closures. The ability of public location policies to influence patterns of employment in a preferred regional reallocation strategy thus depends especially upon those firms, industry groups or tertiary activities which combine economic growth with new job provision and a capacity to relocate further branches of production with the least economic detriment, whether such detriment be actual or merely perceived by the entrepreneur.

Foreign capital and 'know-how' has played an important role in implanting growth industries in postwar France (Guibert *et al.* 1975, 81). Such foreign investment has been concentrated in the more dynamic industrial sectors (petrochemicals, iron and steel, agricultural machinery, machine tools, electrical and electronics) and notably in larger firms or factories, e.g. two-thirds of electrical and electronics investment by foreigners in 1970 was in plants employing more than 1000. Of the 10.7 per cent of the French labour force in foreign firms, 4.6 per cent were in American-owned and 4.7 per cent in firms from the EEC of the 6. In general locational preferences France west of a line from Le Havre to Marseille stands out clearly, together with Ile-de-France, Centre and Côte d'Azur. In such a pattern a balance of forces is evidently operating: market-influenced towards the most affluent areas and the largest markets, in contrast to government-influenced in direction of the Ouest. It would seem that in general foreign firms have responded by going only the minimum required distance.

STRUCTURAL AND SPATIAL MOBILITY

The classification of manufacturing industries according to their structural and spatial mobility performance and potentials has been adapted from a recent French study (Noël 1974). For the period 1954–68 four principal types were identified: I 'growth' industries with a rising momentum of spatial mobility, and thus of particular importance for regional planners; II industries showing a sharp decline in employment and, characteristically, though not universally, a rootedness in place; III slow growth industries, with limited or stagnant mobility potential; and IV slow or fast decline industries which, anomalously, have shown increasing spatial mobility.

I Mobile growth industries

As in Britain the *motor-car* industry (figs. 43 and 44) in France has led in employment growth and export earnings since the late-1940s (La DF

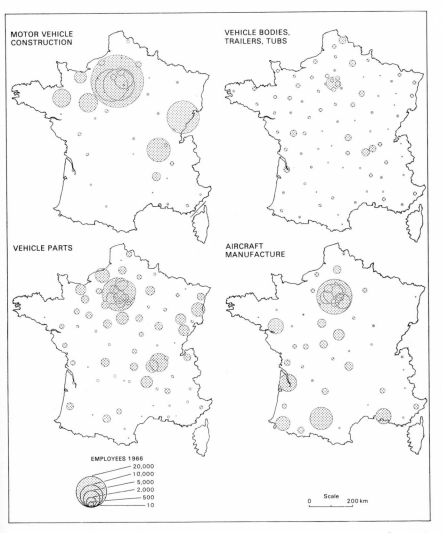

Figure 43   Motor-vehicle construction; vehicle bodies and parts; aircraft manufacture, 1966.

1971B). Inevitably in both countries major new capacity has had to be created, giving a unique opportunity to persuade large-scale entrepreneurs to decentralize new factories to locations beneficial to regional policy. In France the major car producer, Renault, has been nationalized for most of the postwar period, but there is little evidence that this has led to locational decisions other than on sound commercial grounds. It is possible to argue, however, that the chain of new Renault plants downstream from Paris, linked to exports, reinforces the planned industrial growth axis of the Basse-Seine (Part III, ch. 2). An overall assessment of the impact of changing spatial patterns in the car industry is difficult, not least because of

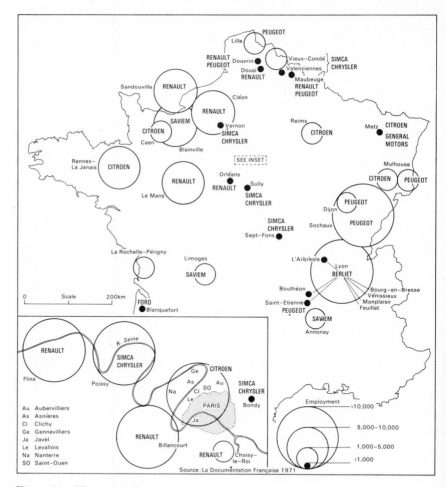

Figure 44   The car industry.

the recurrent recessions of the early 1970s, which are threatening the viability, not only the profitability, of even the larger, traditional centres of car manufacturing. In the mid-1950s the road vehicle industry was strikingly concentrated in and around Paris. Only Peugeot at Sochaux-Montbéliard and Saviem (lorries) at Lyon were substantial producers in the provinces and Renault had only one factory outside Paris, for the manufacture of tractors at Le Mans. Fig. 44 shows a remarkable transformation in the geographical pattern of production (1955 150,000 jobs in Ile-de-France, 79,000 in the provinces; in 1970 183,000 in Ile-de-France and 229,000 in the provinces). Indeed, since 1955 no fewer than 36 car construction plants have been located in the provinces (Durand 1972). Each major company has followed a spatial planning strategy, often in consultation with the government. Nationalized manufacturers, e.g. Renault with Saviem and Berliet, have been more directly influenced by public location policies.

Renault has developed along the Basse-Seine axis with plants at Le Havre, Cléon (Elboeuf), but also in the Nord reconversion region at Douai. Machine shops have been opened at Ruitz (Nord), for the manufacture of gear-boxes at Orléans; a foundry has been built at Lorient, and a rubber factory at Nantes, whilst the prewar plant at Le Mans has been expanded and equipped with assembly lines. Citroën has followed an even more disseminated strategy with a new assembly plant at Rennes, manufacture of gear-boxes at Metz, machine shops at Caen and a foundry at Charleville. Simca (Chrysler) has added to the Paris factory an assembly plant at Bouchain near Valenciennes, and a parts factory at La Rochelle (St Julien 1971). Peugeot built new capacity at Mulhouse, Vésoul and St-Etienne, whilst the two major (nationalized) lorry manufacturing firms also decentralized: Saviem totally to Caen, Annonay and Limoges; Berliet established new factories at Bourg-en-Bresse, St-Etienne and L'Arbresle, all within the regional hinterland of the parent plants in Lyon.

The linkages between vehicle assembly plants and components manufacture are complex, but production of the latter is generally disseminated among major engineering subregions (Nwafor 1974). Even so, the flows of components, even within individual firms, are now much more complex and widespread than twenty years ago. It remains to be seen whether the decentralized pattern of vehicle manufacturing, readily achieved during a period of sustained fast growth, will prove enduring now that world-wide recession has struck the industry.

Figs. 45 and 46 show the fast-growth *electrical and electronics* manufacturing group (La DF 1963). As in the UK, the heavy branches are located in major subregional engineering centres as well as in the capital city, but it is

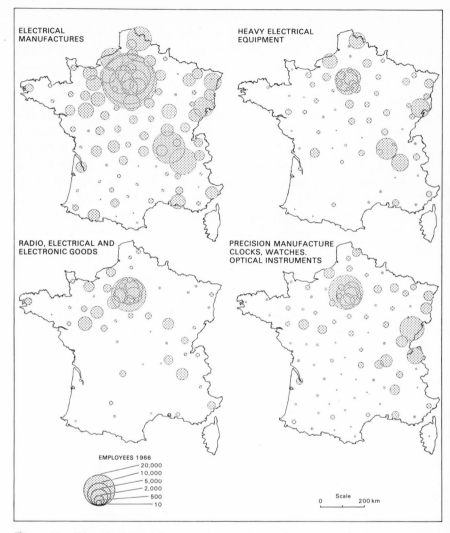

Figure 45   Electrical manufactures; heavy electrical equipment; radio, electrical and electronic goods; precision manufactures, 1966.

the lighter branches which have grown most rapidly and, because they have had high value per unit of weight and bulk, have proved particularly useful in support of decentralization policies. Taking only the *electronics* industry (fig. 46) as an example, the concentration of more than two-thirds of all jobs in Paris during the mid-1950s has now been substantially broken down; Bretagne, Poitou and Basse-Normandie have all benefited. The de-

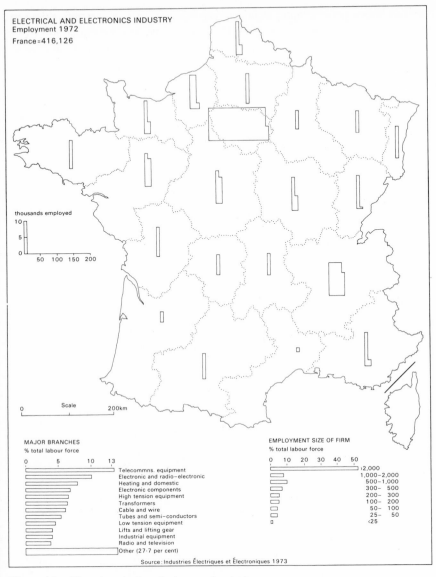

ELECTRICAL AND ELECTRONICS INDUSTRY
Employment 1972
France=416,126

thousands employed

MAJOR BRANCHES
% total labour force

0   5   10   13

Telecommns. equipment
Electronic and radio–electronic
Heating and domestic
Electronic components
High tension equipment
Transformers
Cable and wire
Tubes and semi–conductors
Low tension equipment
Lifts and lifting gear
Industrial equipment
Radio and television
Other (27·7 per cent)

EMPLOYMENT SIZE OF FIRM
% total labour force

0   10   20   30   40   50

>2,000
1,000–2,000
500–1,000
300– 500
200– 300
100– 200
50– 100
25–   50
<25

Source : Industries Électriques et Électroniques 1973

Figure 46   The electrical and electronics industry.

centralization to Bretagne of some 12,000 jobs, including many for women, has been related to three growth poles: Lannion, around the CNET laboratories as a decentralized research establishment; Brest; and Rennes. In all cases the multiplier effect on other jobs and the agglomeration of further firms, for example, in telephone manufacture, electronic tubes and semi-conductors, has added to the benefits of the original transplantations.

In 1954 116,020 jobs in electrical manufactures were in Ile-de-France, 88,220 in the provinces; in 1972 the figures had changed dramatically to 174,175 and 241,950 respectively. Electrical manufactures have proved to be an effective seed-bed for decentralization policy, but there have been difficult problems of education and retraining to overcome, and movement

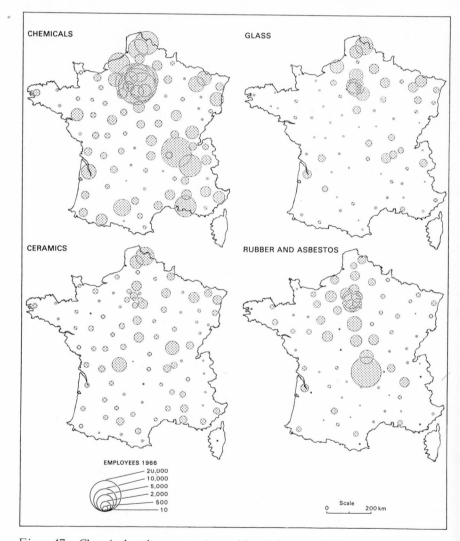

Figure 47   Chemicals, glass, ceramics, rubber/asbestos, 1966.

of a necessary nucleus of highly-skilled workers from Paris to the provinces
has not been easily achieved. The 13 per cent of the market for electronic
and electrical goods which is in the public sector enables the state to
influence many firms intending to expand.

The *chemicals* industry (fig. 47) is extremely variegated with locationally-
tied heavy branches: petrochemicals in port locations or at inland refineries;

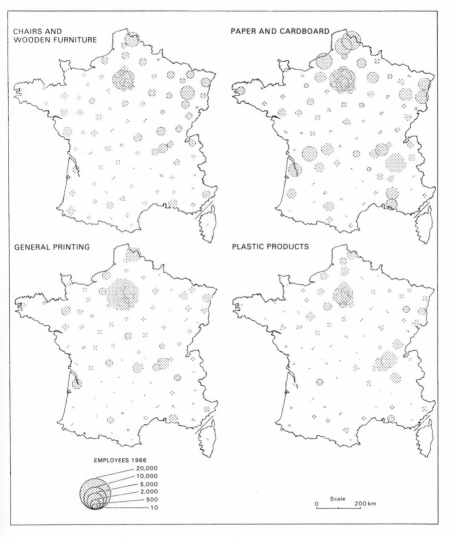

Figure 48   Chairs and wooden furniture; paper and cardboard; general
printing; plastic products, 1966.

coalfield-based complexes; electro-chemical and electro-metallurgical plants in the Alpine and Pyrenean valleys. Lighter branches traditionally concentrated in and around Paris, though there were some centres of marked specialization (e.g. Limoges in ceramics, Clermont-Ferrand in rubber). The impact of chemical industry expansion on regional policies has been limited because many branches are capital- rather than labour-intensive, and there is a strong tendency for new capacity to be located either adjacent to existing centres of manufacture or close to the market. Fig. 48 shows the disseminated pattern of employment in the fast-growth groups of paper and cardboard, printing and plastic products (Bouclier and David 1967). These consumer-orientated branches of chemicals clearly relate directly to the marketing needs of the urban population, both in terms of numbers and also in sophistication of demands.

Almost as polygamous as the chemical industry, the manufacture of machinery (fig. 49) has equally variable potential for further growth and spatial mobility. The fast-changing and rapidly-widening product range has enabled a breakaway from traditional locational ties (coalmining, textile, agriculture, railways for specialized machinery ranges). With vehicles and electrical manufactures light-engineering has proved the third employment sector to respond most directly and substantially to the needs of regional policy. The availability of locally-skilled engineering labour has with time ceased to be a vital locational factor, with an increasing number of women employed and also the spread of automation. Training of semi-skilled operatives often takes but a matter of weeks. Overall in engineering the shift in the balance of jobs between Ile-de-France (IdF) and the provinces is most marked: 1954 IdF 401,660, provinces 604,900; 1968 IdF 426,060, provinces 916,460.

II Fast employment decline, with limited mobility

Locationally constrained by the resources of the soil and subsoil, this category includes, most simply and importantly, agriculture and coalmining. The run-down in mining labour was discussed in Part I, ch. 4 and in Part II, ch. 1; the problem of marginal mining subregions, within the context of industrial reconversion, is treated in Part III.

Though agriculture today contributes only 6 per cent of French GNP and employs a declining 12 per cent of the active population, the remarkable transformations of the rural economy over the past three decades have produced a wide and diversified spectrum of planning problems at all scales from national, through regional and subregional, to the parochial level. The effects of agricultural change on demography, particularly on migration flows, were dealt with in Part I, ch. 4; the problems of rural

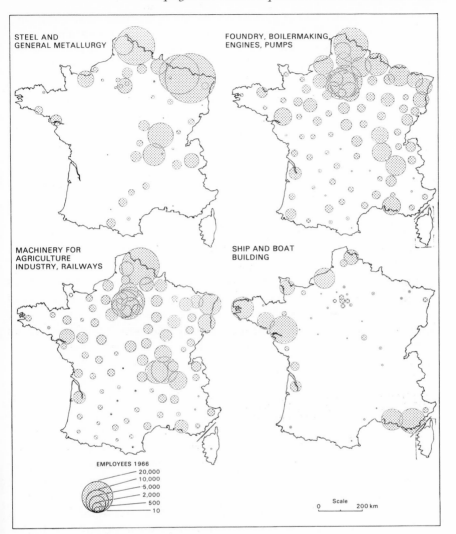

Figure 49 Steel and general metallurgy; foundry, boiler-making, engines, pumps; machinery for agriculture, industry, railways; ship and boat building, 1966.

problem region planning and general management of rural space are left to Part III, ch. 3. Here a brief consideration of the salient features of change and their planning implications must suffice.

Fig. 8 showed the outline land classification of France; fig. 54a shows the reflection of land quality in the value of farmland. Apart from the natural endowment, value relates also to the nature and profitability of farming systems, the size and capitalization of farm-holdings, and entrepreneurial efficiency. On all these counts agriculture in France is extremely diverse and has evolved rapidly during the past thirty years. The relationship between man and land, however, is even more complex, since the numbers in rural areas are rarely in equilibrium with employment opportunities, past or present. In many parts of France there is still a surplus of rural labour in spite of a long history of rural depopulation (Part I, ch. 4).

The problems of French farming may be briefly summarized under five headings (Cazes and Reynaud 1973): technical change, weak economic organization, social malaise, shifts in public agricultural policy, and the context of change in the rural economy. These problems had to be faced in postwar Britain, but the peasant here had long been replaced by the small commercial farmer, land restructuring had progressed further and farm systems were better attuned to both environmental potential and the conditions of demand in a large-scale urban market. In France postwar change has been more traumatic: on the credit side, massive increases in quantum output, productivity per unit area and yield have been achieved with a sharply diminished labour force. This has been made possible by application of fertilizers, seed and animal selection, together with an appropriate level of mechanization and inputs of capital. Stock-rearing now accounts for 57 per cent of agricultural output by value and the surface under arable has diminished accordingly (1963 18.9 million ha. arable, 13.1 m ha. permanent pasture; in 1973 respectively 16.7 and 13.7 million ha.). At the same time there has also been a specialization according to natural comparative advantage (e.g. vines, market garden and horticulture, sugar beets, maize) wherever ecological conditions were particularly suitable.

French farmers have usually been small-scale in production, in productivity per unit area, and in size of holding compared with their West European counterparts. The mean size of farm-holding is 18.8 ha. (fig. 54c), with small-holdings characteristic of the intensive agriculture of the Midi, the valley lands of the mountains and uplands, and the Breton peninsula. Conversely, the large, well-equipped farms are found predominantly in the Bassin Parisien. Unfortunately, but not perhaps surprisingly, owner occupation of farms is dominant in the Midi and the Sud Ouest, regions plagued by excessive land subdivision.

Postwar French farm production has been periodically but persistently affected by large surpluses, of wine, wheat, sugar beet and dairy products in particular. This has in part been true for all of Western Europe, but in France the position was made worse by the myriad small farms in many lines of production, allied with archaic forms of marketing organization,

and a lack of sufficiently well-developed food processing industries
appropriately located. To the instability of production and marketing,
which have periodically led to violent reactions among wine-growers and
market-gardeners, there are to be added the social problems of life on the
land: out-migration of the younger and more able, household income levels
only one-half to two-thirds of those of the towns, poorer housing,

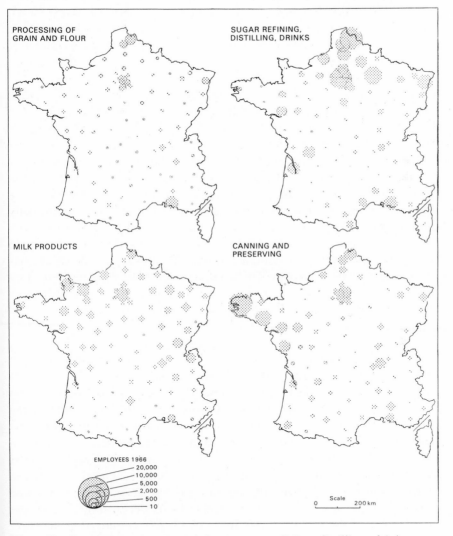

Figure 50   Processing of grain and flour; sugar-refining, distilling, drinks;
milk products; canning and preserving, 1966.

inadequate social or educational provision. Yet it is difficult to generalize upon these conditions, which in the complex rural economies of France may vary within very short distances.

In their rural renovation policies (Part III, ch. 3) successive French governments have sought to diminish built-in economic and social inequalities and to diversify the rural economy, by the introduction of industries (fig. 50), tourism (where appropriate), whilst at the same time tackling the major and widespread problem of modernizing both farms, farming systems and marketing methods. Increasingly and perforce, these more direct agricultural changes have had to be seen within the context of EEC farm policies.

III *Slow employment increase, but declining mobility*

This category includes the building industry, metal-working, glass (fig. 47), ships (fig. 49; La DF 1960) and aircraft (fig. 43), together with the food-processing industries (fig. 50). Except for the coastally- or waterway-tied locations of shipbuilding, with an important part of the national output coming from the industrially weak Ouest region, most industries in the slow growth limited-mobility group are already disseminated very widely throughout France. The aircraft industry (La DF 1971A), traditionally concentrated in and around Paris, benefited from decentralization even before 1939, on strategic grounds, to the Sud-Ouest and Ouest. Since 1945 the aircraft and aerospace complex around Toulouse (Sud Aviation) has been progressively added to. This complex was powerfully reinforced by the decentralization of major research and development establishments from Paris, around which further growth might agglomerate.

IV *Slow or fast employment decline but increasing mobility*

At first sight anomalous, this group includes iron and steel manufacture, textiles, clothing, leather, and the processing of timber.

The *iron and steel* industry (figs. 49 and 51) has experienced fundamental changes in technology since 1945 (Martin 1957, Prêcheur 1961) in the source of its raw materials and fuel, in the fortunes of its traditional manufacturing regions, and since 1966 in the extent of state intervention on location policies. In the course of these changes, major geographical shifts in productive capacity have taken place, with both beneficial and adverse effects upon regional planning, according to the areas affected. Though overall employment in the iron and steel industry declined by only 1.7 per cent between 1964 and 1974, the figure of 157,629 employed in the latter year compares unfavourably with the 198,749 in the industry in 1953.

In July 1966 a planning agreement (*Plan Acier*) under the Vth Plan,

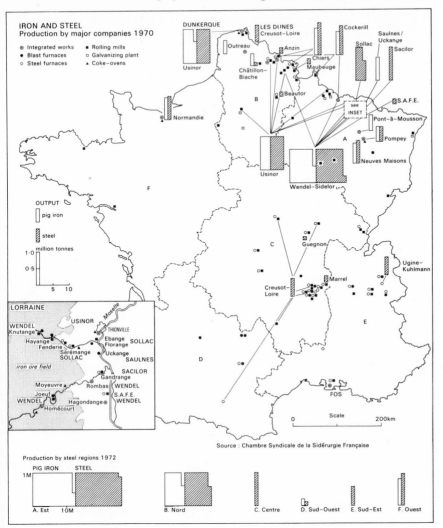

Figure 51   Iron and steel industry, 1970.

between the state and the steel industry, sought to rationalize production, to create complexes of European stature, and to specialize the products according to region: Lorraine, long products; Nord, plates and sheets; Centre-Midi, special steels. The spatial strategy for steel was still national rather than regional in its objectives. In the event, the rationalization to two major groups (Wendel-Sidélor, Usinor) covered 70 per cent of French steel output.

Locally and subregionally, closure of plants and rationalization in older centres accompanied a programmed redistribution of production in new capacity, notably to Dunkerque (Usinor) and, more recently, at Fos (Solmer, Ugine). At both Dunkerque and Fos the steel industry was implanted as a propulsive industry (*industrie motrice*) in the coastal industrial growth complex (Part III, ch. 2). Unemployment in the Lorraine iron-ore mines has been much more dramatic, with the labour force falling from 24,158 (1952) to 14,777 (1969) and 8958 (1975). The economic crisis of the 1970s necessitated even more traumatic readjustments: in April 1977 15,600 redundancies in Lorraine steel were programmed by 1980, 10,000 in 1977 alone. The overall impact would be likely to affect no fewer than 50,000 jobs in ancillary and service industries.

The changing balance between home-produced and imported iron ore has been a principal reason, together with shifts in fuel supplies, underlying both relocation of the iron and steel industry and also its variable fortunes in particular subregions (fig. 51). The low grade French ores (average 30 per cent metal content, 1974), concentrated in Lorraine, have declined in output (1960, 62.7 Mt; 1974, 54.2 Mt). In 1974 18 Mt of Lorraine ore were exported, 10.5 Mt to Luxembourg, 4.6 Mt to Belgium and 3.6 Mt to the Saar; 37 Mt were consumed in the French industry, but on the other hand 16 Mt of foreign ores were landed. In the Nord steel region (fig. 51) 10.1 of a total 10.7 Mt consumed in 1974 were imported and the percentage was even higher at the new steel plant at Fos. 9 Mt of scrap metal was used in steel production (1974), favouring dispersed, market-orientated plants among others. Coal and coke for the industry were increasingly dependent on foreign supplies: in 1974, 3.9 Mt coke from French sources, 4.2 Mt from EEC neighbours (3.2 Ruhr, 0.5 Saar).

French crude steel output has risen sharply since the late 1940s (10.8 Mt 1952; 27.0 Mt 1974); comparable figures for the UK are 16.6 Mt, 22.4 Mt, and for West Germany 18.6 Mt and 53.2 Mt. The technology has changed in dramatic fashion, whilst the increasing scale of production units has been accompanied by closures of older plants and the establishment of 'green-field' integrated iron and steel works (fig. 51). In 1974 58.2 per cent of steel output was by oxygen enriched processes (27.4 per cent by the LD process), only 19.2 per cent by the basic bessemer (Thomas), 10.8 per cent by the open-hearth (Martin) method and 11.5 per cent by electric-arc furnaces.

Shifts in regional significance among steel-producing districts are shown in table 31. Within Lorraine during the Vth and VIth Plans, capacity had been progressively rationalized and an integrated works at Gandrange, with 4 Mt steel-making capacity, completed in 1971. Mergers and linkages in production and marketing have led to the dominance of the Wendel-

Table 31 Iron and steel production, by subregions (fig. 51), 1962, 1974

Mt	pig-iron		crude steel		rolled products	
	1974	1962	1974	1962	1974	1962
Est	13.2	10.6	14.2	11.3	12.1	8.7
Nord	7.1	2.2	9.0	3.9	6.1	3.0
Centre			1.0	0.8	0.9	0.4
Sud Ouest	0.2	0.2	0.1		0.1	
Sud Est	1.0		1.5	0.3	0.6	0.1
Ouest	0.8	0.6	1.0	0.7	1.0	0.7
Total	22.5	13.9	27.0	17.2	20.9	13.0

Sidélor group (created 1968) in Lorraine, producing more than 8 Mt of steel in a normal year; other firms and plants are shown on fig. 51. The major development in the Nord steel region has been the integrated iron and steel plant at Dunkerque (Usinor) with a capacity of 8 Mt crude steel (1975); nearby is the associated rolling-mill at Mardyck. Perhaps most dramatic of all is the 'green-field' integrated iron and steel works at Fos (fig. 67), undertaken by the Solmer subsidiary of Wendel-Sidélor. The first phase of development is complete, with an output potential of 3.5 Mt (1975) and an associated special steels plant (Ugine) with a 200,000 tonne capacity, but in 1976 the main steel plant was working at less than half capacity. By the end of the century, the plant at Fos could theoretically be developed to produce 15 to 20 Mt of steel, though this now seems to be a remote possibility. Indeed, in the current recession a start even on the second phase is likely to be delayed until at least 1980–82. At both Fos and Dunkerque the iron and steel industry is a leader industry in the growth complex (Part III, ch. 3), and in each case an important employer also in its own right (Dunkerque 6000 workers; Fos, estimated 8000 workers in 1975).

Figs. 52 and 53 show the distribution of employment in branches of the *textile, clothing* and *leather* industries, further examples of fast employment decline but not without increasing mobility in some areas during certain periods (La DF 1966, 1968, Boitel 1968). Overall, the textile industries saw a job loss from 536,000 in 1962 to 425,000 in 1971: in cotton manufacture the decline was from 138,000 in 1955 to 72,500 in 1971, in woollens from 100,000 in 1955 to 59,000 in 1971. All these industries are labour-intensive and figs. 52 and 53 bring out clearly the extent of specialization by region. As in the UK during the same period, the decline was due in large measure to competition from cheaper overseas producers and the reactions were

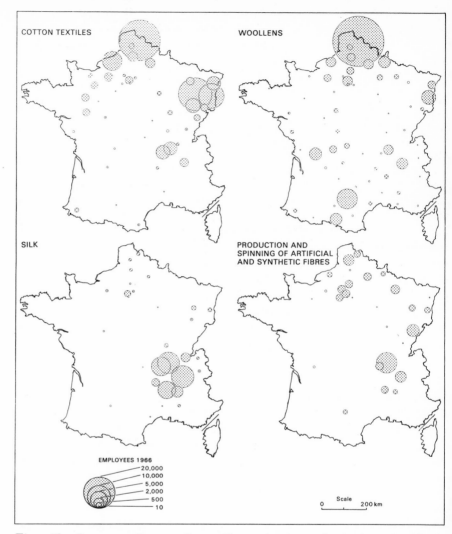

Figure 52　Cotton textiles; woollens; silk; production and spinning of artificial and synthetic fibres, 1966.

similar: government aid in rationalization of production, concentration upon the more competitive higher-value products for western markets, mergers of firms and closures of uneconomic plants, diversification into man-made fibres, and introduction of automation to reduce the labour costs in production. Among the more isolated production centres, as for example the cotton manufacturing towns of the Vosges or the woollen

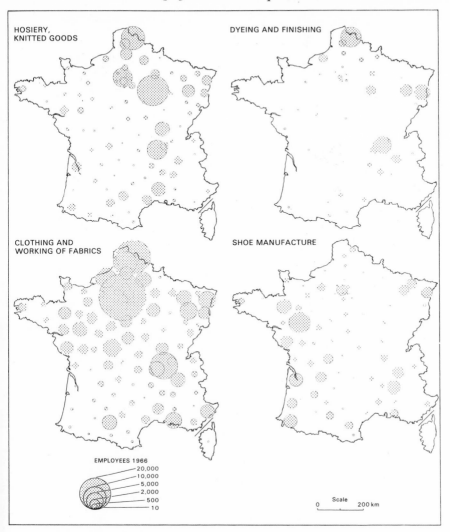

Figure 53 Hosiery, knitted goods; dyeing and finishing; clothing and working of fabrics; shoe manufacture, 1966.

centres of the Massif Central, the problem of industrial reconversion was
particularly acute.

The clothing industry in 1966 (fig. 53) had a strong concentration in and
around Paris; from 1962 to 1970 33,000 jobs were lost nationally. During
the same period, 37,000 jobs were lost in the leather industries, and a
further 6000 in timber processing.

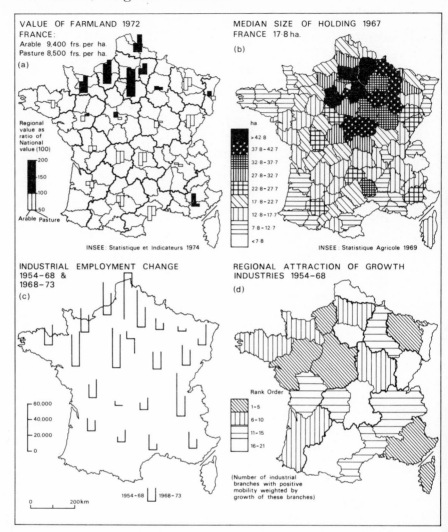

Figure 54   Value of farmland 1972; median size of holding 1967. Industrial employment change 1954–68, 1968–73; regional attraction of growth industries 1954–68.

The brief summary of employment dynamism, or the lack of it in particular branches, together with the spatial patterns of the industry groups (figs. 43–53), is an essential preliminary to an appreciation of government policies on location and their effects. By way of summary, fig. 54b indicates the quantum of industrial employment change 1954–68 and

1968–73 (Noël 1974). Though the rate of change in the latter short period was clearly greater for most regions, it must be remembered that gross change must be set against total employment for each region. It is then seen that in most regions the significance of change is marginal in character, certainly for all major manufacturing areas. Some industries were very mobile throughout the period 1954–73 (cars, electrical manufactures, machinery); others had a persistently low mobility (food, printing). Between 1954 and 1962 there was a considerable employment growth but limited spatial mobility; after 1962 spatial mobility increased markedly, a fortuitous and beneficial trend which both supported and was in turn partly a product of government location policy. For the years 1954–73 Noël calculated the regression of growth on mobility as $r = 0.48$, not a very strong correlation. Clearly other factors were involved, such as technology, concentration policies of firms, inter-industry linkage, and perhaps also the distribution of socio-professional groups.

Fig. 54b further shows marked regional contrasts, reinforced by the evidence of 54d, which classifies the growth-mobility attraction of manufacturing by each economic planning region, 1954–68. The low rank order of Ile-de-France is reflected in the small overall net gain in industrial jobs 1954–68 turned to a net loss in the next five years. The Nord, on the other hand, has staunched the net outflow of the earlier period, though ranking low in attraction of manufacturing. The regions of high attraction are diverse: by market forces (Provence-Côte d'Azur) and through public policy (west and south-west from Paris). The steady attraction of the Bassin Parisien, especially the Centre, is well-seen; regions peripheral to the metropolis often benefited from the first stage of a two-stage de-centralization process by firms from Greater Paris.

It may be wondered if industrial mobility correlates better with urbanization than with general regional development. Noël (1974) found a poor correlation with *level* of urbanization, but a good fit between mobility and *growth* of urban population ($r = 0.94$), particularly for 1962–8. Further tests did not show any significant relationship between mobility leading or lagging behind the urbanization process. Mobility in the electrical manufactures group correlated better with urban growth, but the general conclusion was that urban growth in postwar France was due more directly to growth in the tertiary, rather than in the manufacturing, sector.

Tertiary activities have become a focus of planning attention since the early 1960s, because the potential of fast employment growth in certain branches, particularly in and around Greater Paris, has seemed to offer an increasing prospect of effective decentralization and the promotion of better regional employment balances (Piquard 1971). To achieve regional equilibrium, tertiary supplementation of manufacturing mobility would be needed, and indeed increasingly so as possibilities for further decentralization of manufacturing decrease, and industry in any case becomes more capital- and less labour-intensive.

Definition and classification of the tertiary sector poses certain problems (Tauveron 1974). Certain branches are functionally and unmistakably tertiary: administration; banking, insurance, finance; building societies; commerce (retailing, wholesaling); transport and telecommunications; domestic services; hotels and catering. On the other hand, there is a continuum from decision-taking (research, development, management) to decision-implementing, which means that within manufacturing firms there is an increasing range of occupations which are in effect tertiary in character, but not so classified. Similarly many tertiary activities are tied to production (transport, commerce) whilst others are market- or consumer-orientated (distribution, warehousing, local government, education, domestic service). An alternative classification is into private and public sector tertiary activities. All these different methods of categorizing tertiary employment are important for the development of public location policies.

Fig. 31 shows the great diversity in growth trends among tertiary activities. Since 1962, banking, insurance and finance have grown most rapidly, followed by education, building societies, telecommunications and administration. Transport jobs increased slowly (plus 6 per cent 1962–71), whilst domestic service fell 10 per cent during the same period. Overall tertiary employment in France rose by 1.4 millions 1965–75, plus 300,000 jobs in manufacturing which were really tertiary by nature. Not surprisingly, there were wide regional variations in tertiary growth poles: Ile-de-France set the national trend 1962–8 with +320,000 tertiary jobs (and −100,000 in manufacturing); the greatest positive deviations from the national rates, 1954–68, were in Rhône-Alpes (+11.1 per cent), Provence-Côte d'Azur (+9.0 per cent), Languedoc-Roussillon (+6.8 per cent) and Midi-Pyrénées (+5.9 per cent). The most striking negative deviations were in the northern Massif Central (Limousin −12.1, Auvergne −9.3) and Bourgogne (−8.2 per cent). Most of the Ouest showed modest negative deviations. There is no clear evidence of the kind of the distance-decay from Paris that is outlined later for the decentralization in growth of employment in manufacturing.

Apart from growth trends in employment, tertiary activities vary considerably in the extent to which they are locationally tied. Market-orientation and availability of suitable labour are two strong location elements for many tertiary branches. High mobility potential characterizes research and development units, services directly related to decentralized production units, and those repetitive services requiring a large volume of unskilled labour. Low mobility, on the other hand, typifies all major decision-taking establishments: financial and investment centres, head office organizations, and central government ministries (Rochefort 1972). In principle, the telecommunications system could be a great catalyst for decentralization of decision-taking (Part II, pp. 216–18), but there remain powerful psychological impediments.

Likewise, attitudes to decentralization of tertiary activities from Paris are less favourable than for manufacturing. Directors of firms stress the need for face-to-face contacts with government officials and major clients; they further fear the loss of most able managers or skilled workers. Developers prefer the greater certainty of property value increases in Paris, whilst civil servants resent being transferred to the provinces and feel that tertiary activities in any case provide a poor regional employment multiplier. To local government, industrial plants have greater appeal, and office blocks by comparison are scarcely an electoral asset; if there must be tertiary activities, then only the higher-grade establishments should be attracted and not those with mass cheap office jobs. These attitudes certainly awake echoes of similar thinking in respect of the UK Assisted Areas (House 1977).

PUBLIC POLICIES ON LOCATION AND MOBILITY

Though the Ist Plan introduced a regional dimension to resource allocation (FNAT: *Fonds national d'aménagement du territoire*, operated by *Direction de l'aménagement du territoire*), it was not until 1963 that DATAR, the central *regional* planning organization, was created. In the IInd Plan (1954–7) the concept of redressing regional imbalances was promulgated ('each regional economy was to be able to live from the product of its work'): in 1953 funding bodies for Construction, Equipment of Rural Areas, (FAR) and Economic Expansion came into being; the next year these were complemented by organizations for Industrial Reconversion, Retraining and Industrial Decentralization, to achieve 'the optimum implantation of industry on national soil'. In 1955 FDES was created to promote 'decentralization, industrial reconversion, and regional expansion', leading to the formulation of 'regional action programmes'. The IIIrd Plan (1958–61) was concerned, in the regional dimension, with: 'decentralization and regional equilibrium', 'better management of the French economic map', and 'stabilization of the Paris conurbation', failing which housing, traffic management and public service provision risked becoming unmanageable. The 1960 inter-ministerial committee on regional action problems and management of the national space led to the 1963 creation of DATAR (*Délégation à l'aménagement du territoire et à l'action régionale*).

The objectives of regional planning are: the industrial expansion of the regions (Part III, ch. 3), together with a better distribution of public services, management of the urban system (Part III, ch. 2), tourist development, and finally the formulation of regional and sectoral long-term strategies. Regional *industrial* expansion, in France as in Britain, was regarded as the keystone of regional development. Though financial aid could be given in principle to decentralized tertiary activities from 1955 onwards (*Comité de décentralisation*), only government establishments were decentralized before about 1970. Regional industrial expansion was translated into four types of action: decentralization from Paris, regional balance, industrial reconversion, and rural renovation.

Operational measures

The processes of regional development were eventually modelled at the macro-economic scale (Part III, ch. 1), but in practice the active elements of policy were directed to stimulating or, more rarely, constraining the growth of employment in designated regions, subregions and localities, by specific financial aids or interdictions. Compared with British location policies (House 1977), those in France were operating in a market- rather than in a mixed-economy. Not surprisingly, inducements were more prominent and constraints less frequently employed. In the event, French governments have created a more sophisticated pattern of measures than yet achieved in the UK (fig. 55).

Constraints. The major constraints have been those upon industrial and office growth in Ile-de-France and the City of Paris. From December 1966 to April 1970 there was also a restriction policy by requiring a permit for all growth of more than 1000 m² of industrial floor-space in Greater Lyon, but it was not needed. Industrial, tertiary and spatial strategies for Paris and its region are discussed in Part III, ch. 2. Here only the nature of the locational measures will be outlined. The policy of constraint on development in Paris was not intended to 'sacrifice the future of the capital city to that of the provinces', nor to 'put Paris-based industry at the service of regional requirements'. It was intended as part of a process to implant self-sustaining economic growth in the provincial regions, which would then continue to flourish independent of either the risk or the timing of further decentralizations. Furthermore, it was considered that decentralization of jobs from Paris would continue to be beneficial to that conurbation.

In 1955 (January) a system of licensing was introduced for all creations

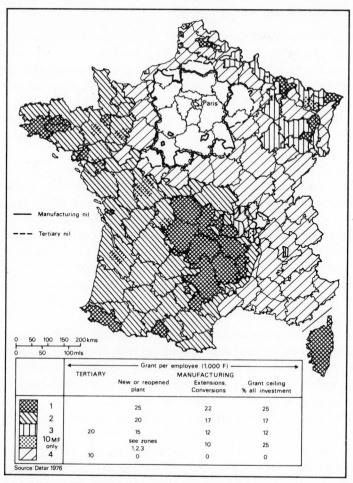

The legend and table within the figure read:

Manufacturing nil ——
Tertiary nil – – –

0 50 100 150 200 kms
0 50 100 mls

| | | Grant per employee (1,000 F) | | |
| | TERTIARY | MANUFACTURING | | |
		New or reopened plant	Extensions, Conversions	Grant ceiling % all investment
1		25	22	25
2		20	17	17
3	20	15	12	12
10 MF only		see zones 1,2,3	10	25
4	10	0	0	0

Figure 55   Regional Development Aids, 1976.

or extensions of more than 500 m² industrial floor-space in Paris, similar to the British IDC policy; in addition, a building permit was required. The policy was strengthened in 1958 (December), and more strictly enforced thereafter. In 1967 (October) the lower limit was raised to 1000 m² for *extensions* only, and in 1972 (April) to 1500 m² for both creations and extensions. The *Comité de décentralisation* (1955) operated the licensing policy and from 1967 onwards had oversight of both the public and the private sectors. In September 1975 warehousing came under the control measures, with a threshold of 5000 m² above which sanction had to be obtained.

Additionally, from 1960 (August) there was a tax on growth of industrial and office floor-space in Paris, of more than 500 m² (1000 m² 1976) for creations, and more than 1000 m² for extensions, or more than 50 per cent of the space previously occupied. The tax varied according to the locality within the city or its environs, and in 1962 was extended out to Meaux and Melun. In 1969 a reduced rate of floor-space tax was introduced for certain underprivileged areas of Paris, whilst in 1971 (July) the development tax was raised to a ceiling of 200 frs (1976, 25–150 frs) per m² for workshops and 500 frs (1976, 100–400 frs) per m² for offices; in the same month a 2 per cent payroll tax was introduced to help subsidize public transport within the city and its commuting area.

In more general terms, from November 1961 onwards there were powers to refuse a building permit to any industrial development proposal anywhere in France thought likely to be contrary to regional planning objectives. In 1964 (April) permission became mandatory for all proposals to create more than an additional 2000 m² of industrial floor-space. Foreign firms willing to locate in France were submitted to the same procedures, whilst for all major companies the sharing of long-term plans with the government, under 'planning agreement' (p. 250), gave the possibility of further influencing major elements of the industrial location pattern.

Incentives. In an essentially market economy, positive aids to *manufacturing* industry have always been more important than constraints. Development premiums have been the most characteristic form of incentive, varying in volume and character, through time and in space, but intended to subsidize the investment costs of movement by firms (Part III, ch. 1).

In 1955 (June) *zones critiques* were designated, in which up to 20 per cent of investment costs of the establishing of transferred plants might be met by government. The zones were diverse in character, but all were districts with problems of declining industry: mining areas (Auchel-Bruay, Alès, St-Etienne, Le Bousquet d'Orb); textile manufacturing towns (Vosges; Amiens; Vienne; Tarare; Bédarieux, Castres; Avesnes-Fourmies); tannery, cutlery, ceramics and shoe manufacturing centres; or individual towns with particular problems, e.g. bituminous shale mining (Autun), or petroleum extraction (Péchelbronn). In 1958 more vigorous action on problem districts was instituted, and in March 1959 *zones spéciales de conversion* were defined, in which premiums of up to 20 per cent of investment on new developments and 15 per cent on industrial extensions might be paid. The designated districts changed somewhat: Nantes-St Nazaire (ship-building), Calais (textiles), Montpellier and Sète (viticulture) were added to the list.

In 1960 (April) there was a break-point in policy. For the first time, the entire national space was reviewed and underemployment was added to unemployment (real or prospective) as a justification for priority aid. Thus the regional aid policy was extended to rural regions and no longer confined solely to the districts with problems of industrial reconversion. In 1964 (May) two categories of designated region were officially recognized: *zones de développement*, mainly rural, in which grants in aid varied from 12 to 25 per cent according to locality; and *zones d'adaptation*, with continuing industrial reconversion problems, in which grants of up to 25 per cent might be made, depending on the severity of employment problems and their associated social manifestations. The policy introduced in 1972 (April) abolished the distinction between the two types of region for aid, in favour of a common PDR (*prime de développement régional*—regional development grant), with a very complex set of levels and mixes of aids. Though flexible aid through the national space was thus indicated, and the levels of aid guaranteed, the time dimension varied. For the duration of the VIth Plan aid was given to the former *zones de développement*, plus certain mining and steel towns in Lorraine, and some frontier localities in the Nord and Est. Aid for 18 months was provided in the former *zones d'adaptation*, to which eight new centres were added.

Fig. 55 shows the pattern of regional development grants (1976), with ceiling levels of grant per job created within a fixed period. The level of grant varies according to the zone and whether the creation of new jobs or addition to existing employment is involved. In exceptional cases grants may be given for non-designated areas, but excluding the Bassin Parisien and Greater Lyon; localities on the borders of designated areas may also be occasionally aided. Agricultural or food industries may receive development grants.

Decisions on grants of up to 10 million francs have been decentralized to *département* level, whilst those of more than 10 million francs are determined by the government on the advice of DATAR, with the interests of the *villes moyennes* very much in mind. Other incentives have included: FDES long-term loans at low interest rates, though these loans were important only during the years 1955–68; payment of an indemnity (40 per cent 1964, 60 per cent 1972) for decentralization costs of firms moving out of the Paris region and the 5 southern *cantons* of Oise, provided a minimum of 500 m² floor-space was released; training and labour relocation grants; and a complex of fiscal aids, such as exceptional depreciation allowed on plant or equipment, exemption from licensing costs (*patente*), reduction of transfer tax (*mutation*), or reduction of value-added tax on property sold if the proceeds were reinvested in projects acceptable to the regional planners (DATAR 1976).

In the *tertiary sector* incentives worked rather differently. During the 1960s there had been a policy of deliberate decentralization of government and semi-official research and development establishments: Toulouse (aerospace), Grenoble (electronics and nuclear energy), Lannion and Rennes (electronics), Lyon (chemicals) and Nice (computers). An associated policy of decentralizing the *grandes écoles* from Paris met with greater resistance, but there were some achievements: Ecole Supérieure d'Electricité (Rennes), Ecole Supérieure d'Aéronautique (Toulouse) and Ecole des Mines (Antibes).

Although aids to office decentralization from Paris became available in 1967 (October), there were only 19 applications in the first three years, compared with 1500 for manufacturing decentralizations during the same period (Durand 1972). All services in direct contact with the public were excluded, and it was necessary to create a minimum of 100 tertiary jobs, or 50 if the proposed decentralization was of a research and development unit, or a head office. The tertiary location grant was restricted to a designated list of towns and there was a ceiling of 15,000 frs aid per job created. At the same time, there was a system of differential taxes on the creation of office space in Paris and its immediate environs. In practice these restraints proved to be inadequate, the disequilibrium between workplace and residence in Paris increased (Part III, ch. 2), both between west and underprivileged east and as between the centre and the periphery; indeed, new tertiary employment in Ile-de-France became heavily concentrated in the city of Paris (57 per cent) and Hauts-de-Seine (14 per cent of all tertiary jobs).

Thus a tougher policy was needed (April 1972). In Paris the flexible floor-space tax to control and steer office development was further refined and strengthened, with a concentric zonal arrangement of bands of diminishing tax outwards. Within the inner bands there were 'islands' of lower tax, intended to concentrate tertiary development either at the 'restructuring poles' (*pôles restructurants*) in eastern Paris, or at major growth poles like La Défense in Hauts-de-Seine. Priority was to be given to tertiary development at the five New Towns (Part III, ch. 2) and within the city and suburbs office development was to have a deliberate role in urban renewal policy. Furthermore, an overall ceiling of 600,000 m² new office space per annum was imposed in Ile-de-France.

In 1972 the tertiary location grant was extended to coincide with the areas designated for priority industrial aid, whilst Caen was added to the list of *métropoles* and towns previously benefiting from aid to the tertiary sector. Within such towns, town planning objectives and social needs should dictate the siting of such new tertiary establishments. The level of the premium was then fixed: 10 per cent of investment costs for administrative or management units, 15 per cent for research and development branches, and 20 per cent for head offices moved out of the Paris region. Firms might restructure or hive-off decentralized parts over a period of time, provided 200 new jobs were created overall (100 if a research and development unit was concerned).

In 1976 (fig. 55) the tertiary location grant became available for all provincial areas other than part of the Bassin Parisien; in Greater Lyon the grant was limited to high level tertiary establishments. Grants were open to new or extended service and tertiary establishments, and to transfers from Ile-de-France. A minimum threshold was imposed of 30 jobs for creations or cases of greater autonomy of decision-powers, and as low as 20 jobs if a head office was created or transferred; for extensions the labour force had to be increased by at least 50 per cent, though creations or moves from Ile-de-France needed only 100 jobs to be eligible for grant. 20,000 frs per job in regional development grant zones and 10,000 frs elsewhere were the grant levels, with an added 5000 frs per job if a head office was involved. Grants were made through the inter-ministerial committee (DATAR) and paid through the Ministère de l'Economie et des Finances.

Additionally in 1976 a research establishment location grant became payable, for the same areas as the tertiary location grant, for private sector firms creating or developing scientific or technical research services. This new grant could not be added to either the regional or the tertiary grants. Certain towns, e.g. Caen, Montpellier, Dijon, together with the eight counterbalancing regional metropoli, were designated research growth poles (20 per cent grant instead of the usual 15).

THE GEOGRAPHICAL IMPACT OF PUBLIC LOCATION POLICIES

Manufacturing decentralization

For reasons given earlier, it is difficult to assess the direct effects of public policies, even at the coarsest aggregate scale (Donolo 1972). It is even more hazardous to attempt an overall evaluation of the indirect or multiplier impact at other than a micro-level of the locality or the firm. In the broadest terms, 450,800 jobs were the result of *industrial* moves notified to the planners between 1955 and the end of 1974, a figure which probably underestimates total employment from moves (St Julien 1973). It concerns the distribution of new growth rather than the displacement of existing activities, and the moves notified include a very wide diversity in terms of the weight of operations transferred within the firm or the extent of devolved decision-taking. Another generalized order of magnitude is the estimate that, 1954–68, the increase in volume of manufacturing jobs in Ile-de-France would have been 459,000 had there been no public location policy, instead of the 8000 increase which in fact took place.

Geographers in France have studied the process of industrial decentralization, both in general terms (George 1961, Gay 1966, Bastié and Trolliet 1967, Bastié 1973, St Julien 1973) and in more localized case-studies of individual *départements* or towns. The study by Palierne and Riquet (1966) highlighted the strong distance-decay in industrial moves from Paris, many of which were only as far as adjacent parts of the Bassin Parisien. Burgel (1965) was concerned with transfer of establishments from Paris to the *département* of Eure; Gouhier (1965) looked at the zone between Seine and Loire, Chesnais (1964) Eure-et-Loir, Babonaux (1959) Loir-et-Cher, Parry (1963) studied the decentralization of the factories of Radiotechnique westwards from Paris, and Frémont *et al.* (1964) made a case-study of the impact of the industrial decentralization process on the town of Argentan. The paper by St Julien (1971) on La Rochelle provides the best example of decentralization to a greater distance, particularly the impact of a Simca (Chrysler) car components plant (suspensions and transmissions) from Poissy. The new plant employed about 3000, a major source of work in an urban economy based on port activity, tourism and commerce.

The case-studies illustrate the complexity of decentralization moves (St Julien 1973). Simple linear transfers, in which a Paris factory is closed and a new one opened in the provinces, are less common than a division of functions between the two production centres, or the development of the provincial plant to give added overall capacity. Moves are often made by stages, and in time the distribution of functions between the parent plant in Paris and the decentralized plant may change. Other moves are multiple in the sense that more than one factory may be closed and regrouping of production may take place on a single provincial site, or one factory from Paris may be split up between several provincial locations. On other occasions the Paris factory may increase in size, even at a time when a new plant is being set up in the provinces, the so-called 'invisible' transfer. Some transfers to the provinces in fact mean no more than the build-up of a factory already there. In France, as in the UK, regional and local authorities are anxious to attract either complete firms, or at least to ensure that decentralized establishments have sufficient decision-taking powers in order that they may have greater stability. The history of the spread of branch plants into the UK Assisted Areas at a time of national economic expansion, and the vulnerability of such plants to early closure at the onset of an economic depression, does not seem to have been repeated in France.

Table 32 summarizes the patterns of industrial decentralization between 1955 and 1974, classified: (a) by distance-decay from Paris; (b) by north-south contrast; and (c) according to regional development prospects (table 4).

Table 32 Industrial decentralizations, 1955–74

(a) Distance-decay from Paris

	jobs (1000s)	%	no of moves	%	Total employment in industry, 1968	Mobile jobs as % all jobs
Zone I	226.5	50.2	1709	56.7	957.0	23.6
II	161.3	35.8	977	32.3	2421.5	6.6
III	63.0	14.0	334	11.0	1069.9	5.9
	450.8	100	3020	100	4448.5	10.1

Zone I   The inner zone: Haute-Normandie, Picardie, Champagne, Bourgogne, Centre
   II   The middle-distance zone: Nord-Pas-de-Calais, Lorraine, Franche-Comté, Rhône-Alpes, Auvergne, Limousin, Poitou-Charentes, Pays de la Loire, Basse-Normandie
   III   The outer zone: Alsace, Provence-Côte d'Azur, Languedoc-Roussillon, Aquitaine, Bretagne

(b) North-south contrasts

	jobs (1000s)	%	no of moves	%	Total employment in industry, 1968	Mobile jobs as % all jobs
North	322.0	71.4	2103	69.6	2214.4	14.5
South	128.8	28.6	917	30.4	2234.1	5.7
	450.8	100	3020	100	4448.5	10.1

North: Nord Pas-de-Calais, Haute-Normandie, Picardie, Champagne, Lorraine, Basse-Normandie, Bretagne, Pays de la Loire, Centre

(c) Regional development prospects (for definitions, see table 4)

	jobs (1000s)	%	no of moves	%	Total employment in industry, 1968	Mobile jobs as % all jobs
Growth	159.6	35.5	1114	37.9	1658.3	9.6
Growth potential	118.6	26.3	1008	33.4	678.7	17.4
Reconversion	47.9	10.6	218	7.2	1118.1	4.2
Developing	124.7	27.6	650	21.5	993.3	12.5
	450.8	100	2990	100	4448.5	10.1

Table 32 (a) clearly establishes the concentric zonal distance-decay outwards from Paris, on all three criteria of total employment, numbers of moves, and contribution by mobile jobs to the total labour force. This deduction corresponds well with the evidence of Palierne and Riquet

(1966) on moves from Paris to locations in the Bassin Parisien. Close territorial linkages with either a Paris-based parent plant or with the metropolitan market, the significantly greater costs of longer-distance transplantation of factories, and the social preferences of both management and workers for proximity to Paris were reasons given in the 1966 study for the marked distance-decay effect. Correlations on the 1955-74 data show that larger establishments have been prepared to move over longer distances, smaller plants opting quite definitely for minimal movement.

If Alsace and Bretagne are reallocated to Zone II, there is no disturbance to the general conclusions. The percentages then read as follows: Zone II 43.4, 36.8 and 7.0; Zone III 6.4, 6.5 and 4.0.

Table 32 (b) brings out the strong correlation between the importance of decentralizations and the needs for new job provision in broadly that part of France north of a line from the mouth of the Loire to the Saar. The northern zone contains the most youthful age structure, and also a spectrum of problem regions of either rural decline or industrial reconversion. The rural regions of Basse-Normandie, Bretagne and Pays de la Loire are characterized by high rural population densities and concealed underemployment coinciding with a youthful regional age structure. In these respects they contrast sharply with the Massif Central to the south.

Table 32 (c) shows an uneven pattern of correlations. The backward regions received an above-average allocation of mobile jobs, but perhaps surprisingly the growth regions or those with growth potential did equally well or better in attracting decentralizations. The highest proportion of mobile to total jobs was for the Centre (33 per cent), a growth potential region, followed by Basse-Normandie (29 per cent); by contrast, the figure for Bretagne was only 15 per cent. The reconversion regions, on the other hand, appear to have received relief at the margin of employment, with only 4 per cent of all employment due to decentralized industry. In terms of the size of establishment (national mean for decentralized firms 149 employed) the reconversion regions (mean 219 employed) and the developing regions (mean 191 employed) attracted the larger units.

Bastié (1972, 1973) analysed the pattern of industrial decentralizations in France in greater detail, for the period 1951–72. He distinguished a considerable zone west and south-west of Paris as one in which decentralization accentuated the growth of industrial employment. By contrast, in Bourgogne, Champagne and Lorraine, decentralization had the effect of counteracting decline in mining and manufacturing, whilst for the Nord/Pas-de-Calais the effect was only to reduce the rate of decline which would otherwise have taken place. According to Bastié (1973) the outer, less industrialized areas, the towns of more than 25,000, absorbed a higher proportion of decentralized firms than was the case for the more disseminated pattern of location in the Bassin Parisien.

Tertiary decentralization

The geographical effects of the decentralization of *tertiary* firms have been less systematically studied, though 18,000 new jobs were created in the provinces (1970–5) by 80 decentralization operations. Apart from the planned dispersal of specialized higher education, research and development centres of governmental or semi-official character, referred to earlier, the main evidence to date is for general office decentralization and that for the banking, insurance and finance group (DATAR 1972). The latter fast growth group is in the private or commercial sector, and its activities penetrate all aspects of national life, from contacts with government and major firms, necessitating an orientation on Paris, to the individual customers throughout France. The strategy of location for banking operations must take into account the data explosion which led to a doubling of items handled 1958–70, a further doubling 1971–6, and prospectively again by 1982. Most head offices of banks are in Paris, with Lyon a secondary but much less significant node. During the past decade, a pattern of banking and financial decentralizations of national significance has taken place, (10,500 jobs 1963–75), with a more or less even distribution among the major towns north of a line from Bordeaux, through Bourges to Reims. Lyon has had seven decentralizations, but all of only regional or local importance. Technical services have most readily been decentralized since neither contact with clients nor decision powers are involved. An alternative form of decentralization is the creation of regional administrative centres for the banks, or computing centres. The efforts by DATAR to establish Lyon as a metropolitan-scale banking centre, with full financial powers to counterbalance Paris, has had some success and has been of particular benefit to industrialists in the fast-growing Rhône-Alpes.

Illustrative of the general trend is the locational pattern of Crédit Lyonnais. The bank has its head offices and highest-level services in Paris, but also four regional administrative centres (Roubaix, Valence, Tours, Melun); to these must be added the bonds office at Bayeux. The computer network of the bank has three centres: Lyon-Rillieux; Limeil-Brétonnes, for the Paris region; and Tours for the north-west and south-west. The computer centres are linked by telecommunications network.

Insurance companies have differentially strengthened their provincial workforce: 1974, 30 per cent outside Paris, compared with 25 per cent in 1968. Few head offices have moved but many regional centres have been set up by firms, each employing several hundreds (only senior staff are normally brought from Paris). For 1975–82 contracts signed with DATAR provide for more than 10,000 further decentralized jobs. Private social security and retirement funds have contributed to decentralization: 5000 jobs from Paris, plus 2000 new jobs, either by movement of head offices, or more commonly expansion of employment in the regions. There has been a marked concentration of such new jobs along the coastlands of Provence, the Loire valley and the Atlantic zone between Loire and Garonne.

Between 1969 and end-1974 one-third of all new office-space approved was for Ile-de-France (which had 40 per cent of all office-space), a much lower proportion than in the 1960s or earlier. The building of speculative office blocks in the provinces, notably at Lille, Lyon and Marseille, was a particular feature of this period; British entrepreneurs were frequently involved (Assoc. Bureaux-Provinces 1975). In many large provincial towns urban renewal operations in the central areas permitted the creation of *centres directionnels* (business centres) with concentration of office blocks and administrative centres: e.g. Part-Dieu (Lyon), Forum (Lille), Mériadeck (Bordeaux). Other grouped office locations have developed on peripheral estates under ZAC designation. Most recently there has been a spreading of smaller office centres to medium-sized towns (office units of up to 2000 m²). For the most part the growth of offices decentralized from Paris has concerned the setting up of regional branches rather than movement of head offices.

The use of major tertiary decentralizations as the focus of an official policy of promoting growth poles is referred to in Part III, ch. 1. Such a policy may be linked to industrial growth, or the nuclei may be used, as in the southern outskirts of Paris, to attract other tertiary establishments. The ability of government to influence location of tertiary employment is greater at the 'downstream' or consumer-orientated end of the spectrum, and also in respect of 'free-standing' units. Thus far there has been little impact on the overcentralization of head offices, or major decision-taking centres in Paris, at least as far as the commercial sector is concerned (Rochefort 1972). The potential for further decentralization is theoretically very considerable and, in principle, tertiary relocation is likely to be more flexible and wide-ranging in space than for manufacturing employment. The major impediments to realization of such potential appear to be psychological or domestic in the first instance.

An interesting example of a deliberately-planned high-level tertiary growth pole, presently unique in France but capable of duplication, is to be found on the Plateau de Valbonne (Sophia-Antipolis) in the immediate hinterland of Nice. On 2400 ha. of woodland and *garrigue* (scrubland) a business and administrative centre is being created, with emphasis on scientific and technological research, advanced and pollution-free manufacturing, and high level tertiary services. The international character of firms already attracted bears witness to the nodal airport location in Europe, and the attractive living environment, planned for an eventual population of 12–15,000 residents.

Two tertiary branches which have been evolving rapidly and largely outside the influence of government are *retailing with wholesaling* and the *tourist industry*.

Retailing with wholesaling

The rapid growth of population, its increasing concentration in urban areas, and the widespread rise in living standards in postwar France, have led to dramatic changes in the volume and diversity of retailing (Smith 1973). Regional variations in the socioeconomic mix in the population, and in the distribution of real incomes, have differentiated the general pattern of change. The geographical implications are threefold: upon the structure of employment, the siting and location of establishments, and the circulation space or hinterland of each.

By tradition, and effectively until the mid-1960s, France had been a country of small shops, the reflection of the localized scale of communities and the persistence of small towns in the urban structure. Wholesaling firms were usually located in or near the central business districts of the larger towns, but there was a well-developed network even down to smaller urban centres. In 1954, 2.3 millions were employed in commerce, half of whom were proprietors or managers. By 1962 the numbers had fallen to 2.0 millions, with only just over one-third proprietors or managers; in 1972 (La DF 1972) employment had risen to 2.5 millions, but proprietors or managers comprised only one-quarter. Many corner-shops, restaurants, pensions and small garages had closed. Retail outlets, furthermore, have grown rapidly in size: in 1976 8 per cent of the retail labour force was in 305 hypermarkets (minimum 2500 m² selling area); in 1972 there were additionally 2334 supermarkets (400–2500 m² selling area). The average hypermarket in 1973 had 5944 m² selling area, 209 employees and 1184 parking spaces; the average supermarket had 741 m² selling area and employed 29 (*Atlas des Hypers et Supermarchés* 1973).

The growth of hypermarkets and supermarkets since 1965 has been uneven (fig. 56). Hypermarket density is greatest in the southern outer suburban ring of Paris, including the largest development in Europe at La Belle Epine (Orly). Other concentrations are around Toulouse, in the towns of the Bassin Parisien and the Nord. Supermarkets are more

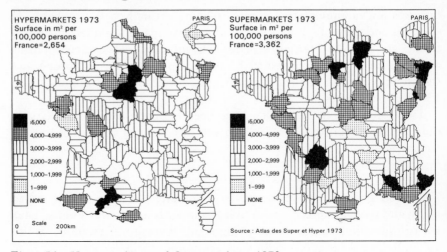

Figure 56   Hypermarkets and Supermarkets, 1973.

widespread, with the greatest density in Hauts-de-Seine, Vaucluse, Alpes-Maritimes and Bas-Rhin (Strasbourg). The out-of-town shopping centre faced less opposition in France, at least until the passing of the Royer law (1973) requiring all major shopping projects to be approved by a committee at *département* level (Dawson 1976, 260). At a time of fast economic growth and rapid urbanization, the competition with city centre shops did not produce serious problems. During 1975–6 fewer hypermarkets were approved, however, and the average size was smaller.

Within existing hypermarkets the trend has been towards diversification of activities, e.g. car accessories, and inclusion of specialized shops. Changes in shopping provision have been accompanied by resiting of wholesaling, either at nodal growth points within the regions, or on the outskirts of the major cities. The movement of the central Paris markets from Les Halles to the 'green-field' site at Rungis-Les Halles is the most prominent example. Inevitably, the redistribution and concentration of retail outlets has affected circulation patterns, and thus the hinterlands of settlements (Bruyelle 1970, Piatier 1971).

Tourism

Tourism, or the taking of residential holidays away from home, has grown very rapidly since the end of the Second World War. Prewar only 5 million French people had residential holidays; in 1974 the figure had risen to 24.9 millions, of whom 22 millions stayed at least four nights away during the summer season. To these numbers must be added the 11 million foreigners

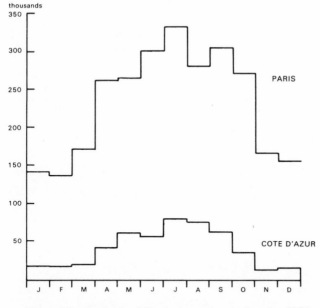

Figure 57   Arrival of foreign tourists in hotels, 1971.

holidaying in France (figs. 57, 58): against them must be set the 5–6 million Frenchmen travelling abroad. Almost 2 million French people patronized winter sports at the home resorts in 1974, supplemented by 260,000 foreigners; 240,000 Frenchmen took a winter holiday outside France. To these residential holiday-makers must be added regular week-enders (3 millions) and casual week-enders (9.9 millions, 1967 already), many of them travelling to second homes at the coast or in the countryside.

The concentrated flood-tide of summer-holiday migrants is but the most dramatic mass manifestation of the growing importance of leisure-time activities. Such activities (Etudes de l'OREAM 1968, Fourastié 1970) have been given great priority in the VIth and, especially, in the VIIth French Plans. The geographical and economic implications are profound at all scale-levels: the neighbourhood and the town, for the development of indoor recreation or cultural facilities: the subregional or regional, in the design of a recreation strategy, including tourism; and nationally, in the designation of tourist or recreation regions or zones, whether as nature reserves, green belts, or national parks, or as economic growth points at resorts, in comprehensively planned coastal, mountain or rural tracts. Among all recreational activities, tourism is the most likely to have the

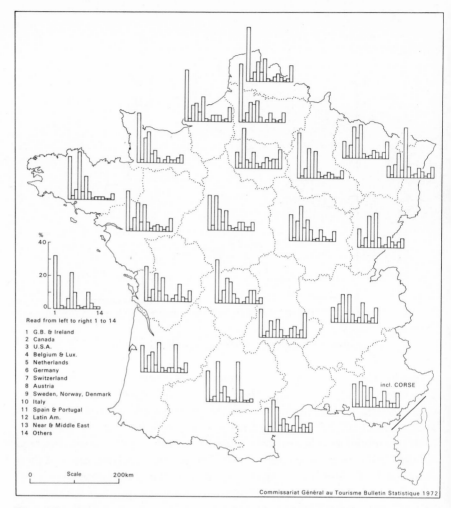

%
40
20
0
1   14
Read from left to right 1 to 14

1 G.B. & Ireland
2 Canada
3 U.S.A.
4 Belgium & Lux.
5 Netherlands
6 Germany
7 Switzerland
8 Austria
9 Sweden, Norway, Denmark
10 Italy
11 Spain & Portugal
12 Latin Am.
13 Near & Middle East
14 Others

incl. CORSE

0   Scale   200km

Commissariat Général au Tourisme Bulletin Statistique 1972

Figure 58   Foreign tourists, 1971: percentage overnight stays.

greatest spatial and sectoral impact, and to justify, indeed even increasingly
to require, the most careful planning and policy commitment at national,
regional and local levels (Clary 1976). Unplanned tourism, conversely, is
capable of the most savage environmental harm, and for both this reason,
and equally to harness the development of the tourist industry as a growth
generator to be manipulated for the benefit of regional planning, there has
been a progressive and large-scale involvement of public policy-making
and controlled investment. The spatial implications, for good or ill, have

led to some of the most dramatic and contested land-use decisions in postwar French planning for the coastline and the uplands.

A geographical interpretation is most logically threefold: first, the magnitude, structure, motivations and trends in the flow of tourists (Cribier 1969, 1973); secondly, the provision of direct facilities and comprehensive infrastructure for the tourist industry (Castex 1972); and, thirdly, the comparative analysis of the spatial impact at the level of resorts or regions, including some assessment of multiplier effects. Together these perspectives may be built into a systems framework (Préau 1973), which in its turn is the most efficient means for monitoring tourism in the interests of regional planning (Madaule *et al.* 1970). It must, however, be admitted that tourist development in postwar France has been part-planned but also partly anarchic (Flament 1975). With the fever of fast growth in the French economy now passing, it is a particularly appropriate time to take stock of the achievements and potentials for further tourist and recreational planning.

In 1974 (May) a new ministry (*Ministère de la qualité de la vie*) was set up, combining the previously separate administrative fields of Environment, Youth and Sport, and Tourism. In November 1974 the Commissariat Général au Tourisme was abolished and a Directorate for the Development of Tourism and the Tourist Trade established under a Secretary of State for Tourism within the new ministry (OECD 1975). As part of regional reforms in the early 1970s (p. 48) regional tourist committees became represented on the new regional economic and social councils, whilst inter-ministerial committees were set up to provide coordinated policy-making for the coastlands (1973), mountain regions, rural areas and 'social' tourism (Dacharry 1965). The stage was thus set for a comprehensive strategy for the further development of tourism, spatial and sectoral allocation of investment and growth possibilities and a proper balance between commercial and environmental interests. Overall there is to be much greater emphasis upon disseminated smaller scale growth, upon the needs of those of modest incomes, and upon sound conservation practices within an increasingly valued national scenic heritage.

Demand. The volume, rhythm, direction, typology and trends of tourist movements are analysed annually (Sec. d'Etat au Tourisme 1975). Table 33 illustrates the trends of the period 1964–74. The overall growth was less than anticipated, but was very unevenly distributed, structurally and in both time and space.

The rise in numbers of holiday-makers is greater than the proportionate rise in total population over the same period, and is due to generally greater

Table 33   Tourism, 1964–74

		1964	1974		1964	1974
Holiday-makers †	(millions)	20.3	24.9	*Type of stay* % holiday-days		
	as % total popn	43.6	50.1	sea	33.9	41.0
Holiday stays	(millions)	31.2	39.1	mountains	13.9	17.8
	, in France	27.4	33.5	countryside	35.2	30.8
	, abroad	3.8	5.6	town	14.2	7.4
				touring	2.8	3.0
				Type of accommodation % holiday-days		
Holiday-days	(millions)	611	745.5	hotel	8.0	7.8
	, in France	541	622	rental accommodation	16.0	15.8
	, abroad	70	123.5	second home	10.7	12.4
% stays	, 28 June-3 July	13.4	15.2	parents and friends		
	, 4 July-3 Aug	48.4	45.9	—main home	44.9	31.4
	, 4 Aug-27 Aug	23.5	23.3	—second home	11.4	8.1
				tent/caravan		18.2
				other	9.0	6.0

† more than 4 days residence away from home
Source: Statistiques du Tourisme

affluence, higher proportions living in towns, and the spread of the 3-week holiday entitlement to new social classes. The proportion of Frenchmen taking holidays abroad has increased sharply, but was more than offset by double the number of foreigners holidaying in France (figs. 57, 58). The severe short holiday peak in the midsummer months has scarcely been reduced, though the fore-peak is now longer, due to the staggering of industrial holidays, and the after-peak spread (September) is mostly the result of foreign visitors in the late season. The attraction of the coastline, with its 200 resorts, increases steadily, but again unevenly (1964–71: +40 per cent Languedoc-Roussillon, +30 per cent Loire-Gironde, +20 per cent Bretagne, less than 20 per cent Côte d'Azur, +10 per cent Normandie, *nil* north of the Baie de Somme [Cribier 1973, 14]). The high proportion of country holidays relates to the disproportionate demand for low-priced 'social' tourism (camping, *colonies de vacances*, etc.), and to the growth of second homes (Clout 1970, La DF 1972). Broadly, the northern half of France, over which tourism has been diffused, is a non-growth area, concentrating mainly on cheaper types of mass social tourism. The mountains and uplands have slow or stable tourist growth rates, but great diversity of trends as between localities.

Winter sports also have increased in popularity: 1968/9 1.4 million stays of more than 4 days, 1973/4 2.3 millions, but there has been a sharply marked altitudinal and social segregation. Most new integral resorts are on 'greenfield' sites above 1500 m, in contrast to village-based winter sports at lower altitudes and summer-based mountain tourism concentrated in the 600–1100 m zone. Camping sites in 1971 had a capacity of 420,000, compared with only 200,000 seven years earlier (fig. 59).

Supply (fig. 59). A pattern of resorts, facilities and infrastructure developed to meet tourist demands progressively from the early origins of the industry. Resorts specialized early in the type of holiday milieu offered, and also in the type of clientèle catered for. The fashionable resorts of the Côte d' Azur and the early winter sports centres, such as Chamonix, catered initially for an *élite* clientèle of foreigners. After the First World War cheaper railway travel encouraged the development of coastal resorts, but on a somewhat haphazard and uncoordinated scale. The introduction of 15 days' statutory holiday in 1936 unleashed a growing flood of visitors to the coast, the mountains and the countryside. It was, however, after 1950 that mass tourism became at all characteristic, with 3 weeks holiday for everyone in 1956 and 4 weeks generally from 1965 onwards. Surprisingly, the growth of tourism was for long accommodated within expansions of traditional centres; of 100 summer resorts in 1973, 96 were already active in

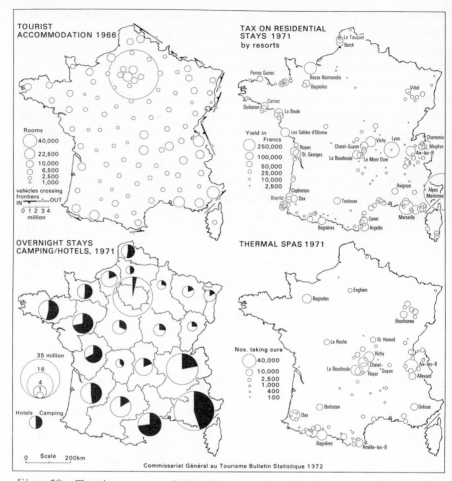

Figure 59   Tourist accommodation 1966; tax on residential stays 1971; overnight stays (camping/hotels) 1971; thermal spas 1971.

1936 (Cribier 1973, 8). Gradually growth was diffused: new coastal and mountain centres were brought into being, whilst camping, caravanning and other aspects of social tourism were disseminated along the coast and throughout the upland countryside. Until the 1950s there was little overview of the growth of tourism and its spatial impact. Planning initiatives have characteristically remained at the level of the commune, in association with developers, even speculators. Many developments have been dramatic, not a few have created major social costs for their communities, and the legacy has inevitably been a mixture of the beneficial (in employment, revenues, land values or multiplier effects) with the unstable, vulnerable to fickle shifts in demand and the trade cycle, traumatic for a highly capitalized industry dependent for its annual profits upon a limited period of a few summer or a few winter months. The environmental impact of sudden urbanization created its own additional problems and, not surprisingly, there has recently been greater public involvement by government in the planning of tourism and the pro-gramming of its spatial patterning and investment.

Apart from the ministerial and inter-ministerial bodies already referred to, public intervention on the supply side of tourism has worked beneficially through the loans and grants scheme of FDES (*Fonds de développement économique et social*) to create new hotel capacity or for modernization or equipment. Since 1974 there has been added emphasis upon 1- and 2-star hotels and the more modest accommodation. At the same time, the areas eligible for grants have been increased to include all mountain regions and districts on the outskirts of national parks. Other FDES loan aid has been made available for camp-sites, holiday villages, ski-lifts and marinas. Additional aid has come from the normal credit institutions and, in more marginal rural areas, from the rural renovation commissions (p. 428), in whose economic strategies tourism is seen as part of coordinated rural development.

Geographical impact. The contribution of tourist planning to regional development is considered later (Part III, ch. 3): attention here is confined to the strategies for tourist development currently active in the major types of region, and the general priorities being followed in public policy-making. The VIth Plan (Rapports des Commissions 1971) defined the priorities: establishment of a better organized, financed and export-orientated tourist industry, with a more highly trained and stable labour force; greater participation by local authorities and bodies in planning tourism; action to develop urban-style resorts and major linear-zonal concentrations on selected parts of the coast, but also a considered programme for social tourism (especially holiday villages, camp and caravan sites).

The most dramatic tourist developments have been at the *coast*, in Languedoc-Roussillon, more recently and prospectively in Aquitaine, and to a subsidiary extent in Corse. The programme for integral urban and recreational development of a coastal zone in Languedoc-Roussillon, 200 km long and 20 km in depth, was ambitiously designed to rival the Côte d'Azur with 1.5 million tourists per annum, or 40 million tourist-nights, bringing in an estimated one milliard francs in revenues and providing an employment multiplier (Barbier 1966) of one job per five beds created. The target is for 600,000 beds, of which 250,000 were available in 1964, 150,000 are to be provided in existing resorts and 250,000 in newly-created centres (Cazes 1972). The urbanization of the coastlands is being carefully controlled by the concentrations of development at 6 localities (*unités*), each to be a self-contained and equipped tourist centre, separated from neighbours by a green belt. Each centre is linked to an inland town and the overall development plan has been entrusted to a *mission d'aménagement* (management corporation). Existing smaller centres are to be incorporated in the plan and there is planned differentiation architecturally, in terms of the balance of hotels, flats, camping, marinas and so forth, and in social composition of the clientèle. The general spatial allocation of growth along the coastlands west of the Rhône is intended to be balanced, though in fact growth to the mid-1970s has created two major nodes, Leucate-Barcarès and St Cyprien close to Perpignan, and La Grande Motte near the Rhône delta.

The transformation of the coastal landscape with the creation of the urban centres has been dramatic, but the long-term future of the project is less assured (Cazes 1972, Barbaza 1970). Within the ZAD mapped out for controlled urban development, the balance between a harmonious and socially just plan and the profit-intentions of speculative developers has not always been satisfactorily achieved. Outside the designated ZAD peripheral, inadequately controlled building has forced up land values undesirably. On the other hand, some architecturally spectacular results have been achieved, new forms of property ownership have been created (co-proprietorship, multi-ownership) and a powerful multiplier effect on the regional economy has been inaugurated.

The integral scheme for the Aquitaine coast (INSEE 1967, Barrère and Cassou-Mounat 1973) was initiated in 1967, to control what had threatened to become an anarchic growth of accommodation for 450,000 by 1980. The planning scheme (fig. 60) divides the 200 km coastline into 16 sectors, with 9 development centres (UPA–*unité principal d'aménagement*) and 7 intervening 'green zones' (SEN–*secteur d'équilibre naturel*). To help unify the environmental elements of sea, forest and lake, the trans-Aquitaine lateral canal axis will link up the Gironde to the Adour and, later, to the southern lakes of the Landes. The accommodation stock by 1980 will include 45 per cent second homes and 26 per cent camp-site places, with 17 per cent hotels and pensions and 6 per cent homes.

In other coastal areas threatened by development (Comité Interministériel 1973, Piquard 1974) preparation of regional planning schemes is active for Provence-Côte d'Azur (61.2 million tourist-days

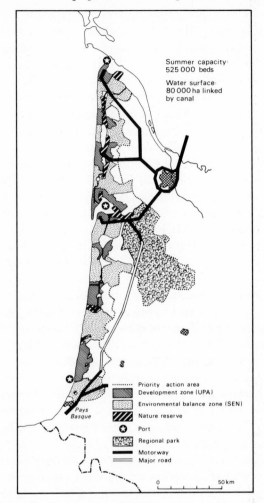

Figure 60   Aquitaine coastal planning scheme for 1980.

1972); Pays de la Loire, Poitou-Charentes (51.7M); Bretagne (54.8M); Basse-Normandie, Haute-Normandie (38.0M); and the Côte d'Opale. For specific proposals a structure plan (*schéma d'aménagement*) is created for rapid provision of infrastructure. The land thus serviced is sold as quickly as possible by the developers until the demand for coastal land becomes exhausted. Thus the development scheme, subject to all the pressures of the market, ironically risks compromising the very planning principles which led to its establishment.

Winter sports. Winter sports tourism is concentrated within the officially defined 'mountain zone' (1967), whose delimitation includes 4263 communes (each with more than 80 per cent of surface above 600 m or a relief difference of more than 400 m for the cultivated area), 9.1 million ha., and 2 million inhabitants (of whom 30 per cent live in settlements of more than 2000 population). Above 1000 m the total population is less than 220,000 practising a decaying pastoralism in the six major mountain massifs, with consequent endemic rural depopulation and inadequate social provision (House 1961, La DF 1970). Between 600 and 1000 m altitude (*moyenne montagne* or *montagne à vaches*) 1.4 millions live in a zone with a more active upland cattle economy and potential for both summer and winter tourism at or near existing settlements. Snow conditions are, however, less reliable and such middle-altitude resorts are thus less competitive with their high-altitude, and in time more fashionable, neighbours. Almost all winter sports resorts lie south of a line from Bayonne to Wissembourg, which puts them beyond weekend range for skiing by about one-third of the French population.

The geographical classification of winter sports centres (La DF 1970, 23; Perrin 1971, 1973) is according to phase of development, morphology and site, equipment and most recently the extent of land-use planning. Early centres grew at climatic or thermal resorts, such as Chamonix, Megève, Mont-Dore. The second pre-1939 generation developed as additions to villages at higher altitudes with more reliable snow, but grew on an uncoordinated pattern with insufficient capital and little regard for impact on the local community (e.g. Les Houches, Serre-Chevalier, Pralognan). After 1930 new 'green-field' stations were established at higher altitudes (e.g. Alpe d'Huez, Val d'Isère, Superbagnères).

During the first three French Plans (1948–60) only Courchevel (1946) was a major new winter sports centre; public involvement was limited to modernization at a selected few stations capable of attracting an international clientèle. Under the IVth Plan the *Commission interministérielle d'aménagement touristique de la montagne* was created (1964), with priority for large-scale developments, grant aid to hotels, infrastructure and equipment. The Vth Plan covered the establishment or modernization of 35 stations, whilst for the VIth and VIIth Plans a '*Plan Neige*' was formulated, with investment emphasis initially upon the high-altitude network of centres with an international reputation. The development of new winter sports resorts since the 1960s has been under a strictly regulated overall plan, e.g. La Plagne, with powers of compulsory land purchase by public authority. The traffic is segregated (pedestrians, skiers, vehicles), buildings and ski-runs are designed integrally (*front de neige*), shopping facilities are located centrally, and overall growth is limited (not more than 5000 beds in all for new centres), to avoid undesirable effects of urbanization; smaller satellite settlements may be established in the heart of the skiing area (La Plagne, Les Arcs).

Apart from residential stations, two other categories are recognized (Perrin 1973): village centres, where skiing is a complement to traditional activities and, as a brake on rural depopulation, has been a growth generator in rural renewal programmes (e.g. Queyras, Massif des Bauges); and weekend stations, used as recreational areas by nearby large towns (e.g. Chartreuse massif north of Grenoble).

During the VIIth Plan (1976–80) priorities for winter sports development are changing: more accommodation at resorts will be in flats (*lits banalisés*, apartments sold on condition that they are let for 5–7 years before being occupied permanently); social segregation by the specialization of accommodation at resorts will be discouraged; less emphasis will be placed on the international clientèle; organized group holidays will be encouraged; and intercommunal planning cooperation for further development will be promoted. The rapid growth of new resorts has permitted a doubling of the winter sports clientèle over the past ten years. It would seem that rural development (p. 428) now has priority (*Commission à la rénovation rurale en montagne*) over the *Plan Neige*, and the future will see much more development of winter sports within the existing rural fabric and less emphasis on large international resorts at high altitude. Planning is now more flexible, and based on the concept that a single resort should be able to cater for skiers of all social classes and abilities (Perrin 1973).

The creation of *second homes* (Clout 1970, Brier 1970, La DF 1972) is one of the most striking developments in postwar recreation: 1954 46,000, 1968 1,255,400. This form of family use of leisure time is paralleled by the rapid growth of 'social tourism' (youth hostels, camps, caravan sites, holiday villages, *colonies de vacances* of firms and municipalities). Including the use of second homes owned by friends or relatives, some 2 million Frenchmen visit second homes each year, along the coast, in the Paris and Lyon urban regions, or along the Paris-Lyon axis. The users of second homes are extremely varied by socio-economic class, age, household composition and type of ownership and tenancy.

A final category of tourism, that of *thermal spas* (fig. 59), has had a long and fashionable history. The number of those taking cures had risen, with fluctuations, from 220,000 (1952) to 378,000 (1968) and 433,500 in 1974, but the proportion of foreign visitors had fallen from 165,000 to 115,000 by 1968. Nevertheless, the significance of revenues from the thermal spas for the French economy is estimated at the equivalent of that from air transport or from the gas industry (Knecht 1971). Brief mention must also be made of pilgrimage traffic, placing Lourdes third in overall tourist night-stays among all French cities.

No more than light industry for dispersal into rural areas is tourism a universal panacea for depressed marginal districts, whether at the coast, in the mountains or in the countryside. Nevertheless, its potential as a growth generator is both considerable and diverse, and it is thus inevitably and increasingly a powerful tool in regional planning policy. The balance between commercial objectives in a fickle and vulnerable industry and planning directed to harmonious and sound conservation allied with tasteful and measured development is a difficult one to strike. With the new ministry (Quality of Life), inter-ministerial groups, regional tourist committees, mixed companies for tourist and general regional development, backed by official research groups and consultant advisers, the French government is uniquely well-equipped to meet the challenge of the 'leisure explosion', and to situate tourism within the general regional development objectives.

Any overall assessment of employment location policies in France, however brief, must emphasize positive achievements. Though regional balance in employment remains a long-term objective (Jouandet-Bernadat 1972), progress has been made in reducing the disequilibrium between Paris and the provinces, and to a much lesser extent between richer and poorer regions. Industrial decentralization from Ile-de-France has broken through the '200 km wall' and the deprived Ouest has been a major beneficiary. In the industrial reconversion regions (Nord, Lorraine) 80,000 new jobs were created 1968–73, though the reconversion has far to go and trans-frontier competition is a potentially serious constraint on growth. Rural areas have benefited considerably, in restructuring of farms, communications, social provision and tourism, whilst rural deprivation has been reduced significantly.

On the other hand, it is possible to argue (Astorg 1973, 33) that the regions to benefit most substantially under the Vth and VIth Plans were those already strong, with a counterbalancing metropolis, major ports or with good motorway connections. In considering the effectiveness of aids to location account must be taken of those moves which might have happened in any case. Nevertheless, 40–50,000 jobs per annum were created 1968–73 (cf. UK 80,000 per annum but at eight times the cost). Decentralization of tertiary activities in the private sector was tardy and both in quality and quantity of employment has lagged behind expectations.

References

Industrial structure and patterns

Boitel, E. (1968) 'L'industrie textile dans le Nord', *Hommes et Terres du Nord*, 2: 9–17.

Bouclier, C. and David, J. (1967) 'La papeterie en Grésivaudan: un problème d'implantation industrielle en montagne', *Revue Géogr. alp.*, 55 (4): 665–91.

Cazes, G. and Reynaud, A. (1973) 'Nécessité et problèmes de l'aménagement de l'espace rural', ch. 10 in *Les mutations récentes de l'économie française*.

Guibert, B. *et al.* (1975) 'La mutation industrielle de la France. Du traité de Rome à la crise pétrolière', *INSEE E* 31–2, 2 vols.

Hirschman, A. O. (1958) *The Strategy of Economic Development*, New Haven, Conn..

House, J. W. (ed.) (1977) *The UK Space* (2nd edn), London, ch. 1.

Jouandet-Bernadat, R. (1972) 'Les expériences d'analyse interindustrielle régionales', *Revue Econ. Sud-Ouest*, 1: 9–33.

La Documentation Française (1960) 'L'industrie française de la construction navale', *Notes et Etudes Documentaires*, 2624.

(1963) 'L'industrie électronique française', *Notes et Etudes Documentaires*, 3042.

(1966) 'L'industrie française des textiles artificiels et synthétiques', *Notes et Etudes Documentaires*, 3263.

(1968) 'L'industrie lainière française', *Notes et Etudes Documentaires*, 3547.

(1971A) 'L'industrie aéronautique et aéro-spatiale en France', *Notes et Etudes Documentaires*, 3764.

(1971B) 'L'industrie automobile en France', *Notes et Etudes Documentaires*, 3811.

Marnet-Leymarie, D. (1974) 'Les relations interindustrielles dans la localisation des industries de croissance', *Revue écon. Sud-Ouest*, 23 (1): 33–94.

Martin, J. (1957) 'Location factors in the Lorraine iron and steel industry', *Trans. Inst. Br. Geogr.*, 23: 191–212.

Myrdal, G. (1957) *Economic Theory and Underdeveloped Regions*, London.

Noël, M. (1974) 'Mobilité spatiale des industries, croissance et urbanisation', *L'Espace géogr.*, III (1): 47–56.

Nwafor, J. C. (1974) 'La structure et l'évolution spatiale de l'industrie française d'équipement automobile', *Annls Géogr.*, LXXXIII (456): 190–203.

Prêcheur, C. (1961) *La sidérurgie française*.

Decentralization

Association Bureaux-Provinces (1975) *La décentralisation des bureaux*.

Astorg, M. (1973) 'Les politiques de développement régional et d'aménagement du territoire en France, de 1954 à 1972', *Commissariat Général du Plan*.

Babonaux, Y. (1959) 'La décentralisation devant le problème de la main d'oeuvre du Loir-et-Cher', *Norois*, 21: 47–52.

Bastié, J. (1972) 'L'évolution récente des localisations industrielles dans une grande agglomération: l'exemple de Paris', *Revue Géogr. alp.*, LX (2): 245–52.

(1973) 'La décentralisation industrielle en France de 1954 à 1971', *Bull. Ass. Géogr. fr.*, 408–9: 561–9.

Bastié, J. and Trolliet, P. (1967) 'Evolution industrielle et décentralisation 1954–63', ch. 73–2 in Bastié, J. and Beaujeu-Garnier, J. (eds) *Atlas de Paris et de la Région Parisienne*.

Burgel, G. (1965) 'La main-d'oeuvre des établissements décentralisés: l'exemple de l'Eure', *Annls Géogr.*, LXXIV (404): 416–31.

Chesnais, M. (1964) 'Bilan de la décentralisation industrielle en Eure-et-Loir', *Norois*, 44: 521–5.

DATAR (1972) *La décentralisation du tertiare: les banques et les assurances.* (1976) *Aides au développement industriel.*

Donolo, C. (1972) *Stratégies de décentralisation et de localisation industrielle.*

Durand, P. (1972) *Industrie et Régions.*

Frémont, A., Ambois, M. and Chesnais, M. (1964) 'Argentan, une petite ville de Basse-Normandie, ranimée par la décentralisation industrielle', *Norois*, 44: 419–37.

Gay, F. J. (1966) *Atlas de Normandie*, E8 'Créations industrielles', Caen.

George, P. (1961) 'Nécessités et difficultés d'une décentralisation industrielle en France', *Annls Géogr.*, LXX (377): 25–36.

Gouhier, J. (1965) 'Notes sur la décentralisation industrielle entre Seine et Loire', *Annls Géogr.*, LXXIV (402): 220–3.

Palierne, J.-L. and Riquet, P. (1966) 'La décentralisation industrielle et le Bassin Parisien', *Cah. IAURP*, 6.

Parry, C. (1963) 'Un exemple de décentralisation industrielle: la dispersion des usines de la Radiotechnique à l'ouest de Paris', *Annls Géogr.*, LXXII (390): 148–61.

Piquard, M. (1971) *Les activités tertiaires dans l'aménagement du territoire*, La DF.

Rochefort, M. (1972) 'La localisation du pouvoir de commandement économique dans une capitale: les sièges sociaux des entreprises dans la région parisienne', *Revue Géogr. alp.*, LX (2): 225–44.

Saint-Julien, T. (1971) 'La Rochelle et la décentralisation industrielle', *Annls Géogr.*, LXXX (442): 687–706.
(1973) 'Signification géographique des implantations industrielles décentralisées en province', *Annls Géogr.*, LXXXII (453): 557–75.

Simonetti, J. O. (1977) 'L'administration de l'espace. L'exemple français', *Annls Géogr.*, LXXXVI (474): 129–63.

Tauvernon, A. (1974) 'Le "tertiaire supérieur", moteur du développement régional?', *L'Espace Géogr.*, III (3): 169–78.

Retailing

Atlas des Hypers et Supermarchés, au janvier 1973

Bruyelle, P. (1970) 'L'influence urbaine en milieu rural dans la région du Nord. Commerce et Services', *CERES*, Lille.

Dawson, J. A. (1976) 'Hypermarkets in France', *Geogr.*, 61 (4): 259–62.

La Documentation Française (1972) *Le commerce intérieur.*

Piatier, A. (ed.) (1971) *Les zones d'attraction commerciale de la région Midi-Pyrénées*, 2 vols.

Smith, B. A. (1973) 'Retail planning in France: the changing pattern of French retailing', *Tn Plann. Rev.*, 44 (3): 279–306.

Tourism and recreation

Barbaza, Y. (1970) 'Trois types d'intervention du tourisme dans l'organisation de l'espace littoral', *Annls Géogr.*, LXXIX (434): 446–69.

Barbier, B. (1966) 'Tourisme et emploi en Provence-Côte d'Azur', *Méditerranée*, 3: 207–28.

Barrère, P. and Cassou-Mounat, M. (1973) 'Le schéma d'aménagement de la côte Aquitaine', *Revue géogr. Pyrénées et Sud-ouest*, 44 (2–3): 303–20.

Brier, M. A. (1970) *Les résidences secondaires.*

Castex, F. (1972) *L'èquipement touristique de la France.*

Cazes, G. (1972) 'Réflexions sur l'aménagement touristique du littoral du Languedoc-Roussillon', *L'Espace géogr.*, I (3): 193–210.

Clary, C. (1976) 'Tourisme et aménagement régional', *Annls Géogr.*, LXXXV (468): 129–54.

Clout, H. D. (1970) 'Social aspects of second-home occupation in the Auvergne', *Plann. Outl.*, 9: 33–49.

Comité Interministériel d'Aménagement du Territoire (1973) *Littoral français*, Rapport au Gouvernement.

Cribier, F. (1969) 'La grande migration d'été des citadins en France', *Mémoires et Documents du CNRS.*

    (1973) 'L'évolution récente des comportements de vacances des Français et la géographie du tourisme', *Trav. Inst. Géogr. Reims*, 13–14: 7–15.

Dacharry, M. (1965) 'Le tourisme social', *Revue Géogr. alp.*, LIII (4): 634–41.

Flament, E. (1975) 'Quelques remarques sur l'espace touristique', *Norois*, 88: 609–21.

Fourastié, J. (1970) *Des loisirs: pour quoi faire?*

Groupe Permanent d'Etudes de l'OREAM (1968) 'Loisirs', *Cah. OREAM*, 6, Lyon.

House, J. W. (1961) 'Western Alpine society in transition', *Plann. Outl,*, V (2): 17–30.

INSEE (1967) *Etude statistique de l'activité touristique en Aquitaine*, 1963–66.

Knecht, M (1971) 'Le thermalisme en France', *Aménagement du territoire et développement régional*, IV, IEP, Grenoble: 509–64.

La Documentation Française (1970) 'Les sports d'hiver en France', *Notes et Etudes Documentaires*, 3701–3702.

    (1972) 'Les résidences secondaires en France', *Notes et Etudes Documentaires*, 3939–3940.

Madaule, M. *et al.* (1970) 'Révolution touristique et aménagement du territoire', *Cah. Hexagone*, 51/52.

OECD (1973, 1974, 1975) *International tourism and tourism policy in OECD member countries.*

Perrin, H. (1971) 'Les stations de sports d'hiver', *L'Administration Nouvelle.*

    (1973) 'La promotion des équipements touristiques en montagne', *Aménagement du territoire et développement régional*, VI, IEP, Grenoble: 231–41.

Piquard, M. (1974) 'Littoral français', *Perspectives pour l'aménagement*, La DF.

Préau, P. (1973) 'L'emprise spatiale du tourisme', *Trav. Inst. Géogr. Reims*, 13–14: 27–33.

Rapports des Commissions du 6e Plan (1971) *Tourisme.*

Sec. d'Etat au Tourisme (1975) 'Les vacances des Français en 1974', *Statistiques du Tourisme*, 6: 2–38.

Part three

Spatial management policies

1 Spatial strategies in the plan process

The term *aménagement du territoire* has no exact English counterpart. It includes regional planning but is perhaps better rendered by spatial management, embracing many forms and different scale levels (Claval 1975). The significance of the term has changed through time as deliberate spatial management has come more to the forefront in planning generally since the early 1960s. Labasse (1960, 390–1) preferred to distinguish between *aménagement* and development: the first, spatial, qualitative, long-term and concerned with reducing territorial disequilibria; the latter, economic and quantitative, shorter-term and often dramatic. Monod (1971) saw spatial management policies as a search for the choices which society makes for the alternative uses of space.

Planning too has changed character from the comprehensive socialist-type, medium-term sector programming of the late 1940s and early 1950s (Carré *et al.* 1975, Fourastié & Courthéoux 1968). There is thus a prime need to evaluate the general change in planning and to situate spatial management policies and town planning measures within this change. No less significant is the need to assess the impact of planning upon changes in French economy and society. It will be seen that such impact has not necessarily been cumulative or directly related to either the increasing sophistication of the plan process or the proliferation of planning organizations. The plan proposals for the VIIth Plan (1976–80) indeed make abundantly clear an abrupt shift both in planning generally and in the collective intentions and the disseminated, more democratic power-base for spatial management policies.

Central planning in postwar France has never been intended as a resource allocation mechanism alternative to that of the market (Holmes and Estrin 1976). Indeed, French planning has been termed 'the best rationalization of the capitalist system yet arrived at' (Boudeville 1966, 153). Planning has been indicative, a framework for government and entrepreneurial decisions, but in only a few instances a binding set of statutory constraints. Such constraints have been partial in time and space, intended to limit industrial or office expansion in and around the metropolis, or to control land speculation in the towns and cities, by the exercise of public rights of pre-emption of land (ZUP, ZAD, ZAC legislation, p. 327). On the other hand the stimuli, collectively substantial, have also been partial and over time somewhat ephemeral. Public action is best regarded as providing a catalyst to change, but overall a powerful catalyst which has had the result of setting some unfavourable national trends into reverse: migration to Paris and the great cities, impoverishment of the countryside, increasing imbalance in regional living standards (though this achievement may be disputed), or decline in older industrial centres (Monod 1974, xiv).

The extent to which such changes would have taken place without the planning organizations is difficult to assess. Critics (Noël 1976) argue that decentralization by firms from Paris would have developed under market forces in any case, to escape congestion and high costs in the metropolis and to search for cheap labour in the provinces. Furthermore, spatial management policies, they argue, have been neither comprehensive, nor responsive to regional and local differences or the views of local people. In such a critique, spatial management is little more than public investment at particular points and the programming of a technostructure (Cognat 1973, 89).

The general context of successive French plans was discussed in Part I, ch. 2. The coverage, intentions, mechanisms and achievements of planning have changed substantially during the course of postwar years within the shifting field of political forces, the state of the economy, and not least the mounting pressure of externalities upon French national life. Through time the spatial dimension in planning has emerged, with regional policy an essential counterpart to incomes policy in attempts to regulate the market system. In the early postwar years, given weak government in France, planning was primarily economic in character, concerned with management of equilibria (balances) of several kinds: between national income, employment, wages and prices; between internal and external trade, reflected in the balance of payments; and between regions in the national space (decentralization policies). The need for spatial management was recognized as early as 1949 by creation of DAT under the *Ministère de la Reconstruction et du Logement* (Housing and Reconstruction). Coherent spatial management was limited to the operation of a system of building licences, together with the requirement of a planning scheme for every urban agglomeration of more than 10,000 population. The FNAT funds (see acronyms) provided financial aid to local authorities, municipalities and chambers of commerce. Additionally, individual ministries had resource management programmes with strong spatial implications (e.g. agriculture: for farm restructuring, drainage, afforestation, rural education, marketing; industry and commerce; labour; transport).

Decentralization from the metropolis was the foundation stone of early spatial management policies (Plans I—III). Indeed it has been said that 'spatial management was at first directed against Paris, but later had to develop in complementary fashion with Paris' (Dischamps 1972, 452). Yet already from 1954 legislation of *regional* significance had been introduced. Indeed as far back as 1949 the problems arising from inequalities among the regions had been recognized and by the mid-1950s regional action programmes for both economic and social development were required by central government, whilst the regions themselves (*régions de programme*, p. 47) had become administratively defined. The regional level had only consultative powers but initiatives in formulating planning proposals were very strong in many of the regions. It was, however, the action of central government which had the greatest spatial impact. Measures of interdiction included controls on all new industrial locations of more than 500 m² in Ile-de-France (1955), a requirement later extended to offices and extensions to industrial premises. Subsequently (p. 274) these measures of interdiction were strengthened and widened in scope, applicable for a few years also to Greater Lyon (1966–70). On the credit side, development premiums, loans, subsidies and equipment bounties (p. 276) were used selectively in both space and time to stimulate firms to locate in zones of unemployment or underemployment. Funding was also available for reconversion operations in industry (redeployment of investment) and for the retraining of the workforce. Problem localities or subregions were identified (p. 276) as *zones critiques*, defined in terms of mining or industrial decline (1955); in 1959 these were redefined as *zones spéciales de conversion* and the list was added to. The relationship of problem localities to the open European frontiers of France became a rising preoccupation.

Planning evolution

During Plans I—III (1947–61) the French economy experienced a rising momentum of boom conditions. The impressive economic growth record of this period was to some extent achieved at the expense of balance, both internally as between employment sectors, and spatially between regions, and externally until 1961 in terms of the balance of trade. From the mid-1950s the prosperity of manufacturing and service industries meant that public stimuli towards relocating production had a diminishing effect. The onset of stronger and more politicized government after 1958 further diminished the effective impact of the planner-technocrats.

Under very different planning institutions Britain experienced some similar trends in the impact of planning between 1947 and 1961 (House 1977, 22–31). A dramatic early postwar effect of Development Area policy was followed by a slackening of controls during the later 1950s and a restriction of priority government economic and social aid to more narrowly defined localities or development districts. There were, however, major substantial differences. The UK lacked the comprehensiveness of successive medium-term economic plans and spatial management policies were more piecemeal and free-standing in character. On the other hand the tight and detailed control over land use under physical planning legislation in Britain (Town and Country Planning Act 1947) had no counterpart in France. Furthermore, the mix of controls and inducements in public location policies in Britain saw a much stronger set of constraints upon industrialists, together with a much more fluctuating, though at times stronger set of selective inducements.

From the onset of the IVth Plan (1962–5) marked changes in the character and significance of French planning took place. More realistic regional and spatial management dimensions were instituted and progressively developed. Planning theory and techniques became greatly sophisticated; in particular, forecasting techniques were markedly improved, whilst the objectives of successive plans were more clearly and quantitatively formulated. Unfortunately for the planners, their influence upon events diminished, for several reasons: particular events such as the mass immigrations from North Africa (1962–5, p. 155), political turbulence in 1968 and its longer-term implications, and the oil crisis of 1973–5; secondly, the influence of external conditions, partly arising from French membership of the EEC (1958), but also due to the break-up of the French Community, and general deterioration in the world trading economy. Moreover, strong governments increasingly controlled the plan process and conditioned its application increasingly in political rather than in technocratic terms. Though this led to pragmatic solutions and distortions of economic logic it had the beneficial effects of making planning more sensitive to human aspirations beyond those of economic rationale or material gain. This process of relating planning more effectively to pursuit of the quality of life and making the plan process focus more deliberately upon social justice and deprived groups culminated in the proposals for the VIIth Plan (1976–80). Planning has thus finally become more macro-economic in emphasis and planning and politics have become increasingly intertwined (Holmes and Estrin 1976, 32). Planning by consent of the people and their representatives at all scale levels, by dialogue and consensus *(concertation)* among sectoral groups in society, and with government acting as the catalyst for private initiatives, has replaced the austere technocratic management of the early postwar years. One result has necessarily been to make more difficult an assessment of the effects of planning policies, diffused as these have become in their application.

With the establishment of DATAR in 1963 spatial management became a central and substantive part of French national planning, on a more coherent and sustained footing. Spatial management was defined as 'an art, a science, a technique and a policy', concerned to 'prepare the future, taking account of space'. The policy was to 'manage mobility' and, whilst 'seeking to steer it for social purposes, not to oppose it'. At regional level spatial management was 'to coordinate and stimulate actions in order to achieve an overall set of objectives for a particular region' (all quotations from Guichard 1965). Durand (1976, 323) saw the purposes of spatial management as 'on the one hand to reduce and if possible eliminate disequilibria generating social problems, financial costs, and technological inefficiencies; on the other, to ensure, within the limits of general development, a diversity of life styles and satisfying working conditions'. The scope of spatial policies was extended to large-scale regional development projects, cities and towns, regional strategies, communications and transport infrastructure, and rural renewal (see below p. 424) (Monod 1974, xiii). DATAR has an interministerial character, with direct access to the prime minister. It has no direct powers but a considerable liaison role and coordinating influence. Decisions on all spatial management policies are taken through the central government apparatus (p. 319) and relayed to regional and more local levels. In return, from these lower levels information and advice is filtered up to central government.

A fundamental need to establish firm regional institutions of planning led to the regional reforms of 1964 (p. 47), creating the regional prefects and the CODER, together with civil service support groups. The further reforms of 1972 widened and strengthened regional representation and participation. The regional net inherited was that created in 1960 (21 *circonscriptions d'action régionale*, p. 47; as from 1956 *régions de programme*); in 1970 Corse was added to the list. It was, however, made clear already in 1964 that the existence of regions did *not* introduce a new level of executive decision-taking between central government and the *départements*. This remains substantially the case today though the right to be consulted at regional level has been greatly extended under the VIth and prospectively the VIIth Plans. The regional CODER was responsible for contributing to and later commenting upon the regional planning programmes, later regional plans, of the *Ministère de la Construction*. Such plans essentially presented the characteristics and trends of geography, demography and economy in the region, and thereafter formulated the objectives of regional development by sector, together with the means of achieving them. The regional prefect acted as guide, overseer and catalyst of these regional plans and since 1961 (IVth Plan) there were instituted *tranches opératoires* (operational slices), later 'regional slices', of the annual national programmes. These provided a list of centrally-approved investments together with some whose allocation could be determined regionally. The 'regional slices' in turn were defined partly in terms of the proposals coming up from the regions, establishing an effective two-way interchange. The regional plans were criticized by geographers among others as being unstructured, lacking in any coordination with those of adjacent regions, and being of little practical effect. It was further argued (Phlipponneau 1968) that regional planning was no more than thinly disguised administrative domination from the centre (*déconcentration* not *décentralisation*), whilst Lafont (1967) spoke of continuing *néocolonialisme*. The potential conflict of interest between national and regional planning remains unresolved. National plans are not the summation of regional plans; nor are regional plans merely subdivisions of a national plan. The relation between the two levels cannot be resolved arithmetically. There are perennial risks of regional bodies seeking illusions of autonomy without taking into account choices and constraints of national plans, whilst national planners may all too easily ignore the coherence of programmes emerging at the regional level (Monier 1965). What is needed is a conciliation between national objectives and the particular or pressing needs of individual regions.

A measure of recognition of differing regional needs was found in the theoretical division (IVth Plan, 1962–5) between policies for *entraînement* (public investment to promote change) or *accompagnement* (complementary to change). In practice a two-fold subdivision was operated (p. 277): *zones de développement* (mainly rural) and *zones d'adaptation* (mainly industrial reconversion). Particular regions had distinctive objectives: relocation of tertiary centres in and around Paris; diversification of manufacturing in the Nord; development of steel-using manufactures in Lorraine; diffusion of light industry, especially electronics, into the Ouest, together with modernization of the rural economy; reconversion of the declining mining districts of the Massif Central and rationalization of traditional industries in difficulty (textiles, shoes); large-scale resources projects in the Midi: water management, tourism, agricultural planning.

Under the Vth Plan (1966–70, pp. 23–4) there were five major spatial management policies: restructuring of Ile-de-France; formulation of the programme for 8 regional metropoli (p. 350), to act as counter-magnets to Paris and in turn the stimuli for more balanced and coherent urbanization within their hinterlands; industrialization of the Ouest; the growth of regions already industrialized, mainly in renewal and diversification programmes in the Nord and Lorraine, together with the creation of an axis of linkage between northern France and the Mediterranean; and finally, the restructuring of rural space, by major management schemes for agricultural, forest or water resources. (The *'sociétés d'économie mixte'*, created earlier, were strengthened for Bas-Rhône-Languedoc (CNABRL —1955), Canal de Provence, Corse (SOMIVAC–1958), the Landes, Côteaux de Gascogne, Friches de l'Est [uncultivated lands] and Auvergne-Limousin (SOMIVAL–1964)).

The VIth Plan (1971–5) continued this package of spatial management programmes, some localized or sectorally defined, but also reinforced the regional level of planning, both in terms of functions and institutions. This Plan will probably be the last to emphasize economic growth as a prime preoccupation, and perhaps the last to formulate programmes in comprehensive, ambitious terms. Political events and the reaction against complex and centralized bureaucratic institutions had already set in. Social priorities and the quality of both life and its environment came to the forefront of planning objectives.

The Plan included 25 objectives, most of which had complex spatial implications. In terms of regional impact there were five groupings: the continuing adjustment of the balance between Paris and the provinces; the Ouest; the frontier regions of the Nord and the Est; the zones of high economic (industrial-urban) density; and the rural areas. The redressing of the metropolis-provinces balance was promoted through the 1972 revision of interdictions and aid measures for industrial and office movement (p. 274), with clear targets for the rate of employment growth in each of the eight ZEAT regions (fig. 4). Priority was given to stimulus in regions undergoing industrial reconstruction, out of declining industries, and areas of large potential agricultural labour surplus. The attraction of foreign firms and their persuasion to locate in priority areas was an element of this policy. The decentralization of decision centres and major tertiary establishments, particularly those in research or education, favoured the countermagnet metropoli and regional capitals. Both public and private establishments were involved (p. 283). The regionalization of the equipment budget in 1972, together with stronger efforts to disseminate ministerial decision-taking, added teeth to these measures.

The development of the Ouest was through employment build-up in the secondary and tertiary sectors, with strong emphasis also on internal and external communications improvement, the growth generating role of the three metropoli and other regional capitals, the attraction of labour-intensive manufacturing jobs, and a balanced programme of stimulus also for small or medium-sized towns (particularly those located along potential small-scale development axes). The older industrial frontier regions of the Nord and Est were given special stimulus, to counteract the adverse pressures from more favoured trans-frontier districts of adjacent countries. Emphasis was laid on continuing industrial renewal in the mining and textile areas, to achieve greater job diversity and a better representation of growth sectors. Infrastructure was once more a key investment, to develop regional interchange, promote the counter-magnet metropoli, and link the regions with proximate hinterlands. Renovation of an outworn urban fabric was a further pressing priority.

Action on the most developed urban-industrial regions concerned the Bassin Parisien with the Basse-Seine, and the Sud-Est. In the Paris ag-glomeration (Part III, ch. 2) redistributive social justice was to relocate growth and improve housing by priority for the deprived eastern sector, to improve workplace-residence relationships generally, and this in part by locating industrial as well as tertiary growth poles in selected sites in the suburban perimeter and beyond. The five New Towns were to be developed with housing, jobs and infrastructure carefully phased. The Bassin Parisien was to benefit from further decentralization of activities to its nine principal towns and the four support zones (*zones d'appui*). Effective transport link-ups were an essential part of the radial strategy and also that for developing the economic growth axis of the Basse-Seine, from Paris through Rouen to Le Havre. Bourgogne, in an intermediate position between the Bassin Parisien and the Sud-Est, was to benefit from dissemination of growth from both directions.

In the Sud-Est the two countermagnet metropoli (Lyon-St Etienne-Grenoble and Marseille-Fos) were planned for fast urban and industrial growth. The potential for linking the metropoli with each other and with their hinterland urban network depended on major communications improvements. Marseille-Fos, with the Basse-Seine and Dunkerque, were the major industrial port complexes, to be developed rapidly in an integral fashion (Part III, ch. 2).

For the rural sector the VIth Plan envisaged continuing the restructur-ing of farms and the diversification of activities, and particularly selective programmes for investment in tourist facilities, some of them (Languedoc, Aquitaine) very dramatic in character, growth and impact (p. 293). In the more remote or poorer marginal rural areas a micro-scale counter-depopulation programme was envisaged, concerned with forms of production, social provision, marketing and improvement in the standards and quality of rural life.

Priorities for the VIIth Plan (1976-80), though not finally translated into plan programmes, are clearly different in scope and kind from earlier plans. Room to manoeuvre in a slow economic growth situation has been limited, whilst problems of inflation, unemployment, and balance of payments have laid further constraints upon an effective plan mechanism under market conditions. Furthermore, the climate has moved against large-scale, complex technocratic and bureaucratic planning. Large firms are now able to finance most of their development without government aid and are less inclined to move production to new locations under slow growth conditions, whilst for the same reason being less susceptible to government pressure to move. Public priorities are to maintain, or rather restore, full employment, and to reduce the more dramatic social inequalities between classes and places. As the prime minister put it: 'It is no longer a question of spatial planning, but of managing planning itself, so that it corresponds to the character, preferences and social choices of the French people' (*Le Monde*, 25 November 1975). Or alternatively, 'the day of the *grands ensembles* (giant housing blocks) and the great city concentrations is over', and the state was to encourage localization of activities more clearly in small and medium-sized towns. Needless migration and depopulation of marginal areas was to be halted. In particular, the isolation of the most poorly-served regions in the Ouest, Massif Central and Sud-Ouest was to be broken, whilst France was to be more closely linked by modern communications into the heartland of the EEC.

A new area planning policy is to respect the characteristics of each region, whilst integrating its development in a framework of national needs. The flight from the land must be slowed down and the spread of suburbs halted, with priority attention to the needs of the inner cities. Apart from action on the underprivileged rural regions already mentioned, particular regional measures include: revitalization of the outer ring of towns and further stimulus for the New Towns of the Bassin Parisien; curbing of the extension of the Lyon and Marseille conurbations in favour of small and medium-sized towns; diversification of farming and industrialization in Languedoc; and construction of the North Sea-Mediterranean waterway (probably during the VIIIth Plan).

There is a widespread emphasis on the doctrine that 'small is beautiful', in settlement, factory, shop or office size, or scale of economic and social organization. In political terms the region is on trial for ten years to 1982, to assess its role in the coordination of economic development, and to decide thereafter whether the region is to continue or to yield to the *département* in that respect. Decentralization must envisage more power at the first rung of democratic life, the *commune*. Already a Commission on Local Government has reported on these possibilities (Guichard 1976). Expenditure on improvements in the quality of life (12 per cent), reduction of social inequalities (15 per cent), restoration of full employment (5 per cent), development of research (5 per cent), regional and local programmes (9 per cent) and economic revitalization (54 per cent) illustrate the balance of priorities in the new planning action programmes.

British planning has seen no such *volte-face* in recent years (House 1977, 41–96). Regional aid policies have continued, with relief of unemployment a persisting barometer of the intensity of regional distress. Economic planning strategies have been put forward by regional economic planning councils, created in 1965 on lines clearly resembling their French counterparts. These strategies, developed in three stages, are not unlike French regional plans of the same era, but there is lacking in Britain both the central planning apparatus (see below) in economic and social terms, and also any specific regional allocation within the national budget. Regional strategies are scarcely interrelated with each other and at best are a shifting backcloth to production of structure plans at the new county level (since 1974). The UK is also lacking in overall spatial appreciations of priorities at regional level, a sad tribute perhaps to the enduring pragmatic strain in these islands, by comparison with the splendid if not always effective regional planning rationale across the Channel.

SOME THEORETICAL CONSIDERATIONS

General equilibrium theory lies implicitly behind successive postwar plans in France. Balanced, harmonious growth has been sought, internationally in trade, nationally in structural terms of production and employment, and regionally in the reduction of first, economic and sectoral and, later, spatial inequalities. The attack on social inequalities, prominent in the VIth and in the forefront of the VIIth Plan, is a further manifestation, but perhaps now more political than theoretical in character. Keynesian policies for demand management came in only during the late 1960s in France (Hough 1976, 27), but even then very modestly. French governments have remained less interventionist and have traditionally relied more on monetarist than upon fiscal policies. Macro-economic planning has taken over from an earlier preoccupation with key sectors and micro-economic projections (Holmes and Estrin 1976, 12). Spatial implications are important at both levels, though macro-economic theory has not been principally concerned with either spatial location or non-economic variables. Spatial and socio-cultural aspects were in practice elaborated at regional level and fed to the national calculations on macro-variables or macro-constants, to limit the zone of indeterminacy in public policy (Della Porta 1960).

Unlike the more pragmatic British version, regional planning in France has had strong theoretical fundaments and those mainly derived from economics, including: economic base theory, related to interregional accounts; cumulative causation theory (Myrdal 1957, Hirschman 1958); and, most notably, theories of polarized growth, including the growth pole concept (Perroux 1964, Boudeville 1966, 1972). These theories have not only afforded powerful conceptual tools for analysis, but have also given rise to families of growth models. Such models have underlain some of the more important planning polices for the diffusion and implantation of economic growth, the harmonious development of interrelated activities in city and region, and, most recently, the interaction of regions within the national framework.

Key concepts in the economist's consideration of non-geographical space include: descriptive homogeneity, the spatial clustering of similarities, in which contiguity plays an important role; polarization, functional relationships crystallizing out in space, as in the nodal points of an urban network, or in the rationalization of selected settlements into growth poles; and decision-space, the units adopted for administrative or executive action (Boudeville 1972, 29). The central concept was earlier expressed by Perroux – 'Economic growth does not appear everywhere at the same time. It is manifest in points or growth poles and expands in different channels with variable intensity throughout the economy' (quoted in Boudeville 1972, 7). These elements of a study of spatial dynamism have variable time dimensions: short-term *conjoncture* (trends of economy, society, or polity); medium-term programmes (e.g. the plan-periods of several years); and longer-term spatial management plans (e.g. 15 years for major transport changes, 30 years for the full development of the regional counter-magnet metropoli). Even two generations may be required to achieve the full objectives of town planning, in the fundamental changes in customs, habits and attitudes (Durand 1976, 326).

For effective spatial planning there is a need to interrelate policies at differing scale levels: the local, with the regional and national; homogeneous regions with polarized urban networks (Charmeil 1975, Perrin 1974, 1975); and the spatial aspects themselves within the macro-economic sectoral policies. Such coherence within spatial planning has never been attempted in Britain, and has only been partially achieved in France since the beginnings of the VIth Plan. The static medium-term planning model for the French economy (FIFI, *Modèle physico-financier*) used 7 employment sectors, 2 with protected prices (food processing; services, building and public works); 1 exposed to international competition (manufacturing); and 4 where prices were 'administered' (agriculture, energy, transport, and housing). A complementary regional-national model (REGINA 1971) was developed to replace simple mechanistic projections of population and employment (Courbis and Prager 1973, Courbis 1972, 1975, Boudeville 1972, 197). REGINA is based upon interregional account tables (TEIR) and for a five-fold regional breakdown of France (each region is also subdivided into rural and two levels of urbanization) determines regional production and regional exchange, on an export-base model, distinguishing 'sheltered' production whose demand is local, from 'exposed' (often propulsive or growth activities), where demand is determined outside and there is freedom to locate activities. Connected to FIFI for the VIIth Plan it will be possible to study the interaction of regional projections with the national, a valid recognition that the regional problem in France is no longer to be considered only by regionalization from national forecasts, but equally by the definition of regional balances to correct parameters of the national model. Most recently REGINA has been modified to include urban problems and also the qualitative growth variables fashionable in the VIIth Plan.

Paradoxically, the increasing sophistication of economic model building has come at a time when planning itself is changing course and in general diminishing in overall impact. Liggins (1975, 1976) defined the IVth and Vth Plans as 'plans of the nation', the search for a consensus being followed by a contract between all the government agencies, including firms, to supplement the market mechanism by reducing uncertainty. The VIth Plan, and even more the VIIth Plan, were 'plans of the government', to test the reactions of various groups to official medium-term policies. The operational aspects were limited to a range of priority programmes for public investment. Planning had become emphatically more political and less technocratic.

Though a few individual French geographers participated significantly in the plan process, including membership of some of the preparatory planning commissions, there was a more widespread scepticism, and on occasion downright political opposition to the regional impact of functions and powers (Phlipponneau 1968). Applied geography itself encountered academic opposition in France, but in time a middle road was defined (Veyret-Verner 1973). Nevertheless the geographical contribution to planning was strongest at the differentiated regional level, perhaps most influential in advice and consultancy on semi-official bodies. As interpreters of the complex realities of space and place geographers offered a healthy and critical corrective to some of the theoretical abstractions of the spatial economists (Labasse 1960). As the focus of planning now shifts to a more pragmatic political basis the potential impact of the geographers should be strengthened thereby. Other social scientists have dissented from the technocratic and on occasion impersonal basis of planning in postwar France (Courthéoux 1968, Decouflé 1972, Biarez 1974), whilst political commentators have not been lacking (Nizard 1972) to deplore the absence of sufficient democratic controls over the plan process. Indeed, the proliferation of democratically-based pressure groups to contest planning decisions has become as characteristic in France as in Britain (Courthéoux 1965).

SPATIAL POLICIES

By way of summary ahead of their more detailed interpretation and interrelation, it is convenient to list the major spatial policies currently active in French planning (fig. 61):

Urban. Management of the growth and spatial differentiation of the urban network (*armature urbaine*), through policies of public investment stimulus at several scale-levels; by comparison, interdiction as a tool of management has been very restricted in both time and space. Urban management policies have been concerned with a better national balance within the French hexagon, notably so between the capital and the provinces, but also within the urban network at lesser scale-levels: provincial metropoli and their satellite towns, down to small towns in a rural hinterland. The policies for promoting eight countermagnet regional metropoli, investing in selected New Towns as satellites for urban decongestion, or the medium-sized towns (*villes moyennes*) policy are all aspects of urban network management. Such management policies have been most directly concerned with setting up the means for disseminating development (Perrin 1968, 223), not simply stimulating the growth of particular size categories of urban centre. Increasingly perhaps, political influences have intruded and bilateral negotiations have disrupted the theoretical elegance of attempted urban systems management, whilst awareness of problems of the inner cities has risen as dramatically in France as in Britain during the past few years.

Other polarized growth policies relate to growth pole identification and selective spatial investment. The concept of industrial growth complexes, as deliberately induced major concentrations at Marseille-Fos, the Basse-Seine, or Dunkerque, is a further distinctive French contribution to planning, whilst the fashionable 'corridor growth' concept awakens echoes of similar thinking in British regional strategies of the 1970s. By comparison, however, the French 'growth corridors' have greater sub-

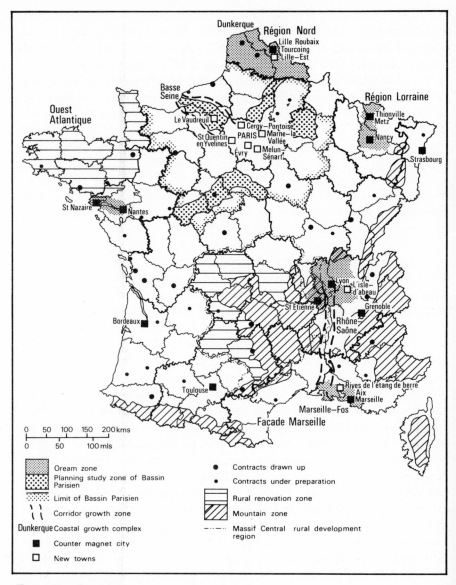

Figure 61   Spatial management policies, 1976.

stance and are a most likely development under the polarizing impact of market forces.

Regional. Regional strategies, programmes or plans have come to play an increasingly important role since the IVth Plan. Earlier disconnected regional 'shopping lists' gave place to the considered views of regional organizations on the desirable nature or likely impact of national planning proposals. Most recently, more formal regional plans have been prepared, the regionalization of the national budget has opened up the financial means, and operational models have helped situate regional plans both in relation to the national plan and to each other. Apart from the 22 homogeneous regions as administrative-decision spaces, there are policies for rural space and for more localized problem regions. Management of rural space is concerned with the stemming of out-migration to the towns, rehabilitation and diversification of the rural economy, together with an improvement in living conditions. The localized problem region approach has been less favoured in France than in Britain, but rural, mining, industrial and coastal areas have been the subject of special public aid policies, though intermittently and temporarily. Even at this delicate political level, planning has sought to work within a market framework rather than clean contrary to longer-term economic forces.

Planning organizations
There is an at times bewildering and seemingly proliferating range of planning bodies, often identified only by their initials (see List of Acronyms). Many are referred to in subsequent sections and attention is here confined to identifying the principal agencies, their roles and interrelationships.

At national level.   (1) Since October 1974, the all powerful *Conseil central de planification* (Central planning council), composed of the prime minister, minister of finance, minister for employment and the planning commissioner (*Délégue à l'aménagement du territoire et à l'action régionale*).

(2) Since the late 1940s, the *Commissariat au Plan*, an initially dominant technocratic body varying between 60 and the present 40 members, with a role ranging over regional as well as sector planning, but also including responsibilities similar to the NEDO in Britain. Lacks its own technical support groups, but relies on INSEE for forecasting and model-building.

(3) DATAR (*Délégation à l'aménagement du territoire et à l'action régionale*), created 1963 as an inter-ministerial service to prepare, and for the central committees to put into effect, policies for spatial management. After many ministerial attachments comes under *Ministère de l'Intérieur*; dependent upon the prime minister for any necessary arbitration. Receives data from regional bodies and disposes of funds for spatial management (FIAT); decentralization (FAD), including public and private institutions; administers FDES funds concerned with regional development premiums. Since 1966 has had charge of regionalizing the national budget.

Five types of regional organization are linked to DATAR:

(a) commissions for industrial reconversion, or industrialization (1967), with responsibilities for attracting firms and improving the industrial environment. In the mid-1970s there were four commissioners: Nord/Lorraine, Ouest Atlantique, Façade Méditerranée, and St Etienne with Alès.

(b) inter-ministerial groups to coordinate actions on major infrastructures (e.g. Fos, Dunkerque; mining basins).

(c) commissions for rural renovation (1967), to improve agricultural production, promote small industries, tourism and accessibility.

(d) interministerial planning commissions for major tourist projects: Languedoc-Roussillon (1963), Aquitaine coast (1967), Corse (1970).

(e) O R E A M for the counterbalancing metropoli (*q.v.*), study organizations to prepare a *schéma directeur* (SDAU) following preparation and discussion of a *livre blanc*.

(4) C N A T (*Commission national de l'aménagement du territoire*), a 'horizontal' commission concerned with long-term spatial management objectives and their formulation into planning perspectives. Representation on CNAT includes the prime minister, ministers, large-scale credit establishments, industrialists, unions, regional bodies, local authorities and the universities.

(5) The *Comité de la régionalisation du plan*, composed of high-level civil servants, issues directives to the regional prefects, prepares the presentation of the 'regional slices' of the Plan for the interministerial committee, and maintains liaison with the regional councils.

At regional level. The regional prefect, and since the 1972 reforms, the *Conseil régional* and the *Conseil économique et social* (p. 48). The regional prefect has powers to propose (investment programmes for *département* or *région*), decide (distribution of regional investment allocated from the centre) and preside over his fellow *département* prefects. He is assisted by a *mission*, or civil service support group, and chairs the *Conférence administrative régionale* of senior civil servants in the region. Among semi-private bodies the *Comité d'expansion* (*économique et sociale*) in most regions has had a long history of research, publicity, promotion and forecasting, often in association with the Chambers of Commerce. Certainly the 1972 regional reform legislation both widened and strengthened democratic participation, a trend likely to be given even greater prominence for decision-taking under the VIIth Plan.

The *financing of regional development* takes place through the national budget and the 'regional slices' of the Plan, but there are additionally funds for special purposes:

at national level:

FDES (*Fonds de développement économique et social*), an overall development fund established as far back as 1955 to advise on the suitability of investment programmes and the availability of aid, with powers to grant loans at reduced interest rates.

FIAT (*Fonds d'intervention pour l'aménagement du territoire*), to finance major development schemes under spatial management policies, and to liaise with regional administrations on objectives and implementation of annual 'regional slices' of the Plan.

FNAFU (*Fonds national d'aménagement foncier et d'urbanisme*), to finance the purchase and equipment of development land, in order to promote town planning, industrial siting and build up reserves of publicly-held land.

FASASA (*Fonds d'action sociale pour l'aménagement des structures agricoles*), to aid in the social restructuring of farming areas, particularly those under marginal conditions.

at regional level:

SDR (*Sociétés de développement régional*), acting as local commercial banks to lend to or to take part in industry.

Sociétés d'équipement, to finance the infrastructure of industrial zones or housing areas, or to undertake major regional development projects (water and agricultural management, construction and operation of toll motorways, tourist equipment at regional level).

SAFER (*Société d'aménagement foncier et d'établissement rural*), to purchase land or holdings, with certain limitations, for restructuring purposes and to resell after regrouping or re-equipment.

References

Biarez, S. (1974) 'Espaces politiques et groupes sociaux', *Aménagement du territoire et développement régional*, VII, IEP, Grenoble: 341–53.

Boudeville, J.-R. (1966) *Problems of Regional Economic Planning*, Edinburgh.
(1972) *Aménagement du territoire et polarisation*.

Carré, J.-J.,Dubois, P. and Malinvaud, E. (1975) *French Economic Growth*, London.

Charmeil, C. (1975) 'Les schémas d'aménagement et d'urbanisme urbains et régionaux, peuvent-ils être soumis à la rationalité économique?', *Econ. appl.*, XXVIII: 13–32.

Claval, P. (1975) 'Planification régionale et aménagement du territoire', *Revue Géogr. Est*, XV: 169–216.

Cognat, B. (1973) 'Une économie dominée' in *La montagne colonisée*.

Courbis, R. (1972) 'The Régina model: a regional-national model of the French economy', *Econ. Plann.*, 12 (3): 133–52.

(1975) 'La comptabilité régionale française', *Econ. appl.*, XXVIII (2–3): 279–330.

Courbis, R. and Prager, J.-C. (1973) 'Analyse régionale et planification nationale: le projet du modèle 'Régina'', *INSEE*, R 12: 9–32.

Courthéoux, J.-P. (1965) 'Groupes de pression face à l'innovation économique: la canalisation de la Moselle', *Revue écon.*, XVI (6): 925–43.

(1968) 'Problèmes sociologiques d'une planification indicative', *Revue écon.*, XIX (5): 785–818.

Decouflé, A.-C. (1972) 'Une anthropologie culturelle de l'aménagement de l'espace', *Cah. int. Sociologie*, 52: 111–22.

Della Porta, G. (1960) 'Planification nationale et planification régionale', *Econ. appl.*, XIII (4): 529–39.

Dischamps, J. C. (1972) 'Rôle et moyens d'action des pouvoirs publics, semi-publics et des institutions privés dans l'aménagement du territoire en France', *Revue Econ. politique*, 82 (3): 443–71.

Durand, P. (1976) 'Prospective et aménagement du territoire', *Futuribles*, 7: 321–33.

Fourastié, J. and Courthéoux, J.-P. (1968) *La planification économique en France*.

Guichard, O. (1965) *Aménager la France*.

(1976) *Vivre ensemble*.

Hirschman, A. O. (1958) *The Strategy of Economic Development*, New Haven, Conn.

Holmes, P. and Estrin, S. (1976) 'French planning today', *Econ. Res. Pap. Ser.*, 76: 4, Univ. Sussex.

Hough, J. R. (1976) 'French economic policy', *Natn. Westminster Q. Rev.*, May 1976: 20–33.

House, J. W. (1977) 'Regions and the system', ch. 1 in House, J. W. (ed.) *The UK Space* (2nd edn), London.

Labasse, J. (1960) 'La portée géographique des programmes d'action régionale français', *Annls Géogr.*, LXIX (374): 371–93.

Lafont, R. (1967) *La révolution régionaliste*.

Le Lannou, M. (1967) *Le déménagement du territoire*.

Liggins, D. (1975) *National Economic Planning in France*, Farnborough.

(1976) 'What can we learn from French planning?', *Lloyds Bank Rev.*, 120: 1–2.

Monier, R. (1965) *Région et économie régionale*.

Monod, J. (1971) Preface to La DF, 'Une image de la France en l'an 2000', *Travaux et Recherches de Prospective*, 20.

(1974) *Transformation d'un pays: pour une géographie de la liberté*.

Myrdal, G. (1957) *Economic Theory and Underdeveloped Regions*, London.

Nizard, L. (1972) 'Le Plan: révélateur d'une définitive impuissance parlementaire?', *Analyse et Prévision*, XIV: 1489–1504.

Noël, M. (1976) 'La crise économique et les limites de la politique d'aménagement du territoire', *L'Espace géogr.*, 5(4): 217–26.

Perrin, J.-C. (1968) 'Schéma d'analyse du développement régional', *Régionalisation et Développement*, CNRS.

(1974) *Le développement régional.*

(1975) 'Les liaisons industrialisation-urbanisation et l'organisation régionale en France', *Econ. appl.*, XXVIII: 77–123.

Perroux, F. (1964) 'La notion de pôle de croissance', *L'economie du vingtième siècle* (2nd edn).

Phlipponneau, M. (1968) *La gauche et les régions.*

Veyret-Verner, G. (1973) 'Aménagement du territoire et géographie. Déterminisme et volontarisme', *Rev. Géogr. alp.*, LXI (1): 5–18.

2 Managing the urban system

TOWN PLANNING: CONTEXT AND CONTENT

The rapidity and widespread nature of urbanization in postwar France has posed planning problems at all scale levels, local, regional and national (Ambassade de France 1972). Urgent in the short term (up to 5 years), solutions to urban problems have also increasingly required medium (12–15 years) and long-term (up to 30 years) strategies. Given the highly centralized planning structure, with major decision powers concentrated inter-ministerially in Paris, the articulation of urban strategies, variegated in both time and space, has been a major, not altogether resolved issue. Town planning, in the meantime, has grown in stature from a limited technical intervention in the built environment, especially concerned with housing, utilities and minimum environmental provision, to a comprehensive management framework for urban economic and social life. It is argued that social justice for those in the French city has lagged behind the economic purposes of town planning. By comparison with Britain, development control of land use has been tardy, partial, and has had but a limited success. On the other hand, town planning at all levels has been better related to regional and national objectives in France and there has been an increasingly effective interrelationship between local, regional and national investment programmes. The translation of national sectoral programmes into spatial terms at different scale levels has been a notable planning achievement. Overall, the development of town planning has been within the 'indicative' philosophy which has likewise characterized planning at regional and national levels. Corresponding to the shifts in emphasis in general planning, however, town planning had a powerful and controlling·impact during early postwar reconstruction, followed by a phase in which planning provided a firm framework for the spatial and structural changes within town and city, leading to a more permissive phase in which market forces operated more freely even within what appeared to be a tighter set of legislative controls (Magnan *et al.* 1973, 8). During the 1970s, finally, an ecological and environmental view has come to the fore in town planning, to match the promotion of the quality of life indicated in the VIIth Plan (1976–80) for national, social, and economic development.

Though the earliest coherent town planning legislation dates from 1919 (management, improvement, and town planning), it was the planning law of 1957 which both required of the larger urban centres a development programme with investment targets for several years ahead and, at the same time, at regional level, instituted the requirement of a regional management plan (*plan d'aménagement régional*, Min. de la Construction) to match the programmes for regional action (*programmes d'action régionale*, Comm. du Plan, 1955). In 1958 the two regional documents were fused to a regional economic and social management plan (*plan régional de développement économique et social et d'aménagement du territoire*). In the same year plans for spatial management were instituted for urban communes or towns, divided into overall plans and detailed proposals (Rouge 1964), whilst for the critical sector of urban housing the ZUP legislation was introduced. Between 1958 and 1967 the ZUP (*zone à urbaniser par priorité*) was the prime means of statutory land use control in urban areas, permitting compulsory purchase and equipment of land required for development (Jamois 1968). Such land could then be resold to developers and, indeed, housing schemes of more than a certain threshold size were normally directed to a ZUP, the major instrument behind the creation of the *grand ensemble* or mass-housing tract. In 1969, however, the requirement to locate major developments within a ZUP was abandoned.

The interrelation of regional plans with town plans, and of both with the national plan, evolved slowly. With the IVth Plan (1962–5) the 'operational slices' for regional investments ('regional slices', Vth Plan) became effectively investment proposals and priorities for the urban areas (PME—*plan de modernisation et d'équipement*). After 1963 the creation of DATAR introduced a further spatial management dimension, on a scale wider than the individual town, or even the region: management of the urban network, creation of conurbation study agencies (OREAM—*organisation d'études d'aménagement d'aires métropolitaines*, 1966) for the regional metropoli; and study agencies for growth areas in the Bassin Parisien (the basin itself; Oise and Aisne valleys; middle Loire valley; and the north Champagne support zone—*zone d'appui nord-champenoise*). Town planning has thus developed within a loosely-articulated relationship with regional and national planning, but in terms of financing and major decisions these have come either from central government direct, or increasingly by delegation from the centre through the regional prefect.

From 1961 a PME covering three plan-periods was required for every major urban centre, the programme to be approved by FDES, the national agency funding economic and social development (Arcy 1970). Preparation of the PME led to in-depth studies of individual towns, on an interdisciplinary basis in many cases. Yet the outcome was very partial, only 15 towns having prepared a long-term programme and only 2 in addition a medium-term plan (Rouen, Amiens) by the end of the Vth Plan (Cornière 1971, 152). By this time, the policy for 8 provincial countermagnet metropoli had been launched and to this was later added the policy for medium-sized towns, both elements of a comprehensive management concept for the national urban network. Under the VIth Plan, decentralization measures for the French economy were intensified, the initiative in urban planning at local level was strengthened, and the PME (1969) gained added importance: more related to the national plan; extended to the 90 urban centres of more than 50,000, covering two-thirds of the urban population; better harmonized with town plans. Town plans, indeed, were required to take account of the wider regional and national contexts and, in turn, the town authorities communicated upwards their assessment of the potential for growth and the limits for further development. Through time, the commitment of investment in towns has increasingly influenced the further course of economic planning.

The Outline Land Act of 1967 (*Loi d'orientation foncière*) provided the essential framework for more comprehensive town planning, in terms of zoning and land use guidance. As in Britain, the land problem continues to be the main obstacle to coherent city planning. The three essential and interrelated elements of the 1967 Act are the SDAU (*schéma directeur d'aménagement et d'urbanisme*), the POS (*plan d'occupation des sols*) and the PME (Magnan *et al.* 1973, 42–50). The SDAU, an overall development and town planning blueprint required for every town of more than 10,000 inhabitants, defines the planning objectives of public policy-makers. As such it is a guidance document, which lays down a framework for the medium- and long-term development of major infrastructures, through which urban growth is stimulated. The SDAU is followed by the first POS, or land use plan. This is legally binding on third parties and is simply an instrument of development control. It establishes the rights, rules and limitations applicable to the use of every plot of land in the short term, subject to periodic revision. These are expressed in ratios of floor space to land for each permitted use (COS —*coefficients d'occupation des sols*). The POS does not programme development, nor does it seek to forecast desirable land use changes; as recently as November 1976 7000 *communes* had not yet established a POS. The PME has already been referred to, an essential financial programme of investments. Until the VIth Plan the PME and the

SDAU were prepared by different commissions under the *département* prefect, the former with a short-term (5 year) perspective, the latter concerned with 10–30 years ahead. In reality, the legislation has been implemented slowly and there is still lacking the overall nationwide coherence typified by the British town and country planning acts of 1947 and 1968.

The ambiguities of 'indicative' planning regionally and nationally are thus reflected at the urban level. Perhaps one-fifth of all investments in towns are directly undertaken by central or local government, whilst private entrepreneurs are subject to stimulus or constraint under SDAU or POS schemes. Since 1968 the possibility of creating a ZAC (*zone d'aménagement concerté*), a concerted development zone, has replaced the former ZUP (1958–67) and ZH (*zone d'habitation*, residential zone) legislation. The ZAC system represents a town planning contract whereby housing, commerce, industry or infrastructure can be programmed as a joint operation involving public bodies and private promoters. Areas designated ZAC are not subject to the POS ordinances, but each has its local plan (PAZ—*plan d'aménagement de zone*), indicating building intentions, densities, heights and ancillary works. The ZAC arrangement is flexible and may involve different balances between public and private investment and initiatives. Areas outside the ZACs may be subject to local taxes, as for the provision of utilities or services (TLE—*taxe locale d'équipement*), or on underdeveloped land (*taxe d'urbanisation*). Similarly, since 1945 the building permit system has been an important tool of the town planner, not required inside a ZAC. In a more constraining sense, the ZAD (*zone d'aménagement différé*, deferred development zone) has been a means since 1962 by which the authorities, or an approved development body, have had rights of pre-emption of designated land initially for 8 years (14 years as from 1971). The ZAD legislation may be used to build up land reserves, as a means of moderating the rise in land prices, or gaining for the community value added by development. Similar procedure, that for sensitive perimeter land (*périmètre sensible*) around major developments, has helped to control speculation in areas fringing the coastal zones of Provence-Côte d'Azur, in Corse and in the Sud-Ouest (Part I, ch. 2).

Urban planning in contemporary France is prompted by a growing social conscience, mitigating the overpowering effects of growth, relating development more to 'human scale', and considering both the quality of life and need for *animation* at neighbourhood or *quartier* level. However, there is still lacking the effective consultation of the public, and local authorities inadequately possess the financial resources to power their own planning initiatives.

PARIS AND THE ILE-DE-FRANCE

The most recent SDAU for Ile-de-France (Préf. Rég. Parisienne 1975) was in direct line of succession from the SDAU of 1965 (Délégation Générale 1965), modified in 1969. All three versions broke away from the containment philosophy of an earlier regional planning scheme, the PADOG (*plan d'aménagement et d'organisation générale de la région parisienne*, Comm. Construction 1960).

The basic propositions of indicative planning within a broadly market system imply that, even for the complexities and scale of the Paris region, it is feasible to set up and implement a blueprint outlining sectoral and spatial objectives for 10–30 years ahead (SDAU). Once approved, the SDAU provides the statutory framework (*loi d'orientation foncière* 1967) for the operational levels of planning at more detailed scales, the 80 SDAU, POS, and PME of the component planning authorities, including those for the city of Paris (1973). The assumptions are, first, that action on the blueprint will enable Paris to continue fulfilling her national and international roles (Beaujeu-Garnier 1974), whilst the city and region also continue to contribute to the overall redistribution of growth by decentralization to the urban network and the other regions of France (District de la Région de Paris 1965). Secondly, and of increasing significance through successive blueprints, the spatial outcome of growth and structural change in Paris and its region could be channelled, in order to diminish some built-in and growing disequilibria: between a more affluent west in the conurbation, with job surpluses and potential for attracting growth and development, and a less privileged east, with deficiency of work, an outworn urban fabric and poorer social provision; between the core of the Paris conurbation and successive radial-concentric zones of the suburban perimeter; and between the Paris conurbation and the thinly peopled rural hinterland of its region. Just as in planning generally in France, there has also been a mounting preoccupation about the quality of urban life, conservation and improvement of the living environment, at work and leisure, and the pressing need for fuller social justice in the city (Merlin 1971).

1960–75
Though attempts at more than minimal town planning go far back in the history of Paris (Sutcliffe 1970, Carmona 1975), it was the PADOG scheme (1960) which for the first time looked comprehensively at the problems of the city and its immediate hinterland. The scheme was for urban containment, a counterpart in this but in no other respect of the Abercrombie plan (1945) for the London region. Containment was to be

effected by controlling the expansion of the urban perimeter, though not by an Abercrombie green-belt type of policy. No overspill schemes were envisaged as for London, and there was no land-use control system for Paris comparable to that of the 1947 Town and Country Planning Act in Britain. In the event, growth pressures in Paris and its region proved too great for the limited constraints available: housing schemes spread beyond the statutory urban perimeter, whilst in-migration to Ile-de-France accelerated to + 160,000 per annum in the early 1960s. The development and equipment of the region became the concern of a district authority created in 1961, whilst a 20-year draft programme was put forward in 1963. It had by then become apparent, however, that the basic assumptions of the PADOG scheme had not proved feasible and a different kind of blueprint would be required. The urban explosion had not been contained, the problems of the suburbs had been aggravated, and the difficult and delicate equilibrium between fulfilling the national and international roles of Paris and achieving greater national balance lacked effective means of achievement.

The 1965 SDAU for the Région Parisienne (Ile-de-France) was introduced at a time when spatial management policies were becoming coherent for the first time, for both the nation and for regions and the urban network (p. 389). Furthermore, the necessary administrative reforms were carried through about the same time: in 1964 the current 7 *départements* were created, and in 1966 the Région Parisienne became one of the 22 statutory economic planning regions. Since 1964 Paris has been a territorial authority, combining the functions of a *commune* with those of a *département*. The 1965 SDAU was founded upon three major spatial principles, which have persisted through later formulations and revisions: unity of the Paris urban region; the creation of new urban centres, the initial 8 New Towns (reduced in 1969 to 5) and within the suburbs the setting up of centres for restructuring the urban fabric and acting as economic and social development nodes; and thirdly the establishment of preferential growth axes, to counteract the peripheral spread and sprawl of the conurbation. These growth axes were aligned in parallel tangential to the conurbation, to the north and south of the Seine valley, in a general direction north-west to south-east. This direction corresponded to the major axis within the central conurbation and permitted controlled urban development to take place on the plateaux flanking the Seine valley.

Essential to the success of the 1965 SDAU were: first, the containment of urban growth to about 14 millions in Ile-de-France by the year 2000, in place of the 16–18 millions forecast by trend extrapolations; secondly, major decentralization of manufacturing, and later of tertiary activities

(p. 283), to other regions and towns of France, but also by redistribution from central Paris within the urban region (*déserrement*); and thirdly, the introduction of an effective land-use control policy (*loi d'orientation foncière* 1967). The policies were essentially concerned with management of growth and its spatial allocation, internally within the region, to counteract growing disequilibria, and externally to achieve a better balance within French economy and society.

Comparison with the South East Study (1964), of similar date, and the South East Strategy (1967) for the London urban region, shows interesting contrasts (House 1977, 89–96). In Britain a radial-concentric strategy for redistribution of urban growth envisaged, first, a second generation of New Towns and major town expansions to accommodate massive overspill from Greater London. Some major growth centres might develop as counter-magnets (cf. French regional metropoli, but these were defined throughout the national space) to the continuing agglomeration around the capital city (1964). The stimulus for counter-magnet cities was increased in the 1967 proposals and corridor growth proposals were also introduced. These corridors were not the tangential growth axes proposed for Greater Paris, but rather radial corridors, each with a major and minor parallel axis to link Greater London with the counter-magnet cities. Within the corridors urban growth was to be concentrated in a few localities, whilst the London green belt was to be preserved. Such redeployment of growth within, and increasingly adjacent to, SE England lacked the French context of an overall economic and social plan, lacked the framework of planning for the national urban network and integration with other regional plans. The British generations of New Towns and expanded towns were more distant from the metropolis, initially programmed to be smaller and more self-contained than their French counterparts. Administrative reform for Greater London (1965) was an essential planning ingredient as it had been for Paris, whilst effective land-use control measures, including development control, building permits for factories and offices, were needed for both metropoli. Faced with a much higher economic growth momentum in Paris, a more indicative planning system and fewer constraints, the outcome was altogether different in the two cases.

In 1969 a major revision of the 1965 SDAU was promulgated, partly due to the findings of the 1968 census, in part to the political turbulence of that year. Demographic growth had been less than anticipated (table 13, p. 137), but radial dispersal trends had caused population losses in Paris, accelerating after 1962. Economic growth had been inadequately managed and more intensive use of constraints was needed, both by permits and through taxes on development. Profound structural changes in employment had set in, as in London, with a marked and uneven loss of manufacturing jobs in particular. The social problems of the city and inner suburbs had become more serious, and intensive urban renewal and slum clearance schemes were started. The balance between growth in the conurbation and at the New Towns was altered: the New Towns were reduced from 8 to 5 (Cergy-Pontoise, Marne-la-Vallée, St Quentin-en-Yvelines, Evry and Melun-Sénart); their population targets were revised downwards to 300–700,000 from 500,000–1 million by the end of the century. There have since been further reductions (table 34, p. 342).

Two major disequilibria had become more serious: that between east and west in the conurbation, in economic, social and political terms; and the centre-periphery, or radial-concentric disparity in growth potential, job availability and general living environment. From 1962–8 two-thirds of the population increase in Paris had taken place in the eastern districts, but only one-quarter of all new jobs; housing standards and urban facilities remained much less favourable there. To counteract this an inner pattern of restructuring poles was defined (p. 338), as employment nuclei and to promote a better living environment. In the west and elsewhere the impact of fast economic growth was widespread: great office complexes were started (e.g. La Défense, Maine-Montparnasse), land prices rocketed and long-distance commuting grew apace. Scarcely controlled economic growth produced manifest social injustice in access to the housing market, driving the poorer classes towards the suburbs. Social housing projects lagged behind and there was a marked polarizing, sociological shift in the structure of the Paris population towards the more affluent on the one hand and the poorer foreign immigrants on the other. The radial-concentric disequilibrium showed up fast and slow growth segments. The policy of restructuring in the inner and outer suburbs was strengthened, to counteract the potential attractions of the New Towns located on the linear growth axes. The Paris airport at Orly and that in construction at Roissy (Charles de Gaulle) were envisaged as major growth generators in close proximity respectively to the northern and southern axes. Transport infrastructure was to link all growth centres with each other and centrally with Paris, while public transport was to have a clearer investment priority over provision for the private car.

Compared with the contemporary Strategic Plan for the South East (1970), there was a stronger and more coherent set of spatial proposals in the 1969 Paris region SDAU, though the Strategic Plan (SPSE) had tested alternative spatial allocations of population and jobs more methodically and more mathematically. Moreover, the Paris region proposals had more direct continuity with those of 1965, whereas the SPSE was markedly less ambitious than the 1967 strategy: the farsighted corridor strategy had been abandoned in favour of more flexible allocations of growth both within and outside the London region. The 1969 SDAU and the 1970 SPSE had, however, a similar commitment to encouraging growth at different levels of the urban hierarchy, especially the medium-sized employment centre which might assist in restructuring the metropolitan region. Both programmes were intended to reduce the necessity for commuting by equalizing residence and job opportunities throughout the respective regions in a more balanced way. The rising preoccupation with environment and the quality of life was a prelude to the most recent revision, the 1975 SDAU for Ile-de-France.

A summing-up on the changes for the decade 1965–75 showed generally creditable achievements in planning. The objective of restraining population growth, difficult to visualize in 1965, had in fact been realized, in the sense that the regional growth rate had fallen to 1.4 per cent p.a., and the traditional net in-migration from the provinces had in fact been set into reverse (p. 137). It nevertheless remained true that this favourable picture was somewhat offset by the continuing migration of foreigners to Paris. The overall employment growth rate had slowed down and net increase in jobs was confined to the tertiary sector. Indeed, by 1975 manufacturing employment had fallen to the levels of 1962, but jobs in the tertiary sector had already reached the target forecast for the year 2000. The spatial mismatch between residence and jobs, already touched upon, became more dramatic: in Paris and the inner western suburbs, decline in manufacturing jobs compensated by the growth in office employment but with little re-employment of displaced factory workers; in the eastern suburbs, aggravated disparity between loss of jobs and availability of housing; in the outer suburbs, on the other hand, the dispersal of workplaces from the central area had improved matters, even though there was a rapid growth in population during the same period.

Urban renewal made rapid strides, 1965–75, but social housing targets remained inadequate, and in all too many cases rehabilitation or renewal of poor housing localities meant rents or house prices which previous residents could no longer afford. Social composition of neighbourhoods thus continued to shift to the disadvantage of the poorer, more deprived households, who were forced towards the periphery of the city. On the credit side, the restructuring of the suburbs had made good progress: the designated centres (La Défense, Bobigny, Rosny, Créteil, Vélizy) had attracted 25,000 houses and one million m² of office space in the ten years.

The industrial poles of St Denis and Rungis had also progressed: the former related to a pre-existing urban centre and in close proximity to the developing university at Villetaneuse; the latter focused upon one million m² of warehousing, markets and industry, plus 200,000 m² of offices, hotels and leisure-time uses. Decentralization of tertiary establishments in the public sector (p. 284) included university campuses, a dozen cultural centres, peripheral location of new hospitals, the opening of one million m² of shopping space, all powerfully strengthening the life of the suburbs.

The New Towns achieved a slower than anticipated rate of take-off (p. 342), but from 1970 had had a new administrative (intercommunal) form of government: 11,000 ha. of land had been acquired (the entire designated areas had been declared ZAD at the outset); two *préfectures* established; numerous shopping, commercial (100,000 m² office space) and educational facilities provided; neighbourhoods constructed (60–70,000 houses in 5 years); and 20 per cent of all industrial growth in Ile-de-France had been attracted. By comparison, one of the most prestigious office complexes, La Défense, took 15 years to create 400,000 m² of office space. The growth corridor concept was reflected in the progress of the New Towns, associated suburban growth poles, and the two Paris airport complexes. It had not, however, been a universally applicable concept. In particular, the widespread designation of ZACs outside the corridor zones had led to a great deal of urban infilling and had somewhat strengthened the radial-concentric model at the expense of corridor polarization. Nevertheless, an incipient policy of green wedges or belts had been sustained, the prelude to the more coherent programme for environmental equilibrium zones (*zones naturelles d'équilibre*) under the 1975 SDAU. Indeed, the unrestrained pursuit of growth by quantification, most of whose targets had in fact been realized, was more generally to be replaced by planning rather for the quality of urban life within its regional setting. Unfortunately, this new trend in planning had to be implemented under conditions of growing economic recession.

The 1975 *schéma directeur*

As in the case of London and the South East, population forecasts for Ile-de-France by the end of the century have been sharply reduced downwards. A low forecast of 12 millions (end-1975, 10.3 millions) would imply that even if foreign immigration was reduced to one-fifth that of recent levels, a steady net exodus of Parisians of 80,000 p.a. to the provinces would be needed. A middle forecast of 13 millions (1965 SDAU 14 millions) would mean a cutback by about one-third in the expected population growth rate for the region by the year 2000. In terms of employment structure the Paris conurbation faces similar problems to those of London, but in some respects more acutely. Both cities have seen a sharp fall in manufacturing jobs, the product of effective regional policies; in both the excessive concentration of tertiary activities gives rise for concern. The 1975 SDAU proposes a slowdown in policy for industrial decentralization, to stabilize numbers in factory employment. The decentralization of tertiary activities is to be principally within the region, to the New Towns and to the suburban restructuring poles. Overall, the regional strategy for Paris is to continue to be set within the policies for achieving better regional and urban balance, through further developments of the eight regional metropoli, and, even more significantly given policy shifts nationally during 1976, by the programmes for the medium-sized towns (*villes moyennes*). Furthermore, the context of a regional strategy for the Bassin Parisien (fig. 62), with its stimulation of a ring of towns and the development of preferential growth corridors and support zones, is to be interpreted in terms of creating self-contained urban centres (workplace—residence association) and of the capacity to take further decentralizations from Paris of those activities which must remain within reasonable proximity of the capital (Centre d'Etudes 1970; DATAR 1969, 1970; Verrière 1972).

The guiding spatial principles of the 1973 SDAU (fig. 63) further elaborated those of 1965, with sophisticated policies for polycentric development at several scale levels. Additionally, there were policies for the protection and management of rural space, particularly through the establishment of environmental balance zones. In the outer rural tracts of the region, a carefully moderated development of small and medium-sized towns was to be encouraged, whilst transport policy favoured a network of bypass routes and selective but minimal development of radial road and rail routes, with special emphasis on linking up the New Towns, the restructuring poles in the suburbs and central Paris. Existing transport infrastructures were to be more intensively used wherever possible, and the ambitious earlier total network plan for transport was modified into a double-cross pattern corresponding to actual demand.

The policy of the parallel tangential growth corridors was to be more effectively sustained: the northern corridor from the valley of the Marne below Meaux to beyond Pontoise (including the New Town of Marne-la-Vallée), the employment growth poles of Le Bourget-Roissy, St Denis-Villetaneuse and beyond the Vallée de Montmorency, the New Town of Cergy-Pontoise; the southern corridor from Melun to the plateaux at Trappes, including the New Towns of Melun-Sénart, Evry and St Quentin-en-Yvelines, in addition to the employment poles of Créteil, Thiais-Rungis and Vélizy (fig. 62).

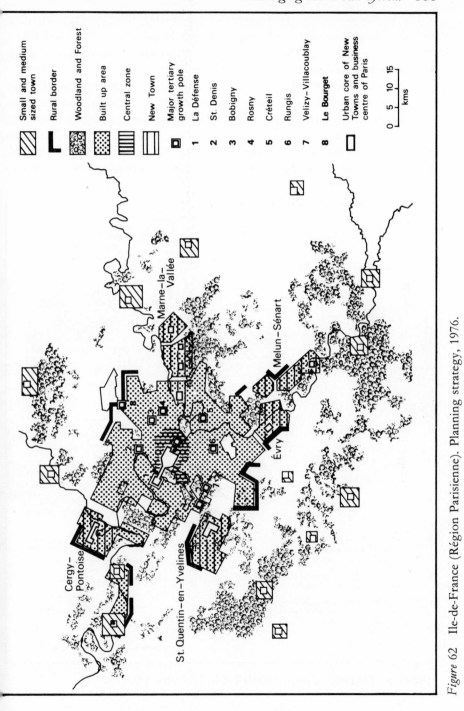

Figure 62   Ile-de-France (Région Parisienne). Planning strategy, 1976.

The policy for stimulating growth poles within the Paris conurbation included those within the city itself, further development of the suburban restructuring poles and the five New Towns, to which latter an overriding priority was to be given.

The SDAU and the POS for the City of Paris (fig. 63) were approved in the spring of 1973 and the zoning characteristics and permitted land-use coefficients for housing, offices and other activities established a control framework for developers and public bodies alike (APUR 1974). Taxes on development were used differentially (p. 278) to stimulate or restrain growth in particular *quartiers* and in relation to a pattern of growth poles,

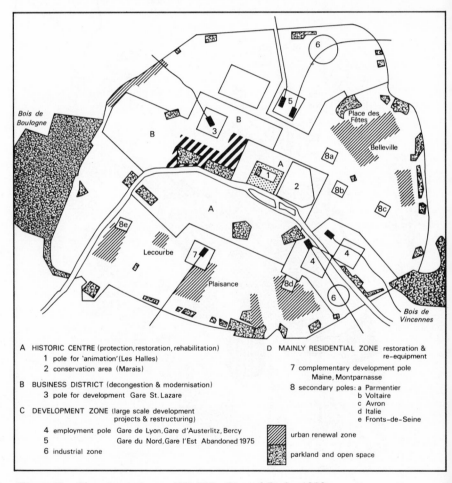

A HISTORIC CENTRE (protection, restoration, rehabilitation)
    1 pole for 'animation'(Les Halles)
    2 conservation area (Marais)

B BUSINESS DISTRICT (decongestion & modernisation)
    3 pole for development Gare St. Lazare

C DEVELOPMENT ZONE (large scale development
                      projects & restructuring)
    4 employment pole Gare de Lyon, Gare d'Austerlitz, Bercy
    5   Gare du Nord, Gare l'Est Abandoned 1975
    6 industrial zone

D MAINLY RESIDENTIAL ZONE restoration & re-equipment
    7 complementary development pole
        Maine, Montparnasse
    8 secondary poles: a Parmentier
                          b Voltaire
                          c Avron
                          d Italie
                          e Fronts-de-Seine

urban renewal zone

parkland and open space

Figure 63   Planning scheme (SDAU), City of Paris, 1973.

favouring the deprived inner eastern suburbs. The historic central area of the city was to be protected from encroachment by offices, its magnificent built environment enhanced by conservation of buildings, vistas and a controlled building line. Urban renewal schemes were developed at several scales: the major sites such as that of the abandoned markets (Les Halles) (Mallett 1967), the Marais district, the Butte Montmartre or the Ile Saint-Louis; and many small-scale schemes for particular *îlots* of high density, poor quality housing. Small-scale schemes included a higher than average proportion of social housing (HLM) and the conscious fostering or preservation of micro-scale industry, workshops, tradesmens' premises or small shops, to sustain living neighbourhoods but on a modernized, viable footing. The redevelopment of the site of Les Halles, following the movement of the markets to Rungis, has involved controversy. Earlier grandiose schemes for an international trade centre, a centre for the arts, commercial and residential development, focused on this nodal com-munications hub on the RER (*réseau express régional* — rapid transit railway). With a more strongly environmentalist perspective, the ratio of open space to development has since been considerably increased. The Centre Georges Pompidou, the cultural complex, was opened in January 1977.

The business quarter is to be contained within its present limits and at its present level, retaining some residential function and concentrating more on high-level decision-taking establishments. As a corollary, there is a positive policy of promoting tertiary growth in centres in the eastern *quartiers*, permitting a better balance of employment, reducing journeys to work and creating complementarity of functions; mere routine business operations in the east, decision-centres in the traditional west. The sector around Gare St Lazare, centred upon the new RER station at Auber, is to act as an inner restructuring pole for a congested district of business and commercial uses.

The so-called 'development zones' are two sectors grouped around Gare de Lyon-Gare d'Austerlitz-Bercy (APUR 1975), and at an earlier stage (now suppressed) Gare du Nord-Gare de l'Est. Both are communications nodes, by rail, *métro*, roads and in the case of the Gare de Lyon also the river. Industrial land is to be redeveloped, major commercial and services development is to be introduced, together with housing and other central area facilities. When fully developed by the end of the century, the Gare de Lyon pole should have 50,000 new jobs, some drawn from the central area. The impact of this pole upon surrounding residential districts will be carefully programmed and creatively fostered, in some contrast to the effects of the massive growth at Maine-Montparnasse. This commercial development around the Montparnasse station will provide 30,000 jobs when completed, but the scheme has had a harsh impact upon the surrounding neighbourhoods. Completion of the office complex at La Défense, commenced as a major tertiary growth pole in the mid-1950s, though outside the city limits, is a counterpart in the west to the Gare de Lyon project in the east. With a congested 'Manhattan' skyline it remains the most spectacular scheme. In 1972 the original target for office space was doubled to a mammoth 1.5 million m^2 (for 100,000 office workers), but the rate of building has fallen sharply since 1974 (296,000 m^2) to only 30,000 m^2 in 1977. Office rents have fallen and early in 1977 145,000 m^2 of office space was empty (cf. 1 million m^2 in Ile-de-France). On orders from the president (1977) further office towers at La Défense were cancelled.

The planning problems of the peripheral *arrondissements* in the city of Paris, on east, south and north, are particularly difficult. There is much substandard old housing, public services are inadequate, and local availability of jobs is limited. Urban rehabilitation with priority for residential improvement is the keynote policy. Unbalanced development during the period of rapid economic growth has left many islands (*îlots*) of deprivation, whilst the closure of factories and workshops created local dereliction. The concept of small-scale integral development schemes (*plans-masse*) was defined already in the 1967 revised Paris town planning proposals (IAURP 1967). Some of the more spectacular schemes are those at Fronts-de-Seine, Belleville, and Italie (the latter halted on orders from the government in 1975): high-rise residential towers alternated with more limited social housing, office blocks (whose workers frequently come from elsewhere), and shopping facilities. The developer certainly seems to have had greater say in many such schemes than either the planner or above all the urban sociologist (Dreyfus 1975). On the other hand, greater concentration on smaller-scale schemes, e.g. Place des Fêtes (Herpin and Pérot 1974), has shown that neighbourhoods can be reanimated, social mixing achieved and a better balance between workplace and residence reintroduced. Such disseminated small-scale renewal and revitalization schemes are to receive greater emphasis at the expense of any further major concentrations disrupting the city skyline or the life of adjacent neighbourhoods. Quality of life in the city requires respect for the innate social diversity and life styles of micro-level communities, of which there has traditionally been a great variegation in the city of Paris.

The 1965 SDAU established the policy of restructuring poles in the *first suburban ring* ('first or little crown') around the city of Paris, with a population of 4.5 millions (1975). This ring had already been transformed in postwar years (Bastié 1972), by in-filling and by extension of the urban area in the form of *grands ensembles* at the periphery, or by individual housing estates. By 1975 (Préf. Région Parisienne 1975, 74 *et seq.*) there was little undeveloped land left and the major planning problem concerned the remodelling of existing urban space rather than the introduction of yet further growth elements. The land use pattern still reflects the long history of unplanned growth searching out low-cost areas for development, in dependence upon central Paris for work and for many services (Vignaux and Lebel 1971). Depressing working-class suburbs alternate with extensive tracts of industry flanking the rivers, warehousing areas, and airfields at Orly and Le Bourget. Administrative fragmentation into a multitude of *communes* hindered coherent planning, but was somewhat improved by the reforms of 1964 creating three new *départements* covering the first suburban ring (Hauts-de-Seine, Seine-Saint-Denis, and Val-de-Marne). Even so, some 30 SDAU are needed to cover 4.5 million people compared with a single SDAU for the city of Paris.

Structural changes in employment in the first suburban ring have reflected those of the city of Paris: loss of factories through the decentralization policy, peripheral spread of offices westwards, and immigration of poorer social classes displaced by renewal operations in the city. Vast tracts of housing are substandard but urban renewal schemes in the suburban ring are costly because of land prices and lack of land for redevelopment. On the other hand, particularly towards the west and south, the characteristic villa type of residential development (*zone pavillonnaire*) offers a better living environment, though in places disrupted by an ill-planned growth of intrusive tower-blocks. Yet the villa estates lack local employment opportunities and service provision of all kinds is often inadequate. Some of the most difficult urban restructuring problems occur in the intermediate zone, with lack of balance between residential and workplace functions, lack of adequate transport, open space or social provision. It is in this tract that the growth of *grands ensembles* has most disrupted neighbourhoods and overburdened the decaying suburban centres. Here, too, the cores of the restructuring poles are located and there has been the most dramatic change as the result of this policy of the 1965 SDAU.

The restructuring poles (fig. 62, eight in number in 1965, Herblay since cancelled and Vélizy added) are to serve several functions: to introduce a better balance between residence and employment, to locate major investments in public facilities (social, educational, transport in particular); and to lighten the concentration of such provision in the city. The term growth pole suggests too coherent and structured a development. The designated areas are rather to be catalysts in the transformation of the urban fabric, taking advantage of every planning opportunity to attract development and facilities. Conceptually (Rousset-Deschamps 1974) there is some doubt as to the practicability of such coherent restructuring proposals within a continuously built-up area. Each urban function tends to locate within its own spatial net, rather than necessarily in close proximity with others. Even where agglomerating tendencies are present, the cost of redeveloping a built-up area and the rates of renewal which are possible may preclude an integrally-planned new central area within a suburb.

To date, the policy has been particularly successful in the creation of shopping centres (Vélizy, Rosny, Belle-Epine, Créteil) and the implanting of two university sites (Créteil and Villetaneuse). Factories (industrial zones of Vélizy, Rosny, Créteil) have been more readily attracted than offices, with exception of the major development at the tertiary growth pole of La Défense, with its unique nodal location on the major westward growth axis from the central Paris business district. Development has been uneven among the eight poles, but three functional types can now be identified: dominantly residential (Bobigny), but lacking an important tertiary or commercial centre; mainly services (Rungis), with food warehousing, industry, hotels and a regional commercial centre dispersed over a wide area; multifunctional (Créteil), with great diversity of well-integrated urban functions. The general verdict (Préf. Région Par. 1975, 164) is that the restructuring poles have had the effect of 'relay-centres' diffusing functions previously sought by suburban residents only in Paris itself, but each pole has adjusted with difficulty to the needs of a hinterland of several hundred thousand people, whilst at the same time seeking to create a more coherent functional structure out of the largely unplanned suburban sprawl. Quality of life has, on occasion, been sacrificed to economic viability and rapidity of development. Furthermore, the designation of the eight poles has affected the fortunes of adjacent non-designated centres in some measure, e.g. Choisy-le-Roi. Finally, the 1975 SDAU proposed that smaller scale, communal or intercommunal centres should be stimulated, each to serve a hinterland population of between 50- and 100,000. This would diffuse the benefits of urban growth and change, and offer the possibility of a better integration between the scale levels of the urban hierarchy, in a more sensitive manner than the more dramatic policy of selective concentration on major restructuring poles has thus far achieved.

The New Towns

Although in principle inspired by British experience, the French programme of New Towns had a different set of objectives from the outset and the operational outcome has been both distinct and diverse (Pressman

1973, Chatin 1975, Merlin 1975, Besnard-Bernadac 1976). The PADOG (1960) planning scheme for Greater Paris (p. 328) came closest to the Abercrombie strategy for Greater London (1945), to contain metropolitan expansion by defining a perimeter to limit the spread of the conurbation and by a policy for decentralizing activities and people. Unlike Abercrombie, however, the PADOG scheme envisaged neither a circumferential green belt nor an 'overspill' programme as such, nor the establishment of a ring of self-contained, medium-scale New Towns beyond the green belt. Both the constraining outer boundary and the green belt concept were considered ineffective ways of stemming French metropolitan expansion, whilst French opinion also regarded the first generation of British New Towns around London as too small, excessively self-contained and artificial in their attempted isolation from the metropolis and the rest of the regional urban network. Nor has there yet been a French counterpart to the policy for the second and subsequent generations of British New Towns intended to act as a prime instrument of regional growth strategies. The five New Towns around Paris are integral and substantial elements in regional strategy, but for redeployment of population and work *within* the city region rather than serving an interregional context. The VIIth Plan, however, provides for strengthening the regional context of the New Towns, and, thereby, their potential for influencing strategic spatial growth and development (Lacaze 1972).

The 1965 SDAU for the Région Parisienne (p. 329) first established the principle of New Towns in France, sustained with differences only in degree through the 1969 revision to the SDAU of 1975 (p. 333). Their role was to help relieve urban congestion in the Paris conurbation, to substitute polycentric development for the excessively monocentric agglomeration of the metropolis, to complement and channel a major part of the inevitable further urban growth, and to have a major multiplier effect by large-scale public investment in selected sites along the preferential growth axes in the outer suburbs. In this latter function the New Towns resembled larger-scale versions of the restructuring poles in the suburbs, e.g. Créteil or La Défense. Indeed, it has been argued (Besnard-Bernadac 1976, 126) that New Towns act within the Paris region in the same manner as the counterbalancing regional metropoli in respect of Paris in relation to the provinces. At no time have the New Towns been seen as fulfilling a role of intercepting or accommodating in-migrants to the region from other parts of France.

The French New Towns collectively represent an enormous potential (table 34), with an ultimate capacity for absorbing rather more than two million people. Although Nardin (1971, 33) dismissed this as but a

Table 34 New Towns, population, 1968–82

1000s	Date of EPA	1968	1975	1982 (est.)	Target popn	Target date	Growth rates 1968=100		land zoning 1974	
							1975	1982	ZAD 1000 ha (2)	central area (ha) (3)
Ile-de-France		263.6	417.9	744.4	—	—	158	282		
Cergy-Pontoise	1969	53.4	84.5	144.2	200	1985	158	270	7.4	75
Evry	1969	33.2	53.6*	103.3*	130*	2000	162	311	3.4	75
St Quentin-en-Yvelines	1970	41.4	103.6	185.8	320	long-term	250	449	11.0	100
Marne-la-Vallée	1972	69.8	81.6	158.8	c.400	"	117	227	10.0	170
Melun-Sénart	1973	65.7	94.5	152.2	300	1985	143	232	8.9	No inf.
Province		147.6	213.9	358.8	—	—	145	243	—	—
Lille-Est (Villeneuve d'Ascq)	1969	26.3	38.6	68.4	100	1985	147	260	3.1	No inf.
Le Vaudreuil	1972	6.3	7.1	34.6	90/140	2000	113	548	4.2	No inf.
L'Isle d'Abeau	1972	38.2	47.5	77.1	250	2000	124	201	14.6	No inf.
Etang de Berre (Ouest)	1973	71.7	107.1	145.6	200	(1)	149	203	22.1	200
" " (Est, Vitrolles)	1973	5.0	13.4	32.8	100/150		265	649		
New Towns, total		411.2	631.9	1,103.2	—	—	153	268		

EPA = *établissement public d'aménagement* (public development corporation)

*project area population: 1974, 240; 1980, 360; 2000, 500

(1) year 2000, 750; (2) cf. Paris 10.0; (3) cf. La Défense 115

Source: Promotions (1976), 99

marginal contribution to French population growth by the end of the century, it is approximately the numbers living in the 33 New Towns of the UK at the end of 1975. New Towns in the provinces are considered later; several have an important growth pole function (L'Isle d'Abeau, 35 km south-east of Lyon, in relation to the new international airport at Satolas; Etang de Berre, the marine industrial development region of Marseille-Fos; and Lille-Est (Villeneuve d'Ascq), centred upon a regional university campus). The Parisian New Towns can be more directly related to redeployment of urban population at the regional level, but within the city region rather than dispersed towards the more distant peripheral towns of the Bassin Parisien. Since their principal objective is to contribute to the restructuring of the city region and, in particular, to accommodate an increasing proportion of the 90–100,000 dwellings built annually in the region (equivalent to a town like Bordeaux every year), they need to develop a balance of internal with external functions. The New Town in this role has been described as 'physical planning at the point where the new urban centre and the preferential axis of urbanization meet' (Rouillier 1970, 2), an 'anchoring ground' for a policy of transforming the configuration of the Paris conurbation. The scale of government action, in space and time, represents a major development from the earlier concept of the ZUP (up to 300 ha, 10,000 dwellings, 6–10 year time scale) to the New Town (10,000 ha. plus, 150,000 dwellings, 30–40 year planning).

The British New Town objective of providing one job locally for each potential worker was totally rejected for the Parisian New Towns. Under a market economy and indicative planning, the Parisian New Towns had to compete for the new industry and tertiary activities. Job diversity and some balance in the ratio of manufacturing to services have been attempted, but until after the abolition of taxes on industrial location at the New Towns in December 1973 (previously 25 frs per m² for factories) local employment lagged behind the potential for residential development (80,000 new jobs provided in all 9 New Towns, end 1974). With the exception of some major public establishments (*préfectures* at Cergy-Pontoise and Evry) and an occasional substantial office headquarters, it has proved difficult for the New Towns to attract tertiary activities out of the inner or suburban tracts of Paris. The need for considerable and continuing commuting is an accepted part of policy and transport planning includes the provision of fast link-up routes to the conurbation, by both road and rail.

On the eve of the VIIth Plan (1976–80) the New Towns were particularly well-poised to fulfil the reformed objectives for urban life (Chatin 1975, 204): abandonment of *gigantisme* (mammoth-scale growth, whether in town-size or architectural forms or *ensembles*), though the longer-term population targets for the New Towns would establish each at a high level in the urban hierarchy; decentralization of employment and of decision-centres; greater use of public transport; planning at human (neighbourhood) scale; improvement of the quality of life (cultural and social facilities; *animation*); and fuller democratic consultation, even participation, in local government. Furthermore, as in the first generation British New Towns, social segregation is to be vigorously controlled. In a sense the social problem is the reverse of that in inner Paris. The New Town populations are predominantly young, with a high proportion of working-class households; to achieve a better social balance more private housing is needed, with policies for attracting skilled workers, professional and managerial families.

There is much less similarity in New Town layout, design or even in balance of functions in France than among British counterparts. Each New Town is related to the needs of its subregional milieu: St Quentin-en-Yvelines, Marne-la-Vallée, and Evry are to grow in close conjunction with the Paris conurbation (cf. Lille-Est); Cergy-Pontoise and Melun-Sénart are to be more physically distinct and in greater measure self-contained (cf. Etang de Berre, L'Isle d'Abeau and Le Vaudreuil). Whereas St Quentin-en-Yvelines, Cergy-Pontoise (Hérin 1973) (fig. 64) and Evry (Darmagnac 1968, IAURP 1969, 1973) came closest to structured development on an urban model, with planned central areas and variegated residential neighbourhoods, Marne-la-Vallée and Melun-Sénart are being pro-grammed along much more flexible lines. Marne-la-Vallée most closely resembles the Milton Keynes type of open structuring, but in linear form with four nodes flanking the new RER fast-transit route (commenced in 1974). Melun-Sénart is focused upon the well-established town of Melun, and is primarily intended to control the strong urbanization pressures between Melun and the Forêt de Sénart. In strong contrast with adjacent Evry, across the Seine, there will be no regional commercial centre and no high-rise development, unlike the spectacular 'pyramids' or the 'Agora' of Evry I. By contrast with British practice, segregation by zoning of land uses is much more flexible in French New Towns, even in the planned central areas. Segregation of factories and residential areas is less necessary for many non-polluting modern industries; indeed, large-scale industrial estates are thought to be undesirable in a harmoniously planned city. Furthermore, the growth of a French New Town is much more of a market operation, in conjunction with a diversity of developers (ZAC procedure), or on a cooperative basis. In either event, zoning rigidities are not practicable. Diversity among residential neighbourhoods, at a wide variety of scales and with contrasts in architectural styles, are a further characteris-

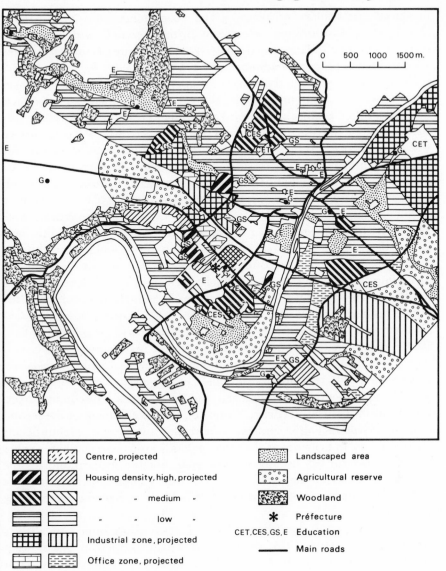

0   500   1000   1500 m.

▦ ▨		Centre, projected
▧ ▨		Housing density, high, projected
▨ ▨		„ „ medium „
▤ ▤		„ „ low „
▦ ▥		Industrial zone, projected
▦ ▦		Office zone, projected

Landscaped area
Agricultural reserve
Woodland
* Préfecture
CET, CES, GS, E Education
——— Main roads

Figure 64   Cergy-Pontoise New Town.

tic feature. All Parisian New Towns incorporate previous urban development, which needs to be harmonized with ongoing growth and equipped in all respects to no-less high standards.

The management and democratic overview of New Towns in France has produced particular problems. The comprehensive New Town Development Corporation beloved of British practice, with powers to plan, programme and develop the New Town from site to completion, was alien to French politics or administration. Initially, 1966–9, *missions d'étude et d'aménagement* (study and planning groups) were set up for each Parisian New Town, but without either legal powers or an independent budget. Their role, often against hostile local government reaction, was to carry out surveys and to coordinate initial land purchases. Each New Town surface was designated a ZAD from the outset, but land purchases of the sites for public equipment were necessary. As the towns developed, the ZAC procedure, for mixed public-private development, became widespread. Once a New Town became operational the *mission* was replaced by a public development corporation (EPA—*établissement public d'aménagement*, table 34), with equal representation of central government officials and local authorities. The EPA was responsible for drawing up and implementing a development programme, often with the aid of consultants, and for providing central services. Guide-lines are established for developers and the EPA is financed by a local government intercommunal syndicate, for public building and works. The syndicate (SCA—*syndicat communautaire d'aménagement*) method of New Town government was introduced in 1970 (*loi Boscher*) to create an intercommunal basis for involvement in decision-taking (only Lille-Est, a single commune, and Le Vaudreuil, a *communauté urbaine*, have different administrations). In effect, divided counsels may prevail and hinder the development of the New Towns. The conflicts over: urbanization at L'Hautil (Cergy-Pontoise), the development of the second stage of Marne-la-Vallée, and even the further progress of Melun-Sénart are often cited in evidence as the price of democratic control. On the other hand, the system has usually worked well, notably in harmonizing the interests of long-standing residents with those of newcomers. Under the VIIth Plan, the voice of the newcomers is likely to become increasingly powerful.

Achievements of the French New Towns programme are already considerable (Chatin 1975, 203): major urban entities in place, well-equipped, growing rapidly (table 34), and attracting an increasing interest among developers; after a slow start and scepticism at both central and local government level, a rising momentum of balanced development, in housing, jobs and public services (though too many speculative office developments had been authorized, and school and hospital provision lagged behind the build-up of population); provision of a technically well-equipped living environment; impressive architectural forms and layout, with harmony between new central areas, residential neighbourhoods and the surrounding area; socially stimulating living conditions reflected in the term *animation*; and, after considerable teething troubles, a more harmonious form of New Town government.

There are, nevertheless, some clouds on the horizon, apart from those attributable to the downturn in national demographic growth and the economic recession of the 1970s. The ability of the Parisian New Towns to develop sufficient employment autonomy, particularly in service activities, remains uncertain. Indeed, the attraction of job opportunities in central Paris may well increase with the building of fast transport links to the New Towns. The prospect of creating balanced social communities is perhaps to be deferred for realization in the next generation. In general, it remains to be seen if the New Towns can sustain their growth momentum in the face of mounting indebtedness and widespread pressures for further ZAC-type additions to the already disturbingly considerable development in non-designated parts of the Paris urban perimeter. Priority for New Towns under the VIIth Plan, together with the environmental management measures (ZNE—p. 348) of the 1975 SDAU, are encouraging portents, but not necessarily altogether reliable under indicative planning in a market economy. The growing political strength of the Left (1977) is intent upon strengthening the New Towns programme, but upon reducing the technocratic influence of non-elected bodies (EPA; central group for the New Towns), whilst at the same time ensuring more effective central government funding for investment under local government control. The New Towns will be smaller than originally envisaged (mostly 300,000 maximum, or less, rather than the 500,000–1 million of the 1965 SDAU), but are likely to be completed more rapidly so long as they are coherently programmed and effectively equipped.

Transport planning

A spatial strategy for apportioning polycentric growth in a complex metropolitan region would be powerless without equal attention to the provision of transport infrastructure. Interregional demand for transport (p. 200) has progressively strengthened the radial-concentric transport network of Ile-de-France. The 1965 SDAU first introduced the polycentric growth concept, with restructuring poles in the suburbs and New Towns located along preferential growth axes (*Paris parallèle*). A necessary counterpart for this was a comprehensive, integrated and interrelated transport network with a balance between continuing radial-concentric growth and the need for new communications links to and between the designated growth poles in the suburbs and beyond. Such new links have been tardily and only partially provided, whilst under the VIIth Plan

(1976–80) no new radial motorways are to be built, public transport on existing infrastructure is to have highest priority and environmental considerations will be taken more fully than ever into account; the Paris left bank expressway was cancelled in 1975. Nevertheless, the transport network must be developed further to serve the needs of 12 million people by the end of the century. Major new growth centres (e.g. the airports at Orly and Roissy, p. 215) will generate the traffic demand, justifying a further disaggregation of the radial-concentric system which has been built up around Paris and cumulatively reinforced through the centuries.

Environmental management (fig. 62)

Though the PADOG scheme (1960) statutorily defined an outer urban perimeter of containment, there was no positive policy for the rural tracts which lay beyond. The 1965 SDAU took a more comprehensive regional view on land use, but did so primarily from an urban standpoint: the need for control measures in the urban-rural fringe belt; and for a policy to define recreational zones in the forests, valleys and water bodies. Though a rural planning scheme for Ile-de-France was published in 1971 (Mission d'Etude 1971), it was the 1975 SDAU which introduced rurally-based policy elements and a full environmental programme (*trame verte*—green open spaces). The environmental pollution, damage and threats inherent in economic growth without adequate control measures in a vulnerable rural zone into which urban spread was being diffused, were the mainsprings behind the policy. There was also a more positive side, to sustain rural life by support measures for agriculture and forestry, monitoring of farm land prices, and the definition of an agricultural 'statute' safeguarding the use of land for agriculture and the farmer as the guardian of the rural landscape. The policy is flexible and does not proscribe all development; it certainly does, however, seek to restrain the proliferation of ZAC outside the designated growth centres of the 1975 SDAU.

The green open space policy is planned on hierarchical lines from the management and development of urban public green space in central and suburban areas to the definition of local or regional environmental balance zones (*zones naturelles d'équilibre*, or ZNE). Recreational, health and aesthetic aspects contributing to the quality of life are to be promoted. Local ZNE are to be developed along principal and secondary (radial) axes of preferred urbanization, whilst regional ZNE are zones deliberately located to break up continuous urbanization along the major preferred growth axes (north-west to south-east). The regional ZNE are similar to the British statutory green belts, but without the same interdictory powers over land use. The major agricultural areas defined for protection include the Plaine de France (with a difficult management problem in the immediate vicinity of Roissy airport), Plateaux de Brie, Plaine de Versailles, Plateaux du Sud and the Hurepoix (fig. 22); the Vexin, to the west of Cergy-Pontoise New Town, has similar qualities though not defined as a ZNE.

With fuller development, the ZNE concept will also be concerned with nature reserves, the historic and cultural landscape heritage, traditional architecture and the stimulation of open-air leisure activities (walks, cycle paths, trails). The growth of small towns within the ZNE is to have particular regard for their qualities of heritage, traditional ways of life and scale. So far as possible urbanization will be directed to existing settlements in ZNE, but even then not at the expense of disturbing their essential characteristics. With 270,000 ha. of forest land in Ile-de-France, 30 per cent of it accessible to the public, there is an immense recreational potential within easy reach of the capital.

The short-term programme for Ile-de-France, 1975–85

Three essential principles are to be fostered: a differentiated spatial strategy to reduce the disequilibrium between residence and place of work; a priority programme for the transport infrastructure which is an essential accompaniment for the polycentric strategy for regional development since the 1965 SDAU; and, thirdly, a particular stimulus to the growth of the New Towns. To reduce the mismatch between residence and workplace will require operational planning through more localized SDAU and POS and a more vigorous application of the system of location taxes (*redevances*) or licensing (*patente*). In spatial terms the objectives are: stabilization rather than development in and around central Paris; renewal in the inner suburban zones, with restructuring by the aid of growth poles in the outer suburbs and at the New Towns; development along the preferential growth axes with designation of ZNE to safeguard rural life and land. To achieve this a 10-year plan for the necessary public investments in housing, equipment and facilities is thought desirable (Préf. Rég. Parisienne 1975, 131), but with a more coherent and sustained framework than the short-term 'regional' slices of the national, social and economic plan permit.

The further development of Ile-de-France cannot be dissociated from wider spatial contexts, first that of the Bassin Parisien (ZEAT region), and then the total national space. In 1966 an interministerial group was formed to study the *Bassin Parisien*, defined as fifteen *départements* around Ile-de-France (fig. 4), parts of seven economic planning regions and including one-quarter of the area and one-third of the population of France. The subsequent studies (DATAR 1969, 1970) clearly defined both the 'spread' and the 'backwash' effects of the growth of Paris upon the Bassin. Backwash effects were shown by the impoverishment of the urban hierarchy throughout the Bassin, with centres at all levels dependent more directly upon Paris than upon any counterbalancing metropolis, or indeed any effective subregional town network. Far from being a coherent region, the Bassin was made up of many small areas, lacking in either economic or geographical unity (Verrière 1972). Drainage of migrants to the metropolis had been traditional, whilst social and cultural life continued to be overshadowed by the capital.

With the progressive development of decentralization policies from the early postwar plans (I—III) to the present, the 'spread' effects of economic growth in Paris have become steadily more apparent. The Bassin received more than half the industrial jobs decentralized from Paris 1955–74 (table 32) (see also IAURP 1966), and more recently a range of important tertiary establishments, both governmental and private (p. 283). Urban population growth in both an inner ring of towns (e.g. Chartres, Sens, Beauvais) and an outer, peripheral ring of larger centres (e.g. Caen, Reims, Rouen) has been dramatic (CEIBAP 1970). In 1970 the principle of apportioning further economic growth between Ile-de-France and the towns of the Bassin was adopted. Economic activities which could be decentralized from the capital, but needed close links with the metropolis, could be moved to the Bassin towns. Elsewhere in the Bassin there were to be regional development schemes focused upon four support zones (p. 373): the Basse-Seine valley, the valleys of the Oise and Aisne, the north Champagne zone, and the Middle Loire valley. Associated with these zones nine regional centres were defined, each with more than 100,000 inhabitants, to act as major stimuli to economic development (Rouen, Le Havre, Tours, Reims, Le Mans, Orléans, Caen, Amiens and Troyes). As gross out-migration from Ile-de-France, already sizeable for the period 1968–75, develops further, the Bassin towns are well-placed to be the major beneficiaries, particularly after 1985. It is important that such growth potential should not be dissipated in a role as dormitory or mere satellite appendages of the metropolitan region.

The national content of urban development in Ile-de-France is reflected in the policies for the regional counterbalancing capitals (*métropoles d'équilibre*), the industrial growth complexes, the medium-sized towns (*villes moyennes*) and in proposals for corridor growth at several scale levels.

COUNTERMAGNET METROPOLI (*métropoles d'équilibre*)

One of the earliest recommendations by DATAR, approved after parliamentary debate in November 1963, was that management of the urban network was the key to effective regional planning in France. Secondly, following upon analysis of the urban system, referred to earlier (Part I, ch. 1), it was officially resolved that the rising demographic and economic fluxes in France should be polarized around eight countermagnet, or counterbalancing metropoli in the provinces. These were to be centred on Lille (with Roubaix-Tourcoing), Nancy (with Metz-Thionville), Strasbourg, Lyon (with St Etienne, and after 1968 Grenoble), Marseille (with Aix and Fos), Nantes-St Nazaire, Bordeaux and Toulouse.

The objectives of the counterbalancing metropoli policy were defined by CNAT (1964) as: creating a demographic counterweight to the attractions of the Paris conurbation; stimulating economic development poles capable of diffusing growth and revitalizing their regions, particularly through enrichment of their urban networks; and, thirdly, building services and decision centres which would diminish recourse to the capital city (La DF 1969A). Not all these objectives were necessarily compatible and, to achieve each or any, inevitably implied complementary policies: sustained decentralization and decongestion of Paris, in terms of decision powers and financial devolution, with both manufacturing and tertiary activities involved as well as government and government-sponsored establishments; a commitment for the longer term, to 1985 for the development of self-sustaining regional metropoli, and to the end of the century for full completion of their metropolitan strategies; a coordinated approach by central and local government to create the major productive, infrastructural, educational and cultural investments, during each successive short-term national economic and social development Plan.

The programme for developing the eight countermagnet metropoli faced difficulties from the outset. Having lived in the metropolitan shadow of the capital for so long none of the eight chosen had sufficient range, volume or rates of growth in the characteristics deemed essential to counterbalance Paris: size of population, commercial services (wholesaling, specialized retailing), independent banking and finance houses, the headquarters of large-scale business organizations, or major services (administration, higher education, medical and hospital facilities, the liberal professions, or cultural provision). In almost all these respects, furthermore, there was a very marked lack of uniformity among the eight. This reflected the course of history, the effects of local resources and location, employment structure, and social characteristics. As a result, there was a varied balance between the internal functions of each city, and its regional, national and in most cases international roles. Quite early in the exposition of the countermagnet metropoli policy, the European context was stressed. George (1967, 105) said the region dominated by a countermagnet metropolis must have the economic stature of a German Land or an Italian province; whilst the metropolis itself should match the 'million' cities beyond the Rhine or the Alps. Only three of the eight proposed (Lille-Roubaix-Tourcoing, Marseille and Lyon-St Etienne) fell within the 'million' city category.

The policy of countermagnet metropoli was thus to build, progressively and substantially, upon the existing provision at the eight centres, to endow each with the capacity to counterbalance Paris, serve the needs and provide the motive force for development in the surrounding region, whilst at the same time making each metropolis and region competitive on the EEC scale. Such wideranging ambitions within the relatively short time-scale, even to the end of the century, meant selective concentration of major investments at the expense of more balanced, wider diffusion of the benefits of national growth throughout the urban system. The policy was in many ways the most dramatic demonstration of the Perroux growth pole hypothesis, and its implementation confidently assumed a continuing national demographic momentum and sustained economic growth over the entire period. In the mid-1960s a doubling of the national population by the year 2000 was confidently forecast, and the limitation on the growth of the Région Parisienne to 14 millions (1965 *schéma directeur*), later to be reduced to 12 millions (1975 *schéma directeur*), would have meant that the countermagnet metropoli would have had to grow differentially very fast (table 35).

In the event, national population growth rates have fallen away, and economic momentum has slackened and become irregular. These changes alone would inevitably have caused some reconsideration of the policy for countermagnet metropoli, but there were other voices raised in criticism. It was feared by some (La DF 1968) that the selective concentration of investment would simply transfer the disadvantages of over-concentration on Paris to eight other centres, which would in their turn prospectively drain the life from their regions, as Paris had done earlier from the rest of France. In this sense it would be undesirable to create at regional level the excessive concentration of population and activities deplored at national level (Noin 1974, 260). In Aquitaine (Région Aquitaine 1976) and Alsace (La DF 1975A) particularly there were strongly expressed views that the countermagnet metropolis concept risked damaging the life and expectations of other towns in the region, whilst seeking, somewhat vainly it was argued, at the same time to fulfil a national and international role.

In theoretical terms all these criticisms suggested that the adverse 'backwash' effects of polarizing growth would outweigh the beneficial 'spread' effects of the diffusion of selectively implanted growth over a wide regional hinterland. The policy of countermagnet metropoli has been in effect for too short a time for a balanced assessment to be attempted. Nevertheless, under the VIIth Plan (1976–80) emphasis in urban programmes is to be transferred more to the smaller and medium-sized towns, though the *schémas directeurs* of the countermagnet metropoli will continue to provide the framework for SDAU, POS and PME, at least until the envisaged economic take-off point for the metropoli around 1985. The dramatic longer-term growth will now no longer be required up to the year 2000, and it is unlikely that further countermagnet metropoli will be designated after 1986, as had originally been a possible intention. Veyret-Verner (1969) argued that France had insufficient population, her demographic growth was too moderate, and her basic geographical character, regions and past history were all unsuited for further large-scale growth at 'superimposed' countermagnet metropoli. Such views are indeed reflected in the VIIth Plan priority for improving living conditions in the large cities, substituting qualitative for the quantitative growth which has for the past ten years powered the policy for countermagnet metropoli.

The policy required major new mechanisms for planning, financing, publicizing, monitoring and administering the countermagnet metropoli. In 1966, on the proposition of DATAR, five metropolitan area planning study groups (OREAM—*Organisation d'études d'aménagement d'aires métropolitaines*) were sanctioned for Lyon-St Etienne, Aix-Marseille, Nantes-St Nazaire, Nancy-Metz, and the Nord, coming into operation during the following year. Each designated metropolitan area was larger than the component urban agglomerations, to allow for more effective survey and more flexible spatial development strategies. The OREAM body was made up of planners, central, regional and local government officials, together with local and regional commissions composed mainly of elected representatives. It had the purpose of defining an outline management strategy (*schéma d'aménagement*) for the metropolitan area, its component sectoral and spatial elements, and the means necessary to achieve a comprehensive development scheme, within existing objectives of regional development policy. Essentially long-term in character, each OREAM produced initially a draft strategy (*livre blanc*) within one year. This was then reviewed by local and regional administrations, chambers of commerce, etc. During 1969 the interministerial committee for spatial management policy (CIAT) took account of these views and also those of the central group for urban planning (GCPU), which had replaced FDES as the arbitrator on equipment programmes. Once the broad strategic principles had been approved by CIAT the second-stage strategy was begun (*schéma d'aménagement d'aires métropolitaines*), translating the broad principles into more detailed sectoral and spatial development options, with time-horizons in the mid-1980s and at the end of the century. The second-stage strategies were also subjected to local and regional consultation and amendment, before going forward for approval by CIAT and parliament. Once finally approved, the *schéma d'aménagement* became, on the one hand, the basis for decisions on projects for public investment (VIth Plan and after, equipment and infrastructure, land reserves, conservation, legislation, financing), on the other, the framework for the more detailed SDAU, POS and PME of the statutory planning authorities (towns and communes).

Reorganization of *local government*, in terms of units, functions and powers in relation to *département*, region and nation, was an essential element for implementing coherent metropolitan planning. Urban communities (*communautés urbaines*) were created in 1966, for Lille, Lyon, Strasbourg and Bordeaux, among the countermagnet metropoli. The urban community (p. 45) exists to coordinate administratively a large number of communes and to provide both financial cohesion, planning and transport services; it does not supplant the legal powers of the component communes. An alternative administrative structure is the formation of intercommunal groupings, most complex around the Etang de Berre: SCA—*syndicat communautaire d'aménagement* (3 communes), SIVOM—*syndicat intercommunal à vocation multiple* (3 communes), and *syndicat mixte* (14 communes). In other metropoli the existing communal structure has persisted without new administrative superstructures.

Table 35 shows the great diversity among the eight countermagnet metropoli, in demographic characteristics (fig. 65), status, trends and preference ratings. Minimum threshold size and sufficient distance from Paris to have generated a range of services and facilities capable of being developed into counterbalancing metropolitan stature explains the peripheral location of all eight chosen centres: close to the land frontiers and thus influenced by conditions and competition in adjacent EEC states, or on the maritime facade of the Atlantic or the Mediterranean. Peripheral location of the countermagnet cities means that very large tracts of France are under the direct influence of the capital, with scant possibility of organizing new metropolitan regions. In eastern France, division between the polycentric Lorraine metropolis and that of Strasbourg respects the historic identity and distinctive economic problems and potentials of Lorraine and Alsace. In western France the choice of metropoli in a region of several towns of similar size and importance in a balanced urban network favoured Nantes-St Nazaire rather than the historic capital of Bretagne.

Table 35 Counterbalancing metropoli (*métropoles d'équilibre*)

	Lille	Nancy-Metz-Thionville	Strasbourg	Lyon-St Etienne-(Grenoble)	Aix-Marseille (Fos)	Bordeaux	Toulouse	Nantes-St Nazaire
Metropolis popn, 1968 (1962), thou.	2400[1]	1050	371[2]	(2088)[3]	1351	810	(400)	(587)
proj. „ „ , 2000 , thou.	3600– 3700	1800– 2000	—	3850[3]	2526– 3356	1250– 1450	1000	1230
2000 as % 1968	150– 154	171– 190	—	184	187– 248	154– 179	250	209
Popn growth rate metropolis (1962–8), regional growth rate = 1.00	1.67	2.74	1.42	1.39	0.89	1.70	2.98	2.43
immigrants (1962–8) as % 1968 popn of metropolis	3.3	7.5	7.9	6.2	4.6	7.6	9.0	8.1
% immigrants to region (1962–8) attracted to metropolis	31.8	31.3	37.6	26.6	16.6	25.6	30.5	22.2
net migration balance, liberal professions and higher management, as % these classes 1968	–5.0	–2.1	–2.5	–1.5	–0.5	–0.3	–2.8	+2.2
FIAT grants, 1963–70, per capita, frs	40.8	28.7	34.4	15.8	26.2	26.7	180.2	66.6
% employment industry	16.9	—	—	16.5	8.6	10.6	9.5	11.3
HQ in metropolis per 10,000 inhabs (1964)	12.4	7.7	9.7	14.7	9.3	9.3	7.0	7.9
HQ wage earners in manufacturing, per 10,000 inhabs, controlled by HQ outside metropolis	233	697	191	447	128	104	111	247
% incr. university popn, 1969–70 to 1973–4	10.0	29.0	—	2.3	5.0	18.8	12.7	36.0
Preference for each metropolis expressed by sample inhabs, Région Parisienne (1969)	7.3	6.0	4.1	3.8	3.4	3.7	2.2	4.9

[1] metropolitan core area
[2] *communauté urbaine*
[3] excl. Grenoble
Source: *Région Aquitaine* 1976; *INSEE*; *SOFRES* 1969

Bordeaux and Toulouse, clearly defined regional capitals, were logical choices for metropoli in the Sud-Ouest, whilst Lyon, Marseille and Lille had the size, status, structure and potential as centres of metropolitan areas which could not be ignored. Curiously enough, though the names of the eight metropoli were included in the Vth Plan, their zones of influence were not then and have not since been defined (George 1967). For each of the five initial OREAMs a study area was designated (fig. 61) but this was rather the site within which metropolitan functions were to be developed and interrelated, than either a zone for preferred development, or any representation of a sphere of influence. Lacking clearly recognizable hinterlands, it is perhaps not surprising that the relationships between the regional and the counterbalancing roles of each metropolis have led to uncertainty, even political controversy.

Lille-Roubaix-Tourcoing

Planning proposals for the Nord metropolis (Lille-Roubaix-Tourcoing) (La DF 1971) come closest to integrating metropolitan with overall regional planning. The OREAM study zone covered the two *départements* of Nord and Pas-de-Calais, the same area as the economic planning region (fig. 71). The approved principles for the *schéma d'aménagement* spoke of restructuring the entire urban network, focused upon the metropolitan capital, to benefit from industrial reconversion programmes and to capitalize upon the potentials of frontier location close to the major EEC growth axes (La DF 1969B). Replanning of the total urban network (Bruyelle 1975) was an inevitable outcome of this uniquely high density concentration of towns, the closest counterpart to North Country con-urbations in Britain but distinctive within France. Furthermore, the serious reconversion problems in coalmining and textiles in particular, together with the effects of the relocation of new steel-making capacity at Dunkerque, meant that metropolitan planning had to be developed in the context of slow economic growth, pockets of serious decline, and in the face of a largely outworn urban fabric. The delicate planning task of counteracting decline whilst at the same time restructuring both the regional economy and living environment is all too familiar to British ears. The potentials for further growth and change which might be unleashed by developing existing transfrontier links within the immediately adjacent EEC are, however, a uniquely French dimension.

Planning of the complex central conurbation (Bruyelle 1975) is a key to the diffusion of growth and change throughout the regional urban system of the Nord. The conurbation takes the form more of an urbanized region than a well-structured, coherent built-up area. There are multiple urban nuclei, each with a distinctive economic pattern and problems. Many nuclei have spread to fuse with others, by diffusion incorporating former rural centres or in ribbons along the main routeways. The restructuring and rehabilitation of the central conurbation (La DF 1968, 36) notably involves: major urban renewal operations, e.g. St Sauveur at Lille, *îlot* Edouard-Anseele at Roubaix; establishment of a major decision-taking centre (*centre directionnel*) at Lille for firms, administration, commerce, banking and finance; and creation of a New Town (Villeneuve d'Ascq) in the eastern suburbs, focused upon the new university of Lille-Est (table 35). The New Town has a target population of 100,000 by the end of the

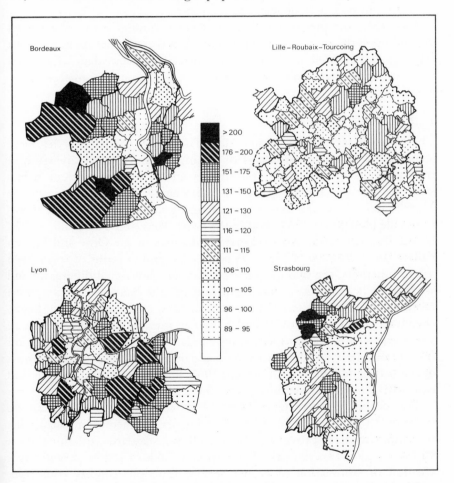

Figure 65   Intra-urban population change, 1968–75: Bordeaux, Lille-Roubaix-Tourcoing, Lyon, Strasbourg.

century, with a function of channelling urban growth in the suburban zone between Lille and Roubaix, whilst at the same time creating a bipolar structure for Lille itself. Between 1968–75 the central areas lost population, whilst the suburban ring (fig. 65) gained, particularly to the east and north.

The stabilization operations and introduction of new growth centres within Lille-Roubaix-Tourcoing will in turn link to urban redevelopment proposals elsewhere in the region: industrial reconversion of the declining coalfield towns with growth poles at Hénin-Liétard, and Lens-Liévin; urbanization of the littoral (Greater Dunkerque, p. 370); and corridor growth along the Escaut valley from Cambrai to Mons in Belgium, centred on a growth pole at Valenciennes.

Inevitably, the progress of metropolitan planning in the Nord must depend upon the successful transformation of the regional economy (Part III, ch. 3), as well as being more directly reliant than any other countermagnet metropolis upon the economic fortunes of adjacent EEC lands.

Lorraine

The Lorraine metropolis (Nancy-Metz-Thionville) shares with the Nord some of the economic problems of mining decline and reconversion in traditional heavy industries, but it has an altogether different urban structure (La DF 1969C, OREAM Lorraine 1971). Focused along the Moselle axis there are two major urban agglomerations: Nancy-Toul-Lunéville (460,000 in 1968); and in the north Metz and Thionville, linked by the iron-ore fields and steel-making districts of the Orne and Fensch valleys (in all 590,000 in 1968). Traditionally, and in terms of specialized urban functions, the two agglomerations have developed differently and with prime linkages in contrasting directions: the Nancy subregion, with more varied manufactures (33 per cent of jobs, steel, engineering, heavy chemicals, consumer goods) and a higher service function, orientated westwards (Paris 300 km) and southwards; the Metz subregion, cut off from France 1871–1919, with a mining and heavy industrial function which developed rapidly between 1945 and 1965, linked mainly northwards and eastwards towards Luxembourg and the Saarland.

The outline strategy (*livre blanc*) 1968, confirmed by the definitive strategy (1970), established the context for development of a metropolis: full employment, improvement of urban living standards, and integration within a regional framework. Three specific fields of action were defined: creation or stimulation of higher service functions (higher education, wholesaling and retailing, leisure and recreation activities, cultural facilities); organization of a coherent transportation network, within and between the cities, and from the cities throughout their hinterlands; and, thirdly, the extension of existing agglomerations, rather than creation of any new urban centres. Each existing town was to retain service functions for its own population and the immediate hinterland. Higher level service functions were to be allocated equitably among the major cities: to Nancy, a 3000 bed university hospital centre, more rapid growth of the local university, the administrative centre for regional education (*académie*); for Metz, the regional *préfecture* and probably the seat of future regional institutions (La DF 1973A). In practice, there have until recently been intense rivalries between Nancy and Metz for preferential allocation of metropolitan-level services, and some resistance by both to the imposition of central government arbitration. Certain facilities, such as the Pannes-Nonsard recreation park, are justified only in relation to the total market of the regional metropolis; the site of the proposed international airport remains in contention.

The creation of a fast-transit rail-link (Métrolor) with regular and frequent services was rejected in its initial form, but on a reduced scale has greatly improved the connections between Nancy and Metz. In a wider positional context, the east-west Paris-Strasbourg axis crosses the north-south axis from the North Sea to the Mediterranean, through the Lorraine metropolis. At present, sections of electrified railway, motorway and canal are the harbingers of the full exploitation of these potentials of position. When fully realized, the Lorraine metropolis can face a European future with greater confidence. At present the limited scale of the metropolis, its restricted range of economic functions, a certain competition with Strasbourg and some overshadowing by the Saar and Luxembourg, pose certain constraints. So, too, does the perennial background problem of further restructuring of the regional industrial economy (Part III, ch. 3).

Strasbourg

Strasbourg is at once the smallest of the countermagnet metropoli and, perhaps by reason of the course of urban development in Alsace leading to a distribution of jealously-guarded functions among several towns (La DF 1975A), the one least likely to dominate or to serve its region in metropolitan terms. In spite of its limited size, it nevertheless fulfils a growing role in tertiary services (commerce, banking, administration, university, cultural facilities, the more specialized professions), but traditionally these are beamed towards the *département* of Bas-Rhin, rather than extending throughout Alsace. Since 1945 the city has added a European dimension to its functions (Council of Europe, international centre for Rhine navigation, congress centre) and has deliberately acquired

metropolitan service institutions (banks, centre for international commerce, national theatre, national library) serving potentially a much larger
area than Alsace and extending across the national frontiers (La DF 1975A,
31). It is precisely the potential conflict of interest between an Alsatian,
Rhineland and European role for Strasbourg that underlies the most recent
local opposition to its development as a primate countermagnet metropolis. Such opposition is, however, deep-seated in the nature and
traditions of the urban system in Alsace.

The SDAU for Strasbourg (La DF 1975A, Nonn 1971) covers an area
wider than the city limits. This long-term scheme stresses the regional role
for the Strasbourg metropolis and urban forms and functions which might
accommodate a doubling of population by the end of the century. Two
models are postulated for the harmonious growth of the conurbation: a
concentration model, with priority axes for development southwards and
westwards to the lower Bruche valley; and a dispersal model, with poles of
secondary growth in the suburbs and in designated outlying settlements.
The dispersal model would have an H-shaped structure of growth axes,
with the short east-west link the means of extending the central city area in
linear fashion. Market forces favour central area redevelopment in
Strasbourg (restructured historic city, tertiary growth) on the one hand,
and major industrial locations on the fringes or outside the SDAU limits
(Offendorf, lower Bruche valley) on the other. In this, as in other matters,
the interests of the city of Strasbourg are to concentrate development,
using available space within the open texture of the city limits (e.g. ZUP at
Hautepierre); neighbouring communes prefer the dispersal of growth, but
also of associated decision-taking functions from the city.

Lyon-St Etienne-Grenoble
The Lyon-St Etienne (and, since 1968, Grenoble) countermagnet metropolis is distinguished by its location within the most prosperous
economic region of France after Paris (Rhône-Alpes), its manufacturing
base with built-in structural problems (in employment proportion similar
to the Nord, table 35), its three regional cities of great economic and social
contrasts, and a nodal location of outstanding potential, both nationally
and internationally. Though Rhône-Alpes does not match the economic
status of Ile-de-France, it attracts migrants from Auvergne and Provence
who might otherwise have gone to the capital, whilst on all counts Lyon is
the second city in France after Paris. Though at first sight this is the most
promising of all eight countermagnet metropoli, there are certain built-in
weaknesses (La DF 1969D, OREAM Lyon 1970): absence of a well-
articulated urban hierarchy and a limited movement of people between the

large towns of the region; rigidity in the allocation and evolution of higher
tertiary functions; weaknesses in the functions of many small towns, and
hence the need for careful location of new urban growth, lest it should have
an adverse effect upon existing settlements. Although the industrial
structure is among the least specialized among French regions (coefficient
0.19, Paris 0.23, Lorraine 0.34) and contains a balance between electrical
and mechanical engineering, textiles, chemicals and consumer goods, it has
a high ratio of firms controlled from outside the region. On the other hand,
it is true that there are many headquarters of smaller businesses in Lyon.
Furthermore, the low ratio of employment in services (37 per cent, national
41) is offset only by the intensity of commercial activity.

The spatial strategy approved in 1968 (fig. 66) rejected both the
concentration of all development at Lyon and the dispersion of growth to
satellite growth points around the Lyon conurbation. Lyon is to be the
principal growth pole, focused upon a metropolitan and regional tertiary
role. The Part-Dieu extension (38 ha.,completed 1976) of the central
business district will accommodate the major new developments, though
the original ambitions for a 'regional decision-taking centre' and a
commercial development of 110,000 m² have both been reduced in scale

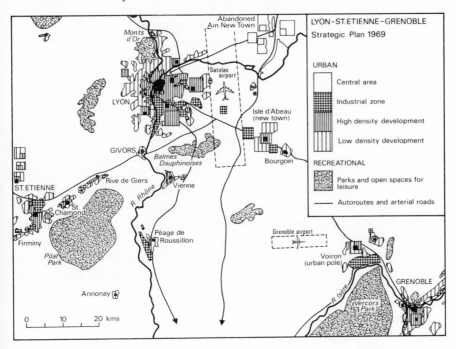

Figure 66　Metropolitan planning: Lyon-St Etienne-Grenoble, 1968.

and scope. The extension of the conurbation will take place eastwards with a secondary centre at Bron, in the direction of the new international airport at Satolas. Two New Towns were approved, to be located along the major highways to Grenoble (L'Isle d'Abeau) and Geneva (Méximieux). The Isle d'Abeau New Town (table 34) is in course of construction, the other proposal deferred; both New Towns are to have important industrial functions to attract incoming firms away from Lyon itself.

Though Grenoble has developed a wide range of science-based growth industries and needs no stimulus from priority government investment, the same is not true for St Etienne. At St Etienne industrial reconversion from mining and heavy industry remains a central issue; development strategy is based on the classic recipe for attraction of new firms in growth industries, a strengthening of the regional (not metropolitan) tertiary sector, and on more efficient transport links (expressway) with Lyon. A major urban extension of St Etienne northwards will provide for a secondary central area, to relieve pressure on the old centre undergoing major urban renewal.

Aix-Marseille

This countermagnet metropolis, the most remote from Ile-de-France and the most urbanized (98 per cent), has the most spectacular growth potential of all, in spite of pressing shorter-term difficulties of matching employment growth with population growth (La DF 1969E, 1975B, OREAM Marseille 1970). The scale of proposed growth envisages a rise in population from 1.3 millions (1968) to 3.3 millions by the end of the century, with no less than a tripling of the annual rate of job provision sustained over a long period. Such an ambitious set of proposals seeks to capitalize upon the major undeveloped assets of the Marseille-Aix region: crossroads location, with a north-south axis linking Western Europe with the Mediterranean, via the Rhône-Saône corridor, and an east-west axis between Spain and Italy; environmental character, climate, water, energy (hydro-electricity, imported oil), space for industrial expansion at tidewater, and for recreation; attractive living conditions. Certain weaknesses need to be overcome: the lack of effective economic or urban unity, partly due to the constraints of relief and the compartmentation into basins; an incoherent spread of uncontrolled urbanization; insufficient integration by Marseille of the regional urban structure, and an unbalanced employment base, with a deficiency in growth manufactures and an excessive concentration of tertiary activities at Marseille.

Development proposals imply the creation of a new regional employment structure, built progressively around a major port-industrial growth pole (Fos) bordering the Etang de Berre (pp. 368–70), and a profound reshaping of urban growth and redistribution of urban functions within a restructured metropolitan region. A deliberate policy of state-supported attraction of growth industries on a considerable scale is an essential ingredient in the rising momentum of population and urbanization intended, first by 1985 and continued to the end of the century. The basis of the urbanization proposals is to effect a symbiosis between two complementary major development poles: Marseille (tertiary) and the port-industrial complex being built west of the Etang de Berre. The pattern of rapid polycentric urbanization will be discontinuous, grouped around existing centres with minimal necessary implantation of New Town type settlements. Marseille, with a target population for the year 2000 of 1.7 millions (950,000 in 1968), will be internally restructured: tertiary activities of metropolitan stature will be located in a redeveloped central area, and secondary centres around the periphery to take services of a regional character; industrial zones will be created (Huveaune valley) to balance the employment structure, and the north-south axis through the conurbation will be one of preferred development. Aix (+ 750,000 by the end of the century) will grow mainly as a tertiary centre, conserving its historic urban character, in association with industrialization of the Arc valley and Gardanne (brown coal). The basin on the south-eastern shores of the Etang de Berre will increase its population by 200,000 in 30 years (to 250,000), with discontinuous urbanization centred on Vitrolles. It is hoped that the present considerable mismatch of jobs and residence will be rectified as the urban centre of gravity moves westwards from Marseille and commuting is reduced. The port-industrial region of Fos and associated urbanization west of the Etang de Berre is to achieve a population target of 500,000 by the year 2000 (presently about 100,000). Urbanization will incorporate existing centres but will be grouped along the major communication gridlines to be established: two principal centres (Martigues-St Mitre in the north and Miramas-St Chamas in the south), a secondary centre at Istres (airfield, port at Fos) and at Salon. About half the proposed regional population growth will thus take place around the Etang de Berre, necessitating a strong environmental management programme if the innate attractiveness of the sites is to be protected (p. 115).

The oil crisis and the economic depression of the mid-1970s have thrown doubt upon the rate of growth and possible long-term targets of population and jobs, particularly at Fos and on the shores of the Etang de Berre. Doubt continues to be expressed about the prospects for a coastal steelworks far removed from coal and iron ore supplies. Nor has the Rhône-Rhine waterway link yet been achieved. Meanwhile the social problems of establishing the urban-industrial complex have proved trying

(Bleitrach and Chenu 1974), whilst the rivalry among local authorities around the Etang de Berre, grouped and financed under two different systems (SCA, SIVOM), has retarded effective and coherent town planning (Vieille 1974).

Nantes-St Nazaire

Not so unambiguous a choice for a counterbalancing metropolis as either Bordeaux or Toulouse, each unrivalled within their regional setting. The case for Rennes would have been virtually as strong, but lacking in the port-based opportunity for attracting new basic industries. All three metropoli of the Ouest have a dominantly rural hinterland, affected by long-term out-migration. The task of balancing a national function in relation to the capital with that of service to the region must give long-term priority to regional benefits, either directly in employment and services or indirectly in the multiplier effects of services of metropolitan character introduced to the counterbalancing cities. A particular objective mentioned for Nantes-St Nazaire is the reduction of out-migration to Paris, a realizable target within a prospective doubling of population (to 1.2 millions) by the year 2000.

The spatial strategy (Minist. du Plan 1970) envisaged two complementary growth poles: Nantes, an existing regional capital, to receive the major metropolitan institutions, but also to develop and diversify its industrial functions (1700 ha. of industrial estates to be created, shipbuilding industry to be relocated westwards); St Nazaire, linked to the new port-industrial zone of Donges-Montoir, to be capable of taking 120,000 dwt vessels, and to develop residential quarters to the west. Smaller-scale urbanization will take place at nodes along the Sillon de Bretagne, linking Nantes with St Nazaire, whilst the Pays de Retz (south of the estuary), a depressed rural tract, has been linked by a new river crossing (1975) and will develop in relation to industrial zones along the river bank. Landscape conservation and development of recreational space (Côte de Jade, Parc régional de la Brière, La Martinière) will have high priority. It is further intended that the new metropolitan region be interlinked by communications along preferential lateral axes and by deliberate road development integrated with the region's needs. A weakness in the scheme may be the confident dependence upon building a more substantial, diversified industrial growth pole and attracting manufacturing from other regions. Lacking the scale of either Marseille-Fos, Dunkerque or the Basse Seine, and prospectively in competition with all three, the proposals may seem optimistic, however theoretically justifiable.

Bordeaux

From the outset the Bordeaux metropolitan pole (La DF 1969F, 1973B, Région Aquitaine 1976) was programmed primarily within the context of the region (Aquitaine), one-quarter of whose population it housed. The economic base for development lies in the chemical and petrochemical industries, particularly envisaging large-scale growth of the latter. Industrial diversification is planned into mechanical and electronic engineering, the aerospace sector, and pharmaceuticals, but there is to be a balance between the regional metropolis and medium-sized towns in allocation of industrial growth. The urban spread of Bordeaux is being controlled, the central areas restructured to accommodate metropolitan functions (Mériadeck 130,000 m² for offices, Quartier du Lac), the public transport system improved and a ringway completed around the conurbation. Progress to date (Région Aquitaine 1976) has been criticized: many of the newer industries are controlled from outside the region (even the aerospace centres of Bordeaux and Toulouse communicate with each other most often via Paris), though table 35 does not confirm this; too many firms have been attracted in a piecemeal fashion without regard to their contribution to regional development or environmental impact; Bordeaux has 'drained' its region, and redistributive allocation of economic growth should favour the medium-sized towns.

Toulouse

Some 250 km from Bordeaux, Toulouse lacks the stimulus of a port-industrial environment and has a hinterland both poorer and less accessible (8 *départements* of Midi-Pyrénées) than Aquitaine in relation to Bordeaux. Nevertheless, the planners (table 35) favour a target of 1 million by the year 2000, a doubling of the present population. Impressive metropolitan-scale additions have been made: the institute for the aeronautical industry (*Ecole supérieure aéronautique*) — in the context of the local aerospace industry, the national aerospace centre, the higher national institute for electrical and hydro-technology, the institute for computing, and a rapid build-up of science-based faculties and institutes in the university. Associated tertiary activities have included cultural, artistic, commercial and tourist provision; the most impressive feature is the build-up of a satellite centre in the Toulouse conurbation (ZUP, Le Mirail, eventually for 100,000). The Toulouse metropolis thus contains a range of high technology industries in strong contrast to diverse traditional manufactures such as heavy inorganic chemicals, food processing, or metal goods. There is little relationship between old and new, and not all the science-based industries, e.g. aircraft manufacture, have proved resistant to depression. The problems of integrating Toulouse with its hinterland are probably greater than for any of the other regional metropoli.

The policy for countermagnet metropoli in the French provinces has no counterpart in British regional planning. The British New Towns policy was also concerned with decentralization of jobs and people, particularly through overspill measures, but not with the implanting of metropolitan functions. The propulsive effect which concentration of public investment in selected major cities might have upon a surrounding hinterland if such implantation took place successfully has been substantially ignored in Britain. Brief flirtation with growth-pole thinking at the time of the 1963 White Papers on Central Scotland and North-East England was not sustained, and in any case lacked both the mechanisms and the selective measures necessary for success. Regional strategy has rather been concerned with unemployment relief and 'worst-first' policies. Ironically, the belated emphasis given in early 1977 to the problems of the inner city areas of the conurbations might have the effect of directing more effective attention to the role which conurbations might have played and might yet play, directly and indirectly, as provincial metropolitan centres and diffusers of growth into a tributary city region.

INDUSTRIAL GROWTH COMPLEXES *(plate-formes industrialo-portuaires)*

Though the counterbalancing metropoli policy laid greatest emphasis upon creation of tertiary facilities and institutions of metropolitan stature, there was nevertheless also an underlying intention in respect of manufacturing. At Lille and in Lorraine industrial reconversion, the attraction of new growth industries, and diversification, afforded the keynotes; at Strasbourg and Lyon diversification, introduction of complementary industries and new growth sectors were stressed; at Toulouse aerospace industries had already provided a new industrial platform. At Marseille-Fos, Nantes-St Nazaire, and Bordeaux, a more deliberate policy of stimulating and building upon port-based industries has been followed. In a more general sense, the policy of industrial decentralization sought to implant firms in the less-industrialized, more remote or least privileged regions (p. 273). Though some spectacular decentralizations were achieved, including major production plants in motor car manufacturing, the policy had no clearcut intention to create carefully structured and articulated industrial growth complexes, polarized upon some central town or towns in the selected regions.

At certain estuarine sites, however, there was just such an intention

(Marseille-Fos, Dunkerque, Basse-Seine), as a deliberate instrument of both urban and regional policy. Based upon selected ports with a major growth potential, the policy of creating industrial growth poles or complexes awakened echoes of the abortive British policy of Maritime Industrial Development Areas (MIDAS), 1967–9. The theoretical justification for such selective, cumulative and coherent public investment in support of, or even anticipatory to, major private investment by leader manufacturing firms in growth industries, lay in the very essence of development pole thinking (Isard *et al.* 1959, Hansen 1970, Dessau and Roth 1971) or in theories of unequal economic growth (Perroux 1961, 152). Creation of an industrial growth complex might result from the collective actions of large-scale entrepreneurs locating major new production capacity or by the policies of public authorities providing the infrastructure, the land, the urbanization for a growth pole associated development. In postwar French planning the state, the local authorities and entrepreneurs have been jointly involved, within a market economy framework.

The ingredients for creating an industrial growth complex (Dessau and Roth 1971, 43) include: a spectrum of propulsive or key industries, well-established elsewhere in the economy and competitive, with a strong representation of growth sectors and probably including large firms in leader industries; existence or the potential for linkages (goods, labour, technology) on an increasingly intensive scale among the industries in the growth pole, or elsewhere in the regional hinterland; geographical proximity of the industries or a well-developed communications system. Secondly, an associated economic and social milieu, with resources and specialized activities: research and development, higher education and vocational training, and a labour market with appropriate skills. Thirdly, a well-articulated network for private and public decision-taking to stimulate, monitor and programme the development of the industrial complex. The definition of propulsive (leading to the accretion of other industries) or key (maximum growth) industries will vary in time and through space, but the essential element is that such industries should support and complement each other during cumulative growth. Failing this, an industrial complex may degenerate into merely a 'potential' pole, or its outward links may be diffused at the expense of central polarized growth ('lateral' pole, Hansen 1970, 143). The test of success for an industrial growth complex lies in the rate of agglomeration, the degrees of linkage, but even more fundamentally the extent of integration within the regional economy. In this sense of intraregional stimulus it resembles the counterbalancing metropolis, and indeed in some cases provides the economic underpinning for a successful counterbalancing policy.

The working of the industrial growth complex policy is most clearly seen at Marseille-Fos, almost equally so at Dunkerque and to a lesser extent in the Basse-Seine (Le Havre, Rouen) and at other estuarine sites (Donges, Bordeaux). Somewhat curiously at first sight, the chosen propulsive or key industries (petroleum and petrochemicals, iron and steel) have certain built-in limitations and have no well-established record of past performance in stimulating, interlinking and integrating growth. In France, the Lorraine steel industry hitherto has had few local multiplier effects, with only a small proportion of output consumed in the region by secondary industries. At Taranto in southern Italy the steel industry, even on a coastal site, has had a limited role in building any industrial growth complex. At Lacq in Aquitaine the natural gas field has not given rise to substantial local manufacturing (Aydalot 1965), and many coastal oil refineries have exported their refined products for manufacture in other regions.

The port-based industrial growth complexes at Fos, Dunkerque and Le Havre, however, must be interpreted in the context of world trading as well as exercising a propulsive role in their regions and for the French economy. With a rising momentum of world trade, industrial products will be needed on ever-increasing scale by developing countries overseas. In this sense the establishment of coastal industrial growth complexes might serve a dual role: processing of imported raw materials and fuels for the French economy; manufacturing both for regional and national consumption, but also for export purposes. In such an export-orientated role, the competitive status of the French ports vis-à-vis their EEC rivals might be enhanced by the government aid given to creation of the industrial growth complex. If Fos is accepted as a relocation of the major growth potential of Marseille, then all three complexes already had substantial assets at the time their priority for accelerated development was announced (Marseille-Fos 1962, Dunkerque steel plant started 1962, Mission de la Basse-Seine 1965).

Marseille-Fos

Marseille-Fos (fig. 67) had a dual objective: to create a port-industrial countermagnet to the over-industrialization of the Channel and North Sea faces of the EEC, and at the same time, as in the case of Taranto (S. Italy), to act as an industrial growth pole for the Mediterranean world, North Africa and the Middle East; secondly, to create a substantive part of the employment base for rapid population growth in the Marseille OREAM by the end of the century (table 35). The scale of intended growth, initially on the port industrial zone at Fos (7250 ha.) and later also on an outlying associated industrial estate, envisages 100,000 new jobs by 1985 (25,000 provided by end-1974), and eventually up to 180,000 jobs. The propulsive

1 Steelworks and rolling mills (SOLMER)
2 Special steels (UGINE)
3 Polyethylene (ICI)
4 Heavy metal structures and boilers (CFEM)
5 Oil refinery (ESSO)
6 Container base
7 Chlorine (UGINE – KUHLMANN)
8 S. European pipeline
9 Gaz de France
10 Liquid air

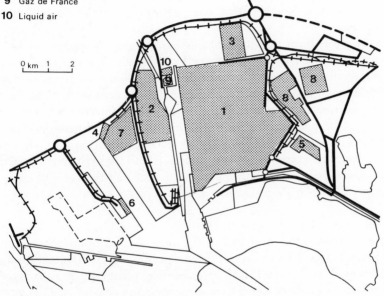

Figure 67   Fos: the industrial zone.

industries are iron and steel, and petroleum with petrochemicals. The steelworks was proposed as far back as 1954, but the site at Fos was confirmed only in 1969, at the time of approval of the *schéma directeur* for the Marseille metropolitan area. Construction of the SOLMER integrated steelworks and slabbing mills started in 1971 with an initial planned capacity of 3.5 million ingot tonnes, to be raised to 7 Mt in a second stage, with a theoretical long-term capacity on site of 20 Mt. By the end of 1974, 6000 men were employed (2200 in-migrants from Lorraine), and a further 1000 nearby at a specialized steel plant (UGINE Aciers) with associated rolling mills (200,000 tonnes specialized steels, 400,000 tonnes rolled products). In the late 1970s there were only small-scale steel-using manufacturing plants (heavy boilers, heavy metallic structures) but it is intended that there should be a proliferation of such plants during the second phase.

The four regional petroleum refineries (Fos, Lavéra, Berre and La Mède, fig. 40) could supply raw materials for a massive petrochemical industry. In 1976 this amounted to no more than a low-density polyethylene plant (ICI, 250 employed 1974) and chlorine production (Ugine-Kuhlmann, 320 employed). Liquefaction of air to oxygen and nitrogen (Air Liquide) is a further chemical starter plant. The methane terminal (1972), for liquefied natural gas from North Africa, has had a negligible effect (40) on local employment.

In the short term, the world recession in steel and the cutback on oil imports after the tripling in price after 1973 will threaten the continued development of the twin pillars of the Marseille-Fos growth complex. Unfortunately, too, closure of traditional firms (engineering at Port-de-Bouc) and reduction of the workforce at others (aircraft manufacture at Istres) have reduced the all too scarce diversity in local manufacturing. In 1977 the Fos complex was working at only 70 per cent capacity, the second stage of the steel complex has been deferred, and the multiplier effects have thus far been below expectations and little to the advantage of the regional economy (Tuppen 1975, Dussart *et al.* 1977).

Dunkerque (*Agence d'Urbanisme* 1971)

Similarly based upon iron and steel production and petroleum refining, Dunkerque already has a greater measure of industrial diversification than at Marseille-Fos. The USINOR iron and steel plant (annual capacity: 8 Mt of cast iron) was one of the earliest in Europe on a coastal site (1962), today employing more than 6000. Some steel is consumed in the local shipyard, a heavy boiler-making plant, and a conventional steel plant; most recently, an oil-rig and offshore equipment manufacturing firm has been established. The bulk of Dunkerque steel production, however, goes elsewhere in the French economy or abroad.

The petroleum refineries (BP, Total) have a throughput capacity of 12 Mt (Marseille-Fos 54 Mt). As yet there is no local petrochemical industry, but in 1978 a 450,000 tonne-capacity steam-cracker for ethylene will be in production, giving a stimulus to the chemical industry throughout northern France. The aluminous cement plant (Lafarge Ltd., 1975) and the Lesieur oil and fats factory represent traditional port-based industries. The prospect of an aluminium plant (PUK) has been mooted for either Dunkerque or Fos, but this valuable additional diversification is linked to the availability of cheap bulk electricity and has been deferred for the present.

Proposals for the development of Dunkerque seem potentially dramatic, with a port industrial zone covering more than 8000 ha., an outer port of 560 ha., with access for vessels of 300,000–450,000 dwt. In time, the entire coastal tract from Dunkerque to Gravelines will become part of the port-industrial growth complex, to be extended in due course to link with Calais. Yet some scepticism is in order: the steel plant cannot expand on site, skilled labour for manufacturing industry is scarce, the port has benefited less than most from processing of intermediate products, North Sea oil is likely to favour ports further north, the port hinterland is limited within France and attraction of steel-using industry from other parts of the Nord has proved difficult (Dussart *et al.* 1977).

Basse-Seine (Mission d'Etudes 1971)
This subregion has no less substantial prospects for developing its industrial growth complex. Le Havre has massive petroleum refineries, the capacity at the outport of Antifer of taking the largest ocean-going tankers, and 8000 ha. of alluvial industrial land flanking the Tancarville canal. The Antifer project in 1977 was landing 45 per cent of French petroleum consumption but the original concept for a rival to Rotterdam, with pipelines to north-west Europe, has been deferred. The industrial estates flanking the canal include motor car plants (Renault at Sandouville; Ford), aeronautical engineering (SNECMA) and other high technology growth industries. Steel manufacture is absent, but petrochemicals have grown strongly on the base of the local oil refineries. Rouen, capable of taking only 30,000 tonne vessels, has developed in complementary fashion, with a wide range of traditional manufactures based on textiles and engineering.

The proposal for a major new port-industrial zone at Donges-Montoir (St Nazaire) has already been referred to (p. 364). In late 1976, a methane terminal was approved for the Loire estuary, in preference to Antifer, the original choice by government.

The policy for massive development at selected coastal industrial growth complexes is essentially long-term (30 years). The initial propulsive industries have been established, with dual but scarcely related growth sectors in iron and steel, petroleum and petrochemicals. The critical second phase of associated linkages has scarcely begun, though all three major sites are linked into the national and international economy. It remains to be seen if the difficult threshold can be crossed from propulsive industry to a widening, growing range of induced manufacturing. In the climate of planning thought (VIIth Plan) against massive concentrations and unrestrained capitalism (Durrieu 1973, Robert 1974) it may be that the agglomerating forces around the coastal growth complexes will be increasingly diffused to the advantages of the regional hinterland, if necessary at the expense of the development pole at the coast.

CORRIDOR GROWTH

The strategy for counterbalancing metropoli, and that for coastal industrial growth complexes, both predicate polarization upon major urban centres. In each case, development of a communications network links the centre to a regional and national hinterland, either diffusing growth to a tributary urban network (relay towns —*centres relais*, medium-sized towns —*villes moyennes*) or assuring the supply of goods and services to and from the centre. Yet the concepts are both essentially polarizing in character: to the extent that communication routes are important, they are so only in the links that they afford to other polarized centres at a lesser or greater order in the urban hierarchy. An alternative spatial growth strategy, however, envisages allocation of growth linearly, along preferential growth axes or corridors, at several scale levels. On the EEC scale the Nord-Belgium-Rhine, the Channel coast-Rhine, the North Sea-Mediterranean, the Basse-Seine-Paris-Est growth axes are often referred to in French regional planning literature. The concept of preferential growth axes at metropolitan scale has figured in the spatial strategies for the Région Parisienne ever since the 1965 *schéma directeur* (p. 329), and remains an essential element in the Nord (Dunkerque-Lille), the Lorraine (Nancy-Metz-Thionville) and the Nantes-St Nazaire strategies. Interestingly, the corridor growth concept had a contemporary British counterpart in the South East Strategy (1967), continued in the Strategic Plan for the South East (1970), found also in the Outline Strategy for the North (1969). Linear stimulation of population and urban growth in France reached its most comprehensive planning form in proposals for the Bassin Parisien (DATAR 1969).

The spatial strategy to be adopted for the Bassin Parisien is a crucial element in both regional and national planning. The policies of decongestion and decentralization of Paris have a particular importance for the 200 km hinterland of the Bassin, which has traditionally been under the economic and social shadow of the capital: low levels of urbanization, lack of an effective independent regional urban hierarchy, persistent net out-migration to Paris; in short, no effective counterpart to the radial-concentric domination by the capital upon the Bassin. Secondly, the links between Paris and the eight counterbalancing metropoli pass through the Bassin and growth pressures might be expected along the major linking corridors. Thirdly, the interregional relationships with the other 21 programme regions include 5 regions wholly and 2 partly within the modified planning definition of the Bassin (1970).

Two underlying and long-standing realities conditioned the spatial strategy to be adopted: first, that the Bassin had neither homogeneity nor unity and, secondly, that its traditional linkages with Paris had been organized in a radial-concentric fashion, to the general detriment of the hinterland region. There is some dispute about the coherence and identity of the Bassin in history and as an entity for resource management (Verrière 1972), but the component programme regions ill accord with either coherence or identity, and in practice the Bassin is organized for social and economic life around perhaps twelve scarcely interrelated towns with their tributary urban fields. Verrière (1972, 267) accepted the Bassin as an entity (structural sedimentary basin, historic unit of royal administration, prime beneficiary of industrial decentralization policies) and saw the planning regions in the Bassin as 'arbitrary, superfluous, and eventually dangerous'. The Bassin offers, indeed, the clearest and at the same time the most substantial example of potential clash of both interests and spatial strategies between the programme regions on the one hand and national spatial management policies on the other: the spatial logic for the Bassin does not often fit well with that for the component regions.

In 1963 the Bassin Parisien was defined as one of the nine large-scale ZEAT regions (fig. 4) grouped around the capital and the eight counterbalancing regional metropoli. The 1965 *schéma directeur* for the Paris region defined broad spatial principles for the urbanization of the Bassin. These were the logical growth areas along the axis of the Seine to the sea, the valleys of the Oise, the Marne and the Seine upstream from Paris. In the same year, the Vth Plan gave priority to a coherent economic development programme for the Bassin, and in 1966 an interministerial planning group was set up to advise on preferential zones for urbanization, location of growth centres, the necessary communications system, and the decon-centration of Parisian employment, especially tertiary activities. The terms of reference for an eventual spatial strategy included the major valleys as support zones (*zones d'appui*) and the towns of more than 100,000 inhabitants as growth centres, offering an alternative to continuing growth in Paris. Planning was to be selectively concentrated and in 1968 four support zones were defined (fig. 61) and nine regional centres (Rouen, Le Havre, Caen, Le Mans, Tours, Orléans, Troyes, Reims and Amiens). Among the four support zones, priority was to be given to: the Basse-Seine axis, and the middle Loire valley. The other two, the Oise-Aisne valleys and the North Champagne support zone, were seen as of lower priority, distinctive but different: the former with neither major towns nor industrial concentrations, the latter with a potential which would not be realized until large-scale communications improvements were undertaken. In the early 1970s the Oise-Aisne valley zone was dropped and it was resolved to give no special priority to any of the remaining three. Four of the nine designated regional centres lay outside the support zones (Caen, Le Mans, Amiens, Troyes), and were to be given particular aid for their development.

The Basse-Seine axis (Mission d'Etudes 1971) linked the Paris region with the port-industrial growth complex of Le Havre-Rouen already described. Such a dual axis, paralleling the Seine valley, was the continuation of the twin preferential growth axes defined for urban redeployment in the Région Parisienne in the 1965 *schéma directeur*, and confirmed in the 1975 SDAU. A *mission d'études* was set up in 1965, publishing a *livre blanc* for the Basse-Seine in 1967, approved in 1969. The guiding spatial principle was for channelled, discontinuous but grouped urbanization along twin corridors flanking the Seine. The dangers were that market forces would perpetuate an uncontrolled sprawl and that Greater Paris would extend its suburban influence progressively downstream. To avoid these twin risks there were to be three major urban-industrial growth nodes: the estuarine zone, with heavy industry extending inland from Le Havre, complemented by the recreational zone of the Calvados coast and the regional tertiary and industrial centre of Caen; the central zone, based on Rouen and the New Town of Le Vaudreuil (table 34), with industrial but increasingly also major regional tertiary functions; and, thirdly, the zone on the approaches to Paris, where the New Town of Cergy-Pontoise and the pressures of suburban spread would dominate, but not to the exclusion of growth at the subregional centre of Evreux. Between the three urbanization nodes, green belts (*coupures vertes*) were to limit urbanization and to conserve high-grade forest and farmland with recreational potential.

Population in the Basse-Seine was to double by the end of the century, mostly through logical growth by market forces, but this is now less likely. Nevertheless, major urbanization will continue: Le Vaudreuil New Town, for example, a re-siting of the 1965 proposal for Mantes, has target population figures of 20,000 by 1984, 90–140,000 by the year 2000. Balancing of urban growth in the three major nodes poses a special planning problem. Controlling possible adverse effects, of polarization of growth into the Basse-Seine corridor, upon the smaller towns and rural society is a no less delicate planning issue.

The middle Loire valley planning scheme, fig. 69, (La DF 1971, Verrière 1972) has an urbanization strategy similar to that of the Basse-Seine: linear allocation of growth, with major urban nodes at each end (Tours, Orléans), and green belts to break up spontaneous trends towards ribbon development of settlement. But the scale and geographical circumstances are altogether different: the Loire is unimportant in terms of waterborne traffic; the road and rail links with Paris are less significant (absence of a motorway; most direct links from Orléans); whilst the industrial potential is of a secondary nature, even though both Tours and Orléans have benefited under decentralization measures from Paris. Nevertheless, the planners propose to synthesize an urban region based along the river banks, uniting the rival centres of Tours and Orléans, with the objective of the high-grade living environment implied in the title 'garden metropolis' (*métropole-jardin*). Verrière (1972) is sceptical of the middle Loire linear city concept: the two major urban centres are at extremities, whilst the central zone around Blois is economically weak; the regional population, and hence the regional market, is too small to nurture a potential sub-metropolitan centre; and the middle Loire remains too firmly and directly under the influence of the capital. Furthermore, though the middle Loire linear urban proposal may satisfy in some measure the radial-concentric decentralization of activities from Paris, it makes less strategic sense in terms of the coherent development of the Centre programme region (p. 401)

The North Champagne support zone (ZANC), based around Reims, Epernay and Châlons-sur-Marne, is somewhat more controversial (La DF 1972). Logically, it lies along the potentially major Channel Coast-Rhine axis, and the approved planning scheme aims to develop a polycentric, agricultural and tertiary growth pole capable of inducing self-sustaining economic growth in the Champagne-Ardennes planning region. The uncertainty on longer-term prospects relates to the high priority given to the New Town of Marne-la-Vallée in the eastern suburbs of Paris, a competitor for activities which might otherwise be decentralized from the capital. Secondly, the completion of the motorways A4 (1976 only Paris-Châlons-sur-Marne open) and the A26 Calais-Dijon will be needed to realize the full potential of the support zone. Indeed, it seems highly likely that the proposals for the support zone will be incorporated into the regional strategy for Champagne-Ardennes.

Corridor growth as a means of synthesizing an urban region flanking a river valley is thus well-established in French planning thinking. The definition of urban nodes and intervening green belts aims to produce a harmonized, discontinuous urbanization, with complementarity of functions between the nodes and an articulation of growth by means of a rapid transit communications network. Such corridor growth proposals concern areas which already face pressure for major development. Alternatives would be uncontrolled urban sprawl or the allocation of growth to regional networks, rather than linearly. The middle Loire proposals bring the linear and the regional allocations most clearly into confrontation.

THE POLICY FOR SMALL AND MEDIUM-SIZED TOWNS *(villes moyennes)*

A logical progression of the decentralization of metropolitan functions to eight regional metropoli, to promote regional balance and avoid centre-periphery disequilibria, was a system of relay-centres to link the regional metropoli effectively with their hinterlands. The benefits of growth at the centre might thus be diffused, whilst the relay-centres or second-order towns would perform a similar function on a lesser scale for their more intimate rural hinterlands. Such an overall policy for managing the national urban hierarchy was a central theme of the Vth Plan (1966–70), and the greatest priority was attached to the rapid growth of the eight regional metropoli. Whilst continuing the policy of the counterbalancing met-ropoli, the VIth Plan (1971–5) laid particular stress upon medium-sized towns, not primarily as relay-centres but as rapidly-growing units, with positive economic and social assets, capable of promoting sound com-munity development at an appropriate human scale emphasizing heritage and the quality of life. Such a set of concepts broke away from a technocratic emphasis on management of the total urban network. A policy for medium-sized towns would treat each case on its merits, with a strong initiative at local authority level. Regional councils would be consulted and relationships with a rural hinterland would be a prime reason for granting state aid to selected towns (Comby 1973).

This change of emphasis in urban planning corresponded with a change in planning generally, towards social priorities and the environmental quality of life; the political events of 1968 and their aftermath strengthened ideas of democratic participation and local scale rather than abstract, remote, centralized, technocratic control. The political advantages likely to accrue to government from such changes could not be and were not ignored. The medium-sized town was ubiquitous in France, was the staple element of traditional and long-standing regional urban networks (Nonn 1975), and had many defenders against the centralization process in planning (Veyret-Verner 1969). During the VIIth Plan (1976–80) the medium-towns policy is to be even more strongly emphasized, in principle with priority over large-scale urban development.

Given the diversity of medium-sized towns, it was difficult at the outset to classify them effectively in terms of their potential for contributing to or benefiting by the new planning policy (Conseil National 1972, Kayser 1972A, B, 1973). In 1973 the *Ministère de l' Aménagement du Territoire* defined the parameters for medium-sized towns which might benefit: a population between 20,000 and 100,000 (165 such towns in 1968 with an aggregate population of 7 millions, or 20 per cent of the then total urban figure); a location outside Ile-de-France, not under the immediate shadow of a regional metropolis, and not primarily a tourist centre. Moreover, to be a candidate for aid by government contract, a medium-sized town had to have an urban environment of quality, with demographic, economic and geographical characteristics permitting a diversified range of functions to be exercised for the benefit of a sufficiently large hinterland. Some paradox was involved since, on the one hand, selected towns were to be encouraged to develop further, but not at the expense of their architectural or social heritage; on the other hand, the growth was ultimately to be restrained, to preserve such urban qualities of life. The greatest risks to the urban heritage were thought to be: the creation of *grands ensembles* out of keeping with the existing urban fabric; an impoverishment of town centres in favour of the periphery or interurban space; and a lack of imagination in using the natural site or the built environment in the course of urban development. A particular set of roles for medium-sized towns was defined: to hold rural migrants who might otherwise drift to the regional metropoli or the capital, by providing services and diffusing the benefits of growth from the regional metropoli (Assocn Bureaux-Provinces 1976).

The many medium-sized towns are unequally equipped to fulfil such roles (Beyer 1971, Kayser 1973). Their pattern in the national space is markedly uneven (fig. 20): constellations around Paris, Lyon and Marseille; groups in southern Alsace, linked to Mulhouse and Bâle, the Lorraine mining basin, the Alpine trough (*sillon alpin*) from Grenoble to Geneva, the Bas-Languedoc coastal plains; in a corridor from Carcassonne to Castres and Carmaux; Poitou-Charentes; and in the north-east Massif Central. Paired medium-sized towns, capable of developing complementary functions, are not uncommon (e.g. Poitiers and Châtellerault), whilst in Bretagne, the middle Loire valley, and southern Aquitaine, there are more numerous isolated examples, over 30 km from an equivalent or larger centre (La DF 1971–2). In the Nord coalfield (Bruyelle 1972) and the Lorraine mining area medium-sized towns commonly have a limited industrial base and are deficient in services. Around the larger cities medium-sized towns have satellite functions (Versailles, Mantes, Vienne) with a high ratio of services, but serving only the local market; commuting to the large town reflects a lack of employment locally. The chief town of a *département* is often a medium-sized centre, linked administratively with the regional metropolis, but often with a balance of employment in both small and medium manufacturing firms and in services. Medium-sized towns directly serving an agricultural hinterland (Rodez, Draguignan) are often the least prosperous, not infrequently remote, and based on a limited range of service functions (Laborie 1974). In general, the links between medium-sized towns and their local hinterlands have weakened as the agricultural population has declined steadily; links with other medium-sized towns and with the regional metropoli have characteristically been strengthened. It is the purpose of the medium-sized towns policy to strengthen both the forward and the backward links.

The great variations in population size further differentiate the medium-sized towns (in 1968 119 had fewer than 50,000 inhabitants, 46 50–100,000). The most positive feature justifying a role in the national urban network for such a heterogeneous group is often said to be their characteristic demographic dynamism, well-sustained since 1954: 1954–68 annual growth rate 2.2 per cent, large towns 1.9 per cent, smaller towns 1.7 per cent; 1968–75, medium-sized towns growth rate 1.3 to 1.5 per cent, a rate higher than that for any other size category. Only in isolated problem mining localities, e.g. Décazeville or Montceau-les-Mines, has there been stagnation or decline (Kayser 1973). The sustained population growth has led to a more youthful population on average but a problem of job availability has emerged. Only the larger towns in the medium-sized category have a diversity of industry; others have mainly a service function, growing in proportion to population size and the improvement in living standards. The building industry in the *villes moyennes* has prospered from population and service growth but clearly there are limits to this continuing without stimulus from the outside.

Other assets of the medium-sized towns are said to be: a community structure in which individuals can feel an identity and which fosters democratic participation; closer residence-workplace relationships; lower housing costs and more individual houses; closer touch with recreational opportunities; less pollution, fewer traffic hazards and better health; a more satisfying general living environment, with a sense of heritage. From a planner's viewpoint it is argued (La DF 1971–2, II–3) that infrastructure costs are often only one-third those of large cities, that factory units employing 300 to 1000 can be effectively decentralized to medium-sized towns (Bastié 1975) where labour costs may be lower, and that social segregation may be reduced.

On the debit side, the 'backwater' outlook of some French provincial towns is likely to resist positive planning. For this reason the initiative rests with the local authority (*commune, municipalité*) to seek a contract for development aid from the *Ministère de l'Aménagement du Territoire*. If accepted in principle, a more detailed scheme is worked out by the local authority, with technical aid; when confirmed, costings are added. Final approval is given by CIAT and financing of the contract is additional to normal local authority grant aid, but is specifically earmarked for particular projects improving the quality of life. By spring 1976, 21 contracts had been signed and a further 60 towns were preparing schemes (fig. 61). The first contract, for Rodez (1973), was for replanning the central area. Since then the range of schemes has widened considerably and changed in emphasis: 'open spaces, conservation of architectural heritage, pedestrian ways' have decreased from 44 to 39 per cent of expenditures in the second 14 medium-sized town contracts compared with the first 14; cultural, social and educational provision has increased from 22 to 34 per cent of expenditure. Local employment difficulties, both in modernizing work-shops and small-scale traditional industries and in the attraction of new firms, have figured increasingly, but an overwhelming impression of uniqueness typifies each contract (DATAR/DAFU 1976).

Since April 1975 (CIAT) the medium-sized town policy has been taken a stage further, by the promotion of aid for even smaller towns or village anchor-points as part of a comprehensive rural planning policy. This is partly in order to sustain the farm-based population and prevent economic drainage from the hinterlands to the stimulated economy and more varied living environments of the state-supported medium-sized towns. To the central government policy of rural planning contracts (*contrats de pays*—a small town 5–15,000 with its rural environs; CAR—*contrats d'aménagement rural*) some of the regional councils have added regional rural planning contracts (e.g. Centre region, CRAR—*contrats régionaux d'aménagement rural*). Both central and regional contracts are concerned to: diversify employment, reinforce local service provision, and improve the quality of life. Since December 1975 the *contrat de pays* and CRAR policies have been consolidated at regional level. Complementary to the latter a *regional* policy for medium-sized towns (*villes moyennes régionales*) has been introduced, for example, in the Centre region (Parant 1976). These towns are of 5–20,000 inhabitants and most of the specific town planning proposals approved for 12 of the 30 regional *villes moyennes* of the Centre concern central area improvements, pedestrian precincts, restoration of historic monuments, social and cultural facilities, or open space provision.

The micro-scale of the regional *villes moyennes* or *village-centres* (anchor-point villages) completes consideration of the French urban hierarchy. It is scarcely more than a decade since French urban policy was directed to management of the hierarchy at all scale levels, to achieve decentralization and thus promote greater balance in economy and society. The towns became the principal instrument for allocating a growth generated by industrialization and polarized by townward movements of people; in turn the rising populations of the towns, at higher living standards, increased consumer demand and stimulated service activities. From the outset it was appreciated that such polarization of growth would create the risk of impoverishment of hinterlands, first those of the counterbalancing metropoli, then those of the relay-centres or the medium-sized towns, and finally those of the regional *villes moyennes* and the anchor-point villages (Barbier 1972). The primacy accorded to economic growth waned during the VIth Plan and has been replaced by concern for the environment and the quality of life under the VIIth Plan. Concurrently the political forces in France have been shifting. The rise of the political Left in the great cities was said by some to have inspired the change of emphasis in urban policy towards the medium-sized towns, in many of which political conservatism remained the order of the day. The 1977 municipal elections, however, had the dramatic outcome that 34 free-standing medium-sized towns, plus 16 in the fringes of the metropoli, passed to the Left. This strengthened an already mounting countertide against centralization and in favour of local decision-taking, against the forces of the market and in favour of social priorities, human scale in planning and identity as well as individuality for regions, towns and people.

On balance, the attempts to manage the urban network have seen outstanding achievements, with public investment and intervention in the most crucial category of large cities dramatically effective. British planners have much to learn from the policies of urban network management practised in France. Coordination and choice of priorities in large-scale investments by public and private capital during a fast growth phase in the economy led to dramatic transformations in the eight regional metropoli. The urban policies were, however, essentially long-term in character, with a 15 to 30 year perspective for completion. The downturn in national circumstances, allied with political shifts and a climate turning against over-centralization, large-scale thinking and untrammelled working of market forces, makes it unlikely that the technocratic elegance of French urban policies will ever be fully realized. The identity, aspirations and character of all towns will have to be fully recognized and planning subjected to more rigorous democratic control, no matter the delays or loss of sophistication which may result.

References

Town planning
Ambassade de France (1972) *Town Planning in France*, London.
Arcy, F. d' (1970) 'Vers un urbanisme volontaire?', *Aménagement du territoire et développement régional*, III, IEP, Grenoble: 33–61.
Cornière, P. (1971) 'Les PME et la planification dans les agglomérations urbaines',

Aménagement du territoire et développement régional, IV, IEP, Grenoble: 147–66.

Jamois, J. (1968) *Les zones à urbaniser par priorité*.

Magnan, R., Bertumé, G. and Comby, J. (1973) 'Conception et instruments de la planification urbaine', *Centre de Recherche d'Urbanisme*.

Rouge, M. (1964) 'L'urbanisation en France et les institutions', *L'urbanisation française*.

Paris and the Ile-de-France

APUR (1974) 'L'avenir de Paris', *Paris-Projet*, 10–11.
——— (1975) 'Paris du sud-est: le projet de schéma de secteur Lyon-Austerlitz-Bercy', *Paris-Projet*, 12: 8–85.

Bastié, J. (1972) 'L'évolution récente des localisations dans une grande agglomération: l'exemple de Paris', *Revue Géogr. alp.*, LX, (2): 245–52.

Beaujeu-Garnier, J. (1974) 'Place, vocation et avenir de Paris et de sa région', *Notes et Etudes Documentaires*, 4142–3.

Carmona, M. (1975) 'Les plans d'aménagement de la Région Parisienne', *Acta géogr. Paris*, 23: 14–46.

Centre d'Etude Interuniversitaire du Bassin Parisien (CEIBAP) (1970) 'Les villes de la couronne du Bassin Parisien', *Colloque de Dourdan* 1969.

Commissaire à la Construction (1960) *Plan d'aménagement et d'organisation générale de la région parisienne* (PADOG).

DATAR (1969) *Projet de livre blanc du Bassin parisien*.
——— (1970) 'Schéma général d'aménagement de la France: aménagement du Bassin Parisien', *Travaux et Recherches de Prospective*, 7.

Délégation Générale au District de la Région de Paris (1965) *Schéma directeur d'aménagement et d'urbanisme de la région de Paris*.

District de la Région de Paris (1965) *Paris en question*.

Dreyfus, J. (1975) 'L'essentiel et le résidu: le cas de la planification urbaine', *Environment & Plann.*, 7 (4): 473–83.

Herpin, I. and Pérot, L. (1974) 'La reconquête du centre', *Archit. d'Aujourd'hui*, 176.

House, J. W. (ed.) (1977) *The UK Space*, London, ch. 1.

IAURP (1966) 'La décentralisation industrielle et le Bassin Parisien', *Cahiers de l'IAURP*, 6.
——— (1967) 'Industrie, artisans et rénovation urbaine; le quartier et la ville', *Cahiers de l'IAURP*, 7.

Mallet, F. (1967) 'Le quartier des Halles de Paris', *Annls Géogr.*, LXXVI (413): 1–28.

Merlin, P. (1971) *Vivre à Paris* 1980.

Mission d'Etude d'Aménagement Rural (1971) *Eléments pour un schéma d'aménagement rural de la Région Parisienne*.

Préfecture de la Région Parisienne (1975) *Schéma directeur d'aménagement et d'urbanisme de la Région Parisienne*.

Rousset-Deschamps, M. (1974) 'Méthode d'approche des centres intermédiaires de la banlieue parisienne', *Annls. Géogr.*, LXXXIII (460): 625–43.

Sutcliffe, A. (1970) *The Autumn of Central Paris. The Defeat of Town Planning 1850–1970*, London.

Verrière, J. (1972) 'Faut-il régionaliser le Bassin Parisien?', *L'Espace géogr.*, I (4): 261–8.

Vignaux, P. and Lebel, N. (1971) 'Hiérarchie spatiale des activités en banlieue de Paris', *Cahiers de l'IAURP*, 22.

New Towns

Besnard-Bernadac, E. (1976) 'Rapport sur l'état de réalisation des villes nouvelles à l'issue du VIe Plan', in 'Les Villes Nouvelles: dix ans après', *Promotions*, 99.

Chatin, C. (1975) '9 villes nouvelles', *Collection Aspects de l'Urbanisme*.

Darmagnac, A. (1968) 'Problèmes de réalisation de villes nouvelles. Le cas d'Evry', *Bull. Ass. Géogr. fr.*, 362–3: 125–40.

Hérin, M. (1973) 'Cergy-Pontoise: une ville nouvelle dans son environnement et son développement', *L'Espace géogr.*, II (2): 127–38.

IAURP (1969) 'Evry—centre urbain nouveau et ville nouvelle', *Cahiers de l'IAURP*, 15.

—— (1973) 'Evry I', *Cahiers de l'IAURP*, 31.

Lacaze, J. P. (1972) 'The role of the French New Towns in regional development and regional life', *VIth Congress, Int. Council of Reg. Econ.*, Warsaw.

Merlin, P. (1975) 'French New Towns', *The Planner*, 61: 3.

Nardin, H. (1971) 'De l'agglomération à la région urbaine: recherche des leviers nouveaux', *Urbanisme*, 129: 31–8.

Pressman, N. (1973) 'French urbanization policy and the new towns programme', *Ekistics*, 36 (212): 17–22.

Rouillier, J.-E. (1970) 'Administrative and financial problems of creating New Towns in the Paris area', *Techqs Archit.*, 5.

—— (1973) 'French New Towns and innovation', 2000 (janvier).

Countermagnet metropoli

Bleitrach, D. and Chenu, A. (1974) 'Aménagement: régulation ou aggravation des contradictions sociales? Fos-sur-Mer et l'aire métropolitaine marseillaise', *Aménagement du territoire et développement régional*, VII, IEP, Grenoble: 187–214.

Bruyelle, P. (1975) 'L'utilisation du sol dans la Métropole du Nord', *Hommes et Terres du Nord*, 1: 113–30.

George, P. (1967) 'Métropoles d'équilibre', *Revue géogr. Pyrénées et Sud-Ouest*, XXXVIII: 105–11.

La Documentation Française (1968) 'L'aménagement du territoire en France', *Notes et Etudes Documentaires*, 3461: 30–4.

—— (1969A) 'Métropoles d'équilibre et aires métropolitaines', *Notes et Etudes Documentaires*, 3633.

—— (1969B) 'Organisation d'études d'aménagement de l'aire métropolitaine du Nord', *Notes et Etudes Documentaires*, 3635–6.

—— (1969C) 'Organisation d'études d'aménagement de l'aire métropolitaine Metz-Nancy-Thionville', *Notes et Etudes Documentaires*, 3637–9.

—— (1969D) 'Organisation d'études d'aménagement de l'aire métropolitaine Lyon-St Etienne', *Notes et Etudes Documentaires*, 3634.

(1969E) Organisation d'études d'aménagement de l'aire métropolitaine marseillaise', *Notes et Etudes Documentaires*, 3640–2.

(1969F) 'Bordeaux et la communauté urbaine de l'agglomération bordelaise', *Notes et Etudes Documentaires*, 3565–6.

(1971) 'Aménagement d'une région urbaine, le Nord-Pas-de-Calais', *Travaux et Recherches de Prospective*, 19.

(1973A) 'Les villes françaises. Nancy et son agglomération', *Notes et Etudes Documentaires*, 4039–40.

(1973B) 'Bordeaux: ville océane, métropole régionale', *Travaux et Recherches de Prospective*, 40.

(1975A) 'Dynamique urbaine et projet régional. Un exemple: la région d'Alsace', *Travaux et Recherches de Prospective*, 56.

(1975B) 'L'aménagement de la région Fos-Etang de Berre', *Notes et Etudes Documentaires*, 4165–6.

Minist. du Plan et de l'Aménagement du Territoire (1970) *Nantes-St Nazaire. Schéma d'aménagement de l'aire métropolitaine.*

Noin, D. (1974) *L'espace français.*

Nonn, H. (1971) 'L'Alsace et son aménagement dans le cadre de la préparation des schémas directeurs', *Revue géogr. Est*, XI (3–4): 353–85.

OREAM Lorraine (1971) *Schéma d'aménagement de la métropole Lorraine*, Pont-à-Mousson.

OREAM Lyon-St Etienne (1970) *La métropole Lyon-St Etienne-Grenoble*, Lyon.

OREAM Marseille (1970) *Schéma d'aménagement de l'aire métropolitaine marseillaise*, Marseille.

Région Aquitaine (1976) *Tableau de bord de développement à moyen terme*, Bordeaux.

Veyret-Verner, G. (1969) 'Plaidoyer pour les moyennes et petites villes', *Revue Géogr. alp.*, LVII (1): 5–24.

Vieille, P. (1974) 'Une séquence de Kriegspiel méditerranéen, la bataille des rives de l'Etang de Berre, 1972', *Aménagement du territoire et développement régional*, VII, IEP, Grenoble: 377–406.

Industrial growth complexes

Agence d'Urbanisme, Région Dunkerquoise (1971) *SDAU du littoral nord Dunkerque* 2000, Dunkerque.

Aydalot, P. (1965) 'Etude sur les processus de polarisation et sur les réactions des industries anciennes à la lumière de l'expérience de Lacq', *Cahiers de l'ISEA*, 159: 111–64.

Dessau, J. and Roth, E. (1971) 'Le concept de complexe industriel et l'analyse économique régional', *Aménagement du territoire et développement régional*, IV, IEP, Grenoble: 31–69.

Droin, J. C. (1975) *Fos information*, Vitrolles.

Durrieu, Y. (1973) *L'impossible régionalisation capitaliste. Témoignage de Fos et de Languedoc.*

Dussart, F., Hanappe, P., Haumont, B. and Savy, M. (1977) 'Les plate-formes industrielles de Fos et Calais-Dunkerque: approche prospective des perspectives de développement', *Annuaire de l'Aménagement du Territoire*, VIII, IEP, Grenoble: 379–411.

Hansen, N. M. (1970) 'Development pole theory in a regional context', in Richardson, H. W. (ed.) *Regional Economics: a Reader*, London: 134–49.

Isard, W., Schooler, E. and Vietorisz, T. (1959) *Industrial Complex Analysis and Regional Development*, New York.

Mission d'Etudes Basse-Seine (1971) *Schéma d'Aménagement de la Basse-Seine*, 2 vols.

Perroux, F. (1961) 'La notion de pôle de croissance', *L'Economie du vingtième siècle*.

Robert, G. (1974) 'L'opération Fos: un test de l'aménagement capitaliste du territoire', *Urbanisme*, 44: 63–76.

Tuppen, J. N. (1975) 'Fos—Europort of the south?', *Géogr.*, 60 (3): 213–17.

Corridor growth

DATAR (1969) *Projet de livre blanc du Bassin Parisien*.

La Documentation Française (1971) 'Vers la métropole jardin. Livre Blanc pour l'aménagement de la Loire-Moyenne', *Travaux et Recherches de Prospective*, 23.
    (1972) 'L'espace Nord-Champenois', *Travaux et Recherches de Prospective*, 24.

Mission d'Etudes Basse-Seine (1971) *Schéma d'aménagement de la Basse-Seine*, 2 vols.

Verrière, J. (1972) 'Faut-il régionaliser le Bassin Parisien?', *L'Espace géogr.*, 4: 261–8.

Medium-sized towns

Association Bureaux-Provinces *et al.* (1976) *Guide des Villes Moyennes*.

Barbier, B. (1972) 'La survie des petites villes de montagne', *Revue Géogr. alp.*, LX (2): 307–20.

Bastié, J. (1975) 'La décentralisation industrielle et les petites villes' in *Etudes géographiques: mélanges offerts à Georges Viers*, Univ. de Toulouse-Le Mirail: 45–57.

Beyer, M. C. (1971) 'Essai d'étude comparée des formes et tendances de l'organisation de l'espace d'une vingtaine de moyennes et petites villes françaises', *Revue géogr. Est*, 3–4: 399–415.

Bruyelle, P. (1972) 'Les "villes moyennes" dans la région du Nord', *Cérès*, 11: 7–12.
    (1976) 'Délimitation et structure des principales zones urbaines de la région du Nord', *Hommes et Terres du Nord*, 1: 49–96.

Comby, J. (1973) 'Un nouvel aspect de la politique de DATAR: les villes moyennes, pôles de développement et d'aménagement', *Norois*, 80: 647–60.

Conseil National des Economies Régionales (1972) 'Un concours nouveau pour les villes moyennes', *Expansion Régionale*, 62–3: 1–112.

DATAR/DAFU (1976) 'Les contrats d'aménagement des villes moyennes', *Moniteur des Trav. publ. et du Bâtiment*, 14: 45–8.

Kayser, B. (1972A) 'Les petites villes françaises', *Revue Géogr. alp.*, LX (2): 269–84.
    (1972B) 'Problèmes de recherche posés par la croissance des petites villes', *Bull. Ass. Géogr. fr.*, 400–1: 269–95.
    (1973) 'Croissance et avenir des villes moyennes françaises', *Revue Géogr. Pyrénées et Sud-Ouest*, 44 (4): 345–64.

Laborie, J.-P. (1974) 'Industrialisation et croissance démographique de petites villes en milieu rural: l'exemple de Midi-Pyrénées', *Revue géogr. Pyrénées et Sud-Ouest*, 45 (2): 109–31.

La Documentation Française (1971–2) *Les villes moyennes. Dossiers d'étude. Aménagement du territoire.*

Nonn, H. (1975) 'Concerning the notion of 'sub-region': the French case', *Geoforum*, 6 (2): 125–36.

Parant, P. (1976) *Regards sur le Centre: villes moyennes et aménagement rural*, Orléans.

Veyret-Verner, G. (1969) 'Plaidoyer pour les moyennes et petites villes', *Revue Géogr. alp.*, LVII (1): 5–24.

3 Managing the regions

REGIONAL PLANNING: OBJECTIVES

It is increasingly unrealistic to view the region in a detached manner as an instrument or focus of planning, without regard to its more traditional significance in French economy and society, and without taking account of the rising tide of regionalism as either a constructive or, on occasion, a potentially destructive political or cultural force. Even within the more restricted view of the region in planning it is important to distinguish an economic from a geographical viewpoint: the former concerned with abstract programming space, with the region but a convenient interim focus, significant more in its context in the national network than in its specific internal attributes; the latter concerned with a spatial differentiation of complex reality (the economist's *espace banal*), the recognition of formal or functional groupings or interrelationships in space, in physical, economic, social or political terms. The economist's view of the region is also more time-related and flexible on that account. The optimum size of region will vary according to the planning time-horizon (Boudeville 1966, 46): 21 planning regions (22 as from 1970, with Corse) in France for the 4-year National Plans, 8 ZEAT regions (fig. 4) for 15–20 years, and 3 regions (Paris, Est, Ouest) for even longer-term planning. In comparison, the regions of the geographer are seen as more enduring, more tangible, and more programmable within traditionally accepted boundaries in at least some cases. This interdisciplinary distinction corresponds roughly to the differing purposes of economic planning on the one hand and spatial management (*aménagement du territoire*) on the other, and accounts for some of the ambiguities in the regional planning process in France. Put differently, to the economist the region may be an impediment, a constraint upon more efficient deployment of resources nationally, or even internationally; to the geographer the region is often seen as the logical platform for planning, the generator of change on the one hand, the recipient of change from the outside on the other.

At its simplest, administration requires regions for efficiency, convenience or economy, for interpreting government at less than national level. Throughout French history since the Revolution, and in planning since 1945, administrative regions have served the centralizing purposes of the state (Part I, ch. 1), rather than reflecting local or provincial loyalties, the political aspirations of subnational or ethnic minorities, the sense of deprivation or alienation of groups. Furthermore, the hierarchy of administration has scarcely changed with time, in either the levels of responsibility or in the territorial distribution of units. When planning was grafted on to an already complex, centralized administration, there was a grouping of existing territorial entities, without much change of their boundaries, but no powers of substance were transferred from *départements* or *communes*.

The over-concentrated authority of the French state, and its powerful technocratic bureaucracies, have increasingly been questioned. Economically, the reduction of manifest regional inequalities, and the search for a better balance between Paris and the provinces, have been practical objectives in regional planning. In more political terms, the demand for devolution of decision-taking, the belief that through more harmonized regional growth lies a better prospect for sustained national growth, the feeling that for democratic participation to be effective in planning it must work more locally than nationally, and the wish to express the corporate personality of social, cultural or political groupings, helped to reinforce the potential for planning at the regional level. The power behind such a search for regional accommodation necessarily varied with the economic, social, cultural or historical validity of the regional economic planning units concerned (Part I, ch. 1), from the strongest manifestations (Bretagne) to the weaker (Pays de la Loire). Through time the region has nevertheless generally become the focus for rising corporate aspirations as well as discontents. Though admitting that planning has discreetly but progressively developed a corporate mentality in the regions, Brogniart (1971, 127) saw this as mainly negative in character: in opposition to over-centralizing tendencies nationally, or to combat the micro-parochialism of the *commune*, to which might be added the expression of a sense of deprivation and a demand for regional as well as social justice. He felt that these problems might have been ameliorated, if not resolved, by reform of local government on the one hand, and the management of the urban network on the other, without the need for regions. Alternatively, the existence of economic planning regions may have contributed little, given the continuing weak powers allocated and the constant need for compro-mise among conflicting interests within the region. It is equally possible to argue, however, that the regional level is capable of being more than a compromise between the nation and local government, that with satisfactory units and adequate powers the region may synthesize the purposes of efficiency, convenience and economy, without detriment to popular representation, participation in effective decision-taking, or the fuller expression of collective personalities which are the life-blood of democratic life (House 1977). The general trend in regional planning has been to strengthen, if only slowly, the voice, if not the powers, delegated to regions. The VIIth Plan (1976–80), in a more democratic, decentralized perspective on planning, may modestly further the interests of regions, though without apparently any devolution of real powers. It may also be thought by some that the essentials of the VIIth Plan may bypass the region in order to relate planning more directly to the local communities, in city, town or countryside.

Brief mention has already been made of the various networks of planning regions in time and space (p. 42) and the evolution of regional institutions and powers (p. 46). Attention now is concentrated on regional planning procedures and a geographical critique of the kind of regional plan documents which have evolved. No attempt is made to assess comprehensively the resources, economic, social and political characteristics of all French regions; the emphasis is upon the strategy of planning at the regional level, in the face of the manifest diversities of French national life and space. Though difficult to evaluate, the relationship between regional planning and management of the urban network should be borne constantly in mind.

REGIONAL PLANNING: EVOLUTION

In the early phases (1954–8) there was an almost total dissociation between regional programmes and national planning. In 1954 the regional economic expansion committees, many in existence since the 1940s, were officially recognized, with a view to coordinating their efforts. These committees were private survey, research and promotional bodies, often closely linked to the local chambers of commerce or industrial interests. They owed little to outside advice or technical aid and had no representative of local government. In some regions they developed outline growth strategies and problem analyses to press upon the national ministries. Perhaps to re-establish its primacy, the state introduced the principle of regional action programmes (*programmes d'action régionale*) in 1955, initially applicable to any administrative unit, but personified by the 22 planning regions (*régions de programme*) created in the following year. This phase coincided with the establishment of regional development companies (SDR —*sociétés de développement régional*), to stimulate private investment in underdeveloped regions. As a counterpart, public works companies (*sociétés d'équipement*) were to finance and create major infrastructures, whilst by 1958 planning companies (*sociétés d'aménagement*) were formed for resource management for selected areas, but on comprehensive resource management footing (e.g. CNABRL, SOMIVAC). The accent initially was firmly upon action at regional level and upon regionally-derived objectives, but in 1957 the institution of regional management plans, *plans d'aménagement régional* (Minist. de la Construction), implicitly divided regional planning. In 1958, however, the two sets of planning proposals (*programmes d'action régionale, plans d'aménagement régional*) were merged into the requirement for a regional economic, social development and spatial management plan (*plan régional de développement économique et social et d'aménagement du territoire*).

These early regional planning documents have been heavily criticized (Labasse 1960): the regions concerned lacked geographical reality in many cases, the subregions were poorly identified, the early plans (CELIB 1956) lacked adequate demographic analysis and, above all else, they were the work of administrative and technical staffs from central ministries. Local consultation was usually after the event, and the concept of such programmes had a strongly economic sectoral flavour, a true inheritance of the Monnet Plan thinking (1947–52), predating any significant concern for the spatial dimension in planning. Furthermore, the process was long-drawn-out: the Lorraine plan was approved in 1957, that for Bourgogne not until 1966. The plans were long-term strategies but were neither costed with priorities in financial terms, nor effectively linked to the four-year National Plans.

A second phase, 1959–71 (Astorg 1973A), saw the formulation of *programmes d'action régionale* for each of the *circonscriptions* created in 1960 from the former 21 *régions de programme*; in 1970 Corse became the twenty-second *circonscription*. This was a period of proliferation among planning organizations (DATAR 1963; regional reform 1964 creating regional prefects and their consultative committees—CODER; 1966, planning agencies for the coal basins with financial support bodies; 1967, industrial reconversion and rural renovation organizations). Though some of the new bodies had directly spatial responsibilities, many concerned economic sectors or specific rather than regional resource management problems. Under the IVth and Vth Plans economic growth had an accelerating priority, and management of the urban network was increasingly regarded as the key to fast-growth polarized development. Nevertheless, there were two strengthened elements for the regional level of planning: the regionalizing of the National Plan (*tranches opératoires* 1961, *tranches régionales* 1966) provided the financial means for implementing priority public investments in regional or urban development; secondly, the 1964 regional reforms increased the consultation through the CODER, though it must be admitted that the real powers remained with the regional prefect, his technical staff and the central government administrators.

During the VIth Plan (1971–5) modest progress was made in more effective consultation at regional level, especially after the regional reforms of 1972 (Part I, ch. 1, La DF 1974). More coherent regional development and public equipment programmes (PRDE—*programmes régionaux de développement et d'équipement*) were drawn up (1969–72), and a better articulation with both the National Plan and the development aspirations of the diverse local authorities was achieved (Astorg 1973B). The gulf between short-term financial programming and longer-term spatial management or physical planning was reduced in the process. On the other hand, the powers of the regional prefect were undiminished; were, indeed, enhanced in relation to regional and local decision-making. The framework for regional programming, set by the complex skein of spatial management policies at national level, laid constraints upon initiatives at regional level, both conceptually and in terms of the availability of finance for priority projects. This trend towards the dominance by externalities was added to by policies of moving to greater uniformity by region in public investment programmes. In the equation of matching the aspirations and intentions of the regions with the priorities for the nation, the balance remained firmly with national needs. Yet even in curtailed form, or expressed in more uniform terms, the proposals generated by the regions represented a substantive and original contribution to national decision-taking.

State of the game

An assessment of the state of regional planning in the mid-to-late 1970s must consider first the regional inputs, secondly the regional powers of decision and, thirdly, the spatial outcome. Thereafter, the more specific examples of particular regional strategies may be compared in outline. As early as 1968 the regional organizations were asked by CGP for an economic situation report, an assessment of the trends and impact of committed large-scale investments, and some forecast of long-term prospects, taking full account of national planning policies likely to affect the region. These views were consolidated into a regional trend report (RRO—*rapport régional d'orientation*), prepared by the *mission régionale* and presented to CNAT for the guidance of the sector-based national planning commissions. It is argued (Astorg 1973B, 9) that regional objectives tended to be too ambitious, lacking in precision and without adequate regard for the necessary financial means. Furthermore, there was often a built-in ambivalence: claims for economic growth and the jobs it would bring, set against fears of change, of polarization and damage to traditional ways of life. In the event, the sectoral commissions rarely took regional perspectives adequately into account. The key commission, on finance and the general economy, focused on macro-economic and financial equilibria rather than on regional disparities, whilst the employment commission, though compelled to regionalize its forecasts (*fresques régionales de l'emploi*), spent two years in argument with the regions. The commissions on towns and on the countryside, on the other hand, had strong regional perspectives (Astorg 1973B, 4). A basic difference of view concerned the potential spatial impact of policies. Were they to be carried out *in* the region or *by* the region, a recurring aspect of the wider issue of constraining regional boundaries and the wish for autarchy in regional decisions.

The PRDE converted the VIth Plan options into a programme of public works (*équipement*) by the state and by local authorities. National policies (e.g. motorways and urban highways, telecommunications, universities and hospitals) were determined nationally, with advice from the regions, and applied in the regions. The satisfaction of intraregional needs from national investments, on the other hand, was a joint national/regional responsibility for the four-year Plan, but annual decisions devolved to the regions. Regional/*départemental* investments were jointly determined, but the *département* had the power on annual decisions (local public utilities, primary education, sports fields, etc.). *Département/commune* investment (villages, small-scale tourism, local roads) passed to the *commune* as the annual decision-taker. Overall, the provisional PRDE (1972) allocated 80 per cent of global public investment to each region on the basis of population (1971), demographic growth trends (1971–6) and level of urbanization. 20 per cent was reserved, to promote spatial management policies of national concern within particular priority regions. The investment proposals then passed back to regions for consultation (*esquisses régionales*). The regions often preferred to emphasize urban development, transport and health at the expense of other priorities (Astorg 1973B, 18) and arbitration was frequently necessary. Once approved, the PRDE defined the scope, scale and priorities of public investment in the regions, in each of which there followed problems in allocating investment between towns, between regional metropoli and medium-sized centres. Yet on balance the regional/national dialogue worked well. Astorg (1973B, 27) asserted that on balance the regions had a weak influence on industrial and agricultural policies (the latter either national or parochial) but that their influence was stronger on tourism, the countryside and on housing policy. Inevitably, however, the influence of a region on the national scene depended on the personality and dynamism of its leading figures. In general, small regions suffered by comparison with larger and, indeed, it was more difficult for them to have specific, viable policies.

The VIIth Plan (1976–80) has been formulated along similar lines to the VIth in terms of regional participation in three stages: contribution to national draft outline (January-March 1975), RRO September 1975, regional programme (*programme de développement et d'aménagement*) in Autumn 1976.

The comparison with British regional planning (House 1977) highlights more merits than demerits in French policies. Regional strategy formulation was a duty laid on the eight economic planning councils of England when created in 1965. Regional strategies in Britain were formulated in three stages: 1965–7, outline mainly sector-based statements on population and employment trends and forecasts, with emphasis on scarce resources and potential for growth. This first stage may be looked on as the formulation of regional shopping lists by economic planning council and related civil service planning board. The second stage strategy (1967–9) frequently (South East, North, North West) but not invariably had a stronger subregional component, stopping short, however, of attempting to duplicate the physical planning tasks of the statutory local authorities. A third stage, lasting well into the 1970s, was a tripartite exercise (central government, regional council, local authority) laying down guide-lines for development to the 1990s or even beyond. According to the Town and Country Planning Act (1968) the regional strategies, once approved by the Secretary of State for the Environment, became the framework for the formulation of local authority (county) structure plans. In this way, a better link was established between social and economic planning (national, regional) on the one hand, and physical planning (county) on the other. Entirely lacking in British regional strategies is the costing of proposals. Major infrastructural investment decisions have not infrequently been taken at ministerial level without adequate regional consultation. No British counterpart existed for the closely-argued PRDEs of the VIth French plan. British planning councils of the mid-1960s had close parallels with the CODER of similar date, but the powerful regional and central bureaucracies of France were, until recently, foreign to British administrative thinking. Both countries are currently undergoing the pangs of political devolution proposals, with a common reluctance on both sides of the Channel to deconcentrate real powers to either regions or ethnic subnations.

Regional strategies

Table 4 classifies the 22 planning regions, mainly by economic trends, into: growth, growth potential, industrial reconversion and, fourthly, developing categories; Ile-de-France is in a category by itself, in scale, dominance and range of metropolitan problems. The classification matches that by Quelennec (1973), based on principal components analysis of a wide diversity of social and economic parameters. The five-fold categorization is loose, and some regions are marginal or mixed in their characteristics. Nevertheless, it serves as a generally useful basis for the outline indication of problems, priorities and strategies of individual regions. Comprehensiveness is not attempted and for fuller regional statements the reader is referred to Thompson (1970).

GROWTH REGIONS

Attributes shared by the growth regions include: faster and more sustained population growth; higher levels of energy consumption per capita, business receipts, representation of large firms, mean household earnings, male incomes; lower unemployment, and better housing. Not all six regions share the same mix of these attributes, but sufficient to fall within a similar category.

Rhône-Alpes

This is the only French planning region, other than Ile-de-France, to achieve European-scale status and potential (Boudeville 1964). It has the population size (4.78 millions in 1975), the diversity of economy with a strong representation of growth sectors, a balanced urban network including the regional metropolis second in importance only to Paris, and nodal location with powerful transfrontier linkages. Within France, Rhône-Alpes forms part of the Grand Delta (fig. 68), comprising the three south-eastern regions; it flanks the Rhône-Saône corridor and is linked by complementary industries and commercial flows with Switzerland and northern Italy (La DF 1968A).

The regional population has grown steadily since 1945, the product of higher than average natural increase, but equally importantly by sustained in-migration including a strong foreign contingent (11 per cent of the population foreign-born, 1976). Population flows have been consistently polarized towards the large cities, notably Greater Lyon, but the balanced and harmonized network of secondary urban centres has stabilized the life of many subregions. In spite of in-migration, there has been a consistent labour shortage, especially for skilled workers. During the past twenty

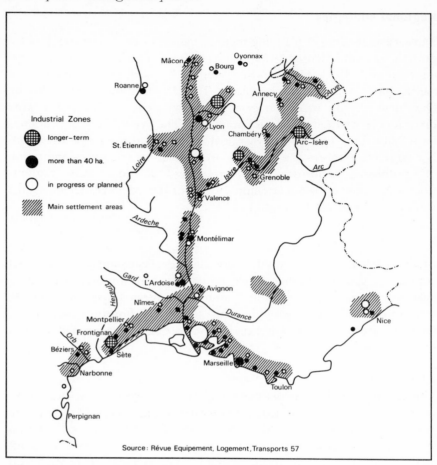

Figure 68   Le Grand Delta: industrial development.

years the industrial structure has changed: 94,000 jobs were lost in coalmining, textiles, clothing manufacture and the leather industry; on the other hand 159,000 were gained in glass, metal manufactures, engineering, electrical machinery and goods, cars and chemicals (Préfet de Région Rhône-Alpes 1976). Pockets of industrial decline or stagnation have developed: Ardèche (textile finishing), St Etienne (coal), and most recently in the upper Arc valley (electrometallurgy). However, a major further asset of Rhône-Alpes lies in the marked degree of industrial specialization within an interdependent urban network, a source of strength for promoting both regional balance and allocating growth at different levels by management of the urban system. As a result, the level of unemployment in Rhône-Alpes has traditionally been one of the lowest in France.

Apart from a diverse industrial heritage, Rhône-Alpes has abundant power resources (HEP, nuclear power at Bugey, Tricastin and Cruas, petroleum products by pipeline from Marseille-Fos), capable of sustaining major exports of power throughout France. Two sources of potential economic weakness, however, lie in the lower than average employment in the tertiary sector, and the dependence of regional industry upon headquarters outside Rhône-Alpes. Under the Vth Plan the Lyon-St Etienne-Grenoble metropolis was designated for the build-up of higher tertiary activities (Part III, ch. 2), with Greater Lyon the major recipient but with complementary interchange between the three cities of very different industrial characteristics. The subsequent growth of the regional metropolis and its attendant problems have already been considered. For the most part, the objectives of the VIth Plan for the region were achieved: the rate of population growth in the regional metropolis was cut back (1962–8, 56 per cent; 1968–75, 38 per cent of regional growth); the rural exodus was restrained (1962–8, − 30,000; 1968–75, + 30,000 net population change).

Under the VIIth Plan (1976–80) Rhône-Alpes needs to achieve about 200,000 new jobs to provide for the expected population, though in the short term economic recession has cut back the immigration of foreigners to a trickle. The relaying of the benefits of economic growth from the metropolis to other parts of the region is perhaps the greatest single planning issue. The diffusion of urbanization from Greater Lyon is to favour the New Town at L'Isle d'Abeau, but also the ring of smaller and medium-sized satellite towns; that from Grenoble to develop the secondary urban centre of Echirolles, whilst St Etienne, to be nourished by medium-sized industry, will concentrate expansion in the northern sector (+ 4.6 per cent p.a. population growth 1968–75). The programme for stimulating growth at medium-sized and smaller 'anchor-point' towns is to relay benefits to the uttermost rural areas, supported by rural planning schemes (PAR) and strategies for the mountain massifs (SOAM —*schémas d'orientation et d'aménagement de massif*).

Given its continuing growth potential, its balanced population and workforce structure and distribution, Rhône-Alpes is well-fitted to develop within the objectives for the VIIth Plan: quality of life (extensive and diverse recreation space; traditional life styles), human-scale planning, and improvement of the living environment.

Provence-Côte d'Azur

This region shares with Rhône-Alpes an attraction for migrants second only to Paris and the Nord, but over a much longer period (1851–1911). It has had the most sustained population growth rate and, 1954–75, the highest regional growth rate in France, at + 2.03 per cent p.a., enriched by the return of North African settlers in large numbers 1962–8. The economic structure of Provence-Côte d'Azur is, however, much less balanced, with less coherent subregional linkages and with serious problems of the lack of regional equilibria of various kinds (La DF 1968B). Though population growth has been rapid, natural increase rates remain low (only one-fifth the growth in numbers 1968–75 was due to surplus of births over deaths) and the population has a built-in welfare problem with above average proportions of those over 65. This is most notably so in the retirement areas of the Côte d'Azur. Of the 3.66 millions in the region in 1975, 11 per cent were foreign-born (cf, Rhône-Alpes) and there are serious problems of social segregation in the larger towns.

Structural changes in employment have done little to diminish the vulnerability of Provence-Côte d'Azur, the most heavily urbanized region of France. Manufacturing industry employs 20 per cent (1976), compared with 29 per cent in France, but there is too great a dependence on declining (food-processing, shipbuilding) or on capital intensive (petroleum, petrochemicals) branches. Tertiary employment has grown more rapidly than population (1968, 58 per cent of jobs, 1975, 61 per cent) but tourism is subject to major fluctuations and growth of services for the regional population will depend on living standards and the economic base. The potential for Marseille-Fos as an industrial growth complex has already been discussed (Part III, ch. 2) but there are two deep-seated problems for regional strategy: to get the balance of employment right between Fos-Etang de Berre and Marseille (1968–74 there were no new industrial jobs in Marseille) and to achieve a better economic cohesion throughout the region.

The four component subregions have contrasting problems and potentials (Préfet de Région, Provence-Côte d'Azur 1976). The coastal zone, Côte d'Azur (fig. 23), has the most concentrated version of an in-migrant, ageing population distributed along a narrow coastal band, with high urban congestion, land values at their highest and a vulnerable employment structure (ODEAM 1971). Control of urban expansion and the conservation of landscape quality are scarcely less pressing problems than the need to increase and diversify local industrial employment. In the mid-1970s the Marseille-Fos industrial growth complex was at a very critical stage in its realization. As a consequence of economic recession the second phase of the complex has been deferred and the multiplier effects of induced, diversified manufacturing have not yet occurred. The third subregion in the triangular delta of the Rhône (Avignon to the sea) has a specialized irrigation agriculture and a balanced network of small to medium-sized towns athwart a nodal cross-roads of the Rhône-Saône valley and the Languedoc-Provence axis. The rural hinterlands of Provence are a vast, thinly-peopled tract, much of it in the middle altitude mountain zone (*moyenne montagne*). The valleys and basins are highly compartmented; the rural exodus has reduced many local communities below levels at which a viable economic and social life can be practised. It is in these areas that disseminated tourism might make the most useful contribution to stabilizing population, diversifying employment, and increasing living standards.

Given the innate subregional diversities and the linear disposition of population, regional cohesion is difficult to achieve, the more so in view of the dramatic contrasts in development potential between west and east and between coast and interior. Moreover, in the wider context of competition with powerful neighbours (Hermitte 1971), the Genoa-Turin-Milan triangle, Catalonia or the subsidized Mezzogiorno, Provence-Côte d'Azur will find more acute specialization of activities difficult to avoid. On all counts, the severe economic and social disparities within the region are likely to prove intractable even within the less growth-orientated strategies of the VIIth Plan.

Franche-Comté

In 1976 the region had a population of only just over one million (cf. 1851 1.0 millions, 1946 0.84 millions), but in spite of this seeming constraint upon flexible planning the economy was remarkably buoyant (Centre d'Etudes 1973, Schmitt 1973). Sixth in income per capita among French regions, and with the most favourable of all regional balances of payment (exports $3\frac{1}{2}$ times imports by value), Franche-Comté is also the second most industrialized region: 50 per cent of the labour force are in manufacturing, though of these as many as 45 per cent are classed as semi-skilled. In its industrial make-up lie both strengths and weaknesses. The range of growth industries is remarkably diverse, including cars (Peugeot); micro-engineering products, e.g. watches (Kelton), dental equipment, glasses, calculating machines (Honeywell-Bull); electric locomotives (Alsthom); chemicals (Solvay, Rhodiacéta). Peugeot has the largest car factory in France at Sochaux-Montbéliard, employing 35,500 in 1975 (50,000 in six factories in the region), almost tripling output 1962–72. However, some local industries have already reached the limits of growth (watches, chemicals), whilst a high proportion of other major firms are controlled either from elsewhere in France or from abroad. Regional tertiary employment (34 per cent) is among the lowest for French regions, though recent growth has been rapid and shopping, for example, has a high ratio of *superettes* and *supermarchés*.

In sharp contrast to the industrial sector, no less than 43 per cent (1968) of the population was classed as rural. Between 1962–8 the rate of outflow by farm-based people was exceeded only by Limousin, though rural population generally has been stable and even increased 1968–75. Median farm income is exceeded only by that for Basse-Normandie, and is concentrated as to 83 per cent of output by value on meat and cheese. 47 per cent of the region is forested and the recreational potential for family tourism is high, and only partially exploited.

In spite of the scale and diversity of industry, there has not been a commensurate urbanization. Half the regional population is in the main centres of Belfort-Montbéliard and Besançon, with two-thirds concentrated along the Doubs corridor. Elsewhere the small town net is balanced in size and distribution. Under the VIIth Plan, the furtherance of the balance in the urban network is a priority: the Doubs axis is to have more diversified manufacturing, but equal emphasis on small towns as tourist or service centres. The opening-out of the region (Rhine-Rhône canal project, A36 motorway, improved rail links between the urban centres) is seen as an essential preliminary to capitalizing upon a nodal European location in relation to Germany, Switzerland and Italy. Commercial competition from the Swiss underlined the purpose of frontier-zone policies under the VIIth Plan.

Haute-Normandie
Haute-Normandie illustrates the somewhat abstract nature of economic region definition; even the historic and cultural province of Normandie had lacked geographical unity. Division of the province into Haute- and Basse-Normandie still did not correspond to the three-fold geographical realities: in the west, the *bocage* country of small dairy farms with a network of service centres (1000–2000 population) and Cherbourg (80,000), the only town larger than 20,000 people; in the centre, a geographically diverse subregion of commercial farming (for beet, wheat, potatoes and more recently maize; cattle rearing), oriented upon the regional administrative and industrial centre of Caen (181,000 in 1975); in the east, Haute-Normandie, the limon-covered chalk plateaux flanking the major urban, industrialized communications axis of the Basse-Seine (La DF 1971). In a 1968 survey only 20 per cent of those interviewed felt an affinity with Haute-Normandie and no more than a further 34 per cent identified with the older provincial Normandie. The inhabitants of Haute- and Basse-

Normandie characteristically had closer links with Paris than with the regional capital of the other subdivision.

The regional planning scheme for a coherent urban, industrialized growth axis, along the Basse-Seine, agreed in 1970, has overwhelmingly dominated spatial strategies for Haute-Normandie. The massive proposed development, with a port-industrial complex centred upon the complementary growth centres of Le Havre and Rouen, has already been considered (Part III, ch. 2). The complex has to be evaluated within the context of planning the Bassin Parisien (p. 373), in which it is outstandingly the most significant among the four designated support-zones (*zones d'appui*), but also in a wider national and international port and trading setting. The heavy public investment in the Basse-Seine supported strong market forces already polarizing industry and urbanization along a logical growth axis. The purpose of the Basse-Seine planning scheme was to regulate and apportion growth along the axis, to safeguard landscapes (*coupures vertes*), and to balance the needs of Greater Paris for diffusion of industrial and tertiary growth with the regional ambitions for a more self-contained urban-industrial development without the satellite connotation which extensions from Paris might suggest. As a 1971 report put it (La DF 1971, 70), Haute-Normandie 'did not wish for expansion at the expense of its regional personality'. In this sense the potential for an interrelated growth of Le Havre, Rouen and Caen was seen as a counterbalance to the influence of the capital.

The future of the Basse-Seine growth corridor, its likely continuing impact upon subregions flanking the axis of urbanization and industrialization, and the need to counteract excessive polarizing trends, are major contemporary planning issues (INSEE 1976, EPR Haute-Normandie 1976). The fast industrial growth along the Basse-Seine has led to vulnerabilities; growth industries, serving mainly an export market, itself now threatened; large-scale firms (1973, 12 per cent of jobs in plants with more than 2000 workers), with two-thirds of investments 1965–75 concentrated in car plants, petroleum refineries and the chemical industry, upon a restricted number of large industrial sites. In 1975 26,000 were employed in car manufacture, some two-thirds of all new jobs in Haute-Normandie 1965–75. The tertiary sector has grown more slowly, under the 'economic shadow' of Paris, and there is a lack of adequate female employment. Industrial strategy is thus to diversify manufacturing along the Basse-Seine, thereby to spread the risks of excessive dependence on a large-scale, export industrial complex, whilst ensuring that there is diffusion of smaller firms to the towns of the flanking plateaux.

Except for the plateaux east of Evreux, benefiting more directly from residential growth pressures and industrial decentralizations from Paris, the plateaux flanking the Seine have traditionally suffered by the polarization of migration on to the Seine axis. In 1962–8, for example, at least 30 per cent of the 20–29 year age group recorded in 1962 had left the plateaux. The Basse-Seine planning scheme spoke of the need for 'transverse equilibrium' to counteract the axial pressures along the growth corridor. Since 1974 the Haute-Normandie EPR has developed a 'policy for the plateaux' to improve regional employment and urban balance, since the hoped-for multiplier effects from the Basse-Seine had not developed. Development of food-processing plants and the dissemination of small engineering firms are being planned for, but this kind of relief at the regional margin has always been a difficult policy to enact in the face of strong regional social and economic disparities and polarization towards major growth centres. The problem towns of Dieppe (relieved by development of engineering, 1970–4) and Fécamp illustrate a further, maritime dimension of the competition of small with notably larger and more dynamic nearby centres.

Picardie and Champagne-Ardennes

It is unrealistic to dissociate *Picardie* and *Champagne-Ardennes* from the overall planning of the Bassin Parisien (p. 373), of which they are so logically and integrally a part. Neither region has a homogeneous or coherent identity, in geographical, economic or historical terms. Both are regions of transit, located between powerful economic neighbours (Paris, Nord, Lorraine), but with the potential for capitalizing upon the long-term advantages of position, once they can escape from the economic shadow of their neighbours. The unrealized potential is both industrial and commercial, but there are already major achievements in the transformation of the economic structure of both regions (La DF 1967A, B). The agriculture of Picardie (wheat, sugar beet, maize) has the highest per capita farm incomes, whilst tripling of cereal yields and doubling of the acreage under beet and of meat production have characterized Champagne-Ardennes. Both regions have been prime beneficiaries of industrial decentralization from Ile-de-France. Traditional manufactures (food, textiles, clothing, wood and furniture) have been well-sustained, whilst valuable diversification has been introduced by decentralization (engineering, electrical manufactures, plastics).

The major strategic planning problem for both regions is to use the benefits of economic growth transplanted from Paris to promote regional cohesion and identity, and to achieve a more balanced urbanization and better linkage between town and countryside. The ability to achieve these purposes depends partly on political strengths, partly on the modification of the planning scheme for the Bassin Parisien (p. 373) to accord more justly with regional aspirations. The concept of support-zones defined the Oise-Aisne valleys and north Champagne (ZANC), one in each region, but neither was given high priority for development. In the event, the Oise-Aisne scheme has been dropped, but the ZANC proposals, for a polycentric city-region based on Reims, Epernay and Châlons-sur-Marne, is being actively developed. The Champagne-Ardennes EPR intends that the benefits of such polarized growth shall be diffused, even as far as the rural problem region of the Ardennes fringe.

POTENTIAL GROWTH REGIONS

Though no sharp dividing line between growth and potential growth regions can be defined, the latter have a narrower or less favourable mix of positive attributes, but nevertheless an underlying potential for substantial improvement under present policies. Two of the potential growth regions, Centre and Bourgogne, are to be differentiated from Picardie and Champagne-Ardennes by lower household incomes and orientation away from the EEC heartland. Languedoc and Aquitaine are two peripheral regions with major growth prospects: coastal tourist development, influence of the regional metropoli of Bordeaux and Marseille-Fos (Provence-Côte d'Azur), and potential for faster growth through trade with Spain and the Mediterranean world respectively.

Centre

Like most of the regions within or flanking the Bassin Parisien, the Centre (fig. 69) is difficult to justify on rational geographical grounds; further-more, it lacks the outline historical justification which ancient provinces might suggest for Picardie or Champagne. Yet during the past two decades the impact of fast economic growth and the rising consciousness of ensuing problems have forced an increasingly strong regional identity 'de facto' (La DF 1972A). In some respects the Centre bears the same problems as Picardie and Champagne-Ardennes, traditionally drained of people and economic life by the attractions of the metropolis but, suddenly, since the mid-1950s, a prime beneficiary of industrial decentralization policies. In the Centre, however, the impact of change has been to increase already disturbing internal disparities, threatening to polarize economic and social activities in a region famed for the tranquillity and quality of life. The concept of the middle Loire support-zone (OREALM p. 375), sought to polarize growth along the major transverse axis. Since 1973 the scheme has

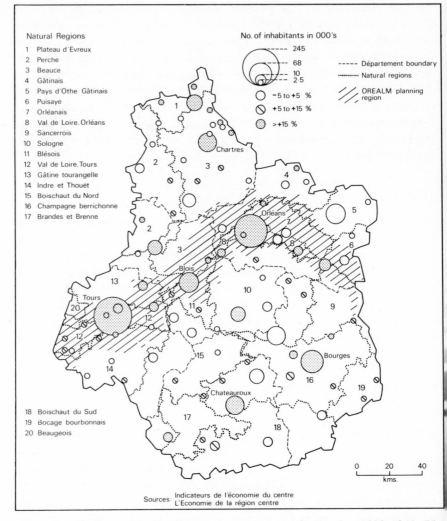

Figure 69　Centre region. Population change, towns of more than 5000, 1968–75; agricultural regions.

been incorporated (OREAC) within a more balanced regional strategy for distributing the benefits of growth more widely.

The reversal of economic fortunes in the Centre was certainly dramatic. For many years an under-peopled, little urbanized region with a traditional net migration loss, the period 1962–8 showed a spectacular reversal of trends. Between 1968 and 1975 the population growth rate (1.1 per cent p.a.) was second only to that of Provence-Côte d'Azur. Furthermore, unlike Picardie and Champagne-Ardennes, where growth was largely due to natural increase, there was a balance between birth surpluses and steady net in-migration. 1968–75, 57,000 new industrial jobs were created (12 per cent of French growth during that period), more than two-thirds in the propulsive industries, cars, chemicals, electrical manufactures, metal working and engineering. Unfortunately, and characteristically for Bassin Parisien regions, control from Paris remained strong (50 per cent of all industrial jobs with headquarters in the capital) and the ratio of semi-skilled to skilled workers was high. There was little commensurate de-centralization of tertiary activities, and that mainly to the twin regional capitals of Tours and Orléans.

The impact of growth within the Centre was uneven. The greatest in-migration and industrialization took place in the northern *départements* (fig. 22), Loiret and Eure-et-Loir, and in Tours and Orléans, increasing already striking north-south gradients in employment and living standards. The suburban areas of the larger towns grew rapidly, but during the 1970s the rate of urbanization decreased. Conversely, the rural areas which had lost 31,000 1962–8 fared better 1968–75 (only − 16,000).

The regional strategy for the VIIth Plan (Mission Régionale 1976) accords highest priority to strengthening regional cohesion, combatting the inequalities within the region and distributing the lesser growth expected more evenly through the region. The concept of major growth poles with higher tertiary functions at Tours and Orléans and public investment concentrated on these and on development axes, along the middle Loire (A10 motorway) or Paris-Chartres-Le Mans (A11), has given place to a more disseminated policy. The emphasis on social well-being and quality of life favours the medium-sized and smaller town, including regionally-financed schemes (*villes moyennes régionales*). The small town-rural balance is to be strengthened, particularly in the major prosperous farming zones: Val de Loire, the cereal-growing plains of Beauce and the Gâtinais, and the Champagne Berrichonne. Regrouping of holdings, particularly in the southern marginal areas, water resource management, and the promotion of small industries are focal points in rural policy. The Sologne and Forêt d'Orléans will become the major recreational zones.

Intermediate between Ile-de-France and the problem regions of the Massif Central and the Ouest, the Centre region has a delicate role as a planning catalyst, to relay and help diffuse growth to more distant areas, but at the same time to promote its own regional cohesion and safeguard the quality of life summed up for the middle Loire as the 'garden metropolis'. No less demanding is the need to provide more qualified jobs for those leaving higher education establishments, many of whom still need to move to Paris for suitable employment.

Bourgogne

Bourgogne faces the same mix of strategic planning problems as Picardie, Champagne-Ardennes, and Centre: capitalization upon a nodal location within the radial-concentric hinterland of the capital city, and equally in a national and prospectively international context; creation of regional cohesion from disparate geographical circumstances; rectification of an unfavourable urban-rural balance in the direction, on the one hand, of polarization upon a range of growth centres, on the other by dissemination to a widespread network of small towns. Yet Bourgogne has both added strengths and weaknesses, weighted towards the latter.

Though part of an historic province, geographical unity is lacking, and economic interests are fragmented (La DF 1966). The clearest distinction is that of a sill between the Bassin Parisien, the Belfort gap and the Rhône-Saône corridor. Frontiers are fluid and there is no pronounced central focus: Dijon, the capital, is eccentric and bypassed by the A6 motorway; the Morvan upland, according to some (La DF 1966, 6) the central, federating element in Bourgogne, is a thinly-peopled regional nature park, traditionally plagued by rural depopulation. The problems of industrial reconversion in the Le Creusot-Montceau-les-Mines-Blanzy area of coal-mining and metallurgy have nothing in common with the diverse under-peopled, underurbanized rural tracts. Dijon (208,432 inhabitants in 1975) is the classic case of a slow-growing regional city, stimulated by industrial decentralization from Paris and conscious of the as yet unrealized economic potential of location at the intersection of three great growth triangles: le Grand Delta, north-east France, and the Bassin Parisien.

The modest but almost sustained net in-migration since 1962 (+ 0.3 per cent p.a. 1962–8, + 0.2 per cent 1968–75) reversed the traditional outflow from the land, added to town populations, but was insufficient to provide for substantial economic growth. Unlike Picardie or Champagne, Bourgogne has had no large natural reservoir of population within its borders. There is some ambivalence behind regional strategy proposals (Moatti 1972). The intention to strengthen the urban network at all levels, particularly along the main river valleys, to give priority to transverse routes and to balance urban with rural growth (priority areas Puisaye, Hautes-Côtes, Bresse, and north Nivernais) contends with the likely strong polarizing effects of capitalizing upon national and international location. Even under the VIth Plan (1971–6) the CNAT committee on the 'North Sea-Mediterranean axis' forecast rapid population growth in Bourgogne, if the full potential of the axis could be realized. It must, however, remain conjectural how far major through-routes contribute to the well-being of regions of transit. The multiplier effects of the electrified rail route through Dijon have been greater than those of the A6 motorway, but neither has strikingly underpinned the economy of a precariously balanced watershed region.

Aquitaine

In some respects the basic strategic planning problem of Aquitaine is a microcosm of that of France: how to balance the growth of a metropolis (Bordeaux) with an equitable distribution of the benefits of such growth into a diverse hinterland with a range of problem subregions. Excessive distribution of growth may affect the further potential of the metropolis; insufficient diffusion risks polarizing resources and people into the metropolis. Aquitaine also shares with the Nord, Lorraine, Alsace and Provence-Côte d'Azur the problems of frontier location, but in aggravated form: the most remote region on the underdeveloped Atlantic face of France; economic links with Spain as yet scarcely significant, though entry of Spain to the EEC would effect a transformation; as distant from Paris as Marseille-Fos, but lacking the scale and momentum of proposed development; underpeopled and underdeveloped by comparison with other frontier regions.

In the face of such constraints the development of the countermagnet metropolis of Bordeaux (p. 365) has been impressive, and a dramatic change in regional employment structure has been achieved in the region (La DF 1964A, Mission Régionale 1976): 1962–75, employment in agriculture down from 32 to 19 per cent, in manufacturing up from 29 to only 31 per cent, and the tertiary sector from 40 to 50 per cent of the workforce. In 1973 the critical propulsive sector of manufacturing included chemicals and plastics, aerospace, electronics and data-processing equipment (18 per cent of industrial jobs); a further 52 per cent of jobs were in labour- or market-oriented manufactures, likely to be more flexible in location; and the final 28 per cent in jobs tied to raw material locations (agriculture, timber, gas, petroleum). Hitherto the industrial multiplier effects of the Lacq-Parentis oil and natural gas developments have been disappointing at regional level. One-third of government credits and two-thirds of industrial development premiums went to Bordeaux (1965–72), whilst between them Bordeaux, Pau and Bayonne had two-thirds of all employment in capital and intermediate goods manufacture and 37 per cent of those in the petroleum industry; Bordeaux alone had 40 per cent of the jobs in metal-working. By contrast, the more remote *départements* had characteristically small-scale consumer goods firms and a higher than average representation of declining industry (shoes, clothing, furniture). The growth in tertiary activities has also favoured the larger towns, though the integrated coastal development scheme for tourism (p. 295) contributed to the momentum of population growth, 1968–75, from the Gironde to the Spanish frontier.

The proposed spatial strategy under the VIIth Plan (Région Aquitaine 1975) is for more balanced allocation of growth, to designated anchor-zones (*zones d'ancrage*), composed of medium-sized towns and their hinterlands, and to specific rural zones. The ambition is to decrease regional disparities, but the operation will be delicate since Aquitaine has a weak natural increase rate and net in-migration fell from + 0.7 per cent p.a. 1962–8 to only + 0.3 per cent 1968–75. The intention is to reduce further the rural exodus from more marginal areas (565,000 people in 1975 covering one-half the region's land area) by direct intervention in problem localities (Basque areas, Haute-Lande, and north of Périgord, by PAR or by *contrat de pays*—p. 430), more generally by agricultural and rural tourism support policies, and not least by the stabilization effects of the 'anchor-zone' policy. The 'anchor-zone' towns are to focus population and services growth and help local people to remain in the countryside, by providing jobs, better educational facilities and service provision. This concept accords well with the medium-sized towns policy (p. 376) but the mechanism for relaying or diffusing growth from the metropolis remains unclear. Furthermore, there are great disparities already among the rural subregions, notably in population densities and the economic base: wine in the Gironde, cattle rearing in the Pyrénées and south-western Massif Central (fig. 24), timber in the Landes. An intention to diffuse tourism, linking the dramatic coastal developments with disseminated facilities in the mountains and plateaux, is perhaps a more likely prospect than that for light manufacturing as a growth-spreading multiplier from the port-based industrial complex of Bordeaux-Le Verdon. The extent to which a pleasant rural living environment may compensate for lower economic momentum or public investment is a conundrum underlying much of VIIth Plan thinking.

Languedoc-Roussillon

The case for listing Languedoc-Roussillon among regions with growth potential is an arguable one (EPR Languedoc-Roussillon 1976). Demographically, the boost given to population growth 1962–8 by repatriates from North Africa has made for a more youthful and abundant labour force in a region traditionally plagued by low natural increase rates.

Unfortunately, this momentum (+ 1.6 per cent p.a. growth 1962–8, + 1.3 by in-migration) has not been continued 1968–75 (+ 0.7 per cent p.a., + 0.5 by in-migration), though it is true that if arrivals from North Africa during the earlier period are discounted the most recent rate of inflow is, in fact, higher. Unemployment, the product of a low level of industrialization and a vulnerable specialized agriculture, is characteristically among the highest regional totals for France (7.2 per cent, December 1974). Tertiary employment has grown rapidly (54 per cent of all jobs in 1975, 48 per cent in 1968) with coastal tourism a major contributor (p. 293). The region is, however, among the least industrialized in France (29 per cent of jobs in both 1968 and 1975) and 40 per cent of industrial jobs are in the

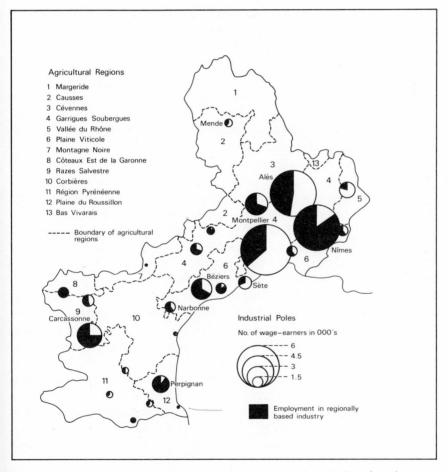

Figure 70   Languedoc-Roussillon. Industrial poles and agricultural regions.

construction sector (fig. 70). Furthermore, the industrial structure is weak, with declining branches (food-processing, textiles, leather and shoes) offset in some measure by spectacular growths of new firms in 'footloose' industries (IBM, Clin-Midy) at Montpellier. In general, most firms are small-scale and industrial growth has relied mainly on the inducements of the PME. The high level of dependence on specialized, vulnerable agricultural products (wine, fruit, vegetables) has been a source of weakness, alternating with periods of high prosperity. Recurrent surpluses have been a problem, whilst marketing and agricultural restructuring have been constraints upon agricultural progress. No fewer than one-half of the farmers in Languedoc-Roussillon have some other part-time job, often in tourism or the service industries.

In many respects availability and good management of water resources are the key to regional advancement (Souchon 1968). The regional development company (CNABRL) has been engaged in multi-purpose projects of water control, irrigation, urban water supply (for inland and coastal centres, and for industry), opening out and helping to interconnect the rural economy of the Languedoc. The impact has been greatest in the already-favoured eastern zones, but under the VIIth Plan extension westwards to the Lauragais and Minervois is intended (for cereals, fodder crops, cattle-rearing and dairying).

Internal imbalances are perhaps the worst handicap for Languedoc-Roussillon: between the coast (34.8 million overnight stays, 1.6 million residential holidays of an average 20 days in 1975) and the mountainous interior (Cévennes), with its traditional impoverishment, rural exodus and the decay of small industrial towns little improved by modest tourism; secondly, between east and west in Languedoc. Uniquely, among southern French regions, Languedoc-Roussillon has no designated countermagnet metropolis. The urban pattern (Dugrand 1960) is well-balanced, with a large town every 20 to 50 km, but an effective regional capital is lacking. Furthermore, the functions, trends and potential among the principal centres are very varied: Montpellier (211,430 in 1975; +2.89 per cent p.a. 1968–75, +2.03 by in-migration) is clearly the most dynamic, the administrative centre (regional council, coastal management headquarters), the largest university town, and the cultural and scientific hub. Nîmes (131,638 in 1975; +0.68 per cent p.a. 1968–75, +0.55 by natural increase) is the commercial and financial centre, has the principal airport, agricultural focus and the seat of CNABRL. Perpignan (117,689 in 1975; +1.23 per cent p.a., +0.77 by in-migration) has its own dynamism, but a very peripheral location.

Most writers (Souchon 1968, Dugrand 1960) attribute the slow industrialization to preference among local entrepreneurs for land rather than factories, and more recently to economic dominance from outside. It is an objective of the VIIth Plan to capitalize upon the attractive living environments of Languedoc-Roussillon, to open up the region by the axial motorway, Orange-Narbonne, to establish the coastal development scheme in a European image of quality, and, more speculatively, to realize the contribution of the region to the Grand Delta and also to the more vigorous trading around the shores of an emerging Mediterranean basin economy (EPR Languedoc-Roussillon 1976).

THE RECONVERSION REGIONS

The Nord, Lorraine and Alsace share the common problems of economic restructuring in a highly competitive frontier location. All three have counterbalancing metropoli, which have already been discussed, and a vigorous agricultural component of the regional economy. Although unemployment is a constant preoccupation, mean household incomes are about the national average, and the *overall* quality of housing and utilities is surprisingly good. The economic recession of the 1970s caught all three regional economies at a very sensitive stage in the reconversion operation. Discussion will be confined to those strategic issues not already considered under the regional metropoli.

The Nord

The Nord is unique in that the definition of the metropolitan area (OREAM Nord) coincides with the economic planning region of the same name (fig. 71). The basic problems are familiar to British planners: the need to achieve major economic restructuring of many outworn mining and industrial towns, for too long based upon a narrow range of predominantly declining industries; the wish to reduce the traditional, even the accelerating net out-migration (1968–75, + 14,000 p.a. overall growth, + 31,000 p.a. by natural increase, − 17,000 p.a by out-migration), and to provide more work locally as a measure of social justice; to use state aid in the difficult reconversion process and to aim for a better diffusion of the benefits of growth throughout the region, not confined to the more logical growth poles or axes. But there are also differences from comparable mining-industrial regions of Britain: unemployment (5.4 per cent February 1977) is only slightly above the national average (5.0 per cent) and, secondly, in spite of a marginal frontier location within the French national space, the potentials of a European link-up are very considerable.

Economic restructuring lies at the heart of the regional problem, both

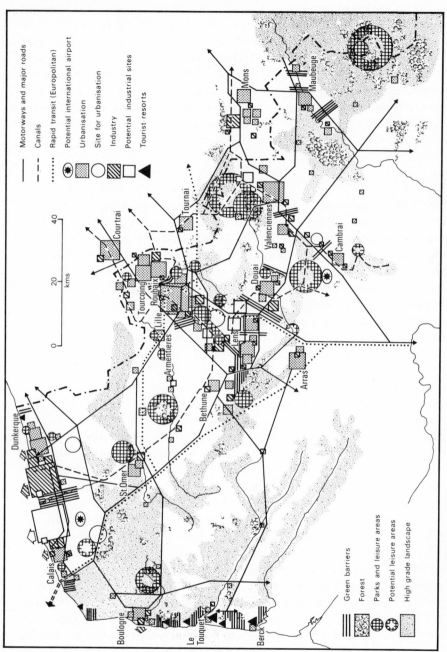

Motorways and major roads
Canals
Rapid transit (Europolitan)
Potential international airport
Urbanisation
Site for urbanisation
Industry
Potential industrial sites
Tourist resorts

Green barriers
Forest
Parks and leisure areas
Potential leisure areas
High grade landscape

Mons
Maubeuge
Tournai
Courtrai
Valenciennes
Cambrai
Tourcoing
Roubaix
Lille
Douai
Armentieres
Lens
Bethune
Arras
Dunkerque
St Omer
Calais
Boulogne
Le Touquet
Berck

0   20   40
kms

Figure 71   Nord regional planning scheme

sectorally and spatially. The most dramatic job declines have been in coalmining (1962 117,400; January 1975 46,500), concentrated in a crescent 110 km from east to west, and likely to close down completely by 1982–5, in coal- and nitrogen-based chemicals, in woollen and cotton textiles, and in certain branches of heavy engineering. In selected localities industrial reconversion began as far back as 1955, and was extended during the 1960s to most of the coalfield: textiles and the clothing industries, with jobs mainly for women, were initially the spearhead of new employment. Since 1967, however, a more coherent and diversified restructuring has taken place, with aid from the state (regional commissioner for industrialization), the coal companies (HBNPC) and local development organizations (Griffon 1972). In eight years to the end of 1974, 200 firms had been attracted, 42,000 new jobs provided (70,000 in the end). The motor car industry, the major propulsive manufacture (p. 255), employed only 4000 in the Nord in 1970, 12,600 by December 1974, and is programmed for 32,000 eventually. Proliferation of little related manufactures has been as characteristic as in the British Assisted Areas. Under the VIIth Plan high priority is put on further deliberate diversification into petrochemicals (steam cracker for 450,000 tonnes ethylene p.a. at Dunkerque), more widely-based engineering to achieve redeployment of skilled workers from declining branches, and into food-processing for the smaller towns in the prosperous rural hinterland (including a regional refrigeration centre at Boulogne).

In spatial terms, growth has been uneven and indeed progressively distorted. The polarizing forces have been concentrated on the Lille countermagnet metropolis (p. 356) and on the Dunkerque port-industrial complex (p. 370). The mining areas have suffered most, whilst Roubaix and Tourcoing have been affected by growth at Lille and the New Town of Lille-Est; rural areas generally have been drained of manpower to meet the needs of the growing cities (fig. 21). The Valenciennes subregion avoided rapid run-down in coalmining, but in 1976 local prosperity was threatened by 2000 redundancies in the steel industry. The VIIth Plan (Préfecture, Nord 1976) intends a better diffusion of growth, but in a largely market economy the operation will be difficult. New industrial growth is to be concentrated whenever possible into the coal-basin towns, containing one million people or one-third of the regional population. Industrial reconversion *in situ* is to be attempted within 20 years rather than the 40–50 years originally intended. Employment increase at Dunkerque is to be limited and multiplier effects in terms of new jobs are to be channelled to the ex-mining towns, where the rate of new job provision has kept pace with decline in mining, but without any real contribution to economic expansion. Though the coal basin is a large, poorly exploited market, underequipped in services and commerce, there must be some doubts as to the ability to 'steer' induced industries from either Dunkerque or the regional metropolis into the underprivileged mining towns.

There is, moreover, some ambivalence in the intended course of a regional development strategy. On the one hand, exploitation of the Lille-Dunkerque axis (1350 t barge canal; electrified rail traction; A25 motorway) is a logical French priority, even though Dunkerque's international hinterland is limited and the Nord-Lorraine coal-steel 'combinaat' is now much reduced in importance. The double marginality (Debeyre 1970) which the Nord has suffered from, within France and also in a European context, may diminish as the illogical political frontier with Belgium ceases to be an economic barrier (Decoster 1969). At the same time, however, the Nord will be opened up to vigorous competition from its neighbours. The potentials are there, but so are the risks of such an enticing set of prospects.

Lorraine

Some of the restructuring problems of Lorraine (fig. 72) are similar to those of the Nord: dependence upon a narrow economic base of coal, steel and cotton textiles and the need to diversify into new forms of manufacturing and tertiary activities; serious out-migration of the young and more able, persisting little checked since 1962 (1962–8, −69,000; 1968–75, −66,000); marked subregional imbalances, reflected in differential economic growth and in unemployment; and the need to modernize outworn urban fabrics and prepare a new living environment. Yet there are significant differences from the Nord, in the mix of problems and their individual significance. The Lorraine coalfield, for example, has more favourable geological conditions than the Nord, higher levels of productivity, a more sustained labour force, and better long-term prospects. Employment in the coal mines has fallen from 38,500 in 1962 to 19,400 (December 1975), but earlier fears of even more drastic contraction under the Bettencourt Plan (1968) have proved unfounded. Production fell to 9 Mt in 1976, but is programmed to rise to 11 Mt by 1985. The scale of reconversion operations on the coalfield is thus less than in the Nord but on the iron-ore field and in the steel industry the position is reversed. Though presently supplying one-half French iron-ore needs, and exporting one-third of output to Benelux and the Saar, the reserves of iron ore will probably be exhausted by the end of the century. Employment on the ore-field fell from 22,700 in 1962 to 9300 in 1975, though iron-ore output fell only from 62.4 to 52.0 Mt during the same period (INSEE 1976A).

The situation in the Lorraine steel industry is much more serious and

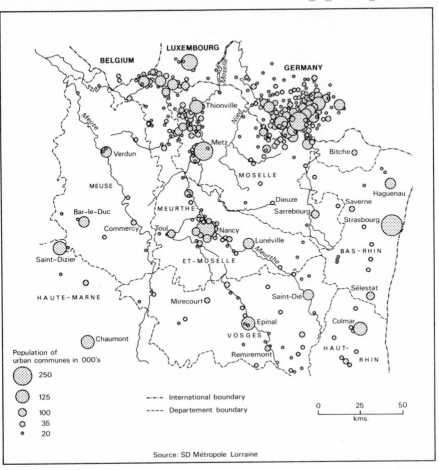

Figure 72   Alsace-Lorraine. Population distribution, 1975.

threatens the stability of the regional economy. In 1974 Lorraine produced 59 per cent of French pig iron and 53 per cent of steel ingots, but major relocations of new steel-making capacity (Dunkerque, Fos) have reduced growth prospects in Lorraine. The 15,600 redundancies in the Lorraine steel industry 1977–80, announced in 1977, with possible negative multiplier effects on 50,000 jobs in all, produced an almost insoluble problem of redeployment and industrial reconversion. Other staple industries have fared better: the cotton spinning and weaving plants on the western slopes of the Vosges; the heavy, capital-intensive chemical industry (soda production from the salt fields; carbo-chemicals and petrochemicals at Carling-Marienau); and general engineering.

Proposals under the VIIth Plan (Préfet de Région, Lorraine 1976) included stabilization of the coal industry, modernization and rationalization in steel production, regrouping of firms in the Vosges textile industry and diversification into new manufacturing branches. Attraction of firms to Lorraine has been modest: 1960–75, 25,000 new jobs in foreign firms (13,000 in firms from Germany); 3500 in French firms (Masson 1976). The coal basin has benefited most fully, whilst the steel-making area attracted little more than 1000 new jobs. Most recently the SAVIEM lorry manufacturing firm has located a plant at Batilly in the steel-making zone, whilst in 1977 the government pressed Renault and Citroën-Peugeot to increase their capacity and thus absorb the growing numbers of displaced steel workers.

There has been criticism (Masson 1976) of the way in which government locational aid policies (PAI, PDR) have been applied in Lorraine. Allocation of aid has been less according to need, which would have favoured districts like Briey and Forbach, and more to reinforce logical growth, as at Epinal; Bar-le-Duc was favoured rather than Verdun, though the latter centre had virtually total economic stagnation; the Vosges textile towns had disproportionately large aid whilst other problem areas in the steel-making basin and the frontier zones were underprivileged. The pattern of aids (fig. 55) is both uneven and changing, difficult to reconcile with the needs of a coherent regional strategy.

The Lorraine regional problem is deep-seated, the result of vulnerability induced by overspecialization in a limited range of staple industries and a sensitivity to competition within the EEC, which is both the major supplier and recipient of Lorraine trade. Apart from male redeployment in mining and manufacturing, there is a dearth of female jobs and both frontier zones and rural areas have their particular intractable problems. The prospects for the countermagnet metropolis (p. 358) must be diminished by the endemic weakness of the economic base. As in the Nord, the opening of Lorraine more fully to EEC contacts, an intention of the VIIth Plan, may prove to be a double-edged weapon, notably so in the current severe economic recession.

Alsace

The justification for including Alsace (fig. 72) among the reconversion regions is three-fold: continuance of the long-standing crisis affecting textile towns in the valleys of the Vosges; more significantly, the necessary adjustment of Strasbourg industries to the decline of coal traffic, the limited growth of petrochemicals, and competition from the Moselle valley routes; thirdly, the frontier economic situation, flanked by more dynamically prosperous neighbours in Germany (Baden) and in Switzerland. Furthermore, traditionally Alsace has been depicted as fragmented into many small *pays* and stratified longitudinally into the Vosges, the piedmont and the plains (La DF 1975A). To these centrifugal forces must be added the subregional differences of language and religion, together with the strongly town-focused and somewhat separatist loyalties. In economic terms there is a broad industrial contrast to be drawn between Bas-Rhin (metal-working, engineering and food-processing industries) and Haut-Rhin (motor cars, chemicals, textiles and clothing). Agriculturally, the wine-growing zone divides the piedmont with intensive arable cultivation (*ackerland*), contrasting with the forests, the more sterile lands (gravel cones-*hardt*) and the river-meadows (*ried*) (Nonn 1972).

As in many peripheral regions undergoing reconversion, there is a unity based upon a sense of deprivation, as well as upon a legacy of provincial culture and life-styles. To these centripetal influences must be added the deliberate regional strategy of polarizing growth upon a balanced urban network, in which, though Strasbourg is the designated regional metropolis (p. 359), it is neither paramount nor dominant. The well-distributed pattern of towns was recognized as the basis for regional planning as far back as 1965, since confirmed in the production of SDAU for urban regions (Nonn 1971). Strasbourg, Colmar and Mulhouse have complementary functions and are linked by the routeways of the Rhine axis. Along this axis of discontinuous urban and economic development, each town in turn polarizes a latitudinal hinterland, stretching from the Vosges, through the Piedmont, to the Rhine lowlands.

THE DEVELOPING REGIONS

The eight regions classified as developing are characterized by some of the following attributes: high ratios of rural population; traditional net out-migration; either slow population growth threatening demographic viability, or fast population growth allied with unemployment or under-employment; low business momentum; the pursuance of policies of industrialization with government aid under decentralization policies; reliance upon a limited range of services oriented to the local population, and with tourism a hoped-for panacea for rural decline in many areas. Social provision is characteristically poorer, though anomalously car ownership is high, largely due to the decline of public transport. Given the similarities among the eight regions, they may be conveniently grouped: Ouest Atlantique (Bretagne, Pays de la Loire, Poitou-Charentes, plus the *département* of Manche) and Basse-Normandie; Massif Central (Auvergne, Limousin); Midi-Pyrénées and Corse.

The creation of an industrial development association for Ouest Atlantique in 1971 recognized some distinctive, in-built and serious problems affecting this entire area: a vulnerably higher ratio still engaged in agriculture (table 4), producing market-sensitive products on uneconomically small family farms (1967–75 farms of 5–10 ha. disappeared at the rate of 7 per cent p.a.); problems of the Atlantic facade of France, with widespread small-scale fishing, but distant from major economic centres in France and the heartland of the EEC, and with only Nantes-St Nazaire a designated port-industrial development complex and a counterbalancing metropolis (government support policy for the maritime facade of France, September 1975); distant from Paris but with a traditional economic draining of people and life from the *départements* most accessible to the metropolis. The risks of drainage towards Paris must be set against the benefits of decentralization, spreading first through adjacent *départements*. For this reason, under the VIIth Plan, the need for a deliberate planning policy to promote further decentralization into the intermediate zones between the Bassin Parisien fringe and the coast has been made a high priority. The common problems of the Ouest Atlantique vary in mix and severity between the component planning regions. Similarly there is some differentiation in recent demographic and economic growth trends (table 36), but the marked surge in employment, especially in manufacturing, clearly identifies the group (fig. 73). Demographic vitality contrasts Bretagne and Pays de la Loire, on the one hand, with national average population growth rates 1968–75 and a welcome and notable reversal of traditional net out-migration, with Poitou-Charentes and the *département* of Manche on the other.

The benefits of government decentralization of industry measures, including notably the electrical and electronics industries (fig. 73), have

Table 36   Population and employment change, Ouest Atlantique, 1968–75

(1968 = 100) Change in:	Popn	Employ- ment	Manu- facturing	Tertiary	Migration (ann. rate)
Bretagne	105	125	136	129	+1.4
Pays de la Loire	107	126	129	132	+1.4
Poitou-Charentes	103	121	126	127	±0
Basse-Normandie (Manche)	100	120	141	120	−4.2
France	105		109		

Source: INSEE, Ouest Atlantique

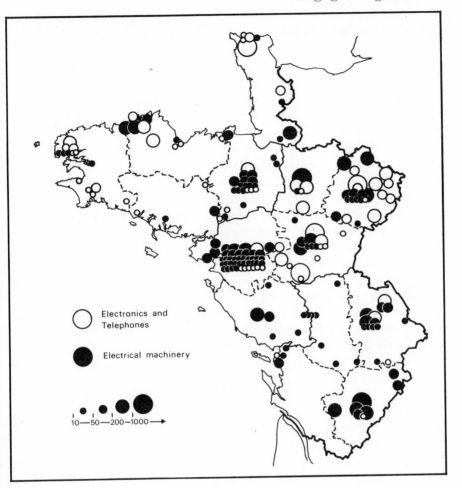

Figure 73   Ouest Atlantique. The electrical and electronics industry, mid-1970s.

faded with increasing distance from Paris and, within each region, away
from the centres of urban polarization. Furthermore, it is argued (CELIB
1971) that much of the industry decentralized was only in search of cheap,
unskilled, and non-unionized labour, there was a lack of decision-taking
powers, and few major enterprises were involved beyond those located in
the nearest, largest urban growth poles (Caen, Rennes, Nantes, Poitiers).
Decentralization of tertiary activities has been tardy, smaller in size and
scarcely diffused once again beyond the major urban centres. Nevertheless,

there have been one or two dramatic transplants, e.g. the CNET (*Centre national d'études des télécommunications*) laboratories to Lannion.

Basse-Normandie

The problems of Basse-Normandie (La DF 1972B, 1973) have earlier been related to those of Haute-Normandie (p. 398). In many respects they are an aggravated version of those of the Ouest Atlantique in general. The divided province of Normandie risks being polarized upon the major growth corridor of the Basse-Seine, or towards Paris. These risks are greater in the east, but conversely the region of Caen has benefited most directly by spin-off of economic growth from both the Basse-Seine and Paris during the 1960s and 1970s; manufacturing has grown more rapidly than tertiary activities. Though Basse-Normandie has a balanced network of secondary urban centres, it has proved difficult to diffuse growth westwards from Caen. Likewise, the endemic social problem of the rural exodus has not yet been stabilized. Cherbourg has emerged as a problem area. The decline of the transatlantic trade, distance from Paris and the unsuitability of the port for large-scale maritime-based industrial developments pose difficult issues of industrial reconversion. The atomic energy plant at La Hague (Cotentin) may be a precursor of new economic growth, but it is food-processing and light engineering which are the hoped-for panaceas, to stabilize the population and enable Cherbourg to act as an urban growth pole for Manche.

Bretagne

Bretagne, a cultural province increasingly politically conscious of its proud traditions and heritage (CELIB 1971), has consistently had the most powerful advocacy for regional strategic planning (Phlipponneau 1970). It was first in the field with a regional action programme (1956) and the principles then enunciated have since held good: to reduce traditional out-migration and improve living standards; concentrate agricultural output on specialities and improve marketing; restructure the fishing industry; renew traditional manufacturing and attract new firms; realize the full tourist potential. Nevertheless, between 1954 and 1962 Bretagne lost 10,000 per annum by net out-migration. The adverse political reaction to inadequate government support policies led to the first wave of sponsored industrialization (CELIB 1971, 15), both locally derived and also by in-migrant firms. The deliberate implantation of an electronics industry growth complex was based on three centres, each with a major research or educational institution: Lannion (CNET laboratories); Brest (*Ecole nationale supérieure des télécommunications*—ENST); Rennes (*Ecole supérieure des télécommunications* (3rd year)). The electronics industry has indeed proved to be the fastest growth branch (3900 in 1968, 14,500 in 1975), but a high proportion of jobs have been only semi-skilled and for women (fig. 73). Between 1964 and 1968 industrial momentum was again lost, leading to an even more dramatic political demonstration by the region.

Strategically, the problems of a peripheral, elongated peninsula with dense rural settlement on the coastal fringes (Armor) and a sparsely populated upland plateau interior (Argoat) must relate to accessibility in the first instance (La DF 1968C). The opening-up of the region needs better latitudinal coastal highways, linking through Rennes to the national motorway system. To achieve a better internal economic equilibrium requires greater diffusion of industrial growth westwards from Rennes, the development of a sizeable secondary coastal growth pole at Brest (ship-repairing, possibly refining and petrochemicals), and greater balance in small-scale manufacturing and tertiary activities in the smaller rural towns (Préfet de Région 1975). Given the significance of the remaining rural population, the rural renovation programme of 1967 (p. 427) for the Ouest, and its supplementation in the more selective pilot-zone (*zones-tests*) policy of 1973, are an essential element of regional planning (Bariou 1975). Under the VIth Plan (1971–5) almost 100,000 new jobs were provided in the Breton economy; under the VIIth (1976–80) 80–90,000 will be needed to sustain growing population numbers and those continuing to leave the land (6–8000 p.a.). Manufacturing industries already established will offer little additional employment, whilst propulsive heavy industries are likely to be attracted only with difficulty. The faster than average growth in per capita income (+ 68 per cent over 15 years, France + 63) will modestly increase service jobs, tourism will continue to develop both coastally and more modestly in the interior. The closer link-up in trade with Britain since the enlargement of the EEC has brought modest dividends in ferry services and agricultural exports. The problems of peripheral location in France and the marginal and vulnerable nature of staple products are likely to prove more enduring.

Pays de la Loire and Poitou-Charentes
Neither Pays de la Loire (INSEE 1976B) nor Poitou-Charentes (La DF 1970, Préfecture de Région Poitou-Charentes 1976) corresponds to clearcut geographical realities. Both are composed of a mosaic of assorted *pays* with distinctive local conditions of soil, land use, rural economy, traditions and contemporary social and economic problems. Superimposed almost upon their diversity is the polarizing influence of large towns and communications corridors.

Pays de la Loire is structured economically around the Loire estuary (p. 364) and along the routeway through Angers to Le Mans. The overall economic momentum of the region depends on the diffusion of growth from the port-industrial complex and counterbalancing metropolis of Nantes-St Nazaire, on the one hand, and decentralization from Paris on the other. Under the VIIth Plan (Région Pays de la Loire 1975) emphasis is laid upon the development of the Atlantic facade, the build-up of the estuarine complex, development of the intermediate zones between the Bassin Parisien and the more remote rural Ouest, and on the more balanced development of small towns serving the 50 per cent of the regional population still classed as rural.

Poitou-Charentes poses a particularly difficult regional task (La DF 1970, 117). The geographical location and historical role both indicate a zone of transit, but peripheral alike to the Paris and Bordeaux spheres of influence. There is no well-established regional capital: Poitiers is eccentric and but one of an ill-distributed group of urban centres, incapable in spite of its university and economic dynamism of catalysing a regional unity. Under the Vth Plan (1966–70) growth was to be polarized along the Poitiers-Châtellerault axis and, secondly, in the coastal zone, by the urban and port functions of La Rochelle and the spread of tourism. The VIth Plan added modestly to the industries of Poitou-Charentes (only 14,300 industrial jobs by decentralization from Paris, 1955–75), but even then in firms controlled from outside, with only a national or regional market, often sub-contracting and paying lower than average wages (La DF 1970, 118). Not surprisingly, out-migration has continued. Under the VIIth Plan (Préfecture de Région Poitou-Charentes 1976) the region is likely to benefit more effectively from policies of small-scale disseminated development to towns (*villes moyennes*) and rural areas (PAR, *contrats de pays*). Agriculture is soundly-based and diversified, including cognac, dairy products, meat. Yet the background problem remains that of a region of transit, with a small total population, a scarcely developed regional consciousness, a polycentric urban network with no nodal capital, liable to the influence of stronger regional centres around its perimeter (Tours, Nantes, Limoges, Bordeaux).

Massif Central

Traditionally looked upon as the 'negative pole' of France, the Massif Central has emerged as collectively her most serious rural problem area (fig. 74). The problems are not new (House 1954), but in the aftermath of rapid national urbanization and industrialization they are more starkly apparent. Furthermore, the continual demographic decline and economic rundown have reduced both people and resources to new critical low thresholds in many parts of the highly diversified Massif. The weaknesses of local economy and society are most clearly expressed demographically (La DF 1964B). Though *Auvergne* increased its population 1962–8 by 40,000, this owed much to foreign-born immigrants and North African repatriates and concealed a loss of some 10,000 local out-migrants. 1968–75 population increase fell to 10,000 and the traditional loss of young people accelerated. *Limousin*, it is true, had slight increases in population in both periods, but these were the lowest growth rates in France. Although there was a net in-migration, a most serious underlying welfare problem lay in the disturbing surplus of deaths over births in both intercensal periods.

Unlike Bretagne, with its high rural population densities, Auvergne (52 persons per km²) and Limousin (44 per km²) are among the most sparsely populated regions of France. Both have low levels of overall urbanization, an ill-distributed and distorted urban network, upon which regional life has become increasingly polarized. In Limousin, for example, 1968–75 urban population increased by 30,000, rural declined by 28,000; in 1962 60 per cent of the people were rurally-based, in 1975 only 52 per cent. In Auvergne (1968–75), the regional capital, Clermont-Ferrand, grew rapidly (+ 1.9 per cent p.a.), medium-sized towns slowly, whilst throughout the mosaic of contrasting rural zones there was demographic stagnation or decline (91 cantons had an overall decline in numbers, 40 of which lost more than 10 per cent of their people).

Agriculture has become more marginal over wide tracts, with the risks of a 'green desert' spreading through the Massif: 1963–70 the farm area declined by 18 per cent; farm labour fell by 6 per cent in Limousin 1968–75 (10 per cent in Creuse) and in Auvergne a further loss of 4 per cent per annum is forecast. High relief, altitude and the profusion of small family farms are the hall-marks of marginal agriculture with high costs and low returns, undercapitalized and distant from markets. Stock-rearing for sheep and hill cattle, dairying for cheese, are staple activities, but there is much wasteland and large tracts given over to scarcely-planned forestry.

Industrial employment in the Massif is low and undiversified by comparison with the national average: in Auvergne 40,000 in rubber and chemicals, 44,000 in general and electrical engineering (50,000 in all supplying the motor car industry with components), but only 8000 in food-processing since most farm products leave the region in the raw state. Recently introduced industrial firms manufacture aluminium and plastics, but 1965–75 there have been no firms coming to Auvergne under the stimulus of government decentralization. In Limousin the traditional porcelain industry and engineering provide a narrow base to manufactur-ing. Throughout the Massif levels of tertiary employment are low, and there have been no significant decentralizations to the area of major public service establishments.

The economic base of the Massif is thus fragile, subject to decision-taking largely from outside, and earliest threatened by the onset of economic depression, since most of the activities are marginal. Furthermore, the disposition of the physical subregions, their innate diversity and their linkages outwards rather than inwards to the Massif, underline intractable internal communications problems and point to the administrative fragmentation of the Massif into parts of five planning regions. Within the contrasting crystalline plateaux, the volcanic or basaltic uplands, or the limestone Causses, there are many 'pays' (*zones défavorisées*) with peculiarly severe economic and social problems.

Faced with such a gamut of deteriorating circumstances, a coordinated three-year planning programme for the Massif Central (fig. 74) was set up in 1975 (La DF 1975B), giving context to the work of other regional development bodies (SOMIVAL, SAFER, etc.). The principles of the 1975 programme are to stimulate economic growth and stabilize population in the region; to diffuse growth more equitably to all levels of settlement; to open up the Massif, both internally and by linkage with the rest of France; and to create a better living environment (*cadre de vie*). The role of the Massif as a great environmental reserve and recreational space (e.g. Parc des Volcans, 273,000 ha., 80,000 inhabitants) is to be enhanced and the tourist trade sustained (24 million overnight stays in 1974). Such a comprehensive revitalization programme would have difficulties even in normal economic circumstances. Growth pressures tangentially, Paris-Lyon, Paris-Bordeaux, are likely to divert people and resources, particularly towards the Grand Delta of the South East (fig. 68). In such competitive conditions, it is understandably the larger towns (Clermont-Ferrand, Limoges) which can most readily stabilize population and attract modest growth. Yet it is the smaller towns and the vast and differentiated marginal rural hinterland which need the most sustained but disseminated and small-scale underpinning, down to the individual *zones défavorisées*. The policy of rural planning agreements (PAR, *contrats de pays*) and the medium-sized town support programme will be more vital here than elsewhere. The Massif Central will be the most demanding test-bed for public planning at the margins within a dominantly market economy (EPR Limousin 1976, Préfecture de Région Auvergne 1976A, B).

Midi-Pyrénées

Midi-Pyrénées is an underdeveloped, remote and peripheral region of both France and the EEC. In spite of the central position of the regional capital,

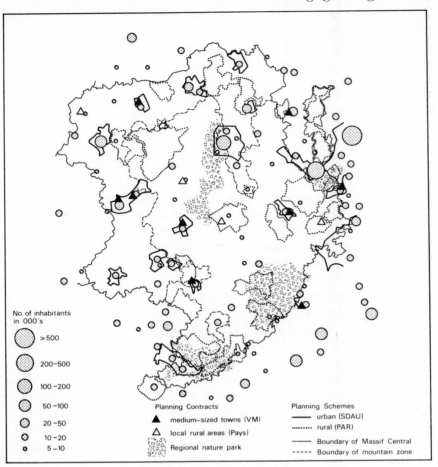

No. of inhabitants
in 000's

> 500

200–500

100 –200

50 –100

20 –50

10 –20

5 –10

Planning Contracts
▲ medium–sized towns (VM)
△ local rural areas (Pays)
Regional nature park

Planning Schemes
—— urban (SDAU)
········· rural (PAR)
—— Boundary of Massif Central
----- Boundary of mountain zone

Figure 74   Massif Central. Planning zones, 1975.

Toulouse, and its status as a counterbalancing metropolis, geographical coherence is lacking in a heterogeneous, thinly-peopled realm larger than Switzerland. 75 per cent of the land is mountainous or upland, with the Pyrénées and the Massif Central encroaching upon the shallow corridor linking the Languedoc coastlands with Aquitaine (La DF 1965). Steady out-migration of younger people has been masked by the inflow of foreign-born and, 1962–8, by repatriates from North Africa. 1968–75 the annual population growth rate was 0.3 per cent, with in-migrants contributing two-thirds. Nevertheless, Midi-Pyrénées has an over-representation of old people and has neither the labour reservoir of Corse nor the degree of self-containedness characteristic of Alsace.

Internally there are serious imbalances, of two principal kinds: between the capital and the more distant rural parts of its hinterland; and between traditional and transplanted elements of the economy. In all sectors and in most parts of the area the mid-1970s were a period of crisis (Idrac and Laborie 1976). After fifteen years of growth, unemployment (7 per cent, September 1975) has become endemic, industrial momentum has been lost in both the intended propulsive industries of aircraft manufacture (Sud-Aviation) and space research. The science-based industrial complex of Toulouse, with its research and development institutes (p. 365), has not had the expected multiplier effect upon other industries. The long-term future of the aircraft industry probably depends on cooperation with the United States, the space centre has been reduced in size, whilst there are also serious threats to the manufacture of electronics. Fortunately, the traditional local manufacturing base is diverse (textiles and clothing, leather, electrometallurgy and electrochemistry, general engineering, food) but, unfortunately, it includes branches in secular decline. Until the depression of the 1970s, useful progress had been made in distributing small-scale industries to country towns.

Unlike Languedoc, Midi-Pyrénées has an unbalanced urban network. Greater Toulouse dominates, growing by 87,000 people 1968–75; the entire region grew by only 84,000 in the same period. 50 per cent of the population is rural, grouped around some 27 small- and medium-sized towns. Depopulation is of long standing, and the small towns have had little influence hitherto in stemming the outflow. Local rural conditions are extremely diverse, with upwards of 50 micro-units of land use within the three-fold division: Pyrénées, stock-rearing; Garonne valley, *polyculture* (wheat, maize, vine, fruit, dairying); south-western Massif Central (fig. 24), sheep (up to 42 per cent in the region 1965–74) and cattle. With 12.7 million overnight stays tourism is a valuable growth generator, but there is a poor correlation with the areas of greatest rural need.

Policies for Midi-Pyrénées under the VIIth Plan (1976–80) (Préfet de Région Midi-Pyrénées 1976A, B) are concentrated on the opening-up of the region, internally and towards both Mediterranean and Atlantic coasts; stimulus to economic growth in all elements of the economy, with less emphasis upon science-based research and development as a propulsive force; and a better balance between Toulouse, the smaller towns and the more remote rural areas. In 1973 a commissioner was appointed to prepare a development programme for the Pyrénées massif; in 1976, a policy was promulgated: disseminated small-scale growth on the basis of individual valleys, but with stock-rearing and forestry to remain the staple forms of employment. It is estimated that the development programme will need 30 years for completion.

As an underdeveloped region, Midi-Pyrénées has merited particular government stimulus. The policy of creating a science-based complex was ambitious, though in part related to the earlier interwar strategic dispersal of aircraft and armaments firms. The association of higher education, research and development institutes was a logical extension and buttress for the industrial complex. Unfortunately, the economy of the region has proved vulnerable at both the most traditional and the most sophisticated ends of the employment spectrum.

Corse

With a 1975 population of only 289,842, a generally mountainous marginal environment, and an island situation closer to Italy (110 km) than to France (Nice 170 km), Corse inevitably has among the most serious and intractable of economic and social problems. Conscious of its late attachment to France (1768), its distinctive culture and traditions, the Corsicans have nurtured an autonomous, even a separatist, political tradition (Savigear 1975). The problems of the island were clearly formulated in the 1957 regional action programme: stemming the out-migrant tide, restructuring farming and forestry, managing underutilized resources of water, the soil and sub-soil, and encouraging the growth of tourism; reduction of the transport disadvantages of island location has been, and continues to be, a perennial theme. In 1957 SOMIVAC was created, a regional development corporation, for agricultural improvement, land reclamation, and water management; in the same year SETCO was established, to develop tourism as a propulsive force for the Corsican economy. In spite of major achievements by these bodies, Corse remained under Provence-Côte d'Azur for regional planning, until 1970 when it was separately identified, and 1972 when it became a full planning region. In 1975 the island was divided, to create two new *départements*: Haute-Corse, Corse du Sud (fig. 4).

Since the late 1950s the economy of Corse has been transformed (La DF 1972C, Préfecture de la Région Corse 1975), but serious imbalances and social tensions have been created (EPR Corse 1975). At first sight the demographic situation seems to have improved: 1962–8, annual growth rate +2.3 per cent (+3.0 if North African repatriates are included); 1968–75, still +0.8 per cent p.a. In practice, out-migration of young Corsicans has been more than replaced by repatriates from North Africa (about 18,000) and by foreign-born (22,000 Italians, 18,000 Moroccans). Immigrants have settled in the larger towns, but particularly on the reclaimed eastern coastal plain (11,000 ha. of farmland created by SOMIVAC, of which 7000 ha. were reclaimed from *maquis* and marsh). Transformation of farming created wealth, most notably for the immigrants: production of wine, largely of common quality (VCC), rose from

231,000 hl in 1962 to 2,100,000 hl in 1973; output of citrus fruits from 2300 tonnes in 1969 to 15,000 in 1974, with a potential for 60,000 tonnes by 1985. Among staple farm products wine contributes 63 per cent of gross agricultural product (1975), citrus fruits 7 per cent, meat 7 and milk 6 per cent. Nevertheless, the wine industry is vulnerable in face of larger bulk producers, all farm production for export suffers from transport costs to the mainland (estimated in 1974 at 20 million francs of extra costs for all farm products), and the new forms of farming have done all too little to help the traditional Corsican small-holders of the upland interior. Between 1955 and 1970 one-third of holdings were given up, arable land fell by 21 per cent, and commercial exploitation of chestnut groves almost ceased. Depopulation of the upland interior has continued, polarizing Corsican life upon the coastline and the principal towns of Ajaccio (50,726 in 1975) and Bastia (50,718 in 1975), which between them accounted for 35 per cent of the island population.

Tourism was looked on initially as a panacea for all rural ills. Certainly the growth rate has been rapid (15 to 18 per cent per annum increase in tourist numbers 1960–74); in 1974 15 million overnight stays were recorded for about 725,000 tourists. Some 22 per cent of the labour force is in the tourist industry, which contributes 28 per cent to gross domestic product in Corse. In spite of a tourist plan since 1957, coastal growth pressures have led to disordered development, mass tourism, risks to the quality of the environment and little contribution to the needs of the interior. Under the VIIth Plan a more harmonious and less ambitious programme of tourist development is intended, with an integral relationship between coastlands and the interior; environmental protection zones will be more strongly safeguarded; social tourism and family holidays will be envisaged at the expense of package-deal tours (EPR Corse 1975).

Strengthening of the small manufacturing base is likely to be modest, as befits a largely underdeveloped primary-producing economy: processing of local raw materials (wood, stone, tiles, perfumes) or foodstuffs; production for local needs (cement, industrialized building); export-oriented textiles, light engineering or electronics, i.e. items with high value per unit and considerable labour inputs.

OTHER AREA POLICIES

Policies for public involvement in location of manufacturing and tertiary activities were considered in Part II, ch. 2, whilst management of the urban network was reviewed in Part III, ch. 2. There remain two kinds of area policy: for the renovation and rehabilitation of rural and mountain zones, and secondly, for the industrial reconversion of declining mining or decaying industrial areas. The very recent tendency to create large informal consultative groups, e.g. for Ouest Atlantique, or the Grand Delta of SE France (Ferraton and Tomczak 1972) is outside formal planning policy, though DATAR often acts as a catalyst in such consultations.

Rural policies

Rural policies have been traditionally directed to relief at the farm-gate, with support for regrouping and enlargement of holdings (*remembrement*), modernization of farming techniques, quality control of products and more efficient marketing arrangements (Viard 1971). Such policies operated nationally and until the late 1950s there was no significant regional perspective. As a complement to the regional economic development programmes from 1955 onwards, rural planning organizations were set up for Bas-Rhône, Languedoc (CNABRL), Provence-Durance, Auvergne-Limousin (SOMIVAL), Corse (SOMIVAC), the Gascony hills (CACG), the Western marshes, and the wastelands of the Est (SAFE). Such organizations were to operate in a more comprehensive way on problems of natural resource use (land, water), but also in stimulating employment alternative to farming in rural areas (forestry, small-scale manufacturing, tourism). Financing was by the state, by public and private bodies, and on occasion by individuals, within the framework of mixed-economy or joint-stock organization.

Acting in a more limited agricultural sector, the rural development boards (SAFER), set up progressively after 1960, have been concerned with farm restructuring, monitoring and influencing land prices, and after 1962 they had powers to acquire land compulsorily in certain circumstances (La DF 1967). With few exceptions all farm sales were subject to intervention by the SAFER if an uneconomic holding would result or be perpetuated. Land bought by the SAFER could be restructured and had to be offered for resale within five years in units sufficient to employ two men throughout the year. By December 1974, 752,000 ha. of land had been acquired by SAFERs and 634,000 ha. had been redistributed in economic holdings. The most prosperous mechanized farming regions (Haute-Normandie, Picardie) never had a SAFER, whilst that for Corse dates from the 1970s. The pattern of SAFERs does not correspond well with either the economic regions, or the rural (1967) or mountain (1973) renovation zones. The rural development board for the Northern Pennines, 1969–71 (House 1976), had features in common with the French SAFER, but also more wideranging powers for achieving a better balance between farming and forestry in the hills, promoting farm- and forest-based tourism, and improving living conditions in the countryside.

By 1967, however, it was clear that in a rapidly industrializing and urbanizing society the gradients in living standards and expectations had moved decisively against rural dwellers (La DF 1972). Not all commentators (Jung 1971) accepted that such a trend justified separate planning policies for the rural areas, yet increasingly the French national conscience required that relief be given at the rural margins, and that in a comprehensive manner. There were, of course, sound political reasons why this should be so. The rural areas had been traditionally conservative and thus a possible counterweight to radicalism or more extreme movements manifesting themselves in the towns in 1968 and thereafter.

Rural depopulation was widespread, with numbers in an increasing range of localities down to a low threshold beyond which social provision could not be sustained and even the livelihood of those who wished to remain on the land risked being threatened (La DF 1970, Faudry 1973). The problems were those of isolation, structural weaknesses in family farming, inadequate alternative employment, and less than satisfactory social facilities. The need for a comprehensive rural policy (Marce 1969, Maquart 1973) to counterbalance those for manufacturing and the towns led in 1967 to the designation of four rural renovation zones (fig. 61): the Ouest (Bretagne, Manche), Limousin, Auvergne, and the mountain zones (initially those *communes* with 80 per cent of their surface higher than 600 m). Together these zones covered 27 per cent of France, had a population of 6.5 millions, and included 550,000 farms (one-third of the national total). For each of the four zones a commissioner was nominated, to carry out research and promote rural well-being, under the direction of the regional prefect. Up to 1970 the Ouest benefited most, but after 1972 the Massif Central (p. 420) had emerged as a problem region for priority treatment. In the Ouest the major fields for public investment were to open up Bretagne (road programme, telephone system), diversify the local employment base, and lay the foundations for modernizing farming and improving the general living environment. Pilot-zones were designated for coordinated rural development and there were programmes to stimulate small-scale, farm-based tourism, the provision of rural workshops, and better transport facilities. In general, efforts were to be concentrated on realizing the greatest economic benefit and the greatest multiplier effects. It was recognized that the mountain zones had a particularly aggravated mix of social and economic problems, and in 1973 a mountain policy was inaugurated.

The 1973 mountain policy (La DF 1974), for *communes* above 600 m or with more then 400 m relief amplitude, covers more than 9 million ha., or one-fifth of France. There are six mountain massifs: three in the middle mountain zone, Massif Central, Jura, Vosges: three in the high mountains, Alpes, Pyrénées, Corse. Administratively, the mountain policy concerns parts of 11 regions, 40 *départements*, and 4800 *communes*, with a population (1975) of about 2.7 millions. Altitude and slope impose particular constraints upon development, whether in the use of land or forest, access to tourist centres, or general circulation. Sparse and thinly-peopled (26 per km²), the mountains have low levels of urbanization concentrated in ribbons along the valleys, a dispersed and ageing demographic structure (18 per cent over 65 years), and a continuing serious depopulation. In some regions population density has fallen as low as 5–10 per km² (2 per km² in the Causse Mégean). Mountain farming is marginal by any criterion; in many areas the traditional pastoral system is stagnating or in decline. Forestry, the second major regenerative resource, is important both for timber, for recreation, and for slope stabilization. Tourism has a major potential, but its impact can be traumatically uneven, as well as dramatic in introducing and imposing alien life styles. Finally, the mountain problem has a European dimension: 1300 km of frontier mountain tracts, with the Alpes shared between five countries. International tunnels, through-routes and passes are further resources for common use and development, but often contribute little to the rural economic base.

In the 1973 and 1974 principles for a mountain policy it is admitted that it is difficult to make a case on strict economic grounds (Brocard 1975). Many of the products from the mountains could probably be made available at lower costs from more favourably endowed or better situated regions. The real justification for a special policy is two-fold: in the name of national solidarity to entitle those continuing to live and work in the mountains to have the same facilities as other Frenchmen; secondly, to conserve the ecological or environmental capital represented by the resources, landscapes and aesthetic appeal of the mountains. In this sense the mountain dweller is the guardian of a precious part of the national estate. Under the VIIth Plan the promotion of the quality of life has a special sense in the mountains. It is the ambition of planning to safeguard this environmental and social quality whilst encouraging multiple-purpose activities and giving those living in the mountains a more decisive say in their own affairs. At the heart of such considerations lies the problem of the marginal farmer. In 1972 the special mountain grant (ISM) was introduced for certain critical localities, and in 1974 was extended to all mountain zones, as an annual subsidy based on the size of flocks or herds.

Four commissioners have been appointed for the mountain zones:

Massif Central; Pyrénées; Alpes, Jura and Vosges; and for Corse. The policy mix to be applied in each mountain zone is likely to be different. As already considered, for the Massif Central (42 per cent of the *communes* and 50 per cent of the mountain population of France) the support for marginal farming is fundamental, to increase and diversify production, and to underpin rural settlement and traditional ways of life. Tourism in a disseminated form will be a valuable complement, as will small-scale industrialization. All mountain massifs face the problem of accessibility; hence the need to open up routes internally and linking to other parts of France. The Alpes (3.2 million ha., 616,000 people) fall into distinct geographical areas: in the north, humid, with dairy and beef cattle-based pastoralism, dramatic but selective development of dominantly winter-sports resorts; in the south, a higher ratio of sheep, poorer pastures, a high rural exodus, lower population density, more limited tourist potential and difficult problems of land restructuring. Mountain agriculture in the Alpes is unlikely to progress further, the general economy is expected to show dramatic but selective growth, and environmental conservation pro-grammes are at last in the forefront of rural planning (House 1961). The Pyrénées (10,500 km², 153,000 inhabitants) are geographically very differentiated over 400 km, physically, economically and in human terms. Administratively, each *département* has hitherto followed its own rural renovation policy, emphasizing the distinctive relationships between the mountains and the plains. The mountain plan for the Pyrénées in 1977 proposes priority for farming, to increase the use of pastoral resources, but in general disseminates aid over tourism, workshops, industry, education. When growth pressures come later, an Alpine-type mixed growth-conservation policy may become more appropriate.

The more localized and widespread rural development programmes (PAR) and contracts for investment in specific rural areas (*contrats de pays*) are a valuable complement to the large-scale, more comprehensive schemes already outlined. A PAR (1970) is prepared by the *département* agricultural directorate (DDA), in concert with local authorities, for a group of problem *communes* forming a geographic or economic entity. The PAR has indeed become obligatory for all cantons preparing a land use plan (POS) with fewer than 10,000 people. Authorized by CIAT, the *contrat de pays* (11 April 1975) is a more recent scheme for modest rural development agreed with local elected representatives.

Mining and industrial margins
The need for locality or subregional policies for industrial reconversion of declining mining or manufacturing areas came later than in Britain and,

until recently, such policies in France have been on a smaller and less coordinated scale. In a rapidly industrializing and urbanizing country, manufacturing in France was early regarded as the most positive and dramatic tool for regional development, both for promoting growth in hitherto dominantly rural regions (Ouest, Sud-Ouest) and for achieving the delicate and difficult employment restructuring of urban areas stagnating or in decline (Nord, Lorraine, and the more isolated coal-basins of the Massif Central, Dauphiné and the Alpes).

The early policies of the mid-1950s concerned isolated mining settlements, e.g. Décazeville (fig. 24) in the south-west Massif Central or St Eloyles-Mines (Pilandon 1971). After the European coal crisis of 1958–9, the run-down of the coalmining labour force began to accelerate and the problem of industrial reconversion became both more widespread and more serious. Coalmine closure programmes affected both the major fields and the more remote pits in Centre-Midi. From 5500 miners in 1946 the colliery labour force at Décazeville, for example, fell to 2700 in 1959 and only 450 in 1966; in 1965 deep-mining closed down. Nationally, employment in the coal mines fell from 242,400 (167,400 underground) in 1952 to 67,400 (42,100 underground) at the end of 1974.

In 1966 'industrial' development associations were created under the guidance of industrial conversion commissioners, appointed in the following year, for the Nord, Lorraine, St Etienne and Alès. The 1967 legislation also led to an industrial commission for the rural Ouest, where the problem was rather to stimulate the introduction of manufacturing into areas of rural overpopulation largely lacking in industrial skills or traditions. The commissioners were catalysts in the economic process, directly responsible to DATAR, rather than the basis for a new planning administration (Durand 1972). In the coalmining regions the colliery companies also had been involved from the mid-1950s in attracting new industry, creating factory sites and retraining ex-miners. The development corporation (SOFIREM), a subsidiary of the Coal Board, had been directly responsible for 11,250 new jobs by the end of 1974, 4000 reserved for ex-miners.

The regional implications of industrial reconversion have been discussed under the Nord (p. 409) and Lorraine (p. 412). The major problems are those of attracting industry to subregions or localities with an outworn social fabric, often substandard housing and living conditions; of retraining ex-miners for the factory or machine skills needed in the new jobs; and of ensuring a sufficiency of male jobs. Such reconversion problems are similar to those experienced from 1957–8 in the British coalfields (House and Knight 1967). At the heart of the wider regional economic problem lie

Table 37   Cévennes coalfield, employment, 1954–74

(1000 *employees*)	1954	1962	1967	1974
Miners	15.1	9.1	7.6	2.8
Total employment	34.9	33.0	33.5	—

Source: ADIRRA 1974

the traumatic effects of rundown and social change at the level of every colliery community.

The recent history of Alès, in the Cévennes, illustrates the general problem of reconversion (table 37, ADIRRA 1974). Between 1947 and 1965 the colliery labour force was steadily run down, with complete closure expected during 1977. The loss of 7500 mining jobs 1954–67 was partly offset by an increase of 3100 in manufacturing, of which 1600 were in government-aided projects, and an additional 1400 jobs in tertiary activities. The unfavourable features were the net loss of 5400 persons by out-migration during the same period and the fact that two-thirds of the factory jobs coming in were for women. Between January 1968 and August 1974 662 ex-miners opted for reconversion and by the time of final closure an additional 940 men needed to be catered for.

The Alès industrial reconversion scheme comes under the commissioner for industrialization of the Mediterranean face of France. By comparison with the port-industrial complex of Marseille-Fos, Alès is small-scale indeed and might in no wise be competitive in a marginal location. Nevertheless, it is argued (ADIRRA 1974, 31) that Alès should be developed as a specialized metal-working industrial pole, concentrating on foundry products, forging, stamping and cold-rolling of iron and steel. By this means the engineering skills and the local labour reservoir could be most efficiently used. Behind this argument is the politically persuasive theme that otherwise the social capital will be run down, out-migration will escalate, and the community will disintegrate. These risks are clear contrary to the welfare thinking behind the VIIth Plan.

References

General
Astorg, M. (1973A) 'Les politiques de développement régional et d'aménagement du territoire en France, de 1954 à 1972', *Comm. Général du Plan*.
   (1973B) 'La régionalisation du VIe Plan', *Comm. Général du Plan*.
Boucher, M. (1973) 'La région', *Cah. fr.*, 158/9.
Boudeville, J.-R. (1966) *Problems of Regional Economic Planning*, Edinburgh.
Brogniart, P. (1971) *La région en France*.

House, J. W. (ed.) (1977) *The UK Space: Resources, Environment and the Future*, London (2nd edn).

Labasse, J. (1960) 'La portée géographique des programmes d'action régionale française', *Annls Géogr.*, LXIX (374): 371–93.

La Documentation Française (1974) 'La réforme régionale, loi du 5 juillet 1972', *Notes et Etudes Documentaires*, 4046.

Thompson, I. B. (1970) *Modern France. A Social and Economic Geography*, London.

Regional

Bariou, R. (1975) 'Problèmes économiques de la Bretagne centrale. L'exemple du Centre Ouest Breton', *Norois*, 85: 5–19.

Boudeville, J.-R. (1964) 'La région Rhône-Alpes comme région européenne', *Cah. INSEE*, 153: 5–74.

CELIB (1956) *Programme d'action régionale pour la Bretagne* (programme officiel du 13 juillet 1956), Rennes.

—— (1971) *Bretagne: une ambition nouvelle*, Rennes.

Centre d'Etudes Economiques Régionales de Franche-Comté (1973) *Connaître la Franche-Comté*, Besançon.

Debeyre, M. G. (1970) 'Aire Métropolitaine, Aménagement Franco-Belge', *Cérès Inf.*, 1.

Decoster, P. (1969) 'Le Nord-Pas-de-Calais, d'une situation géographique à un rôle économique international', *Hommes et Terres du Nord*, 1: 7–12.

Dugrand, R. (1960) *Villes et campagnes en Bas-Languedoc.*

EPR, Corse (1975) *Charte du développement économique de la Corse*, Ajaccio.

EPR, Haute-Normandie (1976) *Réponses au questionnaire sur l'orientation préliminaire du VIIe Plan*, [Rouen].

EPR, Languedoc-Roussillon (1976) *Rapport d'orientation générale pour le 7e Plan* (Comité Economique et Social), [Montpellier].

EPR, Limousin (1976) *Les orientations pour l'avenir du Limousin, VIIe Plan*, 1976–80, Limoges.

Griffon, M. (1972) 'Bassin minier', *Documentation Aménagement Nord*, 32–4.

Hermitte, J. (1971) 'Pour un modèle de développement équilibré de la région Provence-Côte d'Azur-Corse', *Acta géogr. Paris*, 5: 57–67.

House, J. W. (1954) 'A comparative study of the landscapes of the plateau de Millevaches and the Western Cévennes', *Trans. Inst. Br. Geogr.*, 20: 159–80.

Idrac, M. and Laborie, J. P. (1976) 'L'économie de Midi-Pyrénées en crise', *Revue géogr. Pyrénées et Sud-Ouest*, 47 (1): 9–30.

INSEE (1976A) '1975 Bilan d'un crise', *Dossiers de l'Econ. lorraine*, juin, Nancy.

—— (1976B) 'Les hommes et l'espace régional', *Statistique et Développement, Pays de la Loire*, Supplément au no. 20.

INSEE, Dir. Rég. Rouen (1976) *Compte rendu d'exécution du VIe Plan en Haute-Normandie*, [Rouen].

La Documentation Française (1964A) 'L'économie de l'Aquitaine', *Notes et Etudes Documentaires*, 3082.

—— (1964B) 'Economies régionales et planification, Le Limousin', *Notes et Etudes Documentaires*, 3118.

(1965) 'L'évolution économique et sociale de la région Midi-Pyrénées, *Notes et Etudes Documentaires*, 3166.

(1966) 'L'économie de la Bourgogne', *Notes et Etudes Documentaires*, 3350.

(1967A) 'L'économie de la région de Picardie', *Notes et Etudes Documentaires*, 3374.

(1967B) 'L'économie de la région Champagne-Ardennes', *Notes et Etudes Documentaires*, 3436–7.

(1968A) 'L'économie de la région Rhône-Alpes', *Notes et Etudes Documentaires*, 3491–2.

(1968B) 'L'économie de la région Provence-Côte d'Azur-Corse', *Notes et Etudes Documentaires*, 3484–6.

(1968C) 'L'économie de la Bretagne', *Notes et Etudes Documentaires*, 3502–03.

(1970) 'L'économie de la région Poitou-Charentes', *Notes et Etudes Documentaires*, 3731–3.

(1971) 'L'économie de la Haute-Normandie', *Notes et Etudes Documentaires*, 3835–6.

(1972A) 'L'économie de la région du Centre', *Notes et Etudes Documentaires*, 3868–71.

(1972B) 'L'économie de la Basse-Normandie', *Notes et Etudes Documentaires*, 3856–7.

(1972C) 'Schéma d'aménagement de la Corse', *Travaux et Recherches de Prospective*, 32.

(1973) 'L'avenir de la Basse-Normandie,' *Travaux et Recherches de Prospective*, 36.

(1975A) 'Dynamique urbaine et projet régional. Un exemple: la région d'Alsace', *Travaux et Recherches de Prospective*, 56.

(1975B) *Le Massif Central*, 2 vols, DATAR.

Masson, J.-L. (1976) 'Les primes à l'industrialisation ont 20 ans', *Etudes et Statistiques, Lorraine*, 13.

Mission Régionale (Aquitaine) (1976) *Tableau de bord de développement à moyen terme*, Bordeaux.

Mission Régionale (Région du Centre) (1976) *Préparation du VIIe Plan. Programme de développement et d'aménagement*, Pre-Rapport, [Orléans].

Moatti, P.-J. (1972) 'Le PRDE de la Bourgogne pour le VIe Plan', *Bourgogne Expansion*, 55.

Nonn, H. (1971) 'L'Alsace et son aménagement dans le cadre de la présentation des schémas directeurs', *Revue géogr. Est*, XI: 353–86.

(1972) 'Problèmes d'organisation régionale: l'Alsace', *L'Espace géogr.*, I (4): 251–60.

ODEAM (1971) *Schéma d'aménagement de la bande côtière des Alpes-Maritimes*, 2 vols, Nice.

Phlipponneau, M. (1970) *Debout Bretagne*, St Brieuc.

Préfecture de la Région Corse (1975) *Une région française. La Corse*, Ajaccio.

Préfecture de Région (1976) *Présentation de Poitou-Charentes*, Poitiers.

Préfecture de Région, Auvergne (1976A) *VIe Plan. Compte Rendu d'Exécution*, 2 vols, Clermont-Ferrand.

(1976B) *Projet de programme, de développement et d'aménagement*, Clermont-Ferrand.

Préfecture, Nord-Pas-de-Calais (1976) *VIIe Plan. Synthèse des propositions du préfet de région*, Lille.

Préfet de Région, Bretagne (1975) *Rapport d'orientation de la Bretagne pour le VIIe Plan*, Rennes.

Préfet de Région, Lorraine (1976) *Les stratégies de développement et d'aménagement de la région pour le VIIe Plan*, Metz.

Préfet de Région, Midi-Pyrénées (1976A) *Bilan de la réalisation du VIe Plan*, Toulouse.

(1976B) *Contribution à l'élaboration du programme de développement et d'aménagement de Midi-Pyrénées*, Toulouse.

Préfet de Région, Provence-Côte d'Azur (1976) *VIIe Plan. Rapport d'Orientation Générale*, [Marseille].

Préfet de Région, Rhône-Alpes (1976) *Programme de développement et d'aménagement régionale*, Lyon.

Quelennec, M. (1973) 'Différences et ressemblances entre régions économiques', INSEE, R12.

Région Aquitaine (1975) *Rapport d'orientations générales pour le VIIe Plan*, Bordeaux.

Région Pays de la Loire (1975) *Préparation du VIIe Plan*, Première Phase, mars 1975; Deuxième Phase, sept. 1975, Poitiers.

Savigear, P. (1975) 'Corsica 1975: politics and violence', *Wld Today*, 31: 462–8.

Schmitt, C. (1973) *Région de Franche-Comté*, Besançon.

Souchon, M. F. (1968) 'La Compagnie Nationale d'Aménagement de la région du Bas-Rhône-Languedoc', *Cah. Inst. Pol. Grenoble*, 3.

Other area policies

ADIRRA (1974) *L'industrialisation de la zone du bassin minier d'Alès*, Alès.

Brocard, J. (1975) *L'aménagement du territoire en montagne*.

Durand, P. (1972) *Industrie et régions*.

Faudry, D. (1973) 'La désertification de l'espace rurale, sa logique sociale et les conséquences', *Aménagement du territoire et développement régional*, VI, IEP, Grenoble: 147–64.

Ferraton, Y. and Tomczak, W. (1972) 'Le Grand Delta, région d'équilibre d'Europe', *Révue Navigation Fluviale Européenne*: 427–40.

House, J. W. (1961) 'Western Alpine society in transition: the case for regional planning', *Plann. Outlook*, V (2): 17–30.

House, J. W. (1976) 'The geographer and policy-making in marginal rural areas: the Northern Pennines rural development board', ch. 6 in Coppock, J. T. and Sewell, W. R. D., *Spatial Dimensions of Public Policy*, Oxford.

House, J. W. and Knight, E. M. (1967) 'Pit closure and the community', *Papers in Migration and Mobility*, 5, Newcastle upon Tyne.

Jung, J. (1971) *L'aménagement de l'espace rural. Une illusion économique*.

La Documentation Française (1967) 'Les structures agraires en France et les SAFERs', *Notes et Etudes Documentaires*, 3422.

(1970) 'La politique de rénovation rurale', *Notes et Etudes Documentaires*, 3708.

(1972) 'La transformation du monde rural', *Travaux et Recherches de Prospective*, 26.

(1974) *La montagne. Eléments pour une politique.*

Maquart, D. (1973) 'Une politique de conversion rurale, ses principes', *Aménagement du territoire et développement régional*, VI, IEP, Grenoble: 243–68.

Marce, L. (1969) 'Les zones de rénovation rurale', *Aménagement du territoire et développement régional*, II, IEP, Grenoble: 487–518.

Pilandon, L. (1971) 'St Eloy les Mines—crise et tentatives de conversion', *Fac. des Lettres, Clermont-Ferrand*, XLI.

Viard, C. (1971) 'Les structures agricoles et l'action de l'Est', *Aménagement du territoire et développement régional*, IV, IEP, Grenoble: 323–90.

Part four

In conclusion

PROSPECTS, POTENTIALS AND POLITICS

In the late 1970s, in common with other Western urban and industrial nations, France was passing through a deep-seated and structural economic depression. Given the optimistic forecasts for French growth prospects as recently as 1973 (Hudson Institute), it might be thought that the impact of depression would be short-lived, without lasting effects, and that France was on the road to parity in GNP with Western Germany at the latest by 1985, and thereafter would emerge as Western Europe's strongest economic power. The heady forecasts of 1973 coincided with the zenith of technocratic management of the French economy, lasting beyond the political trauma in and after 1968 (Quermonne 1969). Yet it is now becoming clear, precisely because of the rapidity of economic and social change in postwar France, of polarization of regional and national life into towns and industries, that the enforced loss of momentum is a most appropriate time for stock-taking and perhaps for rethinking the onward course, and in it the significance of planning and the management of space. Indeed, many will argue that a turning point has been reached at a critical phase not only in the economy but also in politics, society and the national and international roles of France.

The sense of recharting the future is very evident in political treatises (Giscard d'Estaing 1976), in the writings of planners (Monod 1974), and, most specifically, in the formulation of the VIIth Plan (1976–80). Giscard d'Estaing (p. 17) writes of putting an end to urban proliferation, to giant developments (*gigantisme*) which destroy and degrade. An overriding emphasis in government policy is to be given to improving the quality of life and the living environment (*cadre de vie*). An ecological dimension is to be introduced into the evaluation of all large-scale projects, and an overall policy of environmental protection firmly established. Local levels of government are to be strengthened, the regional level is under suspended judgement (three levels of power considered excessive in a European context) and the role and status of the individual in society is to be magnified through consultation and participation. The battle of ideologies for the possession of men's minds will lead to a pluralist society, tolerant and concerned for the socially underprivileged (whether by class or by place). In town planning home ownership is to be promoted rather than tenancy, individual dwellings rather than collective blocks, rehabilitation rather than new building, small- and medium-sized towns at the expense of conurbations or megalopolis. Economic growth is to be vigorous, with France increasingly opened to EEC and world trade, but growth must respect both life styles and the environment; the president cites the excesses of planning in Paris in this context. In political terms, solidarity, capacity to organize progress, and self-improvement are to be stressed in the pluralist society of the future. As a planning accompaniment, Monod (1971) saw spatial management policies as 'less a search for rationale in the organization of space than for the choices which society will make for its use'. In 1974 (p. 3) he wrote, 'By acting on the distribution of activities and particularly of industry, spatial management responds to the insistent demands for liberty'.

Set against such establishment or technocratic views in a politically highly polarized France in the late 1970s, are views of the Left, such as those of Durrieu (1969): 'The régime of capitalism is not capable of jointly conducting a policy of regional equilibrium and the necessary movements of deconcentration to ensure its productive development'. Indeed, the programme of the political Left in the 1977 municipal elections was rather in the direction of replacing the market economy and indicative planning by a more interventionist type in the pursuit of social justice, which was held also to include regional justice.

The sharply contrasting political testimonies and intentions of the late 1970s are but the latest variation on the perennial theme of the balance between unity and diversity in France (Part I, ch. 2). To the contrast between Paris and the provinces, diminished in a measure by planning but still almost overpowering, there must be added other, changing dualisms in France: the contrasts between resources, problems and potentials divided by a line from Calvados to Marseille; the emerging north-south gradient in demographic vitality, levels of urbanization and potentials for benefit from closer integration into the EEC; the distinctions between polarized and non-polarized zones and regions, or between those with growth potentials and those developing only with government support policies. In a recent forecasting study (La DF 1971), four elements of French society were identified: two in production, agricultural and industrial, two in social organization, rural and urban. The tensions in France were interpreted in their implications for the four-fold differences in society: spatial, as in town/country or interregional contrasts; social, as between workers and management, the state and firms; economic, in the distinctions among industry, agriculture and commerce; educational, on a spectrum from manual worker perhaps to intellectual; in life-styles, as indicated particularly by housing. To these must surely be added the forces of regionalism, perhaps most vividly expressed through ethnicity, and those of political party or ideology.

Acting in a unifying spirit (Part I, ch. 2) in the face of such manifest diversity and potentially fissiparous tendencies, there continues to flourish a strong sense of national ethnic, cultural and historic identity, cemented by a still highly-centralized administration. There is a greater mobility of persons and diffusion of common urban life-styles throughout the managed urban network, the role of regions is seen as still tributary to the national metropolis, and the general, though still uneven, impact of planning policies has made some progress towards reducing the manifest spatial economic and social inequalities. Furthermore, and fundamental to any assessment of the true significance of dramatic changes in postwar France outlined in preceding chapters, the more subtle background threads of long-term continuity in the collective images of the French people must be taken into account. Ardagh (1968, 24) said, 'France is in a sense making a leap straight from the late eighteenth into the twentieth century' and 'Few other nations in the West are so schizophrenic about modernism' (p. 13).

The outward effects of transformation in economy and society may thus disguise underlying tensions, perhaps to be resolved in due course by the re-establishment of older ways and values. The general tenor of the VIIth Plan objectives and the political thinking of M. Giscard d'Estaing (1976) underlines one such reinterpretation of the aspirations of the French people. But there are obverse, less progressive aspects of the continuity of cultural traditions, in uncritical but obstinate resistance to change. As Ardagh (1968, 684) put it, 'France is passing through a more difficult period of transition than almost any other western country'. To Monod (1974, 175), 'Successive generations keep an unchangeability which makes them unable to conceive of the future without breaking with the past'. In this sense change is only accepted as a submission to the inevitable. The 1971 forecasting study (La DF 1971) saw positive merit in the way every national community sought to preserve its particularities, and was self-reinforcing by reproducing subsystems essential both for its survival and its further development. Such strong identification with the long-term perspective on heritage is both conservative and conserving: 'Much the greater part of France has conserved a personality imprinted on the landscapes from very varied past epochs . . . . . a heritage menaced by industrial and urban despoliation' (Monod 1974, 175). An epitaph on the present condition of

France after three decades of indicative planning in a market economy cannot but be that the spectacular transformations achieved by technocracy and materialism must be qualified by their lesser imprint on the values and ways of life of a multitude of Frenchmen. 'Is France fated then to become a more prosperous, efficient and contented country, but also a duller and much less French one?' (Ardagh 1968, 27). To this, or any late 1970s assessment, the answer is surely that this risk has been avoided, but only just and not everywhere.

Like Britain, France has had to adjust painfully to the loss of a colonial empire since 1945, but with some compensation: as a foundation member of the EEC (Treaty of Rome 1958) she has built upon her traditional role of cooperation in Western Europe. In so doing, France has been slow to yield an inch of sovereignty, even for the practical purposes of NATO defence. Apart from a sense of national identity, if not separateness, there may be other more profound geographical reasons for this sustained posture. Though France is geographically a compact hexagon with a radial-concentric disposition of flows and linkages focused upon the national capital, she has important concentrations of population in the frontier zones, both landward and maritime. The landward frontiers in the north and east are open to the dynamic heartland of the EEC and the lower Rhine-Ruhr-Rhine/Main-Switzerland axis; in the south-east the contacts are close with the industrial and urban areas of Piedmont in northern Italy. Inevitably, since her landward neighbours, with possible exception of Italy, are economically more dynamic and France's frontier regions are plagued with industrial reconversion problems, there is the likelihood of an economic polarization outwards, to the benefit of her neighbours and to the disadvantage of France. The inherent risks of such a potential weakening of the internal links and bonds in the French economy are reflected in the degree of ambivalence about the future role of Paris and the Ile-de-France. On the one hand, in the interests of that perennial planning policy of reducing regional inequalities, Paris should continue to distribute part of her growth and limit her further expansion; on the other, any fundamental weakening of her dynamism may accelerate the centrifugal trends in the frontier economies of the Nord, Lorraine, and Alsace. It may be argued that there would be sizeable benefits to France from more open landward frontiers in an era of supranational customs union moving towards economic union in the EEC of the Nine. The risks are that with the present imbalance between French frontier problem regions and their more dynamic neighbours, the terms of trade would move further against France in a polarization of economic life upon an EEC heartland in relation to which so much of France lies marginally (fig. 2). The risks are well-recognized, and in the mid-1970s a deliberate policy of aid to the French frontier regions has been implemented.

The maritime facades of France illustrate perhaps an even more difficult variant of the same kind of problem. The North Sea-Channel face (Dunkerque to Le Havre) continues to be under serious competition from the major European ports further north (Antwerp, Rotterdam-Europort, Amsterdam). Indeed, it has been said (Monod 1974, 101) that the Dunkerque port-industrial complex (p. 370) 'was planned in response to the needs of reconversion in the coalfield *and* the competition from the strong (growth) poles at the mouth of the Rhine'. The port-industrial complex of the Basse-Seine (p. 371) also seeks to divert trade to French advantage and to underpin the industrial base of the Ile-de-France, strengthening the westward linkages from Paris in relation to the logically stronger economic pulls northwards and eastwards from the capital. Marseille-Fos, too, has been described as 'born of the shock at the loss of southern (Mediterranean) markets' (Monod 1974, 101). An alternative view (Hudson Institute 1973) is that the Mediterranean world offers perhaps the greatest growth potential for any maritime face of France, a view difficult to substantiate at least for the medium term. The Marseille-Fos complex stakes out the claims for French participation alongside those of Genoa and northern Italy. In terms of the overall trade strategy of the EEC, Marseille-Fos may continue to be a remote if sizeable and specialist outpost, even when the full communications infrastructure (Rhône-Rhine canal, motorways) has been completed.

The greatest question-mark, however, lies over the Atlantic facade. The chain of ports from Cherbourg to Bordeaux is backed by immediate hinterlands which are economically weak, even though demographic trends in the past decades have improved, industrial decentralization has added usefully to local employment structure, and in Nantes-St Nazaire and Bordeaux there are two counterbalancing regional metropoli, each with an associated port-industrial complex of at least a secondary order. Nevertheless, the Atlantic facade is remote from both the major centres of French life and the EEC heartland, marginal in its resource base *and* in terms of accessibility. Under the VIth Plan, a policy for supporting the Atlantic coast was an integral part of the continuing search for better regional balance. The problems there are deep-seated, however, and similar in many respects to those of developing countries overseas: numerical parity of rural and urban populations, polarization of life upon a few major port towns with a limited range of industries processing either imported petroleum or agricultural products, linked by unfavourable terms of trade to distant, more dynamic urban and industrial economies.

TO THE END OF THE CENTURY

The late 1970s are a particularly difficult time from which to look forward into the future. The essence of forecasting lies in an ability to blend carefully measured trend extrapolations with imaginative insights and judgements. To be effective all forecasting must depart from a firm assessment of present conditions. In France, as in other Western industrial nations, the present is difficult to assess and in particular the distinction between short-run unfavourable trends and their implications for longer-term structural changes is hard to establish. Predictions may be established with confidence only for those few years ahead (to the early 1980s) through which the momentum of present trends will tend to shape the future. The scope for more decisive or different planning interventions will necessarily be limited in the short term and for the achievements of major programmes of metropolitan or regional development some thirty years will be needed, even in normal times. Over the medium- (12–15 years) and longer-term (30 years) futures, measured extrapolations must give place to more generalized and less certain trend scenarios (La DF 1971, Hudson Institute 1973).

The assessment of past successes in spatial management may be most broadly interpreted through demographic change in the first instance, and secondly by analysis of employment structure. The impact of change is in turn writ large in urban and rural landscapes. On all these counts the 1975 census gives credence to the overall success of the VIth Plan (1971–5), in stabilizing regional populations, distributing growth more equitably through the urban network, and in stemming the rural exodus in considerable measure. The achievements in employment structure have been tardy and less decisive, both nationally and regionally, and the significance of public planning interventions more difficult to disentangle from the inexorable march of events in a market economy. To attempt a similar assessment for the period of the VIIth Plan (1976–80) is immediately more hazardous (Passeron 1977). Are the reductions in natural increase, the shifts in interregional migration flows, the restrictions on foreign immigrants, likely to be short- or long-term in their incidence and effects? Will the slow-down in the industrial growth momentum persist and will the outcome be an increase in regional disparities in spite of all that spatial management policies can do? How far will the economic climate impede realization of the spatial objectives for the VIIth Plan: to limit the growth of large towns, and rather than concentrating so emphatically upon reduction of major regional disparities as hitherto, to disseminate growth down to smaller towns and rural areas?

The initial verdict for 1980 is that unless demographic trends in the rural areas (truly rural plus settlements of under 5000 = REC, *rural étendu constant*) can be changed, the objectives of the VIIth Plan will not be reached. The Paris conurbation will need to lose 40,000 per annum, not the 12,000 which would be the trend extrapolation. Other conurbations over 200,000 would need to reduce their growth from 65,000 to 47,000 per annum. Since immigration is not likely to add to the national labour force by 1980, there will be added pressures on rural dwellers to move to the towns for the rising number of jobs available. In interregional terms, the VIIth Plan objective of 'sustaining priority for the western half of France and the reconversion of mono-industrial regions of the Nord and the Est' is likely to be achieved without much change in present trends. That is not to say that all regional inequalities will be reduced: Limousin and Auvergne, for example, will continue to decline in population, and the Nord and Lorraine will barely stabilize their populations.

In employment terms the loss of agricultural jobs will continue at about the rate of the recent past, but the effect of the already much diminished numbers upon regional employment structure is likely to be insignificant. Rural populations will be stabilized more by the dissemination of industrial or tertiary jobs to the small towns. Industrial prospects for most sectors remain uncertain. Fewer decentralizations of firms are likely in conditions of slow economic growth and, furthermore, the social pressures of employees against being transferred to more remote regions are certain to grow. Indeed, the larger firms, notably the multinationals, will be able to press more effectively for the most profitable locations for new capacity, resisting planning influences in the process. It may be that decentralization of tertiary activities will continue more successfully. If there can be a reduction of 50 per cent (− 150,000 jobs) in the tertiary growth rate for Greater Paris, 1976–80, this volume can be distributed equitably among the regions according to their capacity for absorption. The growth in tertiary employment would help counterbalance the declines in industry except in those regions with slow change trends in both sectors (Nord, Rhône-Alpes and Provence-Côte d'Azur-Corse). At all events, tertiary activities will be the major propulsive force for growth until 1980, and the spatial redistributive policies of the VIIth Plan will need to be vigorously implemented.

The longer-range scenarios (La DF 1971) are formulated in a more qualitative manner, to outline the course of development likely to emerge from the extrapolation of present trends over a period of 15 to 30 years. No allowance is made for external circumstances, which seems entirely and increasingly unrealistic, and no account is taken of the potential for planning interventions of any kind. Not surprisingly, the end result is a justification for continuing spatial management policies, failing which the 'unacceptable' will happen.

Assessing the likely trends for industrial, urban, agricultural and rural France to 1985, the scenario is set within regionalization as a regulator for the tensions of society. The expected modernization of smaller, backward French firms in 'archaic' industries (e.g. metal-working, textiles) now seems less likely to occur in the near future, but their important role in labour-intensive stabilization in the developing areas justifies continuing government support policies. Nor is the onset of high technology, capital-intensive industry now expected to proliferate and the propulsive industries so vital to regional development (aerospace, electronics, chemicals) may need more government stimulus if their benefits are to be felt in the most needy areas. The trend for major industrial development to gravitate to the major 'polarization zones' is likely to become more insistent when economic growth is resumed.

The 1971 scenario for the prospects of the towns first distinguishes those west of the Loire where local urban *élites* wish to preserve traditional ways and life styles, to the degree that the rural exodus builds up there without finding adequate or diverse employment. Elsewhere the larger towns would grow rapidly (though the subsequent VIIth Plan objectives are set firmly against this), with intertown rivalries, internal social segregation and tensions arising from immigrants and the elimination of small businesses and shopkeepers. Towards the mid-1980s the privileged status of the counterbalancing metropoli would have been enhanced, but their internal polarization into decaying centre, suburbs and vast housing projects would have been socially even more disruptive. Though the VIIth Plan is intended to restrain such growth, it is unlikely that the massive partial investment already committed will be allowed to go to waste. The medium-sized towns, to which urban policy is now so firmly turned (p. 376), would without it have had very chequered prospects: in the Ouest and Sud-Ouest some 'agro-towns' may have developed, but many would have stagnated; in more prosperous regions the smaller towns would have been more fully integrated into the urban system.

Though agricultural production will continue to vary by the fertility of the land, the social structure and management practice, a broad distinction in prospects is to be drawn either side of a line from Calvados to the Côte d'Azur. In Ile-de-France, Picardie, Champagne, Lorraine and Haute-Normandie, a younger, demographically dynamic farm labour force on viable holdings is adapted to a highly commercialized market economy; the main risks are those of price levels and marketing arrangements. Rhône-Alpes, the Midi, Alsace and the Nord have smaller holdings, but farm consolidation is enabling younger farmers to take up land (except in the Nord). The regional towns offer an assured market and alternative employment for those leaving the land and there is therefore no problem of assimilation to the towns. In the Midi, consolidation of holdings (*remembrement*) will take longer and the scarcity of foreign workers will enforce more mechanization. In other regions the pace of agricultural change will be slower, with an obstinate attachment to outdated systems and holdings, a lack of alternative jobs and of training facilities. By the mid-1980s the rural exodus will have slowed since many uneconomic holdings will have been eliminated, the introduction of modern techniques will have been diffused, but the problem of the middle-sized family farm will emerge, 'squeezed' between the large-scale producer and the marketing monopolies.

Rural society in many areas is already losing content and traditional functions. The *bourg* as a service centre for farms, a residence-workplace unit, with a traditional social structure of *notables*, is already under threat: in some areas (Poitou-Charentes) agriculture has lost people steadily but rural society has increased; in Lozère, Aveyron and Cantal there is recession in both farming and its rural social context. Rural society is becoming politically less significant, with passive resistance growing in areas without economic growth prospects, little tourism and yet strong social consciousness or ethnicity. Change may move in the direction of: decay, adaptation to an urban model, or transformation to new rural forms. The spread of urban values may be the means of further disintegrating rural society, but it is precisely to guard against these risks that the VIIth Plan intends to disseminate growth and social reinforcement with priority for small centres and rural hinterlands.

In the 1971 scenarios for the mid-1980s the region is postulated as the regulator to ensure the permanence and cohesion of the state. Hitherto, regional tensions have often been relieved at regional level, e.g. the rundown of mining in the Nord and Lorraine, the wine-growers of Languedoc, or the Breton market-gardeners. In future the state may be drawn in increasingly as arbitrator. In this sense regional devolution offers a protective screen for the state, but risks further disadvantaging poorer regions and aggravating regional rivalries. Such a scenario is likely to be frustrated by policy-decisions already taken: to put the regional institutions on short-term trial, and to pursue national policies for disseminating growth down to more micro-scale levels.

Beyond 1985 the element of speculation enters in. The 1971 long-term scenarios foresee a priority for urban society, an increasing role for very large industrial groups dominating both national and regional scenes.

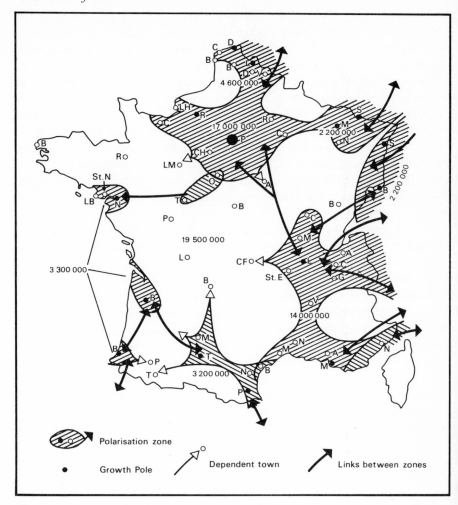

Figure 75   Polarization zones in scenario for 1990–2000.

Administrative power would be devolved to the regions (*déconcentration*), but political power would be retained firmly at the centre. The pressures, congestion and high land values in the large cities would lead to a new phase of decentralizations under market forces. In the cities, particularly the inner cities, the problems of daily living might become increasingly unacceptable. In such a Kafka-like prospect, faced with threats to national unity, by the multinationals governed from abroad and by regional unrest from within, a new phase of regional equilibrium policies would very likely be ushered in. Resources might be abstracted from the richer regions to be shared by the poorer, but an ambivalence creeps in: the large firms pre-empt the most nodal and profitable locations, whilst the state seeks to disseminate growth. Possibly a movement of urban elites to the western coastlands and the frontier regions favours a pattern of localized fast-growth 'micro-polarization' zones.

Towards the end of the century the Lyon region will come to share the economic control of France with Paris. The Midi, the Nord and the Est will be increasingly bound into the economy of adjacent states (fig. 75). Yet on such a speculation there will still be two Frances, which will uneasily co-exist: the subsidized unstable regions contrasting with the European-integrated growth regions. In the industrial-urbanized society of Britain, with its more complex and heavier legacy from earlier industrial re-volutions, the prospect for a continuing regional polarization are not altogether dissimilar (House 1977).

References

Ardagh, J. (1968) *The New France*, Harmondsworth.

Durrieu, Y. (1969) *Régionaliser la France: capitalisme ou socialisme.*

Giscard d'Estaing, V. (1976) *Démocratie française.*

House, J. W. (1977) *The UK Space: Resources, Environment and the Future*, London.

Hudson Institute (1973) *France and its future*, 1973–1985, Stillman Report, Croton-on-Hudson.

La Documentation Française (1971) 'Une image de la France en l'an 2000', *Travaux et Recherches de Prospective*, 20.

Monod, J. (1971) Preface to the above
(1974) *Transformation d'un pays. Vers une geographie de la liberté.*

Passeron, H. (1977) 'Population, emploi et revenus régionaux en 1980', *Econ. et statistique*, 85: 13–28.

Quermonne, J. L. (1969) 'Autonomie régionale et unité nationale', *Aménagement du territoire et développement régional,* II, IEP, Grenoble: 3–37.

Annotated List of Acronyms

ADIRRA	*Association pour le développement industriel et la reconversion de la région alèsenne* Industrial development association (Alès) 15 Sept. 1967
AFPA	*Association (nationale) pour la formation professionnelle des adultes* National Association for Adult Vocational Training. Early 1960s
ANPE	*Agence nationale pour l'emploi* State labour placement organization 1968
AOC	*appellation d'origine contrôlée* wine with registered title
AP	*Autorisations de programme* State investments (normative figures) VIth Plan, 1971–5
APC	*Association des patriotes corses* Policy for autonomy but not separation 1976
APUR	*Atelier parisien d'urbanisme* Working group on planning, City of Paris, 1967
APEILOR	*Association pour l'expansion industrielle de la Lorraine*
APL	*Aide personalisée au logement* Housing policy: transfer of subsidy from the property to the tenant of social housing 1977
ASSEDIC	*Association pour l'emploi dans l'industrie et le commerce* Employment census on 31 Dec. each year; unemployment benefit from non-state funds; included in UNEDIC (q.v.) 31 Dec. 1958
AVTS	*Allocation aux vieux travailleurs salariés* For those over 65 years, with inadequate pension contributions
BAP	*Bénéficiaires de l'aide publique* Unemployment relief
BTP	*Bâtiment et travaux publics* Building and public works
CACG	*Compagnie d'aménagement des collines de Gascogne* Management company for the hills of Gascony 1957–60 *Loi du 24 mai 1951*
CAECL	*Caisse d'aide à l'équipement des collectivités locales* Assistance fund for local authorities 1966
CAP	*certificat d'aptitude professionnelle* 3-year (from 14–15 onwards), in CET (q.v.), 1959; 2-year, second short cycle, in CET (q.v.), 1967; LEP (q.v.) replaced CET 1975

CAR — *Conférence administrative régionale*
1964, 1972 regional reforms; in 1964 replaced *Conférence interdépartementale* (1959)

C(R)AR — *Contrat (régional) d'aménagement rural*
National (regional) contract for rural development. Excludes towns of more than 5000 1975, CIAT (q.v.)

CCES — *Comité consultatif économique et social*
Région Parisienne 1963

CCI — *Chambre de commerce et d'industrie*

CDP — *Centre démocratie et progrès*
Political party: merged 1976 with *Centre démocrate* to form *Centre des démocrates et sociaux* (CDS, q.v.)

CDS — *Centre des démocrates et sociaux*
Political party: by merger of *Centre démocrate* and *Centre démocratie et progrès* (Lecanuet) (CDP, q.v.) 1976

CEA — *Commissariat à l'énergie atomique*
1945

CEE — *Communauté économique européenne*
EEC 1958

CEG — *Collège d'enseignement général (premier cycle)*
College of General Education. First level of secondary education, being replaced by CES (q.v.); 1959

CELIB — *Comité d'étude et de liaison des intérêts bretons*
First regional economic development committee (Bretagne) 1950

CENTREST — *Société de développement régional du Centre-Est*
1957

CEREN — *Centre d'études régionales sur l'économie de l'énergie*
Centre for study of regional energy problems 1955

CES — *coefficient d'emprise des sols*
ratio of land occupied by buildings to total surface

Collège d'enseignement secondaire
First level of secondary education 1963

Conseil économique et social
Economic and Social Council 1973 regional reforms

CET — *Collège d'enseignement technique*
Second cycle, leading to vocational qualifications. Now *lycées d'enseignement professionnel* (LEP); 1945

CETA — *Centre d'enseignement des techniques agricoles; Centre d'études techniques agricoles*
Agricultural technical training centres

CETRAMAR — *Consortium européen de transports maritimes*
Shipping companies' merger (bulk-handling)

CFA — *Centre de formation d'apprentis*
Apprentice training centre
Loi du 16 juillet 1971

CGP	*Commissariat général au Plan* National planning advisory organization (interministerial forum) *Décret du 3 janvier* 1946
CGT	*Compagnie générale transatlantique* French Line 1855
CHR(U)	*Centre hospitalier régional (universitaire)*
CIAM	*Commission interministérielle pour l'aménagement touristique de la montagne* 1964, since replaced
CIAT	*Comités interministériaux pour l'aménagement du territoire et l'action régionale* Consider major infrastructural investments (e.g. Fos, Dunkerque) and approve *schémas directeurs* for regional metropoli or for tourism. Also responsible for rural *contrats de pays* (11 April 1975) *Décret du 19 nov.* 1960
CME	*Commission de modernisation et d'équipement* Preparation of sectoral studies for National Plan
CNABRL	*Compagnie nationale d'aménagement du Bas-Rhône-Languedoc* Irrigation, development and reconversion operations in Gard, Hérault and Aude 1955
CNASEA	*Centre national pour l'aménagement des structures des exploitations agricoles* In charge of public intervention on easing adaptation of agriculturally active population to changes in structure of farm-holdings. Includes IVD (q.v.) *Loi des Finances* 1966
CNAT	*Commission nationale de l'aménagement du territoire* Commission of *Commissariat au Plan*, responsible for regional aspects of planning 1963/4
CNCE	*Centre national du commerce extérieur* Foreign trade centre
CNES	*Centre national des études spatiales* National Centre for Aerospace Studies. Decentralized to Toulouse. 1100 transferred 1961
CNET	*Centre national d'études des télécommunications* Decentralized to Lannion (Bretagne) 1944
CNJA	*Centre national des jeunes agriculteurs* Young farmers' organization (politically active in rural policy since 1960)
CNME	*Caisse nationale des marchés de l'Est* 90% of costs of establishment or development of small or medium-sized firms March 1976
CNR	*Compagnie nationale du Rhône* 1921, restructured 1932

CNRS	*Centre national de la recherche scientifique*
	National Science Research Council 1939
CODER	*Commission de développement économique régional*
	Regional economic development council; 1964 regional reforms
COS	*coefficient d'occupation des sols*
	ratio of total floor-space to plot size
CRAR	*Contrats régionaux d'aménagement rural*
	Regional contracts (state) for rural development 1974
CRCI	*Chambre régional de commerce et d'industrie*
CRP	*Comité de régionalisation du Plan*
	Advice on regionalization of National Economic and Social Development Plan
	Décret du 31 déc. 1958
CSP	*catégorie socio-profesionnelle*
CUMA	*Coopérative d'utilisation de matériel agricole*
	Cooperative for the pooling of agricultural machinery
CUS	*coefficient d'utilisation des sols*
	ratio of land in use to plot size
DAFU	*Direction de l'aménagement foncier et de l'urbanisme*
	Dept. of Land Development and Town Planning
	Décret du 14 fév. 1963, *Ministère de la construction*
DATAR	*Délégation à l'aménagement du territoire et à l'action régionale*
	Centre for coordination and stimulus for area development, attached to *Ministère de l'intérieur* Feb. 1963
DBO5	*demande biologique en oxygène*
	Pollution measure: biochemical oxygen demand (quantity of oxygen necessary to destroy biodegradable organic matter in 5 days)
DCO	*demande chimique en oxygène*
	Pollution measure: capacity of water to absorb oxygen
DDA	*Direction départementale de l'agriculture*
DDE	*Direction départementale de l'équipement*
	Includes GEP, *groupe d'études et de programmation* (planning study group)
DEFM	*demandes d'emploi fin du mois*
	demands for work on record at the end of the month
DENS	*demandes d'emploi non-satisfaites*
	requests for employment still outstanding
DMA	*débit minimum acceptable*
	minimum season discharge (river management)
DUP	*Déclaration d'utilité publique*
	Permit for expropriation by public authority
EDF	*Electricité de France*
	1946
ENST	*Ecole nationale supérieure des télécommunications*
	Transferred to Brest

EPA | *Etablissement public d'aménagement*
Public development corporation (for New Towns). Associates government officials and local (elected) representatives. Replaced *mission d'aménagement* (1969–73)

EPAREB | *Etablissement public d'aménagement des rives de l'Etang de Berre*
March 1973

EPBS | *Etablissement public de la Basse-Seine*
Only EP authorized to levy tax on capital equipment
Décret du 26 avril 1968

EPR | *Etablissement public régional*
3 parts: *Conseil régional, Comité économique et social, Préfet de Région*
1973 regional reform

ETAM | *Employés, techniciens et agents de maîtrise*
Term used in industrial reconversion operations to define retraining and redeployment needs

ETEL | Products pipeline serving Lyon

EURODIF | Enriched uranium factory at Tricastin (French-Belgian-Spanish-Italian and Iranian participation) 1972

FAD | *Fonds d'aide à la décentralisation*
Primarily concerned with tertiary activities 1972

FAL | *Fonds d'action locale*
i) guaranteed minimum support per inhabitant
ii) avoid loss of revenue by tourist or thermal communes
1966, after reform of local tax system

FAR | *Fonds d'action rurale*
From *Ministère de l'agriculture*: agricultural industries, water supply, farm buildings, restructuring of holdings

FAS | *Fonds d'action sociale*
Welfare funds for foreign workers. Early 1960s

FASASA | *Fonds d'adaptation sociale pour l'aménagement des structures agricoles*
Social restructuring of farming areas. Finances IVD (q.v.)
Loi du 8 août 1962

FBCF | *formation brute de capital fixe*
Indicative figure of state plus other public investments (OSPAE q.v.) VIth Plan, 1971–5

FDES | *Fonds de développement économique et social*
For regional development; loans at preferential rates to national organizations whose investments are controlled by the state 1955

FEOGA | *Fonds européen d'organisation et de garantie agricole*
EEC agricultural support fund 1965

FIANE | *Fonds d'intervention et d'action pour la nature et de l'environnement*
Environmental management support fund 1971

FIAT   *Fonds d'intervention pour l'aménagement du territoire*
Fund for territorial planning and development. Finances, by pump-priming, complex equipment operations required by spatial management policies 1963, DATAR (q.v.)

FIC   *Fonds d'intervention culturelle*

FIFI   *Modèle physico-financier*
National economic planning model for the medium-term Formulated 1967–68 for INSEE

FLNC   *Front de libération nationale de la Corse*
More separatist and militant than APC (q.v.)

FNAFU   *Fonds national d'aménagement foncier et d'urbanisme*
Purchase and equipment of development land Feb. 1963, replacing FNAT (q.v.)

FNAT   *Fonds national d'aménagement du territoire*
Financial aid to local authorities, municipalities and chambers of commerce Aug. 1950, replaced Feb. 1963 by FNAFU (q.v.)

FNDA   *Fonds national du développement agricole*
Managed by ANDA (*Assoc. nat. pour le développement agricole*)

FNE   *Fonds national de l'emploi. Ministère du travail*, training grants on the job, 1963; for continuing professional education, 1971

FPA   *Formation professionnelle des adultes*
Adult vocational training

FRR   *Fonds de rénovation rurale*
Rural renovation funds, under DATAR (q.v.) 1971

FSIR   *Fonds spécial d'investissement routier*
Road funds. Annual allocation to priority projects 1952

GAEC   *Groupement agricole d'exploitation en commun*
Cooperative farming group
Loi du 9 août 1962

GCPU   *Groupe central de planification urbaine*
Submits OREAM SDAUs (q.v.) to *Comité interministériel d'aménagement du territoire* (CIAT, q.v.) *Arrêté du 2 juin* 1964, part of DATAR (q.v.)

GCVN   *Groupe central des villes nouvelles*
Central administration of New Towns (interministerial group) 1970

GDF   *Gaz de France*
1946

GEP   *Groupe d'études et de programmation*
Part of DDE (q.v.)

GICAMA   *Groupe interministériel de coordination de l'action en mer des administrations*
Interministerial monitoring and action group for maritime environmental management July 1976

GIE   *Groupement d'intérêt économique*
Part of policy of concentration of firms within French industry. Fiscal inducements
Ordonnance du 23 sept. 1967

GIRZOM   *Groupe interministériel de restructuration des zones minières*
For economic restructuring of coalmining areas; composed of officials 17 Feb. 1972

GOVM   *Groupe opérationnel des villes moyennes*
Central administration for medium-sized towns programme

HBL   *Houillères du bassin de Lorraine*
Coal mines of the Lorraine basin

HBNPC   *Houillères du Bassin Nord-Pas-de-Calais*
Coal mines of the Nord-Pas-de-Calais basin
Ordonnance du 13 déc. 1944

HLM   *habitation à loyer modéré*
dwelling at subsidized rent

IAA   *industries agricoles et alimentaires*
agricultural and food industries

IAURP   *Institut d'aménagement et d'urbanisme de la Région Parisienne*
For long-term planning study of Paris region (1960). IAUIF (Ile-de-France) since 1976

IDI   *Institut de développement industriel*
c.f. Industrial Reorganization Corporation (UK) 1970

IGAME   *Inspecteurs généraux de l'administration en mission extraordinaire*
1947, new regional organization to maintain law and order: 19 military region prefects named IGAME. 1951, other roles might be added.

IGH   *immeuble de grande hauteur*
high-rise block of flats

ILM   *immeuble à loyer moyen*
subsidized flats (by *Caisse de Prêt* or *Crédit Foncier de France*)

ILN   *immeuble à loyer normal*
flats at economic rental

INED   *Institut national pour les études démographiques*
National demographic research institute 1945

INSEE   *Institut national de la statistique et des études économiques*
Government statistical bureau; has regional offices (*observatoires économiques*) 1946

IRAM   *Interventions pour la renaissance agricole de la montagne*
SOMIVAC (q.v.), to improve holdings in mountain zone of Corse

ISM   *Indemnité spéciale montagne*
Annual subsidy on numbers of flock/herd
Loi du 4 janvier 1972, for critical mountain localities
Loi du 20 fév. 1974, extended to *all* mountain zones

IUT   *Institut universitaire de technologie*
Technological university (institute)

IVD   *Indemnité viagère du départ*
Leaving payment for retiring farmers (60 years)
Décret du 26 avril 1968

JAC   *Jeunesse agricole chrétienne*
Started by the priesthood. Grassroots pressure group in rural areas 1929

LEP   See CET

LOF   *Loi d'orientation foncière*
Outline Land Act
Loi du 30 *déc.* 1967

LORDEX   *Société lorraine de développement régional*
1957

MDPNE   *Ministère de la protection de la nature et de l'environnement*
1971–4. Became *Ministère de la qualité de la vie* 1974

MEST   *matières en suspension totales*
Air pollution measure, in tonnes per diem

MIACA   *Mission interministérielle pour l'aménagement de la côte aquitaine*
1967

MIAFEB   *Mission interministérielle pour l'aménagement de la région de Fos-Etang de Berre*
1969–73, MAEB, *Mission d'aménagement de l'Etang de Berre*
March 1973

MIR   *Ministère de l'industrie et de la recherche*

MNDR   *Mouvement national pour la décentralisation et la réforme régionale*
c. 200 parliamentarians, plus regional figures June 1968

MSA   *Mutualité sociale agricole*
Social security for farm-based population

NAE   *nomenclature des activités économiques* (INSEE)
c.f. Standard Industrial Classification (UK) 1949, revised 1958, replaced 1975 by NAP (q.v.)

NAP   *nomenclature d'activités et de produits* (INSEE)
1975, replaced NAE (q.v.)

OENS   *offres d'emploi non-satisfaites*
unfilled employment vacancies

OER   *Observatoire économique régional*
Regional statistical centres (INSEE) 1946

OGAF   *Opérations groupées d'aménagement foncier*
For restructuring or adaptation of farm-holdings 1970

ONI   *Office national de l'immigration*

OP   *ouvrier professionnel*
Possesses a trade qualification, e.g. electrician

OREAC   *Organisation d'études d'aménagement de la région Centre*
Created from OREALM (q.v.) Dec. 1973

OREALM   *Organisation d'études d'aménagement de la Loire moyenne*
Sept. 1968. In Dec. 1973 became OREAC (q.v.)

OREAM   *Organisation d'études d'aménagement d'aire métropolitaine*
Metropolitan area planning study group 1966

OREAV	*Organisme d'études et d'aménagement des vallées (de l'Oise et de l'Aisne)*
	June 1967
OS	*ouvrier spécialisé*
	Specialized worker; in fact many are manual labourers
OSPAE	*Organismes semi-publics d'action économique*
	e.g. Chambers of Commerce, Port Authorities, SAFER, motorway entrepreneurs
OTAM	*Omnium Technique d'Aménagement*
	Planning division of SEMA-METRA INTERNATIONAL Group
PADOG	*Plan d'aménagement et d'organisation générale*
	Regional planning scheme Paris region, *décret du 6 août* 1960
PAF	*Périmètre d'action forestière*
	Zoning for forest management
	Loi du 22 mai 1971
PAI	*Prime d'adaptation industrielle*
	Relocation grant, substituted for earlier *prime spéciale d'équipement* (FDES (q.v.) 1955) 1964–72
PAP	*Programme d'action prioritaire*
	Priority action programme VIIth Plan, 1976–80 See also PAPIN and PAPIR
PAPIN	*Programme d'action prioritaire national*
	VIIth Plan, 1976–80
PAPIR	*Programme d'action prioritaire d'initiative régionale et locale*
	VIIth Plan, 1976–80
PAR	*Plan d'aménagement rural*
	Prepared by DDA (q.v.) in concert with local authorities for group of *communes* forming geographic and economic entity; often for cantons. Obligatory for all cantons with less than 10,000 people and a POS (q.v.)
	Décret du 8 juin 1970
	Programme d'action régionale
	Regional development programme 1955–8. In 1958 became *plan régional*
PAZ	*Plan d'aménagement de zone*
	Local plan, within a ZAC (q.v.). Defines building use, densities and heights, together with constraints 1967
PC	*Parti communiste*
	Political party 1943
PCA	*Prêts de la Caisse nationale du Crédit Agricole*
	For housing loans (HLM, q.v.)
PDA(R)	*Programme de développement et d'aménagement (régional)*
	Replaces PRDE (q.v.) VIIth Plan, 1976–80
PDR	*Prime de développement régional*

Regional development grant Jan. 1972 replaced PAI (q.v.); amended April 1976

PDRE   *population disponible à la recherche d'un emploi*
persons available for work 1962

PDUI   *Plan directeur d'urbanisme inter-communal*
Intercommunal local town plan

PIB   *produit intérieur brut*
gross domestic product

PIC   *Prêts immobiliers conventionnés*
Crédit Foncier makes these loans to banking and financial institutions for property loans. Replaces *prêts spéciaux immobiliers* (PSI, q.v.) originating 1965
Décret du 24 janvier 1972

PLAT   *Prime à la localisation des activités tertiaires*
Tertiary location grant 11 April 1972; amended April 1976

PLD   *plafond légal de densité*
The relationship between the floor-space of a building and the area of the site on which the building is to be constructed; defines the building density. A density equal to 1 defines the legal limit of density (PLD); for Paris this limit is raised to 1.5. The right to build at higher densities, where town planning allows, must be bought from the *commune* 1 April 1976

PLR   *Programme à loyer réduit*
Housing subsidies directly from *Ministère de l'équipement et du logement*

PLSE   *Pipe-line sud-européen*
Rhône valley-south European crude pipeline

PMDRE   *population marginale disponible à la recherche d'un emploi*
Interviewees declaring themselves available for work only at a second stage (prompted by the interviewer)

PME   *Plan (programme) de modernisation et d'équipement*
Programme for modernization and capital equipment; usually 10-year perspective, for towns of more than 50,000. Commitment by ministries and local authorities to future investment in utilities and services
1967, Outline Land Act (LOF, q.v.)

PMI   *Petites et moyennes entreprises industrielles*
Delegate for PMI in *Ministère de l'industrie et de la recherche*
11 March 1976, Presidential Decree

PNB   *produit national brut*
gross national product

POA   *Prime d'orientation agricole*
20%, for improving structure of units, gaining new markets, or better contacts with producers

POS   *Plan d'occupation des sols*

	Zoning and land use constraints, 1: 2,000–1: 5,000 scale 1967, Outline Land Act (LOF, q.v.)
PR	*Préfet de région* 1964
PRDE	*Programme régional de développement et d'équipement* Regional development and public investment programme. *Loi du* 15 *juillet* 1971. Replaced by PDA (R) (q.v.) under VIIth Plan, 1976–80
PS	*Parti socialiste* Political party 1905
PSI	*Prêts spéciaux immédiats* Housing loans
PSR	*Programme social de relogement* Welfare rehousing project
PUD	*Plan d'urbanisme directeur; plan d'urbanisme en détail* Master town plan, or detailed town plan
PUK	*Péchiney-Ugine-Kuhlmann* Chemical firm
RATP	*Régie autonome des transports parisiens* Paris transport authority 1949; since then under *Office régional des transports parisiens*
RCB	*rationalisation des choix budgétaires* c.f. PPB, planned programme budgeting (UK). Planning by objectives
REC	*rural étendu constant* Hypothesis for maintaining rural population at constant numbers VIIth Plan, 1976–80
REGINA	Planning model for simultaneous analysis of problems at both national and regional levels. Commissioned as project 1971 (Courbis, R. and Prager, J. C.); operational for VIIth National Plan (1976–80)
RER	*Réseau express régional* Fast transit suburban rail system (Paris). Planned 1961; first section opened 1969
RPR	*Rassemblement pour la République* Political party, formerly UDR (q.v.), M. Chirac (president) Dec. 1976
RR	*Rénovation rurale* 1 Oct. 1967 policy introduced. 4 commissioners
RRIR	*Réseau routier d'intérêt régional* Regional road network
RRO	*Rapports régionaux d'orientation* Regional trend reports by *Mission régionale*, in preparation of PRDE (q.v.) VIIth Plan, 1976–80
RTM	*Restauration des terres en montagne* Mountain land restoration, under *Office national des forêts*

SAFE   *Société d'aménagement des friches et taillis de l'Est*
Society for the management of the non-cultivated areas and woodland of the Est 1957

SAFER   *Société d'aménagement foncier et d'établissement rural*
To improve agrarian structure, increase size of holdings, aid reclamation, establish farmers on land
Loi d'orientation agricole, 5 *août* 1960

SAM   *Secteurs d'aménagement montagnard*
For agriculture, infrastructure, and local authorities in mountain zones 1974

SAU   *surface agricole (utile*) utilisée*
Farmland, *land capable of being farmed

SCA   *Syndicat communautaire d'aménagement*
Local government (intercommunal) syndicate, 1972
Loi Boscher 1970

SCET   *Société centrale pour l'équipement du territoire*
Branch of *Caisse des dépôts et consignations.* Finances and gives technical advice to local authorities and mixed development companies (SEM) July 1965

SCIC   *Société centrale immobilière de la Caisse des dépôts*
Subsidiary of *Caisse des dépôts*, the state finance house. SCIC France's leading building promoter June 1954

SCP   *Société du canal de Provence et d'aménagement de la région provençale*
Constituted 1957; first land concession 1963

SDAU   *Schéma directeur d'aménagement et d'urbanisme*
(Outline Land Act (LOF, q.v.) 1967). Long-term structure plan, binding on public authorities, for towns of more than 10,000. By defining major national investments, gives framework for town development. 1: 10,000–1: 50,000 scale
Décret du 28 mai 1969

SDR   *Société de développement régional*
For regional economic development; 15 regional authorities cover national territory (excluding Paris region) 1955

SDRSE   *Société de développement régional du Sud-Est*
1957

SEN   *Secteur d'équilibre naturel*
'Green zones' in Aquitaine coastal planning scheme 1967

SESAME   *Système d'études du schéma d'aménagement de la France*
Examines regional effects of sectoral blueprints; population and employment trends; technological forward planning 1969, DATAR (q.v.)

SETCO   *Société pour l'équipement touristique de la Corse*
1957

SICA   *Société d'intérêt collectif agricole*
Marketing groups of farmers 27 Sept. 1967

SIDECO   *Société sidérurgique de participation et de développement économique*

Created by major steel firms to aid deployment of redundant iron-ore miners and steel workers 1966

SIVOM *Syndicat intercommunal à vocation multiple*
In spite of financial aid 1963 and 1966, less favoured by mayors than *syndicats à vocation unique* 1959

SMIC *Salaire minimum industrie et commerce*

Salaire minimum industriel (interprofessionnel) de croissance
Fixed annually in relation to price levels. Covers agricultural wages also; 2 Jan. 1970

SMIG *Salaire minimum interprofessionnel garanti*
Guaranteed minimum wage, replaced by SMIC (q.v.) 1970 1950

SNCF *Société national de chemins de fer*
1937

SNECMA *Société nationale d'étude et de construction de moteurs d'aviation*
Aeronautical engineering company

SOAM *Schéma d'orientation et d'aménagement de massif*
Mountain massif development programmes, under *Commission à l'aménagement de montagne*
Spring 1977

SODECCO *Société de développement régional du Centre et du Centre-Ouest*
1957

SODLER *Société de développement régional de Languedoc-Roussillon*
1957

SOFIREM *Société financière pour favoriser l'industrialisation des régions minières*
Subsidiary of *Charbonnages de France*
Oct. 1967

SOLMER *Société lorraine et méridionale de laminage continu*
Steel plant and rolling mills at Fos. Capital from SACILOR, USINOR, THYSSEN.

SOMIVAC *Société pour la mise en valeur de la Corse*
1957–8

SOMIVAL *Société pour la mise en valeur de l'Auvergne-Limousin*
1964

SPMR *Société du pipe-line Méditerranée-Rhône*
Rhône valley: SPMR products pipeline

SPPPI *Secrétariat permanent pour les problèmes de pollution industrielle (Fos)*
24 Nov. 1971

SRE *Services régionaux de l'équipement*
Urban study programmes, preparation of ZAC (q.v.) programmes; application of urban policy 1967

SRU *Service régional et urbain*
Translates CNAT (q.v.) intentions into employment forecasts and programmes of public equipment 1962

STS   *Sections de techniciens supérieurs*
Technical grammar schools and private technical colleges, 2 years for *brevet*

TC   *transports en commun*
public transport

TEIR   *tableau d'échanges interindustriels interrégional*
inter-regional industrial account table

TGV   *train à grande vitesse*
High-speed train, for Paris-Lyon route. Probably electric traction

TLE   *taxe locale d'équipement*
Local building tax, paid by the contractor, not the landowner, in areas outside ZAC (q.v.) 1967

TOFINSO   *Société toulousaine d'études financières et industrielles du Sud-Ouest*
Creation, decentralization, extension or transformation of firms 20 May 1957

TRAPIL   *Transports pétroliers par pipe-line (Société des)*
Products pipeline serving Basse-Seine-Paris

TVA   *taxe à la valeur ajoutée*
value added tax

UDR   *Union des démocrates pour la République*
Political party (Gaullist) Renamed RPR (q.v.) Dec. 1976

UER   *Unité d'enseignement et de recherche*
University structure since 12 Nov. 1968

UGB   *unité de gros bétail*
Stock or herd units (for agricultural subsidy)

UNEDIC   *Union nationale pour l'emploi et le commerce*
Unemployment insurance fund. Includes ASSEDIC (q.v.) Since early 1950s

UPA   *unité principal d'aménagement*
Aquitaine coastal scheme. 9 integral development units 1967

VCC   *vins de consommation courante*
ordinary quality wines

VDQS   *vins délimités de qualité supérieure*
higher quality wines

VQPRD   *vins de qualité produits dans des régions déterminées*
EEC categorization

ZAC   *Zone d'aménagement concerté*
Concerted development zone
1967 Outline Land Act (LOF, q.v.)

ZAD   *Zone d'aménagement différé*
Concerns urban areas, for deferred development or renovation. Right of public pre-emption of land sales within defined perimeter
Loi du 26 juillet 1962

ZANC   *Zone d'appui Nord-Champenoise*

	Designated in Interministerial Committee (CIAT, q.v.) 26 July 1966
ZEAT	*Zone d'études et d'aménagement du territoire*
	8 long-term planning regions VIth Plan, 1971–5
ZEDE	*Zone d'études démographiques et d'emploi*
	Each homogeneous, with a central place, linkages and a sufficiently large population to achieve balance 1963, designated by INSEE (q.v.)
ZH	*Zone d'habitation*
	Residential zone 1958–67. Incorporated 1967 in ZAC (q.v.)
ZIF	*Zone d'intervention foncière*
	Legal powers of intervention (pre-emption) by *commune* in the land market. For towns of more than 10,000 inhabitants with a town plan. Adjunct to ZAD (q.v.) policy 1976
ZIP	*Zone industrielle prioritaire*
	Priority industrial zone
ZNE	*Zone naturelle d'équilibre*
	Local or regional environmental balance zone 1975 SDAU (q.v.) Ile-de-France
ZOH	*Zone opérationnelle d'habitation*
	Residential development zone
ZPIU	*Zone de peuplement industriel et urbain*
	Groups of *communes*:
	i) homogeneity of settlement, and in particular a small proportion based on agriculture
	ii) important daily residence-workplace movement
	iii) industrial activity, created or developed by proximity to an urban centre, a communications axis, a river, or underground resources
	Census of 1954; designated by INSEE (q.v.)
ZR(U)	*Zone de rénovation urbaine*
	Urban renewal zone
ZSR	*Zone spécifiquement rurale*
	Aquitaine, for rural aid policies VIth and VIIth Plans, 1971–80
ZUP	*Zone à urbaniser par priorité*
	Importance of housing programme requires creation, reinforcement or extension of public capital equipment *Décret du* 1958–1967; replaced by ZAC (q.v.), but term ZUP still in use

Author index

Subject Index